The Aims of Argument

The Aims of Argument

A RHETORIC AND READER

Timothy W. Crusius / Carolyn E. Channell

Southern Methodist University

Mayfield Publishing Company

Mountain View, California

London • Toronto

LIBRARY OF CONGRESS CATALOGING-IN-PUBLICATION DATA

Crusius, Timothy W.

The aims of argument : a rhetoric and reader / Timothy W. Crusius, Carolyn E. Channell.

p. cm.

ISBN 1-55934-114-9

1. English language—Rhetoric. 2. Persuasion (Rhetoric) 3. College readers. I. Channell, Carolyn E. II. Title.

PE1431.C78 1994

808'.0427—dc20 94-8393

CIP

Manufactured in the United States of America

10 9 8 7 6 5 4 3 2 1

Mayfield Publishing Company

1280 Villa Street

Mountain View, California 94041

Sponsoring editor, Janet M. Beatty; production editor, April Wells-Hayes; manuscript editor, Mark Gallaher; text and cover designer, David Bullen; art editor, Susan M. Breitbard; art director, Jeanne M. Schreiber; manufacturing manager, Martha Branch. The text was set in 10½/12 Bembo by Thompson Type and printed on 45# New Era Matte by The Maple-Vail Book Manufacturing Group.

Cover image: Kenneth Noland, *Gift of Reason,* 1986. Acrylic on canvas. 66 × 42". Collection of the artist. Photo by Steven Sloman © 1986.

Acknowledgments and copyrights appear at the back of the book on pages 639–642, which constitute an extension of the copyright page.

For W. Ross Winterowd

PREFACE

In 1980 an author could justify a new argumentation textbook for first-year college students simply by saying that it filled a void; now prospective authors must ask themselves, Does the profession really need yet another book on argumentation? Moreover, they had better have a good answer to a question that experienced instructors of argument will surely ask: How, specifically, is your text different from—and better than—the one I am using?

People write textbooks for many reasons, but probably the most important reason—the one that keeps authors going long after the initial enthusiasm (and advances) are spent—is the chance of satisfying a need. With over thirty years of teaching experience between us, we have tried most of the argumentation texts currently available. Some of them are quite good and we have learned from them. However, we found ourselves adopting a text not so much out of genuine enthusiasm but rather because it had fewer liabilities than any of the others under consideration. True, all textbook selection involves comparisons of the "lesser evil" sort. But we wondered why we were so lukewarm about even the best argumentation textbooks. What was it exactly that put us off?

We found many problems, both major and minor. But our dissatisfaction boiled down to a few major criticisms:

Most treatments were too formalistic and prescriptive.
Most failed to integrate class discussion and individual inquiry with written argumentation.
Apart from moving from simple concepts and assignments to more complicated ones, no book offered a learning sequence.
Despite the fact that argument, like narrative, is clearly a mode or means of development, not an end in itself, no book offered a well-developed view of the aims or purposes of argument.

We thought that these shortcomings had many undesirable results in the classroom, including the following:

The overemphasis on form confused students with too much terminology, made them doubt their best instincts, and drained away energy and interest from the process of inventing and discovering good arguments.

Informal argumentation is not cut-and-dried, but open-ended and creative.

The separation of class discussion from the process of composition created a hiatus (rather than a useful distinction) between oral and written argument so that students had difficulty seeing the relation between the two and using the insights learned from each to improve the other.

The lack of a learning sequence—of assignments that began by refining and extending what students could do without help and then built on these capacities for each subsequent assignment—meant that courses in argumentation were less coherent and less meaningful than they could be. Students did not understand why they were doing what they were doing and could not envision what might reasonably come next.

Finally, inattention to what people actually use argument to accomplish resulted in too narrow a view of the functions of argument and thus in unclear purposes for writing. Because instruction was mainly limited to what we call arguing to convince, too often students saw argument only as a monologue of advocacy. Even when their viewpoint was flexible, too often they assumed a pose of dogmaticism and ignored any true spirit of inquiry.

We set out consciously to solve these problems–or at least to render them less problematical. The result is a book different in notable respects from any other argument text currently available. In Chapter 1 we define and explain four aims of argument:

Arguing to inquire, the process of questioning opinions;
Arguing to convince, the process of making cases;
Arguing to persuade, the process of appealing to the whole person; and
Arguing to negotiate, the process of mediating between or among conflicting positions.

We have found that instructors have certain questions about these aims, especially in terms of how they relate to one another. No doubt we have yet to hear all the questions that will be asked but hope that by answering the ones we have heard, we can clarify some of the implications of our approach.

1. *What is the relative value of the four aims? Since negotiation comes last, is it the best or most valued?* Our answer is that no aim is "better" than any other aim. Given certain needs or demands for writing and certain audiences, one aim can be more appropriate than another for the task at hand. We treat negotiation last because it involves inquiry, convincing, and persuading and thus comes last in the learning sequence.
2. *Must inquiry be taught as a separate aim?* Not at all. We have designed the text so that it may be taught as a separate aim (the use of argument Plato and Aristotle called dialectic), but we certainly do not intend this "may" to be interpreted as a "must." We do think that teaching inquiry as a distinct aim has certain advantages. Students need to learn how to engage in constructive dialogue,

which is more disciplined and more focused than class discussion usually is. Once they see how it is done, students seem to enjoy dialogue with one another and with texts. Dialogue helps students to think through their arguments and to imagine reader reaction to what they say, both of which are crucial to convincing and persuading. Finally, as with the option of teaching negotiation, teaching inquiry offers instructors the option to make assignments in addition to the standard argumentative essay.

3. *Should inquiry come first?* For a number of reasons, inquiry has a certain priority over the other aims. Most teachers are likely to approach inquiry as a prewriting task, preparatory to convincing or persuading. And very commonly we return to inquiry when we find something wrong with a case we are trying to construct, so the relation between inquiry and the other aims is as much recursive as it is matter of before and after.

    However, we think inquiry also has psychological, moral, and practical claims to priority. When we are unfamiliar with an issue, inquiry comes first psychologically, often as a felt need to explore existing opinion. Regardless of what happens in the "real world," convincing or persuading without an open, honest, and earnest search for the truth is, in our view, immoral. Finally, inquiry goes hand-in-hand with research, which, of course, normally precedes writing in the other aims of argument.

    In sum, we would not defend Plato's concept of the truth. Truth is not simply "out there" in some wordless place waiting to be discovered; rather, our opinion is what we discover or uncover as we grapple with a controversial issue and results largely from how we interpret ourselves and our world. We agree, therefore, with Wayne Booth that truth claims ought to be provisional and subject to revision, held for good reasons until better ones change our minds. Moreover, we agree with Plato that rhetoric divorced from inquiry is dangerous and morally suspect. The truth (if always provisional—some person's, some group's, or some culture's version of the truth) must count for more than sheer technical skill in argumentation.

4. *Isn't the difference between convincing and persuading more a matter of degree than of kind?* Fairly sharp distinctions can be drawn between inquiry and negotiation and between either of these two aims and the monologues of advocacy, convincing and persuading. But convincing and persuading do shade into one another, so that the difference is only clear at the extremes, with carefully chosen examples. Furthermore, the "purest" appeal to reason—a lawyer's brief, a philosophical or scientific argument—appeals in ways beyond the sheer cogency of the case being made. Persuasive techniques are typically submerged but not absent in arguing to convince.

    Our motivation for separating convincing from persuading is not so much theoretical as pedagogical. Students usually have so much difficulty with case-making that individual attention to the logical appeal by itself is justified. Making students focally conscious of the appeals of character, emotion, and style while they are struggling to cope with case-making is too much to ask and can overburden them to the point of paralysis.

> Regardless, then, of how sound the traditional distinction between convincing and persuading may be, we think it best to take up convincing first and then persuasion, especially since what students learn in the former can be carried over more or less intact into the latter. And, of course, it is not only case-making that carries over from convincing into persuading. Since one cannot make a case without unconscious appeal to character, emotional commitments (such as values), and style, teaching persuasion is really a matter of exposing and developing what is already there in arguing to convince.

The central tenets of an approach based on aims of argument may be summarized as follows:

> Argumentation is a mode or means of discourse, not an aim or purpose of discourse; consequently,
>
> Our task is to teach the aims of argument.
>
> The aims of argument are linked in a learning sequence, so that convincing builds on inquiry, persuasion on convincing, and all three contribute to negotiating; consequently,
>
> We offer this learning sequence as an aid to conceiving a course or courses in argumentation.

We believe in the learning sequence as much as we do in the aims of argument. We think that anyone giving it an honest chance will come to prefer this way of teaching argument over any other ordering currently available.

At the same time, we recognize that textbooks are used selectively, as teachers and programs need them for help in achieving their own goals. As with any other text, this one can be used selectively, ignoring some parts, playing up others, designing other sequences, and so on. If you want to work with our learning sequence, it is there for creative adaptation. If not, the text certainly does not have to be taught as a whole and in sequence to be useful and effective.

We conclude with some notes on the readings. You will discover that many of the issues around which these essays are organized unavoidably involve students in issues of race, class, and gender difference. This slant is not intended to be political, nor does it reflect a hidden agenda on our part. Rather, we think students can come to feel more deeply about issues of this sort than they do about others we have tried. Class debates are more lively, maybe because such issues hit closer to home—the home and community they came from, the campus they live on now. Whatever the case, we have found that the issues work, both for students and for us.

They work, we think, because such issues help to expose something obvious and basic about argumentation: People differ because they are different, and not just on the basis of race, class, and gender. Without some confrontation with difference, students may miss the deep social and cultural roots of argument and fail to understand why people think in such varied ways about multiculturalism, sexual harassment, homelessness, abortion, and other issues that turn on difference, as well as issues such as the environment, which may seem at first to have nothing to do with difference.

We have consciously avoided the "great authors, classic essays" approach. We have tried instead to find bright, contemporary people arguing well from diverse viewpoints—articles and chapters similar to those that can be found in our better journals and trade books, the sort of publications students will read most in doing research on the issues. We have also tried to bring students into the argument as it currently stands, recognizing that the terms of the debate are necessarily always changing. Finally, we have not presented any issue in a simple pro and con fashion, as if there were only two sides to a question. We want the readings to provide models for writing not too far removed from what students can reasonably aspire to, as well as stimulation toward thinking through and rethinking positions on the issues in question.

Some reviewers and users have called our approach innovative. But is it better? Will students learn more? Will instructors find the book more satisfying and more helpful than what they currently use? Our experience, both in using the book ourselves and in listening to the responses of those who have read it or tested it in the classroom for us, is that they will. Students complain less about having to read the book than they do with others used in our program. They do seem to learn more. Teachers claim to enjoy the text and find it stimulating, something to work with rather than around. We hope your experience is as positive as ours has been. We invite your comments and will use them in the process of perpetual revision that constitutes the life of a text and of our lives as writing teachers.

Included in this range of approaches are arguments made not only with words but with images. Part Two therefore includes some examples of editorial cartoons, advertisements, and photographs; students may want to experiment with making their own nonverbal arguments.

We would like to thank the following reviewers: Betty Bamberg, University of Southern California; Michael C. Flanigan, University of Oklahoma; Nancy L. Joseph, York College; Kate Massey, California State Polytechnic University, Pomona; Michael G. Moran, University of Georgia; Hephzibah C. Roskelly, University of North Carolina, Greensboro; Carol Severino, University of Iowa; Linda K. Shamoon, University of Rhode Island; and especially Doug Hesse, Illinois State University.

We are grateful for all the help given to us by our editors: Jan Beatty, sponsoring editor, who gave enthusiastic support and guidance from the project's beginnings; Mark Gallaher, whose copyediting greatly improved both the style and the content of the text; and April Wells-Hayes, production editor, who gently kept us on time and on track. We also want to thank Pamela Trainer and Julianna Scott for their work on permissions and art.

Here at Southern Methodist University, the Rhetoric Program contributed in many ways. Our thanks go to all the faculty who classroom-tested the text from its earliest stages. For their constructive criticism, we are particularly indebted to Rebecca Innocent and Marilyn Wagner. We are also grateful to the SMU librarians, especially Margaret Bailey, who heads bibliographic instruction here; she made an enormous contribution to the appendix on researching arguments. Our colleagues Ann Shattles, Jo Goyne, and Wendy DeOre deserve special thanks as well, not just for testing our book but for helping us find student essays to include. We want to thank not just the students whose essays appear here, but all of our students who used the text in its draft stages. We learned a great deal from their honest responses. And to the Rhetoric Program's administrative assistant, Linda Graves Lofton, a thousand thank-yous for all the ways you contributed to the project.

Finally, we want to thank Elizabeth Crusius and David Channell for their love, encouragement, and patience.

NOTE TO STUDENTS

Our goal in this book is not just to show you how to construct an argument, but to make you more aware of why people argue, and the purposes that argument serves in our society. Consequently, Part One of this book introduces four specific aims that people may have in mind when they make arguments. Before these chapters on the aims of argument, however, we have placed four relatively short chapters that offer an overview of the four aims and prepare you for working with assignments in the aims.

Chapter 1 explains the aims and how they fit into the larger concept of rhetoric—the persuasive use of language.
Chapter 2 explains what a writer's notebook is and how it can help you cope with writing assignments in any college course;
Chapter 3 offers an approach to reading any argument; and
Chapter 4 shows you, step-by-step, how to analyze the logic of any argument.

Because critical reading and analysis prepare you for the first aim, arguing to inquire, Chapters 3 and 4 lead directly into Chapter 5, and each subsequent chapter on the aims assumes and builds on the previous one.

Part Two of this book consists of readings, most by professional writers. As examples of the aims of argument, they offer something for you to emulate. All writers learn from studying the strategies of other writers. The object is not so much to imitate what some older, more experienced writer does as it is to understand the range of approaches and tactics you might use in your own way and for your own purposes.

Included in this range of approaches are arguments made not only with words but also with images. Part Two therefore includes some examples of editorial cartoons, advertisements, and photographs; you may want to experiment with making your own nonverbal arguments.

The readings serve another function as well. To learn about argument, we have to argue; to argue, we have to have something to argue about. So we have grouped essays around some central issues of current public discussion. We selected these particular issues rather than other widely debated ones for two main reasons. One is that they have worked well in our own classes, better than others we tried and rejected. The other is that most of these issues deal centrally with society and more or less require us to think about difference, about what leads people to disagree with one another in the first place.

Basically, people argue with one another because they do not see the world the same way, and they do not see the world the same way because of different backgrounds. Therefore, in dealing with how people differ, a book about argument must deal with what makes people different, with the sources of disagreement itself—including gender, race, ethnicity, class, and religion. Rather than ignoring or glossing over difference, we hope the readings in Part Two will help you better understand difference—as well as provide interesting and significant subjects to argue about.

This book concludes with two appendices, each a reference that you will want to refer to repeatedly as you work through the assignments in the main parts of the text. Appendix A offers advice about how to do library and field research and how to handle formal documentation. We see such research as a vital component of preparing to write convincingly on any topic, unless you take an extremely personal approach and have had first-hand experiences to draw upon for support. We encourage you to discard the notion of a "research paper" and think instead of how even a brief argument can gain strength from facts or opinions taken from one or two well-selected sources. Appendix B focuses on editing, the art of polishing and refining prose, and on proofreading for some common errors.

Arguing well is difficult for anyone. For many college students it is especially challenging because they have had little experience writing arguments. We have tried to write a text that is no more complicated than it has to be, and we welcome your comments so that we may improve future editions. Please write us at the following address:

The Rhetoric Program
#14 McFarlin
Southern Methodist University
Dallas, Texas 75275

You may also E-mail your comments via the following: cchannel @ sun.cis.smu.edu.

CONTENTS

Part One

THE AIMS OF ARGUMENT

CHAPTER ONE

An Overview of Key Terms

Commonly, the word *argument* refers to a verbal conflict, a dispute involving two or more people. In this book we will use the word in a sense closer to that of the Latin verb from which it derives: *arguere,* "to make clear."

WHAT IS ARGUMENT?

Argument is the process of making what we think clear to ourselves and to others. It takes us from a vague, private viewpoint to a clearly stated position that we can defend publicly in speech or writing. Like any journey, it provides us with discoveries and new knowledge. If we undertake this process in a spirit of honesty and openness, we can compare it to a search for truth.

Argument in this sense of seeking clarity has a two-part form or structure: (1) the statement of an opinion and (2) one or more reasons for holding that opinion. If you say, for example, "Student loans for college ought to be more widely available," you have stated an opinion. In doing so, you have made one thing clear—namely, your position on the issue of student loans. But as yet you have not made an argument in our particular sense of the word. Not until you add to your opinion a reason for holding it—for example, "because rising costs are preventing too many capable but impoverished students from attending"—do you construct an argument. Now you have made something else clear—namely, *why* you take the position you do.

As we will see in detail in later chapters, arguments require more than simply an opinion coupled with a reason. But this basic form is fundamental to accomplishing any of the aims of argument.

WHAT ARE THE AIMS OF ARGUMENT?

Argument is not in itself an end or a purpose of communication. It is rather a *means* of discourse, developing what we have to say. In this book we use the term *aims of argument* to refer to the various purposes that argument helps us accomplish.

We all know people who seem to argue just for the sake of argument, who would "argue with a post," so to speak. But even these people have an aim beyond argument itself. It may be to vent hostility or resentment or outrage. Or it may be to show off, to display what they know, or to dominate (or enliven) a discussion. We may feel that such contentious people are arguing inappropriately, but they are clearly not arguing just to argue. They are arguing to express themselves.

An argument may be almost entirely self-expression. Some speakers and writers are satisfied just to "have their say"; they don't care about winning their opponents over to their side. Consider the letters to the editor in your local paper. A few attempt to influence the viewpoints of others, but most only state an opinion, offering perhaps some minimal justification. Newspaper editors appropriately give these sections titles such as "Sounding Off."

In fact, all arguments are expressive to some degree. Nothing tells us more about people than the opinions they hold and their reasons for holding them. Our opinions play a large role in making us what we are: conservative, liberal, or middle-of-the-road in politics; a believer, an atheist, or an agnostic in religion; and so on. Because what we think is so much what we are, we typically hold our opinions with deep conviction and genuine passion—so much so that we often fail to question our own opinions or to listen to the arguments of other people who disagree with us.

In societies that value freedom of speech, argument as self-expression is common. It is also quite spontaneous: We learn it much as we learned our first language, by just attempting it, with little thought about the form of the argument or the process that brought us to our position. For this reason we have not singled out argument as expression for special concern in this book.

We assume most of your arguments will be expressive, or at least will begin as self-expression. But when you examine your own opinions or the opinions of someone who disagrees with you, when you try to get others to change their positions, when you explore avenues of compromise between competing positions, you have moved beyond self-expression to one of the following four aims of argument, on which we will focus.

Arguing to Inquire

The ancient Greeks called argument as inquiry *dialectic;* today we might think of it as *dialogue,* or serious conversation. But arguing to inquire can also be done in writing and may in fact work best when we can scrutinize our thoughts "out there" on the page.

Arguing to inquire helps us to form opinions, to question opinions we already have, and to reason our way through conflicts or contradictions. It is how we decide what we will accept as the truth about a given issue. It requires an attitude of patient questioning under nonthreatening circumstances and is therefore something we most often do alone or among trusted friends and associates.

In everyday life we most commonly argue to inquire when we face a complicated decision. We can buy only one car, for example, but several appeal to us; or we are interested in several areas of study and cannot decide which to major in. We want to make an intelligent decision, one that seems reasonable to ourselves and to others whose opinions we respect. What do we do? We argue with ourselves, we try out arguments on our friends, we offer a tentative opinion to someone more knowledgeable (the parent who must help us pay for the car or our college tuition, for example).

We also use argument as inquiry when we think through dilemmas, whether personal or public—when one voice inside says one thing, and another says something else that conflicts with the first. For example, we have been taught to be tolerant of others, to respect the opinions of people who disagree with us. But when we encounter opinions that are themselves intolerant, that are racist or sexist in an aggressive and even potentially violent way, we are confronted with a dilemma: How much tolerance is too much tolerance? Where do we draw the line between differences that must be respected, even encouraged, and opinions that are dangerous and should be actively opposed, even suppressed? Should we protest a Nazi group's demonstration on Main Street? Should we support or challenge a campus group that destroys every issue of a school-supported newspaper it finds offensive?

Sometimes college courses ask us to confront such basic philosophical dilemmas as the limits of tolerance. More commonly, though, the purpose of inquiry in college is to help us form opinions about issues requiring some kind of research. We become acquainted with an issue through lectures and assigned reading; then, to assess what we have heard and read, we must seek out additional information and opinions. Argument as inquiry helps us read and listen more critically, so that we can arrive at our own position with confidence. Because inquiry engages us in dialogues with others and with ourselves, its success depends on the art of asking questions, which is the principal concern of Chapter 4.

Finally, argument as inquiry plays a role in our professional lives. A research scientist may devote years, even a lifetime, to formulating, testing, and reformulating hypotheses that explore a single set of phenomena—black holes, for example. Businesspeople must find solutions to practical problems (How can we increase sales in our southern region?), resolve dilemmas based on changing societal and political attitudes (How can we achieve our goals for affirmative action and still hire the best people?), and meet new and often unanticipated challenges that have a direct impact on success or failure (How should we respond to the evolving economic and political conditions in Eastern Europe?). Basic to such research and decision-making is arguing to inquire.

Arguing to Convince

Some inquiry never stops, remaining permanently open-ended; the goal of most inquiry, however, is to reach some kind of conclusion. This conclusion can go by many names, but we'll call it a *conviction,* defining this term as "an earned opinion, achieved through careful thought, research, and discussion." Once we arrive at a conviction, we ordinarily want others to share it—that is, the aim of further argument is to secure the assent of people who do not share our conviction (or who do not share it fully). Such assent is an agreement of minds secured by reason rather than by force.

Arguing to inquire centers on asking questions; we use argument as inquiry to expose and examine what we think. Arguing to convince centers on making a case, which, as we shall see in Chapter 6, involves an elaboration of the basic structure "x because y"; we use argument as convincing in an effort to get others to agree with what we think and to think the same thing. Inquiry is the search for what is true; convincing is the attempt to get others to accept the truths we claim to have reached.

Examples of arguing to convince are all around us. The purest may be found in scholarly and professional writing (for example, when a historian interprets the causes of an event in the past and makes a case for his or her interpretation, or when a judge writes up a justification for a particular ruling). But we see examples in everyday life as well: on editorial pages, where writers make a case for their position on local issues or candidates for office, and even at school, where students may appeal a grade, arguing that the average of the grades received on individual assignments is higher than the grade given for the course.

Whenever we encounter a stance supported by reasons that asks for our assent to the position being argued, we are dealing with argument as convincing. Whenever our intent as writers is primarily to gain the intellectual assent of our reader (when we want a reader to respond with "I agree" or "You're right), we are arguing to convince.

Arguing to Persuade

Persuasion, as we will consider it, is convincing *plus.* More than simply to earn the assent of readers, its aim is to influence their behavior as well, to move them to act upon the conviction to which they have assented. An advertisement for Mercedes-Benz aims not only to convince us that the company makes a high-quality car; it wants us to go out and buy one. A Sunday sermon asks for more than agreement with some interpretation of a biblical passage; the minister wants the congregation to apply the message to their lives. Persuasion asks us to *do* something—spend money, live a certain way, cast a vote, join a movement. Because we don't always act on our convictions, persuasion cannot rely on reasons alone; it must appeal in broader and deeper ways.

Usually persuasion appeals to the reader's emotions. We may be convinced by an argument that starving children deserve our help; but actually getting us to send money may require a photograph of a child with skeletal limbs and a hunger-bloated stomach. The intent of such tactics is clear: to reinforce reasons with pity, the better to move us to action.

To a greater extent than convincing, persuasion also relies on the personal appeal of the writer. To convince readers, a writer must earn their respect and trust; to persuade readers, a writer must get them to identify their own interests with those of the writer. A writer's personal charm may help, but such identification requires much more than that the reader like the writer. Any good feeling must be joined to something "higher" or "larger" than the writer, to something that the writer represents and that the reader would like to be associated with. A majority of Americans identified with Ronald Reagan, for example; his appeal combined personal likeableness with a larger anti-government sentiment, deeply rooted in American history. Similarly, Lee Iacocca managed for a time to get many Americans to identify with him as standing for the revival of American industry. Of course, few of us have the persuasive advantage of being a public figure. Nevertheless, we can ally ourselves with causes and values that our readers find sympathetic. Chapter 7 investigates the resources of identification in more detail.

Finally, in addition to relying on emotional and personal appeals, persuasion exploits the resources of language more fully than convincing does. To convince, our language must be clear and cogent so that readers can follow our case; to persuade, we need language that readers will remember and that will appeal by its sound and by the images it creates. In Chapter 7 we will also explore the persuasive resources of language, traditionally called *style.*

Arguing to Negotiate

By the time we find ourselves in a situation where our aim is to negotiate, we will have already attempted to convince an opponent of our case and to persuade that opponent to settle a conflict or dispute to our satisfaction. Our opponent will no doubt also have used convincing and persuading in an attempt to move us similarly. Yet neither side has been able to secure the assent of the other. At the same time "agreeing to disagree" is not a practical solution because the participants must come to some mutual agreement in order to pursue a necessary course of action.

In most instances of negotiation, the parties involved try to work out the conflict themselves because they have some relationship they wish to preserve—as employer and employee, business partners, family members, neighbors, even coauthors of an argument textbook. Common differences requiring negotiation include the amount of a raise or the terms of a contract, the wording of a bill in a Congressional committee and trade agreements among nations. In private life, negotiation helps roommates live together and families decide on everything from budgets to vacation destinations.

Just like other aims of argument, arguing to negotiate requires sound logic and clear presentation of positions and reasons. However, negotiation challenges our interpersonal skills more than do the other aims. Each side must listen closely to understand not just the other side's case but also the other side's emotional commitments and underlying values. Initiating such a conversation and keeping it going can sometimes be so difficult that an outside party, a mediator, must assist in the process. With or without a mediator, when negotiation works, the opposing sides begin to converge. Exchanging viewpoints and information and building empathy enables all parties to make concessions, to loosen their hold on their original positions, and finally to reach consensus—or at least a resolution that all participants find satisfactory.

As Chapter 8 makes clear, this final aim of argument brings us full circle, back to *dialogue,* to the processes involved in arguing to inquire. The major difference is that in negotiation we are less concerned with our own claims to truth than we are with overcoming conflict, with finding some common ground that will allow us to live and work together.

THE AIMS OF ARGUMENT: A SUMMARY

Argument (the assertion of an opinion, supported by a reason or reasons) is not an end in itself; rather we construct arguments to achieve something else. The major ends or aims of argument are:

Inquiry. *Forming our opinions or questioning those we already have.* The purpose of inquiry is to find and articulate what is true for us. Genuine classroom discussions are good examples of argument as inquiry.

Convincing. *Gaining assent from others through case-making.* In inquiry we look for reasons that convince us; in convincing we look for reasons that will gain the assent of our audience or readership. Good examples of convincing are a lawyer's brief or the justification a newspaper offers for supporting a political candidate.

Persuasion. *Moving others to action through rational, emotional, personal, and stylistic appeals.* Persuasion is convincing *plus;* that is, it uses reasons integrated with the other forms of appeal. Political speeches, sermons, and advertising are instances of arguing to persuade.

Negotiation. *Exploring differences of opinion in the hope of reaching agreement and/or cooperation.* The aim of negotiation is to build consensus, usually by making and asking for concessions. Argument as negotiation is typical of diplomacy, labor relations, and organizational decision-making. It is also common in private life to reduce or eliminate conflict between friends and family members.

WHAT IS RHETORIC?

In this book we will be looking at argument as a rhetorical art. *Rhetoric* originally meant "the art of persuasive *speaking,*" but the term has come to include written discourse as well. Whether oral or written, rhetoric always aims to influence an audience. By *art* we mean not "fine art"—painting, sculpture, music, and so on—but the principles underlying some activity that require education, experience, and judgment—the art of medicine, for example. Like medicine, rhetoric is a practical art: the art of speaking or writing well.

Studying rhetoric involves learning and applying a body of knowledge that originated in ancient Greece and has existed for about 2,400 years. Like all academic and professional fields, this body of knowledge has changed over time as our understanding of language and human nature has evolved. However, in his early analysis of persuasion, the Greek philosopher Aristotle identified three basic types of appeals, which have remained useful to the study of rhetoric through the centuries: *logos,* the use of logic, which appeals to the audience's reason and intellect; *ethos,* the speaker's attempts to project his or her own character as wise, ethical, and practical; and *pathos,* appeals to the emotions or sympathies of the audience.

In addition to these basic concepts, more specific sets of principles have appeared as rhetoric responded to developments in psychology, literature, and philosophy: principles for inventing and organizing arguments, for anticipating the needs of audiences, for building logical cases, and for polishing style and language. Rhetoric has also been influenced by historical developments, such as the spread of democracy and the rise of electronic media. This book combines current principles with the classical tradition to present a contemporary rhetoric for argument.

To a degree, you have been practicing the art of rhetoric all your life. For example, even as a small child you figured out how to convince your parents that you should be able to stay up an hour later or that you "deserved" a certain toy you wanted. Formal rhetoric builds on your aptitudes and experiences, allowing you to develop a more conscious and therefore more discriminating awareness of what you can achieve with argument.

Some people who speak or write well claim to have taught themselves. But most of us need more than our natural ability and experience, and even the talented few can improve by joining natural talents with conscious knowledge and informed, helpful feedback from others. For the purposes of this book, learning rhetoric means consciously applying formal knowledge about arguments and the aims of argument to what you already understand based on your experiences arguing informally. You will become more critical of what you do when you argue. You will also become a more critical listener to and reader of the arguments of others.

We want to stress that arguing well is an ethical act, for the authentic art of rhetoric is, in fact, ethical. The principles of rhetoric oblige a speaker or writer to make the best possible case and to respect the audience, rather than pander to or manipulate it. Too many public speakers and writers today practice an insincere rhetoric that has given the term negative connotations. As we will show, all of the aims of argument require sensitivity to questions of right and wrong.

Each of the major aims of argument has its own rhetoric—its own focus, principles, and methods—and in Chapters 5 through 8 we will take them up one by one, as though they were separate from one another. But we will also explore how they connect with each other and how they often work together in practice. Moreover, we will see how convincing builds on inquiry, how persuasion builds on convincing, and how negotiation integrates inquiry, convincing, and persuading.

Following Through

Recall a recent argument you made, either spoken or written. What was your point? Who was your audience? What was your main aim in arguing? Merely to express your opinion? To convince your audience to assent to your view on the issue? To get your audience to take some action? To negotiate a compromise? Can you think of another recent argument in which your aim was different?

CHAPTER TWO

Keeping a Writer's Notebook

In the past you may have kept a journal, a diary, a lab notebook, or some other written record with daily or weekly entries. A writer's notebook is like these in that it preserves a record of experiences and activities. It differs from them, however, in that it primarily records preparations for writing something else, such as a major essay or a term paper for one of your courses. You may have turned in a lab notebook for a grade; a writer's notebook has no other function than to help you sort out what you learn, accomplish, and think as you go through the stages of creating a finished piece of writing. A writer's notebook contains the writing you do before you write; it is a place to sketch out ideas, assess research, order what you have to say, and determine strategies and goals for writing.

WHY KEEP A NOTEBOOK?

Short, simple, and routine kinds of writing—personal letters, notes to friends, memos, and the like—require little preparation. We just sit down and write them. But much writing in college and professionally demands weeks, months, or—in the case of a book—even years of work. Some projects require extensive research and consultation, which will involve compiling and assessing large amounts of data and working one's way through complex chains of reasoning. Under such conditions even the best memory must fail without the aid of a notebook. Given life's distractions we will forget too much and recall imprecisely what we do manage to remember. With a writer's notebook we can preserve the idea that came to us as we were walking across campus or staring into space over our morning coffee. Throughout this book we will encourage you to use a writer's notebook extensively as you criticize and create arguments.

WAYS OF USING A NOTEBOOK

What sort of notebook entries might be appropriate? The simple answer is anything that helps, whatever you want to write down for future reference. Following are some more specific possibilities for using a writer's notebook.

To Explore Issues You Encounter in and out of Class

Your notebook is a place for freewriting—that is, private exploration for your eyes only. Such writing should not be judged as good or bad. Don't worry about organization, spelling, grammar, or any of the things that might concern you if someone else were to read your entries.

If you have been assigned a topic, write down your first impressions and opinions about it. If you will be choosing some of your own topics in a course, use the notebook to respond to controversial issues in the news or on campus. Your notebook can then become a source of ideas for your essays. Bring it with you to each class session so you can record ideas that come up during class discussions. In fact, a notebook can make you a better contributor to class discussion because it's easier to share your ideas publicly if you have roughed them out in writing first; use your notebook to respond to ideas presented in class and in every reading assignment.

To Copy Down and Analyze Assignments

If your instructor gives you a handout explaining an assignment, staple it to a page in the notebook. If not, write down the assignment word for word from the board or as it is dictated to you. In addition, take notes as your instructor explains the assignment. After class, take time to look over the assignment more carefully. What are the key words? Circle them and make sure you know exactly what they mean. Underline due dates and such information as paper length and format. Record any questions you have about the assignment, and ask your instructor for clarification at the first appropriate opportunity; you may also want to note down your instructor's answers.

To Work out a Timetable for Completing an Assignment

One way to avoid procrastination is to divide the time you have for completing an assignment into blocks: preparation, writing and rewriting, editing, making a final copy, and proofreading. Work out in your notebook how many days you can devote to preparation and research, how many to writing a first draft, how many to revising, how many to editing, and how many to the final typing and proofreading. Draft a tentative schedule for yourself. Your schedule will probably change as you complete the assignment, but mapping one out and attempting to stick to it should help you make steady progress rather than scramble at the last moment to get your paper in on time.

To Make Notes As You Research

No matter the type of research, you should have a place to record ideas, questions, and preliminary conclusions that occur to you as you read, discuss your ideas with others, conduct experiments, compile surveys and questionnaires, consult with experts, and pursue other types of information about your topic. Keep your notebook handy at all times, and write down as soon as possible whatever comes to mind, no matter how promising or unpromising it may initially seem. You can assess the value of your notes later when you have completed your research; but there will be nothing to assess if you do not keep a written record of your thoughts during the process.

To Respond to Arguments You Hear or Read

Your most immediate written responses to what you read are likely to be brief comments in a book's margins. Marginal annotation is a good habit to develop, but an equally good habit is to follow up your reading by jotting down more extended responses in your notebook. You might evaluate a text's strengths and weaknesses, compare the argument with other arguments you have read on the same topic, and make notes about how you might use material in the text to build your own argument (noting down page numbers at this point will make it easier to use such information in your paper later). We'll make more specific suggestions in Chapter 3 about how to read arguments.

To Write a Rhetorical Prospectus

A prospectus details a plan for a proposed work. A rhetorical prospectus gets you thinking not just about *what* you want to say, but about the rhetorical context in which you will say it: *to whom, how,* and—most importantly—*why* you are writing. In real-life arguments these elements are simply a given; but to write a successful argument for a class assignment, you usually have to create a rhetorical situation for yourself. In your notebook, explore

Your *thesis:* What are you claiming?
Your *aim:* What do you want to accomplish?
Your *audience:* Who should read this? Why? What are these people like?
Your *persona:* What is your relationship to the audience? How do you want them to perceive you?
Your *subject matter:* What does your thesis obligate you to discuss? What do you need to learn more about? How do you plan to get the information?
Your *organizational plan:* What should you talk about first? Where might that lead? What might you end with? (This need not be a complete outline; an overview will suffice.)

If you have trouble with the prospectus, discuss it with your instructor at a conference or with a tutor at the writing center, if your school has one.

To Record Useful Feedback

A student writer has at least two sources of feedback on ideas and drafts—other students and the instructor. Many writing classes are now designed to encourage such interaction. Throughout this book, we will suggest points in the writing process when seeking feedback may be a good idea. Examples of such times are:

At the point where your *initial ideas* have taken shape. Seeking feedback now helps you discover how well you can explain your ideas to others and how they respond.

After you and other students have *completed research* on common or similar topics. Feedback at this point allows you to share information and to compare evaluations of the sources.

At the completion of a *first draft*. At this point feedback uncovers what you need to do in a second draft in order to accommodate readers' needs, objections, and questions.

At the end of the *revising process*. This sort of feedback helps eliminate surface problems, such as awkward sentences, usage errors, misspellings, and typos.

You will benefit most from opportunities for feedback if you prepare yourself with specific questions to ask your instructor or classmates. What concerns *you* about how the project is going? Use your notebook to jot down such questions, and leave room to sum up the comments you receive. The suggestion that seems too good to forget during a conference can become elusive as you try to recall it a day or two later at your word processor.

To Assess a Graded Paper

We seldom learn all we could from the comments of instructors. If the comments are positive, we tend to bask in the warmth of praise; if not, we tend to be embarrassed, frustrated, even angry. Neither response is likely to make us better writers.

The best approach is to let the feelings play themselves out: Bask when you can, feel discouraged when you have to. Then resolve to sit down and look over the comments carefully, writing down in your notebook what you find useful for future reference. On the positive side, what did you do well? What did you learn that might carry over to the next assignment? On the not-so-positive side, can you detect any pattern in the shortcomings and errors your instructor has pointed out? If so, make a list of the types of problems you discover, and refer to them at an appropriate time when revising or editing or when composing your next essay. If, for example, you did not develop and support your points well, revise with this in mind or devote special attention to this issue as you plan and draft in the future. If you confuse plural *-s* with possessive *-s* endings, check all *-s* endings in subsequent final drafts.

It is natural to want to be done with a paper once you have turned it in, to get a grade and forget about it. Resist this desire long enough to record anything you can learn from your instructor's comments. In order to apply what you have learned to future assignments in future semesters, you will especially benefit from the self-assessment preserved in your notebook.

Following Through

What issues do you currently have strong opinions about? Although you 0can look to today's newspaper or the evening news for inspiration, think as well about events you've noticed on campus, at your job, or around your town—a change in course requirements for your planned major, for example, or a conflict over some aspect of the work environment or a proposed development on some land near your house. Write a notebook entry in which you list several possible topics for written arguments. Then pick one or two and create the briefest of arguments—a statement of your position followed by a statement of your best reason for holding that position. Think about who the audience for such an argument could be. Think also about your aim: Would you be arguing to inquire, convince, persuade, or negotiate?

CHAPTER THREE

Reading an Argument

Throughout this book you will be reading both professional and student-written arguments that provide examples of ways to argue. Many also offer multiple viewpoints on contemporary issues—conversations you will join when you write arguments of your own. You should read these arguments *critically,* taking on the role of a critic by *analyzing,* to see how the argument is put together, and by *evaluating,* to decide how well the argument achieves its aim and whether it advances a position that merits respect. Critical reading is not casual and should not be undertaken by a tired or distracted mind. Critical reading skills are essential to understanding the aims and methods of argument; we focus now on some specific methods for you to practice.

BEFORE YOU READ

Experts have found that readers who have the greatest success comprehending the ideas in any text meet two criteria: (1) They have some *prior knowledge* of the subject matter, and (2) they are able to see a piece of writing in its *rhetorical context.* Such readers can use context to determine the meaning of unfamiliar words, and they are often able to "read between the lines," recognizing ideas and assumptions that are only implied. Let's look at these two factors with an eye towards argument.

Recalling Prior Knowledge

Virtually every piece of writing about an issue is part of an ongoing conversation, involving a number of participants who represent a range of opinions and who have each contributed a variety of ideas, facts, and authoritative citations to the debate. The greater a reader's familiarity with this background, the easier it is for him or her to approach a new argument from a critical perspective, filling in any gaps of information and recognizing a writer's assumptions and biases.

Therefore, it makes sense to take some time before you start reading to recall what you already know about the topic: the basic issues involved and the perspectives you have read or heard expressed. Use your writer's notebook to record what you remember. And don't neglect to consider your own opinions about the issue. If you are conscious of the attitudes and ideas you bring to your reading, you can better see an argument in its own light and not so much colored by your own biases.

Following Through

You are about to read an argument entitled "Pornography Hurts Women." The three words of this title tell you that the argument will focus on the negative effects of explicit sexual material on women as a group.

In your writer's notebook, jot down some of the arguments you have heard or read on this issue. How would you define pornography? What arguments have been made against it, and by whom? Who defends the publication and sale of pornography, and why? How does pornography depict women? Are men depicted differently?

Considering the Rhetorical Context

Critical readers breathe life into a written argument by seeing it as part of a dynamic activity. They think of the author as a human being with hopes, fears, biases, ambitions, and—most importantly—a purpose that his or her words on the page are intended to accomplish. The argument becomes an action, aimed at affecting a particular audience in a particular place and time.

Publishers' notes and editorial headnotes often include information and clues that can help you answer the following questions about rhetorical context:

When was this argument written? (If not recently, how might it be helpful to know something about the time it first appeared?)

Why was it written? What prompted its creation?

Who is the author, and what is his or her occupation, personal background, political leanings?

Where does the article appear? If it is reprinted, where did it appear originally?

For whom do you think the author is writing?

What purpose does the author have in writing? What does he or she hope to accomplish through the act of making this argument?

Following Through

Read the following editorial headnote for the argument "Pornography

Hurts Women," inferring what you can about its rhetorical context. Use your writer's notebook to record your thoughts. Can you make any connections between the context you infer and your prior knowledge of the topic?

> Susan Brownmiller (b. 1935), a feminist writer and graduate of Cornell University, is founder of the organization Women Against Pornography. This argument is excerpted from her book *Against Our Will: Men, Women, and Rape* (1975).

As you read the essay, you may revise or correct some of your inferences about the rhetorical context. In fact, all reading involves revision of expectations, and it is better to define some initial expectations rather than to begin with none or only vague ones.

AS YOU READ

Critical reading never involves reading a text only once. In fact, critical reading should take you through a text at least three times. Here we will suggest some goals for each of these three readings, but you are likely to have your own way of noting ideas and making connections. Be ready to record whatever thoughts come to mind whenever they do.

The First Reading

Your first reading of any text is an exploration of new territory. You might prefer to start at the beginning and simply read the selection straight through. But it's a good idea to look first at the opening and closing paragraphs, where you will often find explicit statements of the author's thesis and additional clues to help you construct the rhetorical context. You might also scan the text, looking at major headings (if any) and the first sentences of paragraphs. Then read through the essay at a moderate pace.

During this first reading, don't feel compelled to make marks in the text, beyond circling words to look up; but don't hesitate to make marginal notes if thoughts or questions occur to you.

Following Through

Before you read the following argument, "Pornography Hurts Women," look at the first and last paragraphs, and at the first sentence in each paragraph. Try to determine the intended audience and the author's main point and purpose. Is Brownmiller more sympathetic toward conservatives or liberals? Which group is her likely audience? What is her complaint? Finally, read the entire argument. In your writer's notebook add what you have learned or newly inferred about the rhetorical context.

SUSAN BROWNMILLER

Pornography Hurts Women

PORNOGRAPHY HAS been so thickly glossed over with the patina of chic these days in the name of verbal freedom and sophistication that important distinctions between freedom of political expression (a democratic necessity), honest sex education for children (a societal good), and ugly smut (the deliberate devaluation of the role of women through obscene, distorted depictions) have been hopelessly confused. Part of the problem is that those who traditionally have been the most vigorous opponents of porn are often those same people who shudder at the explicit mention of any sexual subject. Under their watchful, vigilante eyes, frank and free dissemination of educational materials relating to abortion, contraception, the act of birth, and female biology in general is also dangerous, subversive, and dirty. (I am not unmindful that frank and free discussion of rape, "the unspeakable crime," might well give these righteous vigilantes further cause to shudder.) Because the battle lines were falsely drawn a long time ago, before there was a vocal women's movement, the antipornography forces appear to be, for the most part, religious, Southern, conservative, and right-wing, while the pro-porn forces are identified as Eastern, atheistic, and liberal.

But a woman's perspective demands a totally new alignment, or at least a fresh appraisal. The majority report of the President's Commission on Obscenity and Pornography (1970), a report that argued strongly for the removal of all legal restrictions on pornography, soft and hard, made plain that 90 percent of all pornographic material is geared to the male heterosexual market (the other 10 percent is geared to the male homosexual taste), that buyers of porn are "predominantly white, middle-class, middle-aged married males," and that the graphic depictions, the meat and potatoes of porn, are of the naked female body and of the multiplicity of acts done to that body.

Discussing the content of stag films, "a familiar and firmly established part of the American scene," the commission report dutifully, if foggily, explained, "Because pornography historically has been thought to be primarily a masculine interest, the emphasis in stag films seems to represent the preferences of the middle-class American male. Thus male homosexuality and bestiality are relatively rare, while lesbianism is rather common."

The commissioners in this instance had merely verified what purveyors of porn have always known: hard-core pornography is not a celebration of sexual freedom; it is a cynical exploitation of female sexual activity through the device of making all such activity, and consequently all females, "dirty." Heterosexual male consumers of pornography are frankly turned on by watching lesbians in action (although never in the final scenes, but always as a curtain raiser); they are turned off with the sudden swiftness of a water faucet by watching naked men act upon each other. One study quoted in the commission report came to the unastounding conclusion that "seeing a stag film in the presence of male peers bolsters masculine esteem." Indeed. The men in groups who watch the films, it is important to note, are *not* naked.

When male response to pornography is compared to female response, a 5
pronounced difference in attitude emerges. According to the commission, "Males report being more highly aroused by depictions of nude females, and show more interest in depictions of nude females than [do] females." Quoting the figures of Alfred Kinsey,[1] the commission noted that a majority of males (77 percent) were "aroused" by visual depictions of explicit sex while a majority of females (68 percent) were not aroused. Further, "females more often than males reported 'disgust' and 'offense.'"

From whence comes this female disgust and offense? Are females sexually backward or more conservative by nature? The gut distaste that a majority of women feel when we look at pornography, a distaste that, incredibly, it is no longer fashionable to admit, comes, I think, from the gut knowledge that we and our bodies are being stripped, exposed, and contorted for the purpose of ridicule to bolster that "masculine esteem" which gets its kick and sense of power from viewing females as anonymous, panting playthings, adult toys, dehumanized objects to be used, abused, broken, and discarded.

This, of course, is also the philosophy of rape. It is no accident (for what else could be its purpose?) that females in the pornographic genre are depicted in two cleanly delineated roles: as virgins who are caught and "banged" or as nymphomaniacs who are never sated. The most popular and prevalent pornographic fantasy combines the two: an innocent, untutored female is raped and "subjected to unnatural practices" that turn her into a raving, slobbering nymphomaniac, a dependent sexual slave who can never get enough of the big, male cock.

There can be no "equality" in porn, no female equivalent, no turning of the tables in the name of bawdy fun. Pornography, like rape, is a male invention, designed to dehumanize women, to reduce the female to an object of sexual access, not to free sensuality from moralistic or parental inhibition. The staple of porn will always be the naked female body, breasts and genitals exposed, because as man devised it, her naked body is the female's "shame," her private parts the private property of man, while his are the ancient, holy, universal, patriarchal instrument of his power, his rule by force over *her.*

Pornography is the undiluted essence of anti-female propaganda. Yet the very same liberals who were so quick to understand the method and purpose behind the mighty propaganda machine of Hitler's Third Reich, the consciously spewed-out anti-Semitic caricatures and obscenities that gave an ideological base to the Holocaust and the Final Solution, the very same liberals who, enlightened by blacks, searched their own conscience and came to understand that their tolerance of "nigger" jokes and portrayals of shuffling, rolling-eyed servants in movies perpetuated the degrading myths of black inferiority and gave an ideo-

[1]Alfred Kinsey was the senior author of two studies of Americans' sexual behavior, published in 1948 and 1953. Known as the "Kinsey Reports," the books were based on interviews with over 10,000 men and women.

logical base to the continuation of black oppression—these very same liberals now fervidly maintain that the hatred and contempt for women that find expression in four-letter words used as expletives and in what are quaintly called "adult" or "erotic" books and movies are a valid extension of freedom of speech that must be preserved as a Constitutional right.

To defend the right of a lone, crazed American Nazi to grind out propa- 10
ganda calling for the extermination of all Jews, as the ACLU[2] has done in the name of free speech, is, after all, a self-righteous and not particularly courageous stand, for American Jewry is not currently threatened by storm troopers, concentration camps, and imminent extermination, but I wonder if the ACLU's position might change if, come tomorrow morning, the bookstores and movie theaters lining Forty-second Street in New York City were devoted not to the humiliation of women by rape and torture, as they currently are, but to a systematized commercially successful propaganda machine depicting the sadistic pleasures of gassing Jews or lynching blacks?

Is this analogy extreme? Not if you are a woman who is conscious of the ever-present threat of rape and the proliferation of a cultural ideology that makes it sound like "liberated" fun. The majority report of the President's Commission on Obscenity and Pornography tried to pooh-pooh the opinion of law enforcement agencies around the country that claimed their own concrete experience with offenders who were caught with the stuff led them to conclude that pornographic material is a causative factor in crimes of sexual violence. The commission maintained that it was not possible at this time to scientifically prove or disprove such a connection.

But does one need scientific methodology in order to conclude that the antifemale propaganda that permeates our nation's cultural output promotes a climate in which acts of sexual hostility directed against women are not only tolerated but ideologically encouraged? A similar debate has raged for many years over whether or not the extensive glorification of violence (the gangster as hero; the loving treatment accorded bloody shoot-'em-ups in movies, books and on TV) has a causal effect, a direct relationship to the rising rate of crime, particularly among youth. Interestingly enough, in this area—nonsexual and not specifically related to abuses against women—public opinion seems to be swinging to the position that explicit violence in the entertainment media does have a deleterious effect; it makes violence commonplace, numbingly routine and no longer morally shocking.

More to the point, those who call for a curtailment of scenes of violence in movies and on television in the name of sensitivity, good taste, and what's best for our children are not accused of being pro-censorship or against freedom of speech. Similarly, minority group organizations, black, Hispanic, Japanese, Italian, Jewish, or American Indian, that campaign against ethnic slurs and demeaning portrayals in movies, on television shows, and in commercials are perceived

[2]Founded in 1917, the American Civil Liberties Union is a nonpartisan organization dedicated to defending the principles stated in the Bill of Rights.

as waging a just political fight, for if a minority group claims to be offended by a specific portrayal, be it Little Black Sambo or the Frito Bandito,[3] and relates it to a history of ridicule and oppression, few liberals would dare to trot out a Constitutional argument in theoretical opposition, not if they wish to maintain their liberal credentials. Yet when it comes to the treatment of women, the liberal consciousness remains fiercely obdurate, refusing to be budged, for the sin of appearing square or prissy in the age of the so-called sexual revolution has become the worst offense of all.

The Second Reading

The goals for your second reading are to recognize the structure of the argument and to wrestle with any difficult passages.

Analyzing Structure

By structure we mean the writer's plan or strategy. Different parts of an argument have different jobs to do, which may include:

Providing background
Offering and developing a reason
Giving an opposing view
Rebutting an opposing view

If the writer's case has been tightly crafted, breaking the essay into its parts can be like breaking a Hershey Bar into its already well-defined segments. Other arguments are more loosely structured, however, and their divisions less readily discernible; even with these, though, close analysis will generally reveal some fault lines that indicate specific divisions, and it will be possible to see the roles played by the various chunks that result. As you read a second time, draw lines across the page between the paragraphs where you detect dividing points. (Some chunks may be single paragraphs, others groups of as many as five or more.) Then try to describe the function of each part. One possible break in Brownmiller's essay occurs between paragraphs 8 and 9. Paragraphs 2 through 8 establish the first reason that liberals should change their position and oppose pornography: Pornography is made by and for men with the purpose of dehumanizing women and is, therefore, "anti-female propaganda," as Brownmiller succinctly states at the beginning of paragraph 9. The audience must first be convinced of this point in

[3]Little Black Sambo is the main character in *The Story of Little Black Sambo*, a children's book written in 1899 by a Scot, Helen Bannerman, who was then living in India. In the original British version, the clever Sambo escapes tigers and other perils in an imaginary jungle-land that blends India and Africa. But the illustrations in twentieth-century American editions portrayed the black characters as racist stereotypes of the pre-Civil War South. The Frito Bandito was a cartoon character used by the Frito-Lay Company in its advertisements during the 1960s. It was withdrawn in the early 1970s after protests that it presented a false and demeaning stereotype of Mexican-Americans.

order to accept the second reason Brownmiller offers for opposing pornography, which she develops from paragraph 9 through the end of the argument: Liberals should see pornography as analogous to films and literature that encourage hatred of and violence toward blacks, Jews, or other religious and ethnic minorities. The conclusion, or main claim, of the argument is that if liberal readers oppose films and literature that demean and attack minorities, they should also oppose pornography that demeans and attacks women.

Looking at Brownmiller's essay in more detail, we can analyze the structure by noting how each reason is developed:

Paragraph 1 introduces the traditional opposing viewpoints in the debate about pornography and shows how the thinking that has led to the taking of these sides is inadequate.

Paragraphs 2, 3, and 4 give evidence that pornography focuses on women as sex objects and establish that men are the producers and consumers of pornography, with women's bodies its subject matter.

Paragraphs 5 and 6 give evidence that pornography dehumanizes women and compare male and female reactions to pornography—respectively, arousal and disgust.

Paragraphs 7 and 8 give evidence that pornography victimizes women just as rape does and compare the motives underlying pornography to those underlying rape.

Paragraphs 9 and 10 first summarize the point that pornography is anti-female propaganda, then argue that pornography is similar to other forms of propaganda that liberals oppose on the grounds that they denigrate and victimize minorities.

Paragraphs 11 and 12 suggest a cause and effect relationship between pornography and violence against women.

Paragraph 13 concludes with a restatement of the appeal for consistency made in paragraphs 9 and 10 (those who oppose hate literature should also oppose pornography).

Working Through Difficult Passages

In order to wrestle with a text's more difficult passages, you should first mark those passages. Then, look up any words or phrases that are obstacles to understanding. Finally, write a paraphrase of the passage, using your own words. Rewriting a complicated idea in your own words makes you think it through and helps you understand it better.

One sort of difficulty can arise because of long sentences with many modifying word groups. As you paraphrase such passages, try rewriting using shorter sentences that will break down the ideas in the original and let you see them more clearly. (See pages 581–584 for more on paraphrasing.)

Another difficulty may result from a writer's use of metaphors. A metaphor is a way of seeing one thing in terms of something else. For example, we commonly describe the act of beginning to love someone in terms of falling: "falling in love." The meanings we associate with literal falling—loss of control, being a victim of circumstance—are carried over into the new context of describing an emotional state. We tend not even to notice such common metaphors, but an unusual metaphor in an unfamiliar context will make us stop to think.

For example, Brownmiller in her first sentence uses the metaphor "patina of chic" to describe the trendy acceptance of pornography. What is a patina, literally? How can we paraphrase "patina of chic?" This metaphor should alert a critical reader to Brownmiller's audience and purpose: She wants to get her liberal readers to see pornography as she sees it.

Remember that metaphors are everywhere, not just in poetry and fiction. You may find a passage of argumentative writing difficult if you try to read a literal meaning into a metaphorical passage.

Following Through

Paragraph 9 of Brownmiller's essay could be described as difficult because it makes a complicated comparison and because it contains an extremely long sentence in which the subject—"liberals"—is repeated three times accompanied by many modifiers before its verb—"maintain"—finally appears. It is also difficult because an abstract concept—the "ideological base" Brownmiller refers to—is central to understanding the point. Can you infer from this paragraph and those that follow what Brownmiller means by "ideological base"? In your writer's notebook, paraphrase paragraph 9.

The Third Reading

Chapter 5 of this book, "Preparing to Write: Arguing to Inquire," explores and explains in depth how a reader can enter into a dialogue with the writer of an argument—by posing questions to the writer and using the text itself as a basis for imagining the writer's responses. Such an extended dialogue is the best inquiry into a written argument, but a faster substitute is to raise questions and anticipate the objections of those with opposing views directly in the margins of the printed text. In your third reading you should raise such questions even if you yourself agree with the writer's argument: It may be easier (and more fun) to challenge arguments you disagree with, but if you are studying arguments as claims to truth, it is even more important to challenge the views you find most sympathetic.

Even if you oppose a writer's position, you should be open in your third reading to recognizing valid points and good reasoning. This kind of critical reading enlarges your understanding of an issue and opens your mind to new perspectives. In fact, it may cause you to change your mind.

Following are some things to look for when annotating an argument.

READING ARGUMENTS CRITICALLY

Note the *main claim,* or *thesis,* of the argument, if it appears explicitly. If it does not, paraphrase it in the margin.

Pick out and mark the *main reasons* in support of the thesis. (Don't expect to find many such major reasons; in a good argument, much space and effort may go toward developing and supporting even one reason.)

Consider the *evidence* offered, and write marginal comments about the reasons themselves and how well they are supported. Question evidence both in terms of quantity and quality.

Note *key terms* and how the writer defines (or fails to define) them. Would most readers agree with the definitions? How would you define or illustrate key terms that need clarification?

If the writer presents any *analogies,* are the things being compared truly similar? Note any problems.

Are there any *contradictions?* Does any evidence cited in the text contradict other evidence in the text or other evidence you know about that is not cited?

Upon what *assumptions* are the thesis and reasons based? Does the argument, or any of its reasons, rest upon an assumption that all readers may not share?

Where, if at all, are *opposing views* represented? Do you think they are depicted fairly?

What is your *personal response?* What do you agree with? What seems true to you? What do you disagree with? Why?

Following Through

Read "Pornography Hurts Women" a third time, making marginal annotations as you go. Consider the following: Does Brownmiller define pornography? If not, why do you think she does not? If she does, would everyone agree with her definition? Do you accept her evidence regarding what pornography depicts? How well does she support her cause-and-effect argument about violence against women? Do you think any of the data and evidence that Brownmiller used in the 1970s has become outdated? How does she represent the viewpoint of her opposition—the liberals—and their motives?

Following, we have annotated the first three paragraphs of "Pornography Hurts Women" as an example.

SUSAN BROWNMILLER

Pornography Hurts Women

PORNOGRAPHY HAS been so thickly glossed over with the patina of chic these days in the name of verbal freedom and sophistication that important distinctions between freedom of political expression (a democratic necessity), honest sex education for children (a societal good), and ugly smut (the deliberate devaluation of the role of women through obscene, distorted depictions) have been hopelessly confused. Part of the problem is that those who traditionally have been the most vigorous opponents of porn are often those same people who shudder at the explicit mention of any sexual subject. Under their watchful, vigilante eyes, frank and free dissemination of educational materials relating to abortion, contraception, the act of birth, and female biology in general is also dangerous, subversive, and dirty. (I am not unmindful that frank and free discussion of rape, "the unspeakable crime," might well give these righteous vigilantes further cause to shudder.) Because the battle lines were falsely drawn a long time ago, before there was a vocal women's movement, the antipornography forces appear to be, for the most part, religious, Southern, conservative, and right-wing, while the pro-porn forces are identified as Eastern, atheistic, and liberal.

But a woman's perspective demands a totally new alignment, or at least a fresh appraisal. The majority report of the President's Commission on Obscenity and Pornography (1970), a report that argued strongly for the removal of all legal restrictions on pornography, soft and hard, made plain that 90 percent of all pornographic material is geared to the male heterosexual market (the other 10 percent is geared to the male homosexual taste), that buyers of porn are "predominantly white, middle-class, middle-aged married males," and that the graphic depictions, the meat and potatoes of porn, are of the naked female body and of the multiplicity of acts done to that body.

Discussing the content of stag films, "a familiar and firmly established part of the American scene," the commission report dutifully, if foggily, explained, "Because pornography historically has been thought to be primarily a masculine interest, the emphasis in stag films seems to represent the preferences of the middle-class American male. Thus male homosexuality and bestiality are relatively rare, while lesbianism is rather common."

AFTER YOU READ

The person who has invested time and effort in critical reading has usually become engaged enough in the text and the issue it deals with to be curious about others' reactions to the same argument. As a student in a college course, you will be able to compare your responses to arguments with the responses of other students and your instructor. Thus, critical reading is a way for you to enter the ongoing conversation that serves to create knowledge itself. For professionals in all fields, conversations about one another's arguments go on all the time—orally, in meetings and at conferences, and in writing, through informal critiques as well as articles in popular and professional journals. Ultimately, such conversations establish and refine the bodies of knowledge that constitute the various disciplines and professions.

Finally, any reading should point you in the direction of further reading. For example, you might find references to other books or articles on the topic; many scholarly arguments conclude with a bibliography showing works the author consulted. Or, you might want to read some more arguments by the same author, which would give you insight into his or her biases and motives for writing. If what you are reading was published some time ago, as is the case with Brownmiller's argument, you could follow up by reading more recent arguments on the same issue. In the debate over pornography, for example, you could read what feminists scholars such as Catharine MacKinnon are saying today. Following any of these paths will improve your critical reading ability by increasing your knowledge of the topic and the context in which it is debated.

Following Through

In your writer's notebook, respond to Brownmiller's argument. Do you accept her argument? If you do, why? If not, why not? If you disagree, is there yet some truth to any of what she claims? What would you have to know more about to arrive at the best position, the position closest to the truth, on the question of whether pornographic material negatively affects the image and treatment of women in our society? Be prepared to discuss your response in class.

CHAPTER FOUR

Analyzing an Argument: A Simplified Toulmin Method

In Chapter 3 we discussed the importance of reading arguments critically: breaking them down into their parts to see how they are put together, noting in the margins key terms that are not defined, raising questions about the writer's claims or evidence. Although these general techniques are sufficient for analyzing many arguments, sometimes—especially with intricate arguments and with arguments that we sense are faulty without being able to define the weakness—we need a more systematic technique.

In this chapter we explain and illustrate such a technique based on the work of Stephen Toulmin, a contemporary philosopher who has contributed a great deal to our understanding of argumentation. This method will allow you to analyze the logic of any argument you encounter, whether written or verbal; you will also find it useful in examining the logic of your own arguments as you draft and revise them. Keep in mind, however, that because it is limited to analysis of logic, the Toulmin method provides an incomplete basis for evaluating an argument. It is also important to question an argument through dialog (see Chapter 5) and to look at the appeals of character, emotion, and style (see Chapter 6).

A PRELIMINARY CRITICAL READING

Before we consider the Toulmin method, first explore the following argument carefully, using the general process for critical reading we described in Chapter 3.

WILLIAM F. MAY

Rising to the Occasion of Our Death

William F. May (b. 1927) is a distinguished professor of ethics at Southern Methodist University. The following essay appeared originally in The Christian Century *(1990).*

FOR MANY parents, a Volkswagen van is associated with putting children to sleep on a camping trip. Jack Kevorkian, a Detroit pathologist, has now linked the van with the veterinarian's meaning of "putting to sleep." Kevorkian conducted a dinner interview with Janet Elaine Adkins, a 54-year-old Alzheimer's patient, and her husband and then agreed to help her commit suicide in his VW van. Kevorkian pressed beyond the more generally accepted practice of passive euthanasia (allowing a patient to die by withholding or withdrawing treatment) to active euthanasia (killing for mercy).

Kevorkian, moreover, did not comply with the strict regulations that govern active euthanasia in, for example, the Netherlands. Holland requires that death be imminent (Adkins had beaten her son in tennis just a few days earlier); it demands a more professional review of the medical evidence and the patient's resolution than a dinner interview with a physician (who is a stranger and who does not treat patients) permits; and it calls for the final, endorsing signatures of two doctors.

So Kevorkian-bashing is easy. But the question remains: Should we develop a judicious, regulated social policy permitting voluntary euthanasia for the terminally ill? Some moralists argue that the distinction between allowing to die and killing for mercy is petty quibbling over technique. Since the patient in any event dies—whether by acts of omission or commission—the route to death doesn't really matter. The way modern procedures have made dying at the hands of the experts and their machines such a prolonged and painful business has further fueled the euthanasia movement, which asserts not simply the right to die but the right to be killed.

But other moralists believe that there is an important moral distinction between allowing to die and mercy killing. The euthanasia movement, these critics contend, wants to engineer death rather than face dying. Euthanasia would bypass dying to make one dead as quickly as possible. It aims to relieve suffering by knocking out the interval between life and death. It solves the problem of suffering by eliminating the sufferer.

The impulse behind the euthanasia movement is understandable in an age 5
when dying has become such an inhumanly endless business. But the movement may fail to appreciate our human capacity to rise to the occasion of our death. The best death is not always the sudden death. Those forewarned of death and given time to prepare for it have time to engage in acts of reconciliation. Also,

advanced grieving by those about to be bereaved may ease some of their pain. Psychiatrists have observed that those who lose a loved one accidentally have a more difficult time recovering from the loss than those who have suffered through an extended period of illness before the death. Those who have lost a close relative by accident are more likely to experience what Geoffrey Gorer has called limitless grief. The community, moreover, may need its aged and dependent, its sick and its dying, and the virtues which they sometimes evince—the virtues of humility, courage, and patience—just as much as the community needs the virtues of justice and love manifest in the agents of care.

On the whole, our social policy should allow terminal patients to die but it should not regularize killing for mercy. Such a policy would recognize and respect that moment in illness when it no longer makes sense to bend every effort to cure or to prolong life and when one must allow patients to do their own dying. This policy seems most consonant with the obligations of the community to care and of the patient to finish his or her course.

Advocates of active euthanasia appeal to the principle of patient autonomy—as the use of the phrase "voluntary euthanasia" indicates. But emphasis on the patient's right to determine his or her destiny often harbors an extremely naïve view of the uncoerced nature of the decision. Patients who plead to be put to death hardly make unforced decisions if the terms and conditions under which they receive care already nudge them in the direction of the exit. If the elderly have stumbled around in their apartments, alone and frightened for years, or if they have spent years warehoused in geriatrics barracks, then the decision to be killed for mercy hardly reflects an uncoerced decision. The alternative may be so wretched as to push patients toward this escape. It is a huge irony and, in some cases, hypocrisy to talk suddenly about a compassionate killing when the aging and dying may have been starved for compassion for many years. To put it bluntly, a country has not earned the moral right to kill for mercy unless it has already sustained and supported life mercifully. Otherwise we kill for compassion only to reduce the demands on our compassion. This statement does not charge a given doctor or family member with impure motives. I am concerned here not with the individual case but with the cumulative impact of a social policy.

I can, to be sure, imagine rare circumstances in which I hope I would have the courage to kill for mercy—when the patient is utterly beyond human care, terminal, and in excruciating pain. A neurosurgeon once showed a group of physicians and an ethicist the picture of a Vietnam casualty who had lost all four limbs in a landmine explosion. The catastrophe had reduced the soldier to a trunk with his face transfixed in horror. On the battlefield I would hope that I would have the courage to kill the sufferer with mercy.

But hard cases do not always make good laws or wise social policies. Regularized mercy killings would too quickly relieve the community of its obligation to provide good care. Further, we should not always expect the law to provide us with full protection and coverage for what, in rare circumstances, we may morally need to do. Sometimes the moral life calls us out into a no-man's-land where we cannot expect total security and protection under the law. But no one said that the moral life is easy.

A STEP-BY-STEP DEMONSTRATION OF THE TOULMIN METHOD

The Toulmin method requires an analysis of the claim, the reasons offered to support the claim, and the evidence offered to support the reasons, along with analysis of any refutations offered.

Analyzing the Claim

Logical analysis begins with identifying the *claim,* the thesis or central contention, along with any specific qualifications or exceptions.

Identify the Claim

First ask yourself, *what statement is the author defending?* In "Rising to the Occasion of Our Death," for example, William May spells out his claim in paragraph 6:

> Our social policy should allow terminal patients to die but it should not regularize killing for mercy.

In his claim, May supports passive euthanasia (letting someone die by withholding or discontinuing treatment) but opposes "regularizing" (making legal or customary) active euthanasia (administering, say, an overdose of morphine to cause a patient's death).

Much popular argumentation is sometimes careless about what exactly is being claimed: Untrained arguers too often content themselves with just taking sides ("Euthanasia is wrong"). Note that May, a student of ethics trained in philosophical argumentation, makes a claim that is both specific and detailed. Whenever an argument does not include an explicit statement of its claim, you should begin your analysis by stating the writer's claim yourself. Try to state all claims fully and carefully in sentence form, as May's claim is stated.

Look for Qualifiers

Next ask, *how is the claim qualified?* Is it absolute, or does it include words or phrases to indicate that it may not hold true in every situation or set of circumstances?

May qualifies his claim with the phrase "on the whole" (paragraph 6), indicating that he recognizes possible exceptions to the application of his claim. Other possible qualifiers include "typically," "usually," and "most of the time." Careful arguers are generally wary of making absolute claims. While unqualified claims are not necessarily faulty in themselves, they do insist that there are no cases or circumstances in which the claim might legitimately be contradicted.

Qualifying words or phrases are often used to restrict a claim and improve its defensibility.

Find the Exceptions

Finally ask, *in what cases or circumstances would the writer not press his or her claim?* Look for any explicit exceptions the writer offers to qualify the claim.

May, for example, is quite clear in paragraph 8 about when he would not press his claim: "I hope I would have the courage to kill for mercy—when the patient is utterly beyond human care, terminal, and in excruciating pain." Once he has specified these conditions in abstract terms, he goes further and offers a chilling example of a case when he believes mercy-killing would be appropriate. Nevertheless, he insists that such exceptions are rare and thus do not justify making active euthanasia legal or allowing it to become common social policy.

Critical readers respond to unqualified claims skeptically—by hunting for exceptions. With qualified claims they look to see what specific exceptions the writer will admit and what considerations make restrictions necessary or desirable.

Summarize the Claim

At this point it is a good idea to write out the claim, its qualifiers, and its exceptions in your writer's notebook, so that you can see all of them clearly. For May they look like this:

(qualifier)	"On the whole,"
(claim)	"our social policy should allow terminal patients to die but it should not regularize killing for mercy."
(exception)	". . . when the patient is utterly beyond care, terminal, and in excruciating pain."

Record the claim and its qualifiers and exceptions in whatever way helps you to see them best, but do not skip this step. Not only will it help you remember the results of your initial claim analysis; you will also be building on this summary as you go on to analyze the argument in more detail.

Analyzing Reasons

Once you have analyzed the claim, you should next identify and evaluate the reasons offered for the claim.

List the Reasons

Begin by asking yourself, *why is the writer advancing this claim?* Look for any statement or statements that are used to justify the thesis.

May groups all of his reasons in paragraph 5:

The dying should have time to prepare for death and to reconcile with relatives and friends.

Those close to the dying should have time to come to terms with the impending loss of a loved one.

The community needs examples of dependent but patient and courageous people who sometimes do "die with dignity."
The community needs the virtues ("justice and love") of those who care for the sick and dying.

When you list reasons, you need not preserve the exact words of the arguer. Often doing so is impossible, since reasons are not always explicitly spelled out but may have to be inferred. Be very careful, however, to adhere as closely as possible to the writer's language; otherwise, your analysis can easily go astray, imposing a reason of your own that the writer did not have in mind.

Note that reasons, like claims, can be qualified. May does not say, for instance, that "the aged and dependent" *always* show "the virtues of humility, courage, and patience." He implicitly admits that they can be ornery and cowardly as well. But for May's purposes, it is enough that they sometimes manifest the virtues he admires.

Use your writer's notebook to list the reasons following your summary of the claim, qualifiers, and exceptions. One possibility is to list them beneath the summary of the claim in the form of a tree diagram (see the diagram on page 34).

Examine the Reasons

There are two questions to ask as you go on to examine the reasons you have listed. First, *are they really good reasons?* A reason is only as good as the values it invokes or implies. A value is something we think is good, worth pursuing for its own sake or because it leads to attaining other goods. For each reason you should specify the values involved and then determine whether you accept those values as generally binding.

Second ask, *is the reason relevant to the thesis?* In other words, does the relationship between the claim and the reason hold up to examination? For example, the claim "You should buy a new car from Fred Freed" cannot be supported by the reason "Fred is a family man with three cute kids" unless you accept a relationship between an auto dealer's having cute children and his or her reliability in dealing with customers.

Be careful and deliberate as you examine whether reasons are good and whether they are relevant. No other step is as important in assessing the logic of an argument, and no other can be quite as tricky.

To illustrate, consider May's first reason: Those who know they are about to die should have time to prepare for death and to seek reconciliation with people from whom they have become estranged. Is this a good reason? Most of us would probably think so, valuing the chance to prepare for death and to reconcile ourselves with estranged friends or family members. Not to do so would seem immature, irresponsible, unforgiving.

But is the reason relevant? May seems to rule out the possibility that a dying person seeking active euthanasia would be able to prepare for death and reconcile with others. But this is obviously not the case. Terminally ill people who decide to arrange for their own deaths may make any number of preparations beforehand, so the connection between this reason and May's claim is really quite weak.

A Toulmin Model for Analyzing Arguments

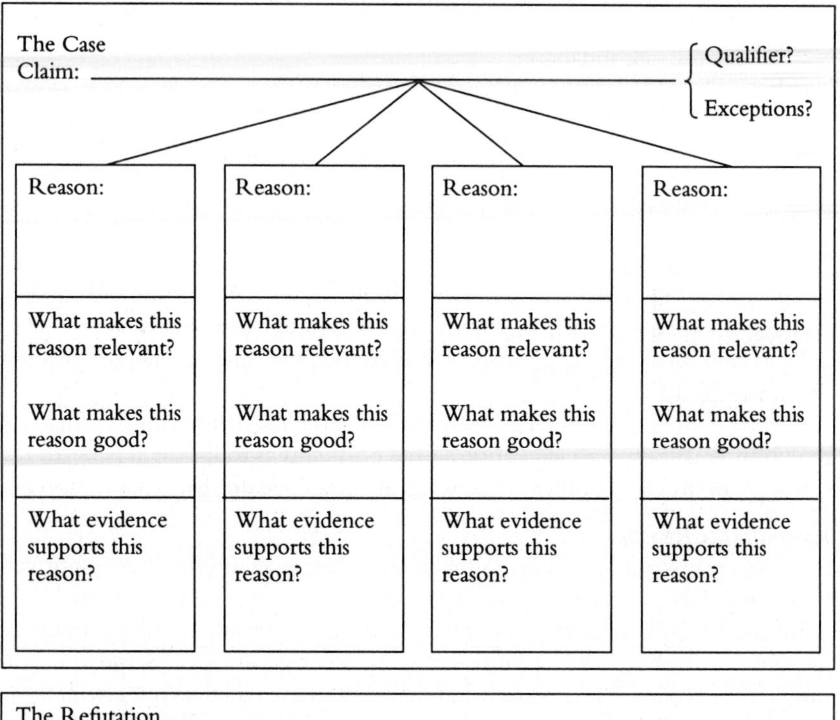

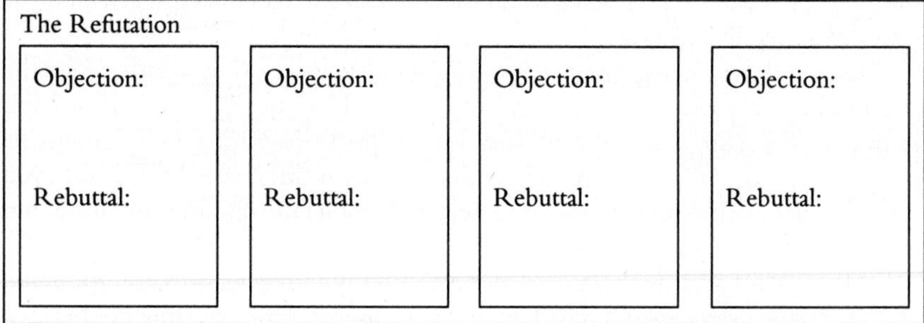

To accept a connection, we would have to assume that active euthanasia necessarily amounts to a sudden death without adequate preparation; since we cannot do so, we are entitled to question the relevance of the reason, no matter how good it might be in itself.

Following Through

Now examine May's second, third, and fourth reasons on your own, as we have just examined the first one. Make notes about each reason, evaluating how good each is in itself and how relevant it is to the thesis. In your notebook, you will be creating your own diagram based on the model on page 34.

Analyzing Evidence

Once you have finished your analysis of the reasons, the next step is to consider the evidence offered to support any of those reasons.

List the Evidence

Ask, *what kinds of evidence (data, anecdotes, case studies, citations from authority, and so forth) are offered as support for each reason.*

Some arguments advance little in the way of evidence. May's argument is a good example of a moral argument from and about principles; such an argument does not require much evidence to be effective. Lack of evidence, then, is not always a fault. For one of his reasons, however, May does offer some evidence: After stating his second reason in paragraph 5—the chance to grieve before a loved one dies can be helpful for those who must go on living after the patient's death—he invokes authorities who agree with him about the value of advanced grieving.

Examine the Evidence

Again, two questions apply. First, *is the evidence good?* That is, is it sufficient, accurate, and credible? Second, *is it relevant to the reason it supports?*

Clearly, the evidence May offers in paragraph 5 is sufficient; any more would probably be too much. We assume his citations are accurate and credible as well. We would generally also accept them as relevant, since apart from our own experience with grieving, we have to rely on expert opinion for such information. (See Chapter 6 for a fuller discussion of estimating the adequacy and relevance of evidence.)

Noting Refutations

A final—and optional—step is to assess an arguer's refutations, his or her effort to anticipate objections and answer them in advance. In a refutation a writer raises a potential objection to his or her position and tries to show why it does not undermine the basic argument. Refutations do not relate directly to claims, reasons, and evidence. A skilled arguer uses them, not as part of the main logic of an argument, but as a separate step to deal with any obvious objections a reader is likely to have.

First ask, *what refutations does the writer offer?* Summarize all refutations and list them on your tree diagram of claims, reasons, and evidence (see the model on page 34). Then ask, *how does the writer attack each objection?*

May's refutation occupies paragraph 7. He recognizes that the value of "free choice" lends weight to the pro-euthanasia position, and so he relates this value to the question of "voluntary euthanasia." Because in our culture individual freedom is so strong a value, May doesn't attack the value itself; rather he forces us to question whether voluntary euthanasia is in fact a matter of free choice. He suggests that unwanted people may be subtly coerced into "choosing" death or may simply be so isolated and neglected that death becomes preferable to life. In this way he refutes the objection that dying people should simply have freedom of choice where death is concerned.

Summarizing Your Analysis

Once you have completed your analysis, it is a good idea to summarize the results in a paragraph or two. Be sure to set aside your own position on the issue and confine your summary to the argument the writer makes. In other words, whether you agree with the author or not, attempt to assess his or her logic fairly.

While May's logic is strong, it doesn't in our view seem fully compelling. He qualifies his argument and uses exceptions effectively, and his single use of refutation is skillful. However, he fails to acknowledge that active euthanasia need not be a sudden decision leading to sudden death. Consequently, his reasons for supporting passive euthanasia can be used to support at least some cases of active euthanasia as well. It is here—in the linkage between his reasons and his claim—that May's argument falls short. Furthermore, we may question whether the circumstances under which May would permit active euthanasia are in fact as rare as he suggests. Experience tells us that many people are beyond human care, terminal, and in pain; and many others suffer acute mental anguish for which they might legitimately seek the relief of death.

Following Through

Following is student-written argument on capital punishment. Read it through once, and then use the Toulmin method as described in this chapter to analyze its logic systematically.

Student Sample: An Argument for Analysis

AMBER YOUNG

Capital Punishment: Society's Self-Defense

JUST AFTER 1:00 A.M. on a warm night in early June, Georgeann, a pretty college student, left through the back door of a fraternity house to walk the ninety feet down a well-lighted alley to the back door of her sorority house. Lively and vivacious, Georgeann had been an honor student, a cheerleader, and Daffodil Princess in high school, and now she was in the middle of finals week, trying to maintain her straight A record in college. That evening several people saw Georgeann walk to within about forty feet of the door of her sorority house. However, she never arrived. Somewhere in that last forty feet, she met a tall, handsome young man on crutches, his leg in a cast, struggling with a brief case. The young man asked Georgeann if she could help him get to his car which was parked nearby. Georgeann consented. Meanwhile, a housemother sleeping by an open window in a nearby fraternity house was awakened by a high-pitched, terrified scream that suddenly stopped. That was the last anyone ever heard or saw of Georgeann Hawkins. Her bashed skull and broken body were dumped on a hillside many miles away, along with the bodies of several other young female victims who had also been lured to their deaths by the good looking, clean-cut, courteous, intelligent, and charming Ted Bundy.

By the time Ted Bundy was caught in Utah with his bashing bar and other homemade tools of torture, he had bludgeoned and strangled to death at least thirty-two young women, raping and savaging many of them in the process. His "hunting" trips had extended into at least five Western states, including Washington, Oregon, Idaho, Utah, and Colorado, where he randomly selected and killed his unsuspecting victims.

Bundy was ultimately convicted of the attempted kidnapping of Carol DeRonche and imprisoned. For this charge he probably would have been paroled within eighteen months. However, before parole could be approved, Bundy was transferred to a jail in Colorado to stand trial for the murder of Caryn Campbell. With Bundy in jail, no one died at his hands or at the end of his savagely swung club. Young women could go about their lives normally, "safe" and separated from Ted Bundy by prison walls. Yet any number of things could have occurred to set Bundy free—an acquittal, some sympathetic judge or parole board, a psychiatrist pronouncing him rehabilitated and safe, a state legislature passing shorter sentencing or earlier parole laws, inadequate prison space, a federal court ruling abolishing life in prison without any possibility for parole, or an escape.

In Bundy's case, it was escape—twice—from Colorado jails. The first time he was immediately caught and brought back. The second time Bundy made it to Florida, where fifteen days after his escape he bludgeoned and strangled Margaret Bowman, Lisa Levy, Karen Chandler, and Kathy Kleiner in their Tallahassee sorority house, tearing chunks out of Lisa Levy's breast and buttock with his teeth. Ann Rule, a noted crime writer who became Bundy's confidant while writing her book *The Stranger Beside Me,* described Bundy's attack on Lisa Levy as like that of a rabid animal. On the same night at a different location, Bundy sneaked through an open window and so savagely attacked Cheryl Thomas in her bed that a woman in the apartment next door described the clubbing as seeming to reverberate through the whole house for about ten seconds. Then, three weeks later, less than forty days after his escape from the Colorado jail, Bundy went hunting again. He missed his chance at one quarry, junior high school student Leslie Ann Parmenter, when her brother showed up and thwarted her abduction. But Bundy succeeded the next day in Lake City where he abducted and killed twelve-year-old Kimberly Diane Leach and dumped her strangled, broken body in an abandoned pig barn.

5 The criminal justice system and jails in Utah and Colorado did not keep Margaret Bowman, Lisa Levy, Karen Chandler, Kathy Kleiner, Cheryl Thomas, Leslie Ann Parmenter, or little Kimberly Leach safe from Ted Bundy. The state of Florida, however, with its death penalty, has made every other young woman safe from Ted Bundy forever. Capital punishment is society's means of self-defense. Just as a person is justified in using deadly force in defending herself or himself against a would-be killer, so society also has a right to use deadly force to defend itself and its citizens from those who exhibit a strong propensity to kill whenever the opportunity and the urge arise.

However, while everyone wants a safe society, some people would say that capital punishment is too strong a means of ensuring it. Contemporary social critic Hendrick Hertzberg often attacks the death penalty, using arguments that are familiar, but not compelling, to those who do not share his absolute value-of-life position. For example, in one article he tries to paint a graphic picture of how horrible and painful even the most modern execution methods, such as lethal injection, are to the prisoner ("Premeditated"). Elsewhere he dismisses the deterrence argument as "specious," since "[n]o one has ever been able to show that capital punishment lowers the murder rate" ("Burning" 4). But the Florida death penalty has, in fact, made certain that Ted Bundy will never again go on one of his hunting trips to look for another young woman's skull to bash or body to ravage. A needle prick in the arm hardly conjures up images of excruciating pain so great as to be cruel and unusual. Thousands of good people with cancer and other diseases or injuries endure much greater pain every day until death. Therefore, waiting for death, even in pain, is more a part of a common life experience than a cruel or unusual punishment.

Of course, the possibility of mistakenly executing an innocent person is a serious concern. However, our entire criminal justice system is tilted heavily toward the accused, who is protected from the start to the end of the criminal justice procedure by strong individual-rights guarantees in the Fourth, Fifth, Sixth, and Seventh Amendments of the U.S. Constitution. The burden of proof in a criminal case is on the government, and guilt must be proved beyond a reasonable doubt. The chances of a guilty person going free in our system are many times greater than those of an innocent person being convicted. Those opposed may ask, "How do we know that the number of innocent people found guilty is really that low?" The number must be low because when the scandal of an innocent person being convicted comes to light, the media covers it from all angles. The movie *The Thin Blue Line* is an example of such media attention. In addition, the story of *The Thin Blue Line* is illustrative in that the U.S. Supreme Court caught the error and remanded the case, and Randall Adams is no longer subject to the death penalty.

If, however, such a mistake should occur in spite of all the protections guaranteed to the accused, such an innocent death would certainly be tragic, just as each of the nearly 50,000 deaths of innocent people each year on our highways are tragic. As much as we value human life, we inevitably weigh and balance that value against social costs and benefits, whether we like to admit it or not. If the rare, almost nonexistent, chance that an innocent person might be executed is such a terrible evil as to require abolition of capital punishment, then why don't we also demand the abolition of automobiles as well? Because we balance the value of those lives lost in traffic accidents against the importance of automobiles in society. In doing so, we choose to accept the thousands of automobile deaths per year in order to keep our cars. It is interesting to note that even opponents of capital punishment, like Hertzberg, do not demand abolition of the automobile, which leads to the observation that even they may not be at the extreme, absolute end of the life-value scale, where preservation of life takes precedence over *all* other social concerns.

Just as we, as a society, have decided that the need for automobiles outweighs their threat to innocent life, we can decide that capital punishment is necessary for the safety and well-being of the general populace. The most legitimate and strongest reason for capital punishment is not punishment, retribution, or deterrence, but simply society's right to self-defense. Society has a right to expect and demand that its government remove forever those persons who have shown they cannot be trusted to circulate in society, even on a limited basis, without committing mayhem. First degree murderers, like Bundy, who hunt and kill their victims with premeditation and malice aforethought must be removed from society permanently as a matter of self-defense.

10 Having made that decision, there are only two alternatives available—life in prison or death. We base our approval or disapproval of capital punishment as an option on fundamental values and ideals relating to life itself, rather than on statistics or factual evidence. Most of us are a long way from the extreme that considers life to have no value; instead, we crowd more closely to the other side, where life is viewed as inviolable. However, few in our society go so far as to believe that life is sacrosanct, that its preservation is required above all else. Our founding fathers wrote in the Declaration of Independence that all men are endowed by their Creator with unalienable rights, including "life, liberty, and the pursuit of happiness." However, there is no indication that life was more sacred to them than liberty. In fact, Patrick Henry, who would later be instrumental in the adoption of the Bill of Rights to the U.S. Constitution, is most famous for his defiant American Revolutionary declaration "I know not what course others may take, but as for me, give me liberty or give me death!"

The sentiment that some things are worse than death remains pervasive in this country where millions of soldiers and others have put themselves in harm's way and even sacrificed their lives to preserve and defend freedom for themselves or for the people they leave behind. Many people will readily or reluctantly admit to their willingness to use deadly force to protect themselves or their families from a murderer. The preservation of life, any life, regardless of everything else, is not an absolute value that most people in this country hold.

In fact, many prisoners would prefer to die than to languish in prison. While some might still want to read and expand their minds even while their bodies are confined, for those who are not intellectually or spiritually oriented, life in prison would be a fate worse than death. Bundy himself, in his letters from prison to Ann Rule, declared, "My world is a cage," as he tried to describe "the cruel metamorphosis that occurs in captivity" (qtd. in Rule 148). After his sentencing in Utah, Bundy described his attempts to prepare mentally for the "living hell of prison" (qtd. in Rule 191). Thus, some condemned prisoners, including Gary Gilmore, the first person to be executed after the U.S. Supreme Court found that Utah's death penalty law met Constitutional requirements, refused to participate in the appeals attempting to convert his death sentence to life in prison because he preferred death over such a life. In our society, which was literally founded and sustained on the principle that liberty is more important than life, the argument that it is somehow less cruel and more civilized to deprive someone of liberty for the rest of his or her life than just to end the life sounds hollow. The Fifth Amendment of the U.S. Constitution prohibits the taking of either life or liberty without due process of law, but it does not place one at a higher value than the other.

The overriding concerns of the Constitution, however, are safety and self-defense. The chance of a future court ruling, a release on parole, a pardon, a commutation of sentence, or an escape—any of which could turn the murderer loose to prey again on society—creates a risk that society should not have to bear. Lisa Levy, Margaret Bowman, Karen Chandler, Kathy Kleiner, Cheryl Thomas, and Kimberly Leach were not protected from Bundy by the courts and jails in Utah and Colorado, but other young women who were potential victims are now absolutely protected from Bundy by the Florida death penalty.

The resolutions of most great controversies are, in fact, balancing acts, and capital punishment is no exception. There is no perfect solution; rather the best answer lies on the side with the greatest advantages. It comes down to choosing, and choosing has a price. Capital punishment carries with it the slight risk that an innocent person will be executed; however, it is more important to protect innocent, would-be victims of already convicted murderers. On balance, society was not demeaned by the execution of Bundy in Florida, as claimed by Hertzberg ("Burning" 49). On the contrary, society is, in fact, better off with Ted Bundy and others like him gone.

WORKS CITED

Hertzberg, Hendrick. "Burning Question." *The New Republic* 20 Feb. 1989: 4+.

---. "Premeditated Execution." *Time* 18 May 1992: 49.

Rule, Ann. *The Stranger Beside Me.* New York: Penguin, 1989.

The Thin Blue Line. Dir. Errol Morris. HBO Video, 1988.

FROM ANALYSIS TO INQUIRY

No method for analyzing arguments is perfect, and no method can guarantee that everyone using it will assess an argument the same way. Uniform results are not especially desirable anyway: What would be left to talk about? The point of argumentative analysis is to step back and examine an argument carefully, to detect how it is structured, to assess the cogency and power of its logic. The Toulmin method helps us move beyond a hit-or-miss approach to logical analysis, but it does not yield a conclusion as compelling as mathematical proof.

Convincing and persuading always involve more than just logic, and, therefore, logical analysis alone is never enough to assess the strength of an argument. For example, William May's argument attempts to discredit those like Dr. Jack Kevorkian, who assist patients wishing to take their own lives. May depicts Kevorkian as offering assistance without sufficient consultation with the patient. Is his depiction accurate? Clearly, we can answer this question only by finding out more about how Kevorkian and others like him work. Because such questions are not a part of logical analysis, they have not been of concern to us in this chapter. But any adequate and thorough analysis of an argument must also address questions of fact and the interpretation of data.

Logical analysis as we have been discussing it here is a prelude to arguing to inquire, the focus of the following chapter. Analysis helps us to find some of the questions we need to ask about the arguments we read and write. Such "stepping back" is good discipline, but we think you will agree that "joining in," contributing to dialogue over arguments, is both more fun and more rewarding. So, not forgetting what we have learned in this chapter, let's move on to the more interesting and more human art of *dialogue.*

CHAPTER FIVE

Preparing to Write: Arguing to Inquire

In Chapter 1 we distinguished four aims or uses of argument: inquiring, convincing, persuading, and negotiating. Argument as inquiry, the focus of this chapter, has the following characteristics.

Its end or purpose is truth. Truth is a claim about what we believe or ought to believe—what we take to be right or correct. When we argue to inquire, we are not attempting to support a belief or position we hold already; rather, we are seeking to define our position on an issue or examining a tentatively held position to discover if it is really the one we should take. Inquiry is a means of finding the position on some issue that both satisfies us personally and holds up under the scrutiny of others.

Its audience is primarily the inquirer along with fellow inquirers concerned with the same controversial issue. In inquiry we argue with ourselves or with other people whose minds are open and who share our interest in some question. Such people might include friends, classmates, counselors, parents, teachers—anyone who will cooperate with us in a patient questioning of opinion.

Its medium is dialogue. Why does inquiry require participating in a conversation instead of simply doing research? Because no claim to truth about a topic exists outside of human conversation, free of opinions and values. Even a factual news report of an event—for example, an assisted suicide—comes to our attention in a way that challenges a set of values, complete with quoted opinions from involved parties and interested authorities. Our opinions result partly from our responses to these other opinions. When we go on to do library research, we extend the conversation as we question and interpret information and arguments in books and articles. Inquiry is interactive, a process of question and answer that can take a variety of forms. The most common of these are one-on-one dialogues and small-group discussions, but inquiry can also take the form of imaginary dialogues that you create with yourself. Further, when you base your inquiry on a written text, you should also engage in "conversation"—listening to what the text says and trying to detect its strengths and weaknesses.

Its art consists of discovering the right questions and the best answers. Inquiry is the process through which we form and test our opinions and earn our claims to truth, our convictions. Therefore, the "right" questions are those that improve our understanding and that reveal weak or misleading parts of an argument. The best answers in inquiry are those that are direct and honest, not evasively convoluted or defensively dogmatic. Inquiry is friendly interrogation, aimed not at proving that we are right and someone else is wrong, but at a disinterested examination of opinion to discover truth.

In sum, then, argument as inquiry is a dialogue with oneself, a person, or a text—a way of examining competing claims of truth through a process of question and answer.

THE IMPORTANCE OF INQUIRY

We begin with argument as inquiry for several reasons. First, inquiry is often where we must start a writing project, especially when we face a topic about which we know relatively little. Even when we know enough about a topic to have formed an opinion about it, we still need to examine what we claim to know and the stance we want to take.

More important, we start with inquiry because, alone among the aims of argument, it has truth as its single goal. Before trying to move an audience toward a position we advocate, we have a moral responsibility to first examine that position and why we hold it. Convincing and persuading become immoral when people have no regard for the truth—when they set out to gain advantage by glossing over or distorting what they know to be true or when they make no effort to distinguish truth from error in the first place. Of course, there is nothing wrong with the desire to influence other people. But we need only look around us to see a world full of irresponsible advocacy. Advertising agencies agree to promote products without questioning their effectiveness or even their safety. Politicians appeal to voters' prejudices and willingly change their positions with shifting winds of public opinion. Television preachers take advantage of the gullible and uneducated, persuading the poor to send money in return for prayers and miracles. Special interest groups thwart the public interest by coercing votes from policymakers fearful of their influence and dependent on their campaign contributions.

Less obviously, perhaps, we each as individuals shirk our moral responsibility when we accept uncritically as received truth the beliefs of others—whether parents, teachers, or so-called experts. Questioning received truths takes effort and may make us uncomfortable, but we must do it if we are to earn our convictions and responsibly exercise our right to free speech.

No amount of thoughtful inquiry can prevent us from being mistaken sometimes. What we take to be true will often turn out to be false or only partly true. But at least if we commit ourselves to serious inquiry we can avoid unethical argumentation, the kind that has no regard for the truth.

Finally, inquiry is fundamental to the academic environment in which you now find yourself. No other contemporary institution is dedicated to inquiry to the extent that higher education is. Here people are valued not only for what they know but also, and more importantly, for the searching questions they ask. Research methods in the various fields of study differ greatly, but all claims to knowledge are arguments, and all arguments are subject to question, to inquiry. Consequently, what we are about to discuss—argument as inquiry—applies to anything you might study in college as well as to the arguments you encounter elsewhere.

QUESTIONS FOR INQUIRY

How do we go about inquiring into our own or someone else's position on an issue? There is no single procedure to follow because a conversation is a natural act and does not run according to a script or pattern. But while every conversation may take its own course, the quality of the dialogue will depend upon the kinds of questions posed. The following list suggests what you should ask when you want to open an argument to scrutiny.

Ask if you have understood the arguer's position on the issue. The best way to do this is to restate, paraphrase, or summarize the thesis. (Face to face you might say, "I believe that you are saying. . . . Am I understanding you?") Be sure to note how strongly the claim is made. Has the arguer qualified it by suggesting conditions or exceptions? If you are inquiring into your own argument, ask if you have stated your own position clearly. Do you need to qualify it in any way?

Ask about the meaning of any words that seem central to the argument. You can do this at any point in a conversation and as often as it seems necessary. When dealing with a written text, try to discern the meaning from context. For instance, if an author's case depends on the "fairness" of a proposed solution, you'll need to ask what "fair" means, since the word has quite a range of possible applications. You might ask, "Fair to whom?"

Ask what reasons support the thesis. Paraphrasing reasons is a good way to open up a conversation to further questions about assumptions, values, and definitions.

Ask about the assumptions on which the thesis and reasons are based. Most arguments are based on one or more unstated assumptions. For example, if a college recruiter argues that the school is superior to most others (thesis) because its ratio of students to teachers is low (reason), the unstated assumptions are (1) that students there will get more attention, and

(2) that more attention results in a better education. As you inquire into an argument, note the assumptions and ask if they are reasonable.

Ask about the values expressed or implied by the argument. For example, if you argue that closing a forest to logging operations is essential even at the cost of dozens of jobs, you are valuing environmental preservation over the livelihoods of the workers who must search for other jobs.

Ask about how well the reasons are supported. Are they offered as opinions only, or are they supported with evidence? Is the evidence recent? Sufficient? What kind of testimony is offered? Who are the authorities cited? What are their credentials and biases? Are there other facts or authoritative statements that might weaken the argument?

Consider analogies and comparisons. If the author makes an argument by analogy, does the comparison hold up? For example, advocates of animal rights draw an analogy with civil rights when they claim that just as we have come to recognize the immorality of exploiting human beings, so we should recognize the immorality of exploiting other species. Do you think this analogy is sound?

Ask about the arguer's biases and background. What past experiences might have led the arguer to take this position? What does the holder of this position stand to gain? What might someone gain by challenging it?

Ask about implications. Where would the argument ultimately lead should we accept what the speaker advocates? For example, if someone contends that abortion is murder, asking about implications would result in the question, "Are you willing to put women who get abortions on trial for murder and, if they are convicted, to punish them as murderers are usually punished?"

Ask whether the argument takes opposing views into account. If it does, are they presented fairly and clearly or with mockery and distortion? Does the author take them seriously or dismiss them? Are they effectively refuted?

Use the preceding questions as a checklist as you inquire into arguments. To keep from overlooking what might be asked, it is a good idea to memorize them or write them down in your writer's notebook for easy reference. Keep in mind, however, that effective inquiry requires much more than a list of questions. First, you must read or listen attentively, taking in what other arguers have to say without being too anxious to assert your own point of view. Of course, you will almost always have some sort of "gut reaction" to any argument you encounter, but be careful to listen rather than rush to judgment, just as you would want others to hear you out. Inquiry is more than an exchange of opinion; it is an exploration of opinion. Clearly no exploration can occur if we are not first listening.

Second, you must ask questions thoughtfully, genuinely engaged with the argument at hand. Because each argument is unique, you cannot apply a checklist of questions mechanically, the same way in every case. In order to open up a particular, individual argument, you must find the "right" questions to ask in each instance, those that reveal the argument's strengths and weaknesses. The art of inquiry, unlike a mechanical process, is a dialogue with one's self, another person, or a text.

INQUIRY AND WRITTEN ARGUMENTS: THE PROCESS OF DIALOGUE

We have said that it is possible to have a "conversation" with writers of written arguments. Doing so requires some imagination on the part of the inquirer, who—in addition to posing questions—must also supply plausible answers from the writer's point of view. Such an imagined dialogue is a good way to evaluate arguments you encounter in your research and to decide which arguments you may want to adapt in support of your own position.

A Preliminary Critical Reading

Suppose that while researching the topic of international terrorism and trying to assess various policies adopted toward it by nations around the world, you encounter the following argument by Michael Levin. First you will read Levin's argument critically, following the procedure discussed in Chapter 3. Start by skimming, reading the first and last paragraphs and the first sentence or two of each paragraph in between in order to get a quick overall idea of Levin's point. Then read the argument sequentially, at a moderate pace. Finally, after putting it aside for awhile, read the argument a second time, underlining whatever seems most important and writing down your responses in the margins and in your writer's notebook. If you find the argument complicated or if you have trouble following its logic, you may want to subject it to a Toulmin analysis as described in Chapter 4. A full critical analysis will help prepare you to enter into a dialogue with the argument.

MICHAEL LEVIN

The Case for Torture

Michael Levin is a philosophy professor at the City College of New York. This argument was written in 1982 and originally published in Newsweek *magazine.*

IT IS generally assumed that torture is impermissible, a throwback to a more brutal age. Enlightened societies reject it outright, and regimes suspected of using it risk the wrath of the United States.

I believe this attitude is unwise. There are situations in which torture is not merely permissible but morally mandatory. Moreover, these situations are moving from the realm of imagination to fact.

Death: Suppose a terrorist has hidden an atomic bomb on Manhattan Island which will detonate at noon on July 4 unless . . . (here follow the usual demands for money and release of his friends from jail). Suppose, further, that he is caught at 10 A.M. of the fateful day, but—preferring death to failure—won't disclose where the bomb is. What do we do? If we follow due process—wait for his lawyer, arraign him—millions of people will die. If the only way to save those lives is to subject the terrorist to the most excruciating possible pain, what grounds can there be for not doing so? I suggest there are none. In any case, I ask you to face the question with an open mind.

Torturing the terrorist is unconstitutional? Probably. But millions of lives surely outweigh constitutionality. Torture is barbaric? Mass murder is far more barbaric. Indeed, letting millions of innocents die in deference to one who flaunts his guilt is moral cowardice, an unwillingness to dirty one's hands. If *you* caught the terrorist, could you sleep nights knowing that millions died because you couldn't bring yourself to apply the electrodes?

Once you concede that torture is justified in extreme cases, you have ad- 5
mitted that the decision to use torture is a matter of balancing innocent lives against the means needed to save them. You must now face more realistic cases involving more modest numbers. Someone plants a bomb on a jumbo jet. He alone can disarm it, and his demands cannot be met (or if they can, we refuse to set a precedent by yielding to his threats). Surely we can, we must, do anything to the extortionist to save the passengers. How can we tell 300, or 100, or 10 people who never asked to be put in danger, "I'm sorry, you'll have to die in agony, we just couldn't bring ourselves to. . . ."

Here are the results of an informal poll about a third, hypothetical, case. Suppose a terrorist group kidnapped a newborn baby from a hospital. I asked four mothers if they would approve of torturing kidnappers if that were necessary to get their own newborns back. All said yes, the most "liberal" adding that she would like to administer it herself.

I am not advocating torture as punishment. Punishment is addressed to deeds irrevocably past. Rather, I am advocating torture as an acceptable measure for preventing future evils. So understood, it is far less objectionable than many extant punishments. Opponents of the death penalty, for example, are forever insisting that executing a murderer will not bring back his victim (as if the purpose of capital punishment were supposed to be resurrection, not deterrence or retribution). But torture, in the cases described, is intended not to bring anyone back but to keep innocents from being dispatched. The most powerful argument against using torture as a punishment or to secure confessions is that such practices disregard the rights of the individual. Well, if the individual is all that important—and he is—it is correspondingly important to protect the rights of individuals threatened by terrorists. If life is so valuable that it must never be taken, the lives of the innocents must be saved even at the price of hurting the one who endangers them.

Better precedents for torture are assassination and preemptive attack. No

Allied leader would have flinched at assassinating Hitler, had that been possible. (The Allies did assassinate Heydrich.[1]) Americans would be angered to learn that Roosevelt could have had Hitler killed in 1943—thereby shortening the war and saving millions of lives—but refused on moral grounds. Similarly, if nation A learns that nation B is about to launch an unprovoked attack, A has a right to save itself by destroying B's military capability first. In the same way, if the police can by torture save those who would otherwise die at the hands of kidnappers or terrorists, they must.

Idealism: There is an important difference between terrorists and their victims that should mute talk of the terrorists' "rights." The terrorist's victims are at risk unintentionally, not having asked to be endangered. But the terrorist knowingly initiated his actions. Unlike his victims, he volunteered for the risks of his deed. By threatening to kill for profit or idealism, he renounces civilized standards, and he can have no complaint if civilization tries to thwart him by whatever means necessary.

10 Just as torture is justified only to save lives (not extort confessions or recantations), it is justifiably administered only to those *known* to hold innocent lives in their hands. Ah, but how can the authorities ever be sure they have the right malefactor? Isn't there a danger of error and abuse? Won't We turn into Them?

Questions like these are disingenuous in a world in which terrorists proclaim themselves and perform for television. The name of their game is public recognition. After all, you can't very well intimidate a government into releasing your freedom fighters unless you announce that it is your group that has seized its embassy. "Clear guilt" is difficult to define, but when 40 million people see a group of masked gunmen seize an airplane on the evening news, there is not much question about who the perpetrators are. There will be hard cases where the situation is murkier. Nonetheless, a line demarcating the legitimate use of torture can be drawn. Torture only the obviously guilty, and only for the sake of saving innocents, and the line between Us and Them will remain clear.

There is little danger that the Western democracies will lose their way if they choose to inflict pain as one way of preserving order. Paralysis in the face of evil is the greater danger. Some day soon a terrorist will threaten tens of thousands of lives, and torture will be the only way to save them. We had better start thinking about this.

A Sample Dialogue

You will begin your dialogue with Michael Levin by questioning the gist of his position in "The Case for Torture." As with any written argument, you must take special care in doing so because the author is not present to correct you

[1]Reinhard Heydrich, deputy chief of the Gestapo in Hitler's Germany, was known as "the Hangman of Europe." He was assassinated by Czech patriots.

if you go wrong. The questioner should always begin with what the answerer has said, gaining the assent of the answerer at every step in the line of reasoning: "Did I understand you to say. . . ?" "Yes." "And did you also assert. . . ?" "I did." These preliminary questions are important because they set the stage for exploring the argument itself and help to insure the mutual understanding necessary for dialogue.

In "The Case for Torture" you don't have to search for a thesis; Levin states his central position explicitly in the second paragraph: "There are situations in which torture is not merely permissible but morally mandatory." You might begin the dialogue by paraphrasing that main idea:

Q: Professor Levin, the way I hear it, you believe that given certain conditions, the *only* right thing to do is to torture someone.

At this point, you can feel confident that Levin would agree.

A: Yes, it would be immoral not to.

Now you are ready to ask another question to explore more fully the point to which Levin has just assented. Asking for definitions is often a good way to probe more deeply. Does anything in Levin's position statement need clarification?

Q: I'd like to know what you mean by situations or conditions in which torture must occur.

Here, again, Levin makes the question relatively easy to answer by stating these conditions explicitly in his essay. You can paraphrase them.

A: Innocent people would be about to die at the hands of terrorists, and the captured terrorist would have to be obviously guilty and have information that would save their lives.

You are now ready to ask Levin a question about his reasons.

Q: Why is it morally mandatory to torture a terrorist under the circumstances you describe above?

This reason is stated most explicitly in paragraph 5.

A: The torture will save the lives of innocent people.

Now that you have elicited Levin's reason, you might ask about the assumptions underlying his position. For example, what is he assuming about the information to be gained through torture?

Q: Aren't you assuming that the person being tortured will tell the truth? If a person is willing to die for a cause, wouldn't he or she also lie—mislead the authorities until the bomb explodes?

By challenging this assumption, have you deflated Levin's whole argument? Recall that in inquiry you are not seeking to destroy an argument, but rather to examine it. This goal requires that you attempt to find the best response to any question. In this case, you must make an honest effort to answer the question as Levin would.

A: The torturer does assume that the terrorist will tell the truth in an effort to get the pain over with as soon as possible. Pain weakens a person's will to resist.

You might press further on this point, particularly if you know something about how the victims of torture generally respond to their captors' demands for information. But you could just as well question at this point the values inherent in Levin's thesis.

Q: I see that while you value civilized behavior over brutality, you value innocent lives most of all. Is that right?

Again you should try honestly to respond as Levin would.

A: Yes. I suggest that we substitute for our current principle, "thou shalt never torture," a new principle: "the decision to use torture is a matter of balancing innocent lives against the means needed to save them" (paragraph 5). In other words, the moral principle underlying my argument is essentially "act always to protect the lives of innocent people."

At this point, remembering that Levin has illustrated his principle with examples—innocent airline passengers and innocent citizens of Manhattan facing nuclear annihilation—you might be ready to say, "Yes, I see that you have a point." But inquiry obligates you to press further: Is it really *right* to accept this principle?

Q: What about our constitutional right to due process, meaning a trial, which pertains even when accused criminals plead guilty?
A: Torture probably is unconstitutional, but the number of lives saved justifies the violation of constitutional rights.
Q: But in paragraph 6, you suggest that if kidnappers threatened to kill even one newborn baby, torture would be justified. Is the number of lives saved through torture a factor or not?

Since an argument must be consistent, finding a satisfactory answer to this question is obviously crucial to defending Levin's position. Levin would probably deny that quantity was a factor.

A: I believe that once you accept the principle that saving innocent lives justifies torture, it does not matter if it is one or one million that you save. I began with the extreme case to persuade you to agree with the principle.

You might also ask a further question about constitutional rights.

Q: The Constitution also guards against the use of cruel and unusual punishment. Obviously, torture is cruel. What specific means are you advocating? Only once do you offer any concrete example of what you have in mind, when you refer in paragraph four to applying electrodes. Let's be more concrete. Is any sort of torture allowable? In addition to electric shock, could we also, say, apply acid to the skin? Or beat the captured terrorist with a rubber hose, perhaps concentrating on the genitalia? Or sever a limb? Furthermore, if one form of torture fails to work, may we try another, more painful one? Exactly how far can we take it? And when do we give up trying to extract the information we want?

You might assume that Levin would step back a bit from his position at this point and respond with some qualification.

A: I am not advocating gruesome or disfiguring forms of torture. Electric shock was what I had in mind. And clearly, we can only take it as far as unconsciousness. We stop when the possibility of saving innocent lives is past.

But this is not in fact consistent with what Levin actually says in paragraph 9, where he suggests that we may use "whatever means necessary" to thwart terrorist activity. To present Levin's position accurately, there is only one consistent response.

A: I set no limits. We should use any means at our disposal. However, I advocate torture not as a punishment, but as a means of preventing the loss of innocent lives.

Once it is clear that the brutality can be unlimited, your next question might center on the issue of determining guilt.

Q: But what if we only *believe* the captured terrorist is guilty? Maybe he or she has been mistakenly identified.

Levin seems to have anticipated this objection. In paragraphs 11 and 12, he answers that we should torture only the "obviously guilty," and claims that terrorists' own desire for publicity makes this error nearly impossible.

Accepting Levin's qualification, you might still be troubled by the fact that others—legitimate soldiers in a war, for example—may cause the death of innocent people. How are terrorists more "guilty" than soldiers?

Q: What are the reasons that terrorists blow up airplanes?

You can paraphrase Levin's response in paragraph 9.

A: Terrorists operate for profit or idealism, that is, out of political motives. Often terrorists are attempting to secure the release of "freedom fighters" or the safety of people fighting for their own political views or disputed land.

Q: Is it possible that terrorists see themselves as soldiers at war?

A: Yes, they might see themselves as guerrillas.

Q: If our country were at war and our military captured enemy soldiers who had information about a planned attack on some American city or base, would our military be able to torture these prisoners of war? Would they not be forbidden to do so under Geneva convention rules?

A: Of course, we should treat our enemies in a declared war according to these principles, but terrorists are not ordinary soldiers; terrorists take the lives of innocent civilians, not other soldiers.

Q: Do not soldiers in declared wars sometimes take the lives of innocent civilians? Would you have advocated that the Japanese torture a captured American who could have given them information about the bombing of Hiroshima?

A: No, I would not advocate torture in a declared war.

Q: So you are saying that in some circumstances, it is mandatory to protect the lives of innocents through torture, but in other circumstances it is immoral to protect the lives of innocents through torture?

A: Yes, that is what I am saying.

The dialogue with Michael Levin could go on indefinitely, exploring the definition of war and the rights of people who fight and kill for political reasons, assuming that both sides were interested in pursuing the truth about whether torture is indeed ever justified.

In your dialogues with texts and other people, try to remember that the point is not to attack or defend, but to probe—to uncover the uncomfortable spots that make both questioner and answerer think harder. Such dialogue tends to reveal the full complexity of a topic, which is exactly what is required to find the best position and make the most truthful argument.

Following Through

1. In your writer's notebook, continue the dialogue with Levin. You might pursue one of the following areas of questioning or another that you have in mind yourself.

   (a) Does Levin offer any evidence? What might you ask him about it? What might he have included that he did not?

   (b) In paragraphs 7 and 8, Levin contrasts torture with capital punishment and also compares it with assassination and preemptive attacks. Continue the dialogue, inquiring into the similarities and differences among these.

2. Select one of the essays from the following list, and do a critical reading as described in Chapter 3 and an analysis as described in Chapter 4. Annotate the text, and make notes in your writer's notebook. With another student or in a small group, create a dialogue with the writer based on the questions outlined on pages 44–45. Then share your questions and answers with the rest of your class, comparing results and focusing on the variety of paths dialogues can take.

   "Rising to the Occasion of Our Death," William May, pages 29–31.

   "Capital Punishment: Society's Self-Defense," Amber Young, pages 36–40

   "Women in Combat," Sara Sabraw, pages 106–107

EVALUATING AN ARGUMENT: AN ANALYSIS BASED ON INQUIRY

A dialogue can take you in many directions and open up a great deal you may not have thought about carefully before. Writing an essay after you conclude a dialogue can help you summarize and reflect upon your total experience and articulate your best insights in order to decide how much of an argument you are willing to accept. Sometimes an informal paragraph or two in your writer's notebook is enough. However, if you want to present your assessment of an argument to other readers, you will need to write a more formal paper, an analysis that evaluates.

The audience for such an evaluation will be other people interested in the issue who, like you, are trying to decide what they think. You may assume that they have read the argument and that they are also trying to evaluate its claim to truth. In other words, think of your audience and yourself as peers, fellow truth-seekers. Your tone should be critical but impartial. Your goal is to evaluate, but you should also be interested in helping your readers understand the argument.

There is no lock-step process for an essay evaluating an argument, but we can offer some suggestions.

Preparing to Write

First, of course, read the argument thoroughly and critically, until you feel confident about your own understanding of it. Review the definition of critical reading (page 16) and our other suggestions in Chapter 3.

As you read, you should mark up the text of the argument (make a photocopy for this purpose, if necessary). Identify the claim, the reasons, and any evidence; mark the sections that the essay breaks down into; note how (and whether) terms are defined; and so on. See Chapter 4 for more advice about analyzing arguments.

If the argument is particularly difficult, summarize and paraphrase the parts you find troublesome (see pages 581–590 for help). Raise questions about these passages in class or in conference with your instructor.

Next, in addition to discussing the essay with others, you should also write out a dialogue with the writer as we have illustrated in this chapter, posing questions and providing careful responses that accurately reflect the writer's position. You will not reproduce the dialogue in your essay, but what you learn and conclude from such dialogue will certainly be useful.

From Dialogue to Draft

Analytical essays are not summaries. You should assume your readers have also read the text you are analyzing, so that rather than a summary they are looking for your insights into the argument and your assessment of the writer's claim to truth. Your thesis, therefore, will be some statement evaluating the overall worth of the argument you are analyzing. To arrive at it, you will review your annotations and recall your dialogue with the text. What strengths and weaknesses did you uncover? Try to consider the larger picture: With respect to the given issue, does the argument shed valuable light on the truth?

You will support your thesis with comments (either negative or positive) that have resulted from your reading of the argument and your dialogue with it. You may focus your critical reading on key aspects of the argument which will form natural topics for paragraphs or groups of paragraphs in your written analysis. For example, you might build a part of your analysis around an evaluation of the argument's main reason, or around an important analogy in the argument, or around an assumption of the writer's that you do not share. One way to discover points to include in your analysis is to recall your dialogue with the writer: What questions proved most fruitful? You will also need to support and develop your comments with specific references to passages in the argument, making use of brief summaries and paraphrases as well as direct quotations.

Remember that you may not be able to include every critical observation in your analysis. Attempting to work in everything can result in an analysis that is more like an inventory or a laundry list—not very readable. It is better to concentrate on related points so that your analysis has unity and focus. Above all, emphasize the main qualities that make the argument succeed or fail in your estimation.

A Sample Analysis

Since we have already illustrated a dialogue with Michael Levin's "The Case for Torture," we follow up with a sample analysis of this argument.

Michael Levin's "The Case for Torture": A Dangerous Oversimplification

TORTURE IS one topic about which the truth seems clear. Enlightened people the world over believe that torture is immoral and barbaric. However, Michael Levin in his essay "The Case for Torture" challenges Americans to rethink their position that nothing could ever justify torture. Levin's case is thought-provoking, but his position is not one that we should accept.

Levin's reason for justifying torture appears in paragraph 5: the end, saving innocent people's lives, justifies the means, denying terrorists their right not to be subjected to cruel and unusual punishment. This reason (and therefore his entire case) rests on two assumptions: that authorities will have terrorists in custody and that torturing them would yield information that would save innocent lives. But if we assent to torture based on these conditions, can we be sure that it will be put into practice only in situations that are equally clear-cut? How would we know, for example, that a "terrorist" was not insane or simply bluffing? What if the terrorist never did speak? And even if he or she did, how would we know that the information was the truth and not a desperate lie aimed at buying time or getting revenge for the torture? No actual situation is likely to be as neat as the one Levin poses, and assenting to torture could result in horrible abuses.

Even if we grant that torture would save lives in such a situation, can we accept Levin's argument? He attempts to win our assent through three hypothetical cases (paragraphs 2–6) in which he claims torture would be "morally mandatory." He first tries to get the reader to accept his argument based on millions of lives being at stake. Levin then extends the principle to a situation where hundreds of lives are at stake and finally to one in which just one life, a newborn baby's, is at stake. By the time he gets to the baby in paragraph 6, he seems to have forgotten that he justified torture's barbarity earlier on the grounds that "millions of lives surely outweigh constitutionality" and that "mass murder" is more barbaric than torture (paragraph 4). Is Levin saying that quantity matters—or not? Because of this inconsistency, Levin's argument here relies more upon emotional appeal than good reasoning.

Another major section of Levin's argument turns on the distinction between torture and punishment. We may agree that torture, unlike the death penalty, might save the lives of potential victims (paragraph 7). However, when Levin says torture is like a preemptive military strike (paragraph 8), he exposes his argument to serious questions. If we can torture a terrorist to save innocent lives, why not torture a soldier to accomplish the same ends? Levin would say the difference is one of guilt and innocence, that the soldier is also an innocent.

However, Levin's use of the terms "guilt" and "innocence" can also be 5
questioned. He defines the innocent as those who have not asked to be put in danger, using newborn babies as one example. Certainly, a soldier, at least one who volunteers to fight, is not innocent according to this definition. Levin would probably argue that soldiers put themselves at risk for better reasons than terrorists do. But Levin admits that terrorists kill for "idealism" (paragraph 9) or to win the release of their "freedom fighters" (paragraph 11). This is killing for political reasons, making a terrorist akin to a soldier. And if we try to make a distinction based on the fact that terrorists kill civilians, we must acknowledge that American soldiers have killed civilians, even infants, in many of our wars, most notably in the bombing of Hiroshima and Nagasaki, but also in Vietnam and more recently in Iraq. Suddenly, Levin's goal of keeping the line clear between "Us and Them" (paragraph 11) becomes more complicated. Just who is eligible for torture?

Admitting that most terrorists are more like soldiers than they are like criminals does not justify terrorism, but it does help us see the problem of terrorism in its political complexity. It also leads us to examine some implications of the decision that torture can be right. Can we assent to using it in warfare? Is torture right depending on whose "civilization," "idealism," and "order" it preserves?

Ultimately, Levin's argument fails to convince. It raises some interesting issues, but even in the most clear-cut situation he presents, Levin is not able to establish the morality of torture. Torture is something we might wish to use given certain circumstances; but defending it as a moral choice, much less as "morally mandatory," does not work.

Following Through

Find an argument on a topic that you are currently researching. Read the argument critically, annotating the text, and write a dialogue with the author. Rather than just pairing questions and answers, try to make chains of questions and answers that follow naturally from one another, as we did earlier with the Levin argument. While you must find justification in the text for every response you have the writer make, you should also push beyond the surface of the text. The dialogue should dig more deeply into the argument, uncovering what is implied, along with what is stated directly. If you get stuck, consult the list of questions on pages 44–45 to help you start a new chain of questioning.

Look over your dialogue and your annotations for points to make about the argument and how well it stands up to inquiry. Finally, draft an analytical essay based on your inquiry. Before you write, you might want to read student Cindy Tarver's analysis of an argument by William Murchison, both of which follow.

WILLIAM MURCHISON

City Shouldn't Ignore Morality

William Murchison is a syndicated columnist whose work appears often in the Dallas Morning News, *where this argument was originally published.*

AND SO another U.S. city bellies up to the gay rights issue. Dallas' City Council asks: Should we or shouldn't we hire gay cops? The answer up to now has been an automatic no. Police work is public in nature. Public law forbids the sexual practices that define homosexuality: in addition to which, police officers function as role models.

Advocates of homosexual rights are nonetheless voluble and persistent. They want action. Americans are having to think carefully about a moral issue long regarded as settled. How should they think? Here is one view.

The homosexual cop issue, it seems to me, is only superficially about civil rights and hiring policy. Deeper down, it is about the legitimation of homosexuality as just another modern "lifestyle."

It is all part of a great design: claim accredited victim status, repeal the anti-sodomy laws, depict practicing homosexuals as appropriate role models, intimidate doubters by smearing them as "homophobic," drop the very word "homosexual" in favor of the positive, upbeat-sounding "gay."

As heterosexuals acquiesce in this design, out of fear or the desire to be politically correct, they move homosexuality further down the road to legitimation. 5

The campaign has succeeded in marked degree. Various cities prohibit various kinds of "discrimination" against homosexuals. The ordination of practicing (as distinguished from celibate) homosexuals is a hot issue among Methodists, Presbyterians, Episcopalians, and others. Traditional prohibitions, such as the military's ban on homosexual personnel, are under legal and political attack.

Non-homophobic foes of homosexual "rights" sometimes don't know what to do. They don't want to injure the feelings of homosexual friends, and they don't want to countenance a radical redrafting of the moral laws. And so they worry.

Why? Can't the moral law be changed by a good old democratic vote? To say so evidences a dramatic misreading of the moral law.

The moral law—peculiar to no religious tradition; rather, innate in the human species—is no set of icky-picky prescriptions made up by kill-joys.

The moral law is an owner's manual for the human body—and soul. You follow it for the reason you change (or should change) your automobile's oil every 3,000 miles: because if you don't, things start to happen, things you may not like. 10

The human "owner's manual" says—always has, actually—that heterosexual monogamy works. It does not work perfectly by the standards of an imperfect world; yet, on the historical record, the alternatives work less satisfactorily and sometimes injuriously. This is as true of, for instance, heterosexual adultery as of other misadventures.

Ten years ago, a well-known homosexual activist paid a call on me to press the case for "gay rights." He grew livid during our visit, all but pounded on the table. Whose business was it, he demanded to know, what sexual preference he evinced? He would do as he wanted. I had never anticipated otherwise. A few years later, he was dead. Of AIDS.

That is not a smug, God-struck-him-dead kind of remark. It is a painful observation about the necessary sequence of cause and effect: If you do "A," expect "B." Or "C." Or "D." Or various permutations and combinations of same.

The great irony of AIDS, the vast majority whose incidences result from anal copulation, is that it occurs in the midst of the ongoing national celebration of the "gay lifestyle." It is like Poe's *Masque of the Red Death.* While inside the nobles whoop it up, the great destroyer enters, unnoticed.

What a waste! My caller of 10 years ago was a talented and probably, when he wasn't yelling at me, genial man. The world was better off with than without him, as could be said of numberless AIDS victims. 15

Anyone who hates or physically torments practicing homosexuals is, in theological or secular terms, a swine. The moral law—remember it?—calls hatred wrong. Wrong likewise is the failure to draw meaningful distinctions among different species of conduct and conviction. American society is being offered that precise temptation today. We should resist to the uttermost.

Student Sample: An Analysis Based on Inquiry

CINDY TARVER

An Appeal to Prejudice

HOMOSEXUALITY EXISTED in biblical times and continues to be viable today. Indeed, the open expression of homosexuality is now so prevalent that gay rights has become a major concern of the American public. Evidence of this concern can be seen specifically in the question recently posed by the Dallas City Council: Should we or shouldn't we drop the ban on gay police officers?

William Murchison, a columnist for the *Dallas Morning News,* states in his editorial "City Shouldn't Ignore Morality" that there is no reason homosexuals should be permitted to serve on the Dallas police force. Nevertheless, Murchison's is not a strong argument as it is based upon faulty reasoning, distorted evidence, and broad assumptions.

Murchison presents several reasons to justify his stance against homosexual cops. His first and most effective reason deals with the questionable legality of allowing gays to serve as officers of the law. Murchison cites the state sodomy law, which declares relations with someone of the same sex a misdemeanor. In doing so, he argues that gays, who must be considered repeat offenders under this law, do not qualify to serve as police.

Murchison's second reason deals with his perception of gay police as poor role models. However, Murchison does not clearly state why he feels homosexual police would be poor role models. One must assume it is because he sees homosexuality as wrong and fears that children would become too accepting of the gay lifestyle were they to embrace gay role models. Moreover, Murchison may fear that children would actually become gay in an effort to imitate their role models. If so, he is assuming that an officer's sexual orientation would be apparent during the performance of his or her professional duties. Furthermore, scientific evidence has begun to point towards a biological basis for homosexuality. If this is in fact the case, society need not worry about children choosing to become homosexual because they think it is "cool."

However, the most destructive flaw in Murchison's argument results from 5
the assumptions upon which he bases his main reason: that homosexuality violates "the moral law." First, Murchison assumes that "moral law" exists. This is a major fault because the existence of moral law cannot be proven. It hinges upon individual beliefs about the human condition. Thus, people who believe that humans are innately good are likely to believe in moral law, while those who believe that humans are innately evil are unlikely to believe in moral law. Thus much of Murchison's argument is ineffective if the audience does not believe in moral law.

Murchison also assumes that all of mankind shares the same moral law. However, this is not necessarily the case. In fact, many would argue that morality is shaped by religion and can thus vary as greatly as do religious beliefs and practices. Another assumption which relates to this concept is the premise that homosexuality is against moral law. If all of humanity does not share the same moral law, then homosexuality may not be against everyone's moral law.

Murchison's final assumption is that homosexuality is a choice, and while that may be, there is mounting evidence that biological factors play a large role in determining sexual orientation. If this is in fact the case and sexual preference is actually determined before birth, then how can homosexuality be considered wrong? Wouldn't it have to become amoral, and of no more consequence than the color of one's eyes?

As evidence to support his point that homosexuality violates the moral law, Murchison argues that AIDS is a logical outcome of engaging in homosexual activities. Evidently, Murchison has forgotten about the tremendous number of people who have contracted AIDS through heterosexual sex, blood transfusions, and sharing needles, as well as the many practicing homosexuals who have not contracted AIDS. The belief that homosexuality and AIDS are intrinsically linked is a massive distortion of the truth.

Thus, what at first appears to be a thoughtful and well executed argument is actually full of weaknesses and contradictions. Murchison's reasoning is faulty, his evidence is distorted, and the assumptions upon which he bases his argument are not necessarily true. It is clear that Murchison designed his argument to appeal to those already entrenched in antihomosexual prejudice. Murchison's argument is nothing more than an emotional appeal, and thus he fails to convince the reader of the validity of his claim.

INQUIRING INTO A RANGE OF POSITIONS

When preparing to write an argument of your own, you should review a variety of published arguments and informative articles about your issue. As you read conflicting points of view, you will discover that the debate surrounding an issue seldom lines up on two distinct sides, for and against. Instead you will find a range of positions, varying with the particular interests and insights of the participants in the debate. Writers who disagree on some points, for example, will agree on others. In order to determine your own best position, you will need to explore a full range of opinions. But sorting through the many positions you encounter can be a challenge.

We suggest that as you inquire into the various positions on an issue, you use your writer's notebook or index cards to record your responses based on the following advice.

Read the sources critically. Be sure that they are addressing the same issue, not just the same topic. For example, one issue growing out of the topic of acquaintance rape is whether incidents of acquaintance rape on college campuses should be handled by college judicial boards or turned over to local police; a different issue on the same topic is whether acquaintance rape can be distinguished from other types of rape. Be able to write a clear statement of the issue being addressed.

Identify the important facts involved in the debate. Factual information can be verified: names, numbers, locations, dates, and so on. You will want to note if any sources disagree about some of the facts. Which sources seem most reliable?

Identify the positions. If your sources are arguments, write a paraphrase of each writer's main claim, or thesis. If you have a source that is an informative article, you may find several positions given, including the names of people or groups who hold those positions. Paraphrase each of these positions as well. Extreme contrasts among positions will be readily apparent; but try to note also more subtle differences among positions that are similar.

Note interactions among the different positions. As you compare arguments on a common issue, you will find topics addressed by several if not all voices in the debate. Cutting across the arguments, you should look at how questions raised by one writer are also addressed by other writers. The idea is to note the threads of conversation that weave through the entire debate and see where the writers agree and where they disagree.

As you move back and forth across the arguments, you may want to work with different colored highlighters to color code the major questions of the debate. Another practical method for making comparisons is to use index cards, recording on one card what writer A has to say on the question of X, on another card what writer B has to say about the same question, and so on.

Conclude your exploration with a tentative position for your own argument. Which sources have contributed to your thinking? What arguments have you accepted, and why?

Following Through

Read two or three arguments on a single issue. Then write a dialogue in which you have the writers set forth their own ideas and challenge each other's. You might also include yourself in the conversation, posing questions and listening to the alternating voices as they agree and disagree (see the questions for inquiry on pages 44–45). You need not take a side, but you do want to be a critical inquirer.

The Exploratory Essay

As a step towards composing an argument of your own, you may be assigned to write an essay that explores the various positions you have encountered in your reading. Such an essay does not begin with a thesis, but rather with a description of the issue under debate and an overview of the conflicting positions. The purpose of the essay is to discover what you accept and reject among the arguments that make up public debate on the issue. Writing such an essay should help you find a position that you can feel confident defending.

Whether your essay is an informal notebook entry or a piece revised for your classmates or instructor, it ought to take the following shape:

Introduction: *Defining and describing the issue.* The paragraphs in this section should introduce the topic and the issue. Include relevant factual information upon which everyone seems to agree. Also paraphrase the positions of the leading voices in the debate.

Inquiry: *Comparing points of disagreement.* The paragraphs in this section should compare the basic points of disagreement among the positions you have just described. Instead of devoting one or two paragraphs to each writer or position, try to organize your paragraphs around particular questions or points upon which the writers differ: "On the question of X, writer A and others who agree with her position argue. . . . Writer B, on the other hand, thinks. . . ." Comment on the strengths and weaknesses of the contrasting views.

Conclusion: *Taking your own position.* Exploratory essays should end with a statement of your own tentative position on the issue, and an explanation of why you think it the best. You may support one of the arguments you have analyzed, modify one of those arguments, or offer a different argument of your own. The important thing is not to leave your readers hanging or yourself sitting on the fence. Make it clear what you think, and why.

Three Opposing Positions

Following are three arguments on the topic of euthanasia. They all address the same issue: Should assisted suicide, what some call active euthanasia, be made legal in the United States? You may already have read the first argument, which appears in Chapter 4; the others offer additional viewpoints on the issue. A sample exploratory essay comparing the three begins on page 69.

WILLIAM F. MAY

Rising to the Occasion of Our Death

FOR MANY parents, a Volkswagen van is associated with putting children to sleep on a camping trip. Jack Kevorkian, a Detroit pathologist, has now linked the van with the veterinarian's meaning of "putting to sleep." Kevorkian conducted a dinner interview with Janet Elaine Adkins, a 54-year-old Alzheimer's patient, and her husband and then agreed to help her commit suicide in his VW van. Kevorkian pressed beyond the more generally accepted practice of passive euthanasia (allowing a patient to die by withholding or withdrawing treatment) to active euthanasia (killing for mercy).

Kevorkian, moreover, did not comply with the strict regulations that govern active euthanasia in, for example, the Netherlands. Holland requires that death be imminent (Adkins had beaten her son in tennis just a few days earlier); it demands a more professional review of the medical evidence and the patient's resolution than a dinner interview with a physician (who is a stranger and who does not treat patients) permits; and it calls for the final, endorsing signatures of two doctors.

So Kevorkian-bashing is easy. But the question remains: Should we develop a judicious, regulated social policy permitting voluntary euthanasia for the terminally ill? Some moralists argue that the distinction between allowing to die and killing for mercy is petty quibbling over technique. Since the patient in any event dies—whether by acts of omission or commission—the route to death doesn't really matter. The way modern procedures have made dying at the hands of the experts and their machines such a prolonged and painful business has further fueled the euthanasia movement, which asserts not simply the right to die but the right to be killed.

But other moralists believe that there is an important moral distinction between allowing to die and mercy killing. The euthanasia movement, these critics contend, wants to engineer death rather than face dying. Euthanasia would bypass dying to make one dead as quickly as possible. It aims to relieve suffering by knocking out the interval between life and death. It solves the problem of suffering by eliminating the sufferer.

The impulse behind the euthanasia movement is understandable in an age 5
when dying has become such an inhumanly endless business. But the movement may fail to appreciate our human capacity to rise to the occasion of our death. The best death is not always the sudden death. Those forewarned of death and given time to prepare for it have time to engage in acts of reconciliation. Also, advanced grieving by those about to be bereaved may ease some of their pain. Psychiatrists have observed that those who lose a loved one accidentally have a more difficult time recovering from the loss than those who have suffered through an extended period of illness before the death. Those who have lost a close relative by accident are more likely to experience what Geoffrey Gorer has called limitless grief. The community, moreover, may need its aged and dependent, its sick and its dying, and the virtues which they sometimes evince—the virtues of humility, courage, and patience—just as much as the community needs the virtues of justice and love manifest in the agents of care.

On the whole, our social policy should allow terminal patients to die but it should not regularize killing for mercy. Such a policy would recognize and respect that moment in illness when it no longer makes sense to bend every effort to cure or to prolong life and when one must allow patients to do their own dying. This policy seems most consonant with the obligations of the community to care and of the patient to finish his or her course.

Advocates of active euthanasia appeal to the principle of patient autonomy—as the use of the phrase "voluntary euthanasia" indicates. But emphasis on the patient's right to determine his or her destiny often harbors an extremely naïve view of the uncoerced nature of the decision. Patients who plead to be put to death hardly make unforced decisions if the terms and conditions under which they receive care already nudge them in the direction of the exit. If the elderly have stumbled around in their apartments, alone and frightened for years, or if they have spent years warehoused in geriatrics barracks, then the decision to be killed for mercy hardly reflects an uncoerced decision. The alternative may be so wretched as to push patients toward this escape. It is a huge irony and, in some cases, hypocrisy to talk suddenly about a compassionate killing when the aging and dying may have been starved for compassion for many years. To put it bluntly, a country has not earned the moral right to kill for mercy unless it has already sustained and supported life mercifully. Otherwise we kill for compassion only to reduce the demands on our compassion. This statement does not charge a given doctor or family member with impure motives. I am concerned here not with the individual case but with the cumulative impact of a social policy.

I can, to be sure, imagine rare circumstances in which I hope I would have the courage to kill for mercy—when the patient is utterly beyond human care, terminal, and in excruciating pain. A neurosurgeon once showed a group of physicians and an ethicist the picture of a Vietnam casualty who had lost all four limbs in a landmine explosion. The catastrophe had reduced the soldier to a trunk with his face transfixed in horror. On the battlefield I would hope that I would have the courage to kill the sufferer with mercy.

But hard cases do not always make good laws or wise social policies. Regularized mercy killings would too quickly relieve the community of its obligation to provide good care. Further, we should not always expect the law to provide us with full protection and coverage for what, in rare circumstances, we may morally need to do. Sometimes the moral life calls us out into a no-man's-land where we cannot expect total security and protection under the law. But no one said that the moral life is easy.

SIDNEY HOOK

In Defense of Voluntary Euthanasia

Sidney Hook (1902–1989) was a philosophy professor at New York University. This essay was originally printed in the New York Times *in 1987.*

A FEW short years ago, I lay at the point of death. A congestive heart failure was treated for diagnostic purposes by an angiogram that triggered a stroke. Violent and painful hiccups, uninterrupted for several days and nights, prevented the ingestion of food. My left side and one of my vocal cords became paralyzed. Some form of pleurisy set in, and I felt I was drowning in a sea of slime. At one point, my heart stopped beating; just as I lost consciousness, it was thumped back into action again. In one of my lucid intervals during those days of agony, I asked my physician to discontinue all life-supporting services or show me how to do it. He refused and predicted that someday I would appreciate the unwisdom of my request.

A month later, I was discharged from the hospital. In six months, I regained the use of my limbs, and although my voice still lacks its old resonance and carrying power I no longer croak like a frog. There remain some minor disabilities and I am restricted to a rigorous, low-sodium diet. I have resumed my writing and research.

My experience can be and has been cited as an argument against honoring requests of stricken patients to be gently eased out of their pain and life. I cannot agree. There are two main reasons. As an octogenarian, there is a reasonable likelihood that I may suffer another "cardiovascular accident" or worse. I may not even be in a position to ask for the surcease of pain. It seems to me that I have already paid my dues to death—indeed, although time has softened my memories they are vivid enough to justify my saying that I suffered enough to warrant dying several times over. Why run the risk of more?

Secondly, I dread imposing on my family and friends another grim round of misery similar to the one my first attack occasioned.

My wife and children endured enough for one lifetime. I know that for 5
them the long days and nights of waiting, the disruption of their professional duties and their own familial responsibilities counted for nothing in their anxiety for me. In their joy at my recovery they have been forgotten. Nonetheless, to visit another prolonged spell of helpless suffering on them as my life ebbs away, or even worse, if I linger on into a comatose senility, seems altogether gratuitous.

But what, it may be asked, of the joy and satisfaction of living, of basking in the sunshine, listening to music, watching one's grandchildren growing into adolescence, following the news about the fate of freedom in a troubled world, playing with ideas, writing one's testament of wisdom and folly for posterity? Is not all that one endured, together with the risk of its recurrence, an acceptable price for the multiple satisfactions that are still open even to a person of advanced years?

Apparently those who cling to life no matter what think so. I do not.

The zest and intensity of these experiences are no longer what they used to be. I am not vain enough to delude myself that I can in the few remaining years make an important discovery useful for mankind or can lead a social movement or do anything that will be historically eventful, no less event-making. My autobiography, which describes a record of intellectual and political experiences of some historical value, already much too long, could be posthumously published. I have had my fill of joys and sorrows and am not greedy for more life. I have always thought that a test of whether one had found happiness in one's life is whether one would be willing to relive it—whether, if it were possible, one would accept the opportunity to be born again.

Having lived a full and relatively happy life, I would cheerfully accept the chance to be reborn, but certainly not to be reborn again as an infirm octogenarian. To some extent, my views reflect what I have seen happen to the aged and stricken who have been so unfortunate as to survive crippling paralysis. They suffer, and impose suffering on others, unable even to make a request that their torment be ended.

I am mindful too of the burdens placed upon the community, with its 10
rapidly diminishing resources, to provide the adequate and costly services necessary to sustain the lives of those whose days and nights are spent on mattress graves of pain. A better use could be made of these resources to increase the opportunities and qualities of life for the young. I am not denying the moral obligation the community has to look after its disabled and aged. There are times, however, when an individual may find it pointless to insist on the fulfillment of a legal and moral right.

What is required is no great revolution in morals but an enlargement of imagination and an intelligent evaluation of alternative uses of community resources.

Long ago, Seneca observed that "the wise man will live as long as he ought, not as long as he can."[1] One can envisage hypothetical circumstances in which one has a duty to prolong one's life despite its costs for the sake of others, but such circumstances are far removed from the ordinary prospects we are considering. If wisdom is rooted in knowledge of the alternatives of choice, it must be reliably informed of the state one is in and its likely outcome. Scientific medicine is not infallible, but it is the best we have. Should a rational person be willing to endure acute suffering merely on the chance that a miraculous cure might presently be at hand? Each one should be permitted to make his own choice—especially when no one else is harmed by it.

The responsibility for the decision, whether deemed wise or foolish, must be with the chooser.

MATTHEW E. CONOLLY

Euthanasia Is Not the Answer

Matthew E. Conolly, a professor of medicine at UCLA, delivered this speech before a 1985 conference sponsored by the Hemlock Society, an organization that advocates voluntary euthanasia.

FROM THE moment of our conception, each of us is engaged in a personal battle that we must fight alone, a battle whose final outcome is never in any doubt, for, naked, and all too often alone, sooner or later we *all* must die.

[1]Seneca (4 B.C.E.–65 C.E.) lived in Rome and taught a philosophy known as Stoicism, which advocated duty, self-discipline, and adherence to the natural order of things.

We do not all make life's pilgrimage on equal terms. For some the path is strewn with roses, and after a long and healthy life, death comes swiftly and easily, for others it is not so. The bed of roses is supplanted by a bed of nails, with poverty, rejection, deformity, and humiliation the only lasting companions they ever know.

I know that many people here today carry this problem of pain in a personal way, or else it has been the lot of someone close to you. Otherwise you would not be here. So let me say right at the outset, that those of us who have not had to carry such a burden dare not criticize those who have, if they should plead with us for an early end to their dismal sojourn in this world.

Hard Cases Make Bad Laws

Society in general, and the medical profession in particular, cannot just turn away. We must do *something;* the question is—what?

The "what" we are being asked to consider today, of course, is voluntary 5
euthanasia. So that there be no confusion, let me make it quite clear that to be opposed to the active taking of life, one does not have to be determined to keep the heart beating at all costs.

I believe I speak for all responsible physicians when I say that there clearly comes a time when death can no longer be held at bay, and when we must sue for peace on the enemy's terms. At such a time, attending to the patient's comfort in body, mind, and soul becomes paramount. There is no obligation, indeed no justification, for pressing on at such a time with so-called life-sustaining measures, be they respirators, intravenous fluids, CPR, or whatever. I believe that there is no obligation to continue a treatment once it has been started, if it becomes apparent that it is doing no good. Also, withholding useless treatment and letting nature take its course is *not* equivalent to active euthanasia. Some people have attempted to blur this distinction by creating the term "passive euthanasia." The least unkind thing that can be said about this term is that it is very confusing.

Today's discussion really boils down to the question—do hard and tragic cases warrant legalization of euthanasia? There can be no doubt that hard and tragic cases do occur. However, the very natural tendency to want to alleviate human tragedy by legislative change is fraught with hazard, and I firmly believe that every would-be lawmaker should have tattooed on his or her face, where it can be seen in the mirror each morning, the adage that HARD CASES MAKE BAD LAWS.

If we take the superficially humane step of tailoring the law to the supposed wishes of an Elizabeth Bouvia (who, incidentally, later changed her mind),[1] we will not only bring a hornet's nest of woes about our own ears, but, at a stroke, we will deny many relatives much good that we could have salvaged from a sad situation, while at the same time giving many *more* grief and guilt to contend

[1] Elizabeth Bouvia, chronically ill with cerebral palsy and crippling arthritis, was well-known in the 1980s for her legal battles for the right to starve herself to death while she was hospitalized.

with. Even worse, we will have denied our patients the best that could have been offered. Worst of all, that soaring of the human spirit to heights of inspiration and courage which only adversity makes possible will be denied, and we will all, from that, grow weaker, and less able to deal with the crisis of tomorrow.

Unleashing Euthanasia

Let's look at these problems one by one. The first problem is that once we unleash euthanasia, once we take to ourselves the right actively to terminate a human life, we will have no means of controlling it. Adolf Hitler showed with startling clarity that once the dam is breached, the principle somewhere compromised, death in the end comes to be administered equally to all—to the unwanted fetus, to the deformed, the mentally defective, the old and the unproductive, and thence to the politically inconvenient, and finally to the ethnically unacceptable. There is no logical place to stop.

The founders of Hemlock no doubt mean euthanasia only for those who 10
feel they can take no more, but if it is available for one it must be available for all. Then what about those precious people who even to the end put others before themselves? They will now have laid upon them the new and horrible thought that perhaps they ought to do away with themselves to spare their relatives more trouble or expense. What will they feel as they see their 210 days of Medicare hospice payments run out, and still they are alive. Not long ago, Governor Lamm of Colorado suggested that the old and incurable have a *duty* to get out of the way of the next generation. And can you not see where these pressures will be the greatest? It will be amongst the poor and dispossessed. Watts will have sunk in a sea of euthanasia long before the first ripple laps the shore of Brentwood. Is that what we mean to happen? Is that what we want? Is there nobility of purpose there?

It matters to me that my patients trust me. If they do so, it is because they believe that I will always act in their best interests. How could such trust survive if they could never be sure each time I approached the bed that I had not come to administer some coup de grace when they were not in a state to define their own wishes?

Those whose relatives have committed more conventional forms of suicide are often afterwards assailed by feelings of guilt and remorse. It would be unwise to think that euthanasia would bring any less in its wake.

A Better Way

Speaking as a physician, I assert that unrelieved suffering need never occur, and I want to turn to this important area. Proponents of euthanasia make much of the pain and anguish so often linked in people's minds with cancer. I would not dare to pretend that the care we offer is not sometimes abysmal, whether because of the inappropriate use of aggressive technological medicine, the niggardly use of analgesics, some irrational fear of addiction in a dying patient, or a lack of compassion.

However, for many, the process of dying is more a case of gradually loosing life's moorings and slipping away. Oftentimes the anguish of dying is felt not by the patient but by the relatives: just as real, just as much in need of compassionate support, but hardly a reason for killing the patient!

But let us consider the patients who do have severe pain, turmoil, and 15
distress, who find their helplessness or incontinence humiliating, for it is these who most engage our sympathies. It is wrong to assert that they must make a stark choice between suicide or suffering.

There is another way.

Experience with hospice care in England and the United States has shown repeatedly that in *every* case, pain and suffering can be overwhelmingly reduced. In many cases it can be abolished altogether. This care, which may (and for financial reasons perhaps must) include home care, is not easy. It demands infinite love and compassion. It must include the latest scientific knowledge of analgesic drugs, nerve blocks, antinausea medication, and so on. But it can be done, it can be done, it can be done!

Life Is Special

Time and again our patients have shown us that life, even a deformed, curtailed, and, to us, who are whole, an unimaginable life, can be made noble and worth living. Look at Joni Earickson—paraplegic from the age of seventeen—now a most positive, vibrant and inspirational person who has become world famous for her triumph over adversity. Time and time again, once symptoms are relieved, patients and relatives share quality time together, when forgiveness can be sought and given—for many a time of great healing.

Man, made in the image of his Creator, is *different* from all other animals. For this reason, his life is special and may not be taken at will.

We do not know why suffering is allowed, but Old and New Testament 20
alike are full of reassurances that we have not been, and will not ever be, abandoned by our God. "Yea, though I walk through the valley of the shadow of death, I will fear no evil *for thou art with me.*"

Call to Change Direction

Our modern tragedy is that man has turned his back on God, who alone can help, and has set himself up as the measure of all things. Gone then is the absolute importance of man, gone the sanctity of his life, and the meaning of it. Gone too the motivation for loving care which is our responsible duty to the sick and dying. Goodbye love. Hello indifference.

With our finite minds, we cannot know fully the meaning of life, but though at times the storms of doubt may rage, I stake my life on the belief that to God we are special, that with Him, murder is unacceptable, and suicide (whatever you call it) becomes unnecessary.

Abandon God, and yes, you can have euthanasia. But a *good* death it can never be, and no subterfuge of law like that before us today can ever make it so.

My plea to the Hemlock Society is: Give up your goal of self-destruction. Instead, lend your energy, your anger, your indignation, your influence and creativity to work with us in the building of such a system of hospice care that death, however it come, need no longer be feared. Is not this a nobler cause? Is not this a better way?

A Sample Exploratory Essay

Exploring the Issue of Voluntary Euthanasia

THE QUESTION I am exploring is whether active euthanasia—assisted suicide—should be legalized as it is in some foreign countries, such as the Netherlands. Debate on this issue has been stirred by the activities of a Michigan pathologist, Jack Kevorkian, who is under criminal indictment for helping several terminally or chronically ill Americans to take their own lives. The arguments that I read are devoted exclusively to the kind of euthanasia in which the patient is conscious and rational enough to make a decision about terminating his or her life.

I encountered two basic positions on this issue. Sidney Hook, a philosopher, represents the view that assisted suicide should be a legal option for the patient. After recovering from a life-threatening illness, Hook decided that each patient must "be permitted to make his own choice" and to ask that his or her suffering be ended. The other two writers take the opposing view that legalizing active euthanasia is bad social policy. However, there their positions differ slightly. Matthew Conolly, a professor of medicine, argues that even the most extreme and tragic cases do not justify legalizing assisted suicide. His view is that proper medical and hospice care totally eliminates suicide as the only alternative to suffering. William May qualifies his opposition to active euthanasia by adding that in extreme cases it would be moral to break the law and to help someone die.

One question all three writers address is whether a patient's suffering justifies giving him or her the right to choose death. Hook argues that suffering can be too horrible to bear, and he supports this reason convincingly with evidence from his own experience with heart failure and stroke. The other writers counter by trying to see some inherent value in suffering. Both argue that it brings out distinctively human virtues, such as courage and patience. I find Hook more convincing on this question; an intelligent man, he did not "soar to heights of inspiration" as Conolly puts it, but rather felt he was drowning in a "sea of slime" as pleurisy filled his lungs. I agree that humans do have great capacity to carry on in spite of adversity, but that does not mean we should demand that they bear it. Their genuine feelings, from my own observations of dying relatives, are more likely fear and impatience, even self-pity.

The writers on both sides agree that the effects on loved ones of a patient's suffering are terrible. Hook offers this as the second of his two reasons for active euthanasia, claiming that his family's life during his illness was "a grim round of misery." Conolly agrees that the family may feel more anguish than the patient. However, when he says that this grief does not justify "killing the patient," he overlooks that the patient would be the one making the choice. And the life the patient is sacrificing for the sake of loved ones is not one he or she finds worth living.

All three writers also touch upon the relationship between the larger com- 5
munity and those within it who are sick and dying. Conolly and May see these people in terms of how they benefit the community, while Hook sees them in terms of what they cost. Conolly and May argue that a civilized society must accept its duty to care for the sick and dying. In this sense, having the sick and dying around gives society a chance to practice a virtue that is in too short supply as it is. Legalizing assisted suicide would make it all too easy for our society to further ignore its duty; as May says, we would "kill for compassion only to reduce the demands on our own compassion." He is right that Americans do not have a good record on compassion for the elderly. Typically, ailing grandparents are institutionalized rather than cared for in the homes of family. And as Conolly points out, the poor suffer the most from our society's indifference. But to argue as May does that a society needs to have sick and dying members in order to bring forth the virtues of caring and compassion asks too much of the sick and dying. It is like saying that we need to have the poor around in order to give the rich an opportunity to be charitable.

Hook agrees that the community has a "moral obligation" to "look after its disabled and aged," but he sees these people more as a burden on community resources; caring for them can become costly, reducing the quality of life for the rest, especially the young. I admire the selflessness of this man, but his argument makes me ask—Is it right to let individuals choose to sacrifice themselves for the sake of the rest?

The answer to this question turns upon one other question that all three writers take up: How freely could one make the choice to die? Hook seems to assume that the choice for everyone would be as unpressured as he feels it would be in his case. But he wrote his argument as an old man with a highly successful life behind him—a man who had enjoyed so much he was in a position to be generous with his life. I tend to agree with Conolly that in poor families, guilt may replace generosity as the motive when insurance or Medicare funds run out. And May argues that elderly people who have lived alone or in institutions for years may choose death out of sheer despair. It is as if the whole society has coerced them into dying.

Hook, Conolly, and May touch on other points in common, but the preceding strike me as the questions most central to the debate. I approached this topic with an inclination to take a position in favor of legalizing assisted suicide. These readings made me see that this policy may bring with it certain dangers.

I agree with Conolly that the medical profession could do more to reduce the suffering of the terminally ill, and I agree with May that society needs to become more compassionate and responsible for quality of life among the aged and terminally ill. However, I do not see either of these desirable goals as alternatives to the option of active euthanasia. Extreme cases of suffering will continue, and they are not as rare as Conolly implies.

However, Conolly and May helped me to see that the apparent individual 10
freedom of choice involved in assisted suicide may be an illusion, so I would want to qualify my position to include a process whereby the courts would be involved to protect the interests of the dying patient. This step may prolong the process of obtaining relief, but I think it ensures justice. Assisted suicide should be a choice, but it must involve more than simply patient, family, and doctor.

USING INQUIRY BY PEERS IN WRITING AN ARGUMENT

After some research into a topic you are preparing to write about, you will find that inquiry by your peers can help you in reaching a position you can defend. We will illustrate how inquiry works in class discussion with an example of one student's presentation of her tentative position and her responses to the questions raised by her classmates.

Dana's topic was harassment codes, which many colleges and universities have recently enacted to restrict language or behavior that is offensive to minorities and other groups by making such behavior a punishable offense. For example, a code in effect at Southern Methodist University states that harassment "directed towards one or more individuals because of race, ethnicity, religion, sex, age, sexual orientation, or handicap is strictly prohibited. Harassment includes but is not limited to physical, psychological, oral, or written abuse." Although such codes have been ruled unconstitutional at some public schools, a number of private schools have been able to defend them successfully.

In preparation for writing an argument on this topic, students did some assigned reading and outside research. Following is a transcript of how Dana presented her initial position to the class in a brief statement.

Dana: I believe the antiharassment code is well-intentioned but dangerous because it threatens the atmosphere of free expression and inquiry that is vital to a great university. The code is vague about what is prohibited, and students will worry too much about expressing opinions that might be described as abusive.

Next, to help Dana think through her argument, her classmates questioned her position, even if they agreed with it, and Dana tried to answer their objections.

Q: Dana, I understand you to say that you are against the code, but you admit it is well-intentioned. So you are saying that it would be a good thing to curb harassment? [question about thesis]

A: I'm saying it is bad to harass, but it is also bad to have these codes because it's hard to draw the line between what should be allowed and what should not. Some opinions may hurt, but people should be allowed to say them. For example, I found a case at one university where a gay student complained because another student in the class said homosexuality was a disease that was treatable. That's an opinion, and to prohibit its expression is a blow against academic freedom.

Q: Are you assuming that our code actually does prohibit students from expressing such opinions? [question about reasons and the assumptions behind them]

A: Our code says psychological abuse is harassment. If a gay person was offended by the opinion that homosexually is an illness, he could claim to be psychologically abused.

Q: So when you said "the spirit of free expression and inquiry" is vital at a great university, you include the right to express offensive opinions? How far would you take that? Would you include the opinions of the Ku Klux Klan? Of Adolf Hitler? [question about definition and implications of the argument]

A: Yes, it has to include offensive opinions—even those of the Klan and Hitler.

Q: Wouldn't these make some people very uncomfortable and even fearful? [question about implications]

A: Yes, but the academic environment requires that there be no restrictions on thought and its expression.

Q: So you are saying that it is more important to have academic freedom at a university than to have a climate where people are not made to feel abused? [question about values]

A: Yes, but to say so makes me sound insensitive. I'm not defending harassment; I just think it is essential that a university guarantees students the right to express opinions.

Q: If the line between offensive opinions and harassment could be drawn more clearly, do you think you could support the code? [question about thesis]

A: I don't think so. Anyway, I don't think it could be done.

Q: Would you say calling someone a "fag" was an opinion that should be protected? Can calling people names possibly be a part of the spirit of academic inquiry? [question about definition]

A: I agree that name-calling and epithets don't belong in an academic environment, but I have to think more about whether that kind of expression should be restricted and how a code might be worded to eliminate that sort of thing, but not free expression. I plan to look at the wording of some codes from other schools.

This dialogue, like all dialogues, could go on indefinitely. But from this brief exchange, you can see that if Dana is to be confident that she has arrived at the best position she can on the issue, she has to think more about her definition of "free inquiry" and her priorities regarding free expression versus protection from harassment. She also will have to consider the meaning of *harassment:* If she can think of examples of expressions and behavior that would constitute clear harassment, she will have to admit that a different wording of the code might be more defensible.

Following Through

If your class has been exploring topics for argument, write a statement of fifty to one hundred words on the position you are planning to take. As Dana did in the preceding example, include in your statement your main claim, or thesis, and explain why you feel the way you do. Then present your statement to a classmate or small group and together construct a written "conversation" about your position. Or present your statement to the whole class for inquiry.

CHAPTER SIX

Making Your Case: Arguing to Convince

The last chapter ended where inquiry ends—with the attempt to formulate a position, an opinion that we can assert with some confidence. Once our aim shifts from inquiry to convincing, everything changes.

The most significant change is in audience. In inquiry our audience is our fellow inquirers, generally friends, classmates, and teachers we can talk with face-to-face; we seek assurance that our position is at least plausible and defensible, a claim to truth that they can respect whether or not they agree with it. In convincing, our audience becomes readers whose positions differ from our own or who have no positions at all on the issue. The audience shifts from a small, inside group that helps us develop our argument to a larger, public audience that will either accept or reject it.

As the audience changes so does the situation or need for argument. Inquiry is a cooperative use of argument. It cannot take place unless people are willing to work together. Convincing, conversely, is competitive. We pit our case against others in an effort to win the assent of readers, who will compare what we say with what others say and ask, "Who makes the best case? With whom should I agree?"

Because of the change in audience and situation our thinking also changes, becoming more strategic and calculated to influence a reader. In inquiry, we try to make a case we can believe in; in convincing, we must make a case that readers can believe in. What we find compelling in inquiry will sometimes also convince our readers, but we will always have to adapt our reasoning to appeal to their beliefs, values, and self-interest. We will also likely offer reasons that did not occur to us at all in inquiry but that come as we attempt to imagine the people we hope to convince. This shift to convincing does not, however, mean abandoning the work of inquiry. Our version of the truth, our convictions, must first be earned through inquiry before we can seek to convince others in the public arena.

In this chapter we will first look at the structure and strategy of complete essays that aim to convince. Then we will provide a step-by-step analysis of the kind of thinking necessary to produce a successful essay which argues to convince.

THE NATURE OF CONVINCING: STRUCTURE AND STRATEGY

In Chapter 1 we defined argument as an assertion supported by a reason. To convince an audience, writers need to expand on this basic plan; they usually have to offer more than one reason, and they must support all reasons with evidence. In this chapter, we will use the term "case structure" to describe a flexible plan for making any argument to any audience that expects good reasoning. We will use the term "strategy" to describe the moves we make to shape a particular argument directed towards a specific audience. Strategic moves include selecting reasons, ordering the reasons, developing evidence, and linking the sections of our argument so that it will have maximum impact on an audience.

Case Structure

All cases have at least three levels of assertion. The first level is the thesis or central claim, which everything else in the case must support. The second level provides the reason or reasons the arguer advances for holding that thesis. The third level is the evidence offered to support each reason, generally drawn from some authoritative source.

In the abstract, then, cases look like this:

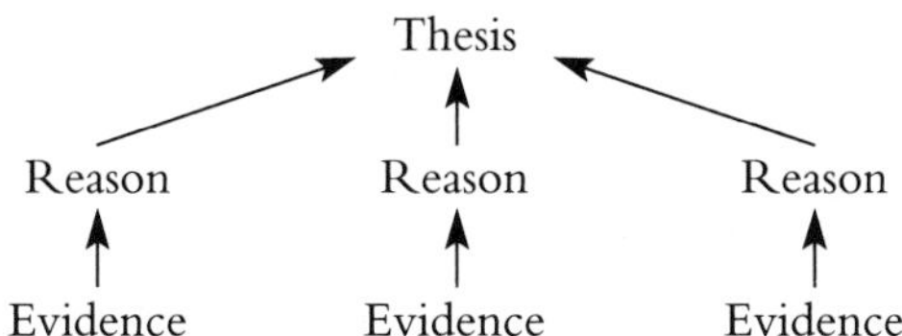

Our illustration shows three reasons, but as we have said, case structure is flexible. A good case could be built with just one reason, or with many more than three.

We refer to this plan as a structure because the parts are built upon each other: The reasons support the thesis and the evidence supports each reason.

Case Strategy

In Chapter 3 on reading arguments, we explained that you can read with greater comprehension if you begin with a sense of the rhetorical context in which the writer worked. Likewise, in preparing to write an argument, you should consider such rhetorical issues as the following:

Who is your intended audience? What preconceptions and biases might they hold about your topic?
What is your aim for writing?
What claim do you want your readers to accept? How strong a claim can you realistically expect them to accept?
What reasons are likely to appeal to this audience?
How should you arrange the reasons to make the greatest impression on your readers?
How should you lead into the argument? How should you conclude it?
What can you do to present yourself as a person the audience can trust and respect?

By working out answers to these questions in your writer's notebook, you will create a rhetorical prospectus which will help you envision a context within which to write and a tentative plan to follow.

To demonstrate case strategy we will look at an argument by Anne Marie O'Keefe, a psychologist and lawyer, that deals with drug testing in the workplace; it was published originally in *Psychology Today* in 1987. As a lawyer, O'Keefe is clearly concerned about employees' rights to privacy; as a psychologist she is sensitive to what drug testing does to human relationships. After careful inquiry, including library research, she has reached the position that, despite the dangers of drugs, the practice of testing people for drug use in the workplace should be prohibited.

Thinking about Audience

In order to make an effective case for her position, O'Keefe keeps in mind an audience that may favor workplace drug screening, and her strategy is to use reasons and evidence to convince readers who initially disagree with her. To do so, she had to consider the likely responses of such readers. Developing a strategy for her argument, then, O'Keefe had to begin with these questions:

Who will my readers be?
How will they be predisposed to view drug testing?
What will they have on their minds as soon as they see that my argument is against testing?

Based on these questions, O'Keefe made the following assumptions about her audience's views:

> Most people feel that drugs are a serious problem in the United States, there is widespread sentiment that something must be done about the problem, and drug testing is a form of specific action. But given Americans' suspicion of authority and high regard for individual rights, support for drug testing cannot run very deep. People may feel that it is necessary under the circumstances but regard it as an invasion of privacy.

Strategy, then, must begin with some thought about the audience, its values and preconceptions. Next we will examine how O'Keefe shapes the elements of case structure—thesis, reasons, and evidence—to appeal to her readers.

Formulating the Thesis

Assuming that her audience shares her esteem for constitutional rights, O'Keefe refines her position to a more specific thesis. While it may not appear word-for-word in the text of the argument, a thesis forecasts how a case will be made. Because you need a clear sense of what you are claiming in order to build the rest of your case, you should always write out a thesis as the first level of your argument's structure. O'Keefe's thesis does not appear explicitly in the text of her argument, but it can be summarized easily: Drug testing in the workplace is an unjustifiable intrusion on the privacy of workers.

Choosing Reasons

O'Keefe's thesis indicates that she will show drug testing to be an invasion of privacy and as such a wrong that cannot be justified. She builds her case on three reasons, aimed strategically at appealing to her audience and undermining their support for drug testing in the workplace.

Thesis: Drug testing in the workplace is an unjustifiable intrusion on the privacy of workers.

Reason 1: Drug abuse is actually declining, and the push for drug-testing in the workplace is motivated solely by politics and profit-making. (Strategy: O'Keefe wants her readers to question the need for testing and the motives of those who advocate testing.)

Reason 2: Drug tests are highly unreliable. (Strategy: O'Keefe wants to undermine any confidence her readers may have in the technology of drug testing.)

Reason 3: Drug testing violates our constitutional right to privacy and destroys employee morale. (Strategy: O'Keefe wants to appeal to American values and the self-interest of employers.)

While O'Keefe does mention the high cost to employers of drug testing, you'll notice that she has not chosen this as a main reason, as she might have had she been writing primarily for the business leaders she criticizes. Rather, she builds her case on values.

As you read O'Keefe's argument, notice how she has arranged her three reasons. We will have more to say later about her strategies for introducing each reason and supporting it with evidence.

ANNE MARIE O'KEEFE

The Case against Drug Testing

DURING 1986, the nation's concern over illegal drug use reached almost hysterical proportions. The U.S. House of Representatives passed legislation that, had the Senate agreed, would have suspended certain constitutional protections and required the death penalty for some drug offenses. The President issued an executive order calling for the mass drug testing of federal employees in "sensitive" positions. Federal courts have deemed such testing to be illegal for some classes of federal workers; however, these decisions are still being appealed, and the administration is determined to forge ahead with its drug-testing program. And private employers have turned increasingly to chemical laboratories to determine who is fit for hiring, promotion, and continuing employment. Between 1982 and 1985, the estimated proportion of Fortune 500 companies conducting routine urinalysis rose from 3 to nearly 30 percent—a figure expected to reach 50 percent by this year or next year.

While there are issues of legitimate concern about drug use and public safety, the speed and enthusiasm with which many of our elected representatives and business leaders have embraced drug testing as a panacea has left many questions unanswered. Why did our national drug problem so rapidly become the focus of political and business decisions? Did this change reflect a sudden, serious worsening of the problem? Why did mass drug testing suddenly gain favor? Was it shown to be particularly effective in detecting and deterring illegal drug use? And finally, what are the costs of making employees and job applicants take urine tests?

Our country has a serious drug problem. The National Institute on Drug Abuse (NIDA) estimates that nearly two-thirds of those now entering the work force have used illegal drugs—44 percent within the past year. But ironically, the drug-testing craze has come just when most types of drug use are beginning to wane. NIDA reports that for all drugs except cocaine, current rates are below those of 1979, our peak year of drug use.

Why the furor now? The drug-testing fad might be viewed as the product of both election-year posturing and well-timed and well-financed marketing efforts by test manufacturers. During the 1970s, the relatively low-cost chemical assay (called EMIT) that promised to detect drugs in urine was first manufactured. In the beginning, these tests were used only by crime laboratories, drug-treatment programs and the military. By the early 1980s, a handful of private employers were also using them. But more recently, sales of drug tests have gotten a big boost from the attitudes and edicts of the Reagan administration. On March 3, 1986, the President's Commission on Organized Crime recommended that all employees of private companies contracting with the federal government be regularly subjected to urine testing for drugs as a condition of employment. Then came the President's executive order on September 15, requiring the head of each executive agency to "establish a program to test for the use of illegal drugs by employees in sensitive positions." It remains unclear how many millions of federal workers will be subject to such testing if the President gets his way.

Strangely, drug testing is becoming widespread despite general agreement 5
that the results of mass tests are often highly inaccurate. Error rates reflect both inherent deficiencies in the technology and mistakes in handling and interpreting test results. In a series of studies conducted by the federal Centers for Disease Control (CDC) and NIDA, urine samples spiked with drugs were sent periodically to laboratories across the country serving methadone treatment centers.

Tests on these samples, which the labs knew had come from CDC, revealed drug-detection error rates averaging below 10 percent. However, when identical samples subsequently were sent to the same laboratories, but not identified as coming from CDC, error rates increased to an average of 31 percent, with a high of 100 percent. These errors were "false negatives," cases in which "dirty" urine samples were identified as "clean."

Independent studies of laboratory accuracy have also confirmed high error rates. One group of researchers reported a 66.5 percent rate of "false positives" among 160 urine samples from participants in a methadone treatment center. False-positive mistakes, identifying a "clean" urine sample as containing an illegal drug, are far more serious in the context of worker screening than are false-negative mistakes. This is because false positives can result in innocent people losing their jobs. Ironically, since the error rates inherent in the drug tests are higher than the actual rate of illegal drug use in the general working population, as reported by NIDA, the tests are more likely to label innocent people as illegal drug users than to identify real users.

Many of the false-positive results stem from a phenomenon known as "cross-reactivity." This refers to the fact that both over-the-counter and prescription drugs, and even some foods, can produce false-positive results on the tests. For example, Contac, Sudafed, certain diet pills, decongestants, and heart and asthma medications can register as amphetamines on the tests. Cough syrups containing dextromethorphan can cross-react as opiates, and some antibiotics show up as cocaine. Anti-inflammatory drugs and common painkillers, including Datril, Advil, and Nuprin, mimic marijuana. Even poppy seeds, which actually contain traces of morphine, and some herbal teas containing traces of cocaine can cause positive test results for these drugs.

Commercial testing companies almost always claim very high accuracy and reliability. But because these laboratories are not uniformly regulated, employers who buy their services may find it hard to confirm these claims or even to conduct informed comparative shopping. Companies that mass-market field-testing kits such as EMITs (which cost an estimated $15 to $25 per test) usually recommend that positive test results be confirmed with other laboratory procedures, which can run from $100 to $200 per test. But relatively few employers seem to be using the expensive back-up procedures before firing employees who test positive. Even when employers do verify positive results, employees who turn out to be drug-free upon retesting will already be stigmatized.

The tests have other critical failings, particularly their limited sensitivity to certain drugs, a shortcoming the drug-test manufacturers readily admit. Consider cocaine, for example. Despite great concern in the 1980s over the use of cocaine, the only illicit drug whose use is on the rise, this is the drug to which the tests are least sensitive since its chemical traces dissipate in a few days. Alcohol, which is legal but potentially detrimental to job performance, is also hard to detect, since traces disappear from within 12 to 24 hours. By contrast, urine testing is, if anything, overly sensitive to marijuana; it can detect the drug's chemical byproducts (not its active ingredient) for weeks after its use and can even pick up the residue of passive inhalation. Drug testing does not indicate the recency of use, nor does it distinguish between chronic and one-time use. Most important, though urinalysis can reveal a lot about off-the-job activities, it tells nothing about job performance.

10 Mass drug testing is expensive, but its greatest costs are not financial and cannot be neatly quantified. The greatest costs involve violations of workers' rights and the poor employee morale and fractured trust that result when workers must prove their innocence against the presumption of guilt.

The most important cost of drug testing, however, may be the invasion of workers' privacy. Urinalysis may be highly inaccurate in detecting the use of illegal drugs, but it can reveal who is pregnant, who has asthma, and who is being treated for heart disease, manic-depression, epilepsy, diabetes, and a host of other physical and mental conditions.

In colonial times, King George III justified having his soldiers break into homes and search many innocent people indiscriminately on the grounds that the procedure might reveal the few who were guilty of crimes against the Crown. But the founders of our nation chose to balance things quite differently. An important purpose and accomplishment of the Constitution is to protect us from government intrusion. The Fourth Amendment is clear that "the right of the people to be secure in their persons . . . against unreasonable searches and seizures, shall not be violated. . . ." Searches are permitted only "upon probable cause, supported by Oath or affirmation, and particularly describing the place to be searched, and the persons or things to be seized."

The U.S. Supreme Court has ruled that extracting bodily fluids constitutes a search within the meaning of this Amendment. Therefore, except under extraordinary circumstances, when the government seeks to test an employee's urine, it must comply with due process and must first provide plausible evidence of illegal activity. People accused of heinous crimes are assured of this minimum protection from government intrusion. Because employees in our government work force deserve no less, most courts reviewing proposals to conduct mass tests on such employees have found these programs to be illegal.

Unfortunately, workers in the private sector are not as well protected. The Constitution protects citizens only from intrusions by government (county, state, and federal); it does not restrict nongovernmental employers from invading workers' privacy, although employers in the private sector are subject to some limitations. The constitutions of nine states have provisions specifically protecting citizens' rights to privacy and prohibiting unreasonable searches and seizures. Several private lawsuits against employers are now testing the applicability of these shields. Local governments, can, if they wish, pass legislation to protect private employees from unwarranted drug tests; in fact, San Francisco has done so. In addition, union contracts and grievance procedures may give some workers protection from mass drug testing, and civil-rights laws could block the disproportionate testing of minorities. Nonetheless, private employees have relatively little legal protection against mandatory drug testing and arbitrary dismissal.

Civil libertarians claim that as long as employees do their work well, in- 15
quiries into their off-duty drug use are no more legitimate than inquiries into their sex lives. Then why has drug testing become so popular? Perhaps because it is simple and "objective"—a litmus test. It is not easily challenged because, like the use of lie detectors, it relies on technology that few understand. It is quicker and cheaper than serious and sustained efforts to reduce illegal drug use, such as the mass educational efforts that have successfully reduced cigarette smoking. And finally, while drug testing may do little to address the real problem of drug use in our society, it reinforces the employer's illusion of doing something.

Apparently some employers would rather test their employees for drugs than build a relationship with them based on confidence and loyalty. Fortunately, there are employers, such as the Drexelbrook Engineering Company in Pennsylvania, who have decided against drug testing because of its human costs. As Drexelbrook's vice president put it, a relationship "doesn't just come from a paycheck. When you say to an employee, 'you're doing a great job; just the same, I want you to pee in this jar and I'm sending someone to watch you,' you've undermined that trust."

Arranging Reasons

Throughout, O'Keefe's strategy is to deal with the likely preconceptions of her readers. After two introductory paragraphs, paragraphs 3 and 4 counter the justification for drug testing based in the belief that the problem of drug abuse is so great that extraordinary measures are required to cope with it. Yes, we have a substance abuse problem, O'Keefe says, but illegal drug use as a whole is declining and has been declining without drug testing. Having weakened this underlying rationale, she goes on to expose what she sees as the genuine motives behind drug testing—hysteria, political advantage, and money. Her strategy here—to discredit the politicians and business leaders who advocate drug testing—plays to the prejudices of many Americans, who view the Washington political establishment and big business as being generally motivated by self-interest.

O'Keefe next seeks to destroy her readers' confidence in the technology of drug testing. She devotes much space (paragraphs 5–9) to this reason, probably because she assumes her readers share the American faith in technology to provide clean, efficient, and relatively simple solutions for complex social problems. Undermining this faith, O'Keefe explicitly points out the "inherent deficiencies" in drug testing technology.

O'Keefe's final reason (paragraphs 10–16) achieves its full force based on reasons one and two. If (1) there is no compelling need for drug testing and the people pushing it are acting out of self-interest and (2) the technology is by nature faulty, then we have to take more seriously the violation of constitutional rights and the undermining of trust between employee and employer that are inherent in drug testing.

Using Evidence

How well has O'Keefe used the third level of case structure, the supporting evidence for each reason? For her first reason she briefly cites National Institute of Drug Abuse reports that the rate of drug use in 1987 was lower than that in 1979, a "peak year." She acknowledges that cocaine is an exception, but the authority of the source and the overall direction of the statistics would sway most readers. She then alleges that businesses and politicians are benefitting from the testing fad; this she supports with a chronological presentation of facts about the advocacy of these tests by the Reagan administration up to 1986, an election year. The strategy here is simply to make the political connection.

O'Keefe offers a wealth of evidence to support her second reason, that drug tests are unreliable (paragraphs 5–9). Her strategy in presenting this evidence is fairly simple but nonetheless effective. She divides her evidence in two parts and begins with the less serious charge: that drug tests can result in false negatives, or failures to detect the presence of illegal drugs. After calling our attention to the failures of drug testing in achieving its primary purpose, to identify users, she goes on to describe the more serious problem of false positives, which can lead to innocent people losing their jobs or being stigmatized in the workplace. She further contrasts error rates in labs that know they are being monitored with error rates in labs that don't, encouraging readers to conclude that the labs are careless and therefore untrustworthy.

In paragraph 8 O'Keefe recognizes a contradictory piece of evidence that defenders of drug testing would be likely to point out: that relatively reliable, more expensive tests exist. In granting the existence of such tests, O'Keefe defends her own case by suggesting that rather than go to the expense of double-checking, most employers will choose simply to fire employees based on the less expensive, less reliable test.

In backing up her third reason, an abstract argument about the right to privacy, O'Keefe appeals strongly and concretely to her readers' fears and their values. Urinalysis reveals "who is pregnant, who has asthma, and who is being treated for heart disease," and so on (paragraph 11), information that has nothing to do with illegal drugs and which most people feel is nobody's business but one's own and one's doctor's. Finally, O'Keefe refers to the authority of history and the Fourth Amendment's protection from unwarranted government intrusion, a basic American value associated with the founders of our nation.

Introducing and Concluding the Argument

We have analyzed O'Keefe's strategic use of the three levels of case structure—thesis, reasons, evidence—to build an argument that will convince her audience not to support drug testing. Arguing to convince also requires that a writer think strategically of ways to open and close his or her presentation of the case.

The Introduction O'Keefe's opening strategy is to cast her argument in terms of reasoned reaction as opposed to emotional overreaction. Note the careful choice of words in her opening sentence: "During 1986, the nation's concern over illegal drug use reached almost hysterical proportions." She goes on in the rest of the paragraph to "prove" her point with sentences that amount to a list: The U.S. House of Representatives did this . . . the President did that . . . private employers have done this. In other words, each of her points after her opening assertion is designed to strengthen our acceptance of "almost hysterical" as an accurate and plausible description of the reaction during 1986 to illegal drug use.

In paragraph 2 O'Keefe poses questions having to do with her three areas of discussion that advocates of drug testing have not answered: Why are the tests being done, how well do they work, and what effects do they have? This opening strategy accomplishes two purposes. First, it provokes the reader to think, to share in her skepticism. Second, it predicts the rest of O'Keefe's essay, which goes on to answer these questions.

The Conclusion O'Keefe's strategy in concluding her complex argument is fairly simple: She attempts to present a fair and rational evaluation of drug testing as a solution to the drug problem. First, in paragraph 15 she again questions why these tests have become so popular. This time her tone is less accusatory, and she seems to be trying to understand her well-intentioned but ill-informed opposition. In the final paragraph she effectively presents a flat alternative: Either we can test employees for drugs, or we can build employer-employee relationships based on mutual respect. She then closes with an image that cannot fail to stick: the undignified position of urinating in a jar while someone watches to make sure the sample is not tampered with. The lack of trust and the cold impersonality of corporate drug testing comes through in a conclusion of real power, made all the more effective because she actually quotes the words of a critical corporate executive.

Following Through

1. A successful essay has smooth transitions between its opening and its first reason and between its last reason and its conclusion, as well as between each of the reasons in the body of the essay. In your writer's notebook, describe how O'Keefe both announces that she is moving on from her introduction to her first reason, from her first reason to her second, and so on, and at the same time links each section with what has come before.
2. Read Gordon Moore's "Let's Provide Primary Care to All Uninsured Americans Now!" (page 310) and Jeffrey Nickel's " Everybody's Threatened by Homophobia" (page 486). Then in your writer's notebook identify the intended audience for each essay, list the thesis and reasons, and discuss each writer's strategies for choosing and arranging reasons, supporting the reasons, and opening and closing the argument.

THE PROCESS OF CONVINCING

Few people draft an essay sequentially, beginning with the first sentence of the first paragraph and ending with the last sentence of the last paragraph. But the final version of any essay must read as if it had been written sequentially, with the writer fully in control throughout the process.

A well-written essay is like a series of moves in a chess game, each made to achieve some end or ends, to gain a strategic advantage, as part of an overall plan to win, in the case of convincing, the agreement of the reader.

While readers may not be fully aware of the moves that make up a convincing argument, the writer probably created most of them through conscious design, or strategy. As the first half of this chapter has shown, we can learn much about how to convince by studying finished essays—polished arguments that convince. However, it is one thing to understand how something works but quite another to produce it ourselves. In part, the difficulty is that we cannot see from the final product everything that went into making it work so well. As the audience for a movie typically cannot imagine all the rehearsals and the many takes and the process of editing that make a scene so powerful, so it is hard for us to imagine all the research and thinking, the many drafts, and the process of editing and proofreading that O'Keefe must have gone through to make "The Case against Drug Testing" worth printing. And yet it is precisely this process you must understand and immerse yourself in if you are to go beyond appreciating the structure and strategies of someone else's writing and actually produce convincing arguments of our own.

The following discussion of the composing process assumes that the work of inquiry (Chapter 5) and research (Appendix A) has been done, and so does not recapitulate these phases of preparing to write. It also assumes that you have worked out a rhetorical prospectus to guide you in combining structure with strategy.

Preparing a Brief

Before you begin to draft, it is a good idea to prepare a brief. Recall that we defined case structure as an abstract form making up the elements of any case. In a brief, you customize and fill in that structure to make a particular argument. The brief shows the thesis and reasons that you plan to use, as well as some indication of how you will support each reason with evidence. The brief ought to indicate a tentative plan for arranging the reasons, but that plan may change as you draft and revise. In the following section, we will take you through the process of creating a brief.

Working toward a Position

First, we need to distinguish a *position* from a *thesis.* A position (or a stance or opinion) amounts to an overall, summarizing attitude or judgment about some issue. "Universities often exploit student athletes" is an example of a position. A thesis is not only more specific and precise but also more strategic, designed to appeal to readers and to be consistent with available evidence. For example, "Student athletes in revenue-generating sports ought to be paid for their services" would be one thesis representing the preceding position, perhaps for an audience of college students. Since a case is nothing more than the reasons and evidence that support a thesis, we cannot construct a case without a thesis. But without a position we do not know where we stand in general on an issue and so cannot experiment with various thesis formulations. Clearly, then, we must have a position before we can have a thesis.

The goal of inquiry is to earn an opinion, to find a stance that holds up in dialogue with other inquirers. What often happens in inquiry, however, is that we begin with a strong opinion, usually unearned, find it failing under scrutiny, discover positions advanced by others that do not fully satisfy us, and so emerge from inquiry uncertain about what we do think. Another common path in inquiry is to start out with no opinion at all, find ourselves attracted to several conflicting positions, and so wind up in much the same condition as the person whose strong initial position collapses under scrutiny—unsure, often even confused and vexed because we can't decide what we think.

In such situations, resolve first to be patient with yourself. Certainty is often cheap and easy; the best, most mature positions typically come to us only after a struggle. Second, take out your writer's notebook and start making lists. Look over your research materials, especially the notecards on which you have recorded positions and evidence from your sources. Make lists in response to these questions:

> What positions have you encountered in research and class discussion? What seems strongest and weakest in each stance? What modifications might be made to eliminate or minimize the weak points? Are there other possible positions? What are their strong and weak points?
>
> What pieces of evidence impressed you? What does each of these imply or suggest? What connections can you draw among the pieces of evidence given in various sources? If there is conflict in the implications of the evidence, state for yourself what the conflict is.

While all this list-making may seem at times to be only doodling, you can often begin to see convergences as your mind begins to sort things out.

Bear in mind that emotional commitment to ideas and values is important to a healthy life but is often an impediment to clear thought and effective convincing. Sometimes we find our stance by relinquishing an opinion to which we are strongly committed but which proves hard to make a case for—perhaps for lack of compelling reasons or evidence that can appeal to readers outside the group that already agrees with us. The more emotional the issue—abortion, pornography, affirmative action, among others—the more likely we are to cling to a position that is difficult to defend. When we sense deep conflict, when we want to argue a position even in the face of strong contradictory evidence and counterarguments we cannot respond to, it is time to reconsider our emotional commitments, perhaps even to change our minds.

Finally, if you find yourself holding out for the "perfect" position, the one that is all strength and no weakness, the best advice is to give up. Controversial issues are controversial precisely because no one's stance convinces everyone, because there is always room for counterargument, and for other positions that have their own power to convince.

Student Sample: Working Out a Position After reading several arguments about animal rights and about ethical treatment of animals by humans, student Carolina Villareal decided on the position "Wearing fur coats is immoral." She had in fact always held this position and became even more convinced when she read defenses of their trade written by members of the fur industry. One furrier, for example, argued that fake furs were not biodegradable like authentic furs and consequently environmentally unsound. Her primary reason for opposing the fur industry, however, was her feeling that people today have many options for warm outer wear that do not require killing animals. In other words, the fur industry is immoral because it takes the lives of animals when there is no necessity.

During inquiry Carolina was questioned by classmates about this reason. How did she define necessity? What about peoples whose cultures and climates traditionally required that furs be worn? Was it wrong for Eskimos and Lapps to wear furs? She decided that it was not. When asked, then, why it was wrong for a woman in New York City to do so, she answered that one can be warm and fashionable without wearing fur. She further stated that most people today wear fur as a status symbol or a fashion statement. She was then asked, what is wrong with fashion? After thinking about it, Carolina decided that fashion is an expression of vanity and, as such, is not as valuable as the lives of animals.

Following Through

Formulate a tentative position on a topic that you have researched and inquired into. Write it up with some brief explanation of why you support this stand. Be prepared to defend your position in class or with a peer in a one-on-one exchange of position statements.

Analyzing Your Audience

Before you decide on a thesis, you need to give some thought to the rhetorical context of the argument you are about to make. Who needs to hear it? What are their values? What common ground might you share with them? How might you have to qualify your position to influence their opinions?

In order to provoke thought, people occasionally make cases for theses that they know have little chance of winning significant assent. A good recent example is the argument for legalizing all drug use. Reasonably good cases have been made for this position, but because it is so radical, most Americans find even the best argument for this position unconvincing. If you want to convince, rather than to provoke thinking or play devil's advocate, you will need to formulate a thesis that both represents your position and creates as little resistance in your readers as possible. Instead of arguing for legalizing drugs, for example, you might argue that much of the staggering amount of money spent on enforcement, prosecution, and prisons be diverted to finance rehabilitation centers and to address the social problems connected with drug abuse.

Most positions allow for many possible theses; writers need to analyze their audience before settling on one. It is helpful to sit down and write an audience profile.

Student Sample: An Audience Profile Carolina, whose position on animal rights we looked at earlier, wisely decided not to write to members of the fur industry, who are unlikely to be persuaded by even the best of arguments. Rather Carolina determined the following audience profile.

> My audience would be potential consumers of fur coats, people considering buying one. These people would be upper-middle class, at least, since they would be able to spend thousands of dollars on a coat. They would probably be thirty years of age or older, mostly women, but some could be men. They socialize a great deal, attending parties, concerts, and plays. They value beautiful things, fashion, and status symbols, which is why they want to wear fur. They have probably not given much thought to animal rights issues, but they are intelligent people who would oppose cruelty to animals. My argument could get them to think twice if it shows that wearing fur is a cruel and unnecessary exploitation of animals.

Following Through

Write a profile of the audience you hope to reach through an argument you are currently planning. Try to be as specific as possible, including any information—age, gender, economic status, and so forth—that may contribute to your audience's outlook and attitudes. What interests, beliefs, and values may be influencing them? How might you have to alter your position or phrase your thesis in order to give your argument a chance of succeeding? What reasons might they be willing to consider? What would you have to rule out?

Refining a Thesis

A good thesis grows out of your position, your research into that position, and your understanding of your audience, including what they will be willing to accept. The thesis must present your position precisely, in language that is specific, not vague. The sentence that you write as a thesis will probably be longer than the one that merely states your position, but it should be clear and direct, making one main point. Below, we show the process one student used to refine her thesis.

Student Sample: Refining a Thesis Carolina's original statement, "Wearing fur coats is immoral," expresses a position, but it is not precise, nor is it aimed at a particular audience. Assuming an audience of fashion-conscious people, possible consumers of fur coats, Carolina needed a thesis statement that would make this group reflective rather than defensive. Also, she does not want readers to think she is taking an extreme animal rights position that would disallow any human use of animals. She refined her position to the following:

> Wearing furs is an unjustifiable use of animals.

This statement is less offensive and more specific, but she wanted to emphasize that her point applies to animals that have been killed for their fur alone, so she refined her position further:

> Killing an animal simply to obtain its fur is unjustifiable.

This statement is better, but it still ignores the problem of some justified uses of fur, such as within an ethnic tradition. She tried one more version.

> The desire to be fashionable does not justify killing an animal to obtain its fur.

Carolina was reasonably satisfied with this version, so she accepted it as a tentative thesis that could guide her in drafting her essay.

Following Through

1. Write at least three versions of a tentative thesis for the essay you are currently working on. For each version, write an evaluation of its strengths and weaknesses. Why is the best version the best?
2. As we saw in analyzing William May's case against assisted suicide (Chapter 4), sometimes a thesis needs to be qualified and exceptions to the thesis need to be stated and clarified. Now is a good time to think about qualifications and exceptions.

   Basically you can handle qualifications and exceptions in two ways. You can do what Carolina did—phrase the thesis in such a way that the qualifications and exceptions are implied. Her stipulation of a specific unacceptable reason ("the desire to be fashionable") implicitly acknowledges that there could be other, legitimate reasons for killing animals for their fur. So, while Carolina's essay must at some point contrast fashion with other, legitimate reasons, her thesis requires no further qualification.

   May's is an example of the other method: He states his claim and then qualifies it with the phrase "on the whole," ultimately spelling out when his claim would not apply.

   Using your best thesis statement from the previous exercise, decide whether qualifications and exceptions are needed. If they are, determine how best to handle them.

Analyzing the Thesis

Once you have a thesis, your next task is to unpack it to determine, given that thesis, what you must argue. Sometimes analyzing the thesis is relatively easy. Anne Marie O'Keefe's "Drug testing in the workplace is an unjustifiable intrusion on individuals' privacy" is a good example. First, you'll notice that her statement implies and thus requires an argument opposing *all* drug-testing in the workplace. Other areas of development required by this thesis are establishing workers' rights to privacy and showing how drug testing is unjustified. Many thesis statements, however, may appear relatively simple but are actually quite complex. We must determine both what they say and what they imply before we can make a case for them.

Let's consider a deceptively simple-sounding thesis on the issue of whether Mark Twain's *Huckleberry Finn* should be taught in public schools. One side has argued that Twain's classic novel should be taken off required reading lists because a number of readers, especially African Americans, find its subject matter and language offensive; in some schools the novel is not assigned at all, while at others it may be assigned, but students have the option of choosing to study another novel of the same period instead. In our example thesis, the writer supports the teaching of the novel: "Mark Twain's *Huckleberry Finn* should be required reading for all high school students in the United States."

Unpacking this thesis, we see that the writer must first argue for *Huckleberry Finn* as required reading—not just as a good book but as one that is *indispensable* to an education in American literature. The writer must show that the book is so valuable it justifies the risk of offending some students and their parents. The writer must also argue that the book be required reading at the high school level, rather than in middle school or at the college level. Finally, although the thesis does not specifically state this point, the writer must defend *Huckleberry Finn* from charges of rascism. Otherwise, these charges stand by default; to ignore them is to ignore the context of the issue.

Thesis statements with two or more parts are very common. Breaking such a thesis down into its parts is a key step towards understanding what an argument requires.

Student Sample: Analyzing the Thesis Analyzing her tentative thesis "The desire to be fashionable does not justify killing an animal just to obtain its fur," Carolina recognized that she would have to devote attention to the key words "fashion" and "justify," defining "fashion" and distinguishing being fashionable from other legitimate motives that would justify taking the lives of animals.

Carolina realized that she would also have to indicate that her other key word, "killing," referred to taking the lives of farm-raised animals such as minks, as well as trapping wild animals. Carolina saw that her thesis was based on the assumption that humans ought to justify any use of animals, an idea which implies that animals deserve moral consideration even if we do not grant them human value.

Following Through

Unpack a tentative thesis of your own, or one that your instructor gives you, to see what key words and phrases an argument based on that thesis must take up. Also consider what an audience would expect you to argue, given general knowledge about the topic and the current context of the dispute.

Finding Reasons

For the most part no special effort goes into finding reasons to support a thesis. They come to us as we attempt to justify our opinions, as we listen to the arguments of our classmates, as we encounter written arguments in research, and as we think about how to reach the readers we hope to convince. Given good preparation to write, we will seldom formulate a thesis without already having some idea of the reasons we will use to defend it. Our problem, rather, is usually selection, picking out the best reasons, and shaping and stating those reasons in a way that appeals to our readers. When we do find ourselves searching for reasons, however, it helps to be aware of the basic sources of reasons.

The Audience's Belief System You should ask yourself, "What notions of the real, the good, and the possible will my readers entertain?" Readers will find any reason unconvincing if it is not consistent with their understanding of reality. For example, people will accept or reject arguments about how to treat illness based on their particular culture's notions about disease. Likewise, people have differing notions of what is good. Some people think it is good to exploit natural resources so that we can live with more conveniences; those who place less value on conveniences see more good in conserving the environment. Finally, people disagree about what is possible. Those who believe it is not possible to change human nature will not accept arguments that certain types of criminals can be rehabilitated.

Special Rules or Principles Another common source of good reasons is a community's accepted rules and principles. For example, in the United States, citizens accept the principle that a person is innocent until proven guilty. The Fifth Amendment states that no one may be "deprived of life, liberty, or property, without due process of law." Americans apply this principle in all sorts of nonlegal situations whenever we argue that someone should be given the benefit of the doubt.

The law is only one source of special rules or principles. We also find them in politics ("one person, one vote"), in business (the principle of "seniority," which gives preference to employees who have been on a job longest), and even in the home, where each family formulates its own "rules of the house." In other words, all human settings and activities have their own norms, and we must ask ourselves in any search for reasons what norms may apply to our particular topic or thesis.

Expert Opinion and Hard Evidence Probably the next most common source of reasons is expert opinion, which we must rely on in dealing with any subject about which we do not have direct experience. Most readers respect the opinion of a trained professional with advanced degrees and prestige in his or her field. And when you can show that experts are in agreement, you have an even better reason.

Hard evidence can also provide good reasons. Readers generally respect the scientific method of gathering objective data upon which conclusions can be drawn. Research shows, for example, that air bags significantly reduce the incidence of death and serious injury in auto accidents. We can, therefore, support the thesis "Air bags should be mandatory for all cars sold in the United States" with the reason "because they have been shown to reduce the rate of death and serious injury significantly."

When you argue about any topic, you will be at a disadvantage if you don't have detailed, current information about it in the form of expert opinion and hard evidence.

Tradition We can sometimes strengthen a position by citing or alluding to well known sources that are part of our audience's cultural tradition: for example, the Bible, the Constitution, and the sayings or writings of people our audience recognizes and respects. Although reasons drawn from tradition may lose their force if many audience members identify with different cultures or are suspicious of tradition itself, they will almost always be effective when readers revere the source.

Comparison A reason based on similarity argues that what is true in one instance should be true in another, as well. For example, we could make a case for legalizing marijuana by showing that it is similar in effect to alcohol, which is legal—and also a drug. The argument might look like this:

> *Thesis:* Marijuana use should be decriminalized.
>
> *Reason:* Marijuana is no more harmful than alcohol.

Many comparison arguments attempt to show that present situations are similar to past ones. For example, many who argue for the civil rights of gay men and lesbians say that discrimination based on sexual preference should not be tolerated today just as discrimination based on race, common thirty years ago, is no longer tolerated.

A special kind of argument based on similarity is an analogy, which attempts to explain one thing, usually abstract, in terms of something else, usually more concrete. For example, in an argument opposing sharing the world's limited resources, philosopher Garrett Hardin argues that requiring the wealthy nations of the world to feed the starving nations is analogous to requiring the occupants of a lifeboat filled to a safe capacity to take on board those still in the water, until the lifeboat sinks and everyone perishes.

Arguments of comparison can also point to difference, showing how two things are not the same, or not analogous. For example, many Americans supported engagement in the 1992 Persian Gulf war by arguing that, unlike the disastrous conflict in Vietnam, this war was winnable. The argument went as follows:

Thesis: America can defeat Iraq's military.

Reason: Warfare in the deserts of Kuwait and Iraq is very different from warfare in the jungles of Vietnam.

The Probable or Likely Of course, all reasoning about controversial issues relies on making a viewpoint seem probable or likely, but specific reasons drawn from the probable or likely may often come into play when we want to defend one account of events over another or when we want to attack or support a proposed policy. For example, defenders of Supreme Court nominee Clarence Thomas attempted to discredit Anita Hill's accusations of sexual harrassment in a number of ways, all related to probability: Is it likely, they asked, that she would remember so clearly and in such detail events that happened as long as ten years ago? Is it probable that a woman who had been harassed would follow Thomas from one job to another, as Hill did?

Because a proposed policy may have no specific precedent, particularly if it is designed to deal with a new situation, speculating about its probable success or failure is sometimes all one arguing for or against the new policy can do. For example, the collapse of communism in eastern Europe and the former Soviet Union has left the United States in the unusual position of having no serious military threat to its own or its allies' security. What, then, should we do? Disband NATO? Drastically reduce our armed forces, especially the nuclear arsenal? Redirect part of what we once spent on defense into dealing with pressing domestic problems? Any proposal for confronting this new situation is defended and attacked based on what we are likely to face in the foreseeable future.

Cause and Effect People generally agree that most circumstances result from some cause or causes, and they also agree that most changes in circumstances will result in some new effects. This human tendency to believe in cause-and-effect relationships can provide reasons for certain arguments. For example, environmentalists have successfully argued for reductions in the world's output of hydroflourocarbons by showing that the chemicals damage the earth's ozone layer.

Cause-and-effect arguments are difficult to prove; witness the fact that cigarette manufacturers have argued for years that the connection between smoking and lung disease cannot be demonstrated. Responsible arguments from cause and effect depend upon credible and adequate hard evidence and expert opinion. And they must always acknowledge the possible existence of hidden factors; smoking and lung disease, for example, may be influenced by genetic predisposition.

Definition All arguments require definitions for clarification. However, a definition can often provide a reason in support of the thesis, as well. If we define a term by placing it in a category, we are saying that whatever is true for the category is true for the term we are defining. For example, Elizabeth Cady Stanton's landmark 1892 argument for women's rights ("The Solitude of Self") was based on the definition "women are individuals":

> *Thesis:* Women must have suffrage, access to higher education, and sovereignty over their own minds and bodies.
>
> *Reason:* Women are individuals.

If Stanton's audience, American congressmen, accepted that all individuals are "endowed with certain inalienable rights," Stanton's definition reminded them that women fit into the category of individual just as much as men do and so deserve the same rights.

Almost all good reasons come from one or some combination of these eight sources. However, simply knowing the sources of good reasons will not result in such reasons automatically. Nothing can substitute for thoughtful research and determined inquiry. Think of each of these sources as an angle from which to think about your thesis statement and the results of your research and inquiry. They can help you generate reasons initially or find better reasons when the ones you have seem inadequate.

Finally, do not feel that quantity is crucial in finding good reasons. While it is good to brainstorm for as many as you can find, you will want to focus on those that you think will appeal most to your audience and that you can develop thoroughly. A good argument may well be based on just one or two good reasons.

Student Sample: Finding Reasons In finding reasons for her argument to convince potential buyers that wearing fur is not justifiable, Carolina began by recalling reasons that occurred to her before her research, based on assumptions and values about what is good and what is possible:

> Fur coats are not necessities, but only status symbols (that is, at most a low-level good, almost trivial).
>
> There are other ways of being both warm and fashionable (the appeal of possible alternatives).

Next, Carolina turned to her research for additional reasons. She saw that those opposing her view argued that wearing fur was the moral equivalent of wearing leather and eating beef. She realized she must argue against the comparison equating fur and leather:

> Killing animals because their fur is fashionable is not the same as killing cows for leather and meat.

Carolina had also found some hard evidence in a magazine article about the cruelty involved in trapping wild animals and raising and killing ranch animals. She decided to include the following reason:

> The fur industry causes unacceptable suffering in animals.

An essay by philosopher Peter Singer, an authority in the field of animal rights, provided a further reason:

> It is immoral not to consider the suffering of any being capable of feeling pain.

Finally, Carolina remembered that she was going to have to define "fashion" and that doing so could offer a reason as well if she thought about it carefully. She decided not to use a dictionary definition but rather came up with her own:

> Fashion is an industry that appeals primarily to human vanity.

Following Through

Here is one way of brainstorming for reasons. First, list the eight sources of good reasons (pages 90–93) in your writer's notebook, perhaps on the inside front cover or on the first or last page—someplace where you can easily find them. Practice using these sources for good reasons by writing the thesis you are working on currently at the top of another page, and then going through the list, writing down reasons as they occur to you.

Exchange notebooks with other class members. See if you can help each other generate additional reasons.

Selecting and Ordering Reasons

Selecting reasons from a number of possibilities depends primarily on two considerations: your thesis and your readers. Any thesis demands a certain line of reasoning. For example, the writer contending that *Huckleberry Finn* should be required reading in high school must offer a compelling reason for accepting no substitute—not even another novel by Mark Twain. Such a reason might be "since many critics and novelists see *Huckleberry Finn* as the inspiration for much subsequent American fiction, we cannot understand the American novel if we are not familiar with *Huckleberry Finn.*" A reason of this kind—one that focuses on the essential influence of the book—is likely to appeal to teachers or school administrators.

It is often difficult to see how to order reasons prior to drafting. Since we can easily reorder reasons as we write and rewrite, in developing our case we need only attempt to discover an order that seems right and satisfies us as an overall sequence.

The writer advocating *Huckleberry Finn,* for example, should probably first defend the novel from the charge that it is racist. Readers unaware of the controversy will want to know why the book needs defending, and well-informed readers will expect an immediate response to the book's critics, since it is the effort to remove the book from classrooms that has created the controversy. Once the charge of racism has been disposed of, readers will be prepared to hear the reasons for keeping it on required reading lists.

The needs and expectations of readers must take precedence in all decisions about sequencing reasons. We should also consider relationships among the reasons themselves, how one may lead to another. For instance, Anne Marie O'Keefe's case against drug testing first establishes the unreliability of the tests, then focuses on the damage such tests inflict on innocent employees and the violation of civil rights they represent. This sequence is effective because each reason prepares the reader for the next one. If drug tests are often inaccurate, then innocent people will be falsely accused; if innocent people are falsely accused, the unwarranted invasion of privacy seems much worse—indeed, indefensible.

Besides thinking about what your readers need and expect and how one reason may gain force by following another one, you should also keep in mind a simple fact about memory. We are likely to recall best what we read last, and next best what we read first. A good rule of thumb, therefore, is to begin and end your defense of a thesis with your strongest reasons, the ones you want to emphasize. A strong beginning also helps to keep the reader reading, while a strong conclusion avoids a sense of anticlimax.

Student Sample: Selecting and Ordering Reasons In selecting reasons, Carolina decided not to use her reason that fur coats were status symbols, because she decided readers might find it too confrontational. She still had to decide in what order to take up the remaining reasons. Recall her thesis ("The desire to be fashionable does not justify killing an animal just to obtain its fur.") and her reasons:

> There are other ways of being both warm and fashionable.
> Killing animals because their fur is fashionable is not the same as killing cows for leather and meat.
> The fur industry causes unacceptable suffering in the animals.
> It is immoral not to consider the suffering of any being capable of feeling pain.
> Fashion is an industry that appeals primarily to human vanity.

In creating her brief, Carolina decided to take up the last assertion first, to establish fashion as an indulgence, something not wrong but not really necessary. Having established that point, she could have gone on to almost any of her other reasons, but she decided that a good strategy would be to save for last her reason that there are other ways of being warm and fashionable; this, she felt, would allow her to end on an upbeat note.

Carolina next chose as her second reason that fur coats cannot be produced without causing animals to suffer, whether they are trapped or raised on farms. As part of her strategy, she wanted the evidence about animal suffering to directly follow the point about human vanity, emphasizing the idea of suffering by putting it in the context of unnecessary exploitation. She also realized the reason "It is immoral not to consider the suffering of any being capable of feeling pain" would make concrete the implications of her first and second reasons and allow her to establish an important general principle about the moral and immoral uses of animals. She decided to include it third in the sequence. With this general principle established, she could then defend herself from the charge of being an extreme animal rightist by bringing up her point about the use of cattle for beef and leather; she would then conclude, as she had already decided, by emphasizing options, including fake furs, to indicate that the desire to be fashionable need not be sacrificed to prevent unnecessary animal suffering.

Following Through

We call the case structure a flexible plan because as long as you maintain the three-level structure of thesis, reasons, and evidence, you can change everything else at will: throwing out one thesis for another or altering the wording of a thesis, adding or taking away reasons or evidence, reordering both to achieve the impact you want. So when writing your brief, don't feel that the order in which you have found your reasons and evidence should determine their order in your essay. Rather, make your decisions based on the following questions:

What will my audience need or expect to read first?
Will one reason help to set up another?
Which of my reasons are strongest? Can I begin and conclude my argument with the strongest reasons I have?

To a thesis you have already refined, now add the second level of your brief, the reason or reasons. Be ready to explain your decisions about selection and arrangement. Final decisions about ordering will often be made quite late in the drafting process—in a second or third writing. Spending a little time now, however, to think through possible orderings can save time later and make composing less difficult.

Using Evidence

The skillful use of evidence involves many complex judgments. Let's begin with some basic questions.

What Counts as Evidence? Because science and technology rely on the hard data of quantified evidence—especially statistics—some people assume that hard data is the only really good source of evidence. Such a view, however, is far too narrow for our purposes. Besides hard data, evidence includes

Quotation from authorities: expert opinion, statements from people with special knowledge about an issue, and traditional or institutional authorities such as respected political leaders, philosophers, well known authors, and people who hold positions of power and influence. Besides books and other printed sources, you can gather both data and quotations from interviews with experts or leaders on campus and in the local community.

Constitutions, statutes, court rulings, organizational by-laws, company policy statements, and the like.

Examples and case histories (that is, extended narratives about an individual's or organization's experience).

The results of questionnaires, which you devise and administer.

Personal experience.

In short, evidence includes anything that confirms a good reason or anything that might increase your readers' acceptance of a reason advanced to justify your thesis.

What Kind of Evidence Is Best? What evidence is best depends on what particular reasons call for. To argue for air bags in all new cars by saying they will save lives and reduce injury in auto accidents, we need to cite facts and figures—hard data—to back up our claim. To defend *Huckleberry Finn* by saying that it is an indictment of racism will require evidence of a different kind: quoted passages from the novel itself, statements from respected interpreters, and so forth.

When you have many pieces of evidence to choose from, what is best depends on the quality of the evidence itself and its likely impact on readers. In general—especially for hard data—the best evidence is the most recent. Also the more trusted and prestigious the source, the more authority it will have for readers. Arguments about the AIDS epidemic in the United States, for example, often draw on data from the Centers for Disease Control in Atlanta, a respected research facility that specializes in the study of epidemics. And since the nature of the AIDS crisis changes relatively quickly, the most recent information would be more authoritative than that of a year ago.

Finally, always look for evidence that will give you an edge in winning reader assent. For example, given the charge that *Huckleberry Finn* is offensive to blacks, its vigorous defense by an African-American literary scholar would carry more weight than its defense by a white scholar, even one considered the world's leading expert on Twain.

How Much Evidence Do I Need? The amount of evidence required depends on two judgments. The more crucial a reason is to your case and the more resistant readers are likely to be to a reason, the more evidence you need.

Most cases have at least one pivotal reason, one point upon which the whole case is built and upon which, therefore, the whole case stands or falls. Anne Marie O'Keefe's case against drug testing in the workplace turns on our accepting the inherent inaccuracy of the tests themselves. Such a pivotal reason needs to be supported at length, regardless of the degree of reader resistance to it, and about one third of O'Keefe's essay supports her contention that drug tests are unreliable. Compare this with the relatively small amount of space she devotes to showing that drug use is in decline.

Of course, our pivotal reason may also be the reason to which readers will be most resistant. For instance, many arguments supporting women's right to choose abortion turn on the reason that a fetus cannot be considered a human being until a certain point in its development and, therefore, does not qualify for protection under the law. This reason is obviously both pivotal and likely to be contested by many readers, so devoting much space to evidence for the reason would be a justified strategy.

Student Sample: Using Evidence Carolina added to her brief some indication of the evidence she would use to support each of her points, including the sources from which she took it.

Thesis: The desire to be fashionable does not justify killing an animal just to obtain its fur.

Reason: Fashion is an industry that appeals primarily to human vanity.

Evidence: Support from personal observations, ads, and so forth.

Reason: The fur industry causes unacceptable suffering in animals.

Evidence: Ranching: no laws regulating farms, death by carbon monoxide, anal electrocution (Source: Kasindorf).
Trapping: stress, mutilation, drowning (Source: Kasindorf).

Reason: It is immoral not to consider the suffering of any being capable of feeling pain.

Evidence: A well-known philosopher's argument (Source: Singer).
Humans should have "moral superiority." (Source: Shyer).
We should not inflict pain for "frivolous purposes" (Source: Greenfield).

Reason: Killing animals because their fur is fashionable is not the same as killing cows for leather and meat.

Evidence: Examples of leather not being easily replaced.
Animals' bodies should be used, not seen as waste products (Source: Shyer).
Examples of multiple purposes of carcasses.
Humane Society President Laura Chapin on the difference between killing farm animals and killing for fur (Source: Kasindorf).

Reason: There are other ways of being both warm and fashionable.

Evidence: Designers Blass, Herrara, Armani, who use fake but not real fur (Source: Kasindorf).

Models and actresses who refuse to wear fur (Source: Kasindorf).
Worldwide decline of fur industry, statistics showing fur going out of style (Source: Burns).

Following Through

Prepare a complete brief for an argument. Include both reasons and some indication of the evidence you will use to support each one, with a note about sources. Remember that a brief is a flexible plan, not an outline engraved in stone. The plan can change as you begin drafting.

From Brief to Draft

Turning a rough outline, or brief, of your argument into a piece of prose is never easy. Even if you know what points you will bring up and in what order, you still must introduce the argument, determine how many paragraphs to devote to each reason, work evidence from sources into your own writing, and conclude without simply rehashing all that you have said before. Here we offer some suggestions, with examples, that you may find helpful as you begin to draft.

Introductions

Some writers must work through a draft from start to finish, beginning every piece of writing with the introductory paragraph. They ask, how could you possibly write the middle unless you know what the beginning is like? Other writers feel they can't write the introduction until they have written the body of the argument. They ask, how can you introduce something until you know what it is you are introducing? Either approach will eventually get the job done, as long as the writer takes the rhetorical context and strategy into account when drafting the introduction and goes back to revise it when the draft is completed.

Introductions are among the hardest things to write well. As you look at the suggestions below, remember that an introduction need not be one paragraph but is often two or even three short ones.

A good introduction (1) meets the needs of the audience by setting up the topic with just enough background information, and (2) goes right to the heart of the issue as it relates to the audience's concerns. For example, our student writer Carolina might ask whether she needs to tell her readers that humans have exploited animals from prehistoric time and even whether she needs to inform them that the fur industry has become the target of animal rights advocates. Most readers, however, would find the first point irrelevant, the second unnecessary. What would readers need to know from the introduction? Essentially, only that if they are thinking of buying a fur coat, they should think again.

Should the introduction end with the thesis statement? This strategy works well in offering the easiest transition from brief to draft; it immediately sets the stage for the reasons. However, the thesis need not be the last sentence in the introduction, and it may not appear explicitly until much later in the draft—or even not at all, providing that the reader can tell what it is from the title or from reading the essay.

A good introduction does not state as established truth an assumption that readers are not likely to share and that the essay must argue. For example, Carolina opened her original draft with this sentence: "When God gave man 'dominion over all the living things that move on the earth,' He did not intend for man to abuse the rights of animals." She later deleted the sentence because she realized that this early in her essay, some readers would not be ready to concede that animals even had rights.

Rather than confronting readers, the introduction should attempt to establish some common ground with them. One of Carolina's sources did just that, as the author used her own experience to show her shift in perspective on the issue:

> Ten years ago, I finally got the full-length mink coat I'd wanted for years. It was then considered the elegant, mature woman's symbol of taste and class, and had the unique advantage of "fitting in" wherever it was worn, whether over a pair of jeans to the supermarket, to a funeral, or covering sequins on their way to a New Year's Eve formal.
>
> —MARLENE SHYER, "Changing Thoughts on Furs"

Shyer recognizes that some readers may want a fur coat for all the reasons she did; by spelling out their own viewpoint so clearly, she draws them in. They will want to know what made this woman change her mind.

Finally, a good introduction attracts the interest of the reader. This is done best through specifics rather than generalizations, such as the specifics of jeans and sequins in Shyer's introduction.

Student Sample: The Introduction Let's look at how Carolina finally opened her argument against wearing fur coats:

> "Can I afford it?" is the only question women used to ask when considering buying a fur. Now they might also be asking, "Do I have the courage to wear it?" Just walking down the street, fur coat wearers commonly have to endure disapproving looks and hostile comments about animal blood and animal pain. Is it rude to remind the woman or man in a fur coat that animals died, and perhaps suffered, in the making of it? Is it wrong to ask them to justify this human use of animal life? I do not encourage such rudeness, but I would ask fur buyers, paying for a fashion statement with their gold cards, not to ignore the cost in terms of animal life. Animal life is not worthless. The desire to be fashionable does not justify killing an animal merely to obtain its fur.

Carolina's strategy in her introduction was to anticipate the attitude of her audience. Knowing that they would be aware of the protests, she guessed they might be thinking of facing public disapproval and maybe even questioning their own decision: "I want a fur coat, but should I really want one?" She decided first to criticize those who make rude comments on the street but also to insist on the importance of the ethical questions these comments raise.

Presenting Reasons and Evidence

We now turn to drafting the body paragraphs of the argument. While it is possible in a short argument that one paragraph could fully develop one reason, avoid thinking in terms of writing only one paragraph per reason. Multiple paragraphs are generally required to develop and support a reason.

The key thing to remember about paragraphs is that each one is a unit that performs some function in presenting the case. You ought to be able to say what the function of a given paragraph is—and your reader ought to be able to sense it. Does it introduce a reason? Does it define a term? Does it support a reason by setting up an analogy? Does another paragraph support the same reason by offering examples or some hard data or an illustrative case?

Not all paragraphs need topic sentences announcing their main point. Worry instead about opening each paragraph with some hints to allow readers to recognize the function of the paragraph. For example, some transitional word or phrase could announce to readers that you are turning from one reason to a new one. When you introduce a new reason, be sure that readers can see how it relates to the thesis. Repeating a key word or offering a synonym for one of the words in the thesis is a good idea.

Student Sample: Reasons and Evidence As an example let's look at some paragraphs from the middle of Carolina's draft on the fur question. These follow several paragraphs about the relationship of fashion to human vanity, contrasting human vanity with human need. In her brief Carolina had planned next to take up the cruelty of the fur industry, but in drafting the paragraphs about vanity, she realized that she was moving more naturally to the reason she had planned to take up third: that it is immoral to cause unnecessary suffering to animals. Notice how she uses a number of paragraphs and multiple sources to develop her reason. (See Appendix A for guidelines on quoting and citing sources.)

> We can accept that vanity is part of the human pursuit of happiness for most people. The difficult question I want to ask is this: Do animals have any rights at all, and if so, how do these compare to human rights?
>
> Extreme animal rights advocates such as the philosopher Peter Singer argue that animals have rights equal to those of humans, especially the right to be left alone and the right not to be made to suffer. Singer says, "If a being suffers, there can be no moral justification for refusing to take that suffering into consideration, and indeed, to count it equally with the like suffering . . . of any other being" (187). To Singer, it is therefore immoral to exploit animals for any human use, including medical research and eating meat.

But other advocates of animal rights recognize that some human interests overrule animal interests. Meg Greenfield, a *Newsweek* columnist, writes:

> [I]t is possible to remain stalwart in your view that the human claim comes first and in your acceptance of the use of animals for human betterment and *still* to believe that there are some human interests that should not take precedence. For we have become far too self-indulgent, hardened, careless, and cruel in the pain we routinely inflict upon these creatures for the most frivolous, unworthy purposes. (394)

Singer's view is extreme, but we need to recognize that animal suffering matters, and that we need to weigh animals' interests against humans' interests in every case where we exploit them. If we look into the cruelty inflicted in raising, ranching, trapping, and killing animals for fur, and weigh that suffering against whatever "human betterment" we get from a fur coat, we will find it hard to justify the coat.

Notice that at this point Carolina is ready to take up her next reason: The fur industry causes unacceptable suffering in animals. She has simply reversed the order of two reasons in her brief. Because writing assumes a momentum and often a direction of its own, drafting involves some back-and-forth movement between brief and draft. Having the brief as a guide to drafting will keep you on track, but don't be afraid to make changes in the brief, even to add new reasons or to subtract some.

Conclusions

Once you have presented your case, what else is there to say? You probably do not need to sum up your case; going over your reasons one more time is not generally a good strategy and will likely bore your readers. And yet you know that the conclusion is no place to introduce new issues.

Strategically, you want to end by saying, "Case made!" Here are some suggestions for doing so:

Look back at your introduction. Perhaps some idea that you used there to attract your readers' attention could come into play again as you close, providing a sort of frame for the argument. A question you posed has an answer, a problem you raised has a solution.

Think about the larger context your argument fits into. For example, an argument about why *Huckleberry Finn* should be taught in public high schools, even if some students are offended by its language, could end by pointing out that education becomes diluted and artificial when teachers and administrators design a curriculum that avoids all controversy.

Ending with a well worded quotation discovered in your research is sometimes effective, but try to follow it up with some words of your own, as you normally would whenever you quote.

Too many conclusions run on after their natural endings. If you have written a conclusion that you feel dissatisfied with, try lopping off the last one, two, or three sentences. You may uncover the real ending.

Pay attention to style, especially in the last sentence. An awkwardly worded sentence will not have a sound of finality, but one with some rhythmic punch or consciously repeated sounds can wrap an essay up neatly.

Student Sample: The Conclusion Let's see what strategies Carolina used in concluding her case against wearing fur. She decided to return to the idea about courage raised in her introduction.

> In November of 1991, "brave" women in London staged a "National Wear Your Fur Day," when they confronted public opinion and marched to demonstrate their right to wear fur. But were they really brave? The right to wear fur, as I have shown, is actually the right to make animals pay for our vanity, at the cost of their suffering and lives. What these women were demonstrating was not a show of courage, but a lack of conscience.

Carolina ends by reminding her readers of her thesis as she answers one of the questions raised in her opening: "Do I have the courage to wear fur?" The answer, she seems to say, is that this question of courage is irrelevant and ignores the real issue—the ethics of wearing fur. Notice too how her stylistic choices work: The "not x, but y" pattern gives balance to her closing words.

Revising the Draft

Too often revising is confused with editing. Revising, however, implies making large changes in content and organization, not simply sentence-level corrections or even stylistic changes, which fall into the category of editing.

To get a sense of what is involved in revising, look at the following paragraph, which represents Carolina's original conclusion to her argument against wearing furs (the revised version of which you read earlier):

> On "National Wear Your Fur Day" in London, brave women wore their furs. But were they really brave? I think not. They were just flaunting their right to drape dead animals over their shoulders.

This ending has punch, but it is too strong in denouncing those who wear fur. As a classmate who read Carolina's draft pointed out, a backlash response from her audience at the end could undo all the progress she had made in convincing them up to that point.

Revision means literally "seeing again," and that is hard to do if you are too close to your draft. Try to let it rest for at least twenty-four hours before you reread with an eye to revision.

When you are ready to revise, the following suggestions ought to be helpful.

Read Your Own Writing Critically

As we explained in Chapter 3, being a critical reader of arguments means being an analytical reader. In that chapter, we made suggestions for reading any argument; here, we show what to look for in reading your own writing critically.

Read with an Eye Toward Structure Remember, different parts of an argument perform different jobs. Read to see if you can divide your draft easily into its strategic parts, and be sure you can tell yourself what role each group of paragraphs plays in the overall picture. The draft should reflect your brief, or you should be able to create a new brief from what you have written. If you have trouble identifying the working parts and how they fit together, you need to see where points are overlapping, where you are repeating yourself, what distant parts actually belong together. This may be the time for scissors and paste, or electronic cutting and pasting if you are working at a computer.

Read with an Eye Toward Rhetorical Context You may need to revise to make the rhetorical context clearer—why you are writing, with what aim, and to whom. You establish this reader awareness in the introduction, and so you need to think about your readers' values and beliefs, as well as any obvious personal data that might help explain their position on the issue—age, gender, race, occupation, economic status, and so on. You may need to revise your introduction now, finding a way to interest your readers in what you have to say. The more specific you can make your opening, the more likely your success.

Inquire into Your Own Writing Have a dialogue with yourself about your own writing. Some of the questions that we listed on pages 44–45 will be useful here:

Ask what you mean by the words that are central to the argument. Have you provided definitions when they are needed?

Find the reasons, and note their relation to the thesis. Be able to state the connection, ideally linked with "because": *Thesis* because *Reason*.

Be able to state what assumptions lie behind your thesis and any of your reasons. Ask yourself, "What else would someone have to believe to accept this as valid?" If your audience is unlikely to share the assumption, then you must add an argument for it—or change your thesis.

Look at your comparisons and analogies. Are they persuasive?

Look at your evidence. Have you offered facts, expert opinion, illustrations, and so on? Have you presented these in a way that would not raise doubts but eliminate them?

Consider your own bias. What do you stand to gain from advocating the position you take here? Is your argument self-serving or truth-serving?

Get Feedback from Other Readers

Because it is hard to be objective about your own work, getting a reading from a friend, classmate, teacher, or family member is a good way to see where revision would help. However, an unfocused reading usually isn't critical enough; casual readers may applaud the draft too readily if they agree with the thesis and condemn it if they disagree. Therefore, we suggest that readers use a revision checklist, such as the following.

READER'S CHECKLIST FOR REVISION

First be sure you understand the writer's intended audience, either by discussing this with the writer or reading any notes the writer has provided. Then read through the entire draft. It is helpful to number all the paragraphs, so you can later refer to them by number.

If you can find an explicit statement of the author's thesis, underline or highlight it. If you cannot find one, do you think it is necessary that the thesis be stated explicitly, or would any reader be able to infer it easily? If the thesis is easily inferred, put it in your own words at the top of the draft.

How could the thesis be improved? Is it offensive, vague, or too general? Does it have a single focus? Is it clearly stated? Suggest more concrete diction, if possible.

Circle the key terms of the thesis—that is, the words most central to the point. Could there be disagreement about the meaning of any of these terms? If so, has the author at some point in the essay offered clarification of what he or she means by these terms?

Look for the structure and strategy of the argument. Underline or highlight the sentences that most clearly present the reasons, and write Reason 1, Reason 2, and so forth, in the margin. If doing so is not easy, indicate this problem to the author. Do the reasons not stand out as reasons? Do you think the author has arranged the reasons in the best order? Make suggestions for improvement.

Which is the author's best reason? Why would it appeal to the audience? Has the author strategically placed it in the best position for making his or her case?

Look for any weak parts in the argument. What reasons need more or better support? Next to any weakly supported reasons, write questions to let the author know what factual information seems lacking, what sources don't seem solid or credible, what statements sound too general, what reasoning—such as analogies—seems shaky. Are there any reasons for which more research is in order?

Does the author show an awareness of opposing arguments? Where? If not, should this be added? Even if you agree with this argument, take the viewpoint of a member of the opposition: What are the best challenges you can make to anything the author has said?

Evaluate the introduction and conclusion.

Editing and Proofreading

The final steps of writing any argument are editing and proofreading, which we take up in Appendix B.

Following Through

In the following essay student Sara Sabraw aims to convince her readers that women in the military should not serve in the front lines of combat. The audience for this argument would most likely be women who believe gender should be no barrier to any type of military service and would possibly include women who had undergone training for combat. Use the checklist for revision on page 105 and determine the argument's effectiveness. Which are the strongest reasons? The weakest? Can you think of other reasons or evidence that would make the case more convincing?

STUDENT SAMPLE: AN ESSAY TO CONVINCE

SARA SABRAW

Women in Combat

WOMEN'S ROLES in the home, the work place, and even the military have changed remarkably in the past fifty years. In the armed forces women hold a number of vital positions such as medics, computer operators, and even F-15 fighter pilots. Although roles continue to expand, women are still prohibited from hand-to-hand combat, and this restriction should continue. Our collective best interest demands that women not serve on the front lines.

Physical, brute force is a necessity for ground combat, and women are not as physically strong as men. Even though some extreme feminists would not like to believe it true, women and men are created differently. Even some military training is based on an acknowledgement of these differences. For example, according to U.S. Army Colonel David Hackworth, "To pass the Marines' combat-conditioning test, men must climb 20 feet of rope in 30 seconds; women can take 50 seconds" (26). But by setting the scale lower for women, the military is not developing the strongest possible army. And in war the enemy does not give women an extra twenty seconds to escape. A plethora of war stories throughout the ages tell of men carrying their fellow soldiers to safety. And, although a woman might believe she could and would want to do this, her lack of upper body strength would not permit it. "A 110-pound woman with the heart of a lion can't pack out a wounded 200-pound comrade" (Hackworth 25). The front lines require physical strength and brawn that the average woman does not possess.

Also, there is a psychological element that raises questions regarding women in the military. For years, one of the strongest arguments against women in combat has been that the presence of women would interfere with male bonding. Army Captain Carol Barkalow states that during her service in Desert Storm she "saw a new type of relationship forming between men and women; it was a nurturing relationship based on respect" ("Women Have"). But most male soldiers would refute this idea and proclaim that the bonding just isn't the same. Specialist Peter Cardin of the elite XVIII Airborne Corps states that "I couldn't handle being in a tank or infantry squad with a woman. It would blow unit esprit and destroy male bonding" (Hackworth 26). Colonel Hackworth adds, "male bonding is an abstract thing, yet it is the glue that holds fighting units together and allows them to do the impossible" (26). This sort of teamwork and unity is essential for achieving success.

Undoubtedly, emotional problems arise when women and men are together on the front lines. Working in such close quarters with men, combined with the stress of wartime combat, increases the chances of emotional relationships forming. But in a combat situation, the outcome of such relationships could be disastrous. Soldiers might be more apt to put themselves in a risky position for the welfare of a lover, possibly endangering other troops. The emotional outcome might hinder the mental judgment and fighting capability of the soldier. Also, jealousy may become a factor when men and women work so closely on the front lines, causing problems for the whole military unit. If soldiers have personal vendettas with fellow soldiers over male/female relationships, maximum effectiveness will be virtually unattainable.

Possibly the most significant social factor concerning women in combat 5
roles is the possibility of pregnancy. When men and women are thrown together under stress in close army quarters, the chances of their becoming sexually involved certainly exists. Obviously, soldiers are going to be carrying guns and grenades before condoms. In fact, the "destroyer tender Acadia returned from the Persian Gulf with 36 female crew members—a tenth of its female complement—in the family way" (Murchison). The possibility of pregnant soldiers poses a major problem to the unit's effectiveness because these women would have to be sent home and replaced.

Modern warfare has made combat exceedingly complex and difficult. These complexities and difficulties would be exacerbated by expanding the role of women to include front-line combat. The stresses of men and women together on the front lines would reduce the overall effectiveness of our military in time of war.

WORKS CITED

Hackworth, David H. "War and the Second Sex." *Newsweek* 5 Aug. 1991: 24–28.

Murchison, William. "An Idea Whose Time Won't Come." *Dallas Morning News* 2 Jan. 1988: 31a.

"Women Have What It Takes." *Newsweek* 5 Aug. 1991: 30.

CHAPTER SEVEN

Appealing to the Whole Person: Arguing to Persuade

In Chapter 1 we defined persuasion as convincing *plus,* to suggest the three forms of appeal in addition to reason required for persuasion: the appeals to the writer's character; to the emotions of the audience; and to style, the artful use of language itself. Building on what you learned about making cases in Chapter 6, in this chapter your goal will be to understand and control this wider range of appeals. But why? Shouldn't reason be enough?

Perhaps it would be if human beings were like *Star Trek*'s Dr. Spock, truly rational creatures. But human beings are only sometimes rational—and even then imperfectly. We often agree with an argument but lack the courage or motivation to translate our assent into action.

Persuasion, then, aims to close the gap between assent and action. Because persuasion seeks a deeper and stronger commitment from readers, it appeals to the whole person, to our full humanity, not just to the mind. It offers reasons, of course, because people respond to good reasons. But it also encourages the reader to identify with the writer, because people respond not just to the quality of an argument but also to the quality of the arguer. In addition, the persuader wants to stir the reader's emotions, because strong feelings reinforce the will to act; persuasion works on the heart as much as the mind. Finally, choices about style matter in persuasion, because human beings are language-using animals whose response to what is said depends on how well it is said.

A MATTER OF EMPHASIS: WHEN TO CONVINCE AND WHEN TO PERSUADE

When should you aim to persuade rather than to convince? Always notice what an academic assignment calls for, because the full range of persuasive appeal is not always appropriate for written arguments in college. In general, the more academic the audience or the more purely intellectual the issue, the less appropriate it is to appeal to the whole person. A philosophy or science paper might often require you to convince but rarely to persuade. In such cases, you should confine yourself primarily to thesis, reasons, and evidence.

But when you are working with public issues, with matters of policy or questions of right and wrong, persuasion's fuller range of appeal is usually appropriate because such topics address a broader readership and involve a more inclusive community. Arguments in these areas affect not just how we think but how we act, and the heightened urgency of persuasion goes further in sparking action or fundamental change.

While convincing primarily requires that we control case-making, persuasion asks us to make conscious decisions about three other appeals as well. One, we must gain our readers' confidence and respect through deliberate projection of our good character. Two, we must touch our readers' emotions. And, three, we must focus on language itself as a means of affecting people's thoughts and behavior. The writer who aims to persuade integrates these other forms of appeal with a well-made case, deliberately crafting the essay so that they all work together.

As with convincing, writing a persuasive argument begins with inquiry and research—a patient search for the truth as preparation for earning a claim to truth. However, before you can move from a general idea of your own position to a specific thesis, you must think about the audience you will seek to persuade.

ANALYZING YOUR READERS

Persuasion begins with difference and, when it works, ends with identity. That is, we expect before reading our argument that our readers differ from us not only in beliefs but also in attitudes and desires. A successful persuasive argument brings readers and writer together, creating a sense of connection between parties that were previously separate. But what means can we use to overcome difference and create a sense of identity?

First, we need to focus our attention on our readers, attempting to understand their frame of mind using the following questions.

Who Is the Audience, and How Do They View the Topic?

Who are my readers? How do I define them in terms of age, economic and social class, gender, education, and so forth?

What typical attitudes or stances toward my topic do they have?

What in their background or daily experiences helps to explain their point of view?

What are they likely to know about my topic?

How might they be uninformed or misinformed about it?

How would they like to see the problem, question, or issue resolved, answered, or handled? Why? That is, what personal stake do they have in the topic?

In what larger framework—religious, ethical, political, economic—do they place my topic? That is, what general beliefs and values are involved?

As you answer these questions, you should begin to see possible appeals to your readership. But keep in mind that good persuaders are able to empathize and sympathize with other people, building bridges of commonality and solidarity.

What Are Our Differences?

Audience analysis is not complete until you can specify exactly what divides you from your readers. Sometimes specifying difference is difficult prior to research and detailed formulation of a case, so that understanding exactly what divides you from your readers comes later, at the point of the first draft. But as soon as you can, you must clarify differences; knowing exactly what separates you from your readers tells you what to emphasize in making your case and in choosing other strategies of appeal. These questions can help:

Is the difference a matter of assumptions? If so, how can I shake my readers' confidence in their assumptions and offer another set of assumptions favorable to my position?

Is the difference a matter of principle, the application of general rules to specific cases? If so, should I dispute the principle itself and offer a competing one the audience will also value? Or should I show why the principle should not apply in some specific instance relevant to my case?

Is the difference a matter of a hierarchy of values—that is, do we value the same things, but to different degrees? If so, how might I restructure my readers' values?

Is the difference a matter of ends or of means? If of ends, how can I show that my vision of what ought to be is better or that realizing my ends will also secure the ends my readers value? If a difference of means, how can I show that my methods are justified and effective, more likely to bear fruit than others?

Is the difference a matter of interpretation? If so, how can I shake my readers' confidence in the traditional or common interpretation of something and show them that my interpretation is better, that it accounts for the facts more adequately?

Is the difference a matter of implications or consequences? If so, how can I convince my readers that what they fear may happen will not happen, that it will not be as bad as they think, or that other implications or consequences outweigh any negatives?

What Do We Have in Common?

In seeking to define the common ground you and your readers share, the key point to remember is that no matter how sharp the disagreements that divide you from those you hope to persuade, resources for identification always exist and may be discovered through these sorts of questions:

Do we have a shared local identity—as members of the same organization, for example, or students at the same university?
Do we share a more abstract, collective identity—as citizens of the same region or nation, as worshippers of the same religion, and so forth?
Do we share a common cause—such as promoting the good of the community, preventing child abuse, or overcoming racial prejudice?
Is there a shared experience or human activity—raising children, caring for aging parents, helping a friend in distress, struggling to make ends meet?
Can we connect through a well-known event or cultural happening—a popular movie, a best-selling book, something in the news that would impress or concern both your readers and yourself?
Is there a historical event, person, or document that we both respect?

READING A PERSUASIVE ESSAY

To illustrate the importance of audience analysis, we will turn to a classic essay of the twentieth century, Martin Luther King, Jr.'s "Letter from Birmingham Jail," a brilliant example of the art of persuasion. As we will see, King masterfully analyzed his audience and used the full range of appeals to suit that particular readership.

Background

To appreciate King's persuasive powers, we must first understand the events that led up to the "Letter" and also the actions King wanted to move his readers to take. As president of the Southern Christian Leadership Conference, a civil rights organization dedicated to nonviolent social change, King had been organizing and participating in demonstrations in Birmingham, Alabama, in 1963. He was arrested, and while he was in jail, eight white Alabama clergymen of various denominations issued a public statement reacting to his activities. Published in a local newspaper, the statement deplored the illegal demonstrations of King and his organization as "unwise and untimely":

> We the undersigned clergymen are among those who, in January, issued "An Appeal for Law and Order and Common Sense," in dealing with racial problems in Alabama. We expressed understanding that honest convictions in racial matters could properly be pursued in the courts, but urged that decisions of those courts should in the meantime be peacefully obeyed.
>
> Since that time there had been some evidence of increased forbearance and a willingness to face facts. Responsible citizens have undertaken to work on various problems which cause racial friction and unrest. In Birmingham, recent public events have given indication that

we all have opportunity for a new constructive and realistic approach to racial problems.

However, we are now confronted by a series of demonstrations by some of our Negro citizens, directed and led in part by outsiders. We recognize the natural impatience of people who feel that their hopes are slow in being realized. But we are convinced that these demonstrations are unwise and untimely.

We agree rather with certain local Negro leadership which has called for honest and open negotiation of racial issues in our area. And we believe this kind of facing of issues can best be accomplished by citizens of our own metropolitan area, white and Negro, meeting with their knowledge and experience of the local situation. All of us need to face that responsibility and find proper channels for its accomplishment.

Just as we formerly pointed out that "hatred and violence have no sanction in our religious and political traditions," we also point out that such actions as incite to hatred and violence, however technically peaceful those actions may be, have not contributed to the resolution of our local problems. We do not believe that these days of new hope are days when extreme measures are justified in Birmingham.

We commend the community as a whole, and the local news media and law enforcement officials in particular, on the calm manner in which these demonstrations have been handled. We urge the public to continue to show restraint should the demonstrations continue, and the law enforcement officials to remain calm and continue to protect our city from violence.

We further strongly urge our own Negro community to withdraw support from these demonstrations, and to unite locally in working peacefully for a better Birmingham. When rights are consistently denied, a cause should be pressed in the courts and in negotiations among local leaders, and not in the streets. We appeal to both our white and Negro citizenry to observe the principles of law and order and common sense.

Signed by:

C. C. J. Carpenter, D.D., LL.D., *Bishop of Alabama*

Joseph A. Durick, D.D., *Auxiliary Bishop, Diocese of Mobile, Birmingham*

Rabbi Milton L. Grafman, *Temple Emanu-El, Birmingham, Alabama*

Bishop Paul Hardin, *Bishop of the Alabama-West Florida Conference of the Methodist Church*

Bishop Nolan B. Harmon, *Bishop of the North Alabama Conference of the Methodist Church*

George M. Murray, D.D., LL.D., *Bishop Coadjutor, Episcopal Diocese of Alabama*

Edward V. Ramage, *Moderator, Synod of the Alabama Presbyterian Church in the United States*
Earl Stallings, *Pastor, First Baptist Church, Birmingham, Alabama*

In his cell, King began his letter on the margins of that newspaper page, addressing it specifically to the eight clergymen in the hope that he could move them from disapproval to support, from inaction to a recognition of the necessity of the demonstrations. As a public figure, King knew that his letter would reach a larger audience, including the demonstrators themselves, who were galvanized by its message when 50,000 copies were later distributed by his supporters. In the years since, King's letter has often been published, reaching an audience around the world with its argument for civil disobedience in the service of a higher, moral law.

The Basic Message

King's letter is long; he even apologizes to his readers for having written so much. Its length is not due to its basic message, however, but to its persuasive appeals—to the way the main points are made. Before you read King's "Letter," read the following summary, which differs from King's prose as a nursery song differs from a Beethoven symphony.

> Because I am the leader of an organization that fights injustice, it is most appropriate for me to be in Birmingham, where human rights are being violated. Our campaign of nonviolent civil disobedience was not rash and unpremeditated, but the result of a history of failed negotiations and broken promises. We aim to increase tensions here until the city leaders realize that dialogue must occur. Our actions are not untimely but long overdue, given that blacks have been denied their civil rights in this country for over 340 years.
>
> While we advocate breaking some laws, we distinguish between moral laws and immoral laws that degrade the human personality. The former must be obeyed, the latter disobeyed openly and lovingly.
>
> We may be extremists, but people who accomplish great things are often so labeled, and our nonviolent protests are preferable to inaction.
>
> In failing to support us, white Southern religious leaders such as yourselves fail to meet the challenges of social injustice. You should not praise the police for their work at breaking up the demonstrations, but rather praise the demonstrators for standing up for their human dignity.

MARTIN LUTHER KING, JR.

Letter from Birmingham Jail

April 16, 1963

My Dear Fellow Clergymen:

WHILE CONFINED here in the Birmingham city jail, I came across your recent statement calling my present activities "unwise and untimely." Seldom do I pause to answer criticism of my work and ideas. If I sought to answer all the criticisms that cross my desk, my secretaries would have little time for anything other than such correspondence in the course of the day, and I would have no time for constructive work. But since I feel that you are men of genuine good will and that your criticisms are sincerely set forth, I want to try to answer your statement in what I hope will be patient and reasonable terms.

I think I should indicate why I am here in Birmingham, since you have been influenced by the view which argues against "outsiders coming in." I have the honor of serving as president of the Southern Christian Leadership Conference, an organization operating in every southern state, with headquarters in Atlanta, Georgia. We have some eighty-five affiliated organizations across the South, and one of them is the Alabama Christian Movement for Human Rights. Frequently we share staff, educational, and financial resources with our affiliates. Several months ago the affiliate here in Birmingham asked us to be on call to engage in a nonviolent direct-action program if such were deemed necessary. We readily consented, and when the hour came we lived up to our promise. So I, along with several members of my staff, am here because I was invited here. I am here because I have organizational ties here.

But more basically, I am in Birmingham because injustice is here. Just as the prophets of the eighth century B.C. left their villages and carried their "thus saith the Lord" far beyond the boundaries of their home towns, and just as the Apostle Paul left his village of Tarsus and carried the gospel of Jesus Christ to the far corners of the Greco-Roman world, so am I compelled to carry the gospel of freedom beyond my own home town. Like Paul, I must constantly respond to the Macedonian call for aid.

Moreover, I am cognizant of the interrelatedness of all communities and states. I cannot sit idly by in Atlanta and not be concerned about what happens in Birmingham. Injustice anywhere is a threat to justice everywhere. We are caught in an inescapable network of mutuality, tied in a single garment of destiny. Whatever affects one directly, affects all indirectly. Never again can we afford to live with the narrow, provincial "outside agitator" idea. Anyone who lives inside the United States can never be considered an outsider anywhere within its bounds.

You deplore the demonstrations taking place in Birmingham. But your 5
statement, I am sorry to say, fails to express a similar concern for the conditions that brought about the demonstrations. I am sure that none of you would want to rest content with the superficial kind of social analysis that deals merely with effects and does not grapple with underlying causes. It is unfortunate that dem-

onstrations are taking place in Birmingham, but it is even more unfortunate that the city's white power structure left the Negro community with no alternative.

In any nonviolent campaign there are four basic steps: collection of the facts to determine whether injustices exist; negotiation; self-purification; and direct action. We have gone through all these steps in Birmingham. There can be no gainsaying the fact that racial injustice engulfs this community. Birmingham is probably the most thoroughly segregated city in the United States. Its ugly record of brutality is widely known. Negroes have experienced grossly unjust treatment in the courts. There have been more unsolved bombings of Negro homes and churches in Birmingham than in any other city in the nation. These are the hard, brutal facts of the case. On the basis of these conditions, Negro leaders sought to negotiate with the city fathers. But the latter consistently refused to engage in good-faith negotiation.

Then, last September, came the opportunity to talk with leaders of Birmingham's economic community. In the course of the negotiations, certain promises were made by the merchants—for example, to remove the stores' humiliating racial signs. On the basis of these promises, the Reverend Fred Shuttlesworth and the leaders of the Alabama Christian Movement for Human Rights agreed to a moratorium on all demonstrations. As the weeks and months went by, we realized that we were the victims of a broken promise. A few signs, briefly removed, returned; the others remained.

As in so many past experiences, our hopes had been blasted, and the shadow of deep disappointment settled upon us. We had no alternative except to prepare for direct action, whereby we would present our very bodies as a means of laying our case before the conscience of the local and the national community. Mindful of the difficulties involved, we decided to undertake a process of self-purification. We began a series of workshops on nonviolence, and we repeatedly asked ourselves: "Are you able to accept blows without retaliating?" "Are you able to endure the ordeal of jail?" We decided to schedule our direct-action program for the Easter season, realizing that except for Christmas, this is the main shopping period of the year. Knowing that a strong economic-withdrawal program would be the by-product of direct action, we felt that this would be the best time to bring pressure to bear on the merchants for the needed change.

Then it occurred to us that Birmingham's mayoral election was coming up in March, and we speedily decided to postpone action until after election day. When we discovered that the Commissioner of Public Safety, Eugene "Bull" Connor, had piled up enough votes to be in the run-off, we decided again to postpone action until the day after the run-off so that the demonstrations could not be used to cloud the issues. Like many others, we waited to see Mr. Connor defeated, and to this end we endured postponement after postponement. Having aided in this community need, we felt that our direct-action program could be delayed no longer.

You may well ask: "Why direct action? Why sit-ins, marches and so forth? 10
Isn't negotiation a better path?" You are quite right in calling for negotiation. Indeed, this is the very purpose of direct action. Nonviolent direct action seeks

to create such a crisis and foster such a tension that a community which has constantly refused to negotiate is forced to confront the issue. It seeks so to dramatize the issue that it can no longer be ignored. My citing the creation of tension as part of the work of the nonviolent-resister may sound rather shocking. But I must confess that I am not afraid of the word "tension." I have earnestly opposed violent tension, but there is a type of constructive, nonviolent tension which is necessary for growth. Just as Socrates felt that it was necessary to create a tension in the mind so that individuals could rise from the bondage of myths and half-truths to the unfettered realm of creative analysis and objective appraisal, so must we see the need for nonviolent gadflies to create the kind of tension in society that will help men rise from the dark depths of prejudice and racism to the majestic heights of understanding and brotherhood.

The purpose of our direct-action program is to create a situation so crisis-packed that it will inevitably open the door to negotiation. I therefore concur with you in your call for negotiation. Too long has our beloved Southland been bogged down in a tragic effort to live in monologue rather than dialogue.

One of the basic points in your statement is that the action that I and my associates have taken in Birmingham is untimely. Some have asked: "Why didn't you give the new city administration time to act?" The only answer that I can give to this query is that the new Birmingham administration must be prodded about as much as the outgoing one, before it will act. We are sadly mistaken if we feel that the election of Albert Boutwell as mayor will bring the millennium to Birmingham. While Mr. Boutwell is a much more gentle person than Mr. Connor, they are both segregationists, dedicated to maintenance of the status quo. I have hope that Mr. Boutwell will be reasonable enough to see the futility of massive resistance to desegregation. But he will not see this without pressure from devotees of civil rights. My friends, I must say to you that we have not made a single gain in civil rights without determined legal and nonviolent pressure. Lamentably, it is an historical fact that privileged groups seldom give up their privileges voluntarily. Individuals may see the moral light and voluntarily give up their unjust posture; but, as Reinhold Niebuhr has reminded us, groups tend to be more immoral than individuals.

We know through painful experience that freedom is never voluntarily given by the oppressor; it must be demanded by the oppressed. Frankly, I have yet to engage in a direct-action campaign that was "well timed" in the view of those who have not suffered unduly from the disease of segregation. For years now I have heard the word "Wait!" It rings in the ear of every Negro with piercing familiarity. This "Wait" has almost always meant "Never." We must come to see, with one of our distinguished jurists, that "justice too long delayed is justice denied."

We have waited for more than 340 years for our constitutional God-given rights. The nations of Asia and Africa are moving with jetlike speed toward gaining political independence, but we still creep at horse-and-buggy pace toward gaining a cup of coffee at a lunch counter. Perhaps it is easy for those who have never felt the stinging darts of segregation to say, "Wait." But when you have seen vicious mobs lynch your mothers and fathers at will and drown your sisters and brothers at whim; when you have seen hate-filled policemen curse, kick, and even kill your black brothers and sisters; when you see the vast majority of your twenty million Negro brothers smothering in an airtight cage of poverty in the midst of an affluent society; when you suddenly find your tongue twisted and your speech stammering as you seek to explain to your six-year-old daughter why she can't go to the public amusement park that has just been advertised on television, and see tears welling up in her eyes when she is told that Funtown is closed to colored children, and see ominous clouds of inferiority beginning to form in her little mental sky, and see her beginning to distort her personality by developing an unconscious bitterness toward white people; when you have to concoct an answer for a five-year-old son who is asking: "Daddy, why do white people treat colored people so mean?"; when you take a cross-country drive and find it necessary to sleep night after night in the uncomfortable corners of your automobile because no motel will accept you; when you are humiliated day in and day out by nagging signs reading "white" and "colored"; when your first name becomes "nigger," your middle name becomes "boy" (however old you are), and your last name becomes "John," and your wife and mother are never given the respected title "Mrs."; when you are harried by day and haunted by night by the fact that you are a Negro, living constantly at tiptoe stance, never quite knowing what to expect next, and are plagued with inner fears and outer resentments; when you are forever fighting a degenerating sense of "nobodiness"—then you will understand why we find it difficult to wait. There comes a time when the cup of endurance runs over, and men are no longer willing to be plunged into the abyss of despair. I hope, sirs, you can understand our legitimate and unavoidable impatience.

You express a great deal of anxiety over our willingness to break laws. This 15
is certainly a legitimate concern. Since we so diligently urge people to obey the Supreme Court's decision of 1954 outlawing segregation in the public schools, at first glance it may seem rather paradoxical for us consciously to break laws. One may well ask: "How can you advocate breaking some laws and obeying others?" The answer lies in the fact that there are two types of laws: just and unjust. I would be the first to advocate obeying just laws. One has not only a legal but a moral responsibility to obey just laws. Conversely, one has a moral responsibility to disobey unjust laws. I would agree with St. Augustine that "an unjust law is no law at all."

Now, what is the difference between the two? How does one determine whether a law is just or unjust? A just law is a man-made code that squares with the moral law or the law of God. An unjust law is a code that is out of harmony with the moral law. To put it in the terms of St. Thomas Aquinas: An unjust law is a human law that is not rooted in eternal law and natural law. Any law that uplifts human personality is just. Any law that degrades human personality is unjust. All segregation statutes are unjust because segregation distorts the soul and damages the personality. It gives the segregator a false sense of superiority and the segregated a false sense of inferiority. Segregation, to use the terminology of the Jewish philosopher Martin Buber, substitutes an "I–it" relationship for an "I–thou" relationship and ends up relegating persons to the status of things. Hence, segregation is not only politically, economically, and sociologically unsound, it is morally wrong and sinful. Paul Tillich has said that sin is separation. Is not segregation an existential expression of man's tragic separation, his awful estrangement, his terrible sinfulness? Thus it is that I can urge men to obey the 1954 decision of the Supreme Court, for it is morally right; and I can urge them to disobey segregation ordinances, for they are morally wrong.

Let us consider a more concrete example of just and unjust laws. An unjust law is a code that a numerical or power majority group compels a minority group to obey but does not make binding on itself. This is *difference* made legal. By the same token, a just law is a code that a majority compels a minority to follow and that it is willing to follow itself. This is *sameness* made legal.

Let me give another explanation. A law is unjust if it is inflicted on a minority that, as a result of being denied the right to vote, had no part in enacting or devising the law. Who can say that the legislature of Alabama which set up that state's segregation laws was democratically elected? Throughout Alabama all sorts of devious methods are used to prevent Negroes from becoming registered voters, and there are some counties in which, even though Negroes constitute a majority of the population, not a single Negro is registered. Can any law enacted under such circumstances be considered democratically structured?

Sometimes a law is just on its face and unjust in its application. For instance, I have been arrested on a charge of parading without a permit. Now, there is nothing wrong in having an ordinance which requires a permit for a parade. But such an ordinance becomes unjust when it is used to maintain segregation and to deny citizens the First-Amendment privilege of peaceful assembly and protest.

I hope you are able to see the distinction I am trying to point out. In no 20
sense do I advocate evading or defying the law, as would the rabid segregationist. That would lead to anarchy. One who breaks an unjust law must do so openly, lovingly, and with a willingness to accept the penalty. I submit that an individual who breaks a law that conscience tells him is unjust, and who willingly accepts the penalty of imprisonment in order to arouse the conscience of the community over its injustice, is in reality expressing the highest respect for law.

Of course, there is nothing new about this kind of civil disobedience. It was evidenced sublimely in the refusal of Shadrach, Meshach, and Abednego to obey the laws of Nebuchadnezzar, on the ground that a higher moral law was at stake. It was practiced superbly by the early Christians, who were willing to face hungry lions and the excruciating pain of chopping blocks rather than submit to certain unjust laws of the Roman Empire. To a degree, academic freedom is a reality today because Socrates practiced civil disobedience. In our own nation, the Boston Tea Party represented a massive act of civil disobedience.

We should never forget that everything Adolf Hitler did in Germany was "legal" and everything the Hungarian freedom fighters did in Hungary was "illegal." It was "illegal" to aid and comfort a Jew in Hitler's Germany. Even so, I am sure that, had I lived in Germany at the time, I would have aided and comforted my Jewish brothers. If today I lived in a Communist country where certain principles dear to the Christian faith are suppressed, I would openly advocate disobeying that country's antireligious laws.

I must make two honest confessions to you, my Christian and Jewish brothers. First, I must confess that over the past few years I have been gravely disappointed with the white moderate. I have almost reached the regrettable conclusion that the Negro's great stumbling block in his stride toward freedom is not the White Citizen's Counciler or the Ku Klux Klanner, but the white moderate, who is more devoted to "order" than to justice; who prefers a negative peace which is the presence of tension to a positive peace which is the presence of justice; who constantly says: "I agree with you in the goal you seek, but I cannot agree with your methods of direct action"; who paternalistically believes he can set the timetable for another man's freedom; who lives by a mythical concept of time and who constantly advises the Negro to wait for a "more convenient season." Shallow understanding from people of good will is more frustrating than absolute misunderstanding from people of ill will. Lukewarm acceptance is much more bewildering than outright rejection.

I had hoped that the white moderate would understand that law and order exist for the purpose of establishing justice and that when they fail in this purpose they become the dangerously structured dams that block the flow of social progress. I had hoped that the white moderate would understand that the present tension in the South is a necessary phase of the transition from an obnoxious negative peace, in which the Negro passively accepted his unjust plight, to a substantive and positive peace, in which all men will respect the dignity and worth of human personality. Actually, we who engage in nonviolent direct action are not the creators of tension. We merely bring to the surface the hidden tension that is already alive. We bring it out in the open, where it can be seen and dealt with. Like a boil that can never be cured so long as it is covered up but must be opened with all its ugliness to the natural medicines of air and light, injustice must be exposed, with all the tension its exposure creates, to the light of human conscience and the air of national opinion before it can be cured.

In your statement you assert that our actions, even though peaceful, must 25
be condemned because they precipitate violence. But is this a logical assertion? Isn't this like condemning a robbed man because his possession of money precipitated the evil act of robbery? Isn't this like condemning Socrates because his unswerving commitment to truth and his philosophical inquiries precipitated the act by the misguided populace in which they made him drink hemlock? Isn't this like condemning Jesus because his unique God-consciousness and never-ceasing devotion to God's will precipitated the evil act of crucifixion? We must come to see that, as the federal courts have consistently affirmed, it is wrong to urge an individual to cease his efforts to gain his basic constitutional rights because the quest may precipitate violence. Society must protect the robbed and punish the robber.

I had also hoped that the white moderate would reject the myth concerning time in relation to the struggle for freedom. I have just received a letter from a white brother in Texas. He writes: "All Christians know that the colored people will receive equal rights eventually, but it is possible that you are in too great a religious hurry. It has taken Christianity almost two thousand years to accomplish what it has. The teachings of Christ take time to come to earth." Such an attitude stems from a tragic misconception of time, from the strangely irrational notion that there is something in the very flow of time that will inevitably cure all ills. Actually, time itself is neutral; it can be used either destructively or constructively. More and more I feel that the people of ill will have used time much more effectively than have the people of good will. We will have to repent in this generation not merely for the hateful words and actions of the bad people but for the appalling silence of the good people. Human progress never rolls in on wheels of inevitability; it comes through the tireless efforts of men willing to be co-workers with God, and without this hard work, time itself becomes an ally of the forces of social stagnation. We must use time creatively, in the knowledge that the time is always ripe to do right. Now is the time to make real the promise of democracy and transform our pending national elegy into a creative psalm of brotherhood. Now is the time to lift our national policy from the quicksand of racial injustice to the solid rock of human dignity.

You speak of our activity in Birmingham as extreme. At first I was rather disappointed that fellow clergymen would see my nonviolent efforts as those of an extremist. I began thinking about the fact that I stand in the middle of two opposing forces in the Negro community. One is a force of complacency, made up in part of Negroes who, as a result of long years of oppression, are so drained of self-respect and a sense of "somebodiness" that they have adjusted to segregation; and in part of a few middle-class Negroes who, because of a degree of academic and economic security and because in some ways they profit by segregation, have become insensitive to the problems of the masses. The other force is one of bitterness and hatred, and it comes perilously close to advocating violence. It is expressed in the various black nationalists groups that are springing up across the nation, the largest and best-known being Elijah Muhammad's Muslim movement. Nourished by the Negro's frustration over the continued existence of racial discrimination, this movement is made up of people who have lost faith in America, who have absolutely repudiated Christianity, and who have concluded that the white man is an incorrigible "devil."

I have tried to stand between these two forces, saying that we need emulate neither the "do-nothingism" of the complacent nor the hatred and despair of the black nationalist. For there is the more excellent way of love and nonviolent protest. I am grateful to God that, through the influence of the Negro church, the way of nonviolence became an integral part of our struggle.

If this philosophy had not emerged, by now many streets of the South would, I am convinced, be flowing with blood. And I am further convinced that if our white brothers dismiss as "rabble-rousers" and "outside agitators" those of us who employ nonviolent direct action, and if they refuse to support our nonviolent efforts, millions of the Negroes will, out of frustration and despair, seek solace and security in black-nationalist ideologies—a development that would inevitably lead to a frightening racial nightmare.

30 Oppressed people cannot remain oppressed forever. The yearning for freedom eventually manifests itself, and that is what has happened to the American Negro. Something within has reminded him of his birthright of freedom, and something without has reminded him that it can be gained. Consciously or unconsciously, he has been caught up by the *Zeitgeist,* and with his black brothers of Africa and his brown and yellow brothers of Asia, South America, and the Caribbean, the United States Negro is moving with a sense of great urgency toward the promised land of racial justice. If one recognizes this vital urge that has engulfed the Negro community, one should readily understand why public demonstrations are taking place. The Negro has many pent-up resentments and latent frustrations, and he must release them. So let him march; let him make prayer pilgrimages to the city hall; let him go on freedom rides—and try to understand why he must do so. If his repressed emotions are not released in nonviolent ways, they will seek expression through violence; this is not a threat but a fact of history. So I have not said to my people: "Get rid of your discontent." Rather, I have tried to say that this normal and healthy discontent can be channeled into the creative outlet of nonviolent direct action. And now this approach is being termed extremist.

But though I was initially disappointed at being categorized as an extremist, as I continued to think about the matter I gradually gained a measure of satisfaction from the label. Was not Jesus an extremist for love: "Love your enemies, bless them that curse you, do good to them that hate you, and pray for them which despitefully use you, and persecute you." Was not Amos an extremist for justice: "Let justice roll down like waters and righteousness like an ever-flowing stream." Was not Paul an extremist for the Christian gospel: "I bear in my body the marks of the Lord Jesus." Was not Martin Luther an extremist: "Here I stand; I cannot do otherwise, so help me God." And John Bunyan: "I will stay in jail to the end of my days before I make a butchery of my conscience." And Abraham Lincoln: "This nation cannot survive half slave and half free." And Thomas Jefferson: "We hold these truths to be self-evident, that all men are created equal. . . ." So the question is not whether we will be extremists, but what kind of extremists we will be. Will we be extremists for hate or for love? Will we be extremists for the preservation of injustice or for the extension of justice? In that dramatic scene on Calvary's hill three men were crucified. We must never forget that all three were crucified for the same crime—the crime of extremism. Two were extremists for immorality, and thus fell below their environment. The other, Jesus Christ, was an extremist for love, truth and goodness, and thereby rose above his environment. Perhaps the South, the nation and the world are in dire need of creative extremists.

I had hoped that the white moderate would see this need. Perhaps I was too optimistic; perhaps I expected too much. I suppose I should have realized that few members of the oppressor race can understand the deep groans and passionate yearnings of the oppressed race, and still fewer have the vision to see that injustice must be rooted out by strong, persistent, and determined action. I am thankful, however, that some of our white brothers in the South have grasped the meaning of this social revolution and committed themselves to it. They are still all too few in quantity, but they are big in quality. Some—such as Ralph McGill, Lillian Smith, Harry Golden, James McBride Dabbs, Ann Braden, and Sarah Patton Boyle—have written about our struggle in eloquent and prophetic terms. Others have marched with us down nameless streets of the South. They have languished in filthy, roach-infested jails, suffering the abuse and brutality of policemen who view them as "dirty nigger-lovers." Unlike so many of their moderate brothers and sisters, they have recognized the urgency of the moment and sensed the need for powerful "action" antidotes to combat the disease of segregation.

Let me take note of my other major disappointment. I have been so greatly disappointed with the white church and its leadership. Of course, there are some notable exceptions. I am not unmindful of the fact that each of you has taken some significant stands on this issue. I commend you, Reverend Stallings, for your Christian stand on this past Sunday, in welcoming Negroes to your worship service on a nonsegregated basis. I commend the Catholic leaders of this state for integrating Spring Hill College several years ago.

But despite these notable exceptions, I must honestly reiterate that I have been disappointed with the church. I do not say this as one of those negative critics who can always find something wrong with the church. I say this as a minister of the gospel, who loves the church; who was nurtured in its bosom; who has been sustained by its spiritual blessings and who will remain true to it as long as the cord of life shall lengthen.

When I was suddenly catapulted into the leadership of the bus protest in 35
Montgomery, Alabama, a few years ago, I felt we would be supported by the white church. I felt that the white ministers, priests, and rabbis of the South would be among our strongest allies. Instead, some have been outright opponents, refusing to understand the freedom movement and misrepresenting its leaders; all too many others have been more cautious than courageous and have remained silent behind the anesthetizing security of stained-glass windows.

In spite of my shattered dreams, I came to Birmingham with the hope that the white religious leadership of this community would see the justice of our cause and, with deep moral concern, would serve as the channel through which our just grievances could reach the power structure. I had hoped that each of you would understand. But again I have been disappointed.

I have heard numerous southern religious leaders admonish their worshipers to comply with a desegregation decision because it is the law, but I have longed to hear white ministers declare: "Follow this decree because integration is morally right and because the Negro is your brother." In the midst of blatant injustices inflicted upon the Negro, I have watched white churchmen stand on the sideline and mouth pious irrelevancies and sanctimonious trivialities. In the midst of a mighty struggle to rid our nation of racial and economic injustice,

I have heard many ministers say: "Those are social issues, with which the gospel has no real concern." And I have watched many churches commit themselves to a completely otherworldly religion which makes a strange, un-Biblical distinction between body and soul, between the sacred and the secular.

I have traveled the length and breadth of Alabama, Mississippi, and all the other southern states. On sweltering summer days and crisp autumn mornings I have looked at the South's beautiful churches with their lofty spires pointing heavenward. I have beheld the impressive outlines of her massive religious-education buildings. Over and over I have found myself asking: "What kind of people worship here? Who is their God? Where were their voices when the lips of Governor Barnett dripped with words of interposition and nullification? Where were they when Governor Wallace gave a clarion call for defiance and hatred? Where were their voices of support when bruised and weary Negro men and women decided to rise from the dark dungeons of complacency to the bright hills of creative protest?"

Yes, these questions are still in my mind. In deep disappointment I have wept over the laxity of the church. But be assured that my tears have been tears of love. There can be no deep disappointment where there is not deep love. Yes, I love the church. How could I do otherwise? I am in the rather unique position of being the son, the grandson, and the great-grandson of preachers. Yes, I see the church as the body of Christ. But, oh! How we have blemished and scarred that body through social neglect and through fear of being nonconformists.

There was a time when the church was very powerful—in the time when 40
the early Christians rejoiced at being deemed worthy to suffer for what they believed. In those days the church was not merely a thermometer that recorded the ideas and principles of popular opinion; it was a thermostat that transformed the mores of society. Whenever the early Christians entered a town, the people in power became disturbed and immediately sought to convict the Christians for being "disturbers of the peace" and "outside agitators." But the Christians pressed on, in the conviction that they were "a colony of heaven," called to obey God rather than man. Small in number, they were big in commitment. They were too God-intoxicated to be "astronomically intimidated." By their effort and example they brought an end to such ancient evils as infanticide and gladiatorial contests.

Things are different now. So often the contemporary church is a weak, ineffectual voice with an uncertain sound. So often it is an archdefender of the status quo. Far from being disturbed by the presence of the church, the power structure of the average community is consoled by the church's silent—and often even vocal—sanction of things as they are.

But the judgment of God is upon the church as never before. If today's church does not recapture the sacrificial spirit of the early church, it will lose its authenticity, forfeit the loyalty of millions, and be dismissed as an irrelevant social club with no meaning for the twentieth century. Every day I meet young people whose disappointment with the church has turned into outright disgust.

Perhaps I have once again been too optimistic. Is organized religion too inextricably bound to the status quo to save our nation and the world? Perhaps I must turn my faith to the inner spiritual church, the church within the church, as the true *ekklesia* and the hope of the world. But again I am thankful to God that some noble souls from the ranks of organized religion have broken loose from the paralyzing chains of conformity and joined us as active partners in the struggle for freedom. They have left their secure congregations and walked the streets of Albany, Georgia, with us. They have gone down the highways of the South on tortuous rides for freedom. Yes, they have gone to jail with us. Some have been dismissed from their churches, have lost the support of their bishops and fellow ministers. But they have acted in the faith that right defeated is stronger than evil triumphant. Their witness has been the spiritual salt that has preserved the true meaning of the gospel in these troubled times. They have carved a tunnel of hope through the dark mountain of disappointment.

I hope the church as a whole will meet the challenge of this decisive hour. But even if the church does not come to the aid of justice, I have no despair about the future. I have no fear about the outcome of our struggle in Birmingham, even if our motives are at present misunderstood. We will reach the goal of freedom in Birmingham and all over the nation, because the goal of America is freedom. Abused and scorned though we may be, our destiny is tied up with America's destiny. Before the pilgrims landed at Plymouth, we were here. Before the pen of Jefferson etched the majestic words of the Declaration of Independence across the pages of history, we were here. For more than two centuries our forebears labored in this country without wages; they made cotton king; they built the homes of their masters while suffering gross injustice and shameful humiliation—and yet out of a bottomless vitality they continued to thrive and develop. If the inexpressible cruelties of slavery could not stop us, the opposition we now face will surely fail. We will win our freedom because the sacred heritage of our nation and the eternal will of God are embodied in our echoing demands.

Before closing I feel impelled to mention one other point in your statement 45
that has troubled me profoundly. You warmly commended the Birmingham police force for keeping "order" and "preventing violence." I doubt that you would have so warmly commended the police force if you had seen its dogs sinking their teeth into unarmed, nonviolent Negroes. I doubt that you would so quickly commend the policemen if you were to observe their ugly and inhumane treatment of Negroes here in the city jail; if you were to watch them push and curse old Negro women and young Negro girls; if you were to see them slap and kick old Negro men and young boys; if you were to observe them, as they did on two occasions, refuse to give us food because we wanted to sing our grace together. I cannot join you in your praise of the Birmingham police department.

It is true that police have exercised a degree of discipline in handling the demonstrators. In this sense they have conducted themselves rather "nonviolently" in public. But for what purpose? To preserve the evil system of segregation. Over the past few years I have consistently preached that nonviolence demands that the means we use must be as pure as the ends we seek. I have tried to make clear that it is wrong to use immoral means to attain moral ends. But now I must affirm that it is just as wrong, or perhaps even more so, to use moral means to preserve immoral ends. Perhaps Mr. Connor and his policemen have been rather nonviolent in public, as was Chief Pritchett in Albany, Georgia, but they have used the moral means of nonviolence to maintain the immoral end of racial injustice. As T. S. Eliot has said: "The last temptation is the greatest treason: To do the right deed for the wrong reason."

I wish you had commended the Negro sit-inners and demonstrators of Birmingham for their sublime courage, their willingness to suffer and their amazing discipline in the midst of great provocation. One day the South will recognize its real heroes. They will be the James Merediths, with the noble sense of purpose that enables them to face jeering and hostile mobs, and with the agonizing loneliness that characterizes the life of the pioneer. They will be old, oppressed, battered Negro women, symbolized in a seventy-two-year-old woman in Montgomery, Alabama, who rose up with a sense of dignity and with her people decided not to ride segregated buses, and who responded with ungrammatical profundity to one who inquired about her weariness: "My feets is tired, but my soul is at rest." They will be the young high school and college students, the young ministers of the gospel and a host of their elders, courageously and nonviolently sitting in at lunch counters and willingly going to jail for conscience' sake. One day the South will know that when these disinherited children of God sat down at lunch counters, they were in reality standing up for what is best in the American dream and for the most sacred values in our Judaeo-Christian heritage, thereby bringing our nation back to those great wells of democracy which were dug deep by the founding fathers in their formulation of the Constitution and the Declaration of Independence.

Never before have I written so long a letter. I'm afraid it is much too long to take your precious time. I can assure you that it would have been much shorter if I had been writing from a comfortable desk, but what else can one do when he is alone in a narrow jail cell, other than write long letters, think long thoughts, and pray long prayers?

If I have said anything in this letter that overstates the truth and indicates an unreasonable impatience, I beg you to forgive me. If I have said anything that understates the truth and indicates my having a patience that allows me to settle for anything less than brotherhood, I beg God to forgive me.

I hope this letter finds you strong in faith. I also hope that circumstances *50*
will soon make it possible for me to meet each of you, not as an integrationist or a civil-rights leader but as a fellow clergyman and a Christian brother. Let us all hope that the dark clouds of racial prejudice will soon pass away and the deep fog of misunderstanding will be lifted from our fear-drenched communities, and in some not too distant tomorrow the radiant stars of love and brotherhood will shine over our great nation with all their scintillating beauty.

Yours for the cause of Peace and Brotherhood
MARTIN LUTHER KING, JR.

King's Analysis of His Audience: Identification and Overcoming Difference

King's letter is worth studying for his use of the resources of identification alone. For example, he appeals in his salutation to "My Dear Fellow Clergymen," which emphasizes at the outset that he and his readers share a similar role. Elsewhere he calls them "my friends" (paragraph 12) and "my Christian and Jewish brothers" (paragraph 23). In many other places, King alludes to the Bible and to other religious figures; these references would put him on common ground with his readers.

King's letter also successfully deals with various levels of difference between his readers and himself.

Assumptions

King's readers assumed that if black people waited long enough, their situation would naturally grow better. Therefore, they argued for patience. King, in paragraph 26, questions "the strangely irrational notion . . . that the very flow of time . . . will inevitably cure all ills." Against this common assumption that "time heals," King offers the view that "time itself is neutral," something "that can be used either destructively or constructively."

Principles

King's readers believed in the principle of always obeying the law, a principle blind to both intent and application. King substitutes another principle: Obey just laws, but disobey, openly and lovingly, unjust laws (paragraphs 15–20).

Hierarchy of Values

King's readers elevated the value of reducing racial tension over the value of securing racial justice. In paragraph 10 King's strategy is to talk about "constructive, nonviolent tension," clearly an effort to get his readers to see tension as not necessarily a bad thing, but a condition for achieving social progress.

Ends and Means

King's audience seems not to disagree with him about the ends for which he was working, but they differ with him over means. King, therefore, focuses not on justifying civil rights, but on justifying civil disobedience.

Interpretation

King's audience interpreted extremism as always negative, never justifiable. King counters by showing, first, that he is actually a moderate, neither a "do-nothing" nor a militant (paragraph 28). But then he redefines their interpretation of extremism, arguing that extremism for good causes is justified and giving examples from history to support his point (paragraph 31).

Implications or Consequences

King's readers doubtless feared the consequences of supporting the struggle for civil rights too strongly—losing the support of more conservative members of their congregations. But as King warns, "If today's church does not recapture the sacrificial spirit of the early church, it will . . . be dismissed as an irrelevant social club . . ." (paragraph 42). King's strategy is to turn his readers' attention away from short-term consequences and toward long-term consequences—the loss of the vitality and relevance of the church itself.

Following Through

As a class look closely at one of the essays from an earlier chapter or in Part Two, and consider it in terms of audience analysis. What audience did the writer attempt to reach? How did the writer connect or fail to connect with the audience's experience, knowledge, and concerns? What exactly divides the author from his or her audience, and how did the writer attempt to overcome the division? How effective were the writer's strategies for achieving identification? What can you suggest that might have worked better?

USING THE FORMS OF APPEAL

We turn now to the forms of appeal in persuasion, noting how Martin Luther King, Jr., used them in his letter (pages 114–125).

The Appeal to Reason

Persuasion, we have said, uses the same appeal to reason that we find in convincing; that is, the foundation of a persuasive argument is the case structure of thesis, reasons, and evidence. King, however, seems to have realized that an argument organized like a case would seem too formal and public for his purposes, so he chose instead to respond to the clergymen's statement with a personal letter, organized around their criticisms of him. In fact, most of King's letter amounts to self-defense and belongs to the rhetorical form known as *apologia,* from which our word "apology" derives. An *apologia* is an effort to explain and justify what one has done or chosen not to do, in the face of condemnation or at least of widespread disapproval or misunderstanding.

While his overall organization does not present a case, King still relies heavily on reason. He uses a series of short arguments, occupying from one to as many as eight paragraphs, in responding to his readers' criticisms. These are the more important ones, in order of appearance:

Refutation of "outside agitator" concept (paragraphs 2–4)
Defense of nonviolent civil disobedience (paragraphs 5–11)
Definitions of "just" versus "unjust" laws (paragraphs 15–22)
Refutation and defense of the label "extremist" (paragraphs 27–31)
Rejection of the ministers' praise for the conduct of the police during the Birmingham demonstration (paragraphs 45–47).

In addition to defending himself and his cause, King also pursues an offensive strategy, advancing his own criticisms, most notably of the "white moderate" (paragraphs 23–26) and the "white church and its leadership" (paragraphs 33–44). This concentration on rational appeal is both effective and appropriate: It confirms King's character as a man of reason, and it appeals to an audience of well-educated professionals.

King also cites evidence that his readers must respect. In paragraphs 15 and 16, for example, he enlists the words of Thomas Aquinas, Martin Buber, and Paul Tillich—who represent, respectively, the Catholic, Jewish, and Protestant traditions—to defend his position on the nature of just and unjust laws. He has chosen these authorities carefully, so that each of his eight accusers has someone from his own tradition with whom to identify. The implication, of course, is that King's distinction between just and unjust laws and the course of action that follows from this distinction is consistent with Judeo-Christian thought as a whole.

Following Through

1. Look at paragraphs 2, 3, and 4 of King's letter. What reasons does King give to justify his presence in Birmingham? How well does he support each reason? How do his reasons and evidence reflect a strategy aimed at his clergy audience?
2. King's argument for civil disobedience (paragraphs 15–22) is based on one main reason. What is it, and how does he support it?
3. What are the two reasons that King gives in order to refute his audience's charge that he is an extremist (paragraphs 27–31)?
4. Think about a time in your life when you did (or did not do) something, for which you were unfairly criticized. Choose one or two of the criticisms that were made and attempt to defend yourself in a short case of your own. Remember that your argument must be persuasive to your accusers, not just to you. Ask yourself, as King did, how can I appeal to my readers? What will they find reasonable?

The Appeal to Character

In Chapter 6 on convincing, our concern was how to make a good case. We did not discuss self-presentation explicitly there, but in fact when you formulate a clear and plausible thesis and defend it with good reasons and sufficient evidence, you are at the same time creating a positive impression of your own character. A good argument will always reveal the writer's values, his or her intelligence, knowledge of the subject, grasp of the reader's needs and concerns, and so on. We tend to respect and trust a person who reasons well, even when we do not assent to the particular case being presented.

In terms of the appeal to character, the difference between convincing and persuading is a matter of degree. In convincing this appeal is implicit, indirect, and diffused throughout the argument; in persuading the appeal to character is often quite explicit, direct, and concentrated in a specific section of the essay. The effect on readers is consequently rather different: In convincing we are seldom consciously aware of the writer's character as such; in persuasion the writer's character assumes a major role in determining how we respond to the argument.

The perception of his character was a special problem for King when he wrote his letter. He was not a national hero in 1963 but rather a very controversial civil rights leader, whom many viewed as a troublemaker. Furthermore, of course, he wrote this now celebrated document while in jail—hardly a condition that inspires respect and trust in readers. Self-presentation, then, was very significant for King, something he concentrates on throughout his letter and especially at the beginning and end.

In his opening paragraph, King acknowledges the worst smirch on his character—that he is currently in jail. But he goes on to establish himself as a professional person like his readers, with secretaries, correspondence, and important work to do.

Just prior to his conclusion (paragraphs 48–50), King has offered a strongly worded critique of the white moderate and the mainstream white church, taking the offensive in a way that his readers are certain to perceive as an attack. In paragraph 48, however, he suddenly becomes self-deprecating and almost apologetic: "Never before have I written so long a letter." As unexpected as it is, this sudden shift of tone disarms the reader. Then, with gentle irony (the letter, he says, would have been shorter "if I had been writing from a comfortable desk"), King explains the length of his letter as the result of his having no other outlet for action. What can one do in jail but "write long letters, think long thoughts, and pray long prayers?" King paradoxically turns the negative of being in jail into a positive, an opportunity rather than a limitation on his freedom.

His next move is equally surprising, especially after the confident tone of his critique of the church. He begs forgiveness—from his readers if he has overstated his case, and from God if he has understated his case or shown too much patience with injustice. This daring, dramatic penultimate paragraph is just the right touch, the perfect gesture of reconciliation. Since he asks so humbly, his readers must forgive him. What else can they do? The further subordination of his own will to God's is the stance of the sufferer and martyr in both the Jewish and Christian tradition.

Finally, King sets aside that which divides him from his readers—the issue of integration and his role as a civil rights leader—in favor of that which unifies him with his audience—all are men of God and brothers in faith. Like an Old Testament prophet, he envisions a time when the current conflicts are over, when "the radiant stars of love and brotherhood will shine over our great nation." In other words, King holds out the possibility for transcendence, for rising above racial prejudice to a new age, a new America. In the end, his readers are encouraged to soar with him, to hope for the future.

Here King enlists the power of identification to overcome the differences separating writer and reader, invoking his status as a "fellow clergyman and a Christian brother" as a symbol of commonality. The key to identification is to reach beyond the individual self, associating one's character with something larger—the Christian community, the history of the struggle for freedom, national values, "spaceship Earth," or any appropriate cause or movement in which readers can also participate.

Following Through

1. We have already seen how King associates himself with the Christian community in the essay's final paragraph. Look at the list on page 111 that offers suggestions for creating audience identification with the writer. Find some examples of places in King's letter where he employs some of these resources of identification. Which parts of the letter are most effective in creating a positive impression of character? Why? What methods does King use that any persuader might use?
2. Write an essay discussing the appeal of character in one of the essays in the following list. Begin with a description of the rhetorical context for that essay, paying particular attention to the original place of publication and the writer's original readership. Comment on how the writer uses his or her own background and experience to establish authority and build respect and trust. With what or with whom does the writer identify himself or herself? With what or whom does the writer wish the reader to identify?

    Lame Deer, John (Fire) and Richard Erdoes, "Talking to the Owls and Butterflies," pp. 201–206.
    Hamill, Pete. "Confessions of a Heterosexual," pp. 311–314.
    Marin, Peter. "Virginia's Trap," pp. 242–250.

The Appeal to Emotion

Educated people aware of the techniques of persuasion are often deeply suspicious of emotional appeal. Among college professors—those who will be reading and grading your work—this prejudice can be especially strong, since all fields of academic study claim to value reason, dispassionate inquiry, and critical analysis of data and conclusions. Many think of emotional appeal as an impediment to sound thinking and associate it with politicians who prey on our fears, with dictators and demagogues who exploit our prejudices, with advertisers and television evangelists who claim they will satisfy our dreams and prayers.

Of course, we can all cite examples of the destructive power of emotional appeal. But to condemn it wholesale, without qualification, is to exhibit a lack of self-awareness. Most scientists will concede, for instance, that they are passionately committed to the methods of their field, and mathematicians will confess that they are moved by the elegance of certain formulas and proofs. In fact, all human activity has some emotional dimension, the strongly felt adherence to a common set of values.

Moreover, we ought to have strong feelings about certain things: revulsion at the horrors of the Holocaust, pity and anger over the abuse of children, happiness when a war is concluded or when those kidnapped by terrorists are released, and so on. We cease to be human if we are not responsive to emotional appeal.

Clearly we must distinguish between legitimate and illegitimate emotional appeals, condemning the latter and learning to use the former when appropriate. While distinguishing the two is not always easy, there are certain questions that can help us do so:

> Do the emotional appeals substitute for knowledge and reason?
> Do they work with stereotypes and pit one group against another?
> Do they offer a simple, unthinking reaction to a complex situation?

Whenever the answer is "yes," our suspicions should be aroused.

Perhaps an even better test is to ask, if we act on the basis of how I feel, who will benefit, and who will suffer? We are saddened, for example, to see animals used in medical experiments, but an appeal showing only these animals and ignoring the benefits of experimentation for human life is pandering to the emotions.

On the other hand, legitimate emotional appeal supplements argument rather than substituting for it, drawing on knowledge and often first-hand experience. At its best, it can bring alienated groups together and create empathy or sympathy where these are lacking. Many examples could be cited from Martin Luther King's letter, but the most effective passage is surely paragraph 14:

> We have waited for more than 340 years for our constitutional God-given rights. The nations of Asia and Africa are moving with jetlike speed toward gaining political independence, but we still creep at horse-and-buggy pace toward gaining a cup of coffee at a lunch counter. Perhaps it is easy for those who have never felt the stinging darts of segregation to say, "Wait." But when you have seen vicious mobs lynch your mothers and fathers at will and drown your sisters and brothers at whim; when you have seen hate-filled policemen curse, kick, and even kill your black brothers and sisters; when you see the vast majority of your twenty million Negro brothers smothering in an airtight cage of poverty in the midst of an affluent society; when you suddenly find your tongue twisted and your speech stammering as you seek to explain to your six-year-old daughter why she can't go to the public amusement park that has just been advertised on television, and see tears welling up in her eyes when she is told that Funtown is closed to colored children, and see ominous clouds of inferiority beginning to form in her little mental sky, and see her beginning to distort her personality by developing an unconscious bitterness toward white people; when you have to

> concoct an answer for a five-year-old son who is asking: "Daddy, why do white people treat colored people so mean?"; when you take a cross-country drive and find it necessary to sleep night after night in the uncomfortable corners of your automobile because no motel will accept you; when you are humiliated day in and day out by nagging signs reading "white" and "colored"; when your first name becomes "nigger," your middle name becomes "boy" (however old you are), and your last name becomes "John," and your wife and mother are never given the respected title "Mrs."; when you are harried by day and haunted by night by the fact that you are a Negro, living constantly at tiptoe stance, never quite knowing what to expect next, and are plagued with inner fears and outer resentments; when you are forever fighting a degenerating sense of "nobodiness"—then you will understand why we find it difficult to wait. There comes a time when the cup of endurance runs over, and men are no longer willing to be plunged into the abyss of despair. I hope, sirs, you can understand our legitimate and unavoidable impatience.

Just prior to this paragraph King has concluded an argument justifying the use of direct action to dramatize social inequities and to demand rights and justice denied to oppressed people. Direct-action programs are necessary, he says, because "freedom is never voluntarily given by the oppressor; it must be demanded by the oppressed." It is easy for those not oppressed to urge an underclass to wait. But "[t]his 'Wait' has almost always meant 'Never.'"

At this point King deliberately sets out to create in his readers a feeling of outrage. Having ended paragraph 13 by equating "wait" with "never," King next refers to a tragic historical fact: For 340 years, since the beginning of slavery in the American colonies, black people have been waiting for their freedom. He sharply contrasts the "jetlike speed" with which Africa is overcoming colonialism with the "horse-and-buggy pace" of integration in the United States. In African homelands black people are gaining their political independence; but here, in the land of the free, they are denied even "a cup of coffee at a lunch counter." Clearly this is legitimate emotional appeal, based on fact and reinforcing reason.

In the long and rhythmical sentence that takes up most of the rest of the paragraph, King unleashes the full force of emotional appeal in a series of concrete images designed to make his white, privileged readers feel the anger, frustration, and humiliation of the oppressed. In rapid succession King alludes to mob violence, police brutality, and economic discrimination—the more public evils of racial discrimination—then moves to the personal, everyday experience of segregation, concentrating especially on what it does to the self-respect of innocent children. For any reader with even the least imaginative capacity for sympathy, these images must strike home, creating identification with the suffering of the oppressed and angry impatience toward the evil system that perpetuates this suffering. In short, through the use of telling detail drawn from his own experience, King succeeds in getting his audience to feel what he feels—feelings, in fact, that they ought to share, that are wholly appropriate to the problem of racial prejudice.

What have we learned from King about the available means of emotional appeal? Instead of telling his audience they should feel a particular emotion, he has brought forth that emotion using five specific rhetorical techniques:

concrete examples
personal experiences
metaphors and similes
sharp contrasts and comparisons
sentence rhythm, particularly the use of intentional repetition

We will later consider how style contributes to a persuasive argument.

Following Through

1. We have said that emotional appeals need to be both legitimate and appropriate—that is, honest and suitable for the subject matter, the audience, and the kind of discourse being written. Find examples of arguments from various publications—books, newspapers, magazines, and professional journals. Discuss the use or avoidance of emotional appeal in each. On the basis of this study, try to generalize about what kinds of subjects, audiences, and discourse allow direct emotional appeal and what kinds do not.
2. Write an essay analyzing the tactics of emotional appeal in the editorial columns of your campus or local newspaper. Compare the strategies used with King's. Then evaluate the appeals. How effective are they in moving your emotions? How well do they reinforce the reasoning offered? Be sure to discuss both how the appeals work and their legitimacy and appropriateness.

The Appeal through Style

By style, we mean the choices a writer makes at the level of words, phrases, and sentences. It would be a mistake to think of style as a final touch, put on to dress up an argument. Style actually involves all of a writer's choices about what words to use and how to arrange them. Ideas and arguments do not develop apart from style, and all of the appeals discussed so far involve stylistic choices. For example, you are concerned with style when you consider what words will state a thesis most precisely or make yourself sound knowledgeable or provide your reader with a compelling image. The appeal of style works hand-in-hand with the appeals of reason, character, and emotion.

Further, style makes what we say memorable. George Bush may wish he had never said it, but his statement "Read my lips: no new taxes" was a message that generated high enthusiasm and, to the former President's dismay, remained in people's minds long after he had compromised himself on that stand. Since the persuasive effect we have on readers depends largely on what they remember, the appeal to style matters as much as the appeal to reason, character, and emotion.

Writers with effective style make conscious choices on many levels. One choice involves the degree of formality or familiarity they want to convey. You will notice that King strikes a fairly formal and professional tone throughout most of his letter, choosing words like "cognizant" (paragraph 4) rather than the more common "aware." Writers also consider the connotation of words (what a word implies or what we associate it with) as much as their denotation (a word's literal meaning). For example, King opens his letter with the phrase "While confined here in the Birmingham city jail. . . ." The word "confined" denotes the same condition as "incarcerated" but has less unfavorable connotations, since people can also be "confined" in ways that evoke our sympathy.

Memorable writing often appeals to the senses of sight and sound. Concrete words can paint a picture; in paragraph 45, for example, King shows us "dogs sinking their teeth" into the nonviolent demonstrators. Writers may also evoke images through implied and explicit comparisons (respectively, *metaphor* and *simile*). King's "the stinging darts of segregation" (paragraph 14) is an example of metaphor. In this same paragraph, King refers to the "airtight cage of poverty," the "clouds of inferiority" forming in his young daughter's "mental sky," and the "cup of endurance" that has run over for his people—each a metaphor with a powerful emotional effect.

Even when read silently, language has sound. Therefore, style includes variation of sentence length and the use of rhythmic patterns as well. For example, a writer may emphasize a short, simple sentence by placing it at the end of a series of long sentences or a single long sentence, as King does in paragraph 14. One common rhythmic pattern is the repetition of certain phrases to emphasize a point or to play up a similarity or contrast; in the fourth sentence of paragraph 14, King repeats the words "when you" a number of times, piling up examples of racial discrimination and creating a powerful rhythm that carries readers through this unusually long sentence. Another common rhythmic pattern is parallelism. Note the following phrases, again from the fourth sentence of paragraph 14:

> lynch your mothers and fathers at will
>
> drown your sisters and brothers at whim

Here, King uses similar words in the same places, even paralleling the number of syllables in each phrase. The parallelism here is further emphasized by King's choice of another stylistic device known as alliteration.

Alliteration is the repetition of consonant sounds. In another passage from paragraph 14, King achieves a sound pattern that suggests violence when he describes the actions of police who "curse, kick, and even kill" black citizens. The repetition of the hard "k" sound, especially in words of one syllable, suggests the violence of the acts themselves.

Beyond the level of words, phrases, and sentences, the overall arrangement of an essay's main points or topics can also be considered a matter of style, for such arrangement determines how one point contrasts with another, how the tone changes, how the force of the argument builds. When we discuss style we usually look at smaller units of an essay, but actually all the choices a writer makes contribute in some way to the essay's style.

Following Through

1. Analyze King's style in paragraphs 6, 8, 23, 24, 31, and 47. Compare what King does in these paragraphs with paragraph 14. How are they similar? How different? Why?
2. To an extent style is a gift or talent which some people have more of than others. But it is also learned, acquired by imitating authors we admire, and you can use your writer's notebook to increase your stylistic options. Whenever you hear or read something stated effectively, take a few minutes and copy it down, analyzing why it is effective. Try to make up a sentence of your own using the same choices but with different subject matter. In this way you can begin to use analogy, metaphor, repetition, alliteration, parallelism, and other stylistic devices. Begin by imitating six or so sentences or phrases that you especially liked in King's letter.
3. Write an essay analyzing your own style in a previous essay. What would you do differently now? Why?

DRAFTING A PERSUASIVE ESSAY

Outside of the classroom, persuasion begins, as Martin Luther King's letter did, with a real need to move people to action. In a writing course, you may have to create the circumstances for your argument. You should begin by thinking of an issue that calls for persuasion. Your argument must go beyond merely convincing your readers to believe as you do; now you must decide what action you want them to take, and move them to do it.

Conceiving a Readership

Assuming that the task you have chosen or been assigned calls for persuasion, finding and analyzing your readership is your first concern. Because instructors evaluate the writing of their students, it is probably unavoidable that college writers to some extent tend to write for their instructors. However, real persuasion has a genuine readership, some definite group of people with a stake in the question or issue being addressed. Whatever we say must be adapted for this audience, for moving the reader is the whole point of persuasion.

How can you go about conceiving a readership? First, you should throw out the whole notion of writing to the "general public." Such a "group" is a nearly meaningless abstraction, not defined enough to give you much guidance. If, for example, you are arguing that sex education in public schools must include a moral dimension as well the clinical facts of reproduction and venereal disease, you need to decide if you are addressing students, who may not want the moral lectures; school administrators, who may not want the added responsibility and curriculum changes; or parents, who may not want the schools taking over what they see as the responsibility of family or church.

Second, given the issue and the position you will probably take, you should ask who you would want to persuade. Not, on the one hand, those who already agree with you—there is nothing to be gained by persuading the already persuaded—and not, on the other hand, those so committed to an opposing position that nothing you could say would make any difference. An argument against logging in old growth forests, for example, would probably be aimed neither at staunch environmentalists nor at workers employed in the timber industry, but rather at some readership between these extremes—say, people concerned in general about the environment but not focused specifically on the threat to mature forests.

Third, when you have a degree of choice among possible readerships, you should select your target audience based on two primary criteria. Since persuasion is directly concerned with making decisions and taking action, seek above all to influence those readers best able to influence events. When this group includes a range of readers (and it often will), also consider which of these readers you know the most about and can therefore appeal to best.

Because all appeals in persuasion are appeals to an audience, try to identify your reader early in the process. You can, of course, change your mind later on, but doing so will require considerable rethinking and rewriting. Devoting time at the outset to thinking carefully about your intended audience can save much time and effort in the long run.

Following Through

For a persuasive argument you are about to write on an issue your instructor assigns or you select, determine your audience; that is, decide who can make a difference with respect to this issue, and what they can do to make a difference.

Be sure that you go beyond the requirements of convincing when you make these decisions. For example, you may be able to make a good case that, just as heterosexuals do not "choose" their attraction to the opposite sex, so homosexuality is also not voluntary. Based on this point you could argue to a readership of moderate-to-liberal voters in your home district that they should press state legislators to support a bill extending full citizens' rights to homosexuals. But with such a desire for action in mind, you would have to think even more about your audience, why they might resist such a measure or not care enough to support it strongly.

In your writer's notebook, respond to the questions "Who is my audience?" (pages 109–110) and "What are our differences?" (page 110). Use your responses to write an audience profile that is more detailed than the one you wrote for an argument to convince.

Discovering the Resources of Appeal

With an audience firmly in mind, you are ready to begin thinking about how to appeal to them. Before and during the drafting stage, you will be making choices about

how to formulate a case and support it with research, as needed;
how to present yourself;
how to move your readers' emotions; and
how to make the style of your writing contribute to the argument's effectiveness.

All of these decisions will be influenced by your understanding of your readers' needs and interests.

Appealing through Reason

In both convincing and persuading, rational appeal amounts to making a case or cases—advancing a thesis or theses and providing supporting reasons and evidence. What you learned in Chapter 6 about case-making applies here as well. You may, therefore, wish to review that last chapter as you work on rational appeal for a persuasive paper. Of course, inquiry into the truth (Chapter 5) and research (Appendix B) are as relevant to persuasion as they are to convincing.

One difference between convincing and persuading, however, is that in persuasion you will devote much of your argument to defending a course of action. The steps here are basically a matter of common sense:

You must show that there is a need for action.
If your audience, like that for Martin Luther King's letter, is inclined to inactivity, you must show urgency as well as need—we must act and act now.
Finally, you must satisfy the need, showing that your proposal for action meets the need or will solve the problem; one way to do this is to compare your course of action with other proposals or solutions, indicating why yours is better than the others.

Sometimes your goal will be to persuade your audience *not* to act because what they want to do is wrong or inappropriate or because the time is not right. Need is still the main issue, the difference being, obviously, the goal of showing that no need exists or that it is better to await other developments before a proposed action will be appropriate or effective.

Following Through

Prepare a brief of your argument (see Chapter 5). Be ready to present an overview of your audience and to defend your brief, either before the class or in small groups. Pay special attention to how well the argument establishes a need or motivation to act (or shows that there is no need for action) for your defined audience. If some action is called for, assess the solution in the context of other, common proposals: Will the proposed action meet the need? Is it realistic—that is, can it be done?

Appealing through Character

A reader who finishes your essay should have the following impressions:

The author is well-informed about the topic.
The author is confident about his or her own position and sincere in advocating it.
The author has been fair and balanced in dealing with other positions.
The author understands my concerns and objections and has dealt with them.
The author is honest.
The author values what I value; his or her "heart is in the right place."

What can you do to communicate these impressions? Basically, you must earn these impressions just as you must earn a conviction and a good argument. There are no short cuts, and educated readers can seldom be fooled.

To seem well-informed, you must be well-informed. This requires that you dig into the topic, thinking about it carefully, researching it thoroughly and taking notes, discussing the topic and your research with other students, consulting campus experts, and so on. This work will provide you the hallmarks of being well-informed:

the ability to make references in passing to relevant events and people connected with the issue now or recently
the ability to create a context or provide background information, which may include comments on the history of the question or issue,
the ability to produce sufficient, high quality evidence to back up your contentions

As digging in will make you well-informed, so inquiry (struggling to find the truth) and convincing (making a case for your conviction about the truth) will lend your argument sincerity and confidence. Draw upon personal experience when it has played a role in determining your position, and don't be reluctant to reveal your own stake in the issue. Make your case boldly, qualifying it as little as possible. If you have prepared yourself with good research, genuine inquiry, and careful case-making, you have earned authority; what remains is to claim your authority, essential in arguing to persuade.

Represent other positions accurately and fairly; then present evidence that defeats those positions or show that their reasoning is inadequate or inconsistent. Don't be afraid to agree with parts of other opinions when they are consistent with your own and can help you to make your case. Such partial agreements can play a major role in overcoming reader resistance to your own position.

It is generally not a good idea to subject other positions to ridicule. Some of your readers may sympathize with all or part of the position you are attacking and take offense. Even readers gratified by your attack may feel that you have gone too far. Concentrate on the merits of your own case rather than the faults of others.

Coping with your readers' concerns and objections should present no special problems, assuming that you have found an appropriate audience and thought seriously about both the common ground you share and how their outlook differs from yours. You can ultimately handle concerns and objections in one of two ways: by adjusting your case—your thesis and supporting reasons—so that the concerns or objections do not arise; or by taking up the more significant objections one by one and responding to them in a way that reduces reader resistance. Of course, doing one does not preclude doing the other: You can adjust your case and also raise and answer whatever objections remain. What matters is never to ignore any likely and weighty objection to what you are advocating.

Responding to objections patiently and reasonably will also help us with the last and perhaps most important impression that a reader has of us—that we value what s/he values. Being sensitive to the reasoning and moral and emotional commitments of others is one of those values we can and must share with our readers.

If you are to have any chance of persuading at all, your readers must feel that you would not deceive them, so you must conform to the standards of honesty readers will expect. Leaving readers with the impression of your honesty requires much more than simply not lying. Rather honesty requires reporting evidence from sources accurately and with regard for the original context; acknowledging significant counterevidence to your case, pointing to its existence and explaining why it does not change your argument rather than ignoring it; and pointing out areas of doubt and uncertainty that must await future events or study.

Following Through

You have already prepared an audience profile and explored your key areas of difference with them. Now use the results of that work to help you think through how you could appeal to these readers. Use the questions to help establish commonality with your audience (page 111) to formulate a more specific list of possible areas of common ground and strategies for bringing you and your readership closer together.

Appealing to Emotion

In both convincing and persuading, your case determines largely what you have to say and the order of your presentation. As in King's essay, argument is the center, the framework, while emotional appeal plays a supporting role to rational appeal, taking center stage only here and there. Consequently, your decisions must include these:

what emotions to arouse and by what means
the frequency and intensity of emotional appeals
where to introduce emotional appeals

The first of these decisions is usually the easiest. Try to arouse the emotions that you yourself have genuinely felt: Whatever moved you will probably also move your readers. If your emotions come from direct experience, draw upon that experience for concrete descriptive detail, as King did. Study whatever you heard or read that moved you; you can probably adapt your sources' tactics for your own purposes. (The best strategy for arousing emotions is often to avoid emotionalism yourself. Let the facts, the descriptive detail, the concrete examples do the work, just as King does.)

Deciding how often, at what length, and how intensely to make emotional appeals presents a more difficult challenge. Much depends on the topic, the audience, and your own range and intensity of feeling. In every case you must estimate as best you can what will be appropriate, but the following suggestions may help.

As always in persuasion, your primary consideration is your audience. What attitudes and feelings do they have already? Which of these lend emotional support to your case? Which work against your purposes? You will want to emphasize those feelings that are consistent with your position and show why any others are understandable but inappropriate.

Then ask a further question: "What does my audience not feel or not feel strongly enough that they must feel or feel more strongly if I am to have a chance of persuading them?" King, for example, decided that his readers' greatest emotional deficit was their inability to feel what victims of racial discrimination feel—hence, paragraph 14, the most intense emotional appeal in his letter. Simply put, devote space and intensity to arousing emotions central to your case that are lacking or present only weakly in your readers.

The questions of how often and where to include emotional appeals are both worth careful consideration. Regarding frequency, the best principle is to take your shots sparingly, getting as much as you can out of each effort. Positioning emotional appeals depends on pacing: Use them to lead into or to clinch a key point. So positioned, they temporarily relieve the audience of the intellectual effort required to follow your argument.

It is generally not a good idea to begin an essay with your longest and most intense emotional appeal; you don't want to peak too early. Besides that, you need to concentrate in your introduction on establishing your tone and authority, providing needed background information, and making a clear and forceful statement of your thesis. Conclusions can be effective positions because your audience is left with something memorable to carry away from the reading. But in most cases it is best to concentrate emotional appeals in the middle or near the end of an essay.

Following Through

After you have a first draft of your essay, reread it with an eye to emotional appeal. Use a highlighter to mark the places where you have deliberately sought to rouse the audience's emotions. (You might also ask a friend to read the draft or exchange drafts with another student in your class.)

Decide if you need to devote more attention to your emotional appeal through additional concrete examples, direct quotations, or something else. Consider also how you could make each appeal more effective and intense and whether your position for each appeal is the best possible location in the essay.

Appealing through Style

As we have seen, the style of your argument evolves with every choice you make, even in the prewriting stages. As you draft, it is good to think consciously about how stylistic choices can work for you, but not to agonize over them. In successive revisions, you will be able to make refinements and experiment for different effects.

In the first draft, however, you ought to set an appropriate level of formality. Most persuasive writing is neither chatty and familiar nor stiff and distant. Rather, persuasive prose is like dignified conversation, the way people talk when they care about and respect one another but do not know each other well. We can see some of the hallmarks of persuasive prose in King's letter:

It uses *I, you,* and *we.*
It avoids both technical jargon and slang.
It inclines toward strong, action verbs.
It chooses examples and images familiar to the reader.
It takes care to connect sentence to sentence and paragraph to paragraph with transitional words and phrases like "however," "moreover," "for instance," and the like.

All of these and many other features characterize the middle style of most persuasive writing.

As we discovered in King's letter, this middle style can cover quite a range of choices. King varies his style from section to section, depending on his purpose. Notice how King sounds highly formal in his introductory paragraphs (1–5) where he wants to establish authority, but more plain-spoken when he narrates the difficulties he and other black leaders had in their efforts to negotiate with the city's leaders (paragraphs 6–9). Notice as well how his sentences and paragraphs shorten on average in the passage comparing just and unjust laws (paragraphs 16–20). And we have already noted the use of sound and images in the passages of highest emotional appeal, such as paragraphs 14 and 47.

Just as King matches style with function, so you need to vary your style based on what each part of your essay is doing. This variation creates pacing, or the sense of overall rhythm in your essay. Readers need places where they can relax a bit between points of higher intensity, such as lengthy arguments and passionate pleas to the heart.

As you prepare to write your first draft, then, concern yourself with matching your style to your purpose from section to section, depending on whether you are providing background information, telling a story, developing a reason in your case, mounting an emotional appeal, or something else. Save detailed attention to style, as explained in Appendix B, for later in the process, while editing a second or third draft.

Following Through

Once you have completed a first draft of an argument to persuade, select one paragraph in which you have consciously made stylistic choices to create images, connotations, sound patterns, and so on. It may be the introductory paragraph, the conclusion, or a body paragraph where you are striving for emotional effect. Be ready to share the paragraph with your class, describing your choices as we have done with many passages from Martin Luther King's letter.

READING A DRAFT OF A PERSUASIVE ESSAY WITH AN EYE TOWARD REVISION: A CHECKLIST

The following list of questions will direct you to specific features of a good persuasive essay. You and a peer may want to exchange drafts; having someone else give your paper a critical reading often helps you find weaknesses you may have overlooked. After you have revised your draft, use the suggestions in Appendix B to edit for style and check for errors at the sentence level.

1. Read the audience profile for this essay. Then read the draft all the way through, projecting yourself as much as possible into the role of the target audience. After reading the draft, find and mark the essay's natural divisions. You may also want to number the paragraphs, so that you can refer to them easily.

2. Persuasive arguments must be based on careful inquiry and strategic case-making. Inspect the case first. Begin by underlining the thesis and marking the main reasons in support. You might write "Reason 1," "Reason 2," and so forth in the margins. Circle any words that need clearer definition. Also note any reasons that need more evidence or other support, such as illustrations or analogies.

3. Evaluate the plan for organizing the case. Are the reasons presented in a compelling and logical order? Does the argument build to a strong conclusion? Can you envision an alternative arrangement? Make suggestions for improvement, referring to paragraphs by number.

4. Persuasion demands that the writer make an effort to present himself or herself as worthy of the reader's trust and respect. Reread the draft with a highlighter or pen in hand, marking specific places where the writer has sought the identification of the target audience. Has the writer made an effort to find common ground with readers by using any of the ideas on page 111? Make suggestions for improvement.

5. Persuasion also requires that the writer make conscious efforts to gain the audience's emotional support through concrete examples and imagery, analogies and metaphors, first-person reporting, quotations, and so on. How many places can you find where a conscious emotional appeal is made? Are the efforts at emotional appeal uniformly successful? What improvements can you suggest? Has the writer gone too far with emotional appeal? Or should more be done?

6. Conscious stylistic appeals may be added later, in the editing stage, because style involves refinements in word choice and sentence patterns. However, look now to see if the draft exhibits a middle style appropriate to the targeted audience. Mark any instances of the following:

poor transitions between sentences or paragraphs

wordy passages, especially those containing the passive voice (see pp. 615–616) and overuse of the verb "to be"

awkward sentences

poor diction—that is, the use of incorrect or inappropriate words

7. Note any examples of effective style—good use of metaphor, repetition, or parallelism, for example.

8. Describe the general tone. Does it change from section to section? How appropriate and effective is the tone in general and in specific sections of the essay?

9. After studying the argument, are you sure what the writer wants or expects of the audience? Has the writer succeeded in persuading the audience? Why or why not?

Following Through

Read the following argument, which was written by a first-year student at a private university. Be ready to discuss its effectiveness as persuasion; you might build your evaluation around the preceding list of considerations for revising a persuasive essay.

STUDENT SAMPLE: AN ESSAY TO PERSUADE

The following essay was written in response to an assignment for a first-year rhetoric course. The intended audience was other students, eighteen to twenty-two years old and for the most part middle-class, who attended the same large, private university as the writer. Within this group, Shanks was trying to reach those who might sit in class and disagree with the opinions of more outspoken students but, for whatever reasons, fail to express their own dissenting viewpoints.

JOEY SHANKS

An Uncomfortable Position

I SAT quietly in my uncomfortable chair. Perhaps it was my position, I thought, and not the poly-wood seat that tormented me; so I sat upright, realizing then that both the chair and my position were probably responsible for my disposition. But I could do nothing to correct the problem.

Or maybe it was the conversation. I sat quietly, only for a lack of words. Usually I rambled on any subject, even if I knew nothing about it. No one in my rhetoric class would ever accuse me of lacking words, but today I was silent. The opinions of my classmates flew steadily across the room with occasional "I agree's" and "that's the truth's." My teacher shook her head in frustration.

She mediated the debate, if it was a debate. I could not imagine that a group of white college students angrily confessing that we all were constantly victims of reverse racism could provide much of a debate. In order for our generalizations to have formed a legitimate debate, there should have been two opposing sides, but the power of the majority had triumphed again. I sat quietly, knowing that what I heard was wrong. The little I said only fueled the ignorance and the guarded, David Duke-like articulations.

Did everyone in the class really think America had achieved equal opportunity? I could only hope that someone else in the classroom felt the same intimidation that I felt. I feared the majority. If I spoke my mind, I would only give the majority a minority to screw with.

But what about the young woman who sat next to me? She was Hispanic 5
with glasses and no name or voice that I knew of. She was the visible minority in a class full of Greek letters and blonde hair. She must have been more uncomfortable than I was. She sat quietly every day.

The individual in society must possess the courage and the confidence to challenge and oppose the majority if he or she feels it necessary. In the classroom I had not seen this individualism. My classmates may have had different backgrounds and interests, but eventually in every discussion, a majority opinion dominated the debate and all personalities were lost in a mob mentality. In rhetoric class, we read and discussed material designed to stimulate a debate with many sides; however, the debate was rendered useless because the power of the majority stifled open discussion and bullied the individual to submit or stay quiet.

De Tocqueville wrote of the dangerous power of the majority in his book *Democracy in America:* "The moral authority of the majority is partly based upon the notion that there is more intelligence and wisdom in a number of men united than in a single individual" (113). De Tocqueville illustrated a point that I witnessed in class and that history has witnessed for ages. The majority rules through the power of numbers. No matter how wrong, an opinion with many advocates becomes the majority opinion and is difficult to oppose. The majority makes the rules; therefore, we accept that "might makes right."

The true moral authority, however, lies in the fundamental acceptance that right and wrong are universal and not relative to time and place. Thomas Nagel, a contemporary philosopher, states, "Many things that you probably think are wrong have been accepted as morally correct by large groups of people in the past" (71). The majority is not right simply because it is a large group. An individual is responsible for knowing right from wrong, no matter how large the group appears. Ancient philosophers such as Aristotle and Socrates have defied generations of majorities. They preached that morality is universal and that the majority is not always right.

In our classroom after the first week, all the students chose their chairs in particular areas. Certain mentalities aligned, acknowledging similar philosophies on politics, hunting, sports, African Americans, welfare, and women. Debate on *The Awakening* awoke the beefcake majority with confused exclamations: "She's crazy! Why did the chick kill herself?" The majority either misunderstood the book or was not willing to accept another opinion.

Mark Twain, a pioneer of American literature, fought an empire of slavery 10
with his book *The Adventures of Huckleberry Finn.* Twain saw through the cruelty of racism and spoke against a nation that treated men and women like animals because of the color of their skin. Twain possessed the confidence and individualism to fight the majority, despite its power. Mark Twain protected individualism when he opposed racism and the institution of slavery. He proved that the single individual is sometimes more intelligent than men united.

Ramsey Clark, a former attorney general and now a political activist, expressed a great deal of distress over the Persian Gulf war. He spoke for the minority, a position of peace. In an interview in *The Progressive,* Clark stated, "We really believe that might makes right, and that leads us to perpetual war" (qtd. in Dreifus 32). Clark was referring to the United States' foreign policy of peace through intimidation, but his words can be taken on a universal level. We will never accomplish anything if might makes right and humanity is in a perpetual war of opinions. Clark is an example of individualism against the majority, though he will never be considered an American hero; few may remember his words, but like Mark Twain, he fought the majority's "moral authority."

In the classroom, or in the post-slavery South, or in the deserts of the Middle East, the majority has the power, and whoever has the power controls the world and may even seem to control all the opinions in it. As a country we abuse the power of the majority. America, the spokesperson for the world majority, manipulates its position while flexing and growling, "Might makes right!" This situation is a large scale version of a rhetoric seminar in which students too frequently align with or submit to the majority opinion. In rhetoric seminar we lack champions, individuals who see wrong and cry, "Foul!" Maybe the young Hispanic woman who quietly sits is just waiting for the right moment. Perhaps I had my chance and lost it, or maybe the majority has scared all the individuals into sitting quietly in their uncomfortable chairs.

WORKS CITED

De Tocqueville, Alexis. *Democracy in America.* 1835. New York: Penguin, 1956.

Dreifus, Claudia. "An Interview with Ramsey Clark." *The Progressive* Apr. 1991: 32–35.

Nagel, Thomas. *What Does It All Mean?* Oxford: Oxford UP, 1987.

THE APPEALS OF PERSUASION IN VISUAL ARGUMENTS

Arguments to persuade are often primarily visual. Advertisements, editorial cartoons, news photographs, and some art works—paintings, films, sculpture, architecture—are fundamentally arguments. Their creators' aim is to make the audience see their subject as they do—and often to act in accord with a particular point of view. As we become familiar with the images and styles used in a particular visual medium, such as photography, we become more adept at "reading" the images critically, just as we read written texts critically.

As with critical reading, our understanding of a visual argument depends on certain prior knowledge as well as on our ability to see the image in a rhetorical context. Further, we should be able to inquire into a visual argument just as we do a written text, seeing not just surface features but also the rhetorical appeals to reason, character, emotion, and style.

An Example from Advertising

The advertisement for Silver Jeans on page 147 is a good example of how the appeals of persuasion apply to nonverbal arguments. The prior knowledge that helps us understand this advertisement is based both in current events within our culture and in current advertising trends, particularly trends in clothing advertisements. First, we recognize that, in the United States in the early 1990s, the image touches on current issues involving racial tension and ethnic separatism, and we understand the idea being sold as something more specific and contemporary than "Peace on Earth": The embrace shared by the young couple suggests that romantic love is, or should be, blind to differences of race.[1] Second, we know from experience that contemporary clothing advertising often argues indirectly,

[1]We should note, however, that this is a Canadian advertisement for a Canadian product. Readers in Canada, which has a more culturally diverse society would be unlikely to see the image as a strong political statement.

selling an idea in order to sell a product, so we have no difficulty understanding that this is an argument for buying a particular brand of jeans.

PEACE ON EARTH
PH. IAN MCCAUSLAND DESIGN: THE BRAINSTORM GROUP
S
SILVER™
SILVER JEANS U.S. **CHARLES COFFEY** 1466 BROADWAY, SUITE 211, NY,NY 10036 (212) 575-1975
SILVER JEANS CANADA **MICHAEL SILVER** 555 LOGAN AVENUE, WINNIPEG, MANITOBA (204) 788-4249

The rhetorical context that helps us understand the ad is that it appeared in the December 1993/January 1994 issue of *Vibe* magazine, which is aimed at an audience of men and women of all races in their late teens and early twenties and which focuses on popular African-American music. The magazine has a liberal perspective, appealing to people interested in the arts.

While the advertisement argues that the readers should buy Silver Jeans, it does not make a case, either verbally or visually, with reasons for doing so. It does not state or show that Silver offers good fit or good value. In fact, the viewer could almost miss the jeans hanging on a clothesline in the background.

Instead of through rational appeal, the Silver advertisement sells the product by associating it with values and emotions that would appeal to *Vibe* readers. Just as verbal persuasion may appeal through character, with the writer presenting himself or herself as sharing some common ground with readers, so may visual advertisements depict the product as having something in common with the target audience's lives and values. The Silver advertisement identifies the product with youth and racial tolerance. While nondenominational, the verbal text "Peace on Earth" reiterates the message of brotherly love.

As a visual representation of these values, the couple photographed must appeal to *Vibe* readers, and there are several factors that present the couple sympathetically. First, the advertisement suggests that these are real lovers, not models striking a pose. They are attractive, but not glamorous; for example, the freckles on the woman's arm have not been airbrushed away. Also, the camera seems to have intruded upon a private moment. Notably, it is a sexual moment, but the couple is not blatantly sexy in either pose or dress.

As in verbal persuasion, style pervades all of the other appeals, affecting selection, arrangement, emphasis, tone, and so on. In this advertisement, some stylistic choices seem deliberately artistic, such as the decision to print the ad in black and white, rather than color. We might also notice how the arrangement of text, the inset oval photograph, and the couple's forehead-to-forehead pose emphasize the man's and woman's eyes; as the viewer looks at the couple, they seem to be looking back. Their gazes invite interpretation. The most notable thing about the style, however, is the decision to sell jeans indirectly, rather than directly, to a young, sophisticated audience.

Following Through

1. Find other advertisements that use an indirect approach, selling an idea in order to promote a product. For each, determine the audience, and write an analysis of how the ad appeals to that audience through reason, character, emotion, and style.
2. Analyze the two advertisements for jeans printed on pages 369–370, which originally appeared in fashion magazines such as *Vogue* and *Elle,* whose readers are middle and upper-middle class women, twenty to fifty, who have an interest in clothes, beauty products, fitness, cooking, and the arts. Within this large audience, can you infer a smaller target audience for each ad? Analyze the forms of appeal that each ad uses to persuade the target audience.

Two Examples from Public Art

Public sculptures, such as war memorials, are rhetorical; they aim to teach an audience about a nation's past and to represent the values for which its citizens

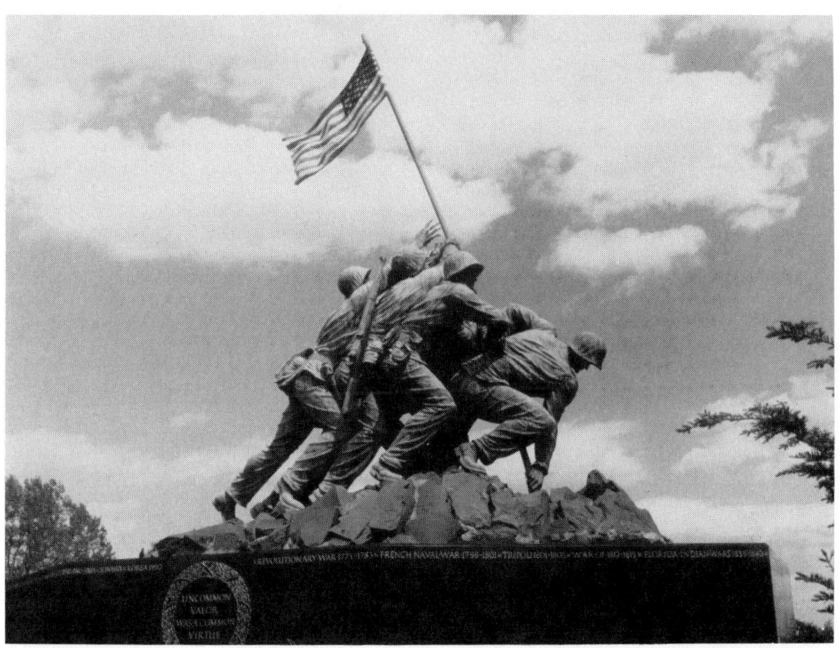

were willing to die. Consider, for example, the Marine Corps memorial (better known as the Iwo Jima memorial), which was erected in 1954 on the Mall in Washington, D.C. (see the photograph above). The Marine Corps memorial honors all Marines who have given their lives for their country through a literal depiction of one specific act of bravery, the planting of the American flag on Iwo Jima, a Pacific island that the United States captured from the Japanese in 1945. The argument of the statue is unambiguous. Charles Griswold, a philosopher, describes the Iwo Jima memorial as ". . . a classic war memorial. The soldiers strain every muscle toward one end only, the raising of the flag. The monument shouts this imperative: Honor your country, act as nobly as these men have."

In addition to the reasoned argument, the monument stirs patriotic feelings by its choice of subject matter—the raising of the flag, a symbol of Americans' common values and identity, on what was formerly enemy soil. Through our citizenship, we share in the victory and the glory that is depicted. The Marine Corps memorial has emotional appeals as well, because it portrays real people, their faces and bodies straining to the task. It invites the viewer to relive the experience. Style is an important consideration here, because the sculpture is a realistic representation of the people and the event.

In November 1982, a very different memorial was dedicated in Washington, the Vietnam War memorial, which has become popularly known as "the Wall" (see the photographs on pages 150 and 151). Designed by Maya Lin when

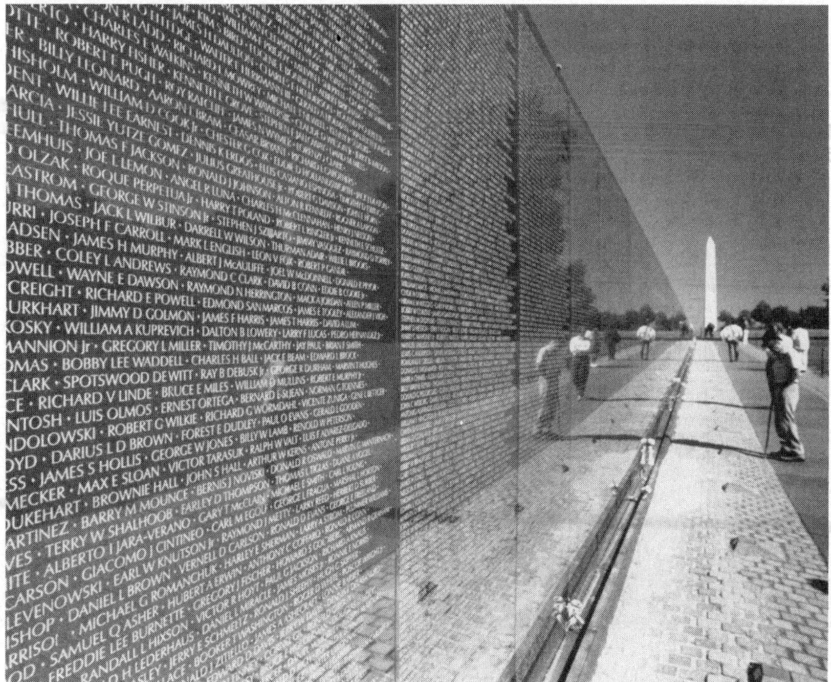

she was an undergraduate architecture student at Yale, the monument aroused controversy because it was so untraditional in its design and its argument. However, the context for this visual argument was also untraditional; it did not honor a victory but rather those who died in a war that tore the nation apart. Abstract rather than literal, ambiguous rather than direct, it nevertheless makes an argument with the appeals of reason, character, style, and, perhaps above all, emotion.

Following Through

The Vietnam War memorial invites interpretation and analysis. How do you "read" the argument of the Wall? How would you describe the visual argument in terms of its thesis and its appeals of style, reason, character, and emotion?

Two Editorial Cartoons

Unlike most cartoons on the comics pages, editorial cartoons comment on issues in the news. They can be seen as brief arguments, expressing the cartoonist's

opinion, along with a reason or reasons in support of it. While editorial cartoons often make their point very effectively, we might question how persuasive they are. The cartoonist's aim may be merely to express his or her opinion with creativity and humor. Editorial cartoonists prefer to mock their opposition rather than appeal to it, and their humor can be biting, as the two cartoons reproduced on page 152 illustrate.

The first one comments on extremists of the antiabortion movement, some of whom expressed no regrets over the shooting death of a Florida doctor by a fanatic protestor in 1993. The second comments on the position, held by many in the pro-choice movement, that a girl under the age of eighteen should not have to obtain the consent of a parent if she wishes to have an abortion. Instead, the minor may request that a judge grant a release for the surgery.

Following Through

How do you read the arguments made by the two editorial cartoons reproduced here? Would either be at all persuasive to a reader who disagreed with the perspective of the cartoonist? Why, or why not?

SCOTT STANTIS
Courtesy Grand Rapids Press

CHAPTER EIGHT

Negotiation and Mediation: Resolving Conflict

Argument with the aims of convincing and of persuading is a healthy force within a community. Whatever the issue, people hold a range of positions, and debate among advocates of these various positions serves to inform the public and draw attention to problems that need solution. Yet, while some issues seem to be debated endlessly—the death penalty, abortion, gun control, the U.S. role in the affairs of other nations—a time comes when the conflict must be resolved and a particular course of action pursued.

But what happens after each side has made its best effort to convince and persuade, yet no one position has won general assent? If the conflicting parties all have equal power, the result can be an impasse, a stalemate. More often, however, one party has greater authority and is able to impose its will, as, for example, a university dean or president may impose a policy decision on students or faculty. But imposing power is costly—especially in terms of the worsened relationships that result—and it is often temporary. Foes of abortion, for example, have been able to influence policy significantly under conservative administrations, only to see their policy gains eroded when more liberal politicians gain power. If conflicts are going to be resolved—and stay resolved—each side needs to move beyond advocating its own positions and start arguing with a new aim in mind: negotiation.

Arguing to negotiate aims to resolve—or at least reduce—conflict to the mutual satisfaction of all parties involved. But negotiation involves more than simply making a deal in which each side offers a few concessions while retaining a little of its initial demands. As this chapter will show, through the process of negotiating, opposing sides come to a greater understanding of their differing interests, backgrounds, and values; ideally, negotiation builds consensus and repairs relationships that may previously have been strained.

NEGOTIATION AND THE OTHER AIMS OF ARGUMENT

You may find it difficult to think of negotiation as argument if you see argument only as presenting a case for a particular position or persuading an audience to act in accordance with that position. Both of these aims clearly involve advocating one position and writing an argument for it, addressed to those with different viewpoints. But recall that one definition of argue is "to make clear." As we discussed in Chapter 5, sometimes we argue in order to learn what we should think; that is, we argue to inquire, trying out an argument, examining it critically and with as little bias as possible for an audience of non-threatening partners in conversation such as friends or family.

Arguing to negotiate shares many of the characteristics of arguing to inquire. Like inquiry, negotiation most often takes the form of dialogue, although writing plays an important role in the process. Also, whether a party in the conflict or an outside mediator among the various parties, the negotiator must inquire into the positions of all sides. Further, anyone who agrees to enter into negotiation, especially someone who is a party to the conflict, must acknowledge his or her bias and remain open to the positions and interests of others, just as the inquirer does. Negotiation differs from inquiry, however, in that negotiation must find a mediating position that accommodates at least some of the interests of all sides. The best position in negotiation is the one all sides will accept.

As we shall see in more detail, argument as negotiation draws upon the strategies of the other aims of argument as well. Like convincing, negotiation requires an understanding of case structure, as negotiators must analyze the cases that each side puts forth, and mediators often need to build a case of their own for a position acceptable to all. And like persuasion, negotiation recognizes the role of human character and emotions, both in the creation of conflict and in its resolution.

To illustrate the benefits to be gained through the process of negotiation, we will concentrate in this chapter on one of the most heated conflicts in the United States today: the debate over abortion. A wide range of positions exists on this issue. Extremists for fetal rights, who engage in sometimes violent acts of civil disobedience, and extremists for the absolute rights of women, who argue that a woman should be able to terminate a pregnancy at any time and for any reason, may not be amenable to negotiation; however, between these poles lie the viewpoints of most Americans, whose differences could possibly be resolved.

Negotiation has a chance only among people who have reasoned through their own position, through inquiry, and who have attempted to defend it, not through force, but through convincing and persuasive argumentation. And negotiation has a chance only when people see that the divisions caused by their conflict are counterproductive. They must be ready to listen to each other. They must be willing to negotiate.

THE PROCESS OF NEGOTIATION AND MEDIATION

As a student in a writing class, you can practice the process of negotiation in at least two ways. First, you and several other students who have written conflicting arguments on a common topic may negotiate among yourselves to find a resolution acceptable to all, perhaps bringing in a disinterested student to serve as a mediator. Or, your class as a whole may act as a mediator in a dispute among writers whose printed arguments offer conflicting viewpoints on the same issue. Here we illustrate the mediator approach, which is easily adapted to the more direct experience of face-to-face negotiation.

Understanding the Spirit of Negotiation

In arguing issues of public concern, it is a mistake to think of negotiation as the same thing as negotiating the price of a car or a house or even a collective bargaining agreement. In such dialogues between a buyer and seller, both sides typically begin by asking for much more than they seriously hope to get, and the process involves displays of will and power as each side tries to force the other to back down on its demands. Negotiation as rhetorical argument, however, is less adversarial; in fact, it is more like collaborative problem-solving, where various opposing parties work together not to rebut one another's arguments, but to understand them. Negotiation leads to the most permanent resolution of conflict when it is based on an increased understanding of difference rather than on a mere exchange of concessions. Negotiators must let go of the whole notion of proving one side right and other sides wrong. Rather, the negotiator says, "I see what you are demanding, and you see what I am demanding. Now let's sit down and find out *why* we hold these positions—what are our interests in this issue? Maybe, together we can work out a solution that will address these interests."

Unlike negotiators, mediators are impartial, and if they have a personal viewpoint on the issue, they must suppress it and be careful not to favor either side.

Understanding the Opposing Positions

Negotiation begins with a close look at opposing views. As in inquiry, the first stage of the process is an analysis of the positions, the thesis statements, and the supporting reasons and evidence offered on all sides. It is a good idea for each party to write a brief of his or her case, as described on pages 84 and 98–99. These briefs should indicate how the reasons are supported, so that disputants can see where they agree or disagree about data.

The mediator also must begin by inquiring into the arguments presented by the parties in dispute. To illustrate, we will look at two reasoned arguments representing opposing views on the value of the Supreme Court's *Roe v. Wade* decision. That decision, which was handed down in 1973, ruled that the Constitution does grant to citizens a zone of personal privacy, which for women would include the decision regarding whether or not to terminate a pregnancy. The Court did stipulate, however, that the right to abortion was not unqualified, and that states could regulate abortions to protect the fetus after viability.

The first argument, "Living with *Roe v. Wade,*" is by Margaret Liu McConnell, a writer and mother of three, who herself had an abortion while she was in college. This experience led McConnell to decide that abortion on demand should not have become a constitutional right. To those who applaud abortion rights, McConnell argues that *Roe v. Wade* has had serious social and moral consequences for our nation. She does not call for the decision to be overturned, but she does want abortion rights supporters to take a closer look at the issue and recognize that abortion is fundamentally an immoral choice, one that should result in a sense of guilt. This essay originally appeared in 1990 in *Commentary,* a journal published by the American Jewish Committee.

The second argument is by Ellen Willis, also a mother who once had an abortion. For Willis, abortion is very much a right, in fact, the foundation of women's equality. Willis defends *Roe v. Wade* as the "cutting edge of feminism." Her audience is liberals who oppose abortion—"the left wing of the right-to-life movement"—specifically, the editors of *Commonweal,* a liberal Catholic journal. Her audience could also include people like Margaret Liu McConnell, who see abortion as a moral question rather than as a political question framed in terms of equal rights. "Putting Women Back into the Abortion Debate" originally appeared in the left-leaning *Village Voice* in 1985.

MARGARET LIU MCCONNELL

Living with Roe v. Wade

THERE IS something decidedly unappealing to me about the pro-life activists seen on the evening news as they are dragged away from the entrances to abortion clinics across the country. Perhaps it is that their poses remind me of sulky two-year-olds, sinking to their knees as their frazzled mothers try to haul them from the playground. Or perhaps it is because I am a little hard put to believe, when one of them cries out, often with a Southern twang, "Ma'am, don't keel your baby," that he or she could really care that deeply about a stranger's fetus. After all, there are limits to compassion and such concern seems excessive, suspect.

Besides, as pro-choice adherents like to point out, the fact that abortion is legal does not mean that someone who is against abortion will be forced to have one against her wishes. It is a private matter, so they say, between a woman and her doctor. From this it would follow that those opposed to abortion are no more than obnoxious busybodies animated by their own inner pathologies to interfere in the private lives of strangers.

Certainly this is the impression conveyed by those news clips of antiabortion blockades being broken up by the police. We pity the woman, head sunk and afraid, humiliated in the ancient shame that all around her know she is carrying an unwanted child. Precisely because she is pregnant, our hearts go out to her in her vulnerability. It would seem that those workers from the abortion clinic, shielding arms around her shoulders, their identification vests giving them the benign look of school-crossing guards, are her protectors. They are guiding her through a hostile, irrational crowd to the cool and orderly safety of the clinic and the medical attention she needs.

But is it possible that this impression is mistaken? Is it possible that those who guide the woman along the path to the abortionist's table are not truly her protectors, shoring her up on the road to a dignified life in which she will best be able to exercise her intellectual and physical faculties free from any kind of oppression? Is it possible that they are serving, albeit often unwittingly, to keep her and millions of other women on a demeaning and rather lonely treadmill—a treadmill on which these women trudge through cycles of sex without commitment, unwanted pregnancy, and abortion, all in the name of equal opportunity and free choice?

Consider yet again the woman on the path to an abortion. She is already a 5
victim of many forces. She is living in a social climate in which she is expected to view sex as practically a form of recreation that all healthy women should pursue eagerly. She has been conditioned to fear having a child, particularly in her younger years, as an unthinkable threat to her standard of living and to the career through which she defines herself as a "real" person. Finally, since 1973, when the Supreme Court in *Roe v. Wade* declared access to abortion a constitutional right, she has been invited, in the event that she does become pregnant, not only to have an abortion, but to do so without sorrow and with no moral misgivings. As the highly vocal proabortion movement cheers her on with rallying cries of "Freedom of Choice," she may find herself wondering: "Is this the great freedom we've been fighting for? The freedom to sleep with men who don't care for us, the freedom to scorn the chance to raise a child? The freedom to let doctors siphon from our bodies that most precious gift which women alone are made to receive: a life to nurture?"

My goal here is not to persuade militant pro-choicers that abortion is wrong. Instead, it is to establish that abortion cannot and should not be seen as strictly a matter between a woman and her doctor. For the knowledge that the law allows free access to abortion affects all of us directly and indirectly by the way it shapes the social climate. Most directly and most easy to illustrate, the realization that any pregnancy, intended or accidental, may be aborted at will affects women in their so-called childbearing years. The indirect effects are more difficult to pinpoint. I would like tentatively to suggest that *Roe v. Wade* gives approval, at the highest level of judgment in this country, to certain attitudes which, when manifest at the lowest economic levels, have extremely destructive consequences.

But to begin with the simpler task of examining *Roe*'s questionable effect on the world women inhabit: I—who at thirty-two am of the age to have "benefited" from *Roe*'s protections for all my adult years—offer here some examples of those "benefits."

It was my first year at college, my first year away from my rather strict, first-generation American home. I had a boyfriend from high school whom I liked and admired but was not in love with, and I was perfectly satisfied with the stage of heavy-duty necking we had managed, skillfully avoiding the suspicious eyes of my mother. But once I got to college I could think of no good reason not to go farther. For far from perceiving any constraints around me, I encountered all manner of encouragement to become "sexually active"—from the health center, from newspapers, books, and magazines, from the behavior of other students, even from the approval of other students' parents of their children's "liberated" sexual conduct.

Yet the truth is that I longed for the days I knew only from old movies and novels, those pre-60's days when boyfriends visiting from other colleges stayed in hotels (!) and dates ended with a lingering kiss at the door. I lived in an apartment-style dormitory, six women sharing three bedrooms and a kitchen. Needless to say, visiting boyfriends did not stay in hotels. By the end of my freshman year three out of the six of us would have had abortions.

How did it come to pass that so many of us got pregnant? How has it come 10
to pass that more than one-and-one-half million women each year get pregnant in this country, only to have abortions? Nowadays it is impossible to go into a drugstore without bumping into the condoms on display above the checkout counters. And even when I was in college, contraception was freely available, and everyone knew that the health center, open from nine to four, was ready to equip us with the contraceptive armament we were sure to need.

Nevertheless, thanks to *Roe v. Wade,* we all understood as well that if anything went wrong, there would be no threat of a shotgun marriage, or of being sent away in shame to bear a child, or of a dangerous back-alley abortion. Perhaps the incredible number of "accidental" pregnancies, both at college and throughout the country, finds its explanation in just that understanding. Analogies are difficult to construct in arguments about abortion, for there is nothing quite analogous to terminating a pregnancy. That said, consider this one anyway. If children are sent out to play ball in a yard near a house, a responsible adult, knowing that every once in a while a window will get broken, will still tell them to be very careful not to break any. But what if the children are sent into the yard and told something like this: "Go out and play, and don't worry about breaking any windows. It's bound to happen, and when it does, no problem: it will be taken care of." How many more windows will be shattered?

There were, here and there, some women who seemed able to live outside these pressures. Within my apartment one was an Orthodox Jewish freshman from Queens, another a junior from Brooklyn, also Jewish, who was in the process of becoming Orthodox. They kept kosher as far as was possible in our common kitchen, and on Friday afternoons would cook supper for a group of friends, both men and women. As darkness fell they would light candles and sing and eat and laugh in a circle of light. I remember looking in at their evenings from the doorway to the kitchen, wishing vainly that I could belong to such a group, a group with a code of behavior that would provide shelter from the free-for-all I saw elsewhere. But the only group I felt I belonged to was, generically, "young American woman," and as far as I could see, the norm of behavior for a young American woman was to enjoy a healthy sex life, with or without commitment.

A few months later, again thanks to *Roe v. Wade,* I discovered that the logistics of having an abortion were, as promised, extremely simple. The school health center was again at my service. After a few perfunctory questions and sympathetic nods of the head I was given directions to the nearest abortion clinic.

A strange thing has happened since that great freedom-of-choice victory in 1973. Abortion has become the only viable alternative many women feel they have open to them when they become pregnant by accident. Young men no longer feel obligated to offer to "do the right thing." Pregnancy is most often confirmed in a medical setting. Even though it is a perfectly normal and healthy state, in an unwanted pregnancy a woman feels distressed. The situation thus becomes that of a distressed woman looking to trusted medical personnel for relief. Abortion presents itself as the simple, legal, medical solution to her distress. A woman may have private reservations, but she gets the distinct impression that if she does not take advantage of her right to an abortion she is of her own accord refusing a simple solution to her troubles.

That is certainly how it was for me, sitting across from the counselor at the 15
health center, clutching a wad of damp tissues, my heart in my throat. The feeling was exactly parallel to the feeling I had had at the beginning of the school year: I could be defiantly old-fashioned and refuse to behave like a normal American woman, or I could exercise my sexual liberation. Here, six weeks pregnant, I could be troublesome, perverse, and somehow manage to keep the baby, causing tremendous inconvenience to everyone, or I could take the simple route of having an abortion and not even miss a single class. The choice was already made.

Physically, also, abortion has become quite a routine procedure. As one of my grosser roommates put it, comforting me with talk of her own experiences, it was about as bad as going to the dentist. My only memory of the operation is of coming out of the general anesthesia to the sound of sobbing all around. I, too, was sobbing, without thought, hard and uncontrollably, as though somehow, deep below the conscious level, below whatever superficial concerns had layered themselves in the day-to-day mind of a busy young woman, I had come to realize what I had done, and what could never be undone.

I have since had three children, and at the beginning of each pregnancy I was presented with the opportunity to have an abortion without even having to ask. For professional reasons my husband and I have moved several times, and each of our children was born in a different city with a different set of obstetrical personnel. In every case I was offered the unsolicited luxury of "keeping my options open": of choosing whether to continue the pregnancy or end it. The polite way of posing the question, after a positive pregnancy test, seems to be for the doctor to ask noncommittally, "And how are we treating this pregnancy?"

Each one of those pregnancies, each one of those expendable bunches of tissue, has grown into a child, each one different from the other. I cannot escape the haunting fact that if I had had an abortion, one of my children would be missing. Not just a generic little bundle in swaddling clothes interchangeable with any other, but a specific child.

I still carry in my mind a picture of that other child who was never born, a picture which changes as the years go by, and I imagine him growing up. For some reason I usually do imagine a boy, tall and with dark hair and eyes. This is speculation, of course, based on my coloring and build and on that of the young man involved. Such speculation seems maudlin and morbid and I do not engage in it on purpose. But whether I like it or not, every now and then my mind returns to that ghost of a child and to the certainty that for seven weeks I carried the beginnings of a being whose coloring and build and, to a large extent, personality were already determined. Buoyant green-eyed girl or shy, dark-haired boy, I wonder. Whoever, a child would have been twelve this spring.

I am not in the habit of exposing this innermost regret, this endless remorse 20
to which I woke too late. I do so only to show that in the wake of *Roe v. Wade* abortion has become casual, commonplace, and very hard to resist as an easy way out of an unintended pregnancy, and that more unintended pregnancies are likely to occur when everyone knows there is an easy way out of them. Abortion has become an option offered to women, married as well as unmarried, including those who are financially, physically, and emotionally able to care for a child. This is what *Roe v. Wade* guarantees. For all the pro-choice lobby's talk of abortion as a deep personal moral decision, casting abortion as a right takes the weight of morality out of the balance. For, by definition, a right is something one need not feel guilty exercising.

I do not wish a return to the days when a truly desperate woman unable to get a safe legal abortion would risk her life at the hands of an illegal abortionist. Neither could I ever condemn a woman whose own grip on life is so fragile as to render her incapable of taking on the full responsibility for another life, helpless and demanding. But raising abortion to the plane of a constitutional right in order to ensure its accessibility to any woman for any reason makes abortion too easy a solution to an age-old problem.

Human beings have always coupled outside the bounds deemed proper by the societies in which they lived. But the inevitable unexpected pregnancies often served a social purpose. There was a time when many young couples found in the startling new life they had created an undeniable reason to settle down seriously to the tasks of earning a living and making a home. That might have meant taking on a nine-to-five job and assuming a mortgage, a prospect which sounds like death to many baby boomers intent on prolonging adolescence well into middle age. But everyone knows anecdotally if not from straight statistics that many of these same baby boomers owe their own lives to such happy (for them) accidents.

When I became pregnant in college, I never seriously considered getting married and trying to raise a child, although it certainly would have been possible to do so. Why should I have, when the road to an abortion was so free and unencumbered, and when the very operation itself had been presented as a step on the march to women's equality?

I know that no one forced me to do anything, that I was perfectly free to step back at any time and live by my own moral code if I chose to, much as my Orthodox Jewish acquaintances did. But this is awfully hard when the society you consider yourself part of presents abortion as a legal, morally acceptable solution. And what kind of a world would it be if all those in need of a moral structure stepped back to insulate themselves, alone or in groups—ethnic, religious, or economic—each with its own exclusive moral code, leaving behind a chaos at the center? It sounds like New York City on a bad day.

This is not, of course, to ascribe the chaos reigning in our cities directly to 25
Roe v. Wade. That chaos is caused by a growing and tenacious underclass defined by incredibly high rates of drug abuse, and dependence on either crime or welfare for financial support. But sometimes it does seem as though the same attitude behind abortion on demand lies behind the abandonment of parental responsibility which is the most pervasive feature of life in the underclass and the most determinative of its terrible condition.

Parental responsibility can be defined as providing one's offspring at every level of development with that which they need to grow eventually into independent beings capable of supporting themselves emotionally and financially. Different parents will, of course, have different ideas about what is best for a child, and different parents will have different resources to draw upon to provide for their children. But whatever the differences may be, responsible parents will try, to the best of their ability and in accordance with their own lights, to raise their children properly. It is tedious, expensive, and takes a long, long time. For it is not a question of fetal weeks before a human being reaches any meaningful stage of "viability" (how "viable" is a two-year-old left to his own devices? A five-year-old?). It is a question of years, somewhere in the neighborhood of eighteen.

Why does any parent take on such a long, hard task? Because life is a miracle that cannot be denied? Because it is the right thing to do? Because there is a certain kind of love a parent bears a child that does not require a calculated return on investment? Because we would hate ourselves otherwise? All these factors enter into the powerful force that compels parents to give up years of their free time and much of their money to bring up their children. Yet the cool, clinical approach *Roe v. Wade* allows all of us—men no less than women—in deciding whether or not we are "ready" to accept the responsibility of an established pregnancy seems to undermine an already weakening cultural expectation that parents simply have a duty to take care of their children.

A middle- or upper-class woman may have high expectations of what she will achieve so long as she is not saddled with a baby. When she finds herself pregnant she is guaranteed the right under *Roe v. Wade* to opt out of that long and tedious responsibility, and does so by the hundreds of thousands each year. By contrast, a woman in the underclass who finds herself pregnant is not likely to have great expectations of what life would be like were she free of the burden of her child; abortion would not broaden her horizons and is not usually her choice.

Yet she often lacks the maternal will and the resources to take full responsibility for the well-being of her child until adulthood.

To be sure, these two forms of refusing parental responsibility have vastly different effects. But how can the government hope to devise policies that will encourage parental responsibility in the underclass when at the highest level of judgment, that of the Supreme Court, the freedom to opt out of parental responsibility is protected as a right? Or, to put the point another way, perhaps the weakening of the sense of duty toward one's own offspring is a systemic problem in America, present in all classes, with only its most visible manifestation in the underclass.

The federal Family Support Act of 1988 was the result of much study and 30
debate on how to reform the welfare system to correct policies which have tended to make it easier for poor families to qualify for aid if the father is not part of the household. Among other provisions intended to help keep families from breaking up, states are now required to pay cash benefits to two-parent families and to step up child-support payments from absent fathers. New York City, for example, has this year begun to provide its Department of Health with information, including Social Security numbers, on the parents of every child born in the city. Should the mother ever apply for aid, the father can be tracked down and child-support payments can be deducted from his paycheck. Such a strict enforcement of child-support obligations is a powerful and exciting legal method for society to show that it will not tolerate the willful abandonment of children by their fathers.

It is evident that there is a compelling state interest in promoting the responsibility of both parents toward their child. The compelling interest is that it takes a great deal of money to care for a child whose parents do not undertake the responsibility themselves. For whatever else we may have lost of our humanity over the last several decades, however hardened we have been by violence and by the degradation witnessed daily in the lost lives on the street, we still retain a basic decent instinct to care for innocent babies and children in need.

It is also evident that parental responsibility begins well before the child is born. Thus, the Appellate Division of the State Supreme Court of New York in May of this year ruled that a woman who uses drugs during pregnancy and whose newborn has drugs in its system may be brought before Family Court for a hearing on neglect. Yet how can we condemn a woman under law for harming her unborn child while at the same time protecting her right to destroy that child absolutely, for any reason, through abortion? Is the only difference that the first instance entails a monetary cost to society while the second does not?

There is another kind of behavior implicitly condoned by *Roe v. Wade,* which involves the value of life itself, and which also has its most frightening and threatening manifestation in the underclass. Consensus on when human life begins has yet to be established and perhaps never will be. What is clear, however, is that abortion cuts short the development of a specific human life; it wipes out the future years of a human being, years we can know nothing about. Generally we have no trouble conceiving of lost future years as real loss. Lawsuits routinely place value on lost future income and lost future enjoyment, and we consider the death of a child or a young person to be particularly tragic in lost potential, in the waste of idealized years to come. Yet under *Roe v. Wade* the value of the future years of life of the fetus is determined by an individual taking into account only her own well-being.

Back in 1965, justifying his discovery of a constitutional right to privacy which is nowhere mentioned in the Constitution itself, and which helped lay the groundwork for *Roe v. Wade,* Justice William O. Douglas invoked the concept of "penumbras, formed by emanations" of constitutional amendments. Is it far-fetched to say that there are "penumbras, formed by emanations" of *Roe v. Wade* that grant the right to consider life in relative terms and to place one's own interest above any others? This same "right" when exercised by criminals is a terrifying phenomenon: these are people who feel no guilt in taking a victim's life, who value the future years of that life as nothing compared with their own interest in the victim's property. Of course, one might argue that a fetus is not yet cognizant of its own beingness and that, further, it feels no pain. Yet if a killer creeps up behind you and blows your head off with a semi-automatic, you will feel no pain either, nor will you be cognizant of your death.

Roe v. Wade was a great victory for the women's movement. It seemed to 35
promote equality of opportunity for women in all their endeavors by freeing them from the burden of years of caring for children conceived unintentionally. But perhaps support for *Roe v. Wade* should be reconsidered in light of the damage wrought by the kind of behavior that has become common in a world in which pregnancy is no longer seen as the momentous beginning of a new life, and life, by extension, is no longer held as sacred.

At any rate, even if one rejects my speculation that *Roe v. Wade* has at least some indirect connection with the degree to which life on our streets has become so cheap, surely there can be no denying the direct connection between *Roe v. Wade* and the degree to which sex has become so casual. Surely, for example, *Roe v. Wade* will make it harder for my two daughters to grow gracefully into womanhood without being encouraged to think of sex as a kind of sport played with a partner who need feel no further responsibility toward them once the game is over.

For me, that is reason enough not to support this elevation of abortion to the status of a constitutional right.

ELLEN WILLIS

Putting Women Back into the Abortion Debate

SOME YEARS ago I attended a New York Institute for the Humanities seminar on the new right. We were a fairly heterogeneous group of liberals and lefties, feminists and gay activists, but on one point nearly all of us agreed: The right-to-life movement was a dangerous antifeminist crusade. At one session I argued that the attack on abortion had significance far beyond itself, that it was the linchpin of the right's social agenda. I got a lot of supporting comments and approving nods. It was too much for Peter Steinfels, a liberal Catholic, author of *The Neoconservatives,* and executive editor of *Commonweal*. Right-to-lifers were not all right-wing fanatics, he protested. "You have to understand," he said plaintively, "that many of us see abortion as a *human life issue.*" What I remember best was his air of frustrated isolation. I don't think he came back to the seminar after that.

Things are different now. I often feel isolated when I insist that abortion is, above all, a *feminist issue.* Once people took for granted that abortion was an issue of sexual politics and morality. Now, abortion is most often discussed as a question of "life" in the abstract. Public concern over abortion centers almost exclusively on fetuses; women and their bodies are merely the stage on which the drama of fetal life and death takes place. Debate about abortion—if not its reality—has become sexlessly scholastic. And the people most responsible for this turn of events are, like Peter Steinfels, on the left.

The left wing of the right-to-life movement is a small, seemingly eccentric minority in both "progressive" and antiabortion camps. Yet it has played a critical role in the movement: By arguing that opposition to abortion can be separated from the right's antifeminist program, it has given antiabortion sentiment legitimacy in left-symp and (putatively) profeminist circles. While left antiabortionists are hardly alone in emphasizing fetal life, their innovation has been to claim that a consistent "pro-life" stand involves opposing capital punishment, supporting disarmament, demanding government programs to end poverty, and so on. This is of course a leap the right is neither able nor willing to make. It's been liberals—from Garry Wills to the Catholic bishops—who have supplied the mass media with the idea that prohibiting abortion is part of a "seamless garment" of respect for human life.

Having invented this countercontext for the abortion controversy, left antiabortionists are trying to impose it as the only legitimate context for debate. Those of us who won't accept their terms and persist in seeing opposition to abortion, antifeminism, sexual repression, and religious sectarianism as the real seamless garment have been accused of obscuring the issue with demagoguery. Last year *Commonweal*—perhaps the most important current forum for left antiabortion opinion—ran an editorial demanding that we shape up: "Those who hold that abortion is immoral believe that the biological dividing lines of birth or viability should no more determine whether a developing member of the species is denied or accorded essential rights than should the biological dividing lines of sex or race or disability or old age. This argument is open to challenge. Perhaps the dividing lines are sufficiently different. Pro-choice advocates should state their reasons for believing so. They should meet the argument on its own grounds. . . ."

In other words, the only question we're allowed to debate—or the only one 5
Commonweal is willing to entertain—is "Are fetuses the moral equivalent of born human beings?" And I can't meet the argument on its own grounds because I don't agree that this is the key question, whose answer determines whether one supports

abortion or opposes it. I don't doubt that fetuses are alive, or that they're biologically human—what else would they be? I do consider the life of a fertilized egg less precious than the well-being of a woman with feelings, self-consciousness, a history, social ties; and I think fetuses get closer to being human in a moral sense as they come closer to birth. But to me these propositions are intuitively self-evident. I wouldn't know how to justify them to a "nonbeliever," nor do I see the point of trying.

I believe the debate has to start in a different place—with the recognition that fertilized eggs develop into infants inside the bodies of women. Pregnancy and birth are active processes in which a woman's body shelters, nourishes, and expels a new life; for nine months she is immersed in the most intimate possible relationship with another being. The growing fetus makes considerable demands on her physical and emotional resources, culminating in the cataclysmic experience of birth. And child-bearing has unpredictable consequences; it always entails some risk of injury or death.

For me all this has a new concreteness: I had a baby last year. My much-desired and relatively easy pregnancy was full of what antiabortionists like to call "inconveniences." I was always tired, short of breath; my digestion was never right; for three months I endured a state of hormonal siege; later I had pains in my fingers, swelling feet, numb spots on my legs, the dread hemorrhoids. I had to think about everything I ate. I developed borderline glucose intolerance. I gained fifty pounds and am still overweight; my shape has changed in other ways that may well be permanent. Psychologically, my pregnancy consumed me—though I'd happily bought the seat on the roller coaster, I was still terrified to be so out of control of my normally tractable body. It was all bearable, even interesting—even, at times, transcendent—because I wanted a baby. Birth was painful, exhausting, and wonderful. If I hadn't wanted a baby it would only have been painful and exhausting—or worse. I can hardly imagine what it's like to have your body and mind taken over in this way when you not only don't look forward to the result, but positively dread it. The thought appalls me. So as I see it, the key question is "Can it be moral, under any circumstances, to make a woman bear a child against her will?"

From this vantage point, *Commonweal*'s argument is irrelevant, for in a society that respects the individual, no "member of the species" in *any* stage of development has an "essential right" to make use of someone else's body, let alone in such all-encompassing fashion, without that person's consent. You can't make a case against abortion by applying a general principle about everybody's human rights; you have to show exactly the opposite—that the relationship between fetus and pregnant woman is an exception, one that justifies depriving women of their right to bodily integrity. And in fact all antiabortion ideology rests on the premise—acknowledged or simply assumed—that women's unique capacity to bring life into the world carries with it a unique obligation that women cannot be allowed to "play God" and launch only the lives they welcome.

Yet the alternative to allowing women this power is to make them impotent. Criminalizing abortion doesn't just harm individual women with unwanted pregnancies, it affects all women's sense of themselves. Without control of our fertility we can never envision ourselves as free, for our biology makes us constantly vulnerable. Simply because we are female our physical integrity can be violated, our lives disrupted and transformed, at any time. Our ability to act in the world is hopelessly compromised by our sexual being.

Ah, sex—it does have a way of coming up in these discussions, despite all. 10
When pressed, right-to-lifers of whatever political persuasion invariably point out that pregnancy doesn't happen by itself. The leftists often give patronizing lectures on contraception (though some find only "natural birth control" acceptable), but remain unmoved when reminded that contraceptives fail. Openly or implicitly they argue that people shouldn't have sex unless they're prepared to procreate. (They are quick to profess a single standard—men as well as women should be sexually "responsible." Yes, and the rich as well as the poor should be allowed to sleep under bridges.) Which amounts to saying that if women want to lead heterosexual lives they must give up any claim to self-determination, and that they have no right to sexual pleasure without fear.

Opposing abortion, then, means accepting that women must suffer sexual disempowerment and a radical loss of autonomy relative to men: If fetal life is sacred, the self-denial basic to women's oppression is also basic to the moral order. Opposing abortion means embracing a conservative sexual morality, one that subordinates pleasure to reproduction: If fetal life is sacred, there is no room for the view that sexual passion—or even sexual love—for its own sake is a human need and a human right. Opposing abortion means tolerating the inevitable double standard, by which men may accept or reject sexual restrictions in accordance with their beliefs, while women must bow to them out of fear . . . or defy them at great risk. However much *Commonweal*'s editors and those of like mind want to believe their opposition to abortion is simply about saving lives, the truth is that in the real world they are shoring up a particular sexual culture, whose rules are stacked against women. I have yet to hear any left right-to-lifers take full responsibility for that fact or deal seriously with its political implications.

Unfortunately, their fuzziness has not lessened their appeal—if anything it's done the opposite. In increasing numbers liberals and leftists, while opposing antiabortion laws, have come to view abortion as an "agonizing moral issue" with some justice on both sides, rather than an issue—however emotionally complex—of freedom versus repression, or equality versus hierarchy, that affects their political self-definition. This above-the-battle stance is attractive to leftists who want to be feminist good guys but are uneasy or ambivalent about sexual issues, not to mention those who want to ally with "progressive" factions of the Catholic church on Central America, nuclear disarmament, or populist economics without that sticky abortion question getting in the way.

Such neutrality is a way of avoiding the painful conflict over cultural issues that continually smolders on the left. It can also be a way of coping with the contradictions of personal life at a time when liberation is a dream deferred. To me the fight for abortion has always been the cutting edge of feminism, precisely because it denies that anatomy is destiny, that female biology dictates women's subordinate status. Yet recently I've found it hard to focus on the issue, let alone summon up the militance needed to stop the antiabortion tanks. In part that has to do with second-round weariness—do we really have to go through all these things twice?—in part with my life now.

Since my daughter's birth my feelings about abortion—not as a political demand but as a personal choice—have changed. In this society, the difference between the situation of a childless woman and of a mother is immense; the fear that having a child will dislodge one's tenuous hold on a nontraditional life is excruciating. This terror of being forced into the sea-change of motherhood gave a special edge to my convictions about abortion. Since I've made that plunge voluntarily, with consequences still unfolding, the terror is gone; I might not want another child, for all sorts of reasons, but I will never again feel that my identity is at stake. Different battles with the culture absorb my energy now. Besides, since I've experienced the primal, sensual passion of caring for an infant, there will always be part of me that does want another. If I had an abortion today, it would be with conflict and sadness unknown to me when I had an abortion a decade ago. And the antiabortionists' imagery of dead babies hits me with new force. Do many women—left, feminist women—have such feelings? Is this the sort of "ambivalence about abortion" that in the present atmosphere slides so easily into self-flagellating guilt?

Some left antiabortionists, mainly pacifists—Juli Loesch, Mary Meehan, 15
and other "feminists for life"; Jim Wallis and various writers for Wallis's radical evangelical journal *Sojourners*—have tried to square their position with concern for women. They blame the prevalence of abortion on oppressive conditions—economic injustice, lack of child care and other social supports for mothers, the devaluation of childrearing, men's exploitative sexual behavior and refusal to take equal responsibility for children. They disagree on whether to criminalize abortion now (since murder is intolerable no matter what the cause) or to build a long-term moral consensus (since stopping abortion requires a general social transformation), but they all regard abortion as a desperate solution to desperate problems, and the women who resort to it as more sinned against than sinning.

This analysis grasps an essential feminist truth: that in a male-supremacist society no choice a woman makes is genuinely free or entirely in her interest. Certainly many women have had abortions they didn't want or wouldn't have wanted if they had any plausible means of caring for a child; and countless others wouldn't have gotten pregnant in the first place were it not for inadequate contraception, sexual confusion and guilt, male pressure, and other stigmata of female powerlessness. Yet forcing a woman to bear a child she doesn't want can only add injury to insult, while refusing to go through with such a pregnancy can be a woman's first step toward taking hold of her life. And many women who have abortions are "victims" only of ordinary human miscalculation, technological failure, or the vagaries of passion, all bound to exist in any society, however utopian. There will always be women who, at any given moment, want sex but don't want a child; some of these women will get pregnant; some of them will have abortions. Behind the victim theory of abortion is the implicit belief that women are always ready to be mothers, if only conditions are right, and that sex for pleasure rather than procreation is not only "irresponsible" (i.e., bad) but something men impose on women, never something women actively seek. Ironically, left right-to-lifers see abortion as always coerced (it's "exploitation" and "violence against women"), yet regard motherhood—which for most women throughout history has been inescapable, and is still our most socially approved role—as a positive choice. The analogy to the feminist antipornography movement goes beyond borrowed rhetoric: the antiporners, too, see active female lust as surrender to male domination and traditionally feminine sexual attitudes as expressions of women's true nature.

This Orwellian version of feminism, which glorifies "female values" and dismisses women's struggles for freedom—particularly sexual freedom—as a male plot, has become all too familiar in recent years. But its use in the abortion debate has been especially muddleheaded. Somehow we're supposed to leap from an oppressive patriarchal society to the egalitarian one that will supposedly make abortion obsolete without ever allowing women to see themselves as people entitled to control their reproductive function rather than be controlled by it. How women who have no power in this most personal of areas can effectively fight for power in the larger society is left to our imagination. A "New Zealand feminist" quoted by Mary Meehan in a 1980 article in *The Progressive* says, "Accepting short-term solutions like abortion only delays the implementation of real reforms like decent maternity and paternity leaves, job protection, high-quality child care, community responsibility for dependent people of all ages, and recognition of the economic contribution of childminders"—as if these causes were progressing nicely before legal abortion came along. On the contrary, the fight for reproductive freedom is the foundation of all the others, which is why antifeminists resist it so fiercely.

As "pro-life" pacifists have been particularly concerned with refuting charges of misogyny, the liberal Catholics at *Commonweal* are most exercised by the claim that antiabortion laws violate religious freedom. The editorial quoted above hurled another challenge at the proabortion forces:

> It is time, finally, for the pro-choice advocates and editorial writers to abandon, once and for all, the argument that abortion [*sic*] is a religious "doctrine" of a single or several churches being imposed on those of other persuasions in violation of the First Amendment. . . . Catholics and their bishops are accused of imposing their "doctrine" on abortion, but not their "doctrine" on the needs of the poor, or their "doctrine" on the arms race, or their "doctrine" on human rights in Central America. . . .
>
> The briefest investigation into Catholic teaching would show that the church's case against abortion is utterly unlike, say, its belief in the Real Presence, known with the eyes of faith alone, or its insistence on a Sunday obligation, applicable only to the faithful. The church's moral teaching on abortion . . . is for the most part like its teaching on racism, warfare, and capital punishment, based on ordinary reasoning common to believers and nonbelievers. . . .

This is one more example of right-to-lifers' tendency to ignore the sexual ideology underlying their stand. Interesting, isn't it, how the editorial neglects to mention that the church's moral teaching on abortion jibes neatly with its teaching on birth control, sex, divorce, and the role of women. The traditional, patriarchal sexual morality common to these teachings is explicitly religious, and its chief defenders in modern times have been the more conservative churches. The Catholic and evangelical Christian churches are the backbone of the organized right-to-life movement and—a few Nathansons and Hentoffs notwithstanding—have provided most of the movement's activists and spokespeople.

Furthermore, the Catholic hierarchy has made opposition to abortion a 20
litmus test of loyalty to the church in a way it has done with no other political issue—witness Archbishop O'Connor's harassment of Geraldine Ferraro during her vice-presidential campaign. It's unthinkable that a Catholic bishop would publicly excoriate a Catholic officeholder or candidate for taking a hawkish position on the arms race or Central America or capital punishment. Nor do I notice anyone trying to read William F. Buckley out of the church for his views on welfare. The fact is there is no accepted Catholic "doctrine" on these matters comparable to the church's absolutist condemnation of abortion. While differing attitudes toward war, racism, and poverty cut across religious and secular lines, the sexual values that mandate opposition to abortion are the bedrock of the traditional religious world view, and the source of the most bitter conflict with secular and religious modernists. When churches devote their considerable political power, organizational resources, and money to translating those values into law, I call that imposing their religious beliefs on me—whether or not they're technically violating the First Amendment.

Statistical studies have repeatedly shown that people's views on abortion are best predicted by their opinions on sex and "family" issues, not on "life" issues like nuclear weapons or the death penalty. That's not because we're inconsistent but because we comprehend what's really at stake in the abortion fight. It's the antiabortion left that refuses to face the contradiction in its own position: you can't be wholeheartedly for "life"—or for such progressive aspirations as freedom, democracy, equality—and condone the subjugation of women. The seamless garment is full of holes.

These preceding essays by McConnell and Willis represent the two sides on which most Americans fall regarding the issue of legalized abortion. Since abortion is likely to stay legal, what is the point of trying to reconcile these positions? One benefit is that doing so might help put to rest the controversy surrounding abortion, a controvery that rages at abortion clinics and in the media, distracting Americans from other issues of importance and causing devisiveness and distrust, and that also rages within millions of Americans, who want abortion to remain legal but at the same time disapprove of it. In addition, reaching some consensus on abortion might resolve the contradiction of its being legal but unavailable to many women, as extremist opponents have caused many doctors to refuse to perform abortions and the access of poor women is limited by restrictions on public funding for abortion. Finally, some consensus on abortion will be necessary to formulate decisions of public policy: What restrictions, if any, are appropriate? Should parental notification or consent be required for women under eighteen? Should public funds be available for an abortion when a woman cannot otherwise afford one?

We have said that the first step in resolving conflict is to make sure that we understand what the parties in conflict are claiming, and why. Using the outline form that we have called the brief, we can describe the positions of each side as follows:

McConnell's position: She is against unrestricted abortion as a woman's right.

Claim (or thesis): The right to abortion has hurt the moral and social climate of our nation.

Reason: It has put pressure upon young single women to adopt a "liberated" lifestyle of sex without commitment.
Evidence: Her own college experiences.

Reason: It has caused an increase in unintended pregnancies.
Evidence: The analogy of children playing ball.

Reason: It has taken questions about morality out of the decision to end a pregnancy.
Evidence: Her own experiences with doctors and clinics.

Reason: It has allowed middle- and upper-class men and women to avoid the consequences of their sex lives and to evade the responsibilities of parenthood.
Evidence: None offered.

Reason: It has reduced people's sense of duty toward their offspring, most noticeably in the lower classes.
Evidence: Legislation has become necessary to make fathers provide financial support for their children and to hold women legally culpable for harming their fetuses through drug use.

Willis's position: She is for unrestricted abortion as a woman's right.

Claim (or thesis): The right to abortion is an essential part of feminism.

Reason: Without control of their reproductive lives, women constantly fear having their lives disrupted.
Evidence: A fetus makes immense demands on a woman's physical and mental resources. Her own pregnancy is an example.

Reason: Without abortion, women must live according to a sexual double standard.

Evidence: Sex always carries the risk of pregnancy.
The fear of pregnancy puts restrictions on women's ability to enjoy sex for pleasure or passion, rather than procreation.

Following Through

If you and some of your classmates have written arguments taking opposing views on the same issue, prepare a brief of your position, to share with those other classmates. (You each might also create briefs of your opponents' positions to see how well you have understood one another's written arguments.)

Alternately, write briefs summarizing the opposing positions offered in several published arguments as a first step toward mediating these viewpoints.

Locating the Areas of Disagreement

Areas of disagreement generally involve differences over facts and differences in interpretation.

Differences over Facts

Any parties involved in negotiation, as well as any mediator in a dispute, should consider both the reasons and evidence offered on all sides in order to locate areas of factual agreement and, particularly, disagreement. Parties genuinely interested in finding the best solution to a conflict rather than in advocating their own positions ought to be able to recognize where more evidence is needed, no matter the side. Negotiators and mediators should also consider the currency and the authority of any sources. If new or better research could help resolve factual disparities, the parties should do it collaboratively rather than independently.

Following Through

In the preceding arguments on abortion, the writers do not present much factual evidence, as their arguments are relatively abstract. Are there any facts that they agree on? Would more facts make a difference in getting either side to reconsider her position? How could you gather more solid evidence or hard data?

Differences in Interests

Experts in negotiation have found that conflicts most often result from interpretive differences rather than from factual differences; that is, people in conflict look at the same situation differently depending on their values, their beliefs, and their interests. McConnell opens her argument with this very point by showing, first, how most women's rights advocates would interpret the scene at a typical antiabortion protest, and then offering a second perspective, affected by her view that legalized abortion has victimized women.

What kinds of subjective differences cause people to draw conflicting conclusions from the same evidence? To identify these differences, we can ask the same questions that are useful in persuasion to identify what divides us from our audience (see the box below). In negotiation and mediation, these questions can help uncover the real interests that any resolution must address. It is in identifying these interests that the dialogue of negotiation begins, because only when the interests that underlie opposing positions are identified can creative solutions be formulated. Often, uncovering each party's real interests leads to the discovery of previously ignored common ground. Finding these interests should be a collaborative project, one which negotiation experts compare to problem-solving through teamwork.

QUESTIONS ABOUT DIFFERENCE

1. Is the difference a matter of *assumptions*? As we discussed in Chapter 4 on the Toulmin method of analysis and in Chapter 5 on inquiry, all arguments are based on some assumptions.
2. Is the difference a matter of *principle*? Are some parties to the dispute following different principles, or general rules, than others?
3. Is the difference a matter of *values,* or a matter of having the same values but giving them different *priorities*?
4. Is the difference a matter of *ends or means*? That is, do people want to achieve different goals, or do they have the same goals in mind but disagree on the means to achieve them?
5. Is the difference a matter of *interpretation*?
6. Is the difference a matter of *implications* or *consequences*?
7. Is the difference a result of *personal background, basic human needs,* or *emotions*? To our list of questions about difference in persuasive writing we add this further question, because negotiation requires the parties involved to look not just at one another's arguments but also at one another as people, with histories and feelings. It is not realistic to think that human problems can be solved without taking human factors into consideration. Negotiators must be open about their emotions and such basic human needs as personal security, economic well-being, and a sense of belonging, recognition, and control over their own lives. They can be open with each other about such matters only if their dialogue up to this point has established trust between them. If you are mediating among printed texts, you must use the texts themselves as evidence of these human factors.

Here we apply the questions about difference to McConnell's and Willis's positions on abortion rights.

Is the Difference a Matter of Assumptions? Both arguments make the assumption that legalizing abortion removed constraints on women's sexuality. McConnell blames abortion for this presumed effect, but Willis credits abortion with enabling women to enjoy sex as men have traditionally been able to do. A mediator could begin by pointing out that this assumption itself could be wrong, that it is possible, for example, that the introduction of birth control pills and the political liberalism of the 1970s contributed more to the increased sexual activity of women. McConnell wants young women not to feel pressured to have sex, while Willis's interest is in freeing women from a sexual double standard.

McConnell also assumes that abortion becomes guilt-free for most women because it is legal. Willis insists that women should not feel guilty. A mediator might ask what interest McConnell has in making women feel guilty, and what Willis means when she says she would now feel "conflict and sadness" over choosing an abortion. What is the difference between "conflict and sadness" and "guilt"?

The main assumption these writers do not share concerns the motives of those who cast abortion as a moral issue. Willis assumes that any question about the morality of abortion is part of an effort to repress and subordinate women. This assumption makes Willis see those who disagree with her as a threat to her chief interest—women's rights. McConnell, on the other hand, challenges the feminist assumption that abortion has liberated women. To her, the legalization of abortion, rather than protecting women's rights, has actually contributed to the further exploitation of women sexually, which she sees as immoral.

Is the Difference a Matter of Principle? The principle of equal rights for all individuals is featured in both arguments, but in different ways. Willis is interested in equal rights among men and women. McConnell is concerned with the equal rights of the fetus, as a potential human being.

Is the Difference a Matter of Values or of Priorities? The question of priorities brings us to a key difference underlying the positions of McConnell and Willis. Willis puts the value of a woman's well-being above the value of a fetus's life (paragraph 5). In paragraph 8, she states, ". . . in a society that respects the individual, no [fetus] in *any* stage of development has an 'essential right' to make use of someone else's body . . . without that person's consent." For Willis, it is immoral to force any woman to bear a child against her will. For McConnell, however, the interests of the fetus have priority over the interests of the pregnant woman. Denying the fetus's rights in this case is denying nothing less than life itself; therefore, the woman has a duty and responsibility to bear the child, even at great sacrifice to her well-being. For McConnell, it is immoral for a woman to refuse this obligation (paragraph 4).

In addition, these two writers have very different values regarding sex. For McConnell, sex for pleasure, without commitment, is "demeaning" to women, something that they acquiese to only because they have been told that it is normal and healthy. For Willis, sexual passion "for its own sake is a human need and a human right" (paragraph 11); she seems to be responding directly to McConnell in paragraph 16: "Behind the victim theory of abortion is the implicit belief . . . that sex for pleasure is not only 'irresponsible' (i.e., bad) but something men impose on women, never something women actively seek."

Is the Difference a Matter of Ends or Means? McConnell and Willis both claim to have the same end in mind—a society in which women are truly free and equal, able to live dignified and uncompromised lives. However, they differ over legalized abortion as a means to this end. McConnell does not argue that *Roe v. Wade* should be overturned; rather, she wants her audience to recognize that abortion has cheapened both sex and life, allowing women to be victimized by men who want sex without commitment and encouraging a society that wants rights without responsibilities. Her ultimate goal is higher moral standards for the community. Willis, on the other hand, wants to make sure that freedom and equality for women stay in the forefront of the abortion debate. She resists any compromise on the abortion issue—even the concession that women should feel guilt over having abortions—because she sees the issue of morality as a slope down which women could slide back into a subordinate societal role.

Is the Difference a Matter of Interpretation? These two writers interpret abortion from polar extremes. McConnell sees it as totally negative; to her, abortion is a convenience, a way of avoiding responsibility after an act of sexual carelessness. Willis's definition of abortion stresses its positive political value; it is the "cutting edge of feminism" because it guarantees to women absolute control over their reproductive freedom. Further, as we have seen, they interpret individualism differently: for Willis individualism is positive, the autonomy and freedom to reach one's goals, while for McConnell it is more negative, with connotations of selfishness and immaturity.

Is the Difference a Matter of Implications or Consequences? Both writers are concerned with consequences, but neither entertains the other's concerns. Willis sees the results of legalized abortion as a more just society. McConnell argues that the positive consequences Willis would claim for women are illusory, and that women have been harmed by the easy availability of abortion.

Is the Difference a Result of Personal Background, Basic Human Needs, or Emotions? In their arguments about abortion, both writers are fairly open about some of their emotions. McConnell is quite frank about her "remorse" over her abortion in her first year of college. In her description of that experience, she suggests that she was coerced by the university's health counselors. Notice, too, that she describes herself as the child of "first-generation" Americans, with strict moral standards, a fact that surely influenced her perception of liberated sexual morals.

Willis expresses anger that the arena of debate over abortion has moved from its original focus on women's rights to a new focus on the rights of the fetus. She fears that hard-won ground on women's rights could be slipping from beneath her feet. Yet in discussing her own child, she reveals an emotional vulnerability that could possibly make her rethink her position on the morality of abortion. Note, for example, that she mentions her own abortion only once, in paragraph 14.

In face-to-face negotiation and mediation, having a conversation about underlying differences can go a long way toward helping opposing parties understand each other. Each side must "try on" the position of those who see the issue from a different perspective. They may still not agree or let go of their position, but at this point each side ought to be able to say to the other, "I see what your concerns are." Progress toward resolution begins when people start talking about their underlying concerns, or interests, rather than their positions.

As a student mediating among written texts, you must decide what you could say to help each side see the point of view of the other, and to loosen the commitment each has to his or her own position.

Following Through

If you are negotiating between your own position and the arguments of classmates, form groups and use the questions on page 172 to identify the interests of each party. You may ask an outside student to act as a mediator to direct the discussion. As a group, prepare a report on your conversation: What are the main interests of each party?

If you are mediating the views of printed arguments, write an analysis based on applying the questions to two or more arguments. You could write out your analysis in list form, as we did in analyzing the differences between McConnell and Willis, or you could treat it as an exploratory essay (see pages 60–61).

As a creative variation for your analysis, write a dialogue with yourself as mediator, posing questions to each of the opposing parties. Have each side respond to your questions just as we demonstrated in our sample dialogue in Chapter 5 on inquiry (pages 48–52).

Defining the Problem in Terms of the Real Interests

As we have said, while it is important in negotiating to see clearly what each side is demanding, successful negotiation looks for a solution that addresses the interests that underlie the positions of each side. Uncovering those interests is the first step. The next is summing them up, recognizing the most important ones which a solution must address. Meeting these underlying interests is the task that negotiators undertake collaboratively.

To illustrate, let's look at the two arguments over legalized abortion. While McConnell criticizes abortion and those who choose it, she admits that she would keep it legal. Her real interest is in reducing what she sees as the consequences of legalized abortion: irresponsible sex and disregard for life.

Willis is not totally unwilling to consider the moral value of the fetus as human life, admitting that it begins to acquire moral value as it comes to term; her problem with the moral question is the possibility that considering it at all will endanger women's right to choice about abortion. Her real interest is in equality of the sexes.

A mediator between these two positions would have to help resolve the conflict in a way that guarantees women's autonomy and control over their reproductive lives at the same time that it promotes responsibility and respect for the value of life. Any resolution here must ensure the rights of the individual and the good of the community at the same time.

Following Through

For the conflict among classmates' positions that you have been negotiating or the conflict among written texts that you have been mediating, write a description of the problem that a resolution must solve: What are the key interests that must be addressed? If you are negotiating, come to a collaborative statement.

Inventing Creative Options

Parties can work together to come up with solutions to a problem collaboratively, each party can brainstorm solutions alone, or an individual mediator can take on this task. Collaboration can either help or hinder the invention process, depending on the relationship of the negotiators, and since coming up with possible solutions means making some concessions, you might want to do so privately rather than state publicly what you would be willing to give up. Whether you are a mediator or a negotiator, this is the stage for opening the options, for exploring wild ideas, for experimenting without making any judgments.

With respect to the abortion issue, Willis might be willing to consider counseling for women contemplating abortion and admit that the issue inevitably involves some ethical concerns. McConnell might be willing to take a less judgmental position and concede that it is not really fair to impose either motherhood or guilt on every woman with an unwanted pregnancy.

Following Through

1. What do you think might be a possible compromise on the issue of legalized abortion? Your ideas should address the interests of both Willis and McConnell. How likely do you think the two writers would be to accept your compromise?
2. For a class assignment on negotiating or mediating a dispute, brainstorm possible solutions either independently or collaboratively. Try to make your list of options as long as you can, initially ruling out nothing.

Gathering More Data

Once a mediator has proposed a solution or negotiators have created a tentative resolution, some or all of the parties might be thinking that they could accept it if only they had a little more information. For example, one side in the abortion issue might want to know not just that there are approximately one and one-half million abortions performed each year in the United States, but how many of them are second or third abortions for the same women. If Willis learned that many women have abortions repeatedly, she might agree that the right is being abused—and that some counseling might help. If McConnell were to find out that most women have only a single abortion, she might decide that women do not interpret the right to abortion as nonchalantly as she had imagined. Professionals in the field of negotiation suggest that information-gathering at this point be done collaboratively. The trust and spirit of collaboration built so far can be damaged if each side tries to gather data favorable to its own original position.

Following Through

1. If you have an idea for a compromise that would address the interests of Willis and McConnell, what additional data do you think either or both of these authors would want to have before accepting your solution?
2. If you have invented a proposal for resolving a conflict that you and some classmates have been negotiating or that you have been mediating, decide together if additional information could help you reach consensus. What questions need to be answered? Try to answer these collaboratively, with a joint visit to the library.

Reaching a Solution Based on Agreed-Upon Principles

It is important to see that the kind of negotiation we have been talking about in this chapter is not of the "I-give-a-little, you-give-a-little" sort that occurs between a buyer and seller or, for example, in a hostage situation when terrorists trade a number of hostages for an equal number of released prisoners. Such a resolution involves no real principle other than that concessions ought to be of equal value. It brings the opposing sides no closer to understanding why they differed in the first place.

Instead, negotiated settlements on matters of public policy such as abortion or sexual harassment or gun control ought to involve some principles that both sides agree are fair. For example, Willis might agree that abortion ought to be a real choice, not something a woman is railroaded into as McConnell feels she was at age eighteen. On this principle, Willis might agree that professional counseling about ethics and options ought at least to be available to women considering abortion.

Following Through

1. If you have been mediating or negotiating a conflict with classmates, formalize your resolution, if possible. Be ready to explain what principles you have agreed on as the basis for the compromise.
2. After reading about mediatory essays in the following section, decide if the example offered, "How to End the Abortion War" by Roger Rosenblatt, would move Willis and McConnell—and others who hold similar views—closer to consensus about how to view abortion. What is Rosenblatt's proposed solution? Could you improve upon it? Then read another essay which attempts to mediate the same question, "Ending the Abortion War: A Modest Proposal" by Frances Kissling, on pages 431–437. Decide which of the two mediatory essays is more effective.

THE MEDIATORY ESSAY

Arguments that appear in newspapers and magazines for the general public usually seek to convince or persuade the audience to accept the author's position. Sometimes, however, the writer assumes the role of mediator and attempts to negotiate a solution acceptable to the opposing sides. The writer of such an essay moves beyond the stated positions and the facts of the dispute to expose the underlying interests, values, and beliefs of those in opposition. The goal is to show what interests they may have in common, to increase each side's understanding of the other, and to propose a solution to the dispute, a new position based on interests and values that will be acceptable to both sides. The following essay by Roger Rosenblatt aims to mediate one of the most deeply entrenched conflicts of our day—the issue of legalized abortion. As you read it, keep in mind the arguments of Margaret McConnell and Ellen Willis. Do you think that reading this mediatory essay might bring them closer to some consensus on the question of how to live with legalized abortion?

ROGER ROSENBLATT

Ending the Abortion War

Roger Rosenblatt is a writer who regularly contributes to the New York Times Magazine, *where this essay originally appeared.*

THE VEINS in his forehead bulged so prominently they might have been blue worms that had worked their way under the surface of his skin. His eyes bulged, too, capillaries zigzagging from the pupils in all directions. His face was pulled tight about the jaw, which thrust forward like a snowplow attachment on the grille of a truck. From the flattened O of his mouth, the word "murderer" erupted in a regular rhythm, the repetition of the r's giving the word the sound of an outboard motor that failed to catch.

She, for her part, paced up and down directly in front of him, saying nothing. Instead, she held high a large cardboard sign on a stick, showing the cartoonish drawing of a bloody coat hanger over the caption, "Never again." Like his, her face was taut with fury, her lips pressed together so tightly they folded under and vanished. Whenever she drew close to him, she would deliberately lower the sign and turn it toward him, so that he would be yelling his "murderer" at the picture of the coat hanger.

For nearly twenty years these two have been at each other with all the hatred they can unearth. Sometimes the man is a woman, sometimes the woman a man. They are black, white, Hispanic, Asian; they make their homes in Missouri or New Jersey; they are teenagers and pharmacists and college professors; Catholic, Baptist, Jew. They have exploded at each other on the steps of the Capitol in Washington, in front of abortion clinics, hospitals, and politicians' homes, on village greens and the avenues of cities. Their rage is tireless; at every decision of the United States Supreme Court or of the President or of the state legislatures, it rises like a missile seeking only the heat of its counterpart.

This is where America is these days on the matter of abortion, or where it seems to be. In fact, it is very hard to tell how the country really feels about abortion, because those feelings are almost always displayed in political arenas. Most ordinary people do not speak of abortion. Friends who gladly debate other volatile issues—political philosophy, war, race—shy away from the subject. It is too private, too personal, too bound up with one's faith or spiritual identity. Give abortion five seconds of thought, and it quickly spirals down in the mind to the most basic questions about human life, to the mysteries of birth and our relationship with our souls.

We simply will not talk about it. We will march in demonstrations, shout 5
and carry placards, but we will not talk about it. In the Presidential election of 1992, we will cast votes for a national leader based in part on his or her position on abortion. Still, we will not talk about it.

The oddity in this unnatural silence is that most of us actually know what we feel about abortion. But because those feelings are mixed and complicated, we have decided that they are intractable. I believe the opposite is true: that we are more prepared than we realize to reach a common, reasonable understanding on this subject, and if we were to vent our mixed feelings and begin to make use of them, a resolution would be at hand.

Seventy-three percent of Americans polled in 1990 were in favor of abortion rights. Seventy-seven percent polled also regard abortion as a kind of killing. (Forty-nine percent see abortion as outright murder, 28 percent solely as the taking of human life.) These figures represent the findings of the Harris and Gallup polls, respectively, and contain certain nuances of opinion within both attitudes. But the general conclusions are widely considered valid. In other words, most Americans are both for the choice of abortion as a principle and against abortion for themselves. One has to know nothing else to realize how conflicted a problem we have before and within us.

The fact that abortion entails conflict, however, does not mean that the country is bound to be locked in combat forever. In other contexts, living with conflict is not only normal to America, it is often the only way to function honestly. We are for both Federal assistance and states' autonomy; we are for both the First Amendment and normal standards of propriety; we are for both the rights of privacy and the needs of public health. Our most productive thinking usually contains an inner confession of mixed feelings. Our least productive thinking, a nebulous irritation resulting from a refusal to come to terms with disturbing and patently irreconcilable ideas.

Yet acknowledging and living with ambivalence is, in a way, what America was invented to do. To create a society in which abortion is permitted and its gravity appreciated is to create but another of the many useful frictions of a democratic society. Such a society does not devalue life by allowing abortion; it takes life with utmost seriousness and is, by the depth of its conflicts and by the richness of its difficulties, a reflection of life itself.

Why, then, are we stuck in political warfare on this issue? Why can we not 10
make use of our ambivalence and move on?

The answer has to do with America's peculiar place in the history of abortion, and also with the country's special defining characteristics, both ancient and modern, with which abortion has collided. In the 4,000-year-old history extending from the Greeks and Romans through the Middle Ages and into the present, every civilization has taken abortion with utmost seriousness. Yet ours seems to be the only civilization to have engaged in an emotional and intellectual civil war over the issue.

There are several reasons for this. The more obvious include the general lack of consensus in the country since the mid-60's, which has promoted bitter divisions over many social issues—race, crime, war, and abortion, too. The sexual revolution of the 60's resulted in the heightened activity of people who declared themselves "pro-choice" *and* "pro-life"—misleading terms used here principally for convenience. The pro-life movement began in 1967, six years before *Roe v.*

Wade. The women's movement, also revitalized during the 60's, gave an impetus for self-assertion to women on both sides of the abortion issue.

But there are less obvious reasons, central to America's special character, which have helped to make abortion an explosive issue in this country.

Religiosity. America is, and always has been, a religious country, even though it spreads its religiosity among many different religions. Perry Miller, the great historian of American religious thought, established that the New England colonists arrived with a ready-made religious mission, which they cultivated and sustained through all its manifestations, from charity to intolerance. The Virginia settlement, too, was energized by God's glory. Nothing changed in this attitude by the time the nation was invented. If anything, the creation of the United States of America made the desire to receive redemption in the New World more intense.

Yet individuals sought something in American religion that was different, 15
more emotional than the religion practiced in England. One member of an early congregation explained that the reason he made the long journey to America was "I thought I should find feelings." This personalized sense of religion, which has endured to the present, has an odd but telling relationship with the national attitude toward religion. Officially, America is an a-religious country; the separation of church and state is so rooted in the democracy it has become a cliché. Yet that same separation has created and intensified a hidden national feeling about faith and God, a sort of secret, undercurrent religion, which, perhaps because of its subterranean nature, is often more deeply felt and volatile than that of countries with official or state religions.

The Catholic Church seems more steadily impassioned about abortion in America than anywhere else, even in a country like Poland—so agitated, in fact, that it has entered into an unlikely, if not unholy, alliance with evangelical churches in the pro-life camp. In Catholic countries like Italy, France, and Ireland, religion is often so fluidly mixed with social life that rules are bent more quietly, without our personal sort of moral upheaval.

Americans are moral worriers. We tend to treat every political dispute that arises as a test of our national soul. The smallest incident, like the burning of the flag, can bring our hidden religion to the surface. The largest and most complex moral problem, like abortion, can confound it for decades.

Individualism. Two basic and antithetical views of individualism have grown up with the country. Emerson, the evangelist of self-reliance and nonconformity, had a quasi-mystical sense of the value of the individual self.[1] He described man as a self-sufficient microcosm: "The lightning which explodes and fashions planets, maker of planets and suns, is in him." Tocqueville had a more prosaic and practical view.[2] He worried about the tendency of Americans to

[1]Ralph Waldo Emerson (1803–1882) was an essayist and leader of New England transcendentalism.

[2]Alexis de Tocqueville (1805–1859) was a French aristocrat and magistrate who toured the United States in 1831 to study the effects of democracy. His classic work *Democracy in America* was first published in 1835.

withdraw into themselves at the expense of the public good, confusing self-assertion with self-absorption.

Abortion hits both of these views of the individual head on, of course; but both views are open to antipodal interpretations. The Emersonian celebration of the individual may be shared by the pro-choice advocate who sees in individualism one's right to privacy. It may be seen equally by a pro-life advocate as a justification for taking an individual stance—an antiliberal stance to boot—on a matter of conscience.

20 The idea of the independent individual may also be embraced by the pro-life position as the condition of life on which the unborn have a claim immediately after conception. Pro-life advocates see the pregnant woman as two individuals, each with an equal claim to the riches that American individualism offers.

Tocqueville's concern with individualism as selfishness is also available for adoption by both camps. The pro-life people claim that the pro-choice advocates are placing their individual rights above those of society, and one of the fundamental rights of American society is the right to life. Even the Supreme Court, when it passed *Roe v. Wade,* concluded that abortion "is not unqualified and must be considered against important state interests in regulation."

To those who believe in abortion rights, the "public good" consists of a society in which people, collectively, have the right to privacy and individual choice. Their vision of an unselfish, unself-centered America is one in which the collective sustains its strength by encouraging the independence of those who comprise it. Logically, both camps rail against the individual imposing his or her individual views on society at large, each feeling the same, if opposite, passion about both what society and the individual ought to be. Passion on this subject has led to rage.

Optimism. The American characteristic of optimism, like that of individualism, is affected by abortion in contradictory ways. People favoring the pro-life position see optimism exactly as they read individual rights: Every American, born or unborn, is entitled to look forward to a state of infinite hope and progress. The process of birth is itself an optimistic activity.

Taking the opposite view, those favoring abortion rights interpret the ideas of hope and progress as a consequence of one's entitlement to free choice in all things, abortion definitely included. If the individual woman wishes to pursue her manifest destiny unencumbered by children she does not want, that is not only her business but her glory. The issue is national as well as personal. The pro-choice reasoning goes: The country may only reach its ideal goals if women, along with men, are allowed to achieve their highest potential as citizens, unburdened by limitations that are not of their own choosing.

25 Even the element of American "can-do" ingenuity applies. The invention of abortion, like other instruments of American optimism, supports both the pro-life and pro-choice stands. Hail the procedure for allowing women to realize full control over their invented selves. Or damn the procedure for destroying forever the possibility of a new life inventing itself. As with all else pertaining to

this issue, one's moral position depends on the direction in which one is looking. Yet both directions are heaving with optimism, and both see life in America as the best of choices.

Sexuality. The connection of abortion with American attitudes toward sexuality is both economic and social. The American way with sex is directly related to the country's original desire to become a society of the middle class, and thus to cast off the extremes of luxury and poverty that characterized Europe and the Old World. The structure of English society, in particular, was something the new nation sought to avoid. Not for Puritan America was the rigid English class system, which not only fixed people into economically immobile slots but allowed and encouraged free-wheeling sexual behavior at both the highest and lowest strata.

At the top of the English classes was a self-indulgent minority rich enough to ignore middle-class moral codes and idle enough to spend their time seducing servants. At the opposite end of the system, the poor also felt free to do whatever they wished with their bodies, since the world offered them so little. The masses of urban poor, created by the Industrial Revolution, had little or no hope of bettering their lot. Many of them wallowed in a kind of sexual Pandemonium, producing babies wantonly and routinely engaging in rape and incest. Between the two class extremes stood the staunch English middle class, with its hands on its hips, outraged at the behavior both above and below them, but powerless to insist on, much less enforce, bourgeois values.

This was not to be the case in America, where bourgeois values were to become the standards and the moral engine of the country. Puritanism, a mere aberrant religion to the English, who were able to get rid of it in 1660 after a brief eighteen years, was the force that dominated American social life for a century and a half. Since there has been a natural progression from Puritanism to Victorianism and from Victorianism to modern forms of fundamentalism in terms of social values, it may be said that the Puritans have really never loosened their headlock on American thinking. The Puritans offered a perfect context for America's desire to create a ruling middle class, which was to be known equally for infinite mobility (geographic, social, economic) and the severest forms of repression.

Abortion fits into such thinking more by what the issue implies than by what it is. In the 1800's and the early 1900's, Americans were able to live with abortion, even during periods of intense national prudery, as long as the practice was considered the exception that proved the rule. The rule was that abortion was legally and morally discouraged. Indeed, most every modern civilization has adopted that attitude, which, put simply, is an attitude of looking the other way in a difficult human situation, which often cannot and should not be avoided. For all its adamant middle-classedness, it was not uncomfortable for Americans to look the other way, either—at least until recently.

When abortion was no longer allowed to be a private, albeit dangerous, 30
business, however, especially during the sexual revolution of the 60's, America's basic middle-classedness asserted itself loudly. Who was having all these abor-

tions? The upper classes, who were behaving irresponsibly, and the lower orders, who had nothing to lose. Abortion, in other words, was a sign of careless sexuality and was thus an offense to the bourgeois dream.

The complaint was, and is, that abortion contradicts middle-class values, which dictate the rules of sexual conduct. Abortion, it is assumed, is the practice of the socially irresponsible, those who defy the solid norms that keep America intact. When *Roe v. Wade* was ruled upon, it sent the harshest message to the American middle class, including those who did not oppose abortion themselves but did oppose the disruption of conformity and stability. If they—certainly the middle-class majority—did not object to *Roe v. Wade* specifically, they did very much object to the atmosphere of lawlessness or unruliness that they felt the law encouraged. Thus the outcry; thus the warfare.

There may be one other reason for abortion's traumatic effect on the country in recent years. Since the end of the Second World War—American society, not unlike modern Western societies in general, has shifted intellectually from a humanistic to a social science culture; that is, from a culture used to dealing with contrarieties to one that demands definite, provable answers. The nature of social science is that it tends not only to identify, but to create issues that must be solved. Often these issues are the most significant to the country's future—civil rights, for example.

What social science thinking does not encourage is human sympathy. By that I do not mean the sentimental feeling that acknowledges another's pain or discomfort; I mean the intellectual sympathy that accepts another's views as both interesting and potentially valid, that deliberately goes to the heart of the thinking of the opposition and spends some time there. That sort of humanistic thinking may or may not be humane, but it does offer the opportunity to arrive at a humane understanding outside the realm and rules of politics. In a way, it is a literary sort of thinking, gone now from a post-literary age, a "reading" of events to determine layers of depth, complication, and confusion and to learn to live with them.

Everything that has happened in the abortion debate has been within the polarities that social science thinking creates. The quest to determine when life begins is a typical exercise of social science—the attempt to impose objective precision on a subjective area of speculation. Arguments over the mother's rights versus the rights of the unborn child are social science arguments, too. The social sciences are far more interested in rights than in how one arrives at what is right—that is, both their strength and weakness. Thus the abortion debate has been political from the start.

A good many pro-choice advocates, in fact, came to lament the political 35
character of the abortion debate when it first began in the 60's. At that time, political thinking in America was largely and conventionally liberal. The liberals had the numbers; therefore, they felt that they could set the national agenda without taking into account the valid feelings or objections of the conservative opposition. When, in the Presidential election of 1980, it became glaringly apparent that the feelings of the conservative opposition were not only valid but were politically ascendant,

many liberals reconsidered the idea that abortion was purely a rights issue. They expressed appreciation of a more emotionally complicated attitude, one they realized that they shared themselves, however they might vote.

If the abortion debate had risen in a humanistic environment, it might never have achieved the definition and clarity of the *Roe v. Wade* decision, yet it might have moved toward a greater public consensus. One has to guess at such things through hindsight, of course. But in a world in which humanistic thought predominated, abortion might have been taken up more in its human terms and the debate might have focused more on such unscientific and apolitical components as human guilt, human choice and human mystery.

If we could find the way to retrieve this kind of conflicted thinking, and find a way to apply it to the country's needs, we might be on our way toward a common understanding on abortion, and perhaps toward a common good. Abortion requires us to think one way and another way simultaneously. Americans these days could make very good use of this bifurcated way of thinking.

This brings me back to the concern I voiced at the beginning: Americans are not speaking their true minds about abortion because their minds are in conflict. Yet living with conflict is normal in America, and our reluctance to do so openly in this matter, while understandable in an atmosphere of easy polarities, may help create a false image of our country in which we do not recognize ourselves. An America that declares abortion legal and says nothing more about it would be just as distorted as one that prohibited the practice. The ideal situation, in my view, would consist of a combination of laws, attitudes, and actions that would go toward satisfying both the rights of citizens and the doubts held by most of them.

Achieving this goal is, I believe, within reach. I know how odd that must sound when one considers the violent explosions that have occurred in places like Wichita as recently as August of last year, or when one sees the pro-life and pro-choice camps amassing ammunition for this year's Presidential campaign. But for the ordinary private citizen, the elements of a reasonably satisfying resolution are already in place. I return to the fact that the great majority of Americans both favor abortion rights and disapprove of abortion. Were that conflict of thought to be openly expressed, and were certain social remedies to come from it, we would not find a middle of the road on this issue—logically there is no middle of the road. But we might well establish a wider road, which would accommodate a broad range of beliefs and opinions and allow us to move on to more important social concerns.

What most Americans want to do with abortion is to permit but discourage 40
it. Even those with the most pronounced political stands on the subject reveal this duality in the things they say; while making strong defenses of their positions, they nonetheless, if given time to work out their thoughts, allow for opposing views. I discovered this in a great many interviews over the past three years.

Pro-choice advocates are often surprised to hear themselves speak of the immorality of taking a life. Pro-life people are surprised to hear themselves defend individual rights, especially women's rights. And both sides might be surprised to learn how similar are their visions of a society that makes abortion less necessary through sex education, help for unwanted babies, programs to shore up disintegrating families and moral values, and other forms of constructive community action. Such visions may appear Panglossian, but they have been realized before, and the effort is itself salutary.

If one combines that sense of social responsibility with the advocacy of individual rights, the permit-but-discourage formula could work. By "discourage," I mean the implementation of social programs that help to create an atmosphere of discouragement. I do not mean ideas like parental consent or notification, already the law in some states, which, however well-intentioned, only whittle away at individual freedoms. The "discourage" part is the easier to find agreement on, of course, but when one places the "permit" question in the realm of respect for private values, even that may become more palatable.

Already 73 percent of America finds abortion acceptable. Even more may find it so if they can tolerate living in a country in which they may exercise the individual right not to have an abortion themselves or to argue against others having one, yet still go along with the majority who want the practice continued. The key element for all is to create social conditions in which abortion will be increasingly unnecessary. It is right that we have the choice, but it would be better if we did not have to make it.

Were this balance of thought and attitude to be expressed publicly, it might serve some of the country's wider purposes as well, especially these days when there is so much anguish over how we have lost our national identity and character. The character we lost, it seems to me, was one that exalted the individual for what the individual did for the community. It honored and embodied both privacy and selflessness. A balanced attitude on abortion would also do both. It would make a splendid irony if this most painful and troublesome issue could be converted into a building block for a renewed national pride based on good will.

For that to happen, the country's leaders—Presidential candidates come to 45
mind—have to express themselves as well. As for Congress, it hardly seems too much to expect our representatives to say something representative about the issue. Should *Roe v. Wade* be overturned, as may well happen, the country could be blown apart. To leave the matter to the states would lead to mayhem, a balkanization of what ought to be standard American rights. Congress used to pass laws, remember? I think it is time for Congress to make a law like *Roe v. Wade* that fully protects abortion rights, but legislates the kind of community help, like sex education, that would diminish the practice.

Taking a stand against abortion while allowing for its existence can turn out to be a progressive philosophy. It both speaks for moral seriousness and moves in the direction of ameliorating conditions of ignorance, poverty, the social self-destruction of fragmented families, and the loss of spiritual values in general. What started as a debate as to when life begins might lead to making life better.

The effort to reduce the necessity of abortion, then, is to choose life as wholeheartedly as it is to be "pro-life." By such an effort, one is choosing life for millions who do not want to be, who do not deserve to be, forever hobbled by an accident, a mistake or by miseducation. By such an effort, one is also choosing a different sort of life for the country as a whole—a more sympathetic life in which we acknowledge, privileged and unprivileged alike, that we have the same doubts and mysteries and hopes for one another.

Earlier, I noted America's obsessive moral character, our tendency to treat every question that comes before us as a test of our national soul. The permit-but-discourage formula on abortion offers the chance to test our national soul by appealing to its basic egalitarian impulse. Were we once again to work actively toward creating a country where everyone had the same health care, the same sex education, the same opportunity for economic survival, the same sense of personal dignity and worth, we would see both fewer abortions and a more respectable America.

Analyzing a Mediatory Essay

Rosenblatt's argument poses a possible resolution of the abortion controversy, and in so doing, analyzes the opposing positions and interests, as all mediation must. The following analysis shows how Rosenblatt takes his readers through the process of mediation.

Understanding the Spirit of Negotiation

A mediator has to be concerned with his or her own ethos as well as with helping the opposing parties achieve an attitude that will enable negotiation to begin. The mediator must sound fair and even-handed; the opposing parties must be open-minded.

Rosenblatt, interestingly, opens his essay in a way that invites commentary. In his first two paragraphs he portrays both sides at their worst, as extremes in no frame of mind to negotiate—and, in fact, in no frame of mind even to speak to each other. In his third paragraph he relates the history of their debate, describing their emotions with words like "hatred" and "rage" and their behavior with metaphors of war and destruction. Readers who see themselves as reasonable will disassociate themselves from the people in these portraits.

Following Through

Do you think that Rosenblatt's introduction is a good mediation strategy? In your writer's notebook, describe your initial response to Rosenblatt's opening. After reading the whole essay, do you think it is an effective opening? Once he has presented these "warriors" on both sides, do you think he goes on to discuss the opposing positions and their values in an even-handed, neutral way? Can you cite some passages where you see either fairness or bias on his part?

Understanding the Positions

Rosenblatt establishes the opposing positions, already well-known, in the first two paragraphs: the "pro-life" position that abortion is murder, the "pro-choice" position that outlawing abortion violates women's rights. Interestingly, Rosenblatt does not wait until the close of the essay to suggest his compromise position. Rather, he presents it in paragraph 9, although he goes into more detail about the solution later in the essay.

Following Through

In your writer's notebook, paraphrase Rosenblatt's compromise position on abortion. Do you think this essay would have been more effective if Rosenblatt had postponed presenting his solution?

Locating Areas of Disagreement over Facts

Rosenblatt points out that both sides' focus on the facts alone is what has made the issue intractable. As he points out in paragraph 34, the opposing sides have adopted the "objective precision" of the social sciences: The pro-life side has focused on establishing the precise moment of the beginning of life; the pro-choice side has focused on the absolute rights of women, ignoring the emotions of their conservative opponents.

Following Through

Reread paragraph 33. In your writer's notebook, paraphrase Rosenblatt's point about humanistic thinking as opposed to social science thinking. If you have taken social science courses, what is your opinion?

Locating Areas of Disagreement in Interests

Rosenblatt perceives that the disagreement over abortion may in fact be a disagreement over certain underlying interests and emotions held by each side, involving their perceptions about what life should be like in America. His aim is to help the two sides understand how these "less obvious reasons" have kept them from reaching any agreement. At the same time, he points out that many of the differences which seem to put them at odds are tied to common values deeply rooted in American culture. Thus, Rosenblatt attempts to show each side that the other is not a threat to its interests and perceptions of the American way of life.

Rosenblatt notes that both sides share an assumption that is keeping them apart: they both assume that there is one answer to the question of abortion rights, rather than a solution that accepts ambivalence. He locates the source of this assumption in what he calls "social science" thinking, which leads both sides to think that problems can be objectively studied and solved apart from human subjectivity. Thus, both sides are ignoring the very thing that we find so vital to the process of negotiation and mediation.

Rosenblatt further shows how different principles underly the arguments of each side. One side bases its argument on the right to privacy and free choice, while the other bases its argument on the right to life. Both principles are fundamental to American society—and neither is completely unqualified.

In addition, Rosenblatt shows how each side values the rights of the individual, but interprets these rights differently. For example, antiabortion advocates see the fetus as an individual with the right to life, while pro-choice advocates argue for the individual right of the mother to privacy. In paragraphs 18 through 22, Rosenblatt shows how two perceptions or interpretations of individualism, one positive (emphasizing self-reliance) and one more critical (emphasizing selfishness), are traceable throughout American culture. In fact, he shows how both sides embrace individualism as an element of their arguments.

In addressing the main difference between the opposing parties over values, Rosenblatt shows how legalized abortion could be perceived as a threat to traditional middle-class economic and social values, and he traces middle-class sexual repression back to the Puritans. Rosenblatt may be stepping outside of the neutral stance of a mediator here, as he suggests that antiabortionists are somewhat prudish. He makes no corresponding remarks about the sexual values of the pro-choice side.

Rosenblatt points out that both sides see different consequences of legalizing abortion. Antiabortion advocates see abortion as destabilizing society and undermining the middle-class American way of life. These people worry not just about abortion but rather about an "unruly" society. Pro-choice advocates, on the other hand, see abortion as the route to a better society; as Rosenblatt paraphrases their vision, "the country may only reach its ideal goals if women, along with men, are allowed to achieve their highest potential as citizens . . ." (paragraph 24).

In addressing the emotional characteristics of those involved in the dispute over abortion, Rosenblatt points to the role of religion in America. He explains that Americans have historically been more emotional about religion and morality than people of other nations, even ones where Catholicism is a state religion.

Following Through

Recall the chief areas of difference between Ellen Willis and Margaret McConnell in their respective arguments on the value of abortion rights. In your writer's notebook, indicate which of their stated concerns correspond to points in Rosenblatt's analysis of the differences that fuel the abortion war. Does Rosenblatt say anything that might help to bring Willis and McConnell closer together?

Defining the Problem in Terms of the Real Interests

Rosenblatt finds the real issue in the abortion controversy to be not whether abortion should be legal or illegal but rather how fundamental conflicting interests in American society can be addressed—in other words, how can we create laws and institutions that reflect the ambivalence most Americans feel on the topic of abortion? How do we permit abortion legally, in order to satisfy our traditional values for privacy and individual rights, but also discourage it morally, in order to satisfy the American religious tradition that values life, respects fetal rights, and disapproves of casual and promiscuous sex.

Following Through

In your writer's notebook, give your opinion of whether or not Rosenblatt has defined the abortion debate in terms of the opposing sides' real interests. Would his definition of the problem affect related abortion rights issues, such as making the "abortion pill," or RU486, available in the United States?

Inventing Creative Options

Rosenblatt's solution is based on what he calls humanistic thinking, that is, thinking that permits conflict and rejects simple solutions to complicated human problems. He shows that a great number of individual Americans think that abortion is both right and wrong, but cannot even talk about their feelings because they are so contradictory. His creative option is for us to accept this ambivalence as a society and pass legislation that would satisfy both "the rights of citizens and the doubts held by most of them" (paragraph 38). In paragraph 45, Rosenblatt suggests that Congress pass a law legalizing abortion but at the same time requiring various activities, such as sex education, that with time promote respect for life and strengthen community moral standards.

Following Through

Reread paragraphs 39 through 48, and explore in your writer's notebook your opinion of Rosenblatt's proposed solution. Should he have made it more specific?

Gathering More Data

Before opposing sides can reach an agreement based on the real issues, they often need to get more information. Rosenblatt's mediatory argument is short on actual data. In response to his proposed solution, the antiabortion side might have severe doubts that the social programs proposed could in fact reduce the number of abortions performed.

Following Through

In your writer's notebook, make suggestions as to what kind of evidence Rosenblatt might have to offer to convince the antiabortion side that sex education and other social programs could reduce the number of abortions performed.

Reaching a Solution Based on Agreed-Upon Principles

Rosenblatt attempts to get those who support abortion rights and those who oppose them to reduce their differences by accepting the principle of "permit but discourage." This is a principle that American society applies to other areas, such as marital infidelity, which is legal, but certainly discouraged through social institutions and customs.

Following Through

1. Reread, if necessary, the two arguments on abortion by McConnell and Willis beginning on page 156. Would each writer accept the principle of "permit but discourage"?
2. Draft a letter to the editor of the *New York Times Magazine,* where Rosenblatt's argument originally appeared. In no more than three paragraphs, evaluate the argument as an attempt at mediation. Then read the following letters to the *Times Magazine,* responding to Rosenblatt's essay.

   Alternatively, write a letter or letters to the editor of the *New York Times,* playing the role of either Willis or McConnell, or both, responding as you think each would.

> Roger Rosenblatt's essay on abortion is timely and welcome ("How to End the Abortion War," Jan. 19). However, his belief that Americans can coalesce on a policy that "discourages" abortion without making it illegal is probably too optimistic. The polarization of Americans on this issue results from some pretty deep differences. Differences in life style, for one thing, can dictate profound political polarization. Many American women derive their most fundamental sense of self-worth from child-rearing and care of the family; many others find theirs in lives that include participation in the larger society, particularly the work place. For women in "traditional" families (and their husbands), untrammeled access to abortion constitutes a form of permissiveness that threatens the things they hold most dear. For women whose identities are tied to work outside the home, the right to control reproductive lives is essential.
>
> So I'm afraid these wars will continue. Rosenblatt and others should not tire in their efforts to find middle ground, but it would be unrealistic to think that we will be able to occupy it together anytime soon.
>
> —PHILIP D. HARVEY *Cabin John, Md.*

I don't want to "permit but discourage" abortion. I want to stop abortion the way the abolitionists wanted to stop slavery. I believe slavery is wrong: that no one has the right to assure his or her quality of life by owning another. In the same way, and for the same reasons, I believe abortion is wrong: that no one has the right to assure her quality of life by aborting another.

—ANITA JANDA *Kew Gardens, Queens*

Your article states that "most of us actually know what we feel about abortion." It is true that most people have a position on abortion, but that position is seldom an informed one in this era of the 10-second sound bite and the oversimplification of issues.

Few people understand that *Roe v. Wade* gives the interests of the woman precedence over those of the embryo early in the pregnancy, but allows Government to favor the fetus once it has attained viability.

Were a poll to propose full freedom of choice for women during the early stages of pregnancy, and prohibition of abortion during the later stages, except in cases of fetal deformity or a threat to a woman's life, I believe that the response of the American public would be overwhelmingly positive. Rosenblatt is right on the mark in saying that the public "simply will not talk about abortion." With thoughtful and dispassionate discussion, we might lay aside the all-or-nothing attitude that currently prevails.

—RICHARD A. KELLEY *Rumson, N.J.*

Following Through

Analyze the preceding letters to the *New York Times Magazine* critiquing Rosenblatt's article. What values does each contribute to the debate? How might Rosenblatt respond to each?

Writing a Mediatory Essay

Prewriting

If you have been mediating the positions of two or more groups of students in your class or two or more authors of published arguments, you may be assigned to write a mediatory essay in which you argue for a compromise position, appealing to an audience of people on all sides.

In preparing to write such an essay, you should work through the steps that make up the process of negotiation and mediation, as described on pages 155–156. In your writer's notebook, prepare briefs of the various conflicting positions, and note areas of disagreement; think hard about the differing interests of the conflicting parties, and respond to the questions about difference on page 172.

If possible, give some thought to each party's background—age, race, gender, and so forth—that might contribute to his or her viewpoint on the issue. For example, in a debate about whether *Huckleberry Finn* should be taught and read aloud in U.S. high schools, an African-American parent whose child is the only minority student in her English class might well have a different perspective from that of a white teacher. Can the white teacher be made to understand the embarrassment that a sole black child might feel when the white characters speak with derision about "niggers"?

In your notebook work out a description of the problem that reveals the conflict in terms of the opposing sides' real interests rather than the superficial demands each side might be stating. For example, considering the controversy over *Huckleberry Finn,* you might find some arguments in favor of teaching it anytime, others opposed to teaching it at all, others suggesting that it be an optional text for reading outside of class, and still others proposing that it be taught only in twelfth grade when students are mature enough to understand Mark Twain's satire. However, none of these suggestions addresses the problem in terms of the real interests involved: a desire to teach the classics of American literature for what they tell us about the human condition and our country's history and values; a desire to promote respect for African-American students; a desire to insure a comfortable learning climate for all students; and so on. You may be able to see that people's real interests are not as far apart as they might seem. For example, those who advocate teaching *Huckleberry Finn* and those who are opposed may both have in mind the goal of eliminating racial prejudice.

At this point in the prewriting process, you may be able to think of some solutions that would satisfy at least some of the real interests on all sides. It might be necessary for you to do some additional research. What do you anticipate that any of the opposing parties might want to know more about in order to accept your solution?

Finally, write up a clear statement of your compromise. Can you explain what principles it is based on? In the *Huckleberry Finn* debate, we might propose that the novel be taught at any grade level provided that it is presented as part of a curriculum to educate students about the African-American experience, with the involvement of African-American faculty or visiting lecturers.

Drafting

As the essays by Roger Rosenblatt and Frances Kissling on the abortion controversy indicate, there is no set form for the mediatory essay. In fact, it is an unusual, even somewhat experimental, form of writing. The important thing, as with any argument, is that you have a plan for arranging your points, and that you provide clear signals to your readers.

One logical way to organize a mediatory essay is in three parts:

Overview of the conflict. The introductory paragraphs should present a description of the conflict and the opposing positions.

Discussion of differences underlying the conflict. Here, your goal is to make all sides more sympathetic to each other as well as to sort out the important real interests that must be addressed by the solution.

Proposed solution. Here you make a case for your compromise position, giving reasons why it should be acceptable to all—that is, showing that it does serve at least some of their interests.

Revising

When revising a mediatory essay, you should look for the usual problems of organization and development that you would be looking for in any essay to convince or persuade. You want to be sure that you have inquired carefully and fairly into the conflict, and that you have clearly presented the cases for all sides, including your proposed solution. At this point, you also need to consider how well you have used the persuasive appeals:

The Appeal to Character. What kind of character have you projected as a mediator? Have you maintained neutrality? Do you model openmindedness and genuine concern for the sensitivities of all sides?

The Appeal to Emotions. To arouse sympathy and empathy, which we have said are needed in negotiation, you should take into account the emotional appeals discussed in Chapter 7 (pages 130–133). Your mediatory essay should be a moving argument for understanding and overcoming difference.

The Appeal through Style. As in persuasion, you should put the power of language to work for you. Pay attention to concrete word choice, striking metaphors, and phrases that stand out because of repeated sounds and rhythms.

For suggestions about editing and proofreading, see Appendix B.

Student Sample: A Mediatory Essay

ANGI GRELLHESL

Mediating the Speech Code Controversy

THE RIGHT to free speech has raised many controversies over the years. Explicit lyrics in rap music and marches by the Ku Klux Klan are just some examples that test the power of the First Amendment. Now, students and administrators are questioning if, in fact, free speech ought to be limited on university campuses. Many schools have instituted speech codes to protect specified groups from harassing speech.

Both sides in the debate, the speech code advocates and the free speech advocates, have presented their cases in recent books and articles. Columnist Nat

Hentoff argues strongly against the speech codes, his main reason being that the codes violate students' First Amendment rights. Hentoff links the right to free speech with the values of higher education. In support, he quotes Yale president Benno Schmidt, who says, "Freedom of thought must be Yale's central commitment. . . . [U]niversities cannot censor or suppress speech, no matter how obnoxious in content, without violating their justification for existence. . . ." (qtd. in Hentoff 223). Another reason Hentoff offers against speech codes is that universities must teach students to defend themselves in preparation for the real world, where such codes cannot shield them. Finally, he suggests that most codes are too vaguely worded; students may not even know they are violating the codes (216).

Two writers in favor of speech codes are Richard Perry and Patricia Williams. They see speech codes as a necessary and fair limitation on free speech. Perry and Williams argue that speech codes promote multicultural awareness, making students more sensitive to the differences that are out there in the real world. These authors do not think that the codes violate First Amendment rights, and they are suspicious of the motives of those who say they do. As Perry and Williams put it, those who feel free speech rights are being threatened "are apparently unable to distinguish between a liberty interest on the one hand and, on the other, a quite specific interest in being able to spout racist, sexist, and homophobic epithets completely unchallenged—without, in other words, the terrible inconvenience of feeling bad about it" (228).

Perhaps if both sides trusted each other a little more, they could see that their goals are not contradictory. Everyone agrees that students' rights should be protected. Hentoff wishes to ensure that students have the right to speak their minds. He and others on his side are concerned about freedom. Defenders of the codes argue that students have the right not to be harassed, especially while they are getting an education. They are concerned about opportunity. Would either side really deny that the other's goal had value?

Also, both sides want to create the best possible educational environment. Here, the difference rests on the interpretation of what benefits the students. Is the best environment one most like the real world, where prejudice and harassment occur? Or does the university have an obligation to provide an atmosphere where potential victims can thrive and participate freely without intimidation?

I think it is possible to reach a solution that everyone can agree on. Most citizens want to protect constitutional rights; but they also agree that those rights have limitations, the ultimate limit being when one person infringes on the rights of others to live in peace. All sides should agree that a person ought to be able to speak out about his or her convictions, values, and beliefs. And most people can see a difference between that protected speech and the kind that is intended to harass and intimidate. For example, there is a clear difference between expressing one's view that Jews are mistaken in not accepting Christ as the son of God, on the one hand, and yelling anti-Jewish threats at a particular person in the middle of the night, on the other. Could a code not be worded in such a way as to distinguish between these two kinds of speech?

Also, I don't believe either side would want the university to be an artificial world. Codes should not attempt to ensure that no one is criticized or even offended. Students should not be afraid to say controversial things. But universities do help to shape the future of the real world, so shouldn't they at least take a stand against harassment? Can a code be worded that would protect free speech and prevent harassment?

The current speech code at Southern Methodist University is a compromise that ought to satisfy free speech advocates and speech code advocates. It prohibits hate speech at the same time that it protects an individual's First Amendment rights.

First, it upholds the First Amendment by including a section that reads, "due to the University's commitment to freedom of speech and expression, harassment is more than mere insensitivity or offensive conduct which creates an uncomfortable situation for certain members of the community" (*Peruna* 92). The code therefore should satisfy those, like Hentoff, who place a high value on the basic rights our nation was built upon. Secondly, whether or not there is a need for protection, the current code protects potential victims from hate speech or "any words or acts deliberately designed to disregard the safety or rights of another, and which intimidate, degrade, demean, threaten, haze, or otherwise interfere with another person's rightful action" (*Peruna* 92). This part of the code should satisfy those who recognize that some hurts cannot be overcome. Finally, the current code outlines specific acts that constitute harassment: "Physical, psychological, verbal and/or written acts directed toward an individual or group of individuals which rise to the level of 'fighting words' are prohibited" (*Peruna* 92).

The SMU code protects our citizens from hurt and from unconstitutional censorship. Those merely taking a position can express it, even if it hurts. On the other hand, those who are spreading hatred will be limited as to what harm they may inflict. Therefore, all sides should respect the code as a safeguard for those who use free speech but a limitation for those who abuse it.

WORKS CITED

Hentoff, Nat. "Speech Codes on the Campus and Problems of Free Speech." *Debating P.C.* Ed. Paul Berman. New York: Bantam, 1992. 215–224.

Perry, Richard, and Patricia Williams. "Freedom of Speech." *Debating P.C.* Ed. Paul Berman. New York: Bantam, 1992. 225–230.

Peruna Express 1993–1994. Dallas: Southern Methodist University, 1993.

Part Two

READINGS: ISSUES AND ARGUMENTS

CHAPTER NINE

Environmentalism

Environmentalists are concerned with a variety of closely related problems: acid rain, global warming, deforestation, air and water pollution, and loss of natural habitats, among others. All are complicated problems with multiple causes and no easy solutions, and each is worth investigating on its own and in relation to the whole.

Rather than focus on one or several specific environmental problems, we have chosen instead to spotlight the environmental movement itself. Over the last twenty years or so, it has become a highly organized, well-financed, and powerful political force. In Washington, D.C., alone ten major organizations lobby for environmental causes, and countless grass roots organizations have sprung up on the local level. Vice-President Albert Gore's 1992 book about global environmental problems, *Earth in the Balance,* was a national best-seller, while the actions of radical environmental groups like Greenpeace and Earth First! help to keep environment issues in the news and therefore at the forefront of public attention.

To some extent, almost everybody is an environmentalist, concerned with issues that affect the earth and its atmosphere. The real issue is not whether ecology matters, but rather what courses of action to take in dealing with the environment. In broad terms, we can distinguish three basic approaches to environmentalism.

The first can legitimately be called "radical" (from the Latin *radix,* meaning root), for it sees itself as striking to the root of the problem. These so-called "deep" ecologists believe that only revolutionary changes in how we live and what we value can save the planet. In this view technology and industry are the source of the crisis and each day push us a little closer toward ecological disaster; the only solution is to reject our dependence on technology, return to the land, and live in harmony with nature. Groups like Greenpeace and Earth First! subscribe to this approach and often resort to direct action—including civil disobedience—to protest what they see as threats to the environment. But the radical viewpoint is hardly confined to fringe organizations. Some scientists see themselves as deep ecologists, much of the rapidly growing "green press" (environmental newsletters, magazines, and so forth) moves in this direction, and radical environmentalism is common on college campuses.

In contrast, mainstream environmentalism seeks to improve the environment by raising public consciousness and by influencing public policy. Whereas radicals see the system as the problem, mainstreamers see themselves as part of a system that must be reformed, but not rejected wholesale. In part by winning the support of many major corporations, this approach has attracted most of the funding for environmental causes, and its advocates have played a significant role in the passage of environmental legislation, such as the Clean Air Act and measures to preserve wild places and endangered species. Organizations such as the Sierra Club and the National Audubon Society are at the heart of the environmental mainstream, which also includes most grass roots environmentalists and indeed most Americans insofar as they care about the environment and act on its behalf but are unwilling to desert the comforts of modern technological society.

A third approach might be called "independent" or "skeptical." Unlike those who oppose any form of environmental action, the independents (generally individuals, not groups) think concern for the environment is justified. However, they are scornful of the radicals and question many of the assumptions of the mainstreamers. For example, they want proof that global warming is a reality rather than merely a theory. They argue that some government regulation intended to improve the environment has had no effect—or even a negative effect—and they criticize some policies (such as the Clean Air Act) as costing too much for too little benefit. In general, the independents ask that we stand back, analyze environmental problems, and seek practical solutions regardless of ideology, whether radical or mainstream. They also tend to see concern for the environment as something of a manufactured crisis that deflects attention from more pressing human problems, such as poverty and illiteracy.

As you read the articles in this chapter and do further research into the vast literature on environmental issues, you will probably find yourself moving toward one of these basic positions. Which attracts you most will depend primarily on your answers to the following questions:

How serious is the environmental problem?

How does the environment rate in degree of importance to other concerns, such as crime, the economy, public education, and the like?

In what ways and to what degree must we as a society change to guarantee a quality environment for ourselves and for future generations?

How likely is it that current economic and political institutions and technical innovation can address and solve environmental problems?

One last point: Environmentalism cannot be detached from other causes and issues. Because the poor have little political clout, environmental degradation can be greatest where they live and work, so concern for the environment is often tied to programs aimed at greater social justice. Also women's issues and the environment come together in ecofeminism, which holds that traditional male domination and power structures underlie much social inequity and disregard for ecology. In taking up the question of environmentalism, then, you should think about the meaning of the environment in the broadest sense—both natural and social.

JOHN (FIRE) LAME DEER and RICHARD ERDOES

Talking to the Owls and Butterflies

The history of environmentalism extends at least as far back as the eighteenth century. (See, for example, Richard H. Grove's "Origins of Western Environmentalism" in the July 1992 issue of Scientific American.*) Many cultures have contributed, and women have for a long time played a major role. But Native Americans were the first radical environmentalists; they provide a model for living in harmony with nature as well as a philosophy of living generally that contrasts sharply with the rationale of modern industrial society.*

It is only fitting, then, to begin with the thoughts of John (Fire) Lame Deer, a Sioux medicine man (1900–1976). The following powerful critique of European civilization comes from Lame Deer, Seeker of Visions *(1972), a collaboration between Lame Deer, who spoke his story, and Richard Erdoes, who transformed their conversations into prose. Their fruitful work together is an impressive example of cultural interaction and cooperation.*

LET'S SIT down here, all of us, on the open prairie, where we can't see a highway or a fence. Let's have no blankets to sit on, but feel the ground with our bodies, the earth, the yielding shrubs. Let's have the grass for a mattress, experiencing its sharpness and its softness. Let us become like stones, plants, and trees. Let us be animals, think and feel like animals.

Listen to the air. You can hear it, feel it, smell it, taste it. *Woniya waken*—the holy air—which renews all by its breath. *Woniya, woniya waken*—spirit, life, breath, renewal—it means all that. *Woniya*—we sit together, don't touch, but something is there; we feel it between us, as a presence. A good way to start thinking about nature, talk about it. Rather talk to it, talk to the rivers, to the lakes, to the winds as to our relatives.

You have made it hard for us to experience nature in the good way by being part of it. Even here we are conscious that somewhere out in those hills there are missile silos and radar stations. White men always pick the few unspoiled, beautiful, awesome spots for the sites of these abominations. You have raped and violated these lands, always saying, "Gimme, gimme, gimme," and never giving anything back. You have taken 200,000 acres of our Pine Ridge reservation and made them into a bombing range. This land is so beautiful and strange that now some of you want to make it into a national park. The only use you have made of this land since you took it from us was to blow it up. You have not only despoiled the earth, the rocks, the minerals, all of which you call "dead" but which are very much alive; you have even changed the animals, which are part of us, part of the Great Spirit, changed them in a horrible way, so no one can recognize them.

There is power in a buffalo—spiritual, magic power—but there is no power in an Angus, in a Hereford.

There is power in an antelope, but not in a goat or in a sheep, which holds still while you butcher it, which will eat your newspaper if you let it. There was great power in a wolf, even in a coyote. You have made him into a freak—a toy poodle, a Pekingese, a lap dog. You can't do much with a cat, which is like an Indian, unchangeable. So you fix it, alter it, declaw it, even cut its vocal cords so you can experiment on it in a laboratory without being disturbed by its cries.

A partridge, a grouse, a quail, a pheasant, you have made them into chick- 5
ens, creatures that can't fly, that wear a kind of sunglasses so that they won't peck each other's eyes out, "birds" with a "pecking order." There are some farms where they breed chickens for breast meat. Those birds are kept in low cages, forced to be hunched over all the time, which makes the breast muscles very big. Soothing sounds, Muzak, are piped into these chicken hutches. One loud noise and the chickens go haywire, killing themselves by flying against the mesh of their cages. Having to spend all their lives stooped over makes an unnatural, crazy, no-good bird. It also makes unnatural, no-good human beings.

That's where you fooled yourselves. You have not only altered, declawed, and malformed your winged and four-legged cousins; you have done it to yourselves. You have changed men into chairmen of boards, into office workers, into time-clock punchers. You have changed women into housewives, truly fearful creatures. I was once invited into the home of such a one.

"Watch the ashes, don't smoke, you stain the curtains. Watch the goldfish bowl, don't breathe on the parakeet, don't lean your head against the wallpaper; your hair may be greasy. Don't spill liquor on that table: it has a delicate finish. You should have wiped your boots; the floor was just varnished. Don't, don't, don't. . . ." That is crazy. We weren't made to endure this. You live in prisons which you have built for yourselves, calling them "homes," offices, factories. We have a new joke on the reservation: "What is cultural deprivation?" Answer: "Being an upper-middle-class white kid living in a split-level suburban home with a color TV."

Sometimes I think that even our pitiful tar-paper shacks are better than your luxury homes. Walking a hundred feet to the outhouse on a clear wintry night, through mud or snow, that's one small link with nature. Or in the summer, in the back country, leaving the door of the privy open, taking your time, listening to the humming of the insects, the sun warming your bones through the thin planks of wood; you don't even have that pleasure anymore.

Americans want to have everything sanitized. No smells! Not even the good, natural man and woman smell. Take away the smell from under the armpits, from your skin. Rub it out, and then spray or dab some nonhuman odor on yourself, stuff you can spend a lot of money on, ten dollars an ounce, so you know this has to smell good. "B.O.," bad breath, "Intimate Female Odor Spray"—I see it all on TV. Soon you'll breed people without body openings.

I think white people are so afraid of the world they created that they don't 10
want to see, feel, smell, or hear it. The feeling of rain and snow on your face,

being numbed by an icy wind and thawing out before a smoking fire, coming out of a hot sweat bath and plunging into a cold stream, these things make you feel alive, but you don't want them anymore. Living in boxes which shut out the heat of the summer and the chill of winter, living inside a body that no longer has a scent, hearing the noise from the hi-fi instead of listening to the sounds of nature, watching some actor on TV having a make-believe experience when you no longer experience anything for yourself, eating food without taste—that's your way. It's no good.

The food you eat, you treat it like your bodies, take out all the nature part, the taste, the smell, the roughness, then put the artificial color, the artificial flavor in. Raw liver, raw kidney—that's what we old-fashioned full-bloods like to get our teeth into. In the old days we used to eat the guts of the buffalo, making a contest of it, two fellows getting hold of a long piece of intestines from opposite ends, starting chewing toward the middle, seeing who can get there first; that's eating. Those buffalo guts, full of half-fermented, half-digested grass and herbs, you didn't need any pills and vitamins when you swallowed those. Use the bitterness of gall for flavoring, not refined salt or sugar. *Wasna*—meat, kidney fat, and berries all pounded together—a lump of that sweet *wasna* kept a man going for a whole day. That was food, that had the power. Not the stuff you give us today: powdered milk, dehydrated eggs, pasteurized butter, chickens that are all drumsticks or all breast; there's no bird left there.

You don't want the bird. You don't have the courage to kill honestly—cut off the chicken's head, pluck it and gut it—no, you don't want this anymore. So it all comes in a neat plastic bag, all cut up, ready to eat, with no taste and no guilt. Your mink and seal coats, you don't want to know about the blood and pain which went into making them. Your idea of war—sit in an airplane, way above the clouds, press a button, drop the bombs, and never look below the clouds—that's the odorless, guiltless, sanitized way.

When we killed a buffalo, we knew what we were doing. We apologized to his spirit, tried to make him understand why we did it, honoring with a prayer the bones of those who gave their flesh to keep us alive, praying for their return, praying for the life of our brothers, the buffalo nation, as well as for our own people. You wouldn't understand this and that's why we had the Washita Massacre, the Sand Creek Massacre, the dead women and babies at Wounded Knee. That's why we have Song My and My Lai now.[1]

To us life, all life, is sacred. The state of South Dakota has pest-control officers. They go up in a plane and shoot coyotes from the air. They keep track of their kills, put them all down in their little books. The stockmen and sheepowners pay them. Coyotes eat mostly rodents, field mice, and such. Only once in a while will they go after a stray lamb. They are our natural garbage men cleaning up the rotten and stinking things. They make good pets if you give them a chance. But their living could lose some man a few cents, and so the coyotes are killed from

[1]The first three refer to massacres of Native Americans in the nineteenth century, the last two to massacres of Vietnamese by American military in the 1960s.

the air. They were here before the sheep, but they are in the way; you can't make a profit out of them. More and more animals are dying out. The animals which the Great Spirit put here, they must go. The man-made animals are allowed to stay—at least until they are shipped out to be butchered. That terrible arrogance of the white man, making himself something more than God, more than nature, saying, "I will let this animal live, because it makes money"; saying, "This animal must go, it brings no income, the space it occupies can be used in a better way. The only good coyote is a dead coyote." They are treating coyotes almost as badly as they used to treat Indians.

15 You are spreading death, buying and selling death. With all your deodorants, you smell of it, but you are afraid of its reality; you don't want to face up to it. You have sanitized death, put it under the rug, robbed it of its honor. But we Indians think a lot about death. I do. Today would be a perfect day to die—not too hot, not too cool. A day to leave something of yourself behind, to let it linger. A day for a lucky man to come to the end of his trail. A happy man with many friends. Other days are not so good. They are for selfish, lonesome men, having a hard time leaving this earth. But for whites every day would be considered a bad one, I guess.

Eighty years ago our people danced the Ghost Dance, singing and dancing until they dropped from exhaustion, swooning, fainting, seeing visions. They danced in this way to bring back their dead, to bring back the buffalo. A prophet had told them that through the power of the Ghost Dance the earth would roll up like a carpet, with all the white man's works—the fences and the mining towns with their whorehouses, the factories and the farms with their stinking, unnatural animals, the railroads and the telegraph poles, the whole works. And underneath this rolled-up white man's world we would find again the flowering prairie, unspoiled, with its herds of buffalo and antelope, its clouds of birds, belonging to everyone, enjoyed by all.

I guess it was not time for this to happen, but it is coming back, I feel it warming my bones. Not the old Ghost Dance, not the rolling-up—but a new-old spirit, not only among Indians but among whites and blacks, too, especially among young people. It is like raindrops making a tiny brook, many brooks making a stream, many streams making one big river bursting all dams. Us making this book, talking like this—these are some of the raindrops.

Listen, I saw this in my mind not long ago: in my vision the electric light will stop sometime. It is used too much for TV and going to the moon. The day is coming when nature will stop the electricity. Police without flashlights, beer getting hot in the refrigerators, planes dropping from the sky, even the President can't call up somebody on the phone. A young man will come, or men, who'll know how to shut off all electricity. It will be painful, like giving birth. Rapings in the dark, winos breaking into the liquor stores, a lot of destruction. People are being too smart, too clever; the machine stops and they are helpless, because they have forgotten how to make do without the machine. There is a Light Man coming, bringing a new light. It will happen before this century is over. The man who has the power will do good things, too—stop all atomic power, stop wars, just by shutting the white electro-power off. I hope to see this, but then I'm also afraid. What will be will be.

I think we are moving in a circle, or maybe a spiral, going a little higher every time, but still returning to the same point. We are moving closer to nature again. I feel it. . . . It won't be bad, doing without many things you are now used to, things taken out of the earth and wasted foolishly. You can't replace them and they won't last forever. Then you'll have to live more according to the Indian way. People won't like that, but their children will. The machine will stop, I hope, before they make electric corncobs for poor Indians' privies.

We'll come out of our boxes and rediscover the weather. In the old days 20
you took your weather as it came, following the cranes, moving south with the herds. Here, in South Dakota, they say, "If you don't like the weather, wait five minutes." It can be 100 degrees in the shade one afternoon and suddenly there comes a storm with hailstones as big as golf balls, the prairie is all white and your teeth chatter. That's good—a reminder that you are just a small particle of nature, not so powerful as you think. . . .

But all animals have power, because the Great Spirit dwells in all of them, even a tiny ant, a butterfly, a tree, a flower, a rock. The modern, white man's way keeps that power from us, dilutes it. To come to nature, feel its power, let it help you, one needs time and patience for that. Time to think, to figure it all out. You have so little time for contemplation; it's always rush, rush, rush with you. It lessens a person's life, all that grind, that hurrying and scurrying about. Our old people say that the Indians of long ago didn't have heart trouble. They didn't have that cancer. The illnesses they had they knew how to cure. But between 1890 and 1920 most of the medicines, the animal bundles, the pipes, the ancient, secret things which we had treasured for centuries, were lost and destroyed by the B.I.A.,[1] by the Government police. They went about tearing down sweat lodges, went into our homes, broke the pipes, tore up the medicine bags, threw them into the fire, burned them up, completely wiped out the wisdom of generations. But the Indian, you take away everything from him, he still has his mouth to pray, to sing the ancient songs. He can still do his *yuwipi* ceremony[2] in a darkened room, beat his small drum, make the power come back, make the wisdom return. He did, but not all of it. The elk medicines are gone. The bear medicine, too. We had a medicine man here, up the creek, who died about fifteen years ago. He was the last bear medicine man that I knew about. And he was good, too. He was really good. . . .

As for myself, the birds have something to tell me. The eagle, the owl. In an eagle there is all the wisdom of the world; that's why we have an eagle feather at the top of the pole during a *yuwipi* ceremony. If you are planning to kill an eagle, the minute you think of that he knows it, knows what you are planning.

[1]The Bureau of Indian Affairs enforces U.S. government policy regarding Native Americans.

[2]*Yuwipi* is a religious ceremony designed to cure illness and promote the health of the community.

The black-tailed deer has this wisdom, too. That's why its tail is tied farther down at the *yuwipi* pole. This deer, if you shoot at him, you won't hit him. He just stands right there and the bullet comes right back and hits you. It is like somebody saying bad things about you and they come back at him.

In one of my great visions I was talking to the birds, the winged creatures. I was saddened by the death of my mother. She had held my hand and said just one word: "pitiful." I don't think she grieved for herself; she was sorry for me, a poor Indian she would leave in a white man's world. I cried up on that vision hill, cried for help, stretched out my hands toward the sky and then put the blanket over myself—that's all I had, the blanket and the pipe, and a little tobacco for an offering. I didn't know what to expect. I wanted to touch the power, feel it. I had the thought to give myself up, even if it would kill me. So I just gave myself to the winds, to nature, not giving a damn about what could happen to me.

All of a sudden I hear a big bird crying, and then quickly he hit me on the back, touched me with his spread wings. I heard the cry of an eagle, loud above the voices of many other birds. It seemed to say, "We have been waiting for you. We knew you would come. Now you are here. Your trail leads from here. Let our voices guide you. We are your friends, the feathered people, the two-legged, the four-legged, we are your friends, the creatures, little tiny ones, eight legs, twelve legs—all those who crawl on the earth. All the little creatures which fly, all those under water. The powers of each one of us we will share with you and you will have a ghost with you always—another self."

25 That's me, I thought, no other thing than myself, different, but me all the same, unseen, yet very real. I was frightened. I didn't understand it then. It took me a lifetime to find out.

And again I heard the voice amid the bird sounds, the clicking of beaks, the squeaking and chirping. "You have love for all that has been placed on this earth, not like the love of a mother for her son, or of a son for his mother, but a bigger love which encompasses the whole earth. You are just a human being, afraid, weeping under that blanket, but there is a great space within you to be filled with that love. All of nature can fit in there." I was shivering, pulling the blanket tighter around myself, but the voices repeated themselves over and over again, calling me "Brother, brother, brother." So this is how it is with me. Sometimes I feel like the first being in one of our Indian legends. This was a giant made of earth, water, the moon and the winds. He had timber instead of hair, a whole forest of trees. He had a huge lake in his stomach and a waterfall in his crotch. I feel like this giant. All of nature is in me, and a bit of myself is in all of nature.

Questions for Discussion

1. Lame Deer speaks directly to his audience of white Americans, attempting to change their perspective on a way of life they take for granted by comparing it to the ways of Native Americans. How has white civilization separated humans from nature? How does Lame Deer seek to convince us that our separation from nature is bad and that his culture's closeness to it is good?

2. Read and discuss the first two chapters of *Genesis.* Compare this biblical understanding of humankind's place in creation with Lame Deer's. How does the Old Testament God differ from Lame Deer's Great Spirit? Lame Deer speaks of "the terrible arrogance of the white man" (paragraph 14). What does he mean?
3. In paragraph 13, Lame Deer connects incidents in which Native Americans were massacred with massacres of Vietnamese by American troops during the Vietnam war. What relationship does he suggest exists between being close to nature and the value of one's life? Evaluate this argument.
4. In paragraph 21, Lame Deer mentions the *yuwipi* sacred ritual, which was designed to secure the health and well-being of the entire tribe. He also mentions the part that the eagle and the deer play in the ritual. Do some research on the folk medicine of Native American culture. Compare such methods of healing to modern technological medicine. Without forgetting the advantages of modern medicine, do you see anything missing from modern practices? How do these differences in culture relate to ecology?
5. As prophets everywhere do, Lame Deer foresees a future where the deficiencies of the present will be overcome—"We are moving closer to nature again" (paragraph 19). Do you see this happening? If so, in what ways exactly? How meaningful is this movement insofar as improving the environment is concerned?

For Research and Inquiry

Collect some literature from Greenpeace and Earth First!, as well as some examples of writing from the green press. What arguments do you find? In what ways are they similar to and different from Lame Deer's? Assess the reasoning and critical perspectives of both. Which is more convincing? Why? What weaknesses do you find in any of the reasoning?

For Convincing

The American literary critic Kenneth Burke (1897–1993) claimed that we "create new problems and call it progress when we find the remedies." Do you think this is an accurate assessment of progress in technological society?

Write a critique of modern technology as you live in and with it daily. To what extent is technology to blame for our ecological difficulties?

For Persuasion

Lame Deer writes from the perspective of one not enmeshed in the civilization he criticizes. Do you consider yourself an insider in a technology-dependent society? If so, write a criticism or defense of technology-dependent society, aimed at persuading an appropriate audience.

UNION OF CONCERNED SCIENTISTS

World Scientists' Warning to Humanity

Signed by over 1600 scientists, 102 of them Nobel prize winners, the following statement first appeared on November 18th, 1992, and has since been reprinted a number of times in journals such as Scientific American. *The "Warning" is for obvious reasons a significant document of the environmental movement and cannot be dismissed as the extremism of "greenies" on the fringe of society.*

The Union of Concerned Scientists was established in 1969 and "is dedicated to advancing responsible public policies in areas where technology plays a critical role." Scientists from 70 countries have signed the document so far.

INTRODUCTION

Human beings and the natural world are on a collision course. Human activities inflict harsh and often irreversible damage on the environment and on critical resources. If not checked, many of our current practices put at serious risk the future that we wish for human society and the plant and animal kingdoms, and may so alter the living world that it will be unable to sustain life in the manner that we know. Fundamental changes are urgent if we are to avoid the collision our present course will bring about.

THE ENVIRONMENT

The environment is suffering critical stress.

The Atmosphere

Stratospheric ozone depletion threatens us with enhanced ultraviolet radiation at the earth's surface, which can be damaging or lethal to many life forms. Air pollution near ground level, and acid precipitation, are already causing widespread injury to humans, forests, and crops.

Water Resources

Heedless exploitation of depletable ground water supplies endangers food production and other essential human systems. Heavy demands on the world's surface waters have resulted in serious shortages in some 80 countries, containing 40 percent of the world's population. Pollution of rivers, lakes, and ground water further limits the supply.

Oceans

Destructive pressure on the oceans is severe, particularly in the coastal 5
regions which produce most of the world's food fish. The total marine catch is now at or above the estimated maximum sustainable yield. Some fisheries have

already shown signs of collapse. Rivers carrying heavy burdens of eroded soil into the seas also carry industrial, municipal, agricultural, and livestock waste—some of it toxic.

Soil

Loss of soil productivity, which is causing extensive land abandonment, is a widespread by-product of current practices in agriculture and animal husbandry. Since 1945, 11 percent of the earth's vegetated surface has been degraded—an area larger than India and China combined—and per capita food production in many parts of the world is decreasing.

Forests

Tropical rain forests, as well as tropical and temperate dry forests, are being destroyed rapidly. At present rates, some critical forest types will be gone in a few years, and most of the tropical rain forest will be gone before the end of the next century. With them will go large numbers of plant and animal species.

Living Species

The irreversible loss of species, which by 2100 may reach one-third of all species now living, is especially serious. We are losing the potential they hold for providing medicinal and other benefits, and the contribution that genetic diversity of life forms gives to the robustness of the world's biological systems and to the astonishing beauty of the earth itself.

Much of this damage is irreversible on a scale of centuries, or permanent. Other processes appear to pose additional threats. Increasing levels of gases in the atmosphere from human activities, including carbon dioxide released from fossil fuel burning and from deforestation, may alter climate on a global scale. Predictions of global warming are still uncertain—with projected effects ranging from tolerable to very severe—but the potential risks are very great.

Our massive tampering with the world's interdependent web of life— 10
coupled with the environmental damage inflicted by deforestation, species loss, and climate change—could trigger widespread adverse effects, including unpredictable collapses of critical biological systems whose interactions and dynamics we only imperfectly understand.

Uncertainty over the extent of these effects cannot excuse complacency or delay in facing the threats.

Population

The earth is finite. Its ability to absorb wastes and destructive effluent is finite. Its ability to provide food and energy is finite. Its ability to provide for growing numbers of people is finite. And we are fast approaching many of the earth's limits. Current economic practices which damage the environment, in both developed and underdeveloped nations, cannot be continued without the risk that vital global systems will be damaged beyond repair.

Pressures resulting from unrestrained population growth put demands on the natural world that can overwhelm any efforts to achieve a sustainable future. If we are to halt the destruction of our environment, we must accept limits to that growth. A World Bank estimate indicates that world population will not stabilize at less than 12.4 billion, while the United Nations concludes that the eventual total could reach 14 billion, a near tripling of today's 5.4 billion. But, even at this moment, one person in five lives in absolute poverty without enough to eat, and one in ten suffers serious malnutrition.

No more than one or a few decades remain before the chance to avert the threats we now confront will be lost and the prospects for humanity immeasurably diminished.

WARNING

We the undersigned, senior members of the world's scientific community, 15
hereby warn all humanity of what lies ahead. A great change in our stewardship of the earth and the life on it is required, if vast human misery is to be avoided and our global home on this planet is not to be irretrievably mutilated.

WHAT WE MUST DO

Five inextricably linked areas must be addressed simultaneously:

1. **We must bring environmentally damaging activities under control to restore and protect the integrity of the earth's systems we depend on.** We must, for example, move away from fossil fuels to more benign, inexhaustible energy sources to cut greenhouse gas emissions and the pollution of our air and water. Priority must be given to the development of energy sources matched to Third World needs—small-scale and relatively easy to implement. We must halt deforestation, injury to and loss of agricultural land, and the loss of terrestrial and marine plant and animal species.
2. **We must manage resources crucial to human welfare more effectively.** We must give high priority to efficient use of energy, water, and other materials, including expansion of conservation and recycling.
3. **We must stabilize population. This will be possible only if all nations recognize that it requires improved social and economic conditions, and the adoption of effective, voluntary family planning.**
4. **We must reduce and eventually eliminate poverty.**
5. **We must ensure sexual equality, and guarantee women control over their own reproductive decisions.**

The developed nations are the largest polluters in the world today. They must greatly reduce their overconsumption, if we are to reduce pressures on resources and the global environment. The developed nations have the obligation to provide aid and support to developing nations, because only the developed nations have the financial resources and the technical skills for these tasks.

Acting on this recognition is not altruism, but enlightened self-interest: Whether industrialized or not, we all have but one lifeboat. No nation can escape from injury when global biological systems are damaged. No nation can escape from conflicts over increasingly scarce resources. In addition, environmental and economic instabilities will cause mass migrations with incalculable consequences for developed and undeveloped nations alike.

Developing nations must realize that environmental damage is one of the gravest threats they face, and that attempts to blunt it will be overwhelmed if their populations go unchecked. The greatest peril is to become trapped in spirals of environmental decline, poverty, and unrest, leading to social, economic, and environmental collapse.

Success in this global endeavor will require a great reduction in violence 20
and war. Resources now devoted to the preparation and conduct of war—amounting to over $1 trillion annually—will be badly needed in the new tasks and should be diverted to the new challenges.

A new ethic is required—a new attitude towards discharging our responsibility for caring for ourselves and for the earth. We must recognize the earth's limited capacity to provide for us. We must recognize its fragility. We must no longer allow it to be ravaged. This ethic must motivate a great movement, convincing reluctant leaders and reluctant governments and reluctant peoples themselves to effect the needed changes.

The scientists issuing this warning hope that our message will reach and affect people everywhere. We need the help of many.

We require the help of the world community of scientists—natural, social, economic, political;
We require the help of the world's business and industrial leaders;
We require the help of the world's religious leaders; and
We require the help of the world's peoples.
We call on all to join us in this task.

Sponsored by
The Union of Concerned Scientists
26 Church Street
Cambridge, MA 02238

Questions for Discussion

1. In paragraph 11 uncertainty about the exact extent of environmental damage is acknowledged, but the statement claims that uncertainty "cannot excuse complacency or delay in facing the threats." Do you see uncertainty being used as an excuse for inaction? In what ways can lack of certainty be a genuine problem even for those not inclined toward complacency or delay?
2. The causes of environmental stress are numerous. What does the "Warning" name as the primary cause? What other contributing causes are mentioned? Do you think the document's causal analysis is adequate?

3. The scientists link environmental degradation to various social and political problems. What problems do they mention? Is it realistic to make saving the environment dependent upon solving these other problems on a global scale?

For Research and Convincing

Select one of the environmental problems discussed in paragraphs 3–8 and attempt to discover what is known about the problem. For example, what do most experts believe about the nature and seriousness of ozone depletion? What exactly is uncertain or disputed?

Arguing from "scientific fact"—that which scientists themselves take to be established knowledge—propose and defend a course of action for dealing with the environmental problem you have selected. If you think there is no need for action or no need for further action, explain why and defend your explanations.

For Persuasion

The United States is clearly one of the developed nations in which we find evidence of overconsumption. What, to your mind, constitutes overconsumption? Do you agree with the "Warning" that overconsumption results in pollution (paragraph 17)? If so, write an argument to persuade offenders to reduce their consumption. Does this mean asking them to reduce their standard of living?

H. PATRICIA HYNES

Beyond Global Housekeeping

Author of two books on the environment and Director of the Institute on Women and Technology, Patricia Hynes teaches at the Massachusetts Institute of Technology. The following article appeared in Ms. *magazine in a section headed "Ecofeminism," a term discussed in the introduction to this chapter. Following the article we include a brief essay, also by Hynes, about Ellen Swallow and Rachel Carson, whom she calls "ecofounders."*

We tend to live and think compartmentally—women's rights are one thing, the environment another. Hynes challenges such dissociations of thought and action, as well as such intellectual distinctions as separate gender-based roles and the separation of public from private life. Whether or not we accept her case for seeing environmentalism and feminism as a unified concern, her holistic view encourages us to relate issues we often divorce from one another.

"THE EARTH fighting back" is how one commentator described the acute environmental events of 1988. That year medical and human waste floated onto public beaches in North Jersey, Long Island, Connecticut, and Massachusetts. That summer a drought persisted in the Midwest agricultural belt with a severity not felt since the Dust Bowl of the 1930s. The drought coincided with a heat wave throughout much of the country. For more than a decade, climate researchers have predicted the results of a buildup of "greenhouse" gases generated largely from the burning of fossil fuels: drought in mid-continental areas; extended heat waves; more frequent and severe forest fires; flooding in India and Bangladesh; and superhurricanes. In 1988, the planet experienced all five.

But who really believes that extended heat waves and superhurricanes are the Earth fighting back? On the contrary, they are dramatic evidence that environmental protection is not working and cannot be left to government agencies and small numbers of activists. This breakdown of the vast, seemingly untouchable systems of climate and atmosphere can make us feel powerless and often hopeless about solutions. Faced with our seeming powerlessness, I contend that it is we who can and must fight back, but we must do more than mop up the waste—a public version of what most women already do in the domestic sphere. We must exact environmental justice, and ensure that the enormous global activity of women to preserve life on Earth does not reduce to global housekeeping after men—their governments and their companies—who do not know how, and *do not want to know how,* to clean up after themselves.

A profound political alchemy is that women—the people with the least formal power, the poorest and most illiterate in virtually every country—are everywhere catalysts and initiators of environmental activism. In Kenya, anatomist Wangari Maathai founded the Green Belt Movement in 1977, after observing that the desert spread when trees removed for fuel were not replaced. Using the tree to spearhead environmental protection, she has involved schoolchildren and upward of 15,000 small-scale farmers, many of them women, in planting more than 2 million trees.

In the 17th century, more than 300 Indian people led by a woman named Amitra Devi lost their lives trying to save their sacred trees by clinging to them. This is the ancient taproot of the modern Chipko movement of primarily rural women who protest the destruction of their forests and water resources through commercial forestry. The diversified forests used by women and their animals for food, fuel, and fodder are being turned into privately owned, single-species tree farms run by local men. Chipko means "to hug." Indian women have embraced trees so loggers could not cut them, placed themselves between chain saws and trees where intense logging was destroying primeval forests, and formed human chains across roads to keep out logging equipment.

In the surging Green Parties of Europe and the dozens of U.S. nonprofit 5
environmental organizations, women's membership equals and often surpasses men's. Judie Nielson of the Oregon Department of Natural Resources translated her concern about plastic debris on the Oregon coast into a 350-mile beach cleanup. On an October Saturday in 1984, more than 2,000 people participated, some driving from 75 miles inland. Nielson's project inspired beach cleanups in other states, and along the Mediterranean Sea in Egypt, France, Greece, Israel, Jordan, Spain, and Turkey.

The grass-roots antitoxics movement in the United States is symbolized in Lois Gibbs, a housewife and mother who organized her blue-collar neighborhood at Love Canal in 1978, and forced the government to evacuate 900 families. Gibbs then founded the Citizen's Clearinghouse on Hazardous Waste that now advises 6,000 citizen groups (the majority organized by women like herself) fighting to close leaking landfills and stop the siting of incinerators in their neighborhoods.

But has this enormous activity of women gone beyond global housekeeping? Or are we concentrating on household hazardous waste collection, beach cleanups, closing landfills, keeping out incinerators, and staffing voluntary recycling centers while men institutionalize environmental protection and situate themselves in well-financed and powerful organizations and lobbies? If women are so central in the movement, why is the national leadership in the U.S.—the experts quoted, the people historicized—preponderantly white males? Why, if we are so numerous, are we not setting the agendas and developing the strategies? Why, if we are already so effective, *need* we also set the agendas?

If women do not frame the problems and define the solutions, then we risk inheriting an environmental movement disconnected from and detrimental to our own liberation movement.

For example, the first serial rights of *Green Rage* (Little, Brown), by Christopher Manes of the radical environmental organization Earth First!, have been sold to *Penthouse,* a men's magazine that has featured women bound and hanging from trees. Earth First! prides itself on challenging "human" domination of nature through civil disobedience and ecoterrorism to save trees. Yet how vacant and baseless is a "green" radicalism that rages against the razing of forests, in a forum that eroticizes the bondage and torture of women, then sanitizes this degradation with "intellectual" and "political" articles printed on recycled paper.

10 In a 1987 British edition of *The Green Consumer* (Penguin), a best-selling guide to purchasing "environmentally friendly" products, authors John Elkington and Julia Hailes recommend Playboy deodorant because it does not contain ozone-depleting chlorofluorocarbons. Already accused of being little more than "green capitalism," this brand of consumer movement will advance nothing if pornographic images and sexist messages stay intact in "green" products.

The issue of increasing population and decreasing agricultural yields features critically on the global environmental agenda. If men dominate this issue, we will see population planning continue to be defined as controlling women's bodies with risk-laden chemical contraceptives instead of undoing the inequality of women in culture.

What strategies can we use to ensure that the worldwide movement of environmental justice we build is wholly and substantively just?

- Define environment in its fullest sense: the human and the natural. Saving the environment cannot be cut off from the liberation of women, just as the rain forest movement aims to save rain forests and also the culture of the rain forest people.
- Make global housekeeping, like local housekeeping and cooking, everyone's job. Otherwise we may end up with a movement that mirrors the economy of house and society: women in neighborhoods organizing to clean up hazardous waste, and men in think tanks negotiating to limit nuclear arms, ozone-depleting chemicals, and global warming.
- Challenge the roots of environmental problems by focusing on eliminating toxic materials *in* products as well as minimizing the toxic waste generated by manufacturing them.
- Demand environmental responsibility of all companies and public institutions. Every workplace can reduce and recycle materials and buy recycled products; conserve energy and water; reward employees using public transportation and car pools; minimize pesticides and toxic solutions used in maintenance; invest in environmentally responsible companies and funds, and in research for alternatives to toxic products and animal experimentation; support environmental education in local schools.

Environmental justice goes much further than environmental protection, a passive and paternalistic phrase. Justice requires that industrial nations pay back the environmental debt incurred in building their wealth by using less of nature's resources. Justice prescribes that governments stop siting hazardous waste facilities in cash-poor rural and urban neighborhoods and now in the developing world.

Justice insists that the subordination of women and nature by men is not only a hazard; it is a crime. Justice reminds us that the Earth does not belong to us; even when we "own" a piece of it, we belong to the Earth.

ECOFOUNDERS

At the turn of this century, Ellen Swallow was the first woman student at MIT and the first woman faculty. Distinguishing herself as a water chemist, an industrial chemist, a metallurgist, an expert in food and nutrition, and an engineer, she conducted water and sewage surveys that are credited with initiating modern water and waste treatment. Swallow created the first curriculum of ecology and environmental engineering, but she and her science of ecology were squeezed out of MIT in turf battles, and her laboratory was closed. Men she educated, however, were named "father" of their respective disciplines.

In the last 15 years of her life, Swallow took the idea of ecology to the only audience that listened to and received her: professional women's associations and institutions concerned with women in the domestic sphere. She renamed her science "home ecology" or "domestic science." Unwelcomed as the "Founder of Ecology," Ellen Swallow was heralded instead as the "Mother of Home Economics."

For her acclaimed 1962 book, *Silent Spring,* on the indiscriminate use of pesticides, Rachel Carson is credited with precipitating the modern environmental movement. Politicians who represented agricultural interests suggested that she concentrate on nature writing and leave running the world to them. The agrichemical industry and some government officials said she wasn't a scientist, so her science was unsound (she was a marine biologist); and that she was an animal lover, implying she preferred them to humans and so was inhumane. On the other hand, remarked one critic, "Isn't she a spinster? Why is she so concerned about genetics?"

Although Carson's work was ultimately vindicated, her papers lay uncataloged until recently in the basement of the Beinecke Library at Yale. Because of Yale's neglect, some think, this great woman's work has not grown into a "school," as has happened with men of much less stature.

Questions for Discussion

1. Hynes cites many examples of women's involvement in and leadership of grass roots movements for environmental cleanups. Would you agree that these activities parallel women's traditional housekeeping role in domestic life? What more is Hynes asking women to do? What does she say has prevented them from taking these steps?

2. In paragraphs 7 through 11, Hynes describes some problems resulting from the fact that the leadership of the environmental movement is largely male. What evidence does she offer for her assertion that the movement is "disconnected from and detrimental to" women's liberation (paragraph 8)? Assess her evidence and reasoning in paragraphs 9, 10, and 11.
3. In paragraphs 12–16 Hynes lists her strategies for achieving environmental justice. What is "environmental justice"? How would each strategy contribute to achieving this justice? Would you characterize Hynes's suggestions as radical or as mainstream, as we defined these terms in the chapter introduction?

For Research and Convincing

Find out as much as you can about the lives, professional careers, and writings of Ellen Swallow and Rachel Carson. Hynes alleges that a male-dominated power structure essentially thwarted their careers and minimized their achievements. Are her allegations true? If so, to what extent did Swallow and Carson suffer from gender discrimination? To what extent has the environmental cause been set back by sexism?

For Persuasion

If you agree with the basic point of Hyne's article, write an essay addressed to your peers encouraging them to link women's rights with environmentalism. You may borrow some ideas and information from Hynes, but be sure to design your appeals for first-year college students or to your own age group or generation.

If you disagree with Hynes, write an essay directed at classmates who agree with Hynes—or write an essay responding to Hynes herself. Conceive your essay as a contribution to the editorial page of your campus newspaper or to the letters to the editor section of *Ms.*, whichever is appropriate.

VIRGINIA I. POSTREL

The Environmental Movement: A Skeptical View

Virginia Postrel, a much-published writer, is also the editor of Reason, *a journal of public affairs. The following documented argument opposing environmental extremism appeared in* Chemtech, *a journal published by the American Chemical Society.*

Postrel's argument is directed against both radical and mainstream environmentalists. She accuses the former of inhumaneness, of a disregard for people that, at its worst, amounts to misanthropy; she accuses the latter of strangling technical innovation that could improve the environment. Her position is that common sense, economic incentives, and individual initiative, if unimpeded, will find solutions to our environmental problems without sacrificing growth and prosperity.

On Earth Day 1990, Henry Allen of the *Washington Post* published a pointed and amusing article.[1] In it, he suggested that we've created a new image of Mother Nature:

> A sort of combination of Joan Crawford in *Mildred Pierce* and Mrs. Portnoy in *Portnoy's Complaint,* a disappointed, long-suffering martyr who makes us wish, at least for her sake, that we'd never been born.
>
> She weeps. She threatens. She nags. . . . She's a kvetch who makes us feel guilty for eating Big Macs, dumping paint thinner down the cellar sink, driving to work instead of riding the bus, and riding the bus instead of riding a bicycle. Then she makes us feel even guiltier for not feeling guilty enough.
>
> "Go ahead, use that deodorant, don't even think about me, God knows I'll be gone soon enough, I won't be here to see you get skin cancer when the ozone hole lets in the ultraviolet rays. . . ."

All of us can see that Allen is on to something. There's a lot of truth in his picture of the new Mother Nature.

Where did this new Mother Nature come from? We Americans have historically been a can-do people, proud of our Yankee ingenuity. We believe in solving problems. Based on our history, you'd expect to see us tackling environmental problems the way John Todd took on sewage sludge.

Todd is an environmental biologist who became concerned about the toxic sludge that comes out of sewage plants. Through his biological research, he realized that the sludge could be cleaned up by mixing it with certain microbes. The microbes would metabolize it and produce clean water. Todd now has a pilot plant in Providence, Rhode Island, and he estimates that such a system could handle all of that city's sludge with 120 acres of reaction tanks—a modest number.

Now, if you're like me, you think this is great. Here is a bona fide environ- 5
mental problem. An ingenious man with an environmental conscience has come

along, put his ingenuity and training to work, and solved the problem. But rather than applauding Todd's solution, many of his friends in the environmental movement have stopped speaking to him. "By discovering a solution to a man-made offense," writes Gregg Easterbrook in *The New Republic,* "he takes away an argument against growth."[2]

Todd's practical environmentalism has run up against what I refer to as "green ideology." This ideology is distinct from the common desire for a cleaner world—that's why it can lead people to condemn solutions like Todd's. It is also different from the traditional doctrines of either the left or the right: It combines elements from each with a value system of its own.

Know the Theory

This green ideology underlies many of the environmentalist critiques and policy recommendations we see today. Now, I'm not suggesting that environmentalists are engaged in some sort of grand conspiracy or are governed by some lockstep system of thought. What I am suggesting is that if you want to understand a political movement, it's a good idea to read its theorists and find out who its intellectual heroes are.

Green ideology is not some fringe theory cooked up in California. Like many important ideas in American history, it is largely imported from Britain and Germany. It is, increasingly, one of the most powerful forces in our culture. We may even adopt parts of it without realizing their origins. To be informed citizens, we ought to know something about it.

First of all, a caveat. Ideologies are messy. They tend to associate disparate ideas in unexpected ways. What's more, people who share the same general ideological viewpoint rarely agree about everything. No two conservatives or liberals or libertarians or even Marxists believe exactly the same thing. And political movements are almost always riven by internal conflict (you should read some of the things the abolitionists said about each other).

The environmental movement is no different. Purist greens who distrust 10
political compromise berate Washington-based groups that lobby for legislation. The Green-Greens, who aren't leftist, attack the Red-Greens, who are. Grassroots activists criticize the "Gang of 10," the large, well-funded environmental groups.

Perhaps the biggest philosophical split is between "deep ecology" and other forms of environmentalism. Deep ecologists advocate a mystical view of the natural world as an end in itself, not made for human beings. They criticize traditional conservationism, as well as leftist "social ecology," for emphasizing the environment's value to people.

Most environmental activists—the rank and file—combine some of each outlook to create a personal viewpoint. They can do this because, deep down, the greens aren't as divided as they sometimes like to think.

Every ideology has a primary value or set of values at its core—liberty, equality, order, virtue, salvation. For greens, the core value is stasis, or "sustainability," as they put it. The ideal is of an Earth that doesn't change, that shows little or no effects of human activity. Greens take as their model of the ideal society the notion of an ecosystem that has reached an unchanging climax stage. "Limits to growth" is as much a description of how things should be as it is of how they are.

That is why there is no room in the green world for John Todd and his sewage-cleaning microbes. Todd hasn't sought to stop growth. He has found a way to live with it.

The static view has two effects on the general environmental movement: 15
First, it leads environmentalists to advocate policies that will make growth hard on people, as a way of discouraging further development. Cutting off new supplies of water, outlawing new technologies, and banning new construction to increase the cost of housing are common policies. Second, the static view leads environmentalists to misunderstand how real environmental problems can be solved.

Consider how we regulate air pollution. Americans spend some $30 billion a year just to comply with the 1977 Clean Air Act—with very little to show for it. Current policy dictates specific technologies—for example, smokestack scrubbers for coal-burning power plants. The plants can't just use cleaner coal. And cars have to have catalytic converters. If someone comes up with a cheaper or more efficient way to get the same result, the government says, "Sorry. We've picked our one true technology. You can't sell yours."

For decades economists have suggested that we take a different approach to regulating pollution. Set an overall allowable level, they say, then let companies decide how to achieve it. Let them buy and sell permits that regulate the amount of pollution they can emit: If you wanted to build a new plant, you'd have to buy some permits from somebody else who was closing their plant or reducing their pollution. The economy could grow without increasing the total amount of pollution. Companies would have to pay a price for the pollution they put out. And plant managers would have an economic incentive to adopt—or even develop from scratch—pollution-saving technologies.

Most environmentalists, however, call this a "license to pollute." Emissions trading treats pollution as a cost, a side effect to be controlled, rather than an outright evil, a sin. It allows growth. And it lets individual choice, not politics, determine exactly which technologies will be adopted to control pollution. It takes a dynamic view rather than a static one. Over time, it assumes, people will come up with better and better ways to deal with pollution. And, it assumes, we ought to encourage those innovations. (The 1990 Clean Air Act, in a departure from its predecessor's static philosophy, makes room for some emissions trading and other market-oriented programs.)

People rarely adopt a new technology because it makes life worse. But nowadays we tend to pay more attention to the dangers of pollution from new technologies. We take the old technologies' disadvantages for granted. So, for example, we forget that the automobile actually made city life cleaner.

By creating a market for petroleum-derived gasoline, the car also encour- 20
aged the production of heating oil and natural gas—much cleaner fuels than the

coal people used to use to heat homes and businesses. And, thanks to the automobile, cities no longer have to dispose of tons of horse manure every day.

FACTS VS. VALUES

A dynamic view sees the pluses of change as well as the minuses. And it appreciates how new, unforeseen technologies or social changes can allay current problems. By contrast, the environmental movement has been built on crisis.

Contrary to the doomsayers, both past and present, people have a knack for innovating their way out of "crises"—if they have both the permission and the incentive to do so. We find that people developed petroleum as whale oil became scarce, that farmers turned to drip irrigation as water prices rose, and that drivers bought fuel-efficient cars when gas prices went up.

To a large degree, however, green ideology is not about facts. It is about values, and the environmental movement is about enforcing those values through political action. Green politics, write British greens Jonathon Porritt and David Winner,[3] "demands a wholly new ethic in which violent, plundering humankind abandons its destructive ways, recognizes its dependence on Planet Earth, and starts living on a more equal footing with the rest of nature. . . . The danger lies not only in the odd maverick polluting factory, industry, or technology, but in the fundamental nature of our economic systems. It is industrialism itself—a 'super-ideology' embraced by socialist countries as well as by the capitalist West—which threatens us."

If we look around, we can see the effort to remake "violent, plundering humankind" in a number of current initiatives. Take recycling. On one level, it seems like common sense. Why waste resources? That's certainly true with aluminum, which takes huge amounts of electricity to make in the first place and very little energy to recycle. But then there's glass. Both making glass in the first place and melting it down for recycling take about the same amount of energy. The only other thing new glass takes is sand—and we have plenty of that. Unless you're worried about an imminent sand crisis, there's little reason to recycle glass. It doesn't even take up much room in landfills.

Getting people to recycle glass is a way to remind them of the evils of 25
materialism and the folly of convenience. As Jeremy Rifkin's little booklet *The Greenhouse Crisis: 101 Ways to Save the Earth*[4] advises shoppers: "Remember, if it's disposable and convenient, it probably contributes to the greenhouse effect." On a scientific level, this is ridiculous. But as a value statement it conveys a great deal. Convenient, disposable products are the creations of an affluent, innovative, industrial society that responds to consumer demands. In a static green world, we would forego incandescent lighting for fluorescent bulbs and clothes dryers for clothes lines. We would give up out-of-season fruits and vegetables, disposable diapers (of course), free-flowing shower heads, and other self-indulgent pleasures.

If green ideology is guilt transformed into politics, we might wonder why people adopt it. Partly, I think, green ideology appeals to many people's sense of frustration with modern life. Technology is too complicated, work too demanding, communication too instantaneous, information too abundant, the pace of life too fast. Stasis looks attractive, not only for nature but also for human beings.

To slow the economy and the society to the approved adagio,[5,6] the greens have some fairly straightforward prescriptions: Restrict trade to the local area. Eliminate markets where possible. End specialization. Anchor individuals in their "bioregions," local areas defined by their environmental characteristics. Shrink the population. Make life simple again, small, self-contained.

It is a vision that can be made remarkably appealing, for it plays on our desire for self-sufficiency, our longing for community, and our nostalgia for the agrarian past. We will go back to the land, back to the rhythms of seedtime and harvest, back to making our own clothes, our own furniture, our own tools. Back to barn raisings and quilting bees. Back to a life we can understand without a string of Ph.D.s.

"In living in the world by his own will and skill, the stupidest peasant or tribesman is more competent than the most intelligent workers or technicians or intellectuals in a society of specialists," writes Wendell Berry, an agrarian admired by both greens and cultural conservatives.[7] Berry is a fine writer; he chooses words carefully; he means what he says. We will go back to being peasants.

These are, of course, harsh words. And we aren't likely to wake up as subsistence farmers tomorrow. But an economy, like an ecology, is made up of intricate connections. Constantly tinkering with it—cutting off this new technology here, banning that product there—will have unintended consequences. And sometimes, one suspects, the consequences aren't all that unintended.

Take electricity. Environmentalists, of course, rule out nuclear power, re- 30
gardless of the evidence of its safety. But then they say coal-powered plants can cause acid rain and pollution, so they're out, too. Oil-fired plants release greenhouse gases (and cost a bundle, too). Hydroelectric plants are no good because they disrupt the flow of rivers.

Solar photovoltaic cells have always been the great hope of the future. But making them requires lots of nasty chemicals, so we can expect solar cells to be banned around the time they become profitable. Pretty soon, you've eliminated every conceivable source of electricity. Then your only option is to dismantle your industry and live with less: The environmentalist warning of impending shortages becomes a self-fulfilling prophecy.

And, make no mistake about it, many environmentalists have a truly radical agenda. "It is a spiritual act to try to shut down Du Pont," says Randall Hayes, director of the Rainforest Action Network.[4] From the appealing ads his group runs to solicit donations to save the rainforests, you'd never guess he had that goal in mind.

Consider the remarkably frank book, *Whatever Happened to Ecology?,* by longtime environmental activist Stephanie Mills, published last year by Sierra Club Books.[8] Mills garnered national attention in 1969, when she delivered a college commencement address entitled "The Future Is a Cruel Hoax" and declared she'd never have children. The book traces the evolution of the environmental movement and of her ideas since then. Today, she and her husband live on a farm in northern Michigan, where they pursue their bioregionalist ideal of "reinhabiting" the land by restoring some of its wildness and blocking future development. A journalist, not a theorist, Mills speaks not only for herself but for the intellectual movement of which she is a part. Her words are chilling: "We young moderns resort to elaborate means of getting physical experience. Yogic practice, fanatical running, bicycling, competitive sports, bodybuilding. All of these recreations are voluntary and may not cultivate the endurance necessary for the kind of labor required to dismantle industrial society and restore the Earth's productivity."

She continues: "One summer afternoon a few days after a freak windstorm, I made a foray out to buy some toilet paper. (Every time I have to replenish the supply of this presumed necessity, I wonder what we're going to substitute for it when the trucks stop running.)"

When the trucks stop running. There is a history of the future buried in those 35
words, fodder for several science-fiction novels—but no explanation of when and why the trucks will stop. Or who will stop them.

What Future?

People don't want to be peasants: The cities of the Third World teem with the evidence. And certainly, the typical subscriber to the *Utne Reader* (a sort of green *Reader's Digest* with a circulation of 200,000 after only six years of publication) doesn't envision a future of subsistence farming—much less the hunter-gatherer existence preferred by deep ecologists. More to the reader's taste is, no doubt, the cheery vision offered by Executive Editor Jay Walljasper:[9]

It's 2009. Nuclear weapons have been dismantled. Green publications have huge circulations. Minneapolis has 11 newspapers and its own currency ("redeemable in trout, walleye, or wild rice"). Sidewalk cafés sell croissants and yogurt. A local ordinance decrees a 24-hour workweek. Cars are nearly nonexistent (a delegation from the "People's Independent Republic of Estonia" is in town to help design better ski trails for commuters). Citizens vote electronically. The shopping mall has become a nature preserve.

Walljasper is clearly having fun—after all, he puts Aretha Franklin's face on the $10 bill—and he doesn't consider any of the tough questions. Like how all those magazines and newspapers exist without printing plants or paper mills. How the Estonians got to town without airplanes or the fuel to run them (Jeremy Rifkin specifically names the Boeing 747 as the kind of product that can't be produced in the small-is-beautiful factories of the coming "entropic age"[10]). How the chips to run the electronic voting got etched without chemicals. Where the chips were made. How a 24-hour workweek produced the sustained concentration needed to write software or the level of affluence that allows for restaurant croissants.

And, above all, Walljasper doesn't explain why after millennia of behaving otherwise, humans simply gave up wanting stuff. If the Walljasper of 2009 still overloads on reading material, why should we assume that people whose fancy runs toward fast food and polyester (or fast cars and silk) would be struck with a sudden attack of bioregionally approved tastes? How exactly did that shopping mall disappear?

"The root of the solution has to be so radical that it can scarcely be spoken 40
of," says movie director and British green John Boorman.[11] "We all have to be prepared to change the way we live and function and relate to the planet. In short, we need a transformation of the human spirit. If the human heart can be changed, then everything can be changed."

We have heard this somewhere before—in, for example, the promise of a "New Soviet Man." People are forever seeking to change the human heart, often with tragic results.

The greens want people to give up the idea that life can be better. They say "better" need not refer to material abundance, that we should just be content with less. Stasis, they say, can satisfy our "vital needs." They may indeed convince some people to pursue a life of voluntary simplicity, and that is fine and good and just the kind of thing a free society ought to allow. Stephanie Mills is welcome to her organic farm.

But most of us do not want to give up 747s, or cars,[12] or eyeglasses,[13] or private washing machines,[14] or tailored clothing,[15] or even disposable diapers. The "debased human protoplasm" that Stephanie Mills holds in contempt for their delight in "clothes, food, sporting goods, electronics, building supplies, pets, baked goods, deli food, toys, tools, hardware, geegaws, jim-jams, and knick-knacks" will not happily relinquish the benefits of modern civilization. Many ordinary human beings would like a cleaner world. They are prepared to make sacrifices—tradeoffs is a better word—to get one. But ordinary human beings will not adopt the Buddha's life without desire, much as E. F. Schumacher might have ordained it.

At its extreme, green ideology expresses itself in utter contempt for humanity. Reviewing Bill McKibben's *The End of Nature* in the *Los Angeles Times,* National Park Service research biologist David M. Graber concluded with this stunning passage:[16]

> Human happiness, and certainly human fecundity, are not as important as a wild and healthy planet. I know social scientists who remind me that people are part of nature, but it isn't true. Somewhere along the line—at about a billion years ago, maybe half that—we quit the contract and became a cancer. We have become a plague upon ourselves and upon the Earth. It is cosmically unlikely that the developed world will choose to end its orgy of fossil-energy consumption, and the Third World its suicidal consumption of landscape. Until such time as *Homo sapiens* should decide to rejoin nature, some of us can only hope for the right virus to come along."

It is hard to take such notions seriously without sounding like a bit of a 45
kook yourself. But there they are—calmly expressed in the pages of a major, mainstream, establishment newspaper by an employee of the federal government.

When it is acceptable to say such things in polite intellectual company, when feel-good environmentalists tolerate the totalitarians in their midst, when sophisticates greet the likes of Graber with indulgent nods and smiles rather than arguments and outrage, we are one step farther down another bloody road to someone's imagined Eden.

REFERENCES

1. Allen, H. *Washington Post,* April 21, 1990.
2. Easterbrook, G. *The New Republic,* April 30, 1990, p. 26.
3. Porritt, J.; Winner, D. *The Coming of the Greens,* Fontana: London, 1988.
4. Rifkin, J. *The Greenhouse Crisis: 101 Ways to Save the Earth;* The Greenhouse Crisis Foundation: Washington, D.C. 1990.
5. Schumacher, E. F. *Small Is Beautiful;* Harper & Row: New York, 1973, p. 157.
6. Rifkin, J. *Utne Reader,* Sept. 1987, p. 57.
7. Berry, W. *The Unsettling of America;* Avon: New York, 1977, p. 21.
8. Mills, S. *Whatever Happened to Ecology?* Sierra Club Books: San Francisco, 1989, p. 190.
9. Walljasper, J. *Utne Reader,* Nov./Dec. 1989, p. 142.
10. Rifkin, J. *Entropy: A New World View;* Bantam: New York, 1980, p. 216.
11. Boorman, J., quoted in Porritt and Winner, p. 266.
12. Sale, K. *Resurgence,* Jan./Feb. 1989, p. 33.
13. McIntyre, J., quoted in Mills, p. 106.
14. Bookchin, M. *The Progressive,* Aug. 1989, p. 22.
15. Schumacher, p. 57.
16. Graber, D. M. *Los Angeles Times Book Review;* Oct. 22, 1989, p. 9.

Questions for Discussion

1. Perhaps the most valuable section of this essay is "Know the Theory," paragraphs 7–20. What does Postrel say about the nature of all ideology? Paraphrase her explanation of stasis as the central value of environmentalism. Do you think Postrel is fair and accurate in her critique of environmental ideology?
2. Whenever anyone analyzes someone else's ideology, we need to ask about the ideology of the analyst. Postrel's argument is based on growth, in opposition to stasis, as a central value. What do you understand her to mean by growth? Which value is more likely to appeal to her readership? Why?
3. Postrel attempts to explain the attraction of green ideology as an appeal "to many people's sense of frustration with modern life" (paragraph 26). How does she elaborate on this explanation? Read or reread the essay by John (Fire) Lame Deer earlier in this chapter. Is frustration with modern life enough to account for the appeal of his arguments?

For Negotiation

Postrel makes an obvious but nevertheless important point near the end of her essay: Most people are not about to give up the benefits of modern living to embrace a lifestyle closer to nature. Lame Deer's values may appeal to us, but not many of us would want to live as Native Americans did before Columbus.

And yet the way all of us live clearly contributes to the degradation of our environment. Clearly we have to mediate between what we want and what the environment needs, giving up some things and reducing and modifying our reliance for other things most damaging to the environment.

Write an essay indicating exactly what you are willing to forego or restrict your use of in the interest of a better environment. Also indicate what positive action you are willing to take on behalf of the environment. Compare your essay with those of other members of the class. Attempt to negotiate your differences and arrive at a class consensus about how to be environmentally responsible.

For Research and Convincing

Look into the practice of "emissions trading," which Postrel explains in paragraphs 17–19. Write an argument making a case for or against this practice.

SNEED B. COLLARD III

The Environment: Us Versus It?

The following article appeared, just prior to the 1992 Presidential election, in The Humanist, *a journal which "presents a nontheistic, secular, and naturalistic approach to philosophy, science, and broad areas of personal and social concern." Sneed Collard is a freelance writer with a special interest in science and the environment. He argues here that our tendency to view the relationship between human beings and the environment as an adversarial one misconceives the whole issue: "We" are part of "it," and there can be no choice between a healthy economy and a healthy environment because, in the long run, we need both and both depend on each other.*

Collard is critical of industry and government. But he does see hope in the environmental awareness of some corporate executives (such as Samuel Johnson of Johnson Wax) and some political leaders (such as soon-to-be Vice President Gore). Clearly mainstream in his viewpoint, Collard believes that we can improve the environment and sustain economic growth if we are willing to make some difficult choices and work together for the benefit of all.

People or Spotted Owls?

We've all seen the choice. In election-year essays, news features, political speeches—even on bumperstickers—environmental protection is increasingly being portrayed as an "unnatural" obstacle to jobs and economic growth. As our economy struggles, Americans are more and more being pressured to support one extreme or the other. It's people versus the environment; us versus it.

This kind of thinking has reached a critical stage in many areas. In the Pacific Northwest, protection of old-growth forests and the spotted owl is billed as the doom of the logging industry. In Alaska, the opening of the Arctic National Wildlife Refuge to oil drilling is marketed as a solution to the state's economic woes. Even in California, stereotypical mecca of environmentalism, state senators are trying to undermine environmental regulations to stanch "the flight of business."

These and similar arguments, however, are misleading. Even cursory examination reveals that our nation's economic problems have grown over many years and that no quick dissolution of environmental policy will solve them. The threat to jobs in the Pacific Northwest, for example, stems from sawmill modernization, export of wood-processing to Japan, and long-term overcutting of forests. Alaska's financial problems are a result of shrinking natural resources and lack of economic diversification. California's "business flight" has roots in the state's overdependence on defense industries, the collapse of the real-estate market, and the decreasing quality of life.

Ironically, the solution to these problems is not the abandonment of environmental protection but a better, more sophisticated understanding of the environment and how we fit into it.

Environmental Protection, Natural Resources, and the Economy

Economic growth cannot persist without environmental protection. One 5
can cite facts and figures, but the truth is a matter of common sense. Take an industry—*any* industry—and ask, "What do I need for this business to prosper?" You may start with answers like money and office space and computers, but if you keep breaking it down into basics, the bottom line will be that business depends on two things: people and natural resources. Not people *or* natural resources. People *and* natural resources. Further analysis will even merge people into the natural resources category. After all, people need food, water, and air to survive; no natural resources, no people.

The connection between natural resources and environmental protection hit me on a visceral level when I visited Haiti in November 1990, just before that country's first democratic election. The poorest nation in the Western hemisphere, Haiti is populated by six million people, many of whom cannot obtain adequate food, water, and shelter.

Once a forested paradise, Haiti's mountains now resemble the exposed bones of giant dinosaurs. Trees have been cleared for firewood, lumber, and farmland, eliminating the country's main source of fuel and building materials. The destruction of forests has led to severe soil erosion and changed rainfall patterns, triggering frequent droughts. When clouds do burst, the water quickly races down treeless slopes and out to sea where it becomes unavailable for drinking, washing clothes, fish farming, and crop irrigation.

Without the basic raw materials to support life, half a million Haitians have been forced into the squalor of the capital, Port au Prince, to eke out any kind of living they can find. In one of the world's worst slums, Cité Soleil, I saw people packed into tin sheds without running water or sewers. Diarrhea-stricken children defecated in a putrid garbage dump while they picked for scraps of food. Men, unable to afford other transportation, carried enormous loads of firewood on their backs. Economic activity consisted of a desperate scramble to obtain enough food, water, and fuel to get through the day. The near-total destruction of natural resources in Haiti has occurred due to a lack of environmental protection. Haiti can no longer sustain its people and, as a result, its economy is in a shambles.

Of course, Haiti's oppressive political history is primarily responsible for today's situation; as a result, Haitians have been forced to cash in their forests and other resources for short-term survival. Tragically, in doing so, the country has forfeited its future.

The United States—A Third World Economy?

What has happened in Haiti is happening on a global scale—including in 10
the United States. Americans are also cashing in our forests, oil, air, agricultural

land, wildlife, water, and, in the long run, our very economy. Each year, immense swaths of farmland wash away or are paved over, federally mismanaged forests and rangelands are destroyed or become less fertile, and clean water and other natural resources become scarcer. And, despite growing demands for these resources, our government actually *gives* them away to a few favored clients. For example, the Bureau of Land Management allows select ranchers to graze their herds on public lands and charges only a fraction of what the grazed land is actually worth. Worse, one study found that at least 71 percent of BLM rangelands had been overgrazed, reducing their long-term viability for cattle and wildlife and removing yet another key support for our foundering economy.

Yet, despite the interdependence of natural resources and economic health, politicians and pundits nevertheless persist in attacking environmental protection. This has been particularly evident in election-year posturing by the presidential candidates. This past January, George Bush bowed to pressure from the far right and proclaimed a moratorium on all new business regulations. These included not only environmental regulations, such as those to protect workers from exposure to toxic chemicals, but regulations to safeguard children from dangerous toys, increase banks' fiscal responsibility, and ensure the adequacy of car safety belts.

Ex-independent candidate Ross Perot joined Bush in toeing an extremist line. When asked about the logging controversies in the Pacific Northwest, Perot replied, "Nobody will think about the spotted owl if they're starving, except maybe to eat him"—a clever retort but one which exposed Perot's simplistic view of environmental issues and effectively ignored the vast economic advantages to environmental protection.

Democrats generally perform better than Republicans on environmental issues, but last spring's slate of candidates revealed an astonishing dearth of environmental awareness. Of the Democrats, only Jerry Brown seemed to realize the importance of developing a sustainable economy which protects our natural resources. His proposals to improve mass transit and promote alternative energy disclosed a good overall grasp of economic and environmental issues. Unfortunately, the man who beat the rest of the field—smooth-talking Bill Clinton—has been no environmental messiah as governor of Arkansas. In that office, he caved into logging interests that are bent on clear-cutting Arkansas' national forest lands and has failed to force his state's poultry industry to stop polluting rivers. When Clinton was forced, early in the campaign, into mentioning environmental issues, he seemed to treat them on a par with welfare and social security—more of those pesky social issues.

Special Interests—The Source of the Sludge

The shortage of political environmental awareness has clear roots in business perceptions. Clearly, our current ways of doing business must change. But this change threatens a number of major industries which have thrived on the old ways of doing business. An instructive example can be found in that symbol of American capitalism, the gas-powered automobile.

15 Gasoline-powered cars were a decidedly luxurious transportation option when they were first invented—back when there were still only a couple billion people on the planet. But as mass production put them within reach of the multitudes and as the global population rose to almost five-and-a-half billion people, our reliance upon cars as a primary means of transportation has now acquired nightmare ramifications for both our economy and the environment.

Automobiles are a leading contributor to greenhouse gases, which produce global warming and are predicted to have disastrous effects on climate patterns, sea levels, and our ability to produce food. Roads for cars also take up an inordinate amount of space—space which we need for agriculture, housing, and recreation. Cars produce excessive noise and directly kill over a quarter-million people per year worldwide. To keep these motorized monsters fed, we poke holes all over the planet—polluting water and air, harming aboriginal societies, and chewing up biodiversity.

And those are just the gas-powered car's "environmental" impacts. Direct economic losses from automobile use are staggering. U. C. Davis researchers estimate that economic costs from vehicle-generated air pollution annually run between *$10 billion and $200 billion*. To keep us driving comfortably, state and federal governments directly spend about $71 billion per year in road construction and maintenance. Businesses and taxpayers spend $175 billion for additional road maintenance, police, fire, and ambulance services, and parking. Military activities to safeguard oil supplies cost another $50 billion. In Los Angeles, Houston, Chicago, and many other cities, traffic jams strangle productivity to the tune of between $124 billion and $140 billion *per year.* And if you want to figure in accident-related bills from property damage, medical expenses, court costs, and emergency services, tack on another $350 billion. All told, we're out almost a *trillion* dollars—the size of our federal budget—*every year* because of our love affair with the automobile.

Clearly, this is one affair which has got to end.

Yet, the automobile and petroleum industries are so dependent upon gas-powered transportation for profits that they stubbornly resist any attempt to redirect these industries from their current economic "highways"—even though this resistance threatens the very economy upon which they depend. Why can't they see the folly of their present course? Perhaps they do. But these industries also realize they've got a good thing going, at least in the short run. After all, *we* are the ones picking up that trillion-dollar price tag—not them. Whatever their thinking, auto and oil industries exert enormous pressure on politicians and the media to maintain the status quo. The result is that politicians such as ex-oilman George Bush devise high-profile, quick-fix solutions like regulation moratoriums instead of creating environmentally responsible, economically smart programs such as mass transit and urban planning.

Dawn of a New Business Ethic

20 Fortunately, not all businesses are as shortsighted as the auto and oil industries. *Beyond Compliance,* a recent book from the World Resources Institute, documents a refreshing shift of values among several of the world's largest corporations. Displaying what must be one of corporate America's most enlightened attitudes, Samuel Johnson, the chairman of S. C. Johnson Wax, philosophizes:

> When we set aside the obvious business benefits of being an environmentally responsible company, we are left with the simple human truth that we cannot lead lives of dignity and worth when the natural resources that sustain us are threatened or destroyed. We must act responsibly and we must act now.

Johnson Wax and many other corporations have begun ambitious programs to do more than obey current laws. In 1990, chemical giant Monsanto announced its goal of aggressively eliminating 90 percent of its toxic air emissions by 1992. Xerox pledged to reduce waste by 50 percent and "has adopted a 'cradle-to-grave' requirement for product design architectures that addresses environmental concerns throughout a product's life," according to the World Resources Institute report. Dozens of other companies have also begun extensive environmental programs.

How are these changes affecting business? Positively, in both publicity and economic terms. Savings from 3M's Pollution Prevention Pays program have amounted to over *$530 million* since 1975. In eliminating chlorofluorocarbon use, the Zytech Corporation found that it improved product quality, used fewer raw materials, and reclaimed expensive floor space. Dow, one of the country's leading producers of toxic waste, discovered that simply by fine-tuning the operation of one of its plants it saved money, reduced toxic discharges by millions of pounds, and increased efficiency.

These examples confirm that humans can have *both* a healthy environment and a vigorous economy—that, in fact, the two can go together. Moreover, these examples strongly suggest that the simple-minded gutting of environmental regulations is not the answer; almost all of the companies listed in *Beyond Compliance* cited regulations and public opinion as prime motivators in their recent environmental turns. And certainly, as our knowledge about the environment deepens, new regulations will have to be adopted.

People *and* Spotted Owls

The answer from a farsighted business standpoint is clearly not to get rid of existing regulations but to bring together businesses, government, citizens' groups, and scientists to work out what kinds of regulations will accomplish concrete results while creating the fewest costs for companies. One possible model for this kind of cooperation is the 1990 air-pollution accord, which allows companies to find their own ways to reduce air pollution as long as they get the job done.

25 Corporations also need to continue to work on their powers of long-term vision. Going back to my earlier example, auto and oil companies are in for a rough ride, but they can make it easier on themselves. By taking the initiative and working with Congress, they can ensure that they get first crack at developing and implementing new transportation and energy technologies such as high-speed trains, electric cars, and solar power. To allow their market foothold to grow, they could negotiate financial incentives and interim protection from foreign competitors. By responsibly using global resources and taking serious measures to protect the environment, businesses would not only garner public approval; they would help cement America's economic vitality far into the future.

Meanwhile, you and I have a very real opportunity to speed things along. Although neither of the presidential candidates has demonstrated a deep understanding of environmental-economic relationships, Clinton's choice of Al Gore for vice-president shows a willingness to broaden his approach. Pat Buchanan, George Will, and other Republican propagandists have tried to slur Gore as an "environmental extremist" (although, as a Comedy Central commentator recently pointed out, Buchanan's view of an environmental extremist is "anyone in favor of shade"). In fact, Gore just displays the realistic attitude toward our economic future that we so desperately need. Furthermore, the Democrats' platform includes a number of proposals which will both protect our environment *and* reinvigorate our economy. These include redirecting funds for weapons programs into renewable energy and mass transit initiatives, insisting on environmental and health provisions in free-trade agreements, and providing financial incentives for buying fuel-efficient automobiles.

This November—and in every future election—we have a real opportunity to cast a skeptical, critical eye at the simplistic, panic-promoting slogans that claim to address our environmental and economic dilemmas. Instead of voting for a manufactured extreme—either people *or* spotted owls—we can send a clear signal to politicians at all levels. We must insist on a new choice: the economy *and* a world we can live in.

Questions for Discussion

1. The course of action we take in dealing with environmental problems depends almost completely on where we place the blame for the problems. Whom does Collard blame? How does his analysis compare with that of the concerned scientists in their "Warning to Humanity" (pages 208–211)? Whom do they blame? How do the courses of action proposed by both arguments differ? Which do you find more persuasive? Why?
2. Do you think it is either necessary or desirable to reduce our dependency on automobiles and oil, as Collard so strongly recommends? Is better mass transit the answer? Is it accurate and fair to say that our love affair with cars is sustained by "special interests"?
3. "World Scientists' Warning to Humanity" claims that human civilization and the environment are on a "collision course," exactly the kind of thinking ("us"

versus "it") that Collard deplores. In your view, who is closer to the truth? Does Collard underestimate the ecological problems we face and what will be necessary to solve them?

For Research and Convincing

Collard notes almost casually that "Haiti's oppressive political history" has much to do with that country's desperate condition (paragraph 9). Do some research on Haiti, on other developing countries, and on the underlying causes of rain forest destruction. How much does past and present political oppression account for the destruction of the land? What other causes play significant roles?

Write an essay that takes a stand on the importance of political and social reform in solving the global environmental problem. Address it to an audience of concerned American citizens whose environmental approach ranges from mainstream to skeptical.

For Research and Convincing

Collard sees the automobile as one of the worst contributors to urban air pollution and to our nation's environmental problems. In contrast, Postrel claims that the automobile has made U. S. cities cleaner. Look into the facts and make a case for or against the rise of the gasoline-powered car on the American transportation scene.

GUY BADEAUX

Cartoon

The preceding selection by Sneed Collard III suggests that we do not need to choose between economic growth and environmental preservation, provided that business and industry increase their environmental awareness. The following cartoon by Guy Badeaux suggests what will happen if we continue to exploit the Earth's resources with no thought to the future.

For Discussion

Badeaux's argument is made through a visual analogy. Comment on its logic and effectiveness.

For Further Research and Discussion

1. Make a list of environmental problems, and in small groups choose one for in-depth study. Try to answer the following questions:

   How serious is the problem now?
   Is it getting better or worse?
   Who or what is to blame?
   What, if anything, is being done?
   What should be done?
   What social, political, and economic factors affect the problem or will be affected by the solution you propose?

   Each group should present to the class a summary of its findings. Then, as a class, try to formulate a comprehensive environmental policy for the United States, including what role or roles we should take in advancing global ecology.
2. Read, discuss, and assess Albert Gore's book *Earth in the Balance,* either in small groups or as a class. Answer the following questions:

   How does Gore see environmental problems as a whole?
   What depth of change in dealing with these problems does he think will be necessary?
   What measures does he propose and why?

   Based on your answer, assess Gore's approach to the environment. Is his understanding and vision adequate? Is his approach practical, likely to produce results? Can his measures be implemented? If they are, what effect will they have on us all?

Additional Suggestions for Writing

1. *Convincing and Persuasion.* After completing 1 under For Further Research and Discussion, write an essay focusing on the environmental problem your group addressed. Choose an appropriate audience and construct a case that will move your audience to see the problem as you do and that will draw their support for whatever course of action you advocate. Of course, you may defend existing policy if it seems adequate to you.
2. *Inquiry.* Many people feel that we must develop an entirely different way of relating to nature and to each other if modern civilization is to survive. "World Scientists' Warning to Humanity," for example, calls for a "new ethic." Select any three attempts to formulate such a new vision or ethic and assess the reasoning and persuasiveness of each. Conclude with a defense of your own view of how we must change and why.

CHAPTER TEN

Homelessness

Not long ago people we now call "homeless" were mostly out of sight and out of mind—segregated on "skid row." Today most Americans have had at least some first-hand experience with homeless people, sleeping on public property or asking for handouts on city streets; and for those who have not had personal encounters, the media's concentration on the homeless in recent years has made it impossible to be unaware of the problem.

Two questions go to the heart of the issue:

What should our attitude toward the homeless be?

What action or actions should be taken to solve or alleviate the problem of homelessness?

Clearly these questions are closely related, since our general stance toward homeless people governs the policies we choose to support; so the articles in this chapter focus on questions of attitude and policy. The greater challenge, however, is to understand homelessness, without which our attitudes are likely to be inappropriate and our policies ineffectual.

Understanding the problem of homelessness and its ramifications is complicated by the lack of reliable, undisputed data. For example, so basic a matter as determining the number of homeless people in the United States has not been settled: Estimates range from 300,000 to several million. These estimates vary so greatly because "homeless" may be defined in different ways, because counting such people presents obvious difficulties, because the homeless population itself is not stable, and because individual researchers may have a vested interest in making the total count appear high or low.

Even when there is general agreement about facts, interpretation varies enormously. For instance, recent research shows clearly that the older stereotype of the homeless as "bums" or "tramps" does not characterize the current population. That is, most homeless people are not single, white, male alcoholics. The majority now are blacks, many are women, and some are children. So much is clear, beyond dispute.

But how do we explain the rise in homelessness, for instance, among blacks? Is racism to blame? Or is the determining factor not race so much as poverty and a slumping economy that leaves a disproportionate number of blacks unemployed or working at jobs that do not pay a living wage? Some would say that there is a culture of homelessness, habits and values that make certain groups of people more likely to become homeless. Others say that government policy is the culprit, especially the welfare system, the lack of public housing, and local regulations governing rental property.

Thinking through the problem of homelessness is indeed a significant challenge to both our critical abilities and our value system. Bear in mind as you read the following articles that very little of significance can be said about homeless people in general. The population is as diverse as the causes of homelessness. Simple, sweeping remedies, therefore, are unlikely to convince an informed audience. Also try to think about homelessness in context—as part of the housing situation in the United States generally and as part of our continuing struggle with poverty, racism, and social instability.

L. CHRISTOPHER AWALT

Brother, Don't Spare a Dime

An example of the popular "My Turn" columns in Newsweek, *"Brother, Don't Spare a Dime" is an effective piece of persuasion. Note, for example, how Awalt appeals to our irritation with homeless people in the first paragraph, how he builds his own authority through appeal to personal experience (especially in paragraphs 3 and 8), and how he appeals to skeptics to test his conclusions in paragraph 9. Note also how his distinction between the temporarily homeless and the chronically homeless (developed in paragraphs 4, 5, and 6) helps to deflect criticism of his case.*

The essay as a whole appeals to a deeply felt set of American values. The United States is the land of opportunity. Each of us, as individuals, is responsible for what we are. Hence, if you are down and out, it is your fault. Fundamentally it is up to the individual to improve his or her situation.

HOMELESS PEOPLE are everywhere—on the street, in public buildings, on the evening news and at the corner parking lot. You can hardly step out of your house these days without meeting some haggard character who asks you for a cigarette or begs for "a little change." The homeless are not just constant symbols of wasted lives and failed social programs—they have become a danger to public safety.

What's the root of the homeless problem? Everyone seems to have a scapegoat: Advocates of the homeless blame government policy; politicians blame the legal system; the courts blame the bureaucratic infrastructure; the Democrats blame the Republicans; the Republicans, the Democrats. The public blames the economy, drugs, the "poverty cycle," and "the breakdown of society." With all this finger-pointing, the group most responsible for the homeless being the way they are receives the least blame. That group is the homeless themselves.

How can I say this? For the past two years I have worked with the homeless, volunteering at the Salvation Army and at a soup kitchen in Austin, Texas. I have led a weekly chapel service, served food, listened, counseled, given time and money, and shared in their struggles. I have seen their response to troubles, and though I'd rather report otherwise, many of them seem to have chosen the lifestyles they lead. They are unwilling to do the things necessary to overcome their circumstances. They must bear the greater part of the blame for their manifold troubles.

Let me qualify what I just said. Not everyone who finds himself out of a job and in the street is there because he wants to be. Some are victims of tragic circumstances. I met many dignified, capable people during my time working with Austin's homeless: the single father struggling to earn his high-school equivalency and to be a role model for his children; the woman who fled a good job in another city to escape an abusive husband; the well-educated young man who had his world turned upside down by divorce and a layoff. These people deserve every effort to help them back on their feet.

But they're not the real problem. They are usually off the streets and resum- 5
ing normal lives within a period of weeks or months. Even while "down on their luck," they are responsible citizens, working in the shelters and applying for jobs. They are homeless, true, but only temporarily, because they are eager to reorganize their lives.

For every person temporarily homeless, though, there are many who are chronically so. Whether because of mental illness, alcoholism, poor education, drug addiction, or simple laziness, these homeless are content to remain as they are. In many cases they choose the streets. They enjoy the freedom and consider begging a minor inconvenience. They know they can always get a job for a day or two for food, cigarettes, and alcohol. The sophisticated among them have learned to use the system for what it's worth and figure that a trip through the welfare line is less trouble than a steady job. In a society that has mastered dodging responsibility, these homeless prefer a life of no responsibility at all.

Waste of time. One person I worked with is a good example. He is an older man who has been on the streets for about 10 years. The story of his decline from respectability to alcoholism sounded believable and I wanted to help. After buying him toiletries and giving him clothes, I drove him one night to a Veterans Administration hospital, an hour and a half away, and put him into a detoxification program. I wrote him monthly to check on his progress and attempted to line up a job for him when he got out. Four months into his program, he was thinking and speaking clearly and talking about plans he wanted to make. At five months, he expressed concern over the life he was about to lead. During the sixth month, I called and was told that he had checked himself out and returned home. A month later I found him drunk again, back on the streets.

Was "society" to blame for this man? Hardly. It had provided free medical care, counseling, and honest effort. Was it the fault of the economy? No. This man never gave the economy a chance to solve his problems. The only person who can be blamed for his failure to get off the streets is the man himself. To argue otherwise is a waste of time and compassion.

Those who disagree will claim that my experience is merely anecdotal and that one case does not a policy make. Please don't take my word for it. The next time you see someone advertising that he'll work for food, take him up on it. Offer him a hard day's work for an honest wage, and see if he accepts. If he does, tell him you'll pay weekly, so that he will have to work for an entire week before he sees any money. If he still accepts, offer a permanent job, with taxes withheld and the whole shebang. If he accepts again, hire him. You'll have a fine employee and society will have one less homeless person. My guess is that you won't find many takers. The truly homeless won't stay around past the second question.

So what are the solutions? I will not pretend to give ultimate answers. But 10
whatever policy we decide upon must include some notion of self-reliance and individual responsibility. Simply giving over our parks, our airports, and our streets to those who cannot and will not take care of themselves is nothing but a

retreat from the problem and allows the public property that we designate for their "use" to fall into disarray. Education, drug, and alcohol rehabilitation, treatment for the mentally ill, and job training programs are all worthwhile projects, but without requiring some effort and accountability on the part of the homeless for whom these programs are implemented, all these efforts do is break the taxpayer. Unless the homeless are willing to help themselves, there is nothing anyone else can do. Not you. Not me. Not the government. Not anyone.

Questions for Discussion

1. Are the homeless "a danger to public safety," as Awalt claims (paragraph 1)? In what sense? To what degree? Does Awalt support this claim?
2. Is it true that the homeless themselves are blamed least for their condition? Do you blame them? What have you heard others say? How important is it to determine degree of fault for a social problem like homelessness?
3. Awalt qualifies his argument by acknowledging that there are exceptions to his position that most homeless are irresponsible (paragraphs 4 and 5). How well does he make the case that the majority are irresponsible?
4. "In a society that has mastered dodging responsibility," Awalt says, "these [chronically] homeless prefer a life of no responsibility at all" (paragraph 6). Do you think our society "dodges" responsibility? Based on other essays you read in this chapter, do you think that most homeless people are totally irresponsible?

For Research and Critique

In paragraph 10 Awalt offers no solution for the problem of homelessness but does claim that "whatever policy we decide upon must include some notion of self-reliance and individual responsibility (paragraph 10)." In short, "[u]nless the homeless are willing to help themselves, there is nothing anyone else can do." Contact some local charities and agencies that deal with the homeless. Visit shelters and talk to program directors, to people working closely with the homeless, and to homeless people themselves. How do they respond to Awalt's statements?

After class discussion of what those involved in local charities and agencies say, write an essay responding to Awalt's final paragraph.

PHOTOGRAPH

Bruce Young

News photography offers more than a visual recording of current events. The photographer's choice of subjects and manipulation of camera angles and other artistic elements allow him or her to interpret reality. In turn, readers interpret the visual image that appears in the paper. After a snowstorm hit Washington, D.C., in January of 1994, shutting down government operations, photographer Bruce Young captured this image of homeless people huddled on benches.

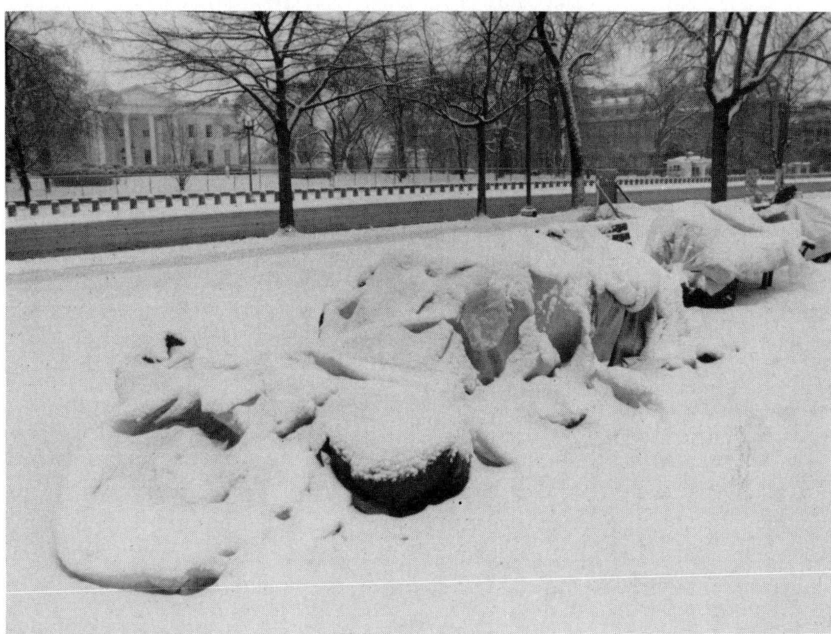

For Discussion

What elements contribute to your reading of this photograph?

PETER MARIN

Virginia's Trap

The previous argument distinguished the temporarily from the chronically homeless and reinforced a stereotypical view of homeless people by selecting an older, alcoholic male as its only extended example. In the following argument, Peter Marin calls our attention to another kind of homelessness, especially common among the urban poor: recurrent or cyclical homelessness, characterized by frequent, forced changes of residence and brief periods on the streets between periods of having a place to live. He chooses a black woman with children as his primary example, one of the "new" homeless population discussed in the chapter introduction. Further, unlike Awalt, Marin sees homelessness in several contexts—influenced by government policy, racism, the economic conditions of the poor, and the culture of the American South. You will also notice that Marin, a poet and essayist, uses narrative as a means of persuasion rather than the more openly argumentative structure of thesis and reasons.

"Virginia's Trap" appeared in Mother Jones, *a San Francisco-based magazine that describes itself as "the best of the alternative press." The "alternative press" includes publications not controlled by major media corporations and espousing more radical viewpoints than those appearing in more widely read newspapers and magazines. In the United States, the alternative press is usually leftist and often dedicated to social reform or causes like environmentalism.*

SEVERAL YEARS ago in New Orleans, I met a young African-American woman, Virginia,[1] who at the age of twenty-one was on her own in the world with two small children. She had just gotten out of a shelter after being homeless for a year, and over the coming twelve months she and her boys would become homeless several times again. Even when they had somewhere to stay, Virginia was so close to the edge, so precariously situated, that it took only the slightest mishap or misstep to send her back onto the street.

Michael Harrington once wrote that we should not talk about "poverty," but about poverties. He meant that there are so many ways of being poor that no single description or analysis can apply to them all. Virginia's situation shows that the same thing is true of homelessness. There are in actuality a variety of homelessnesses, each one different from the others in terms of causes, particulars, and solutions. Furthermore, the kind Virginia endures—a recurrent homelessness so much a part of the cycle of poverty that it becomes a predictable part of people's lives—gets much less attention than it deserves.

Too often, most of us think of homelessness as the result of a long downward slide (as with alcoholics, for example), or else of a catastrophic event—

[1]The names of the people in the story have been changed. [Author's footnote]

serious illness, mental collapse, the sudden loss of a job or a home. In both cases, it seems like a sudden and forced exile, almost a falling off the earth, something that places people beyond our ordinary social or economic orders and into another reality altogether.

But Virginia's kind of homelessness is quite prevalent around us, and very poor people learn, unfortunately, to take it almost for granted. It's a part of our society, part of the poverty that shadows many lives and carries people in and out of homelessness, from low-paying jobs to unemployment to shelters to the street to welfare to low-paying jobs and eventually, again and again, to unemployment and the street.

Race is an important factor in this kind of homelessness, and somewhere 5
between 40 and 50 percent of the homeless population (more, in large cities) is now African American. Virginia is a young single mother without job skills, prospects, or a mate, and many of the families now on our streets or on welfare are headed by women in similar circumstances. So, in a number of ways, her story is a representative one.

I first met Virginia when I was asked to speak in New Orleans at a conference of city planners and administrators concerned about the homeless issue. I asked a local advocate for the homeless to suggest a couple of people who could come to the conference and talk about their lives. One of them turned out to be Virginia, who was then in a short-term church-run program for homeless mothers and was therefore living in an apartment for three months.

One legacy of black-white relations in the South is that there is always some guardedness and masking that goes on. And though my sense of Virginia is limited by what she *let* me see, I liked her from the start. She was tall and slim with a soft face and high cheekbones and her hair cut boyishly short. There was both gentleness and directness in her manner, and a kind of shy diffidence, and she seemed to draw her voice—and her whole being, as well—inward with her breath as she spoke, so that you felt yourself leaning forward, straining to hear, even when you could make her words out clearly.

The audience at the conference liked her, too, when she described her life without self-pity or complaint. Fact followed fact; she didn't editorialize, but, as she went on speaking, becoming more sure of herself, describing what it was like in shelters or walking the streets all day with her children, the people listening were moved by her sorrowful self-possession, perhaps more than they might have been by something more shrill or consciously dramatic.

When the conference ended, Virginia and I kept in touch. Sometimes when she was in financial difficulty, she'd call and I'd wire money. I'd been well paid for my lecture, and I decided to send her whatever she needed until the fee was gone. Month after month, I followed, long-distance, the twists and turns of her fortune. Then, last summer, I went back to New Orleans to learn and write about women who were homeless or on welfare, and had a chance to see, close up, Virginia's struggle to get by.

The economic aspects of that struggle were immediately evident. Virginia's 10
welfare payments were $190 per month—that's what the state of Louisiana gives

to a woman with two children. With one child, you get $138. With three, you get $234. For every additional child, your check increases by an average of $38. Clearly, the total is never enough to lift you out of the worst kind of poverty.

Measure Virginia's payment against her expenses. When the church program ended, she stayed on in her apartment, which cost her $150 a month. Her utilities came to $100. A telephone, which was a necessity both to look for work and to keep in touch with the world, cost another $30 or so, at minimum. Food stamps provided her with food, but, even so, her basic expenses totaled $280 a month; she was $90 behind *before* spending a penny on clothing, toys, or transportation.

Of course, Virginia looked for work. But all she could find were part-time, split-shift jobs at fast-food outlets for minimum wage. Employers in New Orleans prefer such arrangements, because they keep the cost of benefits low and avoid overtime wages entirely. Say that Virginia worked twenty hours a week for $3.35 an hour. That's $60 a week in take-home pay. But she would have to pay someone to watch her kids, and when you deduct that and throw in the cost of transportation—$10 a week—there wouldn't be much left at all.

Moreover, this income would not be allowed as a supplement to welfare, because, under federal law, any money you make must be reported to the welfare office so that the same amount can be deducted from your next monthly check. That means that for every dollar you make you lose a dollar; you're left, always, in the same sorry predicament. And if you don't report your earnings—as Virginia sometimes did not—then you are, according to the law, committing fraud.

What happened to Virginia was predictable and inevitable. She fell further and further behind on her bills. First the telephone was disconnected; then her utilities were cut off. Finally she stopped paying the rent altogether and was evicted. Homeless again, she took the children to the shelter she'd been in before entering the church program. For several months, she kept looking for work but found nothing. And then she chose the only option left open to her and did what almost everyone on welfare in New Orleans ends up doing: She put her name down on the waiting list for an apartment in the city's "projects" and took the first one that became available.

There are about a dozen projects scattered throughout New Orleans— 15
huge federally funded developments that were built in the 1930s and 1940s and are now administered by the city. Official estimates put the number of people in the projects at anywhere from 40,000 to 60,000, almost all of them black and most on welfare. But homeless-advocates estimate that, when you add in illegal residents and doubled-up families, the total is even higher, perhaps as much as a quarter of the city's African-American population of 330,000.

Old picture postcards of the projects show neat lawns and tidy two- and three-story brick buildings surrounded by trees, street lamps, and wrought-iron benches. These days they're dusty, run-down wastelands, largely ignored by the city government that manages them. In some projects, a third of the apartments have been gutted and abandoned; drugs and guns abound; violence is commonplace, and at night you often hear gunfire. When Virginia lived in the projects, she kept her windows boarded up and wouldn't let her children play outside.

"Minute I'd let them out," she said, "I'd hear shootin' and they come runnin' inside. I always told them to git down low and don't be scared."

For those who live in the projects, it's the meanest kind of life. The only reason for moving in is economic, and once you're there it isn't easy to get out. Again, the numbers reveal why: Rents are geared to income, and an apartment like Virginia's, utilities included, costs $60 a month. Figure again $30 for a phone, and assume that food stamps provide food. That leaves approximately $25 a week for all other expenses—more than you'd have living outside the projects. And if you teach yourself to need little and expect nothing, you can last there forever, though impoverished and in constant danger.

But Virginia didn't last. She missed a couple of welfare appointments and her checks stopped arriving. She fell behind in her rent and was evicted again. Homeless once more, she went to stay with an older woman friend, whose one-bedroom apartment was paid for by a lover. Virginia and her boys slept on a fold-out couch in the living room and got all of their meals, in return for which Virginia signed over her now-restored welfare checks to her friend. She was, she told me later, a virtual prisoner. But even that didn't last. The boyfriend grew tired of her presence, and her friend told her to leave.

When Virginia was growing up in New Orleans—to hear her and others tell it—the city was more prosperous, neighborly, orderly, and livable than it is now. The black neighborhoods were thriving, whites had not yet fled the city for the suburbs, and inexpensive housing and decent jobs were easier to come by.

Virginia had three sisters and two brothers, a mother who took good care 20
of them, and a father who drank a bit too much but worked steadily on the docks as a foreman. He had managed to buy a small house, and their life was stable and ordinary. But when Virginia was seven, her mother died. Her father's drinking increased. Her two older sisters and a brother moved out, and at eleven she was left in the house with a younger brother and sister. "My daddy was gone all the time," she says. "We was in the house by ourselfs many a night. Sometimes he came home and sometimes not. We never knew where he was, 'cause he didn' want us knowin' his business."

Then, Virginia's father was shot and wounded in a bar by a jealous woman. He lost his job on the docks, and the house was sold at auction. Virginia and the other two children moved in with an older sister, who sent Virginia to a Catholic day school. Their father disappeared on the streets of the city, and Virginia's oldest brother became her surrogate father—until he was shot five times and killed in a barroom brawl.

Virginia managed to graduate from high school, but in her senior year she fell in love with a boy and was soon pregnant. She had the baby, stayed on with her sister, met another man, and got pregnant again. Neither of the men could take care of her or wanted to marry her. Both went off, but Virginia showed no anger when talking about them: "I don't bear them no grudge in my mind."

Of the first one, she said, "He tried. He wanted to be a man. But he couldn't find no job or nothin'. He got discouraged and got hisself in trouble. I think he was misled to wrongness."

Of the second, "He never had no chance. He grew up in the projects not carin' about things. That was his lifestyle. Now he got another baby by a woman younger than me."

When I asked about birth control, she said, "See, when you're just startin' 25
out, you don't know what you do now. I was only nineteen and a good girl and my sister—she kept that stuff quiet."

When Virginia had her second child, her sister told her she couldn't take care of her anymore, it cost too much, there was too little space. So Virginia went to a Salvation Army shelter and, after several months, into the church program she was in when I met her.

There's nothing unusual in this story—at least not in terms of what I heard in New Orleans. Most of the stories I heard had many of the same elements as Virginia's: early or adolescent pregnancies, men drifting in and out, little preparation for work or the world, little family support, and, perhaps most importantly, personal tragedies that had destroyed an orderly world or deprived people of the sustenance they needed.

For instance, there was Lobelia, a thirty-five-year-old woman in the projects who had had eight children by six different men. She was tough and outwardly cheerful, and had been twice hooked on drugs but was clean when I met her and trying hard to replace crack with Christ. She had a twenty-inch scar on her thigh from a recent fight with a neighbor over a man, and she wouldn't, she told me, let any male visitor into the house unless he brought whiskey, food, or money. "I ain't no whore," she said.

I didn't quite know what to make of her until she told me one day that her father, whose favorite she was, died when she was thirteen. "I went so wild with grief," she said, "there wasn't no controlling me. My mama had the doctor declare me crazy and they put me away for a year." When she got out, she immediately started having sex and children, and soon her mother would have nothing to do with her. So she went from one relative to the next until, homeless and on welfare, she moved to the projects.

Mixed in with economic troubles, there are always these other difficulties— 30
sorrows of the heart and grievances of the soul—that isolate men and women and take away their ability to maintain order in their lives. Is that a surprise? In perhaps the best book ever written about the near-homeless poor, *People of the Abyss,* Jack London[1] speculated that, in a competitive and individualized economic system, those who fail soonest are those without the energy and will, as well as the means, to survive. What I'm suggesting here is that those at the bottom are neither the weakest nor the worst but often those with the least sense of human connectedness or the strongest sense of betrayal: the wounded, the abandoned, the excluded, the abused—all those who cannot on their own and without the help of others discover how to fit into the world or even a reason for trying. I remember once asking Virginia what she most wanted in the world, expecting her to say

[1]Jack London (1876–1916) was a celebrated journalist and novelist.

something about safety or money or a job or a man. Instead she said, in a voice so soft I had to bend to hear, "I want my momma to be livin'."

There's something else worthy of attention in Virginia's story, particularly because you hear it so often from women in trouble. All of the women I spoke with in New Orleans have been forced to care for their children without help from men, and almost all have had two or sometimes three sets of children by different men, all of them outside of marriage. Most women had their first children in their middle or late teens, often with men they say they loved. Birth control isn't much talked about or used; abortion hasn't much appeal; and since most of the men involved are without money, jobs, skills, or prospects, going on welfare is, for most of these women, the only possible choice. And since family aid goes only to households without men, welfare regulations have destroyed or nullified the cultural sanctions that keep men and women together.

Once on welfare, women are almost like hostages: bored and isolated from the larger world, with little hope of changing their lives. They become stationary targets for disenfranchised men for whom sex is an anodyne and a consolation and a way of proving one's worth or simply that one *exists.* Out of boredom and the human need for attention and pleasure, more children are born. In the South, especially among poor, black people, children are valued in a way that makes abortion virtually unthinkable.

I talked to a woman who was in her late twenties, Tanya, a second-generation project dweller. She had had three children by two different men friends and was still nursing one of them. Now she was pregnant again. The father was a man she hardly knew and didn't like; she had slept with him while drunk and without precautions, believing, falsely, that she couldn't conceive as long as she kept suckling her infant. "It wasn't quite rape," she said. "But it was, almost. I just lay there, not ready, not caring, feeling nothing. But I didn't bother to say no." Still, she could not bring herself to have an abortion. She had intended to get one, but, after her doctor let her listen to the fetal heartbeat with a stethoscope, she "couldn't do nothing. It was like my own heart I heard." She sat there, musing, and asked me: "Would someone like you like me if I had an abortion? Do you think God would like me?"

It's easy to see the children as echoes of the large families from which these beleaguered women come, and they provide at least some sense of connection to the past and to a larger world, some sense of purpose, and someone to love, in lives that might otherwise be too empty and crimped to bear.

Tanya's two older children—a boy of ten, a girl of eight—told me that 35
between them they had two "daddies" and considered one of Tanya's long-term boyfriends a third. They felt that all of their daddies' other children by other women were their brothers and sisters—eight in all, they said, toting it up on their fingers. And the mothers of those children were in many cases surrogate aunts, and the children of those women by still *other* men were, they thought, their cousins, all part of a network extending outward or expanding by the collapse and formation of sexual relationships and the birth of new babies.

It is true, of course, that, within this network, relationships are not always determined by biology. Tanya's son, for instance, told me he felt closer to his sister's natural father than to his own. They went fishing and spent part of the summer together. The sister, in turn, spent much of her time with her brother's daddy's new girlfriend, whom she was, she said, growing to love.

When I asked the kids if they would rather have had one permanent father there all the time, they wistfully nodded yes. But nonetheless, these families *work*. They aren't just a breakdown of "normal" family life, but a variation—a system of kinship and connection, which acts as a buffer against loneliness and isolation, creating a meaningful, social world. Viewed one way, they seem evidence of a culture in decline or trouble; but in another sense, they are continuing and extending a culture, keeping it alive.

Among the critical elements at work in lives like Virginia's and Tanya's are culture and racism. I link them together because they are not easily separated in the South. Everywhere, you see poor black men and women clinging to certain aspects of traditional black culture: large families, language, music. But because these people are surrounded by a still-racist society, you cannot tell precisely what they would leave or keep if they were free to choose. In general, the overriding sense in the projects is of people caught between the remnants of African-American traditions and the demands of the "mainstream" American order that they're expected to join in order to survive. The problems of "assimilation," of mediating between a cultural past and an economic future, seem as painful for many African Americans as they do for Native Americans.

For decades now, African-American intellectuals have argued that entry into mainstream American life, whether voluntary or forced, has involved terrible losses for black people in terms of culture, community, and identity. Though nobody in the projects articulated that problem to me in precise terms, it was nonetheless at work wherever I looked. Yet even in the midst of despair and individual tragedy, many of the traditions of black culture have remained sufficiently intact to exert a hold on people and partially sustain them. There's a whole world alive in the projects about which outsiders understand very little. Though this world cannot be entered, you can sense and hear it from a distance, from the outside. It's there in the dialogue, a patois so private that when spoken fast it sounds like a foreign language. It's there in the music, in the systems of kinship, in the perceptions of time and space, in the assignment of values, in the attitudes toward pleasure, work, leisure, family, and friendship. It's there in the still-astonishing capacity for generosity, sweetness, and sacrifice; in the tenacity in the face of suffering; in the passion for relationships rather than competition; and in a system of meaning that somehow raises life itself—its complexities, joys, and griefs—to a crowning position unchallenged by personal success or material accumulation.

This is the surviving culture of the rural South that I'm trying to describe. 40
Obviously, it is a culture in disarray, and many cling to it because they have little choice. But if others hold tight to it, willingly, is that so surprising? Look around. There's something so joyless and pained about the individualized sink-or-swim

economy we expect people to enter, something so empty of community and vitality—it is not difficult to understand why some are reluctant to enter it, or to trade away the little they have for the little it offers in return.

All of this is part of Virginia's story, in the background of the more obvious issues of wages and rents. At the point last summer when I was visiting her, Virginia was on the verge of returning to the streets. She was about to leave her friend's apartment, with absolutely nowhere to go.

Had I not been there, she might have become homeless again. But she had one welfare check in hand and asked me for a loan of $200. With the total, she said, she'd be able to move into an apartment of her own. I tried to tell her that, even if she got a place, she'd be unable to keep up the rent payments and would be out on the street in two months and we both would have wasted our money. "I don't care," she said. "I ain't going back to the shelter. And I got a feeling this time that somethin' good is gonna happen."

One Sunday, with newspaper in hand, we went hunting for apartments. Virginia wanted to get as far away from the projects as possible, so we drove out to an area on the city's edge. Over the last three decades, developers had moved into what had been rural territory to build apartment complexes for an anticipated invasion of baby boomers, which never materialized. The rents are low and there are still open spaces and stands of trees and, at twilight, a whole host of country smells, though it is only twenty minutes by bus—"a straight shot," in Virginia's words—to downtown New Orleans.

We only had to look at two places before Virginia found what she wanted: a rather dingy one-bedroom apartment in a colonial-style complex with a dirty pool, a laundry room, and both black and white tenants. The ad in the paper mentioned something about moving in for $199, but Virginia talked to the manager alone, and when she emerged she had handed over all of her money—$400—for the first month's rent plus what he had mysteriously told her were "one-time unrefundable charges."

The apartment was on the first floor, out on the edge of the complex, 45
where all the black tenants lived. The living room had a glass door, which slid open to a swampy common that had once been a lawn. The whole place smelled of the mildew and mold growing on the wall a couple of feet above the damp shag carpet. But Virginia loved it. It was the nicest place she'd lived in, she said, "since my daddy's house." The manager, who had overcharged her, took a liking to her, and dragged out of storage an old box spring and two torn high-backed velvet chairs and a lopsided table. Said Virginia, "It's my own, my first real home."

And then, to my surprise, and right before I left New Orleans, something good *did* happen. Virginia had a friend who worked at a downtown hotel, and for more than a year had called the hotel every few weeks to see if a job was available. Three days after she moved into the apartment, she called again and they told her that someone had quit and that, if she came in to be interviewed, they would put her to work.

Within a week, she had a steady job and had found someone to watch her kids free of charge. It was a good job, as such jobs go. The hotel was old and locally owned and the owners treated their employees in a familial way. The pay was close to five dollars an hour, and there were scheduled raises and a health plan and below-cost hot lunches in the cafeteria. It was clear, Virginia told me, that, if you did your work and showed up on time and didn't mess up, you could stay there a lifetime. "You're gonna have to show me," she said excitedly, "how to open a bank account and *save.* I never done it before."

But there was a hitch. The hours and pay weren't steady. In the winter, when the hotel was full, you might work seven hours a day, six days a week—forty-two hours in all. But in the summer, when the flow of tourists slowed, you might work only three or four days a week, and five or six hours a day.

During the busy season, Virginia could clear $175 a week for rent, food, clothing, toys, etc.—enough to get by and perhaps save a bit. But during the off-season, her take-home pay would be lower than her expenses. She could get some food stamps, as long as she reapplied for them every time her income dipped. But what about other expenses? She'd no doubt fall behind, just as before; then the phone would be cut off, the lights would go, there would be a monthly struggle to come up with the rent—and, sooner or later, she'd be homeless again.

I can't help worrying that that's exactly what has happened to Virginia. 50
When I talked to her several months ago, work had slowed and she was having terrible problems. And recently, I tried to track her down but failed. The phone at her apartment had been disconnected. At the hotel, they told me that Virginia didn't work there anymore, and they didn't know where she'd gone.

Questions for Discussion

1. Marin works hard to generate sympathy for "Virginia" and, through her, for others in similar plights. How exactly does he do so? Are his tactics effective as persuasion—that is, are you persuaded that Virginia is trapped in her cycle of poverty and hopelessness? Why, or why not?
2. The focus of Marin's article is not government policy; nevertheless, in several places government policy is clearly under attack (for example, paragraphs 13, 16, and 32). Assuming that the article depicts Virginia's situation and actions accurately, what changes in policy would you suggest that might do more to help people in similar conditions?
3. How do you evaluate the "extended family" arrangements described and explained in paragraphs 32–37? Do you agree with Marin that the relationships "aren't just a breakdown of 'normal' family life"?
4. In paragraphs 39–40 Marin attempts to give readers some sense of the "surviving culture of the rural South." Do some reading or consult with campus experts about current African-American culture in the South and elsewhere. What role would you say culture plays in producing "Virginia's trap"?
5. Marin uses the narrative of Virginia's life to illustrate the homeless problem as he sees it. Where does Marin interrupt the story to offer analysis? How do you evaluate this organizational strategy?

6. How does Marin's style—word choice, imagery, sentence patterns—contribute to the persuasiveness of his essay?

For Convincing or Persuading

Peter Marin claims that people such as Virginia cling to their culture—despite its obvious disadvantages—because "there's something so joyless and pained about the individualized sink-or-swim economy we expect people to enter, something so empty of community and vitality" (paragraph 40). Do you agree that we have an "individualized sink-or-swim economy"? Obviously, you must cope with our economic system somehow, but are you *attracted* to its demands, responsibilities, and rewards, or do you feel that American capitalism destroys "community and vitality"?

Drawing on Marin's essay, your own experience, and class discussion, write an essay that responds to his statement.

JAMES D. WRIGHT

Address Unknown: Homelessness in Contemporary America

The first two essays in this chapter offer highly personal and deeply felt views of the homeless. James Wright's stance in the following essay is far cooler, more detached, the voice of an expert assessing a complex problem—as one would expect from a Tulane University professor of human relations writing for the social science journal Society. *In the course of his research, Wright has probably encountered more homeless people than either Awalt and Marin; but, unlike them, he does not mention individuals or create case histories to support his points. If Wright's argument lacks the passion and concreteness of the first two, it has other strengths characteristic of good academic writing: command of the available data coupled with an awareness and acknowledgment of what is not known; analytical precision; carefully worded conclusions with strong supporting evidence; and a "big picture" view of the whole problem.*

At first this article may seem more informative than argumentative. But Wright is not merely presenting data; he is interpreting and drawing conclusions. Blocked out by subheadings, each section in fact argues a specific thesis. For instance, Wright's introduction doesn't simply tell us about stereotypes; rather, it argues that none of the stereotypes fit all homeless people. The essay as a whole is not neutral, but committed—as sympathetic toward the homeless as Marin's, if less critical of capitalism and more practical in assessing what must be done and the political resistance to accomplishing these goals.

THE PAST decade has witnessed the growth of a disturbing and largely unexpected new problem in American cities: the rise of what has been called the "new homeless." Homeless derelicts, broken-down alcoholics, and skid row bums have existed in most times and places throughout our history. But the seemingly sudden appearance of homeless young men, women, children, and whole families on the streets and in the shelters was, in retrospect, a clear signal that something had gone very seriously wrong.

The sudden intensity and new visibility of the homelessness problem took most observers by surprise. Ten or fifteen years ago, a walk along the twenty-odd blocks from Madison Square Garden to Greenwich Village would have been largely uneventful, a pleasant outing in an interesting part of New York City. The same walk today brings one across an assortment of derelict and indigent people—old women rummaging in the trash for bottles and cans, young kids swilling cheap wine from paper bags, seedy men ranting meaninglessly at all who venture near. Who are these people? Where did they come from? What, if anything, can or should be done to help?

Many stereotypes about the homeless have sprung up in the last decade. One of the most popular is that they are all crazy people who have been let loose from mental hospitals. A variation is that they are all broken-down old drunks. One writer has described them as the "drunk, the addicted, and the just plain shiftless"; the implication is that most of the homeless could do better for themselves if they really wanted to. Still another view is that they are welfare leeches, living off the dole. A particularly popular view that sprang up during the Reagan years was that most of the homeless are, as Reagan put it, "well, we might say, homeless by choice," people who have chosen to give up on the rat race of modern society and to live unfettered by bills, taxes, mortgage payments, and related worries. In truth, all of these stereotypes are true of some homeless people, and none of them are true of all homeless people. As with any other large group in the American population, the homeless are a diverse, heterogeneous lot. No single catch phrase or easy myth can possibly describe them all.

As in times past, most homeless people in America today are men, but a sizable fraction are women and a smaller but still significant fraction are the children of homeless adults. All told, the women and children add up to between one-third and two-fifths of the homeless population. Indifference to the plight of homeless adult men comes easily in an illiberal era, but indifference to the plight of homeless women and children, groups society has traditionally obligated itself to protect, comes easily only to the coldhearted.

Likewise, alcohol abuse and homelessness are tightly linked in the popular 5
stereotype, but recent studies confirm that less than 40 percent of the homeless population abuses alcohol to excess; the majority, the remaining 60 percent, do not. Focusing just on the adult men, the studies show that alcohol abuse still runs only to about 50 percent: About half the men are chronic alcoholics, but then, the other half are not.

In like fashion, mental illness is certainly a significant problem within the homeless population, but severe chronic psychiatric disorder characterizes only about a third; the remaining two-thirds are not mentally ill, at least not according to any meaningful clinical standard.

Being among the poorest of the poor, it is also true that many homeless people receive governmental assistance in the form of general assistance (welfare), food stamps, disability pensions, and the like. Yet, nationwide, the studies show that only about half the homeless receive any form of social welfare assistance; the remaining half survive on their own devices, without government aid of any sort.

And so: Some of the homeless *are* broken-down alcoholics, but most are not. Some *are* mentally impaired, but most are not. Some *are* living off the benefit programs made available through the social welfare system, but most are not. Clearly, the popular mythologies do not provide an adequate portrait of the homeless in America today.

On Definitions and Numbers

Defining homelessness for either research or operational purposes has proven to be a rather sticky business. It is easy to agree on the extremes of a definition: An old man who sleeps under a bridge down by the river and has nowhere else to go would obviously be considered homeless in any conceivable definition of the term. But there are also many ambiguous cases. What of persons who live in rooming houses or flophouses? Even if they have lived in the same room for years, we might still want to consider them homeless in at least some senses of the term. What of persons who live in abandoned buildings? In tents or shacks made from scrap materials? In cars and vans? What of a divorced woman with children who can no longer afford rent on the apartment and who has an offer from her family "to live with us for as long as you need"? What of people who would be homeless except that they have temporarily secured shelter in the homes of their families or friends? Or those that would be homeless except that they are temporarily "housed" in jails, prisons, hospitals, or other institutions? What of the person on a fixed income who rents a cheap hotel room three weeks a month and lives on the streets or in the shelters for the fourth week because the pension is adequate to cover only three-quarters of the monthly room rent?

Clearly, to be homeless is to lack regular and customary access to a conven- 10
tional dwelling unit. The ambiguities arise in trying to define "regular and customary access" and "conventional dwelling unit."

These examples demonstrate that *homelessness is not and cannot be a precisely defined condition*. A family who sleeps in its pickup truck and has nowhere else to go would be considered homeless by almost everyone. A long-distance trucker who sleeps regularly—perhaps three or four nights a week—in the cab of his $100,000 rig, who earns $30,000 or $40,000 a year, and who has a nice home where he sleeps when he is not on the road, would not be considered "homeless" by anyone. Our long-distance trucker has options; our homeless family living in its pickup does not.

Thus, choice is implied in any definition of homelessness. In general, people who choose to live the way they do are not to be considered homeless, however inadequate their housing may appear to be, while those who live in objectively inadequate housing—in makeshift quarters or cheap flophouses or in the shelters and missions—because they do not have the resources to do otherwise *would* be considered homeless in most definitions, clearly in mine.

"The resources to do otherwise" implies yet another aspect of my definition of homelessness: that true homelessness results from extreme poverty. One hears from time to time of "street people" who are found to have a locker in the bus station stuffed with cash, or of vagabonds who, in a former life, traded stock on Wall Street but cashed in for the unfettered romance of life on the road. In some sense, these people are "homeless," but they are homeless by choice. Ronald Reagan notwithstanding, they comprise no important part of the homeless problem in this nation and I shall say nothing further about them.

Poor people living in objectively inadequate housing because they lack the means to do otherwise number in the tens of millions. Indeed, if we adopt a sufficiently inclusive definition of "objectively inadequate housing," we would capture virtually the entire poverty population of the country, some 35 million people, within the homeless category. And yet, surely, being homeless is more than just being poor, although, just as surely, being poor has a lot to do with it.

My colleagues and I have therefore found it useful to distinguish between 15
the *literally homeless* and the *marginally housed*. By "literally homeless" I mean those who, on a given night, have nowhere to go—no rented room, no friend's apartment, no flophouse—people who sleep out on the streets or who *would* sleep out on the streets except that they avail themselves of beds in shelters, missions, and other facilities set up to provide space for otherwise homeless people. And by "marginally housed" I mean those who have a more or less reasonable claim to more or less stable housing of more or less minimal adequacy, being closer to the "less" than the "more" on one or all criteria. This distinction certainly does not solve the definitional problem, but it does specify more clearly the subgroups of interest.

This discussion should be adequate to confirm that there is no single, best, correct, easily agreed upon definition of "homelessness," and thus, no single correct answer to the question: "How many homeless people are there?" There is, rather, a continuum of housing adequacy or housing stability, with actual cases to be found everywhere along the continuum. Just where in the continuum one draws the line, defining those above as adequately if marginally housed and those below as homeless, is of necessity a somewhat arbitrary and therefore disputable decision.

Nonetheless, despite the unavoidable arbitrariness, the discussion calls attention to three pertinent groups: (1) the poverty population as a whole, (2) the subset of the poverty population that is marginally housed, and (3) the subset of the poverty population that is literally homeless. It is useful to get some feel for the relative sizes of these three groups.

I focus in this brief discussion on the city of Chicago. According to U.S. government statistics and definitions, the poverty population of the city of Chicago amounts to about 600,000 persons. Of these, approximately 100,000 are poor enough to qualify for General Assistance under the rather strict Illinois guidelines. A recent study of General Assistance recipients in Chicago found that fully half resided with relatives and friends—that is, were not literally homeless (mainly because of the largess of their social networks) but who were at high risk of literal homelessness in the face of the merest misfortune. Certainly, we shall not be too far off if we let this group, some 50,000 persons, represent the "marginally housed."

The most recent, systematic, and sophisticated attempt to tally the literally homeless population of Chicago reports about 3,000 literally homeless persons on any given night. Taking these numbers at face value, the ratio of poor persons to marginally housed persons to literally homeless persons, at least in one large American city, is on the order of 600 to 50 to 3.

It is transparent that homelessness is only a small part, indeed, a very small 20
part, of the larger poverty problem in the nation. Most poor people, even most of the very poor, manage to avoid literal homelessness and secure for themselves some sort of reasonably stable housing. Just how they manage to do this given

recent trends in the housing economy is an important question that is yet to be successfully answered.

Also, the number of literally homeless at any one time is much lower than the number of potentially homeless (or marginally housed) people. The evidence from Chicago suggests a pool of 50,000 persons who might easily become homeless on any given day; the actual pool at risk is no doubt even larger. Even with a literally homeless count of 3,000, Chicago is hard-pressed to come up with sufficient shelter space. The point is that however bad the homelessness problem has become, it could easily be worse by one or two orders of magnitude. The *potential* homelessness problem in contemporary America, in short, is many times worse than the *actual* problem being confronted today.

It is also worth stressing that the number of literally homeless *on any given night* is not a true indication of the magnitude of the problem since that number is by definition smaller than the number of homeless *in any given month* or over the span of *any given year.* To illustrate, in the Chicago census of the literally homeless, 31 percent were found to have been homeless less than two months, whereas 25 percent had been homeless for more than two years. Homelessness, that is, is a heterogeneous mixture of transitory short-term and chronic long-term housing problems. Some people became homeless only to reclaim a stable housing arrangement in a matter of days, weeks, or months; some became homeless and remain homeless for the rest of their lives.

The transitory or situational component adds even more ambiguity to the numbers question. The estimate in Chicago, to illustrate, is that the number ever homeless in the span of a year exceeds the number homeless on any given night approximately by a factor of three. A recent study by the Rand Corporation in California gives similar results. Three separate counties were included in that study; the estimated ratios of annual to nighttime homeless in the three counties were about 2 to 1, 3 to 1, and 4 to 1.

Nevertheless, it is still important to have some sense of the approximate dimensions of the homeless problem in America today. Unfortunately, there is no national study that provides this information. However, Martha Burt has published results from a national probability sample of shelter and soup kitchen users suggesting that roughly 200,000 homeless adults used shelters and soup kitchens in the large U.S. cities in a typical week in March, 1987. To provide a *complete* estimate of the "single point in time" number of homeless, one would need to add to this figure all homeless children (who comprise perhaps a tenth of the total), all homeless adults who did not use shelters or soup kitchens during the week in question (an unknown number), and all homeless persons living outside cities with populations of 100,000 or more (also an unknown number). These additions, I think, would bring the final estimate somewhere respectably close to the "best guess" figure given later.

I have reviewed the results from a number of studies done in single cities, 25
discarding those that I felt were obviously deficient and giving the greatest weight to those that I felt had been the most scientifically respectable. Based on these studies and the usual simplifying assumptions, my conclusion is that the total

literally homeless population of the nation on any given night numbers in the hundreds of thousands, although probably not in the millions. As a rule of thumb, we can speak of a half million homeless people in America at any one time. And if the ratio of one-night to annual homelessness estimated for the city of Chicago (about 3 to 1) is generally true, then the *annual* homeless population of the nation is on the order of one-and-a-half millions.

"Reasoned guesses" by advocacy groups invariably posit much larger numbers than these. None of the studies that go into my estimates could be considered definitive, and so it is certainly possible that the true numbers are very much larger than the numbers I have cited. Most of the researchers whose results I have summarized above, however, began their studies expecting to find many more homeless people than they actually found, and almost all of them would have been more satisfied with their results had they done so. In any case, I am aware of no compelling *evidence* that implies numbers of literally homeless people substantially larger than those I have cited.

Worthy and Unworthy Homeless

What have we learned in the research of the past decade about these half-million or so Americans who are homeless on any given night? We have learned, first of all, that they are a very diverse group of unfortunates: men and women, adults and children, young and old, black and white. We have also learned that relatively few of them are chronically homeless. Indeed, only a quarter to a third would be considered chronically or permanently homeless. The majority are *episodically* homeless; that is, they become homeless now and again, with the episodes of literal homelessness punctuated by periods of more or less stable housing situations. And of course, many homeless people on any given night are recently homeless for the first time, so that no pattern is yet established.

Let me digress briefly to a personal reminiscence. A few years ago, I was having dinner with my mother. In the course of our conversation, the subject of my research on the homeless came up, and my mother asked me, "Who are these homeless people anyway?" I began to respond with my standard litany—the average age, the proportion white, the proportion of women, and such—when I was stopped short. "That is not what I want to know," Mother said. "What I want to know is, how many of these people should I really feel sorry for and how many are just bums who could do better for themselves if they tried?" This abrupt question got directly to the heart of the matter.

At the time of this conversation, I was engaged in the national evaluation of the Health Care for the Homeless (HCH) program, a demonstration project that had established clinics to provide health care for the homeless in nineteen large U.S. cities. At the time, we had data on nearly thirty thousand people who had received health care services through this program, and so I tried to tease an answer to my mother's question from these data.

I began with the homeless families, the lone homeless women, and the 30
homeless adolescents already out on their own, figuring that anybody, even

Mother, would find it easy to sympathize with these people. It took her aback to learn that about 15 percent of the HCH clients were children or adolescents aged nineteen or less, and that an additional 23 percent were adult women; the women and children, that is, added up to three-eights of the total. She allowed as how all of these were to be counted among the "deserving homeless." And so I then turned to the lone adult men.

Among the remaining five-eighths of the clients who are adult men, some 3 percent are elderly persons over sixty-five. Being close to sixty-five herself, Mother had no difficulty in adding these to the "deserving" group. Of the remaining non-elderly adult men—and we were now down to about 56 or 57 percent of the client base—fully a third turn out to be veterans of the U.S. armed services. Mother served in the Navy in World War II and found this to be a shocking figure; she just *assumed* that the Veteran's Administration took care of the people who had served their country. And so these too went into the pile of "deserving homeless."

Without the veterans, the elderly, the homeless families, the women, and the children, we were only left with about three-eighths of the client base. Among this three-eighths, I pointed out, fully a third are disabled by psychiatric impairments ranging from the moderate to the profound, and among those without disabling psychiatric impairments, more than a tenth are *physically* disabled and incapable of work. Mother readily agreed that the disabled, either physically or mentally, also deserved our compassion; and we were thus left with fewer than a quarter of the original client base, 22 percent to be precise.

I then pointed out that among this 22 percent—the nonelderly, nonveteran, nondisabled lone adult men—more than half had some sort of job—full-time employment in a few cases, part-time or sporadic employment in most cases, but in all cases jobs whose earnings were not adequate to sustain a stable housing situation. And of those not currently employed, more than half were in fact looking for work. Thus, of the 22 percent of clients remaining at this point, more than 80 percent either had work or were at least looking for work, and Mother, living in a section of Indiana that has been hard hit by the economic developments of the last decade, found it within herself to be sympathetic to these men as well.

We were then left with what she and I both agreed were the "undeserving" or "unworthy" homeless—not members of homeless families, not women or children or youth, not elderly, not veterans, not mentally or physically disabled, not currently working, and not looking for work. My mother's attitude about homelessness in America was altered dramatically when she realized that this group comprised less than 5 percent of the total, barely one homeless person in twenty.

Is Homelessness a "New" Problem?

I began this article by referring to "the growth of a disturbing and largely 35
unexpected new problem." But it is worth asking whether this is a new problem, and whether this is a growing problem.

Strictly speaking, homelessness is definitely *not* a "new problem," in that homeless people have always existed in American society (and, for that matter, in most other societies as well). In the recent past, the homeless were seen to consist mainly of "hobos" (transient men who "rode the rails" and whose style of life was frequently romanticized in the pulp novels of an earlier era) and "skid row bums" (older, usually white, men whose capacity for independent existence had been compromised by the ravages of chronic alcoholism.) Scholarly interest in skid row spawned a large academic literature on the topic, but the homeless received no sustained policy attention; they and their problems were largely invisible to social-policy makers and to the American public at large.

Rather surprisingly, even during the War on Poverty of the middle 1960s, little or nothing was written about the *homeless* poor, although one must assume they existed even then. The most influential book ever written about poverty is probably Michael Harrington's *The Other America,* published initially in 1962. Despite several readings of that fine, sensitive volume, I am unable to find a single word about the homeless poor. Many of the processes that I think have contributed directly to today's homelessness problem, particularly the displacement of the poor to make way for urban renewal and the revitalization of downtown, are taken up by Harrington in considerable detail, but the apparent implication, that some of the displaced would become *permanently* displaced, and therefore *homeless,* goes unstated.

Recent historical research on homelessness confirms that the problem dates back at least to the colonial era, when there were sufficient numbers of "wandering poor" at least to raise popular alarms and enact legal measures to deal with them. In Massachusetts, the chosen mechanism was the process of "warning out." Names of transients, along with information on their former residences, were presented to the colonial courts. Upon judicial review, the person or family could then be "warned out" (that is, told to leave town). Some of the more populous towns actually hired persons to go door-to-door seeking out strangers.

These methods were to the end of controlling the relief rolls; up until 1739, a person was eligible for poor relief in Massachusetts if he or she had not been warned out within the first three months of residency. The modern-day equivalent has come to be known as "Greyhound therapy," whereby transients and derelicts are given a bus ticket that will take them and their problems elsewhere. Transients could also be "bound out," in essence, indentured to families needing laborers or servants: a colonial-era version, perhaps, of what we call "workfare."[1] These methods were used to control homelessness in Massachusetts until they were ended by law in 1794.

As in the present day, the wandering poor of colonial times were largely 40
single men and women, although two-parent families were surprisingly common (comprising between 28 and 68 percent of those warned out across the towns and years covered in these studies). Also as in the present day, the wandering poor

[1]In contrast to welfare, workfare requires that recipients of public assistance work on public projects (such as trash clean-ups) in exchange for aid.

were drawn from the bottom of the social hierarchy: the men were artisans, mariners, or laborers, and the women were domestic servants for the most part. Except for the overseas immigrants (mostly Irish), they came from towns within a ten-mile radius. Interestingly, there were as many women as men among those warned out. Similar findings appear in several historical studies of indigent and homeless populations throughout the nineteenth and early-twentieth centuries.

The Great Depression marked the last great wave of homelessness in this country. Peter Rossi has pointed out that in 1933, the Federal Emergency Relief Administration housed something like 125,000 people in its transient camps around the country. Another survey of the time, also cited by Rossi, estimated that the homeless population of 765 select cities and towns was on the order of 200,000, with estimates for the entire nation ranging upward to perhaps one-and-a-half million (much as the estimates of today). Most of the homeless of the depression were younger men and women moving from place to place in search of jobs.

The outbreak of World War II in essence ended the depression and created immense employment opportunities for men and women alike, an economic boom that continued throughout the post-war decades, certainly well into the middle of the 1960s, and that caused the virtual extinction of homelessness. Certainly, residual pockets of homelessness remained in the skid row areas, but the residents of skid row came less and less to be the economically down-and-out and more and more to be debilitated alcoholic males. Based on the urban renewal efforts of the 1960s and the obvious aging of the residual skid row population, the impending demise of skid row was widely and confidently predicted.

The postwar real growth in personal income ended in 1966, as the Vietnam war heated up. Between the war-related inflation and decay of living standards, the 1973 Arab oil embargo, and other related developments in the world economy, the country entered an economic slump that was to last until 1980. During this period, double-digit inflation *and* double-digit unemployment were not uncommon, and the national poverty rate, which had been steadily declining, began, just as steadily, to climb back up. By 1983, the poverty level was the highest recorded in any year since 1966, and while the rate has dipped back down again slightly since 1983, it is still very much higher than anything witnessed in the 1970s. And thus, by the late 1970s and certainly by the early 1980s, homelessness—the most extreme manifestation of poverty—reappeared as a problem on the national scene.

Homelessness, in short, is not a new problem in the larger historical sweep of things, but the current rash of homelessness certainly exceeds anything witnessed in this country in the last half-century. More to the point, the last major outbreak occurred as a consequence of the worst economic crisis in American history; the current situation exists in the midst of national prosperity literally unparalleled in the entire history of the world.

Not only did homelessness make a "comeback" in the early 1980s, but the character of homelessness also changed; this is another sense in which today's problem could be described as "new." In 1985, my colleagues and I had occasion to review medical records of men seen in a health clinic at the New York City Men's Shelter, in the very heart of the Bowery, for the period 1969–1984. Among the men seen in the early years of this period (1969–1972), almost half (49 percent) were white, 49 percent were documented alcohol or drug abusers, and the average age was forty-four. Among men seen at the end of the period (1981–1984), only 15 percent were white, only 28 percent were documented alcohol or drug abusers, and the average age was thirty-six. Thus, during the 1970s and early 1980s, the homeless population changed from largely white, older, and alcohol-abusive, into a population dominated by younger, non-substance-abusive, nonwhite men. Between the Great Depression and the 1980s, the road to homelessness was paved with alcohol abuse; today, quite clearly, many alternative routes have been opened.

In *Without Shelter* Peter Rossi presents a detailed comparison of results from studies of the homeless done in the 1950s and early 1960s with those undertaken in the 1980s, thus contrasting the "old" homeless and the "new." The first point of contrast is that the homeless of today suffer a more severe form of housing deprivation than did the homeless of twenty or thirty years past. Bogue's 1958 study in Chicago found only about a hundred homeless men sleeping, literally, out on the streets, out of a total homeless population estimated at twelve thousand. Rossi's 1986 survey found nearly fourteen hundred homeless persons sleeping out of doors in a total population estimated at about three thousand. Nearly all of the old homeless somehow found nightly shelter indoors (usually in flophouses and cubicle hotels, most of which have disappeared), unlike the new homeless, sizable fractions of whom sleep in the streets.

A second major difference is the presence of sizable numbers of women among today's homeless. Bogue's estimate in 1958 was that women comprised no more than 3 percent of the city's skid row population; in the middle 1980s, one homeless person in four is a woman. A third important contrast concerns the age distribution, the elderly having disappeared almost entirely from the ranks of the new homeless. Studies of the 1950s and 1960s routinely reported the average age of homeless persons to be somewhere in the middle fifties. Today, it is in the middle thirties.

Rossi points out two further differences: the substantially more straitened economic circumstances and the changing racial and ethnic composition of the new homeless. In 1958, Bogue estimated the average annual income of Chicago's homeless to be $1,058; Rossi's estimate for 1986 is $1,198. Converted to constant dollars, the average income of today's homeless is barely a third of the income of the homeless in 1958. Thus, the new homeless suffer a much more profound degree of economic destitution, often surviving on 40 percent or less of a poverty-level income.

Finally, the old homeless were mostly white—70 percent in Bahr and Caplow's well-known study of the Bowery, 82 percent in Bogue's study of Chicago. Among the new homeless, racial and ethnic minorities are heavily overrepresented.

We speak, then, of the "new face of homelessness" and of the "new homeless" to signify the very dramatic transformation of the nature of the homeless population that has occurred in the past decade. 50

Is Homelessness a Growing Problem?

Granted that the character of homelessness has changed, what evidence is there that the magnitude of the problem has in fact been increasing? Certainly, the amount of attention being devoted to the topic has grown, but what of the problem itself?

Since, as I have already stressed, we do not know very precisely just how many homeless people there are in America today, it is very difficult to say whether that number is higher, lower, or the same as the number of homeless five or ten or twenty years ago. The case that homelessness is in fact a growing problem is therefore largely inferential. The pertinent evidence has been reviewed in some detail by the U.S. General Accounting Office (GAO). Rather than cover the same ground here, let me simply quote GAO's conclusions:

> In summary, no one knows how many homeless people there are in America because of the many difficulties [in] locating and counting them. As a result, there is considerable disagreement over the size of the homeless population. However, there is agreement in the studies we reviewed and among shelter providers, researchers, and agency officials we interviewed that the homeless population is growing. Current estimates of annual increases in the growth of homelessness vary between 10 and 38 percent.

The most recent evidence on the upward trend in homelessness in the 1980s has been reviewed by economists Richard Freeman and Brian Hall. Between 1983 and 1985, they report, the shelter population of New York City increased by 28 percent, and that of Boston by 20 percent. Early in 1986, the U.S. Conference of Mayors released a study of twenty-five major U.S. cities, concluding that in twenty-two of the twenty-five, homelessness had indeed increased. There has also been a parallel increase in the numbers seeking food from soup kitchens, food banks, and the like. Thus, while all indicators are indirect and inferential, none suggest that the size of the homeless population is stable or declining; to the contrary, all suggest that the problem is growing rapidly.

How Did It Come to Be?

To ask how it came to be is to ask of the causes of homelessness, a topic about which everyone seems to have some opinion. *My* opinion is that many of the most commonly cited and much-discussed "causes" of contemporary homelessness are, in fact, not very important after all.

Chief among these not-very-important factors is the ongoing movement to deinstitutionalize the mentally ill. I do not mean to make light of the very 55 serious mental health problems faced by many homeless people, but it is simply wrong to suggest that most, or even many, people are homeless because they have recently been released from a mental hospital.

What is sometimes overlooked in discussions of homelessness and deinstitutionalization is that we began deinstitutionalizing the mentally ill in the 1950s. The movement accelerated in the 1960s, owing largely to some favorable court orders concerning less-restrictive treatments. By the late 1970s, most of the people destined ever to be "deinstitutionalized" already had been. So as a direct contributing factor to the rise of homelessness in the 1980s, deinstitutionalization cannot be that important.

Many also seem to think that the rise of homelessness in the 1980s was the direct responsibility of Ronald Reagan, particularly the result of the many cutbacks that Reagan engineered in human-services spending. This, like the deinstitutionalization theme, is at best a half-truth. Certainly, the Reagan years were not kind or gentle to the nation's poor, destitute, and homeless. A particular problem has been the federal government's absolute bail-out from its commitment to the subsidized construction of low-income housing units, a point that I will return to shortly. But at the same time, many of the factors that have worked to increase or exacerbate the problem of homelessness in the 1980s are rooted in the larger workings of the political economy, not in specific political decisions made by the Reagan administration.

What, then, *has* been the cause of this growing problem? Like most other social problems, homelessness has many complex causes that are sometimes difficult to disentangle. We can begin to get a handle on the complexity, however, by stating an obvious although often overlooked point: Homeless people are people without housing, and thus, the *ultimate* cause of the problem is an insufficient supply of housing suitable to the needs of homeless people. Although this means, principally, an inadequate supply of low-income housing suitable to single individuals, the housing problem cuts even more deeply.

In twelve large U.S. cities, between the late 1970s and the early 1980s, the number of low-income housing units dropped from 1.6 million units to 1.1 million units, a decline of about 30 percent. Many of these "lost" units have been taken from the single room occupancy hotels or flophouse hotels and rooming houses, those that have always served as the "housing of last resort" for the socially and economically marginal segments of the urban poverty population. Many likewise have been lost through arson or abandonment. And many have disappeared as low-income housing only to reappear as housing for the affluent upper-middle class, in a process that has come to be known as gentrification.

Saying that the homeless lack housing, however, is like saying that the poor 60
lack money: the point is a correct one, even a valuable one, but it is by no means the whole story. A second critical factor has been the recent increase in the poverty rate and the growing size of the "population at risk" for homelessness, the urban poor. In the same twelve cities mentioned above, over the same time frame, the poverty population increased from about 2.5 million poor people to 3.4 million, an increase of 36 percent. Dividing poor people into low-income

units, these twelve cities averaged 1.6 poor people per unit in the late 1970s, and 3.1 poor people per unit in the early 1980s. In a five-year span, in short, the low-income housing "squeeze" tightened by a factor of two. Less low-income housing for more low-income persons necessarily predestines a rise in the numbers without housing, as indeed we have dramatically witnessed in the early years of the decade.

My argument is that these large scale housing and economic trends have conspired to create a housing "game" that increasingly large numbers are destined to lose. Who, specifically, will in fact lose at the housing game is a separate question, and on this point, attention turns to various personal characteristics of the homeless population that cause them to compete poorly in this game. Their extreme poverty, social disaffiliation, and high levels of personal disability are, of course, the principal problems. Thus, it is not entirely *wrong* to say that people are homeless because they are alcoholic or mentally ill or socially estranged—just as it is not entirely wrong to blame "bad luck" for losing at cards. Given a game that some are destined to lose, it is appropriate to ask who the losers turn out to be. But it is wrong, I think, to mistake an analysis of the losers for an analysis of the game itself.

Another important factor that is often overlooked in discussions of the homeless is the seemingly endless deterioration of the purchasing power of welfare and related benefits. Converted to constant dollars, the value of welfare, aid to families with dependent children (AFDC), and most other social benefit payments today is about half that of twenty years ago. Twenty years ago, or so it would seem, these payments were at least adequate to maintain persons and families in stable housing situations, even in the face of the loss of other income. Today, clearly, they are not. To cite one recent example, the state of Massachusetts has one of the more generous AFDC programs of any state in the country, and yet the state has been ordered by the courts twice in the past few years to increase AFDC payments. Why? The court compared the average AFDC payment in the state to the average cost of rental housing in the Boston area and concluded that the payment levels, although already generous by national standards, could only be contributing to the homelessness problem among AFDC recipients.

What we witness in the rise of the new homeless is a new form of class conflict—a conflict over housing in the urban areas between that class in the population whose income is adequate to cover its housing costs, and that class whose income is not. In the past, this conflict was held largely in check by the aversion of the middle class to downtown living and by the federal government's commitment to subsidized housing for the poor. As the cities are made more attractive to the middle class, as revitalization and gentrification lure the urban tax base back to the central cities, and as the federal commitment to subsidized housing fades, the intensity of this conflict grows—and with it, the roster of casualties, the urban homeless.

No problem that is ultimately rooted in the large-scale workings of the political economy can be solved easily or cheaply, and this problem is no exception. Based on my analysis, the solution has two essential steps: The federal government must massively intervene in the private housing market, to halt the loss of additional low-income units and to underwrite the construction of many more; and the benefits paid to the welfare-dependent population—AFDC, General Assistance, Veterans Administration income benefits, Social Security, and so on—must approximately double.

Either of the above will easily add a few tens of billions to the annual federal expenditure, and, thus, neither is the least bit likely to happen in the current political environment, where lowering the federal deficit and reducing federal spending are seen as a Doxology of Political Faith, widely subscribed to by politicians of all ideological persuasions. Thus, in the short run, which is probably to say for the rest of this century, the focus will be on amelioration, not on solutions. We will do what we can to improve the lives of homeless people—more and better temporary shelters, more adequate nutrition, better and more accessible health care, and so on. In the process, we will make the lives of many homeless people more comfortable, perhaps, but we will not rid ourselves of this national disgrace. 65

READINGS SUGGESTED BY THE AUTHOR

Rossi, Peter, et al. "The Urban Homeless: Estimating Composition and Size." *Science* 235:4794 (1987).

Rossi, Peter H. *Without Shelter: Homelessness in the 1980s.* New York: Priority Press Publications, 1989.

Rossi, Peter, and James Wright. "The Determinants of Homelessness." *Health Affairs* 6:1 (1987).

U.S. GAO. *Homelessness: A Complex Problem and the Federal Response.* Washington: General Accounting Office, 1985.

Wright, James. "The Worthy and Unworthy Homeless." *Society* 25:5 (1988).

Questions for Discussion

1. In paragraph 15, Wright attempts to distinguish the "literally homeless" from the "marginally housed." Is his distinction clear? Why, or why not? How, for example, would you classify "Virginia," described in the previous article by Peter Marin? If we agree that we have an obligation to help the literally homeless, does society at the same time have an obligation to assist the marginally housed? Why, or why not?
2. How does the distinction between the literally homeless and the marginally housed enable Wright to give readers a sense of the "big picture"? In what other ways has Wright improved your understanding of the homeless problem by placing it in larger contexts?
3. Study carefully paragraphs 28–34, where Wright argues that the "unworthy" homeless constitute "barely one homeless person in twenty." Why does the author use his mother as a measure of how we ought to feel about the homeless? Are you as sympathetic toward each group as she was? Why, or why not?

4. According to Wright, what exactly is "new" about the "new homeless" (paragraphs 44–50)? How does Wright explain these changes in the makeup of the homeless population? Do his explanations seem adequate to you? Would Peter Marin agree with Wright about the causes of homelessness? (Look, especially, at paragraphs 61–63 in Wright's essay for comparison with Marin's analysis.)
5. In paragraph 61, Wright says "it is wrong, I think, to mistake an analysis of the losers for an analysis of the game itself." Does this analogy seem appropriate and persuasive to you? Does Wright's solution address the problems of the "game"? How?

For Exploratory Writing

Although for different reasons, all three authors we have read so far are quite pessimistic about finding a solution to homelessness. Write an essay comparing and contrasting their reasons for pessimism. Which do you find convincing, and why? Do you agree with Wright that, for the near future, "the focus will be on amelioration, not on solutions" (paragraph 65)?

HOMELESSNESS AND RENT CONTROL REGULATION

The honest difference of opinion expressed in the following two articles presents the sort of challenge we face in thinking about any issue of public debate. William Tucker argues that local government regulation of housing—especially rent control—causes homelessness. John Atlas and Peter Dreier, on the other hand, view rent control as a consumer protection policy and contend that it prevents greedy landlords from taking advantage of housing shortages by overcharging tenants. Both arguments are informed and reasonably well-written and thus have roughly the same potential to convince open-minded readers. As concerned citizens with no special expertise regarding the relation of homelessness to rent controls, how are we to decide who is right, or more nearly right?

There are various strategies we use to avoid the challenge of confronting such honest differences of opinion. One is to shrug and say, "Who knows? If the experts disagree, how can I know what to think?" Another is to reduce conflicting viewpoints to simple political motives—to say, for example, as Atlas and Dreier say of Tucker, that his argument only rationalizes conservative economic policies—an attitude which results in cynicism, in dismissing arguments rather than grappling with them. A third response is equally cynical but more opportunistic: We may adopt the argument that supports our own point of view and ignore the other.

Although each of these responses is understandable, the best response is a critique of the sort discussed in Chapter 5 on argument as inquiry: Examine what both authors say, and apply the questions for inquiry to both sides. In short, resolve to avoid any easy way out and rather listen to and critique both sides before deciding which seems most right to you. When you take time to think things through, you can at least claim to have earned your conclusions.

Note that Atlas and Dreier are actually responding to an earlier version of Tucker's basic argument. In the article by Tucker presented here, he has refined his argument from a case against rent control to a case against certain housing regulations in general. This later essay provides a good example of how a writer's case can improve as it responds to opposing voices.

WILLIAM TUCKER

How Housing Regulations Cause Homelessness

THE PROBLEM of homelessness in the 1980s has puzzled liberals and conservatives alike. Both have tended to fit the problem into their preconceived views, without looking at what is new and different about the phenomenon.

For liberals, the issue has been fairly straightforward. Homelessness, they say, stems from a lack of government effort and compassion. Reacting almost reflexively, liberals have blamed homelessness on federal spending cuts and the heartlessness of the Reagan administration. The most commonly cited figure is that budget authorizations for the Department of Housing and Urban Development (HUD) were cut 75 percent in the Reagan years, from $32 billion in 1981 to $8 billion in 1988. Everything else is presumably self-explanatory. This compelling logic has even been repeated in the *Wall Street Journal*.

Conservatives, on the other hand, have taken two approaches. Either they deny the problem's existence or they assert that homelessness is almost always the result of personal pathologies. On the first count, it has often been argued (as in Martin Morse Wooster's June 1987 *Reason* article, "The Homeless: An Adman's Dream") that homelessness is really no worse than it ever was, but that the problem has been exaggerated to justify increases in government spending. On the other, conservatives have also argued that most of the homeless are insane, alcoholics, or drug addicts, and that their personal failings make it impossible for them to find housing, even when it is available.

UNPERSUASIVE EXPLANATIONS

But these arguments, whether liberal or conservative, do not really hold up under close scrutiny.

5 The most obviously flawed explanation lies in the figures that seem to indicate a massive federal cutback in housing assistance. There has been no such cutback. Federal low-income housing assistance actually *increased* from $5.7 billion in 1980 to $13.8 billion in 1988. The number of households receiving low-income housing assistance also rose, going from 3.1 million to 4.2 million during the same period.

The commonly cited "cutback" from $32 billion to $8 billion is the figure for HUD's future authorizations. This figure has nothing to do with actual housing assistance, however, since it only indicates the amount of money that Congress authorized HUD to spend in the future. These authorizations often run forty years in advance—and much of the money is never spent anyway.

The reason for this cutback has been the changeover from a program centered around public-housing construction to one centered around housing vouchers.

When Congress authorizes a unit of new public housing, it must include all future mortgage payments, running decades ahead. In authorizing a housing voucher, Congress pledges money for only five years—the lifetime of the voucher.

In addition, vouchers provide the same housing at only half the price. A unit of public housing costs the federal government $8,000 a year, while a voucher costs only $4,000. Thus, twice as many people can be reached with the same amount of money. This is why HUD has been able to extend housing aid to more low-income people without an equivalent increase in spending.

But if the liberal argument about "spending cuts" is based largely on a misunderstanding of the budgetary process, the conservative argument that homelessness has not really increased at all seems equally ill-founded.

10 There were indeed homeless people long before 1980, and their numbers have always been difficult to count. But it is hard to ignore the almost unanimous reports from shelter providers (many of them old-line conservative church groups) that the problem has been getting steadily worse since 1980. The anecdotal evidence is also abundant. Anyone who has walked the streets of New York or Washington over the last decade knows that there are more beggars sitting on the sidewalks and sleeping on park benches than there were ten years ago.

Although many of the homeless are obviously alcoholics, drug addicts, and people who are clinically insane, large numbers appear only to be down on their luck. The most widely accepted statistical breakdown was first proposed in a 1988 Urban Institute paper: "Feeding the Homeless: Does the Prepared Meals Provision Help?" According to authors Martha Burt and Barbara Cohen, one-third of the homeless can be categorized as released mental patients, one-third as alcoholics and drug abusers, and one-third as people who are homeless for purely economic reasons.

Thus the component of homeless people who are not affected by personal pathologies is large. It should also be noted that being a chronic alcoholic or drug addict does not condemn a person to living in the streets. Even "winos" or "stumblebums" were able to find minimal housing in the past.

And so paradoxes remain. How can we have such a large homeless population at a time when rental vacancy rates are near post-war highs? How can there be plenty of housing but not enough "affordable housing"? In short, how can there be scarcity in the housing market when so much housing is still available?

Variations among Housing Markets

These paradoxes can be resolved when we recognize that the housing market is not a national market but is instead the sum of many regional and local markets. Rental vacancy rates probably serve as the best measure of the availability of affordable housing, since most poor people rent. These rates vary widely from city to city. During the 1980s, rental vacancy rates in Dallas and Houston were rarely below 12 percent—a figure that is about twice what is considered a normal vacancy rate. At the same time, housing has been absurdly scarce in other cities.

New York has not had vacancy rates over 3 percent since 1972. San Francisco had normal vacancy rates during the 1970s, but they plunged to 2 percent during the 1980s, where they remain today.

15 Since the poor tend to be limited in their mobility, vacancy rates significantly affect their ability to find housing. Although southern and southwestern cities claim to receive a regular seasonal migration of homeless people during the winter months, there is little evidence that people are moving from city to city to find housing. Other factors, like work opportunities, proximity to family members, and sheer inertia, seem to dominate people's choice of locale.

What should be far more mobile is the capital that builds housing and has created such a superabundance in specific cities. If it is difficult to find tenants for new apartments in Dallas and Phoenix, why don't builders shift to Boston or San Francisco, where housing is desperately needed?

Once we start asking this question, the impediments in the housing market suddenly become visible. It is obviously not equally easy to build housing in all cities. In particular, the local regulatory climate has a tremendous impact on the housing supply. Dallas and Houston are free-wheeling, market-oriented cities with little or no zoning regulation and negligible antigrowth sentiment. They have been able to keep abreast of housing demand even as their populations grew rapidly. Boston and San Francisco, on the other hand, have highly regulated housing markets. Both are surrounded by tight rings of exclusionary suburbs, where zoning and growth-control sentiment make new construction extremely difficult. In addition, both have adopted rent control as a way of "solving" local housing shortages. As a result, both have extremely high housing prices and extremely tight rental markets. The median home price in each approaches $200,000, while in Dallas and Phoenix the median price is below the national median of $88,000.

Thus it makes little sense to talk about a national housing market's effect on homelessness. Local markets vary widely, and municipal regulation seems to be the deciding factor.

This is what has misled both liberals and conservatives. Conservatives look at the national superabundance of housing and conclude that local problems do not exist. Liberals look at local shortages and conclude that there is a national housing problem. In fact, housing shortages are a local problem created by local regulation, which is the work of local municipal governments.

20 It is not surprising, then, to find that homelessness varies widely from city to city, with local housing policies once again the decisive factor. These conclusions are supported by research that I conducted in 1988: I calculated comparative rates of per-capita homelessness for various cities, using the homelessness figures for the largest thirty-five cities investigated in the 1984 *Report to the Secretary of Housing and Urban Development on the Homeless and Emergency Shelters.* I also added fifteen other large cities that were not included in the initial HUD survey. I then subjected the comparative rates of homelessness to regression analysis, in order to look for possible associations with other factors.

Among the independent variables that I considered were the local unemployment rate, the poverty rate, city size, the availability of public housing, the median rent, annual mean temperature, annual rainfall, the size of the minority population, population growth over the past fifteen years, the rental vacancy rate, the presence or absence of rent control, and the median home price in the metropolitan area surrounding each city.

Of all these variables, only four showed a significant correlation: the median home price, the rental vacancy rate, the presence of rent control, and the size of the minority population. The first three formed an overlapping cluster, with the median home price being the strongest predictor (accounting for around 42 percent of the variation, with a chance of error of less than .001 percent). The size of the minority population added about another 10 percent. The total predictive value for both factors was 51 percent, with a margin of error below .00001 percent.

When combined on a single graph, the figures for the forty cities for which all of the relevant data are available show a strong trendline for median home prices; the cities with rent control are predominantly clustered in the top right-hand quadrant. Of the four major cities with minority populations of more than 60 percent, the two with rent control (Newark and Washington) are right on the trendline, while the two without it (Miami and Detroit) are the sole "outliers"—cities whose rates of homelessness do not seem to correspond with their positions in correlation with median home prices.

Altogether, these data suggest that housing variables are a better indicator of homelessness than are the traditional measures of unemployment, poverty, and the relative size of a city's public housing stock. High median home prices are usually found in cities with strict zoning ordinances and a strong no-growth effort. Cities with a tight ring of exclusionary suburbs (such as Boston, New York, Washington, San Francisco, and Los Angeles) have high home prices. Strangely enough, most have also adopted rent control.

At the same time, rent control is closely correlated with low rental vacancy 25
rates. Every city in the country with rent control (except Los Angeles) has a vacancy rate below 4 percent, while the average for cities without rent control is over 8 percent.

When viewed historically, these low vacancy rates are obviously the result of rent control rather than its cause. When most of these cities adopted rent control in the 1970s, all had vacancy rates around the norm of 6 percent. Rather than being spurred by low vacancies, the rent-control ordinances that swept the East and West Coasts during the 1970s were advertised as a response to inflation. The housing shortages came later. (New York, on the other hand, has had rent control since 1943, when it was imposed as part of World War II price controls. Vacancy rates stood at 10 percent in 1940, but have never been above 5 percent since the war ended; they have been below 3 percent since the late 1960s.)

Given these facts, the most plausible explanation of the relation of homelessness to high median home prices, low rental vacancies, and the presence of rent control seems to be what might be called "intense housing regulation." Many

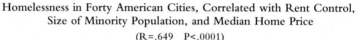

Homelessness in Forty American Cities, Correlated with Rent Control, Size of Minority Population, and Median Home Price
(R=.649 P<.0001)

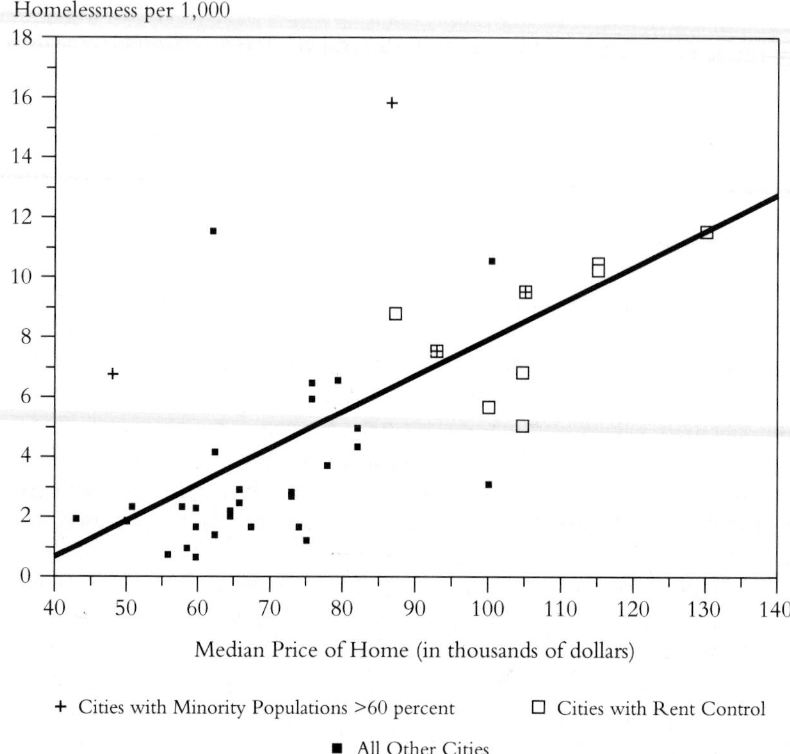

cities, such as San Francisco, Berkeley, and Santa Monica, have adopted rent control as part of municipal efforts to slow growth and stop development. These efforts are often aimed against new housing construction, particularly of apartments and rentals.

Since most communities that adopt no-growth ordinances usually like to think of themselves as liberal-minded, they do not like to admit to limiting housing opportunities for low-income people. So they try to compensate by imposing rent control, which they claim "protects" tenants from rising rents.

But of course rent control makes things only worse, by causing vacancy rates to decline and apartments to become much harder to find. The words of Assa Lindbeck, the Swedish socialist (and now chairman of the Nobel Prize Committee for Economics) can hardly be improved upon:

> The effects of rent control have in fact been exactly what can be predicted from the simplest type of supply-and-demand analysis—"housing shortage" (excess demand for housing), black markets, privileges for those who happen to have a contract for a rent-controlled apartment, nepotism in

the distribution of the available apartments, difficulties in getting apartments for families with children, and, in many places, deterioration of the housing stock. In fact, next to bombing, rent control seems in many cases to be the most efficient technique so far known for destroying cities.

Attacks on Growth and SRO's

30 Perhaps the best place to see this syndrome at work is in the San Francisco area, which has some of the country's most intense and innovative housing regulation and is also generally considered to be the center of some of the nation's worst homelessness.

It may be hard to believe, but housing prices in California in 1970 were no higher than the national average—even though the state experienced astonishing population growth during the 1950s and 1960s. It was not until the wave of environmental regulation and no-growth sentiment emerged in the 1970s that housing prices began to climb. Throughout California, the increase in home prices has consistently outpaced the national average over the last two decades. By 1988, the median price for a home stood at $158,000 there, in contrast to the nationwide figure of $88,000. In the highly regulated San Francisco Bay area, the median was $178,000, more than twice the national median.

California also experienced a wave of rent-control ordinances in the 1970s. Berkeley adopted rent control in 1971, shortly after imposing a "neighborhood preservation ordinance" that all but prohibited new development. The ordinance was eventually overturned in the California courts in 1975. Then in 1978, Howard Jarvis made an ill-fated promise that Proposition 13 would lower rents by reducing property taxes.[1] When rent reductions failed to materialize, angry tenants in more than a dozen cities retaliated by adopting rent control.

As a result, housing in highly regulated metropolitan regions around San Francisco, San Jose, and Los Angeles has become very scarce. At the same time, homelessness has become a pronounced problem. Santa Monica, which imposed rent control in 1979 as part of an intense antidevelopment campaign, has become the homelessness capital of the West Coast.

Once growth control, tight zoning, and rent control are in place, even middle-class people may have trouble finding housing. A municipality in effect becomes a closed community, open only to its current residents (who either experience remarkable run-ups in the value of their homes or live at rents far below market) and people with strong inside connections. Mark Kann's 1986 book *Middle Class Radicalism in Santa Monica,* which generally praised the city's housing policies, speaks of a "woman who tried to get a Santa Monica apartment for more than a year without success[;] . . . she broke into the city, finally, by marrying someone who already had an apartment there."

[1]Proposition 13 was an initiative designed to limit property tax levels; Jarvis spearheaded the initiative, which resulted in cuts in local government spending.

No-growth ordinances and rent control have not, of course, been em- 35
braced everywhere; but city administrations have often produced comparable results through intense housing-code enforcement, designed to drive "undesirable" housing (and the people who live in it) out of their jurisdictions.

In *New Homeless and Old: Community and the Skid Row Hotel,* Charles Hoch and Robert Slayton have traced the disappearance of the single-room occupancy (SRO) and "cubicle" hotels that once provided cheap housing to thousands of marginal tenants in downtown Chicago. Over 8,000 of these hotel rooms—still available to Chicago's low-income transients in 1963—have disappeared, leaving barely 2,000 today. These lost accommodations were all supplied by the private market. Although remarkably inexpensive (often costing only $2 a night), these rooms offered residents exactly what they wanted—security and privacy. Most of the hotels had elaborate security systems, with desk clerks screening visitors and protecting residents from unwanted ones. In addition, the cheap hotels were usually convenient to stores and public transportation, allowing low-income residents with few family connections to lead frugal but relatively dignified lives.

What happened to these old SRO hotels? Almost without exception, they became the target of urban-renewal efforts and municipal campaigns to "clean up downtown." Intense building-code enforcement and outright condemnation drove most of them out of business. Strict zoning ordinances have since made it virtually impossible to build replacements. Hoch and Slayton conclude:

> We do not believe that the demise of Skid Row and the SRO hotels was the inevitable result of market forces, or that Skid Row residents embodied peculiar social and psychological characteristics that produced deviant and pathological social behavior. . . . [Instead,] this loss was the result of decades of antagonism from civic and business leaders, legitimated from the 1950s on by social scientists, and incorporated into dramatic change-oriented programs like urban renewal.

Nor have these policies abated today. Despite the hue and cry over the loss of SRO hotels, their replacement is still generally forbidden by zoning ordinances. In Los Angeles, there is a movement afoot to close down SRO hotels—even those subsidized by the city government—because they are not built to withstand earthquakes. Peter Smith, president of the New York City Partnership for the Homeless, comments: "It's essentially illegal for private developers to build SRO hotels in New York anymore."

Restricting Development

What is causing homelessness, then, is the familiar phenomenon of government regulation. This regulation tends to escape the attention of the public and the enthusiasts of deregulation, because it is done at the local rather than the state or national level.

The truth is that cities and towns do not always welcome new development. 40
At bottom, even the most enthusiastic advocates of progress would often prefer

to see their own neighborhoods remain just as they are. People will usually settle for higher-priced housing, because it raises the value of their own homes; but few want tenements, rentals, or other forms of "low-income" housing.

Through regulation, most cities and towns hold a tight rein on their housing markets. Suburbs are particularly exclusionary, zoning out everything but high-priced single-family homes (which require large lot sizes), and prohibiting the rental of rooms or apartments. Cities themselves, although sometimes offering rhetorical welcomes, often play the same exclusionary games.

An example can be seen in Takoma Park, Maryland, a nineteenth-century "streetcar suburb" of Washington, D.C., which until recently had a long history of tolerant housing policies. Takoma Park is a hodgepodge of two-, three-, and four-family homes within easy commuting distance of Washington. During World War II, homeowners rented attics and spare bedrooms to wartime officials who could not find housing in Washington. This tradition continued after the war, when many returning GI's sought housing while attending nearby Columbia Union College. Many homeowners permanently converted their homes to two- and three-family units.

During the 1970s, however, a group of homeowners living in a recently constructed, more suburban part of the city asked Montgomery County to enforce a sixty-year-old zoning ordinance that prohibited rentals in single-family zones. (Zoning is controlled by county governments in Maryland.) After a long dispute, the city council adopted a compromise in 1978, which permitted anyone who was renting before 1954 to continue to do so for another ten years. In 1988 the reprieve expired, however, and evictions began. More than six hundred tenants were forced to leave their homes.

The Appeal of Utopianism

It is important to realize that housing regulations are to blame for a lot of homelessness. But at the same time, we must acknowledge the impulses that make people want to intervene in the housing marketplace.

About a year ago, I spent a few days in San Francisco's Market Street district, 45
a notorious skid row. Although not particularly dangerous, the surroundings were decidedly unpleasant. Weather-beaten young men, each of whom seemed to have his entire worldly belongings wrapped in a sleeping bag, lounged along the sidewalks. Ragged holdovers from the sixties perched on public monuments, performing drunken imitations of rock singers. Veterans of motorcycle gangs weaved past timid pedestrians, carrying on garrulous arguments with their equally disheveled girlfriends. Along the side streets, tattoo parlors jostled with cheap cafeterias, pornography shops, and the inevitable flophouse hotels.

It was easy enough to imagine some ambitious politician surveying the scene and deciding that it was time to "clean up Market Street." Such campaigns have occurred all over the country and have inevitably produced the disjuncture that we now find between the supply of housing and the price that poor people can afford to pay for it.

Yet distasteful as it may seem, skid rows play a crucial role in providing the poor and near-poor with cheap housing. Not everyone can live in suburban subdivisions or high-rise condominiums. To provide for everyone, we also need rooms for rent, fleabag hotels, tenements, trailer parks—and the "slumlords" who often run them. Although usually imagined to be rich and powerful, these bottom-rung entrepreneurs almost always turn out to be only slightly more affluent than the people for whom they are providing housing.

In the utopian dreams of regulators and "housing activists," such landlords are always eliminated. They are inevitably replaced by the federal government and the "non-profits," orchestrated by the city planners and visionary architects who would "tear down the slums" and replace them with "model tenements" and the "garden cities of tomorrow."

It is not wrong to have such visions. But let us do things in stages. Let us build the new housing *first*—and only then tear down the old "substandard" housing that is no longer needed. If we let the best become the enemy of the good—or even the barely adequate—the homeless will have nothing more substantial to live in than the dreams of the housing visionaries themselves.

JOHN ATLAS and PETER DREIER

The Phony Case against Rent Control

THE NATION'S housing crisis is a manageable problem. It is simply a matter of national priorities. In 1980, for every dollar spent on housing, the Federal Government spent $7 on the military. By 1988, for every housing dollar, Washington spent more than $40 on the military. Federal housing policy needs a major overhaul, based on the premise that decent affordable housing is a basic right.

Today, among the most urgent tasks are to defend rent control and to promote the construction of affordable housing for poor and working-class families.

The National Coalition for the Homeless estimates the homeless population at between two and three million. An increasing percentage of these are families and the working poor who simply can't afford housing on their low wages. Workers near the poverty line are now paying more than half of their limited incomes just to keep a roof over their heads. The only roof that many can find is over a vacant building, or an abandoned car, or an emergency shelter.

"Homelessness is a national tragedy of appalling proportions," said Jack Kemp, George Bush's Secretary of Housing and Urban Development, at his confirmation hearings. But if Kemp pursues the right-wing agenda on housing, he will only deepen that tragedy.

Housing advocates hope that Kemp, who probably harbors greater political 5
ambitions, will take a pragmatic rather than an ideological approach as a way of building a constituency among the poor, the housing industry, and big-city mayors. One early test of Kemp's thinking will be his response to pressure from the real-estate industry, right-wing think tanks, and conservatives in Congress who are waging a holy war against rent control.

Across the country, rents are skyrocketing. According to a recent study by the Harvard Center for Housing Studies, rents are now at their highest level in two decades. Tenants are intensifying their demands for rent control, but the basic premise of rent control is under assault by right-wingers and their allies.

What's behind this new attack on rent control? For landlords, it's a simple matter of greed. While studies demonstrate that rent control allows apartment owners a reasonable profit, it does limit unbridled rent-gouging and real-estate speculation. For New Right thinkers,[1] the battle is part of the larger ideological assault on regulation of the private sector; they view rent control as both an unwarranted interference with private-property rights and a misguided effort to preserve affordable housing. And for some politicians, opposition to rent control

[1]The "New Right" refers to the contemporary conservative movement that seeks to limit government control of business and private life.

is an easy—if obvious—way to curry favor with campaign contributors from the real-estate industry and win plaudits from conservative opinion-leaders.

But the case against rent control is a fraud: Rent control is a scapegoat for the nation's housing ills and for the failure of free-market housing policy.

Rent control has helped slow down gentrification, curb displacement of poor and working-class families, and minimize the disruption of neighborhoods that otherwise would have collapsed under the pressure of free-market forces. In housing, the invisible hand often carries an eviction notice.

The Heritage Foundation[1] claims that rent control actually causes home- 10
lessness. In a recent study prepared by right-wing journalist William Tucker, the Heritage Foundation purported to show that rent control makes housing "more scarce and expensive for everybody."

Tucker looked at fifty cities and found that seven out of nine with rent control also have the largest homeless populations. The fact that forty-one of the cities with sizable homeless problems did *not* have rent control—proving that rent control doesn't cause homelessness—didn't bother Tucker. He noticed a strong correlation between low vacancy rates and rent control. "A 1 per cent decline in the vacancy rate was roughly associated with a 10 per cent increase in homelessness," he said. By some twisted logic, he then concluded that rent control causes homelessness.

In fact, the reverse is true. When there is a severe housing shortage and low vacancy rates, rents begin to escalate. Low-income tenants get pushed into the streets and shelters. Those tenants who can hold on start to push for rent control.

Arguing that rent control causes homelessness is like arguing that the sun comes up because the rooster crows. Tucker concedes that his analysis "cannot prove cause and effect"—it can only demonstrate coincidence. But, he claims, "once correlations have been discovered, however, we can *theorize* about what the causal connections might be."

Despite the obvious holes in Tucker's theorizing, he has become an intellectual stalking horse for the Right. Though he had demonstrated no prior expertise in housing policy, his initial study of rent control was funded by the libertarian Cato Institute and housed at the Manhattan Institute, another right-wing think tank that sponsored Charles Murray, whose *Losing Ground* attacked welfare as the cause of poverty.

Tucker has sold himself as a housing expert, and his articles have appeared 15
in *The American Spectator, The Wall Street Journal,* and *The New Republic,* on the cover of William Buckley's *National Review,* and on the op-ed pages of *The New York Times.*

He is a clever propagandist. In an article in *New York* magazine, he offered readers $50 to send in examples of "rich and famous" New Yorkers living in rent-controlled apartments. When Morton Downey, Jr., did a show on rent control, he invited Tucker, who dutifully bashed tenant activists. Just a few days before

[1]The Heritage Foundation is a conservative think tank.

Bush announced his choice of Kemp for Housing and Urban Development, the Heritage Foundation called a press conference and brought Tucker to the podium to remind the audience that the thousands of New Yorkers sleeping on grates and in shelters only had rent control (and its liberal proponents) to blame.

Tucker and the Right have made headway in their attack. Twice in the last two years, *The New York Times* has run editorials opposing rent control. One of these, attacking Governor Mario Cuomo's plan to retain rent control, was headlined "Mr. Cuomo Promotes Housing Crisis."

And last May, conservative Senator William Armstrong, Republican of Colorado, added a last-minute amendment to the bill reauthorizing McKinney Act funds for the homeless.[1] Armstrong's measure required HUD to study how rent-control laws might be causing homelessness. The amendment passed, and HUD has until October to produce the report.

About 200 cities—including New York, Boston, Los Angeles, Washington, and San Francisco—have adopted some form of rent control. Conservatives are hoping that Jack Kemp will withhold Federal housing funds from these municipalities until they eliminate rent control.

Most people, using common sense, recognize that rent control helps *prevent* 20
homelessness. In fact, the arguments against rent control crumble when confronted with evidence based on experience.

Rent control has had no adverse impact on new construction, housing maintenance, abandonment, or property taxes, conclude two social scientists, Richard Appelbaum of the University of California and John Gilderbloom of the University of Louisville, in their book, *Rethinking Rental Housing.*

For example, in New Jersey, which has about half of all cities in the country with rent control, developers continue to build as many apartments in communities with rent control as in communities without it. Indeed, Appelbaum and Gilderbloom have shown that some cities with rent control actually outpaced those without in the construction of new apartments.

A recent study of local rent control conducted by the Urban Institute to evaluate the program in Washington, D.C., found that rent-control policy primarily benefited the elderly, the poor, and families with children, typically saving households $100 a month. Rent control in Washington was found to have little impact on new construction, repairs, or housing values.

Most local rent-control laws exempt all newly constructed housing, guarantee a fair and reasonable return on investment, and allow annual rent increases as necessary to cover increases in operating costs. Rent control simply limits extreme rent increases where landlords can otherwise take advantage of tight housing markets. And any builder will confirm that the volume of new apartment construction depends less on rent control than on land prices, zoning laws, changes in interest rates, the income and employment of an area, and the availability of Government housing subsidies.

[1]The McKinney Act is federal legislation to aid the poor and destitute.

Still, some neoliberals[1] claim that housing assistance, like Social Security, 25
should be limited to the poor to make it more efficient and equitable; in other words, they favor a means test. But programs that serve only the poor are demeaning and often less efficient, requiring an added bureaucracy to check for cheats and, more importantly, to undercut broad public support for the program itself. Compare Medicare for the middle class with Medicaid for the poor.

In New York City, such critics as William Tucker complain that rent control helps Mia Farrow, Ed Koch, and other affluent tenants. But even in New York City, most tenants pay more than they can afford: 70 per cent of all renters have household incomes of less than $25,000 a year.

Rent control was not designed to be a welfare program but a consumer-protection policy. Appelbaum and Gilderbloom demonstrate that despite the diversity of apartment ownership in many cities, landlords operate as a monopoly, setting price levels through networks such as real-estate boards. In that way, they resemble a local gas or electric utility. And no one asks government utility boards to regulate the price of gas and electricity only for low-income consumers.

Those who attack rent control because it assists the wealthy along with the poor should logically favor Federal housing entitlements for low-income tenants and a beefed-up Federally subsidized housing-production program. But that would cost billions of Federal dollars and probably require a tax increase on the rich—policies conservatives and neoliberals don't like.

And if fairness is the overriding issue, the Government should cap the homeowner tax deductions for mortgage interest and property taxes so that they primarily help poor and working-class families, not the wealthy, whom they currently favor. These deductions cost the Federal Government more than $35 billion last year—four times the HUD budget. About $8 billion of that went to the 2 per cent of taxpayers who earn more than $100,000—with a bonus for those with two expensive homes. Most home owners benefit minimally from such deductions; half do not claim them at all. Tenants, of course, whose incomes are on average half that of home owners, are not eligible.

As President Bush and Secretary Kemp will soon discover, the housing 30
crisis is intensifying not only for the poor but also for the middle class. The level of home ownership is declining for the first time in decades, and the rate of home-mortgage foreclosures is the highest in memory.

The entire housing system—including the savings-and-loan industry—is in shambles, with the homeless only its most visible victims. Ronald Reagan must bear much of the blame. His housing policy was designed to eliminate Federal subsidy programs, particularly those that helped build low-rent housing. Reagan cut housing subsidies more than any other Federal program—from $33 billion in 1981 to $8 billion this year. In the 1970s, Federal assistance

[1]Neoliberals, like President Clinton, believe that government can achieve social goals by making bureaucracy more efficient rather than by increased government spending.

helped to build 200,000 to 300,000 new low-rent apartments a year. This year, the number will barely reach 15,000.

Home ownership has actually declined in the 1980s, the first decade since World War II to register such a drop. Many would-be home owners, especially couples with young children, are now reluctant renters. As a result, demand for apartments has increased and rents have skyrocketed, placing an extra burden on the poor, who now must compete for scarce apartment dwellings.

How will Bush and Kemp respond to the crisis?

At the press conference announcing Kemp's appointment, Bush was asked point-blank whether he intended to expand the housing budget and how he expected to deal with the homeless problem. Bush declined to answer the first question and, in response to the second, reaffirmed his support for the McKinney Act. That law—establishing a small-scale program to help private agencies and church groups create more shelters and soup kitchens—appears to be his favorite solution.

In his Inaugural Address, Bush talked about the tight Federal budget. "Our 35
funds are low," he said. "We have a deficit to bring down. We have more will than wallet; but will is what we need." And though he mentioned the problem of homelessness in his first budget speech in February, Bush continued to slight housing expenditures, implicitly endorsing Reagan's proposed $1 billion cutback.

Kemp, for his part, has pledged to hold the line. "I don't believe we're going to balance the budget by cutting housing," he said at his first press conference with Bush. But Kemp is no New Dealer or Great Society advocate.[1] He told *The Wall Street Journal* on February 16 that he wants to use "the greatest tool that has ever been designed to battle poverty: entrepreneurial capitalism."

Kemp's most likely response will be to expand the Reagan program to give poor people "housing vouchers" to help them pay rent for apartments in the private market. Conservatives like the voucher approach because it relies on private market forces and is obviously cheaper than building new subsidized apartments. In the December 12 *Wall Street Journal,* economist Edgar Olsen claimed that vouchers can serve more poor families for the same money than building new low-rent apartments. But because apartments are so scarce, that's like providing food stamps to the poor when the grocery shelves are empty.

In fact, about half of the low-income tenants who now receive vouchers return them unused because apartments are scarce and most landlords prefer more affluent tenants to the poor—even those with Government vouchers. Despite all the talk about the cost-effectiveness of vouchers, the Reaganites last year provided only 100,000 vouchers nationwide—far from the six or seven million low-income households that potentially need subsidies in the private market.

Even an expanded voucher program won't work unless Washington helps enlarge the overall supply of affordable housing. The National Low-Income

[1]The New Deal was Franklin Roosevelt's legislative program for dealing with the Depression of the 1930s. The Great Society was Lyndon Johnson's program for eliminating poverty and achieving equal opportunity for all Americans in the 1960s. Both involved significant government spending and regulation.

Housing Coalition wants Bush and Congress at least to double the housing budget (to about $20 billion) from its current level of 1 per cent of all Federal spending.

Such an increase—which few housing advocates on Capitol Hill expect will get a friendly reception in the White House—would still leave housing programs far poorer than they were when Reagan took office in 1981. A bill introduced by Representative Barney Frank, Democrat of Massachusetts, calling for an additional $15 billion for affordable housing, is considered a big-spending proposal in today's Gramm-Rudman climate.[1] 40

The challenge for housing activists, however, is not only finding more money to allocate but ensuring that the money is well spent. Here, housing activists have scored some successes. In cities across the country, thousands of community-based nonprofit housing developers are meeting the housing needs of poor and working-class people. With virtually no Federal funding, these nonprofit entrepreneurs have patched together financial support from local governments, private foundations, and churches to build and rehabilitate low-income housing. To turn these local efforts into a successful national housing program will require support from Washington.

Where are we now? Unfortunately, the political conditions do not exist to guarantee that every American has decent and affordable housing. Bush and Congress are in no mood to make additional expenditures. To free up the money, Congress would have to cut the military budget and increase taxes on big business and the wealthy, neither of which seems likely.

Yet, public-opinion polls sponsored by the National Housing Institute and other groups reveal widespread support for a renewed national housing program and even for tax increases to pay for such a program. This sentiment must be transformed into political support before specific legislation can be enacted.

The legislation lies waiting. Representative Ron Dellums, Democrat of California, has sponsored a bill that would provide direct Federal capital grants for public or nonprofit housing, an approach common in Europe. Such a program would represent a radical departure in the nation's housing history as significant as the tenement-reform laws at the turn of the century or the public-housing acts of the 1930s.

But a comprehensive progressive housing program is unlikely to get serious 45
attention in Congress so long as progressive forces are fragmented and isolated. The strategic question is what housing agenda is both politically possible and progressive—a stepping stone toward more fundamental reform.

At the moment, a key strategy must be to defend rent control. On its own, it can't solve the housing crisis; it is, simply, one tool available to local government to deal with astronomical rents and a shortage created in Washington. But rent control can enable large numbers of poor and working Americans to have a roof over their heads. That is the least we can do.

[1]Gramm-Rudman is a legislative initiative that requires the federal government to balance the budget.

Questions for Discussion

1. If you have read the article by James Wright earlier in this chapter, consider whether Wright would side more with Tucker or with Atlas and Dreier. Why? How do you think the other writers in this chapter—Awalt and Marin—would respond to the debate over rent control?
2. Atlas and Dreier urge the principle that "decent, affordable housing is a basic right" (paragraph 1). What do "decent" and "affordable" mean to you? What might these terms mean to "Virginia" in Peter Marin's article? On what basis could we argue that decent, affordable housing is a "right," like free speech? Would Tucker agree with this principle?
3. Near the end of his article, Tucker suggests that urban renewal projects must make provision for the housing of poor people displaced by grand schemes to "clean up downtown." Would Atlas and Dreier agree?
4. Obviously, no national housing policy can work that does not address local conditions because housing problems in San Francisco, for example, are not the same as housing problems in Phoenix, Chicago, or New York. What changes need to occur at the local level? What measures at the Federal level are most likely to be helpful?

For Convincing or Persuasion

Find out which officials in your local community are directly involved with housing policy. Invite one or more to visit your class or interview them at their offices. Ask questions suggested by the two previous articles. You may also seek out published interviews with or statements by such officials.

After discussing what local officials say about the homeless problem in relation to housing policy, write an essay for a local newspaper analyzing the local problem and how best to solve or ameliorate it. Use the articles by Tucker and Atlas and Dreier when they are helpful or appropriate in supporting your own viewpoint.

For Further Research and Discussion

1. Do some research on housing conditions in the United States. How does the housing situation in general help us to understand and explain the problem of homelessness specifically? What, if anything, should be done about the housing problem in general, especially as it effects the poor and young people wanting to buy their first home?
2. There is much talk currently about the breakdown of the American family. Do some research on families in the United States. How has the American family changed in the last thirty years or so? What has caused the changes? Can we describe current conditions as a breakdown? If so, how much do these changes account for the current homeless problem?

Additional Suggestions for Writing

1. *Persuading.* Using any set of classifications that seem appropriate and useful, divide the homeless into groups. Propose measures that will help to deal with each group. Address your proposals to your U.S. Representative or Senator. Be sure to find out about his or her background and basic views and present your proposals appropriately.
2. *Critique and Convincing.* Find out about current housing policy at the Federal level. In the light of what you have learned from research, assess existing policy. As in Suggestion 1, address your assessment and any suggestions you have to one of your U.S. representatives.
3. *Persuading.* What can we, as individuals, do to help the homeless? Write an essay for college students that answers this question.

CHAPTER ELEVEN

National Health Care

Except perhaps for the economy, no other issue has received as much media attention in recent years as health care. Virtually every popular newsmagazine has featured it in cover stories; network news reports have investigated it; talk shows and televised panel discussions have returned to it again and again; and thousands of articles and editorials have been written about it.

Why? One reason is that health care in the United States truly is in crisis. We currently spend about 14 percent of our GNP (that is, our gross national product, the annual estimated value of all goods and services produced in the United States) on health care—more than we spend, for example, on education. Estimates are that the percentage of GNP going towards health care may well increase to 20 percent in a decade or so. Yet, at any one time, about 35 million Americans have no health insurance at all. Many millions more are dangerously under-insured—an extended illness or a serious accident away from financial ruin. Clearly, something is wrong.

That the health-care system is in serious trouble hardly anyone disputes. Unlike the debate over most policy issues, few voices in the health-care debate support the status quo, and almost everyone agrees that current policy must change. But informed analysts disagree about virtually everything else, from what has caused the health-care crisis to what ought to be done.

Dozens of significant proposals have surfaced in the last few years, and we obviously cannot summarize them all here, much less represent more than a fraction of them in the articles included in this chapter. However, most of these proposals fall into one of two categories based on the degree of change advocated: Some aim only to reform the current system, while others aim to overhaul it completely.

We begin with the most widely discussed plan to overhaul the system—national health care based on the Canadian model. We look next at the most common plan for reform—a system requiring employers to provide health insurance for all employees and their families, coupled with extension of Medicaid (currently restricted to the poor) to cover everyone not covered by an employer or by Medicare (restricted to older, mostly retired people). Finally, we include two other proposals that have not been so widely debated and are not so easily classified as reform or overhaul.

Because the issue of health care is complicated, it is easy to get mired in detail and forget what's most important in thinking, talking, and writing about it. These questions may help to maintain focus:

What principles should guide health-care policy?
Which of the many underlying causes of the current crisis are most important?
Which of the solutions grapple best with the underlying causes?
Which of the solutions seem feasible? That is, which have some realistic chance of becoming law and of being administered successfully?

If we keep these basic questions in mind, we stand a better chance of thinking clearly about an issue that affects us all and that urgently requires something we do not have now—a consensus for action.

CONSUMER REPORTS

Does Canada Have the Answer?

The following, which appeared in the September 1992 issue of Consumer Reports, *is excerpted from the final article of a three-part series; we recommend that you consult the September issue for the entire article as well as the articles appearing in the July and August issues. These three reports together (much too long to reprint here) offer, in our opinion, the best introduction to the health-care issue available in the popular press.*

Informed consumers pay special attention to Consumer Reports *because the magazine accepts no advertising and because it is published by the Consumers' Union, an organization that has been conducting research on goods and services marketed to the general public since 1936. Therefore, the information and advice the publication offers have a special authority. Of course, the conclusions it reaches are still disputable in most cases. No journal can address the concerns of all consumers, so we must read the articles in* Consumer Reports *with the same critical eye we bring to any printed material. In fact, most articles in* Consumer Reports *are arguments to convince.*

MORE THAN 30 years ago Canada enacted a program to bring health care within reach of all its citizens. By 1971, Canada's provincial governments were paying the medical bills for everyone in Canada, and few people outside Canada were paying much attention.

As the U.S. health-care system began to creak and groan under the weight of its runaway costs—and as its inability to serve every citizen became increasingly apparent—Americans started to look seriously at Canada's health-care system as a model for reform. At the same time, Canada's system started to come under concerted attack from those special-interest groups—health-insurance companies, medical associations, and hospitals—that profit most from the present nonsystem of health care. This report examines the strengths and weaknesses of the Canadian system and evaluates the criticisms leveled against it.

How the System Works

Contrary to what some in the U.S. health-care industry would have you believe, Canada does not have "socialized medicine." Medicare, as Canada's health-care system is called, is simply a social insurance plan, much like Social Security and Medicare for older people in the U.S. Canada's doctors do not work on salary for the government.

Canadians pay for health care through a variety of federal and provincial taxes, just as Americans pay for Social Security and Medicare through payroll taxes. The government of each province pays the medical bills for its citizens.

Because the government is the primary payer of medical bills, Canada's health-care system is referred to as a "single-payer" arrangement. Benefits vary somewhat among the provinces, but most cover, in addition to medical and hospital care, long-term care, mental-health services, and prescription drugs for people over 65. Private insurance exists only for those services the provincial plans don't cover.

Although each province runs its own insurance program as it sees fit, all are 5
guided by the five principles of the Canada Health Act:

1. *Universality.* Everyone in the nation is covered.
2. *Portability.* People can move from province to province and from job to job (or onto the unemployment rolls) and still retain their health coverage.
3. *Accessibility.* Everyone has access to the system's health-care providers.
4. *Comprehensiveness.* Provincial plans cover all medically necessary treatment.
5. *Public administration.* The system is publicly run and publicly accountable.

Where Doctors Fit In

The role of doctors in the Canadian system is little understood in the U.S. and frequently distorted by the foes of a single-payer system. For example, in announcing his plan for health reform last winter, President Bush declared: "We don't need to put Government between patients and their doctors and create another wasteful federal bureaucracy." Nor should the Government tell doctors how to practice medicine, other opponents of Canadian-style health care often add.

Canada's health-care system does neither. "In the U.S. there's a myth that Canadians have an awful government bureaucracy that tells doctors how to practice medicine," says Dr. Michael Rachlis, a Toronto physician and health-policy consultant. "There's much more interference from third parties [such as insurance companies and utilization-review firms] in the U.S. than from the government in Canada."

Canada's physicians practice in their own offices and work for themselves, just as most U.S. doctors do. The main difference: Canadian doctors may not charge whatever they wish. Their fees are set according to a schedule negotiated by the ministry of health in each province and the provincial medical association. Canadian doctors cannot engage in the common American practice of "balance billing"—billing the patient the difference between what an insurer will pay and what the doctor wishes to charge.

The negotiation process has managed to keep fee inflation in Canada at least modestly in check. Fees tend to be much lower than those commanded by American doctors for the same service. In British Columbia, for example, doctors receive about $349 to remove a gallbladder; in Manitoba, $354; and in Ontario, $348. But in New York City, the customary fee paid by insurance carriers averages about $2,700; in Buffalo, N.Y., $945. (All figures are in U.S. dollars.)

Despite the lower fees, physicians in Canada, like those in the U.S., enjoy 10
high incomes. In British Columbia, the average payment (before overhead) made

by the health ministry to cardiologists last year was $290,500; to ophthalmologists, $240,500; to dermatologists, $200,500; and to general practitioners, $128,000.

Where Patients Fit In

Canadians, like U.S. citizens, can select any doctor they like. Those doctors bill the provincial insurance plans directly and are usually paid within two to four weeks. For patients, there are no bills, claim forms, out-of-pocket costs, or waits for reimbursement from insurance carriers, all common complaints in the U.S.

Roughly half of all Canadian physicians are family practitioners (compared with 13 percent in the U.S.), and Canadians go to them for treatment that Americans might seek from costlier specialists. Most Canadians, for instance, take their children to family practitioners instead of to pediatricians for common childhood illnesses. Most children see pediatricians only for serious problems.

The provinces encourage people who need a specialist's care to obtain a referral from a family doctor, much the way HMOs and other managed-care plans do in the U.S. If a specialist sees a patient who has not obtained a referral, that specialist can bill the Government only the fee that would ordinarily have been paid to a general practitioner.

Those rules, aimed at controlling costs by preventing the overuse of high-priced specialists, do not always have their intended effect. If a patient shows up at a specialist's office without a referral, the specialist need only call the family practitioner, obtain a referral number, and bill the Government the higher fee. Many family doctors are only too glad to send any complicated or time-consuming case to a specialist so they can see more patients and earn more fees. The increased use of medical services is a major reason costs are escalating there as they are here.

Not Enough Hospital Beds?

Canada's rising health-care costs are a favorite target of U.S. critics, who 15
have also made much of the fact that Canadian hospitals have reduced their number of beds in recent months. The implication is that the Canadian health-care system is collapsing and that Canadians now suffer from insufficient hospital facilities. Actually, Canada has too many hospital beds, which is also the case in the U.S. Hospitals proliferated in both countries during the last two decades. Money flowed freely, building new hospitals was good politics, and the public as well as the government came to believe that another hospital bed meant better health.

As health-care costs in Canada rise, the provinces are being forced to rethink how best to spend their health dollars. Most bed closings stem from deliberate government strategies to eliminate waste and duplication of services. In Toronto, for example, where a total of 2,200 beds have been permanently closed, the city's 45 hospitals still have 1,000 beds empty on any given day.

Provincial governments can implement such cost-cutting measures because they control how much money a hospital receives. Every year they negotiate a "global budget" with each hospital in the province. That budget includes money to cover operating costs, increases for inflation and greater utilization, and any special services the ministry wants the hospital to offer. The global budgets set by the provincial governments comprise about 95 percent of a hospital's total funds. Any other money must come from fund-raising and investment earnings. Within the global budgets, hospitals are free to move money around. If, say, a hospital finds the costs of running the emergency room are lower than expected, it can redirect some of the money to increase the number of cataract surgeries, if it chooses to. Canadian hospitals, however, are not allowed to run deficits.

Long Waits for Care?

Perhaps the most frequently heard charge against the Canadian system is that it rations care, and people don't get the treatment they need. The *New York Times* told readers of its editorial page last November that as a result of "rationing," Canadian "women must wait months for a simple Pap smear."

In reality, women in Canada routinely have Pap smears done by their family doctors, who perform them the same way U.S. doctors do. Canada's ambassador to the U.S. traced the tale of Pap smear waits to a brief delay in laboratory processing in Newfoundland some years ago—a problem long since corrected.

20 Canadian men and women routinely have general surgery, diagnostic ultrasound, X-rays, thyroid tests, amniocentesis, EKGs, and hundreds of other procedures and treatments without delay. But Canadians may not have immediate access to the latest technological innovations, such as lithotripters (machines that crush kidney stones with sound waves) and magnetic resonance imagers (MRIs), or to such surgical procedures as a coronary-artery by-pass or hip replacement. Someone who pulls a knee muscle playing soccer isn't likely to get an MRI scan the day after the accident. And those who want bypass surgery to relieve angina symptoms won't be wheeled into the operating room right away. However, anyone requiring emergency care gets it immediately.

Because provincial governments control hospital budgets, they also control the introduction and use of technology. In some cases, they have kept a tight lid on that technology to restrain the high costs associated with overuse, inappropriate use, or duplication. Hospitals denied some piece of equipment by the provincial health ministry are free to buy it with money raised from private contributions, but they can't look to the ministry for funds to operate it.

In Winnipeg, Manitoba, for example, Seven Oaks Hospital purchased a CT scanner with its own funds and is already operating it. The Ministry of Health maintains that the province doesn't need another CT scanner, that the six scanners available at other provincial hospitals are enough to serve the province's needs. The ministry has hinted that it may not cover the $1-million operating and depreciation expenses for the machine.

The ministry has taken a hard line on MRIs as well. The province has just one, and the hospital operating it must follow strict guidelines in deciding when it should be used. The province probably could use another MRI machine, says

Dr. Cam Mustard, an assistant professor of community health sciences at the University of Manitoba. But, he adds, "it's not such a scarce resource that people are coming to harm because they can't get on it. Doctors are very satisfied with the quality of service, and the waiting times are not seen as obstructing their ability to care for patients."

"The alternative [to having such waiting times]," says Dr. Charles Wright, a vice president for medicine at Vancouver General Hospital, "is to have a grossly overbuilt system as in the U.S. If you build for the peaks, you have a hell of a lot of wasted resources."

The published figures on the number of Canadians on waiting lists proba- 25
bly exaggerate the actual delays in receiving care. For the most part, doctors manage the lists, putting people on one or more of them as they deem appropriate. Sometimes doctors put a patient on a list to give him or her hope when a condition is actually hopeless. Sometimes they put patients on just in case their condition worsens and a procedure not now necessary becomes necessary. Queues shift constantly as those needing care immediately move ahead of those whose conditions are less serious. Sometimes queues develop and then disappear. At Wellesley Hospital in Toronto, for example, kidney patients once faced a three-month wait for lithotripsy. Now there's virtually no wait, and the machine doesn't always run at capacity.

When St. Boniface Hospital in Winnipeg investigated its waiting list of 143 people for cardiac angiography, a radiological examination of the arteries surrounding the heart, it found that only 56 people were really candidates for the procedure. Some didn't need it, some didn't want it, and some had already had the procedure done at another hospital. One doctor was accused of packing the list for his own political reasons.

In 1991, a British Columbia Royal Commission on health care investigated all the well-publicized cases of people who claimed to have been harmed by delays in the queue for heart surgery. "When we tracked them down, almost all of the cases crumbled," says Appeals Court Justice Peter Seaton, who chaired the commission.

That finding hasn't stopped opponents of Canadian-style health care from citing waiting lists in British Columbia as evidence that the system is grinding to a halt. "A waiting list of 700 to 800 people for heart surgery is not uncommon," a vice president of the National Center for Public Policy Research, a conservative think tank, wrote in a 1992 *New York Times* column.

A waiting list of that length did exist, but only for a short time. When researchers looked into it, they found that two-thirds of the people on the list were waiting not for the procedure, but for three particular surgeons.

When waiting lists have grown too long, provincial governments have in 30
some instances offered patients the option of going to the U.S. for treatment. The British Columbia Ministry of Health, for example, contracted with hospitals in Seattle to provide 200 heart surgeries. It took more than a year before Canadians filled all 200 slots, raising the question of whether the delays were indeed life-threatening.

Critics like to portray the availability of treatment in the U.S. as a safety valve for Canadians. However, that says as much about the overcapacity of the American system as it does about poor planning on the part of Canada. The British Columbia Health Ministry received many calls from U.S. hospitals eagerly soliciting its heart-surgery business.

Unavailable Operations?

When he was running for the Democratic presidential nomination, Paul Tsongas said that if he had lived in Canada, he would be dead by now. The procedure that arrested his cancer, Tsongas said, was not available there. In fact, the procedure that saved Tsongas' life, autologous bone-marrow transplantation, was indeed available in Canada in 1986 when Tsongas had his operation. In fact, the pioneering research that led to bone-marrow transplants took place at a Toronto hospital 30 years ago.

In making his charge, Tsongas joined the long list of critics of the Canadian health-care system who contend that it denies its citizens appropriate care. The National Center for Public Policy Research, for example, has asserted that "Canadians do not have enough surgery, at least not enough of the surgery they need the most." And Newt Gingrich, the Republican whip in the House of Representatives, has contended that "it is illegal in Canada to get a whole series of operations."

If anything, Canadians are probably getting too much care, just as Americans are. A report prepared for the Conference of Deputy Ministers of Health last year found that a "nontrivial" amount of the medical services Canadians receive are ineffective and inappropriate. The report blamed fee-for-service reimbursements to doctors for much of the problem. The same criticism applies to the U.S., as we detailed in Part 1 of this series.[1]

Surgery rates for some procedures are actually higher in Canada than else- 35
where. Canada is a world leader in the number of gallbladder surgeries and is second only to the U.S. in heart bypass operations. Each year, the French perform 15 to 20 bypass surgeries per 100,000 people; the British, 20 to 30; the Canadians, 50; and the Americans, about 100.

Needless Deaths?

In its health-care reform proposals put forward earlier this year, the Bush Administration asserted that "post-operative mortality is 44 percent higher in Canada than in the U.S. for high-risk procedures, including heart surgery." Dr. Leslie Roos, a professor of community health sciences at the University of Manitoba and

[1]See the headnote.

one of the authors of the study to which the Administration referred, told CU that the statement "seriously distorts our overall findings."

For one thing, the study compared only Manitoba and New England, not the U.S. and Canada. For another, it compared a number of low-risk and moderately risky procedures and only two that were high-risk—repair of hip fracture and concurrent valve replacement with bypass (one kind of heart surgery). The study showed that for the low- and moderate-risk procedures, the number of people who died shortly after surgery was similar in the two regions. The mortality rates for hip-fracture repair in New England were lower than in Manitoba, primarily because many Manitoba patients had to be transported long distances from remote, northern parts of the province.

Roos told CU that later research is showing Manitoba's heart-surgery results "to be fully comparable with those of the leading American centers." He added that three-year survival rates for cardiovascular surgery are better in Manitoba than they are in the U.S.

How Costs Compare

Opponents of a single-payer system also like to claim that health-care costs are rising faster in Canada than in the U.S. A study by the Health Insurance Association of America (HIAA), the insurance companies' trade organization, reported that per capita spending in the U.S. rose, on average, 4.38 percent per year from 1967 to 1987, compared with 4.58 percent in Canada. But Canada's single-payer system wasn't even completely in place until 1971. Although other researchers have refuted the HIAA's findings, the numbers live on in propaganda against the Canadian system.

Health-care costs are lower in Canada than in the U.S., whether measured 40
by per capita spending or as a percentage of gross national product. In 1989, the U.S. spent $2,450 per person on health care, while the Canadians spent $1,800. In 1990, the U.S. spent 12.2 percent of its GNP on health care; Canada spent 9.5 percent.

Before Canada fully implemented its Medicare system in 1971, both it and the U.S. were spending comparable amounts of their respective GNPs on health care. But as Canada's system of universal coverage took hold in all the provinces, spending by the two countries sharply diverged.

Canadian researchers believe that 25 to 35 percent of the difference may be due to Canada's controls on hospitals. One study found that in the early 1980s, for instance, the U.S. spent as much as 50 percent more per person on hospital services, even though Canadians stayed in the hospital longer, on average.

But perhaps the most striking differences are in administrative costs. In 1987, researchers have estimated, the U.S. spent between 19 and 24 percent of its health-care dollars on administrative expenses; the Canadians spent between 8 and 11 percent.

Playing Politics

Much of the ammunition fired at the Canadian system has inadvertently been supplied by the Canadians themselves. When it comes time to negotiate fees or new budgets, doctors and other providers there often assert that the Canadian system is underfunded.

Providers don't hesitate to make waiting lists a political issue or to put their 45
case before the public by writing letters and running advertisements that take their health-care system to task. This spring, a Manitoba Medical Association newsletter featured an open letter to the minister of health headlined "Rationing eye surgery impairs patients' quality of life, MMA President tells Minister." The publication also ran letters from a doctor and a patient's relative pleading for more money for hip-replacement surgery. The British Columbia Medical Association ran newspaper ads warning of the harm that could come from placing a cap on the fees earned by its highest-paid members, such as ophthalmologists, dermatologists, and cardiologists—a strategy the ministry was pursuing to reduce health-care expenditures.

Conflicts between Canada's health-care providers and the government, however, are often overblown in the U.S. Not long ago, Dr. Gur S. Singh, then president of the British Columbia Medical Association, sent a letter to provincial newspapers arguing that Americans should keep their system basically unchanged. Singh said he wanted the U.S. to "continue to provide the necessary safety valve to an overly restrictive Canadian system which will only get worse as further bureaucratic controls are adopted." Health Insurance Association of America president Carl Schramm quoted from Singh's letter in testimony to the U.S. Senate.

At the end of his letter, however, Singh said the Canadian system was "one of the best, and perhaps it still is the best health-care system in the world." That point didn't make it into Schramm's testimony.

An astute Canadian observer would have known that Singh's letter was simply a "piece of negotiating rhetoric intended to bat the minister [of health] over the head," says Dr. Hedy Fry, Singh's predecessor at the medical group. "That letter was for public consumption in B.C."

What Ails the System?

The Canadian health-care system, like every health-care system in the world, has problems, though they're not of the scary sort usually cited by U.S. critics. There is a more-than-adequate supply of doctors in Canada, but there is a shortage of physicians in the remote, northern areas of the country, where few want to practice. The U.S. has the same problem, of course; few doctors care to practice in rural or poverty-stricken areas.

Even though Canada has a greater proportion of family doctors than the 50
U.S., medical-school incentives have steered doctors-in-training to specialties

that command higher fees and result in higher costs to the system. (In Part 1, we noted the same phenomenon in the U.S.) A report presented to Canada's deputy ministers of health last year blamed at least part of this trend on the bad example of the U.S., where 87 percent of all physicians are specialists.

A more fundamental flaw is that through the years, provincial governments have acted more like check-writers than health-care managers. As in the U.S., hospitals and doctors often received generous increases simply by asking for them. In Ontario, for instance, hospital spending has increased 10 percent or more each year for the last 10 years. But that is changing. This year Ontario hospitals are getting just a 1 percent increase in their global budgets, and the ministry is redirecting money to other types of health care.

Canadian patients also may have stayed in hospitals longer than was necessary. In 1989, the average length of stay was 10.5 days, compared to 7.2 days in the U.S. In Canada, patients are still entering hospitals a day or two before their surgeries for preoperative workups, a practice that utilization firms in the U.S. are rapidly putting an end to.

Since 1984, health-care spending by the provinces has increased 80 percent, to about $44 billion. At the same time, the economy that funds that spending has grown less than 20 percent. The Canadian federal government, which once provided about 50 percent of the funding for the provincial health budgets, now supplies only about 35 percent. Eventually it may leave the funding solely to the provinces.

Pushed by rising costs and by pressures on funding, the provinces are redirecting money and starting programs to make better use of their dollars. "We're afraid we're going to lose our system if we don't change it," says Lin Grist, a special assistant to Ontario's minister of health. "It's really quite precious to us."

The U.S. faces similar problems, but Canada is in a better position to solve 55
them. For one thing, it long ago answered the question of whether everyone in the country should be entitled to health care—a question the U.S. seems incapable of resolving. For another, Canada's single-payer system is better suited to the task of redeploying resources as needed. It can decide where to spend its budget for the good of all citizens.

In the U.S., the rhetoric of the day is to contain costs. But few, if any, doctors or other providers embrace limits on their own incomes. And there's no single payer with enough influence to impose the controls necessary to squeeze the billions of dollars of waste out of the system.

One option Canadians are not considering is a move back to a system like the one in the U.S. Of the 1,503 people who testified before the British Columbia Royal Commission in its hearings on health reform, only one favored adopting the American way of paying for health care.

Canadians like their health-care system and expect their government to fix its current problems. But a government that tried to tinker with the basic principles of the Canada Health Act would be a government out of power very soon.

Questions for Discussion

1. The *Consumer Reports* article is unsigned—that is, the person or persons who wrote it are not acknowledged. Why? How does such anonymity contribute to the authority of the argument?
2. Early in the article (paragraph 3), the author or authors claim that "Canada does not have 'socialized medicine.'" What is socialized medicine? Why do the authors put socialized medicine in quotation marks? Why is this claim made so early in the article?
3. Think carefully about the five principles of the Canada Health Act listed in paragraph 5. What is the difference between *universality* and *accessibility*? What does "all medically necessary treatment" mean? Are you comfortable with the idea of a health-care system administered by state and federal agencies?
4. What exactly would change if a Canadian-style health-care system were implemented in the United States? How would such a system alter your behavior as a consumer? How would it effect providers—doctors, hospitals, clinics, and the like? What would happen to American industry, such as those that administer the current system and produce and sell the technology upon which it depends? What impact would national health care have on workers in health-care and supporting industries?

For Inquiry and Persuasion

Talk with anyone who is likely to have had personal experience with the Canadian system—students from Canada, professors and staff members who have lived in Canada, friends and relatives who are Canadians or who reside in Canada, and so forth. Make careful notes about what they say. Compare their experiences with your own and those of American families you know well.

Based on the collective information pooled in class discussion, write an essay either supporting or criticizing the concept of national health care. Deal only with the question of whether such a system is better than the U.S. system, not with the issue of feasibility.

MIKE PETERS

Cartoon

In the preceding selection from Consumer Reports *on the effectiveness of the Canadian health plan, the authors acknowledge that patients in Canada may not have immediate access to the newest and most advanced technology. Critics of the health plan proposed in 1993 by Bill Clinton expressed concern that the latest technologies would also be rationed or reduced in the U.S. under that plan, as suggested in the following editorial cartoon.*

YOU HAVE TO EXPECT SOME CUTBACKS WITH THE CLINTON HEALTH PLAN...

For Discussion

How do you read the aim and argument of this cartoon?

JOHN GOODMAN

An Expensive Way to Die

The previous article is persuasive in part because it appeared in Consumer Reports, *a publication with a reputation for independent and objective judgment of whatever it evaluates. In contrast, the following article was published in* National Review, *a publication closely identified with the strongly conservative political viewpoints of its high-profile editor, William F. Buckley. Further, its author, John Goodman, is president of the National Center for Policy Analysis, a conservative, Dallas-based research organization associated with major corporations, including insurance companies. Clearly, the ideas expressed are grounded in a specific political agenda. Even "considering the source," however, Goodman's case against national health care ought to be taken seriously.*

COUNTRIES WITH national health insurance spend less on health care than the U.S. does. It is all too easy to assume that the U.S. can therefore control health-care costs through national health insurance without any loss of benefits. And this mistake is encouraged by a number of myths.

- *Myth #1: Although the United States spends more on health care per capita than countries with national health insurance, the U.S. does not get better health care for the extra dollars it spends.*

This myth rests upon the fact that life expectancy hardly differs among the developed countries and that infant mortality in the U.S. is actually *higher* than in most other developed countries.

In fact, a population's general mortality is affected by a great many factors over which doctors and hospitals have little influence. For those diseases and injuries for which modern medicine can affect the outcome, however, which country the patient lives in really matters. Life expectancy is not the same among developed countries for premature babies, for children born with spina bifida, or for people who have cancer, a brain tumor, heart disease, or chronic renal failure. Their chances of survival are best in the United States.

Consider the availability of modern technology in the U.S. and in Canada, 5
a country with comprehensive national health insurance. There are eight times more magnetic-resonance-imaging units (the latest improvement on X-rays), seven times more radiation-therapy units (used in the treatment of cancer), about six times more lithoptripsy units (used for nonsurgical removal of kidney stones), and about three times more open-heart surgery units and cardiac-catheterization units per capita in the United States than in Canada.

It is sometimes argued that countries with national health insurance delay the purchase of expensive technology in order to see if it really works and is cost-effective. Even if true, patients will be denied access to life-saving treatment while

Use of Modern Medical Technology in the 1970s

Country	Pacemakers Per 100,000 Population, 1976	CAT Scanners Per Million Population, 1979	Kidney Dialysis And/Or Transplants Per Million Population, 1976
Australia	7.3	1.9	65.8
Canada	2.3	1.7	73.4
France	22.6	0.6	111.3
West Germany	34.6	2.6	105.0
Italy	18.8	NA	102.0
Japan	2.7	4.6	NA
United Kingdom	9.8	1.0	71.2
United States	44.2	5.7	120.0

Source: National Center for Policy Analysis

government bureaucracies evaluate it. For example, during the 1970s, life-saving innovations were made in the fields of renal dialysis, CAT-scan technology, and pacemaker technology. Yet the implant rate of pacemakers in the U.S. during the mid-1970s was more than four times the rate in Britain, and almost twenty times the rate in Canada (see the chart above). The availability of CAT scanners in the U.S. was more than three times that in Canada and almost six times that in Britain. The treatment rate of kidney patients in the U.S. was more than 60 percent greater than in Canada and Britain.

There is considerable evidence that cost effectiveness is not what drives the bias against modern medical technology abroad. CAT-scan technology was invented in Britain, and until recently Britain exported about half the CAT scanners used in the world. Yet the British government has purchased only a handful of CAT scanners for use in the National Health Service. British scientists also co-developed kidney dialysis. Yet Britain has one of the lowest dialysis rates in all of Europe, and as many as nine thousand British kidney patients per year are denied the treatment.

In the United States we pay more for health care. But we also get more. And what we get saves lives.

- *Myth #2: Countries with national health insurance have solved the problem of access to health care.*

10 In Britain and New Zealand, hospital services are completely paid for by government. Yet both countries have long waiting lists for hospital surgery. In Britain, with a population of about 55 million, the number of people waiting for surgery is almost eight hundred thousand. In New Zealand, with a population of three million, the waiting list is about fifty thousand. In both countries, elderly patients in need of a hip replacement can wait in pain for years. Patients waiting for heart surgery are often at risk of their lives.

Average Waiting Time In Newfoundland 1988

Procedure	Average Wait
Mammogram	2½ months
Bone scan	1–1½ months
Myelogram	3–4 months
Brain shunt	5 months
Hip replacement	6–10 months
Cataract surgery	2 months
CAT scan	2 months
Pap smear	2–5 months
Urgent pap smear	2 months

Based on physician surveys by the Fraser Institute. Michael Walker, "From Canada: A Different Viewpoint," *Health Management Quarterly* V11.1 (1989): 12.

In response to rationing by waiting, both Britain and New Zealand have witnessed a growing market in private health insurance—where citizens willingly pay for prompt private surgery, rather than wait for "free" surgery in public hospitals. In Britain, the number of people with private insurance has more than doubled in the last ten years, to about 12 percent of the population. In New Zealand, one-third of the population has private health insurance, and private hospitals now perform 25 percent of all surgical procedures.

Canada has had a national-health program for only a few decades. But because the demand for health care has proved insatiable, and because the Canadian government has resolutely refused to increase spending beyond about 8.5 percent of GNP, the waiting lines have been growing. In Newfoundland the wait for a hip replacement is about six to ten months, the wait for cataract surgery is two months, for pap smears up to five months, for "urgent" pap smears two months (see the chart above). All over Canada, heart patients must wait for coronary bypass surgery, and the Canadian press frequently reports episodes of heart patients dying while on the waiting list. Unlike Britain and New Zealand, however, Canada does not allow patients to turn to the private sector, although Canadian patients who can afford to do so sometimes travel to the U.S. for medical services they cannot get in their own country.

- *Myth #3: Countries with national health insurance hold down costs by operating more efficiently.*

By and large, countries that have succeeded in slowing the growth of health-care spending have done so by *denying people services,* not by making efficient use of resources.

How much does it cost a hospital to perform an appendectomy? Outside 15
the U.S. it is doubtful that there is a public hospital anywhere in the world that could answer that question. One reason for Margaret Thatcher's health-care reforms is that even Britain's best hospitals did not keep adequate records, and it

was not uncommon for the head of a hospital department to be unaware of how many people his department employed.

What about bed management? Consider that while fifty thousand people wait for surgery in New Zealand, one out of every five hospital beds is empty. While nearly eight hundred thousand people wait for surgery in Britain, at any point in time about one out of every four hospital beds is empty. In both Britain and New Zealand, about 25 percent of all acute beds, desperately needed for surgery, are clogged by chronically ill patients who are using the hospitals as nursing homes—often at six times the cost of alternative facilities. In Ontario about 25 percent of hospital beds are occupied by elderly chronic patients. Hospital administrators apparently believe chronic patients are less expensive than acute patients (because they mainly use the "hotel" services of the hospital), and thus are less of a drain on limited budgets.

- *Myth #4: Under national health insurance money is allocated so that it has the greatest impact on health.*

Even when resources are organized efficiently, they are still distributed with random extravagance under systems of national health insurance. These systems take millions of dollars that could be spent to save lives and cure diseases, and spend this money to provide a vast array of services to people who are not seriously ill. Take the ambulance service. English "patients" take more than 21 million ambulance rides each year—about one ride for every two people in all of England. About 91 per cent of these rides are for nonemergency purposes (such as taking an elderly person to a pharmacy) and amount to little more than a free taxi service. Yet for genuine emergencies, the typical British ambulance has little of the life-saving equipment considered standard in most large American cities.

While tens of thousands who are classified as in "urgent need" of surgery wait for hospital beds, the NHS spends millions on items that have only marginal effects on health and which could well be financed either by charges on the patients or by a low-cost limited private insurance. On the average, the NHS spends more than $70 million each year on tranquilizers, sedatives, and sleeping pills; almost $19 million on antacids; and about $21 million on cough medicine. If the NHS did nothing more than charge patients the full costs of the sleeping pills and tranquilizers they consume, enough money would be freed to treat ten thousand to 15,000 additional cancer patients each year and save the lives of an additional three thousand kidney patients.

- *Myth #5: Under national health insurance the elderly in the U.S. will receive at* 20
  least the same benefits they now receive under Medicare.

The elderly have the most to lose from the adoption of national health insurance. Take chronic kidney failure. Across Europe generally, in the late 1970s, 22 percent of dialysis centers reported that they refused to treat patients over 55 years of age. In Britain in 1978, 35 percent of the dialysis centers refused to treat patients over the age of 55; 45 percent refused to treat patients over the age of 65; and patients over the age of 75 rarely received treatment at all for this disease.

How pervasive is denial of life-saving medical technology to elderly patients in other countries? Lacking hard data, one can only speculate. However, a white 65-year-old male in the U.S. can expect to live 1.3 years longer than a 65-year-old British male. A white 65-year-old female in the U.S. can expect to live 1.4 years longer than a 65-year-old British female. For middle-aged males, U.S. mortality rates are higher than European ones. During the retirement years, however, when medical intervention can make much more of a difference, the U.S. mortality rate is significantly below that of European countries.

- *Myth #6: The defects of national-health-insurance schemes in other countries could be easily remedied by a few reforms.*

The characteristics described above are not accidental byproducts of government-run health-care systems. Instead, they are the natural and inevitable consequences of politicizing medical practice.

Why are elderly and poor patients discriminated against in the rationing of 25
acute care under national health insurance? Because national health insurance is always and everywhere a middle-class phenomenon. Prior to the introduction of national health insurance, every country had some government-funded program to meet the health-care needs of the poor. The middle-class working population not only had to pay for its own health care, but it was also paying taxes to fund health care for the poor. National insurance extends the "free ride" to the middle-class working population, and it is designed to serve the interests of this population.

Why do national-health-insurance schemes skimp on expensive services to the seriously ill while providing a multitude of inexpensive services to those who are only marginally ill? Because numerous services provided to the marginally ill create benefits for millions of people (read: millions of voters), while acute and intensive care services concentrate large amounts of money on a handful of patients (read: small number of voters). Democratic political pressures dictate the redistribution of resources from the few to the many.

Why are sensitive rationing decisions left to the hospital bureaucracies? Because the alternative is politically impossible. As a practical matter, no government can afford to make it a national policy that nine thousand people every year will be denied treatment for chronic kidney failure and die. Nor can any government announce that some people must wait for surgery so that elderly patients can use hospitals as surrogate nursing homes, or that elderly patients must be moved so that surgery can proceed. Budgetary decisions made by politicians and administrators are transformed into clinical decisions made by doctors.

- *Myth #7: Since national health insurance is very popular in other countries, it would also be popular in the United States.*

National health insurance remains popular in other countries precisely because it does not function the way its advocates believe it should. It "works" in other countries for three reasons: (1) The wealthy, the powerful, and those who are most skilled at articulating their complaints find ways to maneuver to the front of the lines. (2) Those pushed to the end are generally unaware of the medical technologies denied to them. (3) There are no contingency fees, no generally recognized right of due process, and no lawyers willing to represent those who are systematically discriminated against—though these are beginning to develop, as, for instance, kidney patients learn the facts of their situation and organize into pressure groups on the AIDS model.

"Don't push me around" is a distinctively American phrase. In Europe, 30
people have been pushed around for centuries. In the U.S. we have widespread access to information about modern medical technology, a legal system that encourages litigation, and a strong devotion to basic rights of due process. National health insurance, as it operates in other countries, would not survive the American cultural and legal system.

Questions for Discussion

1. Goodman says that "a population's general mortality is affected by a great many factors over which doctors and hospitals have little influence" (paragraph 4). What might he have in mind? Could such factors explain our higher rate of infant mortality? If so, what are the implications for health care in the United States?
2. "In the United States," Goodman claims, "we pay more for health care. But we also get more" (paragraph 8). What might be questionable in this reasoning? Who, for example, does he mean by "we"? And is more always better?
3. A central point in Goodman's case is that cost-containment in countries with national health care is accomplished "by *denying people services,* not by making efficient use of resources" (paragraph 14). Are there good reasons for denying *some* services? Are there good reasons for delaying others? Based on what you learned from *Consumer Reports'* analysis of the Canadian system, in what other ways does it seem national health-care systems control expenditures?
4. One of the more disturbing points Goodman makes (paragraphs 20–22) is that national health care discriminates against the elderly. Do you find his argument compelling in these paragraphs? Why, or why not? How might you determine whether or not Canada's system is biased against older people?

For Convincing

Many ideas are good in the abstract or sound in principle but not workable. In paragraphs 28–30 Goodman argues that national health care would not work in the United States. Write an essay agreeing or disagreeing with his contentions about feasibility. If you agree with Goodman, propose some reform of the health care system that you think would be popular and effective. (The following article may help you evaluate options besides national health care.)

HENRY J. AARON

The Worst Health Care Reform Plan . . . Except for All the Others

In the headnote to the first article in this chapter, we underscored an obvious but nevertheless important fact: Some organizations have a reputation for independent judgment that increases the authority of whatever they publish under their name. Consumers Union, publisher of Consumer Reports, *is a well-known example. The Brookings Institution is scarcely so popular, but it too has a reputation for scholarly, nonpartisan research in the social sciences and therefore a special authority, especially on matters relating to economics. The following article by Henry J. Aaron, Director of Economic Studies at Brookings, was published in 1991 in* Challenge, *a "magazine of economic affairs" which claims to have a policy of "freedom for diversity," which presumably means that it accepts articles from a wide range of economic viewpoints.*

Aaron rejects national health care as too disruptive of the current U.S. health-care system and favors instead requiring all employers to insure their employees, while extending Medicaid to cover everyone else. Although Aaron does not mention the fact, such a plan is already in effect in the state of Hawaii.

It is hard to open a newspaper or turn on the television without encountering a new proposal to reform the way the United States pays for health care. What should be sad facts have become journalistic clichés—more than thirty million Americans lack insurance and the United States spends more on health care than does any other country. Legislation, one might think, is just around the corner.

That something has to be done is clear. But it will probably not be done soon because two conditions necessary for reform have not been satisfied. First, key groups essential to the formation of a political consensus must come to accept that reform is necessary even if it is not exactly along the lines they prefer. Second, the President must be committed to basic change. Presidential commitment is necessary for action because *every major reform plan is subject to serious and legitimate criticisms.* Only the President can focus the debate on a single plan and effectively make the case that the shortcomings must be accepted for the greater good that the reform can achieve.

Once a sitting President or a successful candidate becomes persuaded that action is necessary and the various interest groups recognize that reform is essential even if not along their preferred lines, the debate about reform will become serious. At that point, Americans will have to grade the major reform alternatives before them.

Any reform must be judged on four broad criteria. First, does the plan assure financial access to care for substantially all Americans? Second, does the

Report Card on Health Reform Proposals

	Access	Cost Control	Needless Winners and Losers	Value Congruence
Incremental Reform	D	D	A	A
Tax Credits	A or F	D	D	A–
National Health Insurance	A	A(?)	F	D
Mandatory Employer-Financed Insurance with Public Backup	A–	A or D	B	B

plan hold the potential to reduce expenditures on low-benefit, high-cost care? Third, to what extent does the new system produce winners and losers for reasons unrelated to either of the first two criteria? Fourth, does the plan support or conflict with important values embodied in American economic or political institutions?

No plan rates top grades in all four categories because changes large enough 5
to assure coverage and to control costs must produce many winners and losers, and are likely to conflict with traditional ways of doing business, as the brief discussion below of major suggested reforms will elucidate. The associated table offers a comparative overview in the form of a "Report Card."

Incremental Reform

The incremental reform strategy comprises many diverse proposals to ameliorate specific problems with the current health care system. "Risk pools," amalgamations of many small groups into large ones, would be established for small employers who often face exorbitant premiums, in part because insurance companies fear that groups with the highest expected costs are most likely to seek insurance. Various proposals have been advanced to set ceilings on allowable premiums and provide public subsidies, if necessary, to offset losses. Some proposals would allow employers to offer lean benefit packages that many states currently prohibit.

The incremental strategy would extend Medicaid coverage and possibly lower the age of eligibility for Medicare. It would encourage the use of "managed care" by private insurers, a set of procedures to encourage patients to choose low-cost providers and to curb the prescription of useless services by hospitals and physicians. It would reform the malpractice insurance system, based on the widely-held, but unsupported view that malpractice insurance and care induced to reduce risk of litigation have contributed significantly to rising costs.

The incremental approach entails no major disturbance in current arrangements. For that reason, it causes few unintended winners and losers and is quite consistent with the prevailing system of voluntary employer-sponsored insurance. This approach does little to offset the tendency of current employer sponsors of health insurance to drop plans because of sharply rising costs of care. As a result, the net increase in the number of people added to the roles of the insured is likely to be negligible. Extensions of Medicaid and Medicare would increase coverage, but incrementalists do not favor large expansions of those programs because of their large budget costs.

Nor does this approach hold out much hope for controlling rising costs. Medical costs are going up principally because of technological innovation, rising labor costs of hospitals, and the aging of the population. When fully insured patients confront physicians paid on a fee-for-service basis, both patient and physician have every incentive to make sure that the patient gets every available beneficial service, regardless of cost. While managed care has achieved some economies and is certain to produce more, it does not change the incentives of the key agents determining how much care is provided—fully insured patients who want everything that is beneficial, and physicians who have every incentive to make sure they get it. Governmental attempts to regulate in the teeth of private incentives almost always fail. There is no reason to think that private attempts at similar regulation will fare any better.

What all this means is that piecemeal reforms may achieve piecemeal suc- 10
cesses in extending insurance coverage and in holding down some costs. But incrementalism will simply put off to a later date reforms that can assure all Americans financial access to care and that promise to cut spending on low-benefit, high-cost care.

Tax Credits

Providing all Americans with refundable tax credits could achieve virtually universal coverage *provided that the tax credit was large enough to cover the full costs of privately purchased insurance.* People would buy the insurance plan that appeals most to them, pay for it, and receive a credit from the government sufficient to cover the costs of a standard plan. People could buy insurance that goes beyond the standard plan, but they would have to do so with after-tax dollars.

Some variants of this approach, however, would limit the credit to a fraction—as little as half—of the cost of typical insurance, the purchase of which would be voluntary. In that event, a system of refundable credits would almost certainly result in much narrower coverage than under current arrangements. Furthermore, this approach has little or no potential for controlling costs. It would do little to encourage insured patients and their physicians to curtail the use of low-benefit, high-cost procedures. And the large inducements to expand sales forces and to proliferate plans would increase the already horrendous administrative costs of the current system. Furthermore, a generous set of tax credits would provide enormous windfalls to employers who currently finance health care for their employees.

Those costs would shift to public budgets, necessitating large increases in taxes. The pattern of tax burdens would inevitably differ from that of premiums. These gains and losses would arise from shifts in the method of financing not from the extension (or contraction) of coverage.

National Health Insurance

For nearly four decades a clutch of elected officials and private analysts has urged that every American be provided health insurance coverage as an incident of citizenship or residence. Supporters of this approach today point to the popularity of the Canadian system among Canadians and its success in providing universal coverage. The costs of national health insurance would be paid for through public budgets and financed from earmarked taxes.

Advocates of these plans have pointed out, correctly, that this approach 15
is the hands-down winner for providing insurance coverage. They have also claimed that it holds out the maximum potential for controlling rising costs, because total costs would be subject to budgetary control. Experience in other countries suggests that central budget control can be effective in limiting the fraction of national income spent on health care. Although faster economic growth abroad partly explains the slower growth in the share of national income spent on health care abroad than in the United States, one cannot be certain that the United States would realize the promise of central control for limiting spending. Still, the potential for cost control is powerful. For starters, national health insurance would obviate most of the private costs of administering the current private insurance system, which some estimate at as much as $100 billion.

The real problem with national health insurance is the enormous disruption it would cause. Establishing national health insurance would require shifting more than $300 billion in financing from private payers to public budgets. Premiums, currently paid by businesses and individuals, would be zeroed out and taxes would have to be increased enough to replace them. The result would be huge windfall gains and losses and complex negotiations over them. The resulting pattern of burdens would almost certainly fall more on those with high incomes than under the current system. While many would find such a shift in burdens an argument for the system, introducing a debate about income redistribution into an already contentious controversy about health care reform can only hinder passage. Tax reform became possible only when both sides agreed to make the plan as nearly neutral as possible in its effects on income distribution.

Furthermore, the shift of health care to public budgets would boost the size of the federal budget by about one-third. A major national activity would be shifted from private to public management. Short of catastrophe or revolution, it is hard to imagine the circumstances under which the American democracy, a system given to slow and incremental change, would embrace such a shift. Even the claimed administrative savings of national health insurance would be a mixed blessing if achieved quickly. They are of the same magnitude as the savings from reductions in defense spending that Congress is finding so difficult to realize because of the simple fact that one person's expense is another person's income.

Mandatory Employer-Financed Insurance

This approach can achieve universal coverage by assuring all workers and their families coverage through their jobs, the way most Americans get their insurance today. A public backup plan would cover everyone else. Whether this approach holds out much promise of controlling growth of spending depends sensitively on how payments to providers are controlled.

Simply extending the current system so that it covers everyone would not fundamentally change the incentives that have relentlessly boosted costs under the current system. But payments to hospitals and physicians could be controlled by regional administrative entities, subject to fixed budget limits set at the national level. New York health commissioner David Axelrod directed the development of one such proposal, and I have outlined a similar plan.

Because this approach builds on the current system of employment based 20
insurance, it is generally consistent with current institutions and arrangements. It violates current norms in mandating employer-financing of insurance. Employers who do not currently offer insurance are strongly opposed to a mandate. Small businesses and employers of low-wage workers are particularly concerned that the added costs of insurance could be ruinous. Defenders of this approach point out that most, although not all, of the sting can be removed by transitional subsidies or gradual introduction. Even those employers who now offer insurance have mixed feelings. They would dearly like to avoid the indirect subsidies they now provide to other firms, because they pay for some of the costs of insurance for dependents of their employees—some of whom work for others. But owners of large companies also deplore interference with managerial autonomy. This approach would necessitate new taxes to pay for increased public coverage for those not insured through work. But the added taxes would be a small fraction of those required to pay for tax credits or national health insurance.

In short, this approach calls to mind Winston Churchill's comment on democracy, which he called "the worst system of government, except for all the others."

Unlike incrementalism, mandatory work-based insurance with a public backup plan can provide insurance to all and can control costs. Unlike the tax-credit approach or national health insurance, it would not entail a massive shift of spending from private to public budgets.

This approach has flaws. Americans do not like mandates. Small business and low-wage employers would have real problems that will demand real answers. The system will not be as neat or as simple as full-scale national health insurance would be. But unlike all of the other systems, *it can work and you can get there from here.*

Questions for Discussion

1. In paragraph 2 Aaron claims that "[o]nly the President can focus the debate on a single plan"; in other words, without leadership from the top nothing will happen. Do you agree? What might work against strong Presidential leadership where health care reform is concerned?
2. In paragraph 9 Aaron alleges that "[m]edical costs are going up principally because of technological innovation, rising labor costs of hospitals, and the

aging of the population." Assume that he is right. How does his own proposal address these three causes? How does a national health-care system respond to them?

For Research and Convincing

Aaron and the author of the preceding article, John Goodman, agree on at least one major point: that national health care won't work in the United States. Aaron says that the chief problem with national health care is "the enormous disruption it would cause" (paragraph 16). Canada, however, went from a system like that in the United States to national health care about twenty years ago. Do some research on what happened. Was there enormous disruption? Write an essay arguing either that Aaron is right or that he overestimates the disruption of shifting from private to public health insurance.

GORDON T. MOORE

Let's Provide Primary Health Care to All Uninsured Americans—Now!

The following is a brief scholarly argument that appeared in 1991 in the Journal of the American Medical Association (JAMA)*; it includes references and endnotes documented according to that journal's style. For obvious reasons,* JAMA *and the* New England Journal of Medicine, *the two most prestigious medical journals in the United States, are much concerned with the health care crisis. Articles on every conceivable aspect of the issue have appeared in these journals over the last few years and are well worth consulting.*

Like the rest of us, doctors are not of one mind about how to solve the crisis. Probably most side with JAMA *in opposing national health care: Understandably, doctors are not cheered by the prospect of having their fees regulated by government agencies. However, a minority of doctors do support national health care, and many of those who do not support national health care seem genuinely disturbed by the lack of access to medical care experienced by millions of uninsured and under-insured Americans.*

In this context we can understand the appeal of Gordon Moore's proposal for extending primary care to all Americans. Since most U.S. doctors are not involved in primary care, his proposal would not effect the vast majority of JAMA*'s readers at all. Yet the proposal would do something significant—provide universal, if severely limited, access to medical services for all Americans—and would, therefore, seem a step in the right direction that his audience could endorse.*

MORE THAN 30 million Americans lack health insurance.[1–3] There is no disagreement that this is a grave national problem; virtually everyone recognizes our need for a workable health-care system that can provide medical care for all Americans. But even amid increasingly intense concern about care for the uninsured, no national policy—or even consensus—has emerged about what to do. The major barrier to decision and change is fear: fear that the price tag to cover medical care for the uninsured will be too high and impossible to control.

Why is it so difficult to find an affordable solution? Our search has been hobbled by a disabling assumption: that any plan must provide comprehensive coverage for virtually all the medical needs of uninsured Americans. Our attempt to insure against the most intensive and costly of services will continue to stymie our efforts to design an affordable program. Since no acceptable plan is likely without agreement about how to contain its costs, we must either ration benefits or, as Relman[4] argues, find methods to make our system perform more economically so we can provide everything. Either will take a long time to agree on, if either is achievable at all.

Why wait to provide help to those without access to medical services? As we continue the national debate about affordability, we should not forgo the solid benefits that small expenditures might make in providing basic, frontline health care services for all uninsured and underinsured citizens. If we cannot, as a nation, easily agree now about how to pay for all-inclusive care, let's at least cover primary health care services.

Primary care is the most economical package of effective medical services we can provide. It is, by definition, accessible, comprehensive, coordinated, continuous, and accountable "first-contact care."[5] Primary care clinicians provide low-cost diagnosis and treatment and bring important benefits to preventing disease and maintaining health. With appropriate insurance to cover primary care, all Americans would have immediate access to medical help when they are sick and to a regular physician who knows them and could coordinate their health care services. Their physician would provide preventive medicine—immunizations, counseling about health risks, and screening for early detection of disease. Even if their patients lacked insurance to pay for hospital and subspecialty care, primary care clinicians could help decide whether a problem beyond their capacity warranted the expense of referral, or they could assist in finding a place where the care might be available inexpensively or at no cost.

Primary care can improve health. Several studies have documented the 5
potential benefits of providing primary care to uninsured Americans. The RAND Health Insurance Study[6,7] demonstrated improved vision, more complete immunization, better blood pressure control, enhanced dental status, and a reduction in predicted mortality among patients given free care vs. groups that had to share health care expenses. The benefits appeared greatest for the poor (exactly the group that now constitutes most of those without insurance), with the most demonstrable gains resulting largely from outpatient primary care types of health services. The study probably underestimated the benefits of free primary care, because the cost-sharing comparison group actually had limited financial risk and received many of these services. Indeed, in a study of Medi-Cal recipients who completely lost their insurance,[8,9] their health care access, satisfaction, and clinical outcomes appeared worse than those of the cost-sharing groups in the RAND study. Thus, poor patients appear to do better when they receive primary care and to deteriorate medically when they lose access to this care.

A primary health care plan would be affordable. In England, for example, half the physicians specialize in primary care and provide more than 80% of the nation's health care visits and associated treatments for less than 20% of its expenditures on health.[10] Extrapolating from expenditure levels in other countries[11] and from actual experience paying for primary care in health maintenance organizations (Gerald Plotkin, M.D., and Michael R. Soper, M.D., oral communication, January 1991), one can estimate that 15% to 20% of what we currently spend on medical care could provide a full range of basic care to every American, including physicians' services and most indicated tests, procedures, and medications needed for good primary medical care. Since the majority of Americans already pay for this through comprehensive insurance or out-of-pocket expenditures, the incremental cost to cover the uninsured would be small—only enough to provide this basic care to the estimated 20% of the population that receives no services now because it has neither insurance nor sufficient income to pay for them.[1,3] At the most, this would add 3% to 4% (a maximum of $28 billion currently) to the nation's yearly health care expenditures, or less than half the current annual rate of increase in health care costs.

In the long run, the net cost of assuring access to primary care services for all Americans might even be lower. Studies have shown that continuity of primary care can enhance quality,[12] improve patient compliance,[13] and decrease use of emergency,[14,15] hospital,[15,16] and subspecialist resources.[15,17] A primary care system, with the proper performance incentives, could pay for itself through improved gatekeeping, better preventive medicine, use of lower-cost primary care physicians rather than subspecialists, and management of more illnesses outside the hospital.

Will entitling the uninsured to primary care cause these costs to escalate over time? Experience suggests that the answer is yes—if we continue to pay physicians by fee-for-service. To keep costs predictable and under control, we could pay primary care physicians in advance to provide a specified package of services to every patient who signed up with them. Such a system is already familiar to the 35 million Americans who use health maintenance organizations. In such prepaid systems, patients pay little or nothing when they use covered services provided by the physician they have selected. Physicians would accept the financial risk for unforeseen variation in use but would benefit by receiving predictable income for patients who now cannot pay.

Improving the access of uninsured Americans to primary care may yield an important side benefit—making a career in primary care a more financially attractive option for medical students. Over the past several decades, the number of physicians choosing to specialize in family practice, general internal medicine, and general pediatrics—the specialties that provide primary care—has declined markedly.[18] The United States now has the lowest ratio of primary care physicians to subspecialists of any country in the developed world, and many observers feel this contributes to our rapidly escalating health care costs. With reliable funding for their services, physicians could choose a career in primary care and have a realistic expectation of steady income. Most experts feel that such a situation would increase the number of medical school graduates who choose to specialize in primary care and would, in turn, make such care more accessible to insured and uninsured alike.

Where can we find the money to start this program? Many funding options 10
exist. An attractive one, for example, would be to cap the special tax-exempt status of employer contributions to health insurance and use the generated tax revenue to cover primary care for uninsured Americans. The treasury estimates the lost tax revenue at $48 billion in 1991, almost twice the largest prediction of costs of the proposed program.[19] This approach to funding would create a disincentive for overly comprehensive coverage among those who have health insurance, while assuring access to primary care for citizens who cannot pay. Those

who could pay for, and who chose to consume, more medical resources would be taxed to help subsidize basic services for those who now get none. The net effect of such a system would be to put a brake on medical cost inflation, encourage a shift of medical expenditures toward primary care, and extend coverage to the uninsured.

Our medical care system is in trouble and getting worse. While the experts try to figure out how to achieve utopian goals at affordable prices, let's do something practical about the suffering on our doorsteps. Primary care is the most affordable safety net we can offer our citizens. By all means, let's continue the debate about universal, comprehensive insurance to cover all medical care costs, but, in the meantime, let's provide primary health care to all uninsured Americans—now!

The author acknowledges the generous support of this work by the Harvard Community Health Plan Foundation, Boston, Mass. and the helpful criticisms of Abby Hansen, Ph.D. and James Sabin, M.D.

References

1. National Leadership Commission on Health Care. *For the Health of the Nation: A Shared Responsibility.* Ann Arbor, Mich: Health Administration Press; 1989.
2. Swartz, K. *The Medically Uninsured: Special Focus on Workers.* Washington, DC: Urban Institute Press; 1989.
3. Weisfeld, V.D., ed. *Access to Health Care in the United States: Results of a 1986 Survey.* Princeton, NJ: Robert Wood Johnson Foundation; 1987. Special Report 2.
4. Relman, A.S. The trouble with rationing. *N Engl J Med.* 1990;323: 911–913.
5. Institute of Medicine. *A Manpower Policy for Primary Health Care: Report of a Study.* Washington, DC: National Academy of Science; 1978.
6. Brook, R.H., Ware, J.E., Jr., Rogers, W.H., et al. Does free care improve adults' health? *N Engl J Med.* 1983;309:1426–1434.
7. Keeler, E.B., Sloss, E.M., Brook, R.H., Operskalski, B.H., Goldberg, G.A., Newhouse, J.P. Effects of cost sharing on physiological health, health practices, and worry. *Health Serv Res.* 1987;22:279–306.
8. Lurie, N., Ward, N.B., Shapiro, M.F., Brook, R.H. Termination from Medi-Cal: does it affect health? *N Engl J Med.* 1984;311:480–481.
9. Lurie, N., Ward, N.B., Shapiro, M.F., Gallego, C., Vaghaiwalla, R., Brook, R.H. Termination of Medi-Cal benefits: a follow-up study one year later. *N Engl J Med.* 1986;314:1266–1268.
10. Office of Health Economics. *Compendium of Health Statistics, 1989.* London, England: Dept. of Health and Social Security; 1989.
11. *Health Care Systems in Transition.* Paris, France: Organization for Economic Cooperation and Development; 1990.

12. Dietrich, A.J., Marton, K.I. Does continuous care from a physician make a difference? *J Fam Pract.* 1982;15:929–937.
13. Charney, E., Bynum, R., Eldredge, D., et al. How well do patients take oral penicillin? a collaborative study in private practice. *Pediatrics.* 1967; 40:188–195.
14. Hochheiser, L.I., Woodward, K., Charney, E. Effect of the neighborhood health center on the use of pediatric emergency departments in Rochester, New York. *N Engl J Med.* 1971;285:148–152.
15. Wasson, J.H., Sauvigne, A.E., Mogielnicki, R.P., et al. Continuity of out-patient medical care in elderly men: a randomized trial. *JAMA.* 1984;252: 2413–2417.
16. Alpert, J.J., Heagarty, M.C., Robertson, L., Kosa, J., Haggerty, R.J. Effective use of comprehensive pediatric care: utilization of health resources. *AJDC.* 1968;116:529–533.
17. Bergman, D.A. The effect of the introduction of a continuity clinic on subspecialty utilization. *J Med Educ.* 1983;58:744–746.
18. Colwill, J.M. Primary care education: a shortage of positions and applicants. *Fam. Med.* 1988;20:250–254.
19. *Reducing the Deficit: Spending and Revenue Options: A Report to the Senate and House Committees on the Budget—Part II.* Washington, DC: Congressional Budget Office; 1990:145.

Questions for Discussion

1. What happens when an uninsured person shows up, seriously ill, in the emergency room of a public hospital in the United States? How could primary health care reduce the demand on the resources of public hospitals?
2. Moore points out (paragraph 6) that in England half of all physicians specialize in primary care. The percentage in the United States is much lower, less than 20 percent. Will there be enough primary care physicians to implement Moore's proposal? How could we find out? Is it reasonable to think, as Moore does (paragraph 9), that providing primary care for all Americans would increase the number of medical students choosing to work in primary care? Why, or why not?
3. How does Moore propose to pay for primary health care (see paragraph 10)? To borrow the language of Henry Aaron in the preceding article, who would be the winners and the losers in Moore's financing system? Are there other ways to pay for primary health care? What advantages might they have over Moore's proposal?

For Inquiry and Convincing

As a class research project, interview local people involved with health care—practicing physicians, hospital administrators, medical school faculty, nurses, managers of health care organizations, and so forth. For each person you interview, first summarize Moore's article and then ask appropriate questions based on Moore's proposal.

After sharing and discussing the results of these interviews in class, write an essay that takes a definite stand on Moore's proposal. Remember that your position can range from enthusiastic support to complete rejection, with many gradations of support or rejection between these extremes. Make your position clear and argue it thoroughly. Respond thoughtfully to any objections to your position.

REGINA HERZLINGER

Healthy Competition

Currently only a small percentage of Americans—mostly those who are self-employed or work for small businesses—buy their own health insurance. Contending that "competition has never been attempted in the health care industry," Regina Herzlinger argues in the following excerpt from a 1991 Atlantic Monthly *article that people not covered by Medicaid or Medicare should all purchase their own insurance. Rather than providing employees with an insurance package, employers would supply funds to employees who would make their own choices about what coverage to buy. Herzlinger's basic idea is that the health-care industry will be made efficient only if it is subject to free market forces.*

As with any simple-sounding solution to a complex problem, Herzlinger's position should provoke some skepticism. Yet it is a fact that no health-care system potentially acceptable to Americans has been fully successful at containing health costs: Increasing costs threaten even Canada's system. It is also true that, while some competition exists in the U.S. health-care industry, for the most part providers experience few of the open market pressures that operate in most other industries.

From the standpoint of the current system, Herzlinger's proposal is the "radical" conservative counterpart of the "radical" liberal solution, national health care.

OUR PRESENT system supports research and freedom of choice, but it does so with ruinous costs, perpetuating the bloated, hospital-centered system that ignores the needs of many Americans. And although national health insurance would provide the uninsured poor with more equitable access to hospitals, it might well drastically reduce the money now spent on research and undermine the freedom of choice that Americans prize. Neither system allows for the much-needed restructuring of the American health-care system.

A better system would control costs, promote health, insure against the costs of long-term health care, and give the poor access to health services. It would provide focused, accessible health services, reduce the hospital sector, and restore confidence to doctors.

I will discuss the outlines of a health-care program that, if it were fleshed out as legislation, could achieve these ends for the great majority of Americans, and I will describe the relatively simple changes in the income-tax codes and the regulation of health-insurance companies that this program would require. The discussion assumes that the current Medicare and Medicaid programs will remain in place.

CONTROLLING COSTS

The American automobile market presents an example of the remarkable cost controls that can be effected by competition. While median U.S. family incomes nearly quintupled from 1965 to 1988, new-car prices increased by only 2.4 times. And current cars are safer, more fuel-efficient and stylish, of better quality, and available in much greater variety than before. How did cars come to be both cheaper and better? For one thing, U.S. consumers became savvy shoppers, with the aid of information ranging from Consumer Reports Buying Guides to Federal government performance disclosures. And the many new, efficient foreign companies that entered the market not only provided better cars but also motivated existing car companies to improve.

Imagine the effect on the automobile industry if American car purchases 5
were "insured," and employers paid for automobiles. Car buyers would no longer be so vigilant; after all, they wouldn't be paying for the car. Pretty soon the cars of yesteryear would reappear, loaded with options that people often don't choose when they have to pay for them. The absence of consumer vigilance in the health-care system has created the health-care equivalent of the seventeen-foot car: overlarge and numerous hospitals loaded with redundant technology.

The gap between consumers and costs could be bridged if employees bought their own health insurance and other health services. Every year employers would transfer the money they now spend on health insurance to their employees, who would use it to buy their own policies. The amount transferred would not be the average cost per employee but would be adjusted for age, sex, and family structure, as it already is for each employee, and increased annually by a medical price index. (The Heritage Foundation[1] has recommended a similar proposal.) So that employees did not pay taxes on money that once was tax-free, those receiving the transfer could deduct qualified health-care expenses from their income, up to the amount of the transfer.

With this change employees would come to treat health-care funds as theirs, and would exercise the vigilance that transformed the American car market. The corporate flexible-spending programs that already give employees some freedom in allocating "their" health-benefit dollars achieve dazzling results. Quaker Oats experienced a compound annual increase of only six percent in its flexible-health-plan costs from 1983 to 1990. And a portion of the increase consisted of cash dividends to employees. Its secret? Quaker Oats employees reduced their hospital usage by 46 percent when they were more closely involved in choosing their health-care plans. From 1986 to 1988 employees in these programs throughout the country kept increases in their health-care costs 27 to 64 percent lower than the national average.

What about employees who took the money but neglected to buy health insurance, and then required the rest of us to pay for their health-care needs? To avoid these free-riders, all currently insured employees would be required to buy

[1]The Heritage Foundation is a conservative think tank.

insurance policies that covered all health-care expenses exceeding a certain percentage of their adjusted gross income; the percentage would be one they could reasonably afford to pay and would be determined by a political process. I will call this a catastrophic-insurance policy, because it pays for all catastrophically expensive health-care services, including nursing-home coverage. Employees would need to demonstrate on their tax returns that they had bought the appropriate amount of health insurance. Failure to do so would be penalized by the Internal Revenue Service as severely as other tax violations.

This system would thus enable Americans to make trade-offs between insurance coverage and other needs. They could retain their present policies, buy more specialized policies, or buy a catastrophic-insurance policy and save the difference or use it for other needs. For example, a woman earning $40,000 who receives the $3,800 cost of her family's current health-insurance policy from her employer could spend it on her present policy or on others, including a catastrophic-insurance policy that covered her family, cost only $2,600, provided nursing-home coverage, and had a deductible of five percent of income. The $1,200 difference in cost between her present policy and the catastrophic one could be saved or used for the other tax-deductible health expenses described below. Whatever their choice, users would be confronted with the cost of their health care—an ingredient critical to a competitive market.

Promoting Health

To promote health, new tax laws would permit deductions for activities 10
that changed life-threatening behaviors such as smoking and heavy drinking. Many experts agree that some health-promotion activities are cost-effective, particularly those that combat smoking, drug and alcohol abuse, morbid obesity, and high blood pressure. Although the success rates in changing behavior are low—after all, it is very difficult to break habits—the savings that successes create, by forestalling diseases like diabetes and lung cancer, more than compensate for their costs. A recent study of 6,000 retirees found that those enrolled in a health-promotion program reduced their medical costs by six or more times the cost of the program.

To protect against unscrupulous providers of health-promotion activities, a licensing authority, functioning like the Joint Commission on Accreditation of Healthcare Organizations, would vet them.

Insuring Against the Costs of Long-Term Care

Unlike present health insurance, which pays primarily for hospital and doctors' expenses and is deductible from taxes only when bought by employers, the mandatory health-insurance policy would be site-neutral and tax-deductible for any buyer. It would pay all catastrophically expensive health costs, whether incurred in the home, a hospital, a hospice, or some other setting (current policies may or may not pay costs incurred outside a hospital), or for one year in a nursing home after the age of sixty-five, after Medicare's limited coverage had been exhausted. This nursing-home insurance would protect the 73 percent of those nursing-home patients over sixty-five who spend less than a year there (44 percent of the others stay until they die). And it would relieve many of the elderly and their caretakers of much of the enormous financial burden created by uninsured long-term-care needs. Yet it would not be terribly costly, because only 4 percent of those reaching age sixty-five in 1991 are expected to spend time in a nursing home before they die, and with this new policy the cost of much of their care would be spread across the entire population. Policies for long-term care lasting more than a year could be bought separately, at a low cost to those under fifty.

Helping the Poor

Many of the 37 million uninsured Americans are poor; in 1986 some 23 million had incomes of less than $20,000 a year. But a large number of the uninsured could well afford to pay for health insurance. Nearly nine million of them had incomes greater than the median household income. The poor uninsured should receive funding for health insurance. To avoid the free-rider problem, the nonpoor uninsured should be required to buy health insurance.

Although these changes would require new tax revenues, they would also generate some tax-revenue savings. The catastrophic insurance including nursing-home costs and the tax-exempt purchase of insurance for long-term care would free up Medicaid funds meant for the poor, by reducing the number of middle-class people who currently rely on Medicaid for their nursing-home services. With the middle class removed from its roster, Medicaid could focus on the poor, its intended recipients.

Questions for Discussion

1. Herzlinger states her goals in paragraph 2. How exactly would her plan achieve each of these goals?
2. Beginning in paragraph 4, Herzlinger compares the automobile industry with the health industry. Is the analogy a good one? Why, or why not?
3. To guard against "free-riders," people who might take their health insurance allotment and spend it on something else, the author proposes a required, minimum level of coverage, to be monitored by the Internal Revenue Service (paragraph 8). Does this part of her plan make sense? Is it appropriate and practical for the IRS to serve such a watchdog function?

For Research and Convincing

Instead of a single plan that enrolls all employees, many employers now offer a number of plans from which their employees choose the one they like best. Do some research on local companies that require their employees to make choices. Based on what you find out and your own response to Herzlinger, write an essay that evaluates the merits of more competition in the health industry.

For Further Research and Discussion

1. Outlays for employee health care constitute a major financial burden for American business. Some argue that these expenses make American products less competitive, contribute to unemployment, and generally hamper economic growth. Do some research on this issue, and discuss its implications for health care reform.
2. What features of the proposals outlined in this chapter do you find most attractive? Make a list of these and, remembering that it is possible to combine parts of various existing and proposed plans, attempt to pull together the features you like best into a coherent proposal. Present your ideas in a class discussion.

Additional Suggestions for Writing

1. *Negotiation.* No plan for reforming or overhauling health care is ideal; all have some serious drawbacks. List as fully as possible the objections to the proposal you like best. Try to think of ways to modify the proposal you favor so as to minimize or eliminate major objections. Present your modified proposal to the class orally, and assess the response of your classmates and instructor. Then write a paper detailing your plan and showing how it would avoid or cope with objections and negative consequences.
2. *Convincing.* In many ways Japan and Germany are our major competitors in the world economy. Find out how these countries approach health care. Assess both the strengths and weaknesses of their existing systems. Then write an essay indicating what aspects of their systems we should emulate in reforming or overhauling health care in the United States, and what aspects we should avoid.

CHAPTER TWELVE

Feminism

In the United States, the struggle for women's rights goes back to the nineteenth century, when the main issues were achieving full rights of citizenship and access to higher education. The women's movement was highly visible during the early part of this century, leading up to the 1920 victory for voting rights. By that time, some women and men realized that the fight for particular rights must be seen as part of a larger and necessary revolution in society's attitudes about the relationship between the sexes. Those who wanted to eliminate the long-standing oppressive and patriarchal attitudes that held women subordinate to men became known as feminists. In its most basic definition, feminism is simply the doctrine that women should enjoy all the rights—political, social, and economic—that men enjoy.

Today, when most people think of feminism, they think of the movement that began in the 1960s and 1970s, taking women out of the domestic sphere into the world of business and politics. This movement downplayed the differences between men and women, arguing that traditional definitions of "femininity" trapped women into dependence on men. Betty Friedan's 1963 book *The Feminine Mystique* was the landmark for this wave of feminism. In it, Friedan analyzed the myth of the "feminine mystique," revealing how it had persuaded women to stop trying to "be like men" and to accept "their own [feminine] nature, which can find fulfillment only in sexual passivity, male domination, and nurturing maternal love." Not surprisingly, the feminists of the 1960s and 1970s advocated liberation from the sexual double standard, independence from men, and achievement in the world outside of the home.

The success of the feminist movement continues today; in 1993, women pilots in the military were granted the opportunity to begin training for combat missions, and in the 1992 elections, women in Congress increased in number from 30 to a record 54. However, feminism has also run into troubled times, as many have begun to question its values and even its relevance in the 1990s. Some people, women as well as men, now argue that early feminist leaders went too far in minimizing the differences between the sexes and in discounting the role of marriage and family in the lives of real women. *Washington Post* columnist Sally Quinn stirred up controversy with her 1992 editorial "Who Killed Feminism?," in which she noted that "many women have come to see the feminist movement as anti-male, anti-child, anti-family, anti-feminine." Quinn charged the leaders of the women's movement with being hypocritical in denying the need of each of the sexes for the other in their personal lives. In response, many feminists argue that this dissatisfaction with feminism is a result of the media's fixation on extremists and society's historical tendency to retrench when its institutions are threatened by rapid change.

The readings in this chapter reveal the many ways in which society is now responding to feminism. More specifically, they pose such questions as

Should feminism have paid more attention to the real needs of the average woman with a husband and children?
Did it go too far in obliterating femininity? Can feminists be feminine?
Must feminism threaten masculinity?
Is there now a backlash that overvalues motherhood and gender differences?

The readings here do not engage many of the questions that feminists themselves are debating: for example, the radical feminist rejection of heterosexual sex and the academic feminist inquiry into whether women have their own way of constructing arguments and knowing the world. We also do not here raise questions of whether feminism is still relevant. Women continue to make seventy cents for every dollar earned by men. Only two of the Fortune 500's chief corporate executives are women. Only 54 of the 535 members of Congress are women. Sexual harassment plagues women at school and in the workplace, and domestic violence threatens them at home. Clearly, feminism is relevant. Indeed, the question these readings pose is, why are we doubting the value of feminism?

KAY EBELING

The Failure of Feminism

Like many young women in the early 1970s, Kay Ebeling embraced the feminist movement. Writing in 1990, she uses the ensuing events of her life as evidence that feminism "backfired" on women, leaving them to struggle alone with work and children while men enjoyed a new freedom from family responsibilities. As you read Ebeling's essay, note what reasons she offers from her personal experiences to support her criticism of feminism. The editor's note in Newsweek, *where this originally appeared as a "My Turn" column, described the author as a freelance writer and single mother of a two-year-old daughter.*

THE OTHER day I had the world's fastest blind date. A Yuppie from Eureka penciled me in for 50 minutes on a Friday and met me at a watering hole in the rural northern California town of Arcata. He breezed in, threw his jammed daily planner on the table, and shot questions at me, watching my reactions as if it were a job interview. He eyed how much I drank. Then he breezed out to his next appointment. He had given us 50 minutes to size each other up and see if there was any chance for romance. His exit was so fast that as we left he let the door slam back in my face. It was an interesting slam.

Most of our 50-minute conversation had covered the changing state of male-female relationships. My blind date was 40 years old, from the Experimental Generation. He is "actively pursuing new ways for men and women to interact now that old traditions no longer exist." That's a real quote. He really did say that, when I asked him what he liked to do. This was a man who'd read *Ms.* magazine and believed every word of it. He'd been single for 16 years but had lived with a few women during that time. He was off that evening for a ski weekend, meeting someone who was paying her own way for the trip.

I too am from the Experimental Generation, but I couldn't even pay for my own drink. To me, feminism has backfired against women. In 1973 I left what could have been a perfectly good marriage, taking with me a child in diapers, a 10-year-old Plymouth, and Volume 1, Number One of *Ms.* magazine. I was convinced I could make it on my own. In the last 15 years my ex has married or lived with a succession of women. As he gets older, his women stay in their 20s. Meanwhile, I've stayed unattached. He drives a BMW. I ride buses.

Today I see feminism as the Great Experiment That Failed, and women in my generation, its perpetrators, are the casualties. Many of us, myself included, are saddled with raising children alone. The resulting poverty makes us experts at cornmeal recipes and ways to find free recreation on weekends. At the same time, single men from our generation amass fortunes in CDs and real-estate ventures so they can breeze off on ski weekends. Feminism freed men, not women. Now men are spared the nuisance of a wife and family to support. After childbirth, if his wife's waist doesn't return to 20 inches, the husband can go out and get a more petite woman. It's far more difficult for the wife, now tied down with a baby, to find a new man. My blind date that Friday waved goodbye as he drove off in his RV. I walked home and paid the sitter with laundry quarters.

5 The main message of feminism was: Woman, you don't need a man. Remember, those of you around 40, the phrase: "A woman without a man is like a fish without a bicycle?" That joke circulated through "consciousness raising" groups across the country in the '70s. It was a philosophy that made divorce and cohabitation casual and routine. Feminism made women disposable. So today a lot of females are around 40 and single with a couple of kids to raise on their own. Child-support payments might pay for a few pairs of shoes, but in general, feminism gave men all the financial and personal advantages over women.

What's worse, we asked for it. Many women decided: You don't need a family structure to raise your children. We packed them off to day-care centers where they could get their nurturing from professionals. Then we put on our suits and ties, packed our briefcases, and took off on this Great Experiment, convinced that there was no difference between ourselves and the guys in the other offices.

Biological thing. How wrong we were. Because like it or not, women have babies. It's this biological thing that's just there, these organs we're born with. The truth is, a woman can't live the true feminist life unless she denies her child-bearing biology. She has to live on the pill, or have her tubes tied at an early age. Then she can keep up with the guys with an uninterrupted career and then, when she's 30, she'll be paying her own way on ski weekends too.

The reality of feminism is a lot of frenzied and overworked women dropping kids off at day-care centers. If the child is sick, they just send along some children's Tylenol and then rush off to underpaid jobs that they don't even like. Two of my working-mother friends told me they were mopping floors and folding laundry after midnight last week. They live on five hours of sleep, and it shows in their faces. And they've got husbands! I'm not advocating that women retrogress to the brainless housewives of the '50s who spent afternoons baking macaroni sculptures and keeping Betty Crocker files. Post-World War II women were the first to be left with a lot of free time, and they weren't too creative in filling it. Perhaps feminism was a reaction to that Brainless Betty, and in that respect, feminism has served a purpose.

Women should get educations so they can be brainy in the way they raise their children. Women can start small businesses, do consulting, write freelance out of the home. But women don't belong in 12-hour-a-day executive office positions, and I can't figure out today what ever made us think we would want to be there in the first place. As long as that biology is there, women can't compete equally with men. A ratio cannot be made using disproportionate parts. Women and men are not equal, we're different. The economy might even improve if women came home, opening up jobs for unemployed men, who could then support a wife and children, the way it was, pre-feminism.

Sometimes on Saturday nights I'll get dressed up and go out club-hopping 10
or to the theater, but the sight of all those other women my age, dressed a little too young, made up to hide encroaching wrinkles, looking hopefully into the crowds, usually depresses me. I end up coming home, to spend my Saturday night with my daughter asleep in her room nearby. At least the NBC Saturday-night lineup is geared demographically to women at home alone.

Questions for Discussion

1. Do you believe that Ebeling's autobiographical account is sufficient to support her claim that feminism has failed to meet its intended goals? If you find her argument convincing, be able to say why. If you do not, say what you would need to know more about—either about her own life or from library or field research.
2. Ebeling's argument appeared originally as a "My Turn" column in *Newsweek;* within that general readership, what specific audience do you think Ebeling was writing to? Was it possibly other women of her generation with similar experiences who nevertheless still have faith in feminism? Or young women who may yet avoid the mistakes she made? Or some other group? Be able to explain the basis for your inference about Ebeling's intended audience.
3. The persuasive appeal of an autobiographical argument depends upon the ability of the writer to build identification and empathy between himself or herself and the audience. How effective is Ebeling at using the ethical and emotional appeals of persuasion?
4. In paragraphs 7 and 9, Ebeling points out that women's biological capacity for child-bearing makes them both different from and "not equal" to men. Do you agree that child-bearing necessarily makes women unable to compete equally in the workplace? Explain.

For Persuasion

Perhaps you have felt personal dissatisfaction over something, as Ebeling has about feminism. Your dissatisfaction may have been over a policy, a social institution, or even a belief or value that has affected your life. Write an argument in which you use your personal experiences to persuade an audience to see the validity of your objections. Try to organize your experience as reasons in support of your position rather than simply presenting a narrative of your experience. Also, try not to sound as if you are merely venting your anger or pleading for sympathy.

BETTY FRIEDAN

The Half-Life of Reaction

In 1963 Betty Friedan's The Feminine Mystique *began a revolution in the way American women thought about success and fulfillment in their lives. Friedan argued that popular culture of the post-World War II era glorified the image of the "happy housewife" who found total satisfaction in housekeeping and meeting the needs of husband and children. This image, the "feminine mystique," suggested that femininity lay in subordinating and even hiding one's real interests and talents. In trying to live up to the mystique, Friedan suggested, American women found only frustration, yet they could not explain why their lives felt so empty. Friedan answered that, in denying their equality with men, women were denying their selves. With this, Friedan—who was one of the founders of the National Organization for Women (NOW)—set the tone for the first stage of feminism, arguing that women should be independent and equal to men, economically, politically, and socially.*

By the 1980s Friedan saw the feminist movement weakening, as women and men questioned whether differences between the sexes could really be ignored and whether feminism, in emphasizing career success, had given too little attention to the role of family and motherhood. In the argument that follows, which is excerpted from her 1981 book The Second Stage, *Friedan offers a revision of feminism. Critics continue to argue whether her revision takes the movement for equality ahead or backward.*

BEFORE WE can come to grips with the practical problems of living, working, and loving in equality in the second stage, we have to understand and transcend the reaction against the family that characterized and distorted the first stage of the women's movement. Otherwise, the modern women's movement could fizzle out in the same stalemate and backlash that aborted the early struggle for women's rights after the winning of the vote in 1920.

Reviewing the history of the original feminist movement and why it failed to alter the lives of most American women, historian William O'Neill, in his book *Everyone Was Brave,* concluded that the trouble was rooted in the movement's unwillingness to tackle the problems of the family. Most of the early American feminists were either young single women opposed to marriage and family or else married professional women who didn't have children or preferred to concentrate on loftier issues, such as the vote. They assumed that winning suffrage would automatically usher in equality and purify society. Yet, wrote O'Neill, since the masses of American women were married or wanted to be, the only way that equality between the sexes could have been achieved was through a "revolution in domestic life" that would reconcile the demands of family and career—a revolution that the first feminists never attempted. And that is why the original feminist movement collapsed after the vote was won in 1920.

Over two million strong in the heyday of their equivalent of NOW, the early feminists' dreams and passions were buried in memory by the backlash of the feminine mystique, as most American women continued to marry, have children, and work briefly before marriage, and in national or domestic emergencies—while a few "exceptional" women had "careers," forgoing marriage or motherhood. Like ghosts of their own truncated dream, the early suffragette leaders grew old and died, a final fiery bitter few living on in Washington in the old house, now a National Historic Landmark, that was headquarters of the National Woman's Party, making a nuisance of themselves with Congressmen about the Equal Rights Amendment, which they had introduced in 1922. Women's rights became an embarrassing dirty joke in Washington, and in the national memory, until we broke through the feminine mystique and began the modern women's movement, nearly fifty years later, starting over from scratch, it seemed.

A few years ago it looked as if the modern women's movement might suffer the same fate as its historical predecessor. The popular (and unpopular) image of the modern feminist was that of a career "superwoman" hellbent on beating men at their own game, or of a young "Ms. Libber" agitating against marriage, motherhood, the family, sexual intimacy with men, and any and all of the traits with which women in the past pleased or attracted men.

That bra-burning image, and other phenomena of "sexual politics"[1] in 5
general, distorted the main thrust of the women's movement for equality and gave its enemies a powerful weapon. For it played into the fears and violated the feelings and needs of a great many women, and men, who still look to the family for security, love, roots in life. And it may have led other women, especially younger women, who ardently embrace the new opportunities and the feminist goal of self-realization, to deny those other needs.

In earlier years I used to blame that bra-burning image on the media or on fringe extremists who did not speak for the women's movement. They were an embarrassment we had to endure, to keep up that solid front of sisterhood. The media did exaggerate the extremist note, but it is necessary now to examine the personal truth of the women who were preaching the most extreme rhetoric of women's lib, and those for whom that note resonated, seductive or threatening. The very extremity of the reaction, and the rage and fear it reflects and elicits, have to be understood now, so that we can transcend reaction and move on to the real work of the second stage, as the first feminists did not.

As long as women remain locked in reaction, they will continue to swing between extreme versions of one half-life or another—the feminine mystique or its feminist reversal—never transcending the terrible split that has tormented women for so long, never embracing the fullness of life that is open to women now, in love and work, as it never was to women before. Or rather, as long as

[1]"Sexual politics" sees the entire history of the relationship between the sexes as one in which men have held the power and have used it to keep women subordinate. The full argument appears in Kate Millett's *Sexual Politics* (1971).

women remain locked in reaction to what was, they will be obsessed with false fears and unreal options instead of confronting the new problems that have to be solved in Stage Two.

It seems to me you can trust feminists—or any other "ists" for that matter—only when they speak from personal truth in all its complexity. Such truth is never black or white. The image of "women's lib" as being opposed to the family was encouraged by women locked in violent reaction against their own identity—in those days when a woman was defined not as a person in herself, but as someone else's wife or mother, defined by her service role in the family as less than a person, "just a housewife," even when she worked outside the home. That feminine mystique had to be broken through so that we might be able to demand and be taken seriously in our demand for equal rights and opportunities in the world. The anger we felt, then, was real enough. But the rhetoric we used to assert our personhood denied—or somehow omitted, skipped over after so many years of overemphasis—other elements of our personal truth.

For instance, the founding mothers of NOW in 1966 averaged more than two children apiece. Kay Clarenbach took care of her three kids in a Quonset hut after World War Two while her husband went to Columbia University on the GI Bill. After her kids went to school, she went back and got her own degree in Wisconsin, where they now lived, and then headed its Continuing Education program. Muriel Fox, high-powered public relations executive, brought her two children along to NOW's founding conference in Washington in 1966, and her surgeon husband put them to bed in the hotel while she stayed up all night getting out our first press release. All the years I was working on *The Feminine Mystique,* I would blithely stop writing when my little daughter came home from school, or my boys were in a Little League or basketball game, or to make a martini when my husband got home, fix dinner, argue, go to the movies, make love, join an expedition to the supermarket or a country auction on Saturday, organize a clambake on the beach at Fire Island, take the kids over the battlefield at Gettysburg, or camping on Cape Hatteras—the stuff of family life. We took all that for granted. But that was supposed to be all of a woman's life, in those days of the feminine mystique. That image had to be corrected. The thrust then, when we started the women's movement, had to be "action to break through the barriers that kept women from participating in the mainstream of society." That meant breaking through the housewife image. Even the demand for equal pay was subverted by that image of women in terms of family—she didn't need the money because she had a husband to take care of her.

I resorted to a rather extreme metaphor at that time, likening the "trap" of 10
the suburban housewife to a "comfortable concentration camp." But even then I realized that it was our fear of risking ourselves in the world that made us cling to the trap. The Statement of Purpose of NOW, as I drafted it, demanded "full equality for women, in truly equal partnership with men." It demanded equality, not only in office, classroom, government, and church, but in marriage and the family. It forswore "enmity to men"; men were members of NOW from the very beginning.

Around 1969, when that anti-man, anti-family, bra-burning image of "women's lib" was built up in *Newsweek* and *Time* cover stories exaggerating the antics of the most extremist voices in the movement, I remember the helpless feeling shared by the founding mothers of NOW: "But that's not what we meant, not at all." For us, with our roots in the middle American mainstream and our own fifties' families, equality and the personhood of women never meant destruction of the family, repudiation of marriage and motherhood, or implacable sexual war against men. That "bra-burning" note shocked and outraged us, and we knew it was wrong—personally and politically—though we never said so, then, as loudly as we should have. We were intimidated by the conformities of the women's movement and the reality of "sisterhood is powerful," as we never would have been by "the enemy."

But in the late sixties and the seventies, young radical women, scarred early by the feminine mystique, and without firm roots in family or career, gave vent to their rage in a rhetoric of sexual politics based on a serious ideological mistake. And they, and later daughters who based personal and political strategies on their distortion, locked themselves and the movement into a reaction that perpetuates, in reverse, the very half-life they were reacting against.

Consider, for instance, the personal reality of some of those valiant women who produced fantasies of mounting Amazonian armies against men, wrote SCUM manifestos (Society for Cutting Up Men), or would shock and titillate suburban matrons at meetings of the League of Women Voters and the National Conference of Christians and Jews by proclaiming, "All married women are prostitutes," and "Only honest prostitutes are heroines." Consider the ones who said women would never be free unless the family was abolished and women forswore motherhood and sexual intercourse with men. "Let babies be bred in test tubes!" they cried. Or they created elaborate rationales reducing every relation of man to woman, and the military and economic depredations of the nation, to rape. The rhetoric ranged from the ridiculous (the members of the consciousness-raising group deciding that if they go home and sleep with their husbands, from now on they must be "on top"; the belief that masturbation or sex with a woman was superior to any "submission" to man's penis) to the sublime (the high preaching of the new feminist theologians against every manifestation of "God, the father," or Mary Daly's image of man as vampire who feeds "on the bodies and minds of women . . . like Dracula, the he-male has lived on woman's blood"). "The personal is political" was the motto: not shaving your legs or underarms, refusing to go to the beauty parlor or wear makeup, not letting him pay the restaurant bill or hold the door open, not making his breakfast or dinner, or washing his socks.

It is easy today for critics to single out the most ludicrous fulminations of radical feminists, and thus to dismiss the entirety of the women's movement and its message as antifamily. Jean Bethke Elshtain, a Massachusetts political scientist, can easily document the case against the women's movement for "mean-spirited denunciations of all relations between men and women and . . . contempt for the female body, for pregnancy, childbirth, child-rearing." She need only cite the following: Man is portrayed as "the oppressor" in Kate Millett's *Sexual Politics;* he is driven by "metaphysical cannibalism" (Ti-Grace Atkinson); he is a "natural predator" (Susan Brownmiller); Pregnancy is "the temporary deformation of the body for the sake of the species," and the fetus is a "parasite," an "uninvited guest" (Shulamith Firestone). Ms. Elshtain could find plenty of feminists who reduced heterosexual sex to "using people, conning people, messing up people, conquering people, exploiting people" (as she put it in "Feminists Against the Family," *The Nation,* November 17, 1979). She found others who treated love itself as a "pathological condition," a "mass neurosis" which must be destroyed. Indeed, there was a time when women like Shulamith Firestone (or before them, Simone de Beauvoir[1]) portrayed motherhood as "a condition of terminal psychological and social decay, total self-abnegation and physical deterioration."

Such rhetorical extremes gave vent to personal rage smoldering under the 15
excessive, self-denying "smotherlove" of countless women who took Dr. Spock[2] literally in that era: the suburban wife whose husband roamed freely in the world and was promoted and rewarded and ate those expense-account lunches while she ate peanut-butter sandwiches with her kids; her younger sister who bought that feminine mystique so completely that she gave up her education at nineteen to get a "nothing" job and put him through medical school (blinding herself to the probability that when he finished his residency, he would leave her for some bright, ambitious intern). "All I wanted was to get married and have four children. I love the kids and Bob and my home. There's no problem you can even put a name to. But I'm desperate. I'm a server of food and putter-on of pants and a bedmaker, somebody who can be called on when you want something. But who am I?" (from *The Feminine Mystique*).

The rhetoric of sexual politics resonated and dignified the mundane, daily buried rage of countless "happy" suburban housewives and sweetly efficient secretaries, nurses, and stewardesses. But its origin was the extreme reaction of the "chicks" and "earth mothers" of the radical student movement of the sixties against their own situation in the so-called revolutionary counterculture where, in fact, the feminine mystique reached its apogee.

The position of women in that hippie counterculture was, as a young radical black male leader preached succinctly, "prone." Tom Hayden and others might like to forget it now, but those early male leaders of the radical student movement and counterculture of the sixties, white and black, were more blatantly male chauvinist pigs than their conservative fathers. From the communes of Haight-Ashbury and Big Sur and Vermont to the seized and trashed academic fortresses of Harvard and Columbia, women were supposed to wash the pots and pans and cook the spaghetti and be good girls at the mimeograph machine—the

[1]Simone de Beauvoir (1908–1986) was a French existentialist and feminist. Her best-known work is *The Second Sex* (1949).

[2]Benjamin Spock (b. 1903) is a pediatrician whose books on child-rearing influenced the parents of the baby boom generation.

"woman trip"—while the men made the revolutionary decisions, smoking their pot around the commune fire and taunting "the pigs" under the television lights.

And when these radical "chicks" were finally infected by our first feminist stirrings, and saw through the feminine mystique in the radical movement itself, and introduced their resolutions for "women's liberation" at Berkeley or Cornell, the radical young men just laughed. So the women walked out of the larger radical "movement" and formed their separate "women's lib" groups—like black separatism, right? No men allowed; man was the *enemy.*

Their personal truth as women in the counterculture or radical student movement of the sixties was doubly humiliating when viewed through the lens of revolutionary equality: the ideology of class warfare they had learned to apply to oppressed races and masses, black, brown, and pink.

They made a simple, though serious, ideological error when they applied 20
the same political rhetoric to their own situation as women versus men: too literal an analogy with class warfare, racial oppression. It was heady, and made headlines, to vent the venom earlier directed against "whitey" or "boss finks" against *men*—your own man and the whole damn sex—and use all that sophisticated Marxist jargon to make a new revolutionary case for destruction of "the patriarchal nuclear family" and the "tyranny" of sexual biology as the source of all oppression. The media seized on the rhetoric. A "revolutionary in every bedroom" was both sexier and less threatening to vested economic and political interests (it was not political at all, merely personal) than the mainstream actions of the women's movement: breaking through sex discrimination in employment, professions, education, the church; gaining women some measure of the economic independence and self-respect they so desperately needed, control over their own bodies and reproductive process, and simple, nonhumiliating police protection against rape.

Even at that time, many of us saw the extremist rhetoric of sexual politics as a pseudo-radical cop-out from the real and difficult political and economic battle for equality for women in society—which would provide a new basis for equality in the family, and for marriage, motherhood, and sexual love without martyrdom, masochism, and denigration of women. We never thought this revolution could be won in the bedroom. The sexual politics was an acting-out of rage that didn't really change anything. When women's position in society changed, sex would take care of itself. Woman's situation with respect to man or the family was *not* the same as that of the worker and boss, the black race and the white. From the totality of our own experience as women—and our knowledge of psychology, anthropology, biology—many feminists knew all along that the extremist rhetoric of sexual politics defied and denied the profound, complex human reality of the sexual, social, psychological, economic, yes, biological relationship between woman and man. It denied the reality of woman's own sexuality, her childbearing, her roots and life connection in the family.

But our voice was drowned out, for a time, in the media, and even in the movement itself, by the more strident, titillating, angry and less politically risky message of sexual politics. And those books *sold.* For they expressed that rage long buried in women out there. It was easier to fulminate against the male chauvinist pig in your own bedroom and liberate yourself from the missionary position than to take the test for law school, get the union to fight for parenting leave, or lobby the state legislature to ratify the Equal Rights Amendment.

Remembering, now, it seems to me the reaction was the most extreme—and deceptive—for those of us who had been, and maybe still were, the most dependent on men. I remember one particularly beautiful and seductive young woman, in those early days, who had quit school at eighteen to marry a successful executive, wearing her fluffy silver fox coat on our first picket lines, and *coming on,* reflexively, to the reporters and politicians she then viciously berated for treating her like a "sex object." When she wrote her treatises, exhorting women to take up arms and kill those male oppressors, she herself was living on alimony.

Another, preaching the doctrine that for women to wear eye makeup, nail polish, a bra, or a dress was to sell out to the enemy, hid behind *Vogue* while she had her own hair streaked at Kenneth's. One who had pronounced categorically that "all married women are prostitutes," outdoing the other sisters in her consciousness-raising group in invectives against the male chauvinist pigs, was so devastated when her own husband, a successful lawyer, left her that she dropped her feminist activities, joined a singles club and a computer-dating service, and came back to the group three months later with a new "fiancé." My own brave words in the early days of the women's movement hid a certain abject terror of making it on my own, in the last days of my self-destructive marriage.

25 The concrete, personal immediacy of the women's movement, the fact that its doctrines were rooted in and immediately applied to the stuff of daily life, was its unique political power—and its danger. For the reactive rhetoric of sexual politics, distorting or denying certain painful or taken-for-granted realities of women's life, hardened into a ritual feminist mystique that triggered an even more distorted and virulent antifeminist reaction. When extremists—both feminists and antifeminists—perpetuate the myth that equality means death to the family, other women, especially younger women, have a hard time figuring out what their real options are, and their own real feelings.

So Phyllis Schlafly and Marabel Morgan[1] make a lot of money pursuing their own careers, going around the country lecturing to women that they don't need equal rights, just husbands to support them (which they'll allegedly stop doing when the Equal Rights Amendment[2] is passed). But Phyllis Schlafly is herself taking advantage of the equal opportunity she says other women don't

[1]Phyllis Schafly is a conservative writer who has been highly critical of the contemporary feminist movement. Marabel Morgan's best-selling book *The Total Woman* (1973) advised women to subordinate their own professional and public lives to the higher priorities of husband, home, and children; it was notorious for suggesting that wives keep their husbands' romantic interest through such tactics as meeting them at the door in provocative costume—for example, covered only with plastic wrap.

[2]The Equal Rights Amendment passed the House (1971) and the Senate (1972) by the required two-thirds margins, but never became law because it was not ratified by at least 38 state legislatures. The amendment stated that "Equality of rights under the law shall not be denied or abridged by the U.S. or any state on account of sex."

need, getting her law degree at a prestigious university which never would have admitted a middle-aged woman like herself before the women's movement. And Marabel Morgan admits to *Time* magazine that she herself no longer has time to deck her naked body in Saran Wrap, ostrich feathers, black-lace garter belt, and baby-white boots, in the manner she prescribes to all those insecure women who pay her for lessons on how to meet their tired husbands at the door, cooing, "I crave your body," to keep them from straying and to keep themselves supported in the style they'd like to stay accustomed to. Marabel Morgan's ability now to contribute her own money to that support may be assumed to be as enticing to her own husband as the Saran Wrap, which in real life does not seem to keep those husbands from straying. Lecturing in Texas recently, several months after Marabel Morgan ran one of her "Total Woman" courses, I heard from some psychologists of the devastation to women, who had flogged themselves on to new depths of self-degradation and denial with those ostrich feathers and Saran Wrap maneuvers, when their husbands, in fact, did run off (maybe faster?) with the younger "chicks" from the office.

Reaction is dangerous in its denial of reality. The underlying reality is no different for the bitterest feminists than for the most stridently fearful defenders of the family. None of us can depend throughout our new long lives on that old nuclear family to meet our needs for nurture, love, and support, but all of us still have those needs. The answer is not to deny them, but to recognize that equality makes it possible, and necessary, for *new* kinds of family. The answer is to recognize, strengthen, or create new family forms that can sustain us now—and that will change, as our own needs change, over time.

But it is not easy to free ourselves from the reaction against past dangers which makes some women so strongly fearful now of marriage or motherhood—and some women fearful of equality, and their own selves, now denying real weakness, now real strength.

Reaction is the blind spot both feminists and antifeminists share about the family, locked in the past. Is the family, in fact, so dependent on women's inequality and denial of self that Phyllis Schlafly and Marabel Morgan, in their accurate recognition of women's deep-rooted feeling about marriage and the family, have to deny the reality of the strong selfhood and freewheeling, rewarding careers they both personally enjoy, while . . . other radical feminists, in their accurate perception of the importance of women's autonomy and self-realization, have to deny the reality of their own and other women's deep personal needs for intimacy and family support?

Perhaps these fears themselves are the main problem now—making us 30
cower behind these masks of blind reaction, resisting the tests of evolving life, at our own needless loss, and peril. For there is evidence already that the new sense of equality and strength of self women are achieving may be better, for women's own health and the strength of the family, than the old abject dependence.

There are also new conflicts, stresses, and problems beyond reaction. Whatever their ideological fix, as more and more women do, in fact, face these tests of life—seizing, or forced by economic necessity to seize, new opportunities in job or profession, dealing with the realities of the families they already have, or making those new choices, to have a baby, or not—the picture that emerges is something quite different from either feminine or feminist mystique, integrating, in new forms, elements recognizable from both. The reality is richer, the problems and the pleasures more complex, interesting, reassuring, surprising, the pains not as unendurable as those fears bred by blind reaction which keep some feminists and antifeminists from risking new life tests.

. . . [N]ew questions have to be asked about women's experience today that may have been hidden or unanticipated by feminist assumptions. These questions couldn't be asked before—and experts, including feminists, can't answer them yet—because women simply didn't have the same choices before.

We may face questions that seem to have no answers today, because the answers involve choices we don't want to make. Beware of that growing dismay that the choices we sought in the sixties and seventies are not so simple as they once seemed. Beware of that return of nostalgia for the simple days when women had no choices. In the fear, and even actual resentment, of the hard choices women face today, beware of the temptation to believe it is even possible, much less desirable, to go back.

We have to ask these new questions to free ourselves from unnecessary conflicts before we can solve other, real problems that we have been evading by sustaining illusions of choice where none exists. It is dangerous for women—or experts or politicians or leaders of women—to kid themselves that there is any real choice that can evade the complex problems women face today in making a new life pattern of family, love, and work.

For instance, confusing the current national discussion of the endangered 35
family—and of women's rights to jobs, Social Security, and child-care aids—is the illusion that it is possible for women to choose not to work outside the home. The idea that it is still possible for young women today to choose to be lifelong, full-time housewives—to look for their whole security, identity, satisfaction, status, and support in marriage and motherhood—lurks underneath much that is written today about women, the family, and children, even by sophisticated young women caught up in uncomfortable conflicts between the feminine and feminist mystiques, such as Linda Sexton in *Between Two Worlds: Young Women in Crisis* and Ellen Goodman in *Turning Points.*

If there is a dangerous denial of reality among some feminists locked in reaction—the ones who would deny their own need as women to love or to have children . . . —there is an equally dangerous denial of reality among those who preach, or secretly believe, that women could solve a lot of complex new problems—from their own emotional fatigue, having to be superwomen on the job and at home, to male impotence, to national unemployment and inflation—by simply "choosing" not to work, to go back home again.

The unreality of much of the talk and thinking about women today in terms of "choice" worries me. If that sense of "either/or" choice was dangerous for women in my generation of the feminine mystique, it is even more dangerous in its denial of reality for women today. That is clearly evident in the conflicts young women now suffer as they reach their late thirties and cannot "choose" to have a child. I don't envy young women who are facing or denying that agonizing choice we won for them. Because it isn't really a free choice when their paycheck is needed to cover the family bills each month, when women must look to their own jobs and professions for the security and status their mothers once sought in marriage alone, and when these professions are not structured for people who give birth to children and take responsibility for their parenting. The superwomen who are trying to "have it all," combining full-time jobs or careers with having children, for whom they still are expected to assume full responsibility, do, in fact, endure such relentless pressure that their younger sisters may not even dare to think about having children.

Even such excellent new discussions of this conflict as Marilyn Fabe and Norma Wikler's *Up Against the Clock* assume it is a simple either/or choice. Feminists like Fabe and Wikler say women can solve it by simply choosing, without guilt, *not to have children*—if only they can get rid of their mothers' expectations (the remnants of the old feminine mystique) that they can't fulfill themselves as women, or will somehow miss out on life, if they don't have children. But isn't motherhood, the profound human impulse to have children, more than a mystique? Is it as lightly denied, by women or men, as much current discussion assumes? On the other hand, the new attacks on feminism, in the name of the family—from Selma Fraiberg (*Every Child's Birthright: In Defense of Mothering*), who says women except those as affluent as herself who can afford full-time nurses and governesses must give up their jobs for full-time mothering, to Jean Elshtain, who blames feminists for encouraging women to work, or even to ask for new child-care arrangements and flexible job hours because it will prevent other women from choosing full-time motherhood (which they assume is a much better "choice" for women and the family than most jobs)—deny the realities of economic survival today, the psychological and economic bottom line, which, in fact, prohibits such "choice" for most women now.

In the U.S., as in all industrialized nations today, an increasingly greater majority of women work outside the home, not just because they want to "fulfill themselves" and assert their independence, but because they must, to survive. They are single and responsible for their own support, divorced and usually responsible for most or all of their children's support, or married and responsible for part of their families' support because one paycheck is not enough.

Yet the U.S. is one of the few advanced nations with no national policy of 40
leaves for maternity, paternity, or parenting at all, no national policy encouraging flexible working arrangements and part-time and shared jobs, and no national policy to provide child care for those who need it. Though most mothers as well as fathers now have to work outside the home, part or full time, the U.S. is spending less on child-care programs now than it did ten years ago. In the name of "preserving the family"—by which they mean that obsolete, traditional family in which mothers, by necessity or choice, stayed home and were supported as housewives by breadwinning fathers—Presidents, both Democratic and Republican, and even distinguished bodies of scholars such as the Carnegie Commission

on Children, investigating the crisis of the American family, have ignored the need for such services, which are now available to parents at all income levels in countries much poorer than ours, with a sliding scale of fees according to a family's ability to pay.

So the question is still treated as the individual woman's "choice"—if she "chooses" to have a child, it is her responsibility to take care of it. Of course, her husband is supposed to help now, share the parenting. But even if he is willing, eager to help, the "choice," the responsibility, is still hers.

The new questions weight that "choice" so heavily that it is no wonder more and more young women say they don't want to have children: "Can we afford for me to stop working?" "Do I have to be a superwoman?" Etc.

But there is another compelling life urge that makes itself heard, drowning out these worrisome questions, as women hit thirty, thirty-five: "Will I miss out in life if I don't have children?"

And if she has the child, and her man is eager, or at least willing, to share as much responsibility as he can (or she will let him) she might ask, "Do I want him to be the important one with the children?"

And then, harassed, when the child comes down with a bug once again at 45
school, and they call her at the office, and she can't get hold of the baby-sitter, she wonders, rushing out—she'll come back later and finish the report, if the baby-sitter comes, after she takes Bobby's temperature, after she talks to the doctor, or when Ralph gets home—but she wonders, "Is it worth it, working full time, always feeling so stretched, for the money I earn?"

And, finally, she might ask, as a new question, "Why can't I just stay home, be a mother, and enjoy it?"

And if, in desperation, she quits her job, and *does* stay home, very soon she will face the reality of that no-win choice: "I feel a pressure to go back to business. Even if you're doing what you want to do, mainly taking care of your own kids, more and more you're the odd woman out. Besides, Jack is beginning to treat me some way I don't quite like. As if he resents my staying home, but doesn't dare say so. The pressure on him is terrible. He's not crazy about his job. His new boss is really riding him, but we can't afford for him to quit. If he gets fired, we won't be able to keep the house. We're a month behind on the mortgage as it is. It was a hassle, working and the house and the two kids, but I'm getting scared, just staying home."

Some of the new questions that have arisen in the wake of the first stage of the women's movement come from defensive reaction against past pain in women's lives; some seem practically unanswerable in terms of social arrangements as they are right now—and women's terrible need to please, to be perfect. Such need makes a woman too slavish a follower of *both* old role models.

The real question, the basic question, has still to be asked: Must—can—women now meet a standard of perfection in the workplace set in the past by and for men who had wives to take care of all the details of living and—*at the same time*—meet a standard of performance at home and as mothers that was set in the past by women whose whole sense of worth, power, and mastery had to come from being perfect, all-controlling housewives and mothers?

From the experience of women in their thirties and forties to whom I have been talking, who have been juggling, trying to put it all together, in the last ten years, or making first one choice, then another—and from the experience of women now in their twenties, facing hard choices, refusing to choose, or on the verge of retreating to impossible, no-win choices again—I get a sense that these new questions have to be pressed further, and new alternatives demanded from society, to give women real choices, easier to work, love, live with. There may be various paths and choices possible for women today, with different tradeoffs and payoffs, in different patterns at different times, rather than that single pattern of lifelong full-time wife and mother, or lifelong male-career pattern, or even a simple combination of those two confining and possibly obsolete patterns. 50

Women's new experience has to lead to further questions to create new standards at home and at work that permit a more human and complete life not only for themselves but also for men. It may be that women's new experience, if we listen to it honestly, with all its dilemmas—instead of retreating in reaction or panic to women's old half-life, or its reversal, aping men's—will converge on new economic and emotional crises, and new technological possibilities in society, and will answer men's new questions in surprising ways.

There is a reconciling of seeming opposites that has to take place now, a dialectical progression from thesis-antithesis (feminine mystique-feminism) to synthesis: a new turn in the cycle that brings us back to a familiar place, from a different vantage. In the second stage, the path that Ibsen's Nora[1] walked to find herself in the world after she slammed that door takes her full circle back—but it's no longer to a Doll's House.

Questions for Discussion

1. Like Kay Ebeling in the preceding essay, Friedan argues here that feminism has failed to address women's real concerns. She calls the first stage of feminism a "half-life of reaction." What was it a reaction against, and why does she see it as a half-life?
2. Friedan wants to establish her own leadership of the movement as having been wise, fair, and realistic, with the aims of the movement distorted by the "sexual politics" of more radical feminists. Find passages where she attempts to establish her own authority and credibility, and where she is critical of other leaders of the movement. Feminist Susan Faludi has charged that *The Second Stage* is "punctuated with the tantrums of a fallen leader." Do you see any evidence to support Faludi's charge in the passages in which Friedan characterizes and criticizes other feminist leaders? (Look at paragraphs 11–14 and 23–24.)
3. In paragraphs 21, 36, 38, and 43, Friedan implies that women are denying reality when they deny their need "to love or to have children" (36). Would most readers share Friedan's assumption that for women, having children is "a

[1]At the end of Norwegian playwright Henrik Ibsen's *A Doll's House* (1879), the main character, Nora, leaves her husband, children, and comfortable home to experience the world and discover her self.

profound human impulse" (38) and "a compelling life urge" (43)? Is Friedan suggesting that this need is greater in women than in men? Do you think it is? If the need is greater in women than in men, does this mean that the responsibility for child raising should be borne mainly by the mother?

4. Friedan argues that the movement became distorted when feminists drew an analogy between oppression based on race and class and the oppression of women by men (19–22). According to Friedan, what was wrong with this analogy?
5. Feminists and antifeminists alike saw Friedan's *The Second Stage* as a strong criticism of feminism and an endorsement of marriage and motherhood. Antifeminist Phyllis Schlafly called it "another nail in the coffin of feminism." Based on this excerpt, would you agree, or would you see Friedan as attempting to mediate between radical feminists and women who want equality with men but feel alienated by the movement? Examine paragraphs 40 and 48–52. What kind of changes is Friedan calling for?

For Persuasion

In the introduction to her argument, Friedan repeats a point made by historian William O'Neill: "the only way that equality between the sexes could have been achieved was through a 'revolution in domestic life' that would reconcile the demands of family and career. . ." (paragraph 2). Do you think such a revolution in domestic life has occurred since the 1950s when women were responsible for nearly all the housework and child-rearing? If not, propose a revolutionary model of domestic life that you think could accomplish domestic equality, and make a case for adopting it. Who would your audience be? What reasons would appeal to them? How could you persuade Americans to adopt it?

For Convincing

Felice N. Schwartz has written articles for the *Harvard Business Review* ("Women as a Business Imperative," March-April 1992, and "Management Women and the New Facts of Life," January-February 1989) in which she argues that corporations that want the greatest return on their investment in training female employees need to provide more flexibility for parenting. She has been criticized by some feminists for suggesting that businesses create a "mommy track" for women who want to combine motherhood and careers, working part-time or sharing time with other workers. Research her suggestions as well as feminist objections, and argue either for or against revolutions in the workplace to make it easier for women wanting to "have it all."

ANNA QUINDLEN

Mother's Choice

As Betty Friedan notes in "The Half-Life of Reaction," many feminists in the 1960s and 1970s devalued the role of motherhood. Even in the 1980s, the "family values" decade, New York Times *columnist Anna Quindlen felt she needed to defend her decision to quit working full-time so that she could stay home and raise her two small sons. In evaluating her purpose for writing, consider to what extent she uses her own experience to persuade other women to make the same choice she did.*

I AM a mom. It's not all I am. But it's the identity that seems to cling to me most persistently right now, like ivy on the walls of an old stone house. Perhaps this is because, just over two years ago, I ditched a perfectly good full-time job in the office for two perfectly good part-time jobs at home, one writing, the other making Tollhouse cookies with assistants who always get eggshell in the batter and praising people who manage to go in the toilet one time out of three. It's a terrific life, but that's not how it's perceived by the outside world. When I quit the job that did not include eggshells and toilet training, there was a kind of solemn attitude toward what I was doing, not unlike the feeling people have about Carmelite nuns. People thought I was Doing the Noble Thing. They also thought I was nuts.

There are valid and complicated reasons why they were wrong, but they haven't been ventilated enough. There has always been a feeling on the part of moms that the Women's Movement has not taken them seriously, has in fact denigrated what they do, unless they do it in a Third World country or do it while running a Fortune 500 company and the New York marathon.

I once felt this same way about moms. Like almost everything else, this feeling had to do with the past. When I was growing up, motherhood was a kind of cage. The moms I knew had more children than they probably would have chosen, spaced closer together than they probably would have liked. Smart, dumb, rich, poor—as soon as you started throwing up in the powder room at parties and walking around in those horrible little pup-tent dresses your life was over. Your husband still went out every day, talked to other adults about adult things, whether it was the Red Sox bullpen or the price of steel. And you stayed home and felt your mind turn to the stuff that you put in little bowls and tried to spoon into little mouths and eventually wound up wiping off of little floors.

By the time I was a grown-up, the answer, if you were strong and smart and wanted to be somebody, was not to be a mom. I certainly didn't want to be one. I wanted my blouses to stay clean. I wanted my plants to have leaves. And I wanted to climb unencumbered up to the top of whatever career ladder I managed to cling to. The Women's Movement was talking about new choices. Being a mom was an old one, and one that reeked of reliance on a man and loss of identity. What kind of choice was that? So I exchanged one sort of enforced role for another, exchanging poor downtrodden mom, with Pablum in her hair, for tough lonely career woman, eating take-out Chinese from the cardboard container. I was neither imaginative nor secure enough to start from scratch. So my choice wasn't about choice at all, only about changing archetypes.

I suppose I only really learned about choice when I chose to devote more 5
of my time to a life I had previously misunderstood and undervalued: that is, when I became a mom. I was finally strong and smart enough to do something that left me vulnerable but made me feel terrific, too. I should say that it's challenging and invigorating, that the future of the next generation is in my hands. But that doesn't have much to do with my real life. About half of being a mom is just like being a mom was for my mother. It's exhausting and grungy and chaotic, and there's an enormous amount of sopping things up with paper towels and yelling things like "Don't you ever stick something like that in his ear again or I will throw you out the window!" It has nothing to do with Doing the Noble Thing.

(Here is the Noble Thing part, at least from a feminist perspective: I am raising boys here. I am teaching them to cook. I am making a game out of putting dirty clothes in the hamper. I am refusing to create Princes. If it kills me, I am going to make at least two sensitive, caring, honest individuals who know what to do with a wire whisk and what wash temperature permanent-press shirts require. Whose idea of the average woman is someone smart, aggressive, and mouthy, with her own surname and checking account.)

I wanted to be somebody, and now I am—several somebodies, to be exact. And one of them is Mom, who has job responsibility for teaching two human beings much of what they will know about feeling safe and secure, about living comfortably with other people, and with themselves. It's a job I'm good at, but that's not really why I chose it. I chose it because, while half of it is exhausting and maddening and pretty horrible, the other half is about as fun as anything has ever been in my life. Going to the playground, picking people up at school, reading "Curious George," a hundred thousand times, building castles at the beach, watching barbershop haircuts in the mirror, making Tollhouse cookies, praising people who go in the toilet: For me, this is about as good as it gets. One of the reasons I became a feminist is because I really believe that, at some level, women are better. And lots of women realize that work is great and work is money and work is ego enhancing. But, at a certain point, it's simply work—no more, no less. They realize that when men are still developing strategies for their careers, along with clogged arteries.

I love my work. Always have. But I have another job now and it's just as good. I don't need anyone to validate me anymore with a byline or a bonus, which is a good thing, because this job still doesn't get much validation, at least until it's over and you've helped raise someone who isn't a cheat or a con man. I don't need validation. I'm having fun instead.

That's why I did what I did. I didn't do it for the kids. I did it for me. Isn't that what we feminists were supposed to be supporting, a little healthy selfishness? I didn't feel guilty about being away all day at work. I just knew I was missing the best time of my life. Like today. Two guys asked me to have pizza and watch *Sleeping Beauty* with them. Do you remember how terrific *Sleeping Beauty* is, with those three fat little fairies named Flora, Fauna, and Merryweather? I could have been at the office, but instead I Did the Noble Thing: two slices with extra cheese and a long discussion of the difference between enchanted sleep and death.

Questions for Discussion

1. In paragraphs 3 and 4, Quindlen presents the opposing view to her position—reasons for not choosing motherhood. What strategies does she use to undermine or discredit women's fears of undertaking the role of "mom"?
2. Quindlen says her reasons for choosing motherhood have nothing to do with self-sacrifice or doing the "Noble Thing." What are her reasons? In particular, what are her reasons for claiming that motherhood is actually superior to other work (see paragraphs 7 and 8)? What assumptions and values are these reasons based on?
3. How is Quindlen's experience with motherhood different from the "cage" she describes in paragraph 3? How does her style of writing help to persuade us that motherhood is fun?
4. What factors in Quindlen's life have enabled her to choose to stay home with her children? How realistic is this choice for most mothers? What factors have helped her to see this lifestyle as a choice rather than a trap?

For Inquiry and Convincing

A sociologist at the University of Illinois, Catherine E. Ross, studied 1,000 families in 1990 to research the effects of parenthood on psychological well-being. Ross found that the happiest women were those with no children and a job, while the most depressed were those who stayed home with their children. Do additional research into the question of whether women in general are happier working outside of the home or staying at home with their young children. Write an argument that uses such broadly based evidence to support or refute Quindlen's case for choosing to stay home.

For Inquiry and Persuasion

Quindlen suggests that women are "better" than men (paragraph 7), and that for this reason, many of them find child-rearing a rewarding experience. Inquire into the issue of whether men can be just as nurturing as women. (As the title of the movie *Mr. Mom* suggests, when men do take on the primary parenting role, are they taking on some sex-specific character traits?) Write a persuasive argument, aimed at men, that will make them willing to put their careers on the back burner while they stay home with their young children.

SUSAN FALUDI

The Backlash against Feminism

In 1991 Susan Faludi published a widely discussed book assessing the climate of opinion about feminism in America. In Backlash: The Undeclared War Against American Women, *she offers evidence from many fronts of attempts to reverse the gains of feminism: from the media's reports of burned-out career women and frustrated husband-hunters; from the beauty industry's silicone implants and diet-plan mania; from films like* Baby Boom *and television shows like* thirtysomething *that glorified motherhood over career; and particularly from the politics of the New Right, which coupled "family values" with women's return to the domestic sphere. Unlike Betty Friedan, Sally Quinn, and others who blame extremist ideology and hypocritical leadership for the "backlash" against feminism, Faludi sees the reaction as a struggle to regain power by interests who feel threatened by the tremendous gains women made in the 1970s and 1980s.*

In the following excerpt from Backlash, *Faludi argues that masculine opposition to feminism, especially among certain socioeconomic groups, is responsible for a counterassault on women's rights.*

> *And when women do not need to live through their husbands and children, men will not fear the love and strength of women, nor need another's weakness to prove their own masculinity.*
>
> —BETTY FRIEDAN, *The Feminine Mystique*

THIS STIRRING proclamation, offered in the final page of Friedan's classic work, is one prediction that never came to pass. Feminists have always optimistically figured that once they demonstrated the merits of their cause, male hostility to women's rights would evaporate. They have always been disappointed. "I am sure the emancipated man is a myth sprung from our hope and eternal aspiration," feminist Doris Stevens wrote wearily in the early 1900s (qtd. in Cott 45). "There has been much accomplishment," Margaret Culkin Banning wrote of women's rights in 1935, ". . . and more than a few years have passed. But the resentment of men has not disappeared. Quietly it has grown and deepened" (358).

When author Anthony Astrachan completed his seven-year study of American male attitudes in the 1980s, he found that no more than 5 to 10 percent of the men he surveyed "genuinely support women's demands for independence and equality" (402). In 1988, the American Male Opinion Index, a poll of three thousand men conducted for *Gentlemen's Quarterly,* found that less than one fourth of men supported the women's movement, while the majority favored traditional roles for women. Sixty percent said wives with small children should stay home (1:2). Other studies examining male attitudes toward the women's movement—of which, regrettably, there are few—suggest that the most substantial share of the growth in men's support for feminism may have occurred in the first half of the '70s, in that brief period when women's "lib" was fashionable, and slowed since. As the American Male Opinion Index observed, while men in the '80s continued to give lip service to such abstract matters of "fair play" as the right to equal pay, "when the issues change from social justice to personal applications, the consensus crumbles" (1:26). By the '80s, as the poll results made evident, men were interpreting small advances in women's rights as big, and complete, ones; they believed women had made major progress toward equality—while women believed the struggle was just beginning. This his-and-hers experience of the equal rights campaign would soon generate a gulf between the sexes.

At the same time that men were losing interest in feminist concerns, women were gaining and deepening theirs. During much of the '70s, there had been little divergence between men and women in polling questions about changing sex roles, and men had even given slightly more support than women to such issues as the Equal Rights Amendment. But as women began to challenge their own internalized views of a woman's proper place, their desire and demand for equal status and free choice began to grow exponentially. By the '80s, as the polls showed, they outpaced men in their support for virtually every feminist position.

The pressures of the backlash only served to reinforce and broaden the divide. As basic rights and opportunities for women became increasingly threatened, especially for female heads of households, the ranks of women favoring not just a feminist but a social-justice agenda swelled. Whether the question was affirmative action, the military buildup, or federal aid for health care, women were becoming more radical, men more conservative. This was especially apparent among younger women and men; it was younger men who gave the most support to Reagan. (Contrary to conventional wisdom, the rise of "the conservative youth" in the early '80s was largely a one-gender phenomenon.) Even in the most liberal baby-boom populations, male and female attitudes were polarizing dramatically. A national survey of "progressive" baby boomers (defined as the 12 million who support social-change groups) found 60 percent of the women called themselves "radical" to "very liberal," while 60 percent of the men titled themselves "moderate" to "conservative." The pollsters identified one prime cause for this chasm: The majority of women surveyed said they felt the '80s had been a "bad decade" for them (while the majority of men disagreed)—and they feared the next decade would be even worse (Craver).

The divergence in men's and women's attitudes passed several benchmarks 5
in 1980. For the first time in American history, a gender voting gap emerged over women's rights issues (Klein 6). For the first time, polls found men less likely than women to support equal roles for the sexes in business and government, less likely to support the Equal Rights Amendment—and more likely to say they preferred the "traditional" family where the wife stayed home (Klein 158–159; Walsh 60).

Moreover, some signs began to surface that men's support for women's rights issues was not only lagging but might actually be eroding. A national poll found that men who "strongly agreed" that the family should be "traditional"—with the man as the breadwinner and the woman as the housewife—suddenly jumped four percentage points between 1986 and 1988, the first rise in nearly a decade (Niemi, et al.). (The same year, it fell for women.) The American Male Opinion Index found that the proportion of men who fell into the group opposing changes in sex roles and other feminist objectives had risen from 48 percent in 1988 to 60 percent in 1990—and the group willing to adapt to these changes had shrunk from 52 percent to 40 percent (2:5).

By the end of the decade, the National Opinion Research poll was finding that nearly twice the proportion of women as men thought a working mother could be just as good a parent as a mother who stayed home. In 1989, while a majority of women in the *New York Times* poll believed American society had not changed enough to grant women equality, only a minority of men agreed. A majority of the men *were* saying, however, that the women's movement had "made things harder for men at home" (Belkin Al). Just as in previous backlashes, American men's discomfort with the feminist cause in the last decade has endured—and even "quietly grown and deepened."

While pollsters can try to gauge the level of male resistance, they can't explain it. And unfortunately our social investigators have not tackled "the man question" with one-tenth the enterprise that they have always applied to "the woman problem." The works on masculinity would barely fill a bookshelf. We might deduce from the lack of literature that manhood is less complex and burdensome, and that it requires less maintenance than femininity. But the studies that are available on the male condition offer no such assurance. Quite the contrary, they find masculinity a fragile flower—a hothouse orchid in constant need of trellising and nourishment. "Violating sex roles has more severe consequences for males than females," social researcher Joseph Pleck concluded (9). "[M]aleness in America," as Margaret Mead wrote, "is not absolutely defined; it has to be kept and reearned every day, and one essential element in the definition is beating women in every game that both sexes play" (318). Nothing seems to crush the masculine petals more than a bit of feminist rain—a few drops are perceived as a downpour. "Men view even small losses of deference, advantages, or opportunities as large threats," wrote William Goode, one of many sociologists to puzzle over the peculiarly hyperbolic male reaction to minuscule improvements in women's rights (137).

"Women have become so powerful that our independence has been lost in our own homes and is now being trampled and stamped underfoot in public." So Cato wailed in 195 B.C., after a few Roman women sought to repeal a law that forbade their sex from riding in chariots and wearing multicolored dresses. In the 16th century, just the possibility that two royal women might occupy thrones in Europe at the same time provoked John Knox to issue his famous diatribe, "The First Blast of the Trumpet Against the Monstrous Regiment of Women."

By the 19th century, the spokesmen of male fears had mostly learned to hide their anxiety over female independence behind masks of paternalism and pity. As Edward Bok, the legendary Victorian editor of the *Ladies' Home Journal* and guardian of women's morals, explained it to his many female readers, the weaker sex must not venture beyond the family sphere because their "rebellious nerves instantly and rightly cry out, 'Thus far shalt thou go, but no farther' " (qtd. in Kinnard 308). But it wasn't female nerves that were rebelling against feminist efforts, not then and not now.

10 A "crisis of masculinity" has erupted in every period of backlash in the last century, a faithful quiet companion to the loudly voiced call for a "return to femininity." In the late 1800s, a blizzard of literature decrying the "soft male" rolled off the presses. "The whole generation is womanized," Henry James's protagonist Basil Ransom lamented in *The Bostonians.* "The masculine tone is passing out of the world; it's a feminine, a nervous, hysterical, chattering, canting age. . . . The masculine character . . . that is what I want to preserve, or rather, as I may say, to recover; and I must tell you that I don't in the least care what becomes of you ladies while I make the attempt!" (290). Child-rearing manuals urged parents to toughen up their sons with hard mattresses and vigorous athletic regimens. Billy Sunday led the clerical attack on "feminized" religion, promoting a "muscular Christianity" and a Jesus who was "no dough-faced, lickspittle-proposition" but "the greatest scrapper that ever lived" (qtd. in Douglas 397). Theodore Roosevelt warned of the national peril of losing the "fiber of vigorous hardiness and masculinity" and hardened his own fiber with the Rough Riders (Kimmel 243). Martial swaggering prevailed on the political platform; indeed, as sociologist Theodore Roszak writes of the "compulsive masculinity" era that culminated in World War I, "The period leading up to 1914 reads in the history books like one long drunken stag party" (92).

The masculinity crisis would return with each backlash. The fledgling Boy Scouts of America claimed one-fifth of all American boys by 1920; its founder's explicit aim was to staunch the feminization of the American male by removing young men from the too powerful female orbit. Chief Scout Ernest Thompson Seton feared that boys were degenerating into "a lot of flat-chested cigarette-smokers, with shaky nerves and doubtful vitality" (qtd. in Hantover 294). Again, in the years following World War II, male commentators and literary figures were panicking over reduced masculine powers. At home, "momism" was siphoning virile juices. Philip Wylie's best-selling *Generation of Vipers* advised, "We must face the dynasty of the dames at once, deprive them of our pocketbooks," before the American man degenerated into "the Abdicating Male" (qtd. in Lynn 60). In what was supposed to be a special issue on "The American Woman," *Life* magazine fixated on the weak-kneed American man. Because women had failed to live up to their feminine duties, the 1956 article charged, "the emerging American man tends to be passive and irresponsible" (qtd. in Lynn 72). In the business world, the *Wall Street Journal* warned in 1949 that "women are taking over" (qtd. in Chafe 182). *Look* decried the rise of "female dominance": First, women had grabbed control of the stock market, the magazine complained, and now they were advancing on "authority-wielding executive jobs" (qtd. in Ehrenreich, *Hearts* 37).

In the '80s, male nerves rebelled once more, as "a decline in American manhood" became the obsession of male clergy, writers, politicians, and scholars all along the political spectrum, from the right-wing Reverend Jerry Falwell to the leftist poet and lecturer Robert Bly. Antiabortion leaders such as Randall Terry rallied thousands of men with their visions of a Christ who was a muscle-bound "soldier," not a girlish "sheep." A new "men's movement" drew tens of thousands of followers to all-male retreats, where they rooted out "feminized" tendencies and roused "the wild man within." In the press, male columnists bemoaned the rise of the "sensitive man." *Harper's* editor Lewis Lapham advocated all-male clubs to tone sagging masculinity: "Let the lines of balanced tension go slack and the structure dissolves into the ooze of androgyny," he predicted (qtd. in Kimmel). In films and television, all-male macho action shows so swamped the screen and set that the number of female roles in this era markedly declined. In fiction, violent macho action books were flying off the shelves, in a renaissance for this genre that Bantam Books' male-action-adventure editor equated with the "blood-and-thunder pulp dime novels of the nineteenth century" (Mehren). In apparel, the masculinity crisis was the one bright spot in this otherwise depressed industry: sales boomed in safari outfits, combat gear, and the other varieties of what *Newsweek* aptly dubbed "predatory fashion" (Conant). In national politics, the '88 presidential campaign turned into a testosterone contest. "I'm not squishy soft," Michael Dukakis fretted, and leapt into a tank. "I'm very tough" (qtd. in McManus and Drogin). George Bush, whose "wimpiness" preoccupied the press, announced, "I'm the pitbull of SDI." He stocked his wardrobe with enough rugged togs to adorn an infantry, and turned jogging into a daily photo opportunity. Two years into his presidency, George Bush's metaphorical martial bravado had taken a literal and bloody turn as his administration took the nation to war; it might be said that Bush began by boasting about "kicking a little ass" in his debate with Geraldine Ferraro and ended by, as he himself put it, "kicking ass" in the Persian Gulf (Warren).

Under this backlash, like its predecessors, an often ludicrous overreaction to women's modest progress has prevailed. "The women are taking over" is again a refrain many working women heard from their male colleagues—after one or two women are promoted at their company, but while top management is still solidly male. In newsrooms, white male reporters routinely complain that only women and minorities can get jobs—often at publications where women's and minorities' numbers are actually shrinking. "At Columbia," literature professor Carolyn Heilbrun has observed, "I have heard men say, with perfect sincerity, that a few women seeking equal pay are trying to overturn the university, to ruin it" (203). At Boston University, president John Silber fumed that his English department had turned into a "damn matriarchy"—when only six of its twenty faculty members were women ("Tenure"). Feminists have "complete control" of the Pentagon, a brigadier general complained (qtd. in Falwell)—when women, much less feminists, represented barely 10 percent of the armed services and were mostly relegated to the forces' lowest levels.

But what exactly is it about women's equality that even its slightest shadow threatens to erase male identity? What is it about the way we frame manhood that, even today, it still depends so on "feminine" dependence for its survival? A little-noted finding by the Yankelovich Monitor survey, a large nationwide poll that has tracked social attitudes for the last two decades, takes us a good way toward a possible answer. For twenty years, the Monitor's pollsters have asked its subjects to define masculinity. And for twenty years, the leading definition, ahead by a huge margin, has never changed. It isn't being a leader, athlete, lothario, decision-maker, or even just being "born male." It is simply this: being a "good provider for his family" (Hayward).

If establishing masculinity depends most of all on succeeding as the prime 15
breadwinner, then it is hard to imagine a force more directly threatening to fragile American manhood than the feminist drive for economic equality. And if supporting a family epitomizes what it means to be a man, then it is little wonder that the backlash erupted when it did—against the backdrop of the '80s economy. In this period, the "traditional" man's real wages shrank dramatically (a 22 percent free-fall in households where white men were the sole breadwinners), and the traditional male breadwinner himself became an endangered species (representing less than 8 percent of all households) (Phillips 18). That the ruling definition of masculinity remains so economically based helps to explain, too, why the backlash has been voiced most bitterly by two groups of men: blue-collar workers, devastated by the shift to a service economy, and younger baby boomers, denied the comparative riches their fathers and elder brothers enjoyed. The '80s was the decade in which plant closings put blue-collar men out of work by the millions, and only 60 percent found new jobs—about half at lower pay (Ehrenreich, *Fear* 207). It was a time when, of all men losing earning power, younger baby-boom men were losing the most. The average man under thirty was earning 25 to 30 percent less than his counterpart in the early '70s. Worst off was the average young man with only a high-school education: He was making only $18,000, half the earnings of his counterpart a decade earlier (Phillips 19, 204). Inevitably, these losses in earning power would breed other losses. As pollster Louis Harris observed, economic polarization spawned the most dramatic attitudinal change recorded in the last decade and a half: a spectacular doubling in the proportion of Americans who describe themselves as feeling "powerless" (33–37).

When analysts at Yankelovich reviewed the Monitor survey's annual attitudinal data in 1986, they had to create a new category to describe a large segment of the population that had suddenly emerged, espousing a distinct set of values. This segment, now representing a remarkable one-fifth of the study's national sample, was dominated by young men, median age thirty-three, disproportionately single, who were slipping down the income ladder—and furious about it. They were the younger, poorer brothers of the baby boom, the ones who weren't so celebrated in '80s media and advertising tributes to that generation. The Yankelovich report assigned the angry young men the euphemistic label of "the Contenders" (Hayward).

The men who belonged to this group had one other distinguishing trait: They feared and reviled feminism. "It's these downscale men, the ones who can't earn as much as their fathers, who we find are the most threatened by the women's movement," Susan Hayward, senior vice president at Yankelovich, observes. "They represent 20 percent of the population that cannot handle the changes in women's roles. They were not well employed, they were the first ones laid off, they had no savings and not very much in the way of prospects for the future." Other surveys would reinforce this observation. By the late '80s, the American Male Opinion Index found that the *largest* of its seven demographic groups was now the "Change Resisters," a 24 percent segment of the population that was disproportionately underemployed, "resentful," convinced that they were "being left behind" by a changing society, and most hostile to feminism (1:17–29).

To single out these men alone for blame, however, would be unfair. The backlash's public agenda has been framed and promoted by men of far more affluence and influence than the Contenders, men at the helm in the media, business, and politics. Poorer or less-educated men have not so much been the creators of the antifeminist thesis as its receptors. Most vulnerable to its message, they have picked up and played back the backlash at distortingly high volume. The Contenders have dominated the ranks of the militant wing of the '80s antiabortion movement, the list of plaintiffs filing reverse-discrimination and "men's rights" lawsuits, the steadily mounting police rolls of rapists and sexual assailants. They are men like the notorious Charles Stuart, the struggling fur salesman in Boston who murdered his pregnant wife, a lawyer, because he feared that she—better educated, more successful—was gaining the "upper hand." They are young men with little to no prospects like Yusef Salaam, one of six charged with raping and crushing the skull of a professional woman jogging in Central Park; as he later told the court, he felt "like a midget, a mouse, something less than a man" (qtd. in Didion 45). And, just across the border, they are men like Marc Lepine, the unemployed twenty-five-year-old engineer who gunned down fourteen women in a University of Montreal engineering classroom because they were "all a bunch of fucking feminists" (qtd. in Kastor).

The economic victims of the era are men who know someone has made off with their future—and they suspect the thief is a woman. At no time did this seem more true than in the early '80s, when, for the first time, women outranked men among new entrants to the work force and, for a brief time, men's unemployment outdistanced women's. The start of the '80s provided not only a political but an economic hair trigger to the backlash. It was a moment of symbolic crossover points for men and women: the first time white men became less than 50 percent of the work force, the first time no new manufacturing jobs were created, the first time more women than men enrolled in college, the first time more than 50 percent of women worked, the first time more than 50 percent of married women worked, the first time more women with children than without children worked. Significantly, 1980 was the year the U.S. Census officially stopped defining the head of household as the husband.

To some of the men falling back, it certainly has looked as if women have 20
done the pushing. If there has been a "price to pay" for women's equality, then it seems to these men that they are paying it. The man in the White House during much of the '80s did little to discourage this view. "Part of the unemployment is not as much recession," Ronald Reagan said in a 1982 address on the economy, "as it is the great increase of the people going into the job market, and—ladies, I'm not picking on anyone but . . .—because of the increase in women who are working today."

In reality, the past decade's economic pains most often took a disproportionate toll on women, not men (Phillips 202). And working women's so-called gains under Reagan had precious little to do with men's losses. If women appeared to be snapping up more jobs in the Reagan era of 1.56 percent annual job growth—the smallest rate under any administration since Eisenhower—that's only because women had few male competitors for these new employment "opportunities." About a third of the new jobs were at or below the poverty level, up from a fourth a decade earlier, and lowly "female" service jobs in retail and service industries accounted for 77 percent of the total net job growth in the '80s. The so-called job growth occurred in such areas as $2-an-hour sweatshop labor, home-based work with subminimum wages, the salesclerk and fast-food career track of no security and no benefits. These were not positions men were losing to women; these were the bottom-of-the-barrel tasks men turned down and women took out of desperation—to support families where the man was absent, out of work, or underemployed (Mishel and Frankel 83–85, 105).

The '80s economy thinned the ranks of middle-income earners and polarized the classes to the greatest extreme since the government began keeping such records in 1946. In this climate, the only way a middle-class family maintained its shaky grip on the income ladder was with two paychecks. Household income would have shrunk three times as much in the decade if women hadn't worked in mass numbers (Phillips 202). And this fact dealt the final blow to masculine pride and identity: not only could the middle-class man no longer provide for his family, the person who bailed him out was the wife he believed he was meant to support.

To the men who were suffering, the true origins of economic polarization seemed remote or intangible: leveraged buyouts that larded up debt and spat out jobs; a speculative boom that collapsed in the 1987 Black Monday stock market crash; a shift to offshore manufacturing and office automation; a loss of union power; the massive Reagan spending cuts for the poor and tax breaks for the rich; a minimum wage that placed a family of four at the poverty level; the impossible cost of housing that consumed almost half an average worker's income. These are also conditions, it's worth noting, that to a large degree reprise economic circumstances confronting American workers in previous backlash eras: Mass financial speculation led to the panic of 1893 and the 1929 crash; under the late-19th-century and Depression-era backlashes, wage earners also reeled under waves of corporate mergers, unions lost their clout, and wealth was consolidated in the hands of the very few.

When the enemy has no face, society will invent one. All that free-floating anxiety over declining wages, insecure employment, and overpriced housing needs a place to light, and in the '80s, much of it fixed itself on women. "There had to be a deeper cause [for the decade's materialism] than the Reagan era and Wall Street," a former newspaper editor wrote in the *New York Times Magazine*—then concluded, "The women's movement had to have played a key role" (Dolan). Seeking effigies to hang for the '80s excesses of Wall Street, the American press and public hoisted highest a few female MBAs in this largely white male profession. "FATS" ("Female Arbitrageurs Traders and Short Sellers") was what a particularly vindictive 1987 column in *Barron's* labeled them (Schwartz). When the *New York Times Magazine* got around to decrying the avidity of contemporary brokers and investment bankers, the publication reserved its fiercest attack for a minor female player: Karen Valenstein, an E. F. Hutton vice president who was one of Wall Street's "preeminent" women (Gross 16). (In fact, she wasn't even high enough to run a division.) The magazine article, which was most critical of her supposed failings in the wife-and-motherhood department, unleashed a torrent of rage against her on Wall Street and in other newspapers (the *New York Daily News* even ran an un-popularity poll on her), and she was ultimately fired, blacklisted on Wall Street, and had to leave town. She eventually opened a more lady-like sweater store in Wyoming (Hopkins 70). Still later, when it came time to vent public wrath on the haves of the decade, Leona Helmsley was the figure most viciously tarred and feathered. She was dubbed "the Wicked Witch of the West" and a "whore" by politicians and screaming mobs, scalded in a *Newsweek* cover story (entitled "Rhymes with Rich"), and declared "a disgrace to humanity" (by, of all people, real-estate king Donald Trump). On the other hand, Michael Milken, whose multibillion-dollar manipulations dwarf Helmsley's comparatively petty tax evasions, enjoyed fawning full-page ads from many admirers, kid-gloves treatment in national magazines such as *Vanity Fair,* and even plaudits from civil rights leader Jesse Jackson.

25 For some high-profile men in trouble, women, especially feminist women, became the all-purpose scapegoats—charged with crimes that often descended into the absurd. Beset by corruption and awash in weaponry boondoggles, military brass blamed the Defense Department's troubles on feminists who were trying "to reduce combat effectiveness" and on "the feminization of the American military" (Mitchell); commanding officers advised the Pentagon that pregnancy among female officers—a condition affecting less than 1 percent of the total enlisted force at any one time—was the armed services' "single biggest readiness problem" (Evans). Mayor Marion Barry blamed a "bitch" for his cocaine-laced fall from grace—and one of his more vocal defenders, writer Ishmael Reed, went further, recasting the whole episode later in a play as a *feminist* conspiracy. Joel Steinberg's attorney claimed that the notorious batterer and child beater had been destroyed by "hysterical feminists" (qtd. in Munk). And even errant Colonel Oliver

North blamed his legal troubles in the Iran-Contra affair on "an arrogant army of ultramilitant feminists" (qtd. in Jaroslavsky).

Once a society projects its fears onto a female form, it can try to cordon off those fears by controlling women—pushing them to conform to comfortingly nostalgic norms and shrinking them in the cultural imagination to a manageable size. The demand that women "return to femininity" is a demand that the cultural gears shift into reverse, that we back up to a fabled time when everyone was richer, younger, more powerful. The "feminine" woman is forever static and childlike. She is like the ballerina in an old-fashioned music box, her unchanging features tiny and girlish, her voice tinkly, her body stuck on a pin, rotating in a spiral that will never grow.

In times of backlash, images of the restrained woman line the walls of the popular culture's gallery. We see her silenced, infantilized, immobilized, or, the ultimate restraining order, killed. She is a frozen homebound figure, a bedridden patient, an anonymous still body. She is "the Quiet Woman," the name on an '80s-vintage wine label that depicted a decapitated woman. She is the comatose woman on display in perfume ads for Opium and many other '80s scents. She is Laura Palmer, the dead girl of "Twin Peaks," whom *Esquire* picked for the cover of its "Women We Love" issue. While there have been a few cases—Murphy Brown on TV, or, to some degree, Madonna in music—where a female figure who is loud and self-determined has successfully challenged the popular consensus, they are the exceptions. More commonly, outspoken women on screen and stage have been hushed or, in a case like Roseanne Barr's, publicly shamed—and applause reserved for their more compliant and whispery sisters. In this past decade, the media, the movies, the fashion and beauty industries, have all honored most the demure and retiring child-woman—a neo-Victorian "lady" with a pallid visage, a birdlike creature who stays indoors, speaks in a chirpy small voice, and clips her wings in restrictive clothing. Her circumstances are, at least in mainstream culture, almost always portrayed as her "choice"; it is important not only that she wear rib-crushing garments but that she lace them up herself.

The restrained woman of the current backlash distinguishes herself from her predecessors in earlier American backlashes by appearing to choose her condition twice—first as a woman and second as a feminist. Victorian culture peddled "femininity" as what "a true woman" wants; in the marketing strategy of contemporary culture, it's what a "liberated" woman craves, too. Just as Reagan appropriated populism to sell a political program that favored the rich, politicians, and the mass media, and advertising adopted feminist rhetoric to market policies that hurt women or to peddle the same old sexist products or to conceal antifeminist views. Bush promised "empowerment" for poor women—as a substitute for the many social-service programs he was slashing (Murray and Wessel). Even *Playboy* claimed to ally itself with female progress. Women have made such strides, the magazine's spokeswoman assured the press, "there's no longer a stigma attached to posing" (Carter).

The '80s culture stifled women's political speech and then redirected self-expression to the shopping mall. The passive consumer was reissued as an ersatz feminist, exercising her "right" to buy products, making her own "choices" at the checkout counter. "You *can* have it all," a Michelob ad promised a nubile woman in a bodysuit—but by "all," the brewing company meant only a less-filling beer. Criticized for targeting young women in its ads, an indignant Philip Morris vice president claimed that such criticism was "sexist," because it suggested that "adult women are not capable of making their own decisions about whether or not to smoke" (Waldman). The feminist entreaty to follow one's own instincts became a merchandising appeal to obey the call of the market—an appeal that diluted and degraded women's quest for true self-determination. By returning women to a view of themselves as devoted shoppers, the consumption-obsessed decade succeeded in undercutting one of the guiding principles of feminism: that women must think for themselves. As Christopher Lasch (who would himself soon be lobbing his own verbal grenades at feminists) observed in *The Culture of Narcissism,* consumerism undermines women's progress most perniciously when it "seems to side with women against male oppression."

> The advertising industry thus encourages the pseudo-emancipation of women, flattering them with its insinuating reminder, "You've come a long way, baby" and disguising the freedom to consume as genuine autonomy. . . . It emancipates women and children from patriarchal authority, however, only to subject them to the new paternalism of the advertising industry, the industrial corporation, and the state. (139–40)

30 The contemporary counterassault on women's rights contributes still another unique tactic to the old backlash strategy books: the pose of a "sophisticated" ironic distance from its own destructive ends. To the backlash's list of faked emotions—pity for single women, worry over the fatigue level of career women, concern for the family—the current onslaught adds a sneering "hip" cynicism toward those who dare point out discrimination or anti-female messages. In the era's entertainment and advertising, aimed at and designed by baby boomers, the self-conscious cast of characters constantly let us know that *they* know their presentation of women is retrograde and demeaning, but what of it? "Guess we're reliving 'Father Knows Best,'" television figures ironically chuckle to each other, as if women's secondary status has become no more than a long-running inside joke. To make a fuss about sexual injustice is more than unfeminine; it is now uncool. Feminist anger, or any form of social outrage, is dismissed breezily—not because it lacks substance but because it lacks "style."

It is hard enough to expose antifeminist sentiments when they are dressed up in feminist clothes. But it is far tougher to confront a foe that professes not to care. Even the unmitigated furor of an antiabortion "soldier" may be preferable to the jaundiced eye of the sitcom spokesmen. Feminism is "so '70s," the pop culture's ironists say, stifling a yawn. We're "postfeminist" now, they assert, meaning not that women have arrived at equal justice and moved beyond it, but simply that they themselves are beyond even pretending to care. It is an affectlessness that may, finally, deal the most devastating blow to American women's rights.

WORKS CITED

The American Male Opinion Index. 2 vols. New York: Conde Nast, 1988.

Astrachan, Anthony. *How Men Feel: Their Response to Women's Demand for Equality and Power.* Garden City, N.Y.: Anchor, 1986.

Banning, Margaret Culkin. "Raise Their Hats." *Harper's* Aug. 1935: 354–358.

Belkin, Lisa. "Bars to Equality Seen as Eroding, Slowly." *New York Times* 20 Aug. 1989: A1+.

Carter, Alan. "Transformer." *TV Guide* 27 Aug. 1988: 20.

Chafe, William H. *The American Woman: Her Changing Social, Economic, and Political Roles, 1920–1970.* New York: Oxford UP, 1972.

Conant, Jennet. "The High-Priced Call of the Wild." *Newsweek* 1 Feb. 1988: 56.

Cott, Nancy F. *The Grounding of Modern Feminism*. New Haven: Yale UP, 1987.

Craver, Roger. Personal interview, 1991, reporting results of 1990 Craver Matthews Smith Donor Survey.

Didion, Joan. "New York: Sentimental Journeys." *New York Review of Books* 17 Jan. 1991.

Dolan, Mary Anne. "When Feminism Failed." *New York Times Magazine* 26 June 1988: 23.

Douglas, Ann. *The Feminization of American Culture.* New York: Avon, 1977.

Ehrenreich, Barbara. *Fear of Falling: The Inner Life of the Middle Class.* New York: Pantheon, 1989.

———. *The Hearts of Men: The American Dream and the Flight from Commitment*. Garden City, N.Y.: Anchor, 1983.

Evans, David. "The Navy's 5000 Pregnant Sailors." *San Francisco Examiner* 15 Aug. 1989: A19.

Falwell, Jerry. *Listen, America!* Garden City, N.Y.: Doubleday-Galilee, 1980.

Friedan, Betty. *The Feminine Mystique.* 1963. New York: Dell-Laurel, 1983.

Goode, William J. "Why Men Resist." *Rethinking the Family.* Ed. Barrie Thorne with Marilyn Yalom. New York: Longman, 1982.

Gross, Jane. "Against the Odds: A Woman's Ascent on Wall Street." *New York Times Magazine* 6 Jan. 1985: 16.

Hantover, Jeffrey P. "The Boy Scouts and the Validation of Masculinity." *The American Man.* Eds. Elizabeth and Joseph H. Pleck. Englewood Cliffs, N.J.: Prentice Hall, 1980.

Harris, Louis. *Inside America.* New York: Vintage, 1987.

Hayward, Susan [senior vice president, Yankelovich Clancy Shulman]. Personal interview, Sept. 1989.

Heilbrun, Carolyn. *Reinventing Womanhood.* New York: Norton, 1979.

Hopkins, Ellen. "The Media Murder of Karen Valenstein's Career." *Working Woman* March 1991: 70.

James, Henry. *The Bostonians.* 1886. Middlesex: Penguin, 1979.

Jaroslavsky, Rich. "Washington Wire." *Wall Street Journal* 2 Feb. 1990: A1.

Kastor, Elizabeth. "When Shooting Stopped, Canada Had Changed." *Washington Post* 10 Dec. 1989: A3.

Kimmel, Michael S. "Men's Responses to Feminism at the Turn of the Century." *Gender & Society* 1.3 (1987).

Kinnard, Cynthia D., ed. *Antifeminism in American Thought: An Annotated Bibliography.* Boston: G. K. Hall, 1986.

Klein, Ethel. *Gender Politics.* Cambridge: Harvard UP, 1984.

Lasch, Christopher. *The Culture of Narcissism.* New York: Norton, 1979.

Lynn, Mary C., ed. *Women's Liberation in the Twentieth Century.* New York: Wiley, 1975.

Mead, Margaret. *Male and Female.* New York: William & Morrow, 1949.

McManus, Doyle, and Bob Drogin. "Democrats and Foreign Policy: Test of Toughness." *Los Angeles Times* 28 Feb. 1988, sec. 1: 1.

Mehren, Elizabeth. "Macho Books: Flip Side of Romances." *San Francisco Chronicle* 2 Aug. 1988: B4.

Mishal, Lawrence, and David M. Frankel. *The State of Working America.* Armonk, N.Y.: M. E. Sharpe, 1991.

Mitchell, Brian. *The Weak Link: The Feminization of the American Military.* Washington: Regnery Gateway, 1989.

Munk, Erika. "Short Eyes: The Joel Steinberg We Never Saw." *Village Voice* 21 Feb. 1989: 20.

Murray, Alan, and David Wessel. "Modest Proposals: Faced with the Gulf War, Bush's Budget Avoids Bold Moves at Home." *Wall Street Journal* 5 Feb. 1991: A1.

Niemi, Richard G., John Mueller, and Tom W. Smith. *Trends in Public Opinion: A Compendium of Survey Data.* New York: Greenwood, 1989.

Phillips, Kevin. *The Politics of Rich and Poor.* New York: Random House, 1990.

Pleck, Joseph H. *The Myth of Masculinity.* Cambridge: MIT Press, 1981.

Roszak, Theodore. "The Hard and the Soft: The Force of Feminism in Modern Times." *Masculine/Feminine: Readings in Sexual Mythology and the Liberation of Women.* Eds. Betty and Theodore Roszak. New York: Harper, 1969.

Schwartz, Steven F. "FATS and Happy." *Barron's* 6 July 1987: 27.

"Tenure and Loose Talk." *Washington Post* 26 June 1990: A20.

Waldman, Peter. "Tobacco Firms Try Soft, Feminine Sell." *Wall Street Journal* 19 Dec. 1989: B1.

Walsh, Doris L. "What Women Want." *American Demographics* June 1986.

Warner, Margaret Garrard. "Fighting the Wimp Factor." *Newsweek* 19 Oct. 1987: 28.

Questions for Discussion

1. Does Faludi offer sufficient hard evidence in paragraphs 2 through 6 to convince you that the majority of American men do not support feminist objectives? Were you surprised by these statistics? Why, or why not? Do you think it would be possible to find other statistics that would indicate more male support for women's equality?
2. What does Faludi mean by "masculinity crisis" (paragraph 11)? What is her strategy in presenting so many historical examples in paragraphs 8 through 12?
3. In paragraph 14, Faludi cites a survey claiming that American society defines masculinity in terms of a person's ability to be a "good provider for his family." Does this mean that women as well as men tend to think of masculinity in economic terms? What social values are revealed by this definition? How would you define the terms "masculinity" and "femininity"?
4. In paragraphs 15 through 23, Faludi attempts to link some of the backlash against feminism with economic conditions in the 1980s. Do you find this cause-and-effect argument convincing? Why, or why not? Can you think of analogous situations where economic insecurity might contribute to a group's attempt to oppress minorities?
5. What images of women do you find in popular culture today? Is it common for magazines, television, and film to portray women as dependent on men,

not serious, even childlike? Do you see any examples of advertisements that promote "sexist products" as feminist choices?

For Inquiry and Convincing

Consider how the terms "masculine" and "feminine" are commonly defined. Does our society define them in ways that assign greater power to men than to women? Do men, in Betty Friedan's words, "need another's weakness to prove their own masculinity"? Does our use of these terms enhance relationships between the sexes, or make them more problematic? Or both? Should we try to even out the differences by playing up androgyny and playing down masculinity and femininity, or does playing up the differences between the sexes make life more interesting? Should we try to change our definitions of "masculine" and "feminine"? Take a position on one of these related issues, refine your thesis, and make a case in support of it.

For Persuasion

Equal rights imply equal access to power. Do gains in power for women necessarily mean a loss of power for men? Regardless of your answer, but keeping your answer in mind, make a case persuading men why they should support feminism. Be specific. For example, why men should support the women's movement when it has "made things harder for men at home" (paragraph 6).

KIRK ANDERSON

Cartoon

The following cartoon appeared in Ms. *magazine in 1993. How common are the attitudes expressed by these characters among your friends and acquaintances?*

THE INCREDIBLE SHRINKING WOMAN

Questions for Discussion

What is the point of the cartoon's title? What definition of "feminism" is being expressed? Evaluate the effectiveness of the cartoon as persuasion.

NAOMI WOLF

The Beauty Myth

Feminist writer Naomi Wolf, a 1984 graduate of Yale, sees a backlash against feminism in our culture's promotion of female beauty. Her controversial book The Beauty Myth: How Images of Beauty Are Used Against Women *(1991) charges that as women's material opportunities have expanded, a psychological force has begun working insidiously to undermine their sense of self-worth. Constantly dissatisfied with their real faces and bodies, women devote inordinate attention, time, and money to pursuing the slender, youthful, unchanging female image dictated by our society as the ideal, some even risking their health to do so through surgery or starvation. Wolf's argument is that the beauty myth is political, not aesthetic; it is imposed upon women by a society threatened by their rise in power. The following excerpt is Wolf's introduction to her book. As you read, decide to what extent Wolf seems to be anti-beauty: Does she seem to oppose all efforts to "look good"?*

AT LAST, after a long silence, women took to the streets. In the two decades of radical action that followed the rebirth of feminism in the early 1970s, Western women gained legal and reproductive rights, pursued higher education, entered the trades and the professions, and overturned ancient and revered beliefs about their social role. A generation on, do women feel free?

The affluent, educated, liberated women of the First World, who can enjoy freedoms unavailable to any women ever before, do not feel as free as they want to. And they can no longer restrict to the subconscious their sense that this lack of freedom has something to do with—with apparently frivolous issues, things that really should not matter. Many are ashamed to admit that such trivial concerns—to do with physical appearance, bodies, faces, hair, clothes—matter so much. But in spite of shame, guilt, and denial, more and more women are wondering if it isn't that they are entirely neurotic and alone but rather that something important is indeed at stake that has to do with the relationship between female liberation and female beauty.

The more legal and material hindrances women have broken through, the more strictly and heavily and cruelly images of female beauty have come to weigh upon us. Many women sense that women's collective progress has stalled; compared with the heady momentum of earlier days, there is a dispiriting climate of confusion, division, cynicism, and above all, exhaustion. After years of much struggle and little recognition, many older women feel burned out; after years of taking its light for granted, many younger women show little interest in touching new fire to the torch.

During the past decade, women breached the power structure; meanwhile, eating disorders rose exponentially and cosmetic surgery became the fastest-growing medical specialty. During the past five years, consumer spending doubled, pornography became the main media category, ahead of legitimate films and records combined, and thirty-three thousand American women told researchers that they would rather lose ten to fifteen pounds than achieve any other goal (Wooley and Wooley). More women have more money and power and scope and legal recognition than we have ever had before; but in terms of how we feel about ourselves *physically,* we may actually be worse off than our unliberated grandmothers. Recent research consistently shows that inside the majority of the West's controlled, attractive, successful working women, there is a secret "underlife" poisoning our freedom; infused with notions of beauty, it is a dark vein of self-hatred, physical obsessions, terror of aging, and dread of lost control (Cash, et al.).[1]

It is no accident that so many potentially powerful women feel this way. We 5
are in the midst of a violent backlash against feminism that uses images of female beauty as a political weapon against women's advancement: the beauty myth. It is the modern version of a social reflex that has been in force since the Industrial Revolution. As women released themselves from the feminine mystique of domesticity, the beauty myth took over its lost ground, expanding as it waned to carry on its work of social control.

The contemporary backlash is so violent because the ideology of beauty is the last one remaining of the old feminine ideologies that still has the power to control those women whom second wave feminism would have otherwise made relatively uncontrollable: It has grown stronger to take over the work of social coercion that myths about motherhood, domesticity, chastity, and passivity, no longer can manage. It is seeking right now to undo psychologically and covertly all the good things that feminism did for women materially and overtly.

This counterforce is operating to checkmate the inheritance of feminism on every level in the lives of Western women. Feminism gave us laws against job discrimination based on gender; immediately case law evolved in Britain and the United States that institutionalized job discrimination based on women's appearances. Patriarchal religion declined; new religious dogma, using some of the mind-altering techniques of older cults and sects, arose around age and weight to functionally supplant traditional ritual. Feminists, inspired by Friedan, broke the stranglehold on the women's popular press of advertisers for household products, who were promoting the feminine mystique; at once, the diet and skin care industries became the new cultural censors of women's intellectual space, and because of their pressure, the gaunt, youthful model supplanted the happy housewife as the arbiter of successful womanhood. The sexual revolution promoted the discovery of female sexuality; "beauty pornography"—which for the first time in women's history artificially links a commodified "beauty" directly and explicitly to sexuality—invaded the mainstream to undermine women's new and

[1]Dr. Cash's research shows very little connection between "how attractive women are" and "how attractive they feel themselves to be." All the women he treated were, in his terms, "extremely attractive," but his patients compare themselves only to models, not to other women. [Author's note.]

vulnerable sense of sexual self-worth. Reproductive rights gave Western women control over our own bodies; the weight of fashion models plummeted to 23 percent below that of ordinary women, eating disorders rose exponentially, and a mass neurosis was promoted that used food and weight to strip women of that sense of control. Women insisted on politicizing health; new technologies of invasive, potentially deadly "cosmetic" surgeries developed apace to re-exert old forms of medical control of women.

Every generation since about 1830 has had to fight its version of the beauty myth. "It is very little to me," said the suffragist Lucy Stone in 1855, "to have the right to vote, to own property, etcetera, if I may not keep my body, and its uses, in my absolute right" (qtd. in Dworkin 11). Eighty years later, after women had won the vote, and the first wave of the organized women's movement had subsided, Virginia Woolf wrote that it would still be decades before women could tell the truth about their bodies. In 1962, Betty Friedan quoted a young woman trapped in the Feminine Mystique: "Lately, I look in the mirror, and I'm so afraid I'm going to look like my mother." Eight years after that, heralding the cataclysmic second wave of feminism, Germaine Greer described "the Stereotype": "To her belongs all that is beautiful, even the very word beauty itself . . . she is a doll . . . I'm sick of the masquerade" (55, 60). In spite of the great revolution of the second wave, we are not exempt. Now we can look out over ruined barricades: A revolution has come upon us and changed everything in its path, enough time has passed since then for babies to have grown into women, but there still remains a final right not fully claimed.

The beauty myth tells a story: The quality called "beauty" objectively and universally exists. Women must want to embody it and men must want to possess women who embody it. This embodiment is an imperative for women and not for men, which situation is necessary and natural because it is biological, sexual, and evolutionary: Strong men battle for beautiful women, and beautiful women are more reproductively successful. Women's beauty must correlate to their fertility, and since this system is based on sexual selection, it is inevitable and changeless.

None of this is true. "Beauty" is a currency system like the gold standard. 10
Like any economy, it is determined by politics, and in the modern age in the West it is the last, best belief system that keeps male dominance intact. In assigning value to women in a vertical hierarchy according to a culturally imposed physical standard, it is an expression of power relations in which women must unnaturally compete for resources that men have appropriated for themselves.

"Beauty" is not universal or changeless, though the West pretends that all ideals of female beauty stem from one Platonic Ideal Woman; the Maori admire a fat vulva, and the Padung, droopy breasts. Nor is "beauty" a function of evolution: Its ideals change at a pace far more rapid than that of the evolution of species, and Charles Darwin was himself unconvinced by his own explanation that "beauty" resulted from a "sexual selection" that deviated from the rule of natural selection; for women to compete with women through "beauty" is a reversal of the way in which natural selection affects all other mammals.[1] Anthropology has overturned the notion that females must be "beautiful" to be selected to mate: Evelyn Reed, Elaine Morgan, and others have dismissed sociobiological assertions of innate male polygamy and female monogamy. Female higher primates are the sexual initiators; not only do they seek out and enjoy sex with many partners, but "every nonpregnant female takes her turn at being the most desirable of all her troop. And that cycle keeps turning as long as she lives." The inflamed pink sexual organs of primates are often cited by male sociobiologists as analogous to human arrangements relating to female "beauty," when in fact that is a universal, nonhierarchical female primate characteristic.

Nor has the beauty myth always been this way. Though the pairing of the older rich men with young, "beautiful" women is taken to be somehow inevitable, in the matriarchal Goddess religions that dominated the Mediterranean from about 25,000 B.C.E. to about 700 B.C.E., the situation was reversed: "In every culture, the Goddess has many lovers. . . . The clear pattern is of an older woman with a beautiful but expendable youth—Ishtar and Tammuz, Venus and Adonis, Cybele and Attis, Isis and Osiris . . . their only function the service of the divine 'womb' " (Miles 43). Nor is it something only women do and only men watch: Among the Nigerian Wodaabes, the women hold economic power and the tribe is obsessed with male beauty; Wodaabe men spend hours together in elaborate makeup sessions, and compete—provocatively painted and dressed, with swaying hips and seductive expressions—in beauty contests judged by women (Woodhead). There is no legitimate historical or biological justification for the beauty myth; what it is doing to women today is a result of nothing more exalted than the need of today's power structure, economy, and culture to mount a counteroffensive against women.

If the beauty myth is not based on evolution, sex, gender, aesthetics, or God, on what is it based? It claims to be about intimacy and sex and life, a celebration of women. It is actually composed of emotional distance, politics, finance, and sexual repression. The beauty myth is not about women at all. It is about men's institutions and institutional power.

[1]See Cynthia Eagle Russett, "Hairy Men and Beautiful Women," *Sexual Science: The Victorian Construction of Womanhood* (Cambridge, Mass.: Harvard U. P., 1989, 78–103.

On page 84 Russett quotes Darwin: "Man is more powerful in body and mind than woman, and in the savage state he keeps her in a much more abject state of bondage, than does the male of any other animal; therefore it is not surprising that he should have gained the power of selection. . . . As women have long been selected for beauty, it is not surprising that some of their successive variations should have been transmitted exclusively to the same sex; consequently that they should have transmitted beauty in a somewhat higher degree to their female than to their male offspring, and thus have become more beautiful, according to general opinion, than men." Darwin himself noticed the evolutionary inconsistency of this idea that, as Russett puts it, "a funny thing happened on the way up the ladder: Among humans, the female no longer chose but was chosen." This theory "implied an awkward break in evolutionary continuity," she observes: "In Darwin's own terms it marked a rather startling reversal in the trend of evolution."

See also Natalie Angier, "Hard-to-Please Females May Be Neglected Evolutionary Force," *New York Times* 8 May 1990; and Natalie Angier, "Mating for Life? It's Not for the Birds or the Bees," *New York Times* 21 August 1990. [Author's note.]

The qualities that a given period calls beautiful in women are merely symbols of the female behavior that that period considers desirable: *The beauty myth is always actually prescribing behavior and not appearance.* Competition between women has been made part of the myth so that women will be divided from one another. Youth and (until recently) virginity have been "beautiful" in women since they stand for experiential and sexual ignorance. Aging in women is "unbeautiful" since women grow more powerful with time, and since the links between generations of women must always be newly broken: Older women fear young ones, young women fear old, and the beauty myth truncates for all the female life span. Most urgently, women's identity must be premised upon our "beauty" so that we will remain vulnerable to outside approval, carrying the vital sensitive organ of self-esteem exposed to the air.

15 Though there has, of course, been a beauty myth in some form for as long as there has been patriarchy, the beauty myth in its modern form is a fairly recent invention. The myth flourishes when material constraints on women are dangerously loosened. Before the Industrial Revolution, the average woman could not have had the same feelings about "beauty" that modern women do who experience the myth as continual comparison to a mass-disseminated physical ideal. Before the development of technologies of mass production—daguerrotypes, photographs, etc.—an ordinary woman was exposed to few such images outside the Church. Since the family was a productive unit and women's work complemented men's, the value of women who were not aristocrats or prostitutes lay in their work skills, economic shrewdness, physical strength, and fertility. Physical attraction, obviously, played its part; but "beauty" as we understand it was not, for ordinary women, a serious issue in the marriage marketplace. The beauty myth in its modern form gained ground after the upheavals of industrialization, as the work unit of the family was destroyed, and urbanization and the emerging factory system demanded what social engineers of the time termed the "separate sphere" of domesticity, which supported the new labor category of the "breadwinner" who left home for the workplace during the day. The middle class expanded, the standards of living and of literacy rose, the size of families shrank; a new class of literate, idle women developed, on whose submission to enforced domesticity the evolving system of industrial capitalism depended. Most of our assumptions about the way women have always thought about "beauty" date from no earlier than the 1830s, when the cult of domesticity was first consolidated and the beauty index invented.

For the first time new technologies could reproduce—in fashion plates, daguerreotypes, tintypes, and rotogravures—images of how women should look. In the 1840s the first nude photographs of prostitutes were taken; advertisements using images of "beautiful" women first appeared in mid-century. Copies of classical artworks, postcards of society beauties and royal mistresses, Currier and Ives prints, and porcelain figurines flooded the separate sphere to which middle-class women were confined.

Since the Industrial Revolution, middle-class Western women have been controlled by ideals and stereotypes as much as by material constraints. This situation, unique to this group, means that analyses that trace "cultural conspiracies" are uniquely plausible in relation to them. The rise of the beauty myth was just one of several emerging social fictions that masqueraded as natural components of the feminine sphere, the better to enclose those women inside it. Other such fictions arose contemporaneously: a version of childhood that required continual maternal supervision; a concept of female biology that required middle-class women to act out the roles of hysterics and hypochondriacs; a conviction that respectable women were sexually anesthetic; and a definition of women's work that occupied them with repetitive, time-consuming, and painstaking tasks such as needlepoint and lacemaking. All such Victorian inventions as these served a double function—that is, though they were encouraged as a means to expend female energy and intelligence in harmless ways, women often used them to express genuine creativity and passion.

But in spite of middle-class women's creativity with fashion and embroidery and child rearing, and, a century later, with the role of the suburban housewife that devolved from these social fictions, the fictions' main purpose was served: During a century and a half of unprecedented feminist agitation, they effectively counteracted middle-class women's dangerous new leisure, literacy, and relative freedom from material constraints.

Though these time- and mind-consuming fictions about women's natural role adapted themselves to resurface in the post-war Feminine Mystique, when the second wave of the women's movement took apart what women's magazines had portrayed as the "romance," "science," and "adventure" of homemaking and suburban family life, they temporarily failed. The cloying domestic fiction of "togetherness" lost its meaning and middle-class women walked out of their front doors in masses.

So the fictions simply transformed themselves once more: Since the wom- 20
en's movement had successfully taken apart most other necessary fictions of femininity, all the work of social control once spread out over the whole network of these fictions had to be reassigned to the only strand left intact, which action consequently strengthened it a hundredfold. This reimposed onto liberated women's faces and bodies all the limitations, taboos, and punishments of the repressive laws, religious injunctions, and reproductive enslavement that no longer carried sufficient force. Inexhaustible but ephemeral beauty work took over from inexhaustible but ephemeral housework. As the economy, law, religion, sexual mores, education, and culture were forcibly opened up to include women more fairly, a private reality colonized female consciousness. By using ideas about "beauty," it reconstructed an alternative female world with its own laws, economy, religion, sexuality, education, and culture, each element as repressive as any that had gone before.

Since middle-class Western women can best be weakened psychologically now that we are stronger materially, the beauty myth, as it has resurfaced in the last generation, has had to draw on more technological sophistication and reactionary fervor than ever before. The modern arsenal of the myth is a dissemination of millions of images of the current ideal; although this barrage is generally seen as a collective sexual fantasy, there is in fact little that is sexual about it. It is summoned out of political fear on the part of male-dominated institutions threatened by women's freedom, and it exploits female guilt and apprehension about our own liberation—latent fears that we might be going too far. This frantic aggregation of imagery is a collective reactionary hallucination willed into being by both men and women stunned and disoriented by the rapidity with which gender relations have been transformed: a bulwark of reassurance against the flood of change. The mass depiction of the modern woman as a "beauty" is a contradiction: Where modern women are growing, moving, and expressing their individuality, as the myth has it, "beauty" is by definition inert, timeless, and generic. That this hallucination is necessary and deliberate is evident in the way "beauty" so directly contradicts women's real situation.

And the unconscious hallucination grows ever more influential and pervasive because of what is now conscious market manipulation: powerful industries—the $33-billion-a-year diet industry (O'Neill), the $20-billion cosmetics industry, the $300-million cosmetic surgery industry (*Standard and Poor's*), and the $7-billion pornography industry ("Crackdown")—have arisen from the capital made out of unconscious anxieties, and are in turn able, through their influence on mass culture, to use, stimulate, and reinforce the hallucination in a rising economic spiral.

This is not a conspiracy theory; it doesn't have to be. Societies tell themselves necessary fictions in the same way that individuals and families do. Henrik Ibsen called them "vital lies," and psychologist Daniel Goleman describes them working the same way on the social level that they do within families: "The collusion is maintained by directing attention away from the fearsome fact, or by repackaging its meaning in an acceptable format" (16–17). The costs of these social blind spots, he writes, are destructive communal illusions. Possibilities for women have become so open-ended that they threaten to destabilize the institutions on which a male-dominated culture has depended, and a collective panic reaction on the part of both sexes has forced a demand for counterimages.

The resulting hallucination materializes, for women, as something all too real. No longer just an idea, it becomes three-dimensional, incorporating within itself how women live and how they do not live: It becomes the Iron Maiden. The original Iron Maiden was a medieval German instrument of torture, a body-shaped casket painted with the limbs and features of a lovely, smiling young woman. The unlucky victim was slowly enclosed inside her; the lid fell shut to immobilize the victim, who died either of starvation or, less cruelly, of the metal spikes embedded in her interior. The modern hallucination in which women are trapped or trap themselves is similarly rigid, cruel, and euphemistically painted. Contemporary culture directs attention to imagery of the Iron Maiden, while censoring real women's faces and bodies.

25 Why does the social order feel the need to defend itself by evading the fact of real women, our faces and voices and bodies, and reducing the meaning of women to these formulaic and endlessly reproduced "beautiful" images? Though unconscious personal anxieties can be a powerful force in the creation of a vital

lie, economic necessity practically guarantees it. An economy that depends on slavery needs to promote images of slaves that "justify" the institution of slavery. Western economies are absolutely dependent now on the continued underpayment of women. An ideology that makes women feel "worth less" was urgently needed to counteract the way feminism had begun to make us feel worth more. This does not require a conspiracy; merely an atmosphere. The contemporary economy depends right now on the representation of women within the beauty myth. Economist John Kenneth Galbraith offers an economic explanation for "the persistence of the view of homemaking as a 'higher calling' ": the concept of women as naturally trapped within the Feminine Mystique, he feels, "has been forced on us by popular sociology, by magazines, and by fiction to disguise the fact that woman in her role of consumer has been essential to the development of our industrial society. . . . Behavior that is essential for economic reasons is transformed into a social virtue" (qtd. in Minton). As soon as a woman's primary social value could no longer be defined as the attainment of virtuous domesticity, the beauty myth redefined it as the attainment of virtuous beauty. It did so to substitute both a new consumer imperative and a new justification for economic unfairness in the workplace where the old ones had lost their hold over newly liberated women.

Another hallucination arose to accompany that of the Iron Maiden: The caricature of the Ugly Feminist was resurrected to dog the steps of the women's movement. The caricature is unoriginal; it was coined to ridicule the feminists of the nineteenth century. Lucy Stone herself, whom supporters saw as "a prototype of womanly grace . . . fresh and fair as the morning," was derided by detractors with "the usual report" about Victorian feminists: "a big masculine woman, wearing boots, smoking a cigar, swearing like a trooper" (qtd. in Friedan 79). As Betty Friedan put it presciently in 1960, even before the savage revamping of that old caricature: "The unpleasant image of feminists today resembles less the feminists themselves than the image fostered by the interests who so bitterly opposed the vote for women in state after state" (87). Thirty years on, her conclusion is more true than ever: That resurrected caricature, which sought to punish women for their public acts by going after their private sense of self, became the paradigm for new limits placed on aspiring women everywhere. After the success of the women's movement's second wave, the beauty myth was perfected to checkmate power at every level in individual women's lives. The modern neuroses of life in the female body spread to woman after woman at epidemic rates. The myth is undermining—slowly, imperceptibly, without our being aware of the real forces of erosion—the ground women have gained through long, hard, honorable struggle.

The beauty myth of the present is more insidious than any mystique of femininity yet: A century ago, Nora slammed the door of the doll's house; a generation ago, women turned their backs on the consumer heaven of the isolated multiapplianced home; but where women are trapped today, there is no door to slam. The contemporary ravages of the beauty backlash are destroying women physically and depleting us psychologically. If we are to free ourselves from the dead weight that has once again been made out of femaleness, it is not ballots or lobbyists or placards that women will need first; it is a new way to see.

WORKS CITED

"Crackdown on Pornography: A No-Win Battle." *U.S. News and World Report* 4 June 1984.

Cash, Thomas, Diane Cash, and Jonathan Butters. "Mirror-Mirror on the Wall: Contrast Effects and Self-Evaluation of Physical Attractiveness." *Personality and Social Psychology Bulletin* 9.3 (1983).

Friedan, Betty. *The Feminine Mystique.* 1963. London: Penguin, 1982.

Goleman, Daniel. *Vital Lies, Simple Truths: The Psychology of Self-Deception.* New York: Simon and Schuster, 1983.

Miles, Rosalind. *The Women's History of the World.* London: Paladin Grafton Books, 1988.

Minton, Michael H., with Jean Libman Block. *What Is a Life Worth?* New York: McGraw, 1984.

Morgan, Elaine. *The Descent of Woman.* New York: Bantam, 1979.

O'Neill, Mollie. "Congress Looking into the Diet Business." *New York Times* 25 July 1988.

Standard and Poor's Industry Survey. New York: Standard and Poor's Corp., 1988.

Reed, Evelyn. *Woman's Evolution: From Matriarchal Clan to Patriarchal Family.* New York: Pathfinder Press, 1986.

Woodhead, Linda. "Desert Dandies." *The Guardian* July 1988.

Wooley, S. C., and O. W. Wooley. "Obesity and Women: A Closer Look at the Facts." *Women's Studies International Quarterly* 2 (1979): 69–79.

Questions for Discussion

1. Wolf seeks to convince her readers that the beauty myth is just that—a myth. What reasons and evidence does she offer to make them see that beauty is not an aesthetic absolute? Do you find her case convincing?
2. What reasons and evidence does Wolf offer to convince her readers that in creating the myth, society is motivated by politics and economics? (To be sure that you understand this part of her argument, you may want to write a paraphrase of paragraph 25.) Explain her analogy between the beauty myth and the medieval Iron Maiden (paragraph 24). How does this analogy reinforce Wolf's argument that the myth is politically motivated?
3. Wolf says in paragraph 14, "The qualities that a given period calls beautiful in women are merely symbols of the female behavior that that period considers

desirable: *The beauty myth is always prescribing behavior and not appearance.*" For example, the quality of thinness might symbolize that our society wants women to deny themselves the pleasures of food, even existing on the daily calorie rations of a person in the Third World or in a prison camp. What other behavior might the beauty myth prescribe?

4. Wolf wrote in a preface to a later edition of *The Beauty Myth* that she was misunderstood by many critics as being anti-beauty. She would like to rewrite the first paragraph to make clear to readers that women should be free to adorn and show off their bodies if they want, celebrating their real beauty. She says it is fine to wear lipstick, but not to feel guilty about not conforming to the ideal image of beauty. Do you find any evidence in the excerpt to suggest Wolf is not against makeup and fashion? That she is against it? Could you write a new first paragraph to introduce Wolf's argument more clearly?

For Convincing

Women know that achieving "beauty" often involves pain and the expenditure of considerable time and money. Do men have their own masculine version of the "beauty myth" that causes them to suffer, to spend time and money for the sake of their appearance? If so, how widely is it subscribed to? Do you think any motives lie behind it other than simple vanity? Write an argument, perhaps addressed to Naomi Wolf, to make the case that excessive concern for one's appearance is not limited to the female sex. If you don't think this is a significant concern for men, write to women, arguing that they should or should not be more like men in this respect.

Two Ads for Women's Jeans

The two advertisements for women's jeans reproduced on the following pages originally appeared in fashion magazines such as Elle *and* Vogue. *What persuasive techniques does each use?*

Created for men.

lingerie catalogs

hair coloring

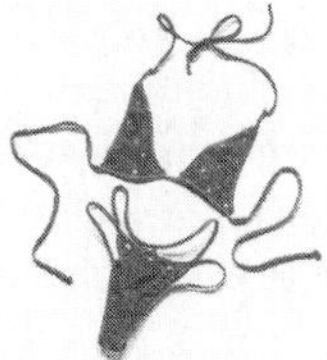

string bikini

breast implants

Created for women.

L A W M A N

J E A N S

They fit who you are.

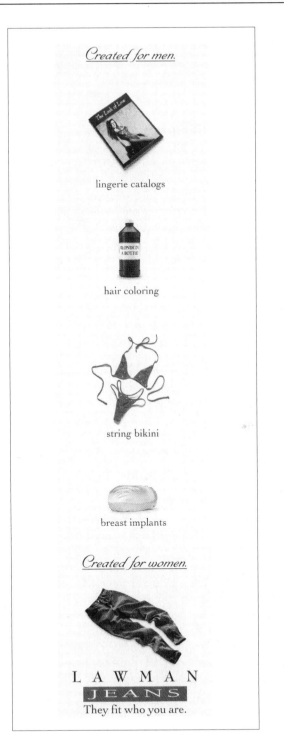

Questions for Discussion

Do you think the two ads—which might have appeared in the same magazine—are actually aimed at the same audience? Discuss the persuasive argument each makes for its audience, and evaluate the effectiveness of each ad.

For Further Research and Discussion

1. Research Elizabeth Cady Stanton's 19th-century arguments for communal living and child-rearing arrangements. What were her objections to traditional marriage and family?
2. One thing that makes it difficult for women in the United States to have a career and a family is that our country is one of the few that does not have some type of government-supported day care. Look into the arrangements that other countries have made that would help working mothers.
3. Read the argument on ecofeminism, "Beyond Global Housekeeping," by H. Patricia Hynes (pages 213–216). Hynes complains that women are commonly involved in "clean-up campaigns" and in organizing citizens for protest; she argues that they are activists but are not represented among the leading ecologists. Look into the numbers of women today who earn degrees in the environmental sciences. Hynes cites the example of Ellen Swallow, an early environmental scientist at MIT, who Hynes argues was discriminated against. Are women still facing discrimination in the sciences? Are they simply discouraged when young by the idea that science is not a feminine pursuit?
4. Since writing *The Beauty Myth,* Naomi Wolf has published another book, *Fire with Fire* (1993), in which she argues for a version of feminism that would make women the equals of men, but that does not deny them their sexuality. Read both Friedan's *The Second Stage* and Wolf's *Fire with Fire,* and compare their suggested revisions to feminism.

Additional Suggestions for Writing

1. *Convincing.* Those who support same-sex education for girls argue that females achieve more when males are not in the academic environment. Look into the arguments for and against sexually segregated education for women. One argument in favor is that women have different learning styles from men; for example, some proponents say that women learn better in less competitive, more collaborative environments. Recent studies have shown that girls' sense of identity and self-confidence is as strong as that of boys until they reach the age of twelve or thirteen. Do girls become less self-assured as they enter puberty? What theories explain this change? Could anxieties about their femininity be behind the problem? You probably have experiences and observations of your own pertaining to these questions. After you have inquired into the subject, make a case for your position on sexually segregated education.
2. *Persuasion.* After considering the goals of feminism and the possible definitions of femininity, decide if it is possible to be feminine and a feminist. As you

inquire, think about who decides what is feminine—men or women or both sexes? Research the biographies of some leading feminists: Would they serve as examples to support your position? Why do so many people have an image (Naomi Wolf calls it a "hallucination") of the Ugly Feminist? Write a persuasive argument aimed at college women, taking either the position that they can be feminists without losing their femininity *or* the position that, at least in our society today, being a feminist necessarily makes a woman appear less feminine.

CHAPTER THIRTEEN

Sexual Harassment

As a concept, sexual harassment has a short history of only about twenty years. Before that, victims of sexual harassment (mostly women harassed by men, but occasionally younger men harassed by women or people harassed by others of the same sex) talked to each other about acts now classified as such but without using the term "sexual harassment" to denote a general problem. Only in 1980, in fact, did prohibitions against sexual harassment become part of federal law, and general awareness and discussion of the problem came even more recently, when in late 1991 Anita Hill charged Clarence Thomas with sexual harassment in her testimony during the confirmation hearings for the seat he now occupies on the Supreme Court.

In one sense, then, sexual harassment is a new issue: Widespread popular debate of the topic is quite recent. In another sense, however, sexual harassment is hardly new. Whenever men and women have associated with one another, even under very controlled conditions, the potential for sexual harassment has existed: Contact between the sexes in a male-dominated society is all that is required. However, conditions that have developed recently have probably made the long-standing problem worse.

Only a half century ago, American society was much more segregated by gender than it now is. Presently women constitute a large percentage of the workforce and of the volunteer armed forces, and they make up over half of college undergraduates in a mostly coeducational system. Rapid integration of the sexes (especially since World War II) has combined with an evolution in attitudes toward traditional morality and sexual roles to provide greater opportunity for sexual harassment. Even now women seldom report abuse, which means that harassers do not have to fear public exposure. No wonder, then, that we have a problem of epidemic proportion.

What is at issue in the debate over sexual harassment? That sexual harassment occurs and that it damages both its victims and society as a whole are points beyond serious dispute. In addition to moral grounds, sexual harassment is generally condemned on practical grounds as well—for instance, for what it costs in terms of absenteeism and diminished productivity for business. But little else about sexual harassment achieves such wide agreement.

Perhaps the major issue for debate is the fundamental question of how to define sexual harassment. Most would agree that a boss who says to an employee, "Sleep with me or I'll fire you," is guilty of sexual harassment. But harassers are rarely so explicit, and harassment is not necessarily limited to requests for sexual favors or even to behavior that is sexual. A male professor who denigrates women in class or who treats female students unfairly or with disrespect may be guilty of sexual harassment according to some statements of university policy.

A further question is whether we should distinguish sexual harassment from what might be called gender prejudice. Should crimes like rape, attempted rape, and obscene phone calls be considered sexual harassment or do they occupy a separate category? Where do we draw the line between generally tolerated behavior—harmless flirtation, say, or gestures of affection, or even overly persistent courtship—and sexual harassment? These are difficult questions that require careful thought.

Even when we agree on a definition of sexual harassment, we are still likely to disagree in answering other questions connected with the topic. For instance.

Should universities, corporations, and other institutions adopt written policy statements and institute procedures to educate faculty, students, employees, and other members about sexual harassment?

Should victims confront their harassers? If so, under what circumstances?

Since a harasser is often a person in authority, with direct power over the victim, what avenues for complaints about sexual harassment ought to exist? What formal procedures for dealing with complaints should be in place?

Since harassment usually goes on in private, without witnesses, what constitutes adequate proof that sexual harassment has occurred? How can we protect people from being falsely accused of harassment?

When guilt has been acknowledged or proven beyond a reasonable doubt, what punishment fits the offense? How do we ascertain the degree of seriousness of the offense, given the spectrum of behavior that might be labeled sexual harassment? What legal and institutional options should society have at its disposal to punish sexual harassment?

Sexual harassment is a slippery and difficult topic, and one that we may find embarrassing to discuss because it involves some of the least attractive of human motives. It also challenges us in uncomfortable ways. A man may ask himself, "Have I been guilty of sexual harassment?" A woman may wonder, "Have I been too tolerant of offenders, lacking the courage to complain, preferring to suffer in silence? "Have I put my career before my self-respect?" It is understandable that people avoid the topic, covering their fears and uncertainties with jokes. But the problem cannot be ignored or minimized; we must strive instead to understand and cope with it as best we can.

EQUAL EMPLOYMENT OPPORTUNITY COMMISSION

Title VII Guidelines on Sexual Harassment

The 1980 Equal Employment Opportunity Commission (EEOC) guidelines on sex discrimination are important for two main reasons. First, because the statement was issued by a federal agency with regulatory power and authority, the guidelines set a nation-wide standard and are often referred to in other policy statements. Second, the statement provides, among other features, a definition of sexual harassment in the workplace and language specifying the extent of employer liability for the conduct of its employees.

SUMMARY: ON April 11, 1980, the Equal Employment Opportunity Commission published the Interim Guidelines on sexual harassment as an amendment to the Guidelines on Discrimination Because of Sex, 29 CFR part 1604.11, 45 FR 25024. This amendment will re-affirm that sexual harassment is an unlawful employment practice. The EEOC received public comments for 60 days subsequent to the date of publication of the Interim Guidelines. As a result of the comments and the analysis of them, these Final Guidelines were drafted.

EFFECTIVE DATE: November 10, 1980.

PART 1604—GUIDELINES ON DISCRIMINATION BECAUSE OF SEX

§ 1604.11 Sexual harassment.

(a) Harassment on the basis of sex is a violation of Sec. 703 of Title VII.[1] Unwelcome sexual advances, requests for sexual favors, and other verbal or physical conduct of a sexual nature constitute sexual harassment when (1) submission to such conduct is made either explicitly or implicitly a term or condition of an individual's employment, (2) submission to or rejection of such conduct by an individual is used as the basis for employment decisions affecting such individual, or (3) such conduct has the purpose or effect of unreasonably interfering with an individual's work performance or creating an intimidating, hostile, or offensive working environment.

(b) In determining whether alleged conduct constitutes sexual harassment, the Commission will look at the record as a whole and at the totality of the

[1]The principles involved here continue to apply to race, color, religion, or other origin. [Original note.]

circumstances, such as the nature of the sexual advances and the context in which the alleged incidents occurred. The determination of the legality of a particular action will be made from the facts, on a case by case basis.

(c) Applying general Title VII principles, an employer, employment agency, joint apprenticeship committee, or labor organization (hereinafter collectively referred to as "employer") is responsible for its acts and those of its agents and supervisory employees with respect to sexual harassment regardless of whether the specific acts complained of were authorized or even forbidden by the employer and regardless of whether the employer knew or should have known of their occurrence. The Commission will examine the circumstances of the particular employment relationship and the job functions performed by the individual in determining whether an individual acts in either a supervisory or agency capacity.

(d) With respect to conduct between fellow employees, an employer is 5
responsible for acts of sexual harassment in the workplace where the employer (or its agents or supervisory employees) knows or should have known of the conduct, unless it can show that it took immediate and appropriate corrective action.

(e) An employer may also be responsible for the acts of non-employees, with respect to sexual harassment of employees in the workplace, where the employer (or its agents or supervisory employees) knows or should have known of the conduct and fails to take immediate and appropriate corrective action. In reviewing these cases the Commission will consider the extent of the employer's control and any other legal responsibility which the employer may have with respect to the conduct of such non-employees.

(f) Prevention is the best tool for the elimination of sexual harassment. An employer should take all steps necessary to prevent sexual harassment from occurring, such as affirmatively raising the subject, expressing strong disapproval, developing appropriate sanctions, informing employees of their right to raise and how to raise the issue of harassment under Title VII, and developing methods to sensitize all concerned.

(g) Other related practices: Where employment opportunities or benefits are granted because of an individual's submission to the employer's sexual advances or requests for sexual favors, the employer may be held liable for unlawful sex discrimination against other persons who were qualified for but denied that employment opportunity or benefit.

Questions for Discussion

1. The EEOC's definition of sexual harassment specifies *unwelcome* sexual advances. Is a sexual advance always simply welcome or unwelcome? How can an initiator know whether his or her act is welcome or unwelcome? Must the subordinate state explicitly that a sexual advance is unwelcome for the act to qualify as sexual harassment?

2. What sort of concrete behavior might qualify as "verbal or physical conduct of a sexual nature"? Should the intent of the initiator matter in determining whether the behavior constitutes sexual harassment?
3. Since individual sensitivities vary a great deal, who can—or should—decide whether a working environment is "intimidating, hostile, or offensive"? Recent court decisions have used the criterion of how "a reasonable woman" would respond to the working environment, eliminating consideration of the harasser's judgment and even that of the person alleging harassment. Does this test help, or not?
4. Reread paragraph 3. Why do the EEOC guidelines put so much emphasis on context and on judging on "a case by case basis"? What different sets of circumstances might make the same act of sexual harassment more or less serious? What sort of evidence or conditions would allow us to say that an employer "knows or should have known" about an employee's conduct? Draw up a list of acts that clearly fall within the definition of sexual harassment. Rank them in order of seriousness. In your opinion, for each kind of act what would constitute "appropriate corrective action" (paragraph 6)?
5. Within the EEOC guideline employer liability for harassment by employees seems almost unqualified. Is this fair or just? Note that in paragraph 8 provision is made for an employee to sue for damages because another employee gained unfair advantages by submitting to sexual advances. Is such a provision reasonable or desirable?

For Inquiry and Research

A number of sexual harassment suits have been filed in state and federal courts. Collect and study reports of several of these, including wherever possible a transcript of the final decision. Choose one, and assess the reasoning of the judge's decision, evaluating the rewards and punishments meted out in the light of the EEOC guidelines.

UNIVERSITY OF MINNESOTA

Policy Statement on Sexual Harassment

Sexual harassment has long been common on college campuses, and concern about the problem is increasing among administrators, faculty, and staff. The desire to take a collective and public stand against sexual harassment has resulted in a number of statements, such as the following from the University of Minnesota. Many schools have instituted other actions designed to condemn and prevent sexual harassment as well, such as having university representatives address the problem during first-year orientation and Panhellenic meetings.

Of course, such statements of policy and other preventative actions also reflect concern for the EEOC guidelines, especially the section about prevention (paragraph 7). Just as companies do, universities worry about the extent of their legal liability in suits alleging sexual harassment.

SEXUAL HARASSMENT in any situation is reprehensible. It subverts the mission of the University, and threatens the careers of students, faculty, and staff. For the purposes of this policy, sexual harassment is defined as follows:

> Unwelcome sexual advances, requests for sexual favors, and other verbal or physical conduct of a sexual nature constitute sexual harassment when (1) submission to such conduct is made either explicitly or implicitly a term or condition of an individual's employment or academic advancement, (2) submission to or rejection of such conduct by an individual is used as the basis for employment decisions or academic decisions affecting such individual, or (3) such conduct has the purpose or effect of unreasonably interfering with an individual's work or academic performance or creating an intimidating, hostile, or offensive working or academic environment.

Sexual harassment is especially serious when it threatens the relationship between student and teacher or the relationship between a supervisor and his or her subordinates. Through grades, wage increases, recommendations for graduate study, promotion, and the like, a teacher or a supervisor can have a decisive influence on a student's or staff member's success and future career at the University and beyond.

When a person is subjected to unwanted sexual attention, a situation is created that may have devastating implications for individual students and staff, and for the academic community as a whole. Through fear of reprisal, a student, staff, or faculty member may submit to unwanted sexual attention at the price of debilitating personal anguish or may withdraw from a course or position and thus be forced to change plans for a life's work.

Conversely, a teacher or supervisor may be inhibited from developing a close and professionally appropriate relationship through fear of initiating a misunderstanding as to sexual harassment. In some cases a person against whom a complaint is directed may be unaware that his or her behavior is inappropriate or coercive, or a person's actions or words may be misinterpreted by another. Such misunderstandings, if not resolved, can interfere with the educational and administrative process even when no actual harassment has taken place.

While sexual harassment most often takes place in a situation of power differential between the persons involved, this policy recognizes also that sexual harassment may occur between persons of the same University status, i.e. student-student; faculty-faculty; staff-staff.

5 Thus, in both obvious and subtle ways, the very possibility of sexual harassment may be deeply destructive to individual students and staff. Academic and career relationships may be poisoned by the subtle and destructive overtones of this problem. For all these reasons, the students, staff, and faculty of the University of Minnesota believe that reaffirmation of a firm stand against sexual harassment and the establishment of procedures specifically designed to resolve complaints of sexual harassment are critically important for this institution.

Questions for Discussion

1. The preceding policy statement was adopted by the University of Minnesota senate, a faculty organization. To what extent would you say its bias or point of view is professorial? The statement calls for "procedures specifically designed to resolve complaints" (paragraph 5) but stops short of suggesting what these procedures might be. What do you make of this omission? What procedures would you suggest?
2. Because of differences in age, maturity, power, and prestige, some people argue that *any* sexual relationship between a professor and a student is necessarily exploitive or coercive. Whether the relationship is consensual or not is irrelevant; the point, so the argument goes, is that sexual relations involving faculty and students are inherently unethical. Do you agree? If not, why not? Under what circumstances could you approve of such a relationship?
3. Being as concrete and specific as you can, explain how you understand the phrase "a close and professionally appropriate relationship" (paragraph 3). Put another way, where do you draw the line between appropriately close and too close? Be prepared to justify your interpretation.

For Convincing or Persuading

1. Find out if your college or university has a written statement about sexual harassment. If not, compose a letter to the editor of your campus newspaper or to an administrator arguing for one. If such a statement exists, get a copy and compare it carefully with the Minnesota policy. Write an essay that explains and defends your assessment of your college's statement. If you have

suggestions for improving the statement, offer them and explain how they would improve the statement.

2. Find out what procedures, if any, exist at your university for handling complaints of sexual harassment. If none exist, write a letter to an appropriate audience arguing for procedures and suggesting what they might be. If procedures do exist, assess them and write an essay explaining and defending your evaluation.

THE NEW REPUBLIC

Talking Dirty

The following brief essay from The New Republic *is a skillful example of the* editorial, *a short argument, often unsigned, that represents the "official" viewpoint of the newspaper or magazine in which it appears. This editorial argues against the "hostile environment" clause of the EEOC guidelines concerning sexual harassment.*

Editorials play a significant role in shaping the reading public's opinions about controversial issues. Although sometimes persuasive—that is, calling for some action on the part of the reader, such as voting for a candidate for public office—many editorials, like this one, are more or less clear instances of arguing to convince, or case-making.

In a world full of issues, all clamoring for attention, in a world of people too busy for extensive reading, the editorial's strength is its potential to convey an informed point of view in a brief format. Its weakness is one with its strength: The need for brevity can easily result in oversimplifying an issue. Do you think the following oversimplifies the issue?

FOR ALL its luridness, absurdity, and brutality, the television trial of Clarence Thomas had at least one laudable side effect. It raised the public's awareness of sexual harassment in the workplace, and may even serve to discourage it in future. As senators not previously known for their concern about women fell over each other to show their sensitivity to the nuances of sexual harassment, men around the country wondered whether they might be guilty of inappropriate conduct themselves. But by also revealing the elasticity of the legal definition of sexual harassment, the hearings could have another effect as well. They could ultimately cause harassment charges to be taken less seriously. Because the legal definition includes any unwanted "verbal conduct" that contributes to an "intimidating, hostile, or offensive working environment," it may lead to an outpouring of charges based less upon legitimate claims of harm than upon an increasingly powerful impulse to censor speech merely because it is offensive.

Invented in the 1970s by the feminist legal theorist Catharine MacKinnon, and endorsed in 1986 by the Supreme Court, the "hostile environment" test threatens to trivialize legitimate claims of sexual harassment by equating sexual assaults with pin-up calendars, and by diverting attention from genuine, harmful sex discrimination. It represents a radical new exception to the First Amendment axiom that speech cannot be punished just because it is offensive. Like restrictions on "hate speech," it punishes expression where it should punish harm. This would present a dilemma for civil libertarians if there weren't any other way to protect victims of real harassment. But there is.

The Civil Rights Act of 1964 says nothing about sexual harassment, and before the 1970s, courts dismissed the idea that offensive words—without physical, psychological, or economic harm—could add up to sex discrimination under Title VII. But in 1980, influenced by Professor MacKinnon's arguments, the Equal Employment Opportunity Commission adopted three tests for deciding whether "unwelcome verbal or physical conduct" violates the Civil Rights Act: First, is it "quid pro quo" behavior that makes submission to sex an implicit or explicit condition of advancement? Second, is it behavior that "unreasonably interferes with an individual's job performance"? And third, is it behavior that creates an "intimidating, hostile, or offensive working environment"?

We have no problems with the first two tests. But the third one is another matter. It relies heavily on the ambiguous term "verbal conduct," obscuring the most important distinction in First Amendment doctrine, which insists that the lines between speech and conduct be drawn as precisely as possible. And in upholding the test, the Supreme Court never explained why unpleasant speech that *didn't* interfere with job performance could be regulated in any way. The ambiguous test then became unintelligible. Courts decided that legality of speech would depend, in retrospect, on whether a "reasonable woman" would have found that it created an "intimidating, hostile, or offensive" environment. This turns the First Amendment on its head. The Supreme Court has traditionally protected offensive speech because "one man's vulgarity is another man's lyric." Under the new rules, speech can be banned whenever one man's lyric becomes a reasonable woman's vulgarity. The fact that men and women often find different things funny (not to mention the fact that women themselves find different things funny) makes the "reasonable woman" standard even more perverse.

To prove the point, a federal appeals court found last January that even 5
"well-intentioned compliments" from officemates can count as sexual harassment. An IRS agent in San Mateo, California, asked a fellow agent out to lunch twice, and after she declined, he declared his love in a poignant note praising her "style and elan," but promising to leave her alone if she asked. She sued and—because the court found that a "reasonable woman" would have found the note unwelcome—won. Days later a Florida district judge ordered the owner of a shipyard to stop his male welders from displaying pin-up calendars and telling dirty jokes. His logic: "[B]anning sexist speech in the workplace does not censor such speech everywhere and for all time."

These cases are disturbing on two levels. First, they suggest that harassment claims tend to be trivial or imagined, when clearly most of them are not. It is impossible to wade through sexual harassment cases without being shocked by the sordidness—and the extent—of the abuse that many women experience at work. The scatology that runs throughout the opinions would make Long Dong Silver blush.[1] But if men are enjoined by courts from writing unwanted love letters, they will find it much harder to take real harassment seriously.

Second, it's scary to suggest that the rights of expression (including the right to ask for dates) should be less protected at work than at home. Work is

[1]Anita Hill claimed that Clarence Thomas referred to "Long Dong Silver," among other inappropriate remarks directed at her.

where most Americans spend most of their waking hours; they must be free to express themselves verbally without fear of prosecution. Professor MacKinnon is correct when she argues that the logic of the "hostile environment" exception cannot be limited to the workplace, which is why it should apply neither in the office nor outside of it.

The solution to this mess is a definition of sexual harassment that excludes verbal harassment that has no other effect on its recipient than to create an unpleasant working environment. Sexual harassment, as the ACLU argues, should be limited to expression that is directed at a specific employee and that "demonstrably hinders or completely prevents his or her continuing to function as an employee." This would refine the existing test for "unreasonable interference." Either version would cover legitimate claims. As a 1989 note in the *Yale Law Journal* points out, *all* women who have successfully sued their supervisors (not their co-workers) for creating a "hostile environment" have also suffered some tangible economic harm, such as being fired. Dropping the hostile environment standard wouldn't permit real harassment by co-workers either. Even though it rarely presents an economic threat, such assaults often interfere with job performance. The law against sexual harassment would be strengthened, not weakened.

Assume, for example, that Anita Hill's charges are true. She would not need a "hostile environment" test to make her case. She might have trouble proving "quid pro quo" harassment, which occurs, according to the EEOC, when submission to (or rejection of) sexual advances is used as the basis for employment decisions. She concedes that her refusal to date Mr. Thomas and to watch bestiality videos didn't stop her from being promoted on schedule. Ms. Hill could argue, however, that Mr. Thomas's advances "unreasonably interfered" with her job performance. She was sent to the hospital with nervous cramps, told her friends she had become depressed, and eventually left the EEOC because she felt unable to continue. The judge in her case would still have to make a difficult, subjective decision about how much the harassment had interfered with her job, and how much interference is "reasonable." But these are the kinds of murky decisions that judges make every day, and they are far more appropriate than decisions about what a reasonable woman would find offensive.

What would be excluded from the legal definition of sexual harassment if 10
the "hostile environment" test were abandoned? Only sexual expression that is offensive but that has no detectable effect on job performance. That would include most pin-up calendars, most well-intentioned compliments, and even some gross remarks. But trivial complaints like these are unusual. Sexual harassment lawyers say that cases of verbal harassment where the woman cannot prove physical or psychological damage are rarely successful in court, even under the "hostile environment" test.

Abandoning the "hostile environment" test is in the best interest of feminists as well as civil libertarians. The only realistic way to narrow the gap between what reasonable women and men perceive as harassment is to persuade men that unwanted advances can hurt women in tangible ways. A definition of harassment that diverts attention from that question makes relief for women all the more remote.

Questions for Discussion

1. Read the stories of college women in the opening of "Sexual Harassment on Campus," the following selection. How many of these reports of sexual harassment would qualify as sexual harassment if the "hostile environment" clause were dropped?
2. Freedom of speech, a basic right upon which democracy depends, is nevertheless not an absolute. Bearing in mind that the job site, office, and campus are all public places, what reasoning could justify restrictions on speech and other forms of expression that some women find offensive or abusive?
3. The *New Republic* writer admits that doing away with the "hostile environment" clause would still leave judges in the position of having to make "difficult, subjective" judgments about whether or not sexual harassment interfered with job performance. The writer contends, however, that such judgments are "more appropriate than decisions about what a reasonable woman would find offensive" (paragraph 9). Do you agree? That is, are judgments of the first kind somehow less murky than judgments of the second kind?

For Negotiation

Whatever your attitude towards it, the "hostile environment" clause of the EEOC guidelines poses genuine problems. Imagine that you are part of a committee charged with drawing up a policy statement to address the problem of sexual harassment on your campus and that you have been given the task of dealing with the "hostile environment" issue. In a written report, explain why the clause may be necessary. Explain also why such a vague notion may be unacceptable. Then attempt to specify what the definition of "hostile environment" should include and exclude.

Submit your proposal to the class for discussion. Based on how they respond, adjust your suggestions until most of the class can accept them.

BILLIE WRIGHT DZIECH AND LINDA WEINER

Sexual Harassment on Campus

Sexual harassment has been investigated and written about fairly extensively in general and specialized journals. However, there are still very few book-length treatments of the subject. Of these few, The Lecherous Professor: Sexual Harassment on Campus *remains, almost ten years after it was published, one of the best. The following excerpt is from Chapter One.*

An essay whose primary purpose is to convey knowledge about something may "argue" by selecting and arranging material to support predetermined conclusions. With varying degrees of explicitness, informative writing attempts to convince or persuade and, therefore, is not as neutral or disinterested as it may sometimes appear to be. Part of our task as critical readers is to find the argument, make it fully explicit, and subject it to inquiry and evaluation. Try to do so as you read the following.

Every sin is the result of a collaboration.

STEPHEN CRANE

SEXUAL HARASSMENT was a way of life. Field trips—a tradition for geographers—were abandoned because women were considered contaminants. One memorable instructor (whose course was required of all graduate students) regularly informed each new generation of graduate students that women are not good for much of anything but sexual exercises. He enjoyed going into graphic description of the trials and tribulations of a journey taken with a group of students during which one female experienced the onset of menstruation. "Blood all over the damn place," our professor told the class, "had to hike miles out of the canyon to find wadding to stuff in her crotch."

I had a typing teacher who used to come up and sit by me when I was typing and touch the side of my breast. He'd make rude comments about my behind and he usually made it a point to pinch me. He'd keep me after class to discuss a paper or show me areas where I needed help. I was an A student, but he always wanted me to stay. If I said no, he'd get very defensive. I was afraid he might not give me the A I deserved. The final straw was when I had gotten ink on my sweater from the typing ribbon and he offered to help me get it off. Well, he put his hands up my shirt, feeling me up, and I pushed him away and yelled. I told my parents, and they said I should go to the Dean. I had my boyfriend come and wait for me after class. I didn't want to start trouble, so I didn't say anything. I decided to change my program and not to have him for a teacher anymore. Even though I wanted to tell the Dean, I was afraid it would just mean more trouble.

I knew that this prof chased his students so when he started flirting with me in class, I just ignored it. I didn't want anything to do with all that and it made me nervous. But one day after class he sort of cornered me as I was leaving. He backed me up against the wall and was touching me and telling me that he wanted me. He was almost shaking and very intense. I was trying to figure out how to get out of there without an awful scene. He started telling me how his wife didn't like oral sex and he felt frustrated because he had so much to give and wanted to give it to me. He was sweating and shaking and said, "I have a magic tongue. That used to be my nickname." I couldn't believe it. I was frightened by him and wanted to laugh at the same time. I pulled away and ran out of the classroom. It still seems a little funny, but he stalks me in the halls and it's still scary to me.

Dr. _____ asked me to come to his office to help him rearrange his books. Maybe it was my fault for going in the first place. He has these high bookcases, and the only way you can reach them is to stand on this little stool. I remember I had on this blue tight skirt that made it hard for me to step off and on that stool, but the skirt was pretty long. After a while, he got up and walked over and started bumping the stool. At first I thought he was just kidding around, and I laughed. Then I got sort of scared because he almost knocked me over. I told him to be careful and that I didn't think he knew I was really scared. "I know you are, but the only way to keep from falling is for you to go about your business while I lay down on the floor here and watch you." I think that's exactly how he said it. I didn't know what else to do. I was afraid to leave, so I just kept on taking books down while he laid on the floor and looked up my dress at my underpants. Then I left, and he said thank you and never ever mentioned anything about it again. I guess I should have reported him to somebody, but I didn't know who. No one would have believed it anyway.

These are stories of American college women. There are thousands like 5
them. Most of the stories are unknown because students rarely tell them, because higher education keeps skeletons in the closet, and because few except the victims understand the seriousness of the problem.

Sexual harassment of college students is not new. A familiar jest is "Where there has been a student body, there has always been a faculty for love." Women were not admitted to the college campus until 1837, when Oberlin became the first to open its doors to them, but it seems likely that sexual harassment has existed as long as there have been women students and male professors. Only in the last few years, however, have women raised their voices in protest. Even now their cries usually fall on curious but uncaring institutional and public ears. Parents worry about tuition increases and financial aid; students worry about grades and job interviews; deans worry about the number of faculty publications and declining enrollments; college presidents worry about budget cuts and collective bargaining; and trustees worry about public images and endowment funds. But until one of their daughters is harassed or news of a case appears in a campus headline or a lawsuit is filed, few are disturbed that women students are sexually intimidated, fondled, propositioned, and even assaulted by their professors.

The silence surrounding sexual harassment is incongruous in light of the last two noisy decades of higher education. The 1960s and '70s were characterized by activism about student representation in governance systems and grievance procedures. During those years, a variety of women's issues were addressed on the campus. Discriminatory policies in admissions, testing, scholarships, and athletics were prohibited. Women's hours were abolished; birth control was incorporated into student health services; abortion ads were placed in student newspapers; and women's centers were established. Women's studies courses, programs, and departments were integrated into academic units. Yet despite all the visibility and public discussion of students' rights and women's concerns on campus, sexual harassment remained in the closet. Women students whispered to roommates about sexual propositions from their professors or hinted of their distress to counselors, but there was little else they could do because until very recently sexual harassment was simultaneously denied, ignored, disputed, discounted, and disregarded.

As late as 1974, there was still no general consensus about sexual harassment. In that year, the American Council on Education published an anthology titled *Women in Higher Education* in which only one essay touched on the experiences of women students as "sex objects." In "Women's Right to Choose, or Men's Right to Dominate," Joan Roberts observed:

> In recent hearings conducted with women students, in research interviews with women students, in discussions with individual women and groups of women, and in their responses to questionnaires, they accused some male faculty members of subtle and even blatant sexism ranging from verbal to physical, sometimes with put-out or get-out connotations. Verbally, a professor aggresses, saying, "Your sweater looks big enough for both of us." Or he may invade the woman's personal space, by touching a pin on her blouse while commenting on its ostensible beauty. (I sometimes wonder what the male professor would do if the woman student made equally personal gestures in public.) Or he may, as in one case reported, make sexual overtures, which, when rebuffed, led him to fail the woman student on her doctoral examination. The same man was later overheard telling a colleague that he did not bother to read her exam. Fortunately, this kind of overt unprofessionalism is infrequently reported.

The assumption at that point in time was that no news—or at least not much news—was good news. Scarcity of information is one key to the historical invisibility of the issue. Because there is no definitive statistical answer to the question "How great is the problem?" it is convenient to deny and ignore the issue. There has been no national study of the frequency of sexual harassment, no data that can set a "standard" against which a campus might measure itself. The National Advisory Council on Women's Educational Programs was established under the 1974 Women's Educational Equity Act. In 1979–1980 it followed its charge to make policy recommendations and circulated "a call for information on the sexual harassment of students." Its results, published in 1980, represented the first attempt to examine the problem on a large scale. The council's report stated firmly that its study was not definitive and that "estimates of frequency [of sexual harassment on the nation's campuses] are beyond the scope of this report."

During the last few years, some organizations and institutions have surveyed 10
themselves and produced statistical indicators of the scope of the problem. These efforts at measuring sexual harassment do not mean that these campuses or organizations have special or unusual problems with harassment; they *do* demonstrate that there is genuine concern about and interest in examining the issue.

- In 1980 at Arizona State University, a joint student/faculty/staff committee distributed a 50-item questionnaire to a random sample of women faculty, staff and students. With an 80% response rate, 13% of the students, 11% of the staff, and 13% of the faculty said they had been sexually harassed. The report pointed out that, lest the 13% student response be considered small, the percent translated to 2,300 women students. Closer scrutiny of the data made it apparent that the real numbers were even higher. Respondents who viewed themselves as victims of harassment were not confined to describing only their *current* situations. Further analysis of the respondents' status at the time of harassment revealed that 46% of the episodes occurred while women were undergraduates and 18% while they were graduate students.
- In 1981, the Iowa State University Committee on Women conducted a detailed study of sexual harassment of college students by faculty members. The survey found that 7% of the women students said faculty had made physical advances toward them; 14% of the women had received invitations for dates; 17% reported receiving verbal sexual advances; 34% had experienced leering or other sexual body language; 43% reported flirtation or undue attention; and 65% said they had been the target of sexist comments. Thirteen percent of the women had avoided courses because the faculty were known sexual harassers. No woman who had experienced one of the three most serious forms of sexual harassment included in the survey reported it to a university official.
- In 1979–80, in response to general discussion on campus and in the press, a campus committee at the University of Rhode Island surveyed students, faculty, and staff about experiences of sexual harassment on campus. The study made distinctions between sexual intimidation, sexual insult, and assault as defined in Rhode Island law. Sexual intimidation was defined as "a threat or a bribe by a person in a position of authority to coerce sexual contact." Citing personal knowledge of such cases, respondents indicated that teachers were initiators in 53% of the cases, graduate assistants in 8%, staff or administrators in 6%, employers in 14%, and students in 14%. Grades or exams were involved in 58% of the cases.

- In 1979, the Michigan State University Student Affairs Office commissioned a survey of women students. A stratified random sample of 998 was contacted, and 47% responded. Twenty-five percent reported that they had been sexually harassed within the last year. A validation study indicated that sexual harassment victims may have been *under*represented in the respondent groups.
- A 1979 University of Florida survey found that 26% of women undergraduate respondents and 31% of graduate respondents said they had been sexually harassed by faculty. Of those who said they had been victims, 70% did not feel free to report it to anyone.
- At the University of California at Berkeley, a 1979 survey of women graduate students found that 20% of the respondents experienced unwanted touches, propositions, or sexual remarks from professors. A 1980 survey of senior women at Berkeley found that 30% of the 269 randomly sampled respondents had experienced "unwanted and objectionable sexual behavior" by at least one male instructor either at Berkeley or at a school from which they had transferred.
- In a 1980 study conducted by the University of Cincinnati Office of Women's Programs and Services, 47% of the women students, faculty, and staff choosing to respond reported several forms of sexual harassment, ranging from leers to assault.
- At East Carolina University, 20% of the 226 women students surveyed in 1979 reported that they had experienced verbal sexual harassment from male instructors.
- A national survey of psychology educators in Division 29 (psychotherapy) of the American Psychological Association in 1979 found that, of a random sample of 481 women, 10% had had sexual contact with their professors. Of those who had received their degrees within the last seven years, 25% reported having sexual contact while they were students of psychology educators.

These individual campus or organizational studies employed different research techniques and slightly different definitions of sexual harassment. Some used random sampling; others reported on self-selected respondents. There clearly is a need for a standardized survey instrument that individual campuses could use to measure frequency so a national profile can be drawn. Yet despite the variations in the surveys, the results are remarkably similar: Again and again 20 to 30 percent of women students report they have been sexually harassed by male faculty during their college years. Campus administrators, student affairs staff, ombudsmen, and consultants who have done workshops on individual campuses affirm the pattern: 20 to 30 percent experience sexual harassment.

Measurement of the problem is elusive, local, and often anecdotal, but the numbers involved are significant. In the fall of 1982, in its annual report on college and university enrollments, the National Center for Educational Statistics reported that 6,374,005 women were enrolled in American colleges and universities. If only *1 percent* of all college women experienced sexual harassment, there would be 63,740 women victims. Twenty percent equals 1,274,800 women. And every year a new group of women enrolls in college to become part of the problem. Higher education faces a problem of epidemic proportion.

Although the numbers are large and indicate the need for serious concern, a conversation between two deans at a meeting reviewing a proposed policy on sexual harassment is a reminder that pressure for change comes only from personal experience. A business administration dean wanted to set his priority by quantifying the problem in his college: "If it's an 80 to 90 percent problem, then we have to do something. But if it's, say, only a 7 percent problem, I would give it less priority." At the other end of the table, a liberal arts dean cited the yearlong struggle he had had with a sexual harassment complaint. He described the pain and confusion of the student victims, the conversations with parents, the disruption within the department, and the time he had spent in hearings and conferences as he tried to resolve the problem. His priority had been set through experience: "One case is enough."

Scarcity of survey information on individual campuses and the national scene is one reason for sexual harassment's invisibility. Equally important is the reluctance of women students to report their experiences. As with rape victims, sexual harassment victims are hesitant to add the pain of self-disclosure and the risk of interrogation to the distress caused by the harassment. Students have several compelling problems when they consider what to do. The National Advisory Council on Women's Educational Programs, after reviewing the information that was sent to them, summarized the complexity:

> Why do victims keep silent or try to cope without involving the authority of the school administration or the courts? Our responses and the work of almost all researchers indicate that there are several primary causes: fear that they—as victims—are somehow responsible for the incident, fear that they will not be believed, shame at being involved in any form of sexual incident, fear that by protesting they will call attention to their sex rather than to their work, a belief that no action will be taken, and fear of reprisals by the initiator and his colleagues.

Students are pragmatic; they know they are subordinate to faculty and administrators. Individually and collectively, they have much less power. Those who are sexually harassed recognize that the professor's role and authority are major reasons for their own victimization, and their experiences with authorities only confirm their powerlessness. A member of a university commission on the status of women expressed the cynicism typical of many students:

> I know, if this is occurring, if there are overtures being made, it's usually from people right over you who control all the power; whether your master's proposal is going to be accepted, how well you are doing on your comprehensives. After all, they are the people who are reading them. These are the people that you have for the majority of your classes,

> they hold your career in their hands. So you can complain about sexual overtures but then because of their rank they can find some way to get rid of you for a million or more reasons; it can be as simple as just undermining your performance. It can just get all mixed together and it's no longer clear what's happening to you.

Students also understand the traditional difference in sex roles and power. One of the earliest survival lessons women learn is that they must handle problems like sexual harassment. Social conditioning leads many to believe that this is the way things are and that there is no point in public protest: No one would believe them. Even if someone did believe them, women are expected—and expect themselves—to resolve such problems.

Diane K., after enduring a yearlong struggle with an English professor, told her parents about his attempts to lure her into an affair.

> I didn't really want them to do anything about it. I was out of his class and was pretty sure I could avoid him on campus. But I felt like I had to explain how it wasn't my fault to Mom and Dad. I didn't want them to think that I wasn't grown-up enough to handle the situation. That's why I didn't tell them at the time it was all happening, even though it really got to me sometimes. I mean, that's the way things are in the real world. I'm going to graduate next year and I'm supposed to be able to deal with all that.

The self-imposed silence of student victims, which contributes to the continued invisibility of the problem, is reinforced by the cloud of confusion that exists—and is sometimes conveniently created—around what sexual harassment actually is. While both rape and sexual harassment are underreported, sexual harassment trades on its victims' uncertainty about how to label their experiences. A woman knows when she has been raped. But there are many forms of sexual harassment, and the term itself is new. Women differ dramatically in their willingness and ability to identify and acknowledge the behavior. A college ombudsman, reflecting on her frustration at hearing students describe blatant acts of sexual harassment and their own ambiguous reactions, commented, "I have to remind myself that the terms are new. Ten years ago, when I was a student, we had the same experiences—a lower grade because you didn't go out with a professor, dropping courses to avoid propositions from the graduate assistant, getting felt up by faculty in their offices. We knew we didn't like what went on, but we didn't have a name for it."

"Sexual harassment" became a commonly used phrase only a few years ago. 25
But the very words "sexual harassment" are ominous to some college women; they seem too legalistic, too political, too combative. Women students resist language that makes them feel set apart from or adversaries of men. Many resist identification with what they consider a "feminist" issue because they aren't comfortable with that label either. Already confused about the uncertain boundaries of male-female and student-teacher relationships, a woman student usually prefaces description of a sexual harassment experience with, "I've never been

sexually harassed, but. . . ." Then she proceeds to give a classic example of the behavior.

Students aren't the only ones bewildered by discussions of sexual harassment. Men and women faculty and administrators assume, are led to believe, or find it convenient to make sexual harassment a confusing topic. Just as discussions of the ERA rapidly deteriorated into arguments about whether women would be drafted or required to share public restrooms with men, attention is quickly distracted from the fundamental issues surrounding sexual harassment to debatable, speculative, or trivial ground. Some people, especially men, worry that sexual harassment is so vague and ill defined that they personally will suffer if the problem is confronted vigilantly. In casual discussions, there is usually a man who asks, "But if we take this harassment stuff too seriously, won't it mean that men and women will never get along again? Won't I have to worry about every look and every gesture and every word I say to a woman?" And there is always another man who adds, "You know, women can really ruin a man with this kind of thing."

Sometimes the confusion is transparent pretense. In the hallway of an undergraduate Midwestern college, a male professor of English observed a scene and commented:

> A group of men faculty—from the math department—were standing in the hallway outside their offices. A fairly attractive girl went up to one of them, apparently her professor, and asked about an assignment. He put his arm around her shoulders, walked a few steps with her, and said, loudly, so everyone could hear, "Let's go in my office and talk about it—and you can take your clothes off." Everyone—except the girl—laughed. One professor asked sarcastically, "Is that harassment?" And someone wisecracked, "Not unless she thinks it is."

Actually, sexual harassment is not that difficult to recognize. Sexual harassment is a professor talking about "wadding in crotches" and about having a "magic tongue." It is grabbing a student's breast or lying on the floor and staring up her skirt. It is not, in the vast majority of cases, ambiguous behavior. It is not, as some imply, a figment of students' imaginations or a weapon women use to damage men's reputations. These worries are usually expressed by men and women who have had little experience dealing with harassment cases or who impose confusion on themselves.

Most of the confusion is attributable to the fact that sexual harassment has only recently been defined as a distinct phenomenon. "Harassment" means to annoy persistently, but "sexual harassment" is a particular type of abuse. The need for a common understanding of the term became pressing in the 1970s as discussions about sexual discrimination and women's positions in the workplace accelerated. If sexual harassment was actionable, whether in the courtroom, the corporate personnel hearing, or the college grievance system, there was a need for precise definitions of what constituted sexual harassment.

As part of its research on the problem in the workplace, the Working Women United Institute in 1975 developed an early working definition. Others followed in rapid succession. Lin Farley's *Sexual Shakedown* and Catharine

MacKinnon's *Sexual Harassment of Working Women* treated sexual harassment as a type of sex discrimination and an abuse of power rather than a sexual issue. Court cases, publications, and policy-makers refined and maintained that position.

This is the heart of the issue. "Sexual harassment" implies misuse of power 30
and role by a faculty member. Although institutions' statements and definitions of sexual harassment are written to accommodate individual circumstances and legal requirements, they should also address this central concept of the power imbalance between students and professors. A sound definition not only sets policy, it also informs and educates the community. It should affirm that sexual harassment is sex discrimination, is illegal, damaging to the academic community, refers to a broad range of behaviors, and may occur as single or repeated incidents.

There is no universally accepted model definition of sexual harassment. The most publicized is that of the National Advisory Council. It describes sexual harassment as:

> objectionable emphasis on the sexuality or sexual identity of a student by (or with the acquiescence of) an agent of an educational institution when (1) the objectionable acts are directed toward students of only one gender; and (2) the intent or effect of the objectionable acts is to limit or deny full and equal participation in educational services, opportunities, or benefits on the basis of sex; or (3) the intent or effect of the objectionable acts is to create an intimidating, hostile, or offensive academic environment for the members of one sex. . . .
>
> Academic sexual harassment is the use of authority to emphasize the sexuality or sexual identity of a student in a manner which prevents or impairs that student's full enjoyment of educational benefits, climate, or opportunities. . . .
>
> [Sexual harassment may be described as] (1) generalized sexist remarks or behavior; (2) inappropriate and offensive, but essentially sanction-free sexual advances; (3) solicitation of sexual activity or other sex-linked behavior by promise of rewards; (4) coercion of sexual activity by threat of punishment; and (5) assaults.

The Modern Language Association's Commission on the Status of Women in the Profession distinguished gender harassment as a specific type of sexual harassment:

> Gender harassment is considerably less dramatic in its manifestations than sexual harassment, but because it is more widespread, it seems more pernicious. It consists of discriminatory behavior directed against individuals who belong to a gender group that the aggressor considers inferior. . . . The forms are often verbal—statements and jokes that reveal stereotypical discriminatory attitudes.

In 1978 the Association of American College's Project on the Status and Education of Women provided a descriptive list of specific actions that might constitute sexual harassment. The list was intended as a guide and identified a broad range of behaviors. Obviously, any single behavior must be evaluated in the context of an individual complaint, as suggested in the EEOC reference to the "totality of circumstances." The list included the following:

verbal harassment or abuse
subtle pressure for sexual activity
sexist remarks about a woman's clothing, body, or sexual activities
unnecessary touching, patting, or pinching, leering, or ogling at a woman's body
constant brushing against a woman's body
demanding sexual favors accompanied by implied or overt threats concerning one's job, grades, letters of recommendation, and so forth
physical assault

Discussion of sexual harassment began in regard to the workplace, where people are unequal in power but more likely equal in age and experience and where professional codes of ethics are few. On the college campus the situation is quite different. Sexual harassment of students involves an individual's decision to violate his professional ethics. To its credit, higher education has always had either written or implied standards of conduct. Colleges, professional associations of academic disciplines, and campus governance groups have lengthy statements on faculty's responsibilities to students. The American Association of University Professors in 1966 adopted a policy statement on professional ethics that outlined professors' responsibilities not to exploit students. In 1983 increasing attention led the AAUP to propose guidelines on sexual harassment and its redress to the national membership.

Intimate relationships between professors and students are regarded with suspicion because they pose conflicts with faculty responsibilities and ethics. The prevailing view among academicians is that the faculty member's job is to teach students. Whenever he chooses to treat his women students differently from the men, to become more man than professor, he manipulates his role and endangers his professionalism. Men professors do not kiss, fondle, or comment on the appearances of male students, and most maintain that there is no reason to treat women differently.

In reality, however, different norms *do* apply for men and women students in everyday campus life. If a male student offers a professor money to alter a grade, all would agree that the professor is wrong if he takes it. But when faculty fantasize about a woman student promising sexual favors in exchange for a better grade, the standard changes. Professional ethics become less important when the issue is sex. It is wrong to take money from students, but sex is another matter.

Discussion of sexual harassment usually includes the "yes, but" view: "Yes, but some women invite ogling, touching, or sexual propositions." Every campus has its real or imaginary tales of beautiful coeds who show their professors nude photographs of themselves or promise they will "do anything" for a better grade. Many are second- or third-hand accounts, more fiction than fact. The implication is that the campus is hazardous for male faculty, that men too are victims of sexual harassment. The underlying message, of course, is that men have a right to harass women because women "ask for it."

The "yes, but" notion distorts the issue. There *are* women who flirt with 35
male faculty and women who cause professors discomfort and embarrassment by pursuing them. Some women *do* get crushes on professors; they *do* engage in seduction. But this has nothing to do with sexual harassment of students by professors. These are two separate problems involving very different dynamics, consequences, and resolutions.

One way to distinguish them is to use clearer terminology. A student is more capable of causing "sexual hassle" than she is of sexually harassing. There is too much difference in role and status of male faculty and female students to make flirtation or even seduction by students harassment. "Harassment" suggests misuse of power, and students simply do not have enough power to harass.

Persistent, unwanted attention from a female student can be extremely disruptive to a male professor. It may embarrass, annoy, and anger him; it may cause turmoil in both his private and professional life. But it cannot destroy his self-esteem or endanger his intellectual self-confidence. Hassled professors do not worry about retaliation and punitive treatment; they do not fear bad grades or withheld recommendations from women students. They are not forced to suffer in silence because of fear of peer disapproval. In fact, many men are eager to discuss being sexually hassled. Their talk may be locker room bragging or a self-protective strategy to prevent gossip.

Even in the most extreme cases of sexual hassle, men faculty seldom suffer the complex psychological effects of sexual harassment victims. They may have to endure unpleasant scenes, disturbed domestic relations, and temporary unease, but they have the power to control the problem. They work in an environment they understand. They are at home in academe as students are not and know how to protect themselves and to discourage students causing them discomfort.

Sexual hassle is not an excuse for tolerating or ignoring sexual harassment. Students do not set the tone or the parameters of interactions with professors. They do not have that kind of authority. No behavior, however seductive, from a student ever legitimizes inappropriate, irresponsible behavior by faculty. Sexual hassle does not give college professors the right to violate responsibilities to students or the ethics of their profession.

When defensive faculty are not bemoaning the vulnerability of professors, 40
they are advocating for openness and sexual health in the academic environment. They worry that prohibition of sexual harassment will become zealous and jeopardize positive interaction between the sexes and make all give-and-take between men and women unacceptable.

The dynamics of men and women working together on the campus and elsewhere is not yet truly understood. Until there is more systematic analysis, the most that can be said is that the presence of both men and women lends a certain excitement and energy to work. Sexual give-and-take—the friendly verbal interaction between colleagues, the acknowledged attraction between coworkers, the accepted physical gesturing of male and female—is a healthy behavior in which individuals of various ages and stations choose to engage.

"Choice" is the critical concept. Give-and-take implies mutual choice by people of equal status. The boundaries of the relationship are understood and accepted by both parties. There is no confusion, no doubt, no feeling of coercion or fear. The effects of jokes, comments, and gestures are that both feel good. The humor and affection in sexual give-and-take may be a way to reduce sexual tensions. It may relieve the monotony of routine work. It may even be preliminary courtship, a kind of testing before proceeding with a more serious relationship.

Whatever the intent, sexual give-and-take is based on mutual consent of equals. This is obviously not the case in sexual harassment. Normal sexual give-and-take is not possible in student-teacher relationships because the power imbalance and role disparity are too great. The legal, public, and institutional concern about sexual harassment is a concern about *unhealthy* sexual dynamics, about behaviors that are exploitive, abusive, and psychologically and academically damaging. In fact, if people become more aware of the sexual harassment problem, a healthier sexual environment for both men and women should result.

Questions for Discussion

1. List each of the explanations the authors offer for the general inattention to sexual harassment on campus. Which of them seems strongest to you, and which weakest?
2. In paragraph 26 the authors seem to dismiss three objections to taking sexual harassment seriously and then claim that "sexual harassment is not that difficult to recognize" (paragraph 27). Is there anything worth considering in the objections? Granted the many clear instances of sexual harassment cited in the selection, can you think of any gray areas or borderline possibilities that might make sexual harassment more difficult to identify?
3. Paragraphs 36–39 develop a key distinction between sexual harassment and sexual hassle. On what do the authors base their distinction? Do you find the distinction useful and convincing?

For Inquiry

Some critics have argued that regulations regarding sexual harassment on college campuses have created an atmosphere in which it is impossible for a legitimate, noncoercive romantic interest to develop between a faculty member and a student. In several recent letters to the *New York Times,* wives who were students when they first became involved with their college professor husbands have suggested that wholesale prohibition of intimate relationships between faculty and students is unrealistic and unfair. What are your ideas about this issue? Is it acceptable for an instructor to flirt with a student when he (or she) has reason to believe that the attraction is mutual, or does the fact that the instructor could be mistaken mean that no flirtation should ever take place? Does the difference in age make a difference, or does the unequal balance of power between the parties always create a serious problem? In an essay explore your thoughts about romantic relationships between teachers and students and how they should be viewed by academic policy-makers.

NICHOLAS DAVIDSON

Feminism and Sexual Harassment

Written for the conservative journal Society, *this essay is both an attack on feminism and an argument that heterosexual men can also be victims—of false allegations of sexual harassment and of male-bashing by aggressive feminists.*

Calling sexual harassment "a feminist issue," Davidson argues, first, that feminist thought is inconsistent and contradictory, and, second, that the logic of feminism leads to a simple-minded "women good, men bad" position. He then attempts to link his critique of feminism with his opposition to the broad definition of sexual harassment, which includes "the creation of a climate of fear, intimidation, and hostility to women" (See the guidelines regarding sexual harassment issued by the Equal Employment Opportunity Commission, pages 374–375.) In the second half of the essay, Davidson contends that feminists are using the charge of sexual harassment as a weapon against men who do nothing more than stare at women or criticize feminist viewpoints. "Just who is harassing whom?" the author asks.

WHEN DEALING with an issue as fraught with emotion and ideology as sexual harassment, it is worth beginning with the obvious. Sexual harassment is a feminist issue. Feminists have raised the issue, defined it, and pushed for the laws and regulations relative to it. Therefore, to understand the issue of sexual harassment, we must first understand the nature of feminism.

Again it is easiest to start with the obvious, the dictionary definition of feminism. According to Webster's New Unabridged Dictionary, feminism is "(a) the theory that women should have political, economic, and social rights equal to those of men; (b) the movement to win such rights for women." Feminism may be more, of course; but we can expect to find some considerable correspondence between this definition and the actual views of contemporary feminists.

Nature of Feminism

With this definition in mind, we can profitably approach a question that has increasingly preoccupied sophisticated feminists, and which can be called "the contradiction." As discussed at length by longtime feminist activist Ann Snitow in a recent article in *Dissent,* and by several feminist academics in two recent anthologies, *Theoretical Perspectives on Sexual Difference* and *Making a Difference: Psychology and the Construction of Gender,* the contradiction consists in this: On the one hand, feminists reject the concept of an inherent gendered human nature. Personality differences between human beings in general, and between men and women in particular, are held to be purely the result of social "conditioning." As Kate Millett wrote in *Sexual Politics,* the book that more than any other established the intellectual respectability of feminism, it is doubtful that there are "any significant inherent differences between male and female beyond the biogenital ones we already know. Conditioning runs in a circle of self-perpetuation and self-fulfilling prophecy." This viewpoint derives from the environmental determinism of modern social science, and of cultural anthropology in particular, which in turn can be traced to John Locke's assertion in the *Essay Concerning Human Understanding* that man is born as a "blank slate." The actual expression Locke used is "white paper." On this paper, society writes whatever it wishes, literally creating human nature. This viewpoint, as applied to the sexes, I propose to call "unisexism"—the belief that there are no inherent differences between the sexes, and that whatever differences exist are socially constructed.

To this viewpoint in the field of human nature corresponds another in the field of public policy: that laws and mores should draw no distinction between the sexes, since such distinctions are, in the final analysis, artificial and to draw such distinctions is to judge individuals unfairly on the basis of arbitrary characteristics. Unisexism is both a theory of human personality and a program for action.

5 Unisexism was the most conspicuous perspective advocated by the modern feminist movement in its initial phase in the late 1960s through the 1970s. Feminists who emphasize unisexism, such as Simone de Beauvoir and Betty Friedan, tend to see women as cut off from the sources of meaning in life, which are monopolized by men. Unisexists display a strong tendency to devalue the feminine and are vulnerable to the charge launched by the antifeminists of yore that they aspire to male imitation. In *The Feminine Mystique,* Friedan went so far as to assert that women, as they presently exist, are "inferior to men, dependent, passive, incapable of thought or decision."

Beginning in the late 1970s, however, awareness of another perspective within feminism began to dawn on sophisticated feminists. This new awareness was brought home to many of them by two books, Nancy Chodorow's *The Reproduction of Mothering* (1978) and, above all, Carol Gilligan's *In a Different Voice* (1982). While environmental determinism remained prominent in the works of these writers, especially in Chodorow's, another perspective was introduced alongside it. Chodorow and Gilligan argued that a male-dominated culture had historically undervalued women's distinct "voice," which constituted an ethic of care, nurturance, and "moral pragmatism" opposed to the abstract, judgmental, and absolutist values they attributed to masculinity. While the emphasis of unisexists tended to be anti-feminine, here the emphasis tended to be anti-masculine and may be called "female chauvinism."

To female chauvinism in the sphere of human behavior corresponds in turn a program for action in the political realm, what is sometimes condemned and sometimes praised as "special rights and privileges for women." With the ascendancy of the female chauvinist perspective in the 1980s, feminist organizations frequently shifted from egalitarian positions, such as no-fault divorce, to sponsoring laws specifically intended to benefit women, such as the automatic assignment of mother custody in divorce along with generous property division and alimony settlements.

Discussing the contradiction in *Theoretical Perspectives on Sexual Difference,* Alison Jaggar argues that "feminists should embrace both horns of this dilemma. . . . They should use the rhetoric of equality in situations where women's interests clearly are being damaged by their being treated either differently from or identically with men." The results of this embrace are visible in many areas of modern life. For instance, colleges for men have been sexually integrated, often forcibly, as in the Justice Department's current suit against the Virginia Military Institute, one of a handful of holdouts. Many all-female colleges, however, remain in existence, including Smith College, which alumna Betty Friedan has aptly described as "the fountainhead of feminism."

Hence we see that the dictionary definition of feminism overlies a more complex reality. Feminism, it seems, is a dual point of view and, on the face of it, these points of view are incompatible. One lauds androgyny, which it tends to see in predominantly masculine terms; the other lauds femininity, rescued from the unisexist devaluation of the feminine, at the price of a devaluation of the masculine. As early as 1973, the antifeminist writer Arianna Stassinopoulos summarized this contradiction in *The Female Woman.* In the final analysis, she stated, feminists "cannot decide whether they want to become men or destroy them."

It would, however, be inaccurate to view the contradiction as an artifact of 10
the 1970s and the 1980s. As Ann Snitow points out in her *Dissent* article, the contradiction is present in what is often regarded as the first statement of modern feminism, Mary Wollstonecraft's 1792 *A Vindication of the Rights of Women.* In Snitow's words: "Wollstonecraft makes demands for women, then doubles back to say that womanhood should be beside the point. . . . So, in the midst of the hopeful excitement, the divide is there, at the beginning of our history." An examination of such later feminist classics as John Stuart Mill's *The Subjection of Women* (1869), Olive Schreiner's *Woman and Labor* (1911), and so forth, quickly reveals that the contradiction is present there too; indeed, it seems to be a constant in feminist writing. Historically, therefore, it appears that feminism is not two points of view, but rather a single point of view that vacillates endlessly between two contradictory poles. Is it possible to find a theoretical explanation for this historical fact? What I would like to suggest—very briefly and without attempting to explore all the ramifications of this view—is that unisexism and female chauvinism are two mutually necessary aspects of the feminist perspective, like twin stars revolving around each other in constant tension and mutual dependency.

The original definition, from which we started, described feminism as "the theory that women should have political, economic, and social rights equal to those of men." This theory presumes that women do not, in fact, have rights equal to men. Rather than dispute this theory, let us explore its implications. If women do not have rights equal to men, the inescapable conclusion, which no feminist will dispute, is that women are oppressed. Feminism thus must include the idea that women are oppressed. Without this idea, feminism would make no sense. However, it also becomes then necessary to explain how women are oppressed, or more specifically, who their oppressors are.

From the perception that women are oppressed follows the perception that men are the oppressors. Society is held to be dominated by men for their selfish benefit. Note that the "oppressed" and the "oppressor" are moral categories—the oppressed are victims who have done nothing to deserve their fate, the oppressors are villains who have done nothing to deserve their privilege. The theory that women lack equal rights inexorably generates the proposition that women are oppressed and that men are oppressors, which, because oppression is a moral category, further implies that women are victims and men are villains. Reduced to simplest terms, this sets up the following equation: women good, men bad—hence women are better than men. Unisexism thus generates female chauvinism, despite the evident contradiction between these two points of view. Feminism is thus not either the belief that women are the same as men, nor the belief that women are different from men and superior to them, but it is both of these beliefs at once. In the final analysis, it is impossible to reject one of these beliefs and remain a feminist. Yet these two beliefs are mutually exclusive.

Consequently, feminism presents a stark choice: Either reason is invalid—as most sophisticated feminists maintain in this "postmodernist" era—or the assumptions of feminism are in fundamental conflict with the nature of things. In the latter event, there is no other choice but to reject feminism and to go back to nature (conceived in an Aristotelian rather than a Rousseauan sense). Since the nature of polylogism, and its implications for feminism cannot be explored within the confines of this essay, let us proceed on the assumption that the reader does not find the rejection of reason plausible and is willing to posit a convergence between metaphysical consistency and reality.[1]

What Is Sexual Harassment?

The question of sexual harassment, as has been noted, is a feminist issue. Three things are already known about sexual harassment: (1) As a feminist issue, it will be an attempt to obtain redress for women from men, with the former seen as victims and the latter as villains; (2) it will be mired in contradictory notions of women's nature; (3) these contradictions are unlikely to delegitimate the issue in the eyes of feminists. Consequently, non-feminists must attempt to evaluate the merits of the issue for themselves, apart from feminist claims.

What, exactly, is "sexual harassment"? For feminists, who are defining the 15
issue, it consists in pressure on a woman to submit to sex with a man, backed up

[1]Davidson here is pointing out what he takes to be a basic contradiction in feminism. Most feminists, he says, hold to feminism by rejecting logic (a "postmodern" accomplishment). He—and he assumes his readers—refuse to reject reason and so recognize that feminism is not consistent with the nature of things in Aristotle's sense of nature as being fixed, unchanging. Polylogism (literally, "many reasons") refers to the notion that there are many logics in speech and writing; Davidson holds to traditional logic, which says that a contradictory view must be rejected.

by psychological, financial, or physical intimidation, short of actual rape. The presumption is that the man holds power with which he is able to coerce the woman, or which persuades him he is able to do so. The attempt to define and punish a crime of "sexual harassment," therefore, is part of a larger effort to fundamentally change the ethos of society, as that ethos is understood by feminists: to wrench power from the male oppressors and create an egalitarian society in which sexual difference will no longer be important and in which sexual hierarchy, in particular, will no longer exist.

Sexual harassment, it is generally accepted, may take place either as an isolated incident or in the context of an ongoing relationship, including a sexual relationship, and regardless of whether or not intercourse actually ensues. A standard scenario involves a male professor who proposes to a female student that she sleep with him in order to get a better grade. Similarly, a male supervisor who demands that a female employee sleep with him as a condition for continued employment is held to be engaging in an act of sexual harassment.

Many feminists, however, take this definition further and argue that "sexual harassment" consists in the creation of a climate of fear, intimidation, and hostility to women. A college student who utters in the classroom the notion that men are better at mathematics than women may be considered guilty of sexual harassment, and may, in fact, be subjected to sensitivity classes at a growing number of universities. (Incidentally, the empirical evidence is overwhelming that men are, on average, better at math than women. For example, the ratio of males to females who score over 700 on the math SAT is thirteen to one.)

Similarly, many feminists also argue that the mere existence of a power differential between a man and a woman introduces an inescapable element of coercion into potential sexual relations. When a male executive proposes a date to a female subordinate, the relationship is inherently coercive. This is one of the principal reasons why the United States military now rigidly prohibits "fraternization," or dating, between personnel of different ranks and genders; the other reason being the effort to retain military hierarchy in the face of the leveling tendencies of Aphrodite.[1]

Threat of punishment for sexual harassment constitutes a growing element in the lives of Americans. It is clear that the oft-predicted demise of feminism is chimerical and feminism continues to represent a major factor in the evolution of society.

As the case of the military suggests, the sexual harassment issue represents 20
in part a reaction to a real problem. With the two sexes cast together in close proximity for long periods of time, the possibilities for sexual contact, and hence for sexual conflict, are vastly multiplied compared to those that exist in a more traditional society. The need to fend off unwanted male advances may well be a greater problem for women today than it was in the past. The sexual revolution, with its rupturing of all traditional sexual taboos that once condemned all sexual

[1]Aphrodite is the Greek goddess of love and sexual desire. Sexual desire "levels" in the sense that it knows no bounds of rank or status.

relations save those between man and wife, has infinitely expanded the field of potential sexual partners for both sexes, rendering all women fair game.

In this sense, women's liberation has produced women's oppression—hence, in part, the turn in feminism from a unisexist emphasis to a female chauvinist one. For women to participate equally in society now seems to many feminists to require special rights and privileges. As feminist writer Sylvia Hewlett argues in *A Lesser Life:* "Women . . . need more than equality with men if they are to attain equal earning power." Ironically, this change is far from unwelcome to many traditionalists, heralding as it does a partial rollback of the sexual revolution. Yet the feminist account of sexual harassment contains some disquieting elements. For one thing, it easily shades into fanaticism, as numerous examples from college campuses indicate. For example, in 1989, a University of Toronto mathematics professor was convicted of "sexual harassment" for allegedly staring at a part-time female student at the university pool. He was severely reprimanded and forced to undergo extended counseling.

This behavior, if it actually took place, is nothing more than Italian or French men do in the street everyday. Such behavior may be rude or intrusive, although anyone who has lived in Italy or France knows that it is considered rude for a man not to notice a beautiful woman. As the Toronto incident illustrates, what feminists are looking for is not simply redress for genuinely objectionable behavior, but a fundamental change of the mores of our society. The issue of sexual harassment extends far beyond questions of law to questions of culture.

A second incident is even more informative of the nature of sexual harassment as understood by feminists. In the spring of 1988, Pete Schaub, a student at the University of Washington at Seattle, was expelled from the university's introductory Women's Studies class for asking questions that were skeptical of some aspects of feminism. Numerous students present have testified that Schaub's demeanor was consistently polite. "What was his crime?" asked one of them, Shirley Hamblin, in a letter to the university newspaper. "He asked questions. He challenged instructors to support their claims." Campus feminists took this expulsion as the signal to start a university-wide campaign, using Schaub as their symbol. They repeatedly accused him in the local press of threatening them. When questioned by reporters about the nature of those threats, they were able to offer nothing more specific than that Schaub, a body-builder, was large and hostile. "If that is threatening," Schaub responded, "I've been threatened many times. I've seen many big people."

Campus feminists, assisted by Seattle feminist groups, proceeded to hold a series of demonstrations against Schaub, whose only crime remained that he had asked questions in class. Schaub showed up at one of the demonstrations to see what was going on. When he was recognized, the crowd encircled him and chanted over and over: "Stop sexual harassment!"

Just who is harassing who? Are alternative conceptions of sexual harassment 25
possible? After all, on the face of it, Schaub was guilty only of being male and having expressed some reservations about feminism. (Despite the treatment he received, Schaub has continued to express support for feminism in general.) On

the face of it—at least by the liberalized definition of harassment as the creation of a hostile or intimidating climate relative to gender—it was Schaub who was sexually harassed.

The nature of the course in which he was enrolled also raises some interesting questions. Several Seattle lesbian feminist activists were brought into the classroom as guest lecturers, where they informed the students about the lesbian lifestyle as an option they might want to consider. The course syllabus contained this assignment: "During the first half of the quarter you are required to take part in an experience of being 'The Other' and to write up a two-page, typewritten, double-spaced summary of your experience. . . ." This experience may fall into two categories:

> 1. The experience of being a minority in a non-white dominant group setting, i.e., being the only white in a group, the only male, only straight person, only English-speaking person, etc.
>
> 2. The experience of becoming "The Other," i.e., ride a Metro bus visibly reading a lesbian book, use a wheelchair for one day, etc.

Not surprisingly, another student project that was suggested in the syllabus was "to join or organize a demonstration."

Schaub recalls that "one of their guest speakers came and taught [the] women how to masturbate. They said that you do not need a man. They proceeded to show them how to masturbate with a feather duster, and they did have a dildo up there." A teaching assistant in the course, Sarah Hirsh, confirms this account and mentions, as do several other students, that at the end of the class the lecturer held up the dildo and joked, "This one has my name on it."

The textbook used in the course, Changing Our Power, included this poem by one of the two course instructors:

> I just love the smell of me
> closest thing I got to
> the taste of you
> now that you've left
> at first I searched my
> cupboards far and wide
> was it Pringles or Mr. Chips
> or would HaagenDazs eaten
> along with tortilla chips
> provide the proper
> salty sweet combination of you
> little did I know I'd
> find your flavor so close to home.

Several students who took the course in previous years report that the 30
course content was identical, right down to the masturbation lecture. It is worth bearing in mind that this was a large lecture course, involving two teachers,

fourteen teaching assistants, and some two hundred students, mostly freshmen and sophomores.

It is reasonable to conclude that these students were sexually harassed by feminists. Indeed, when the Pete Schaub affair became national news, the Washington State Senate held an investigation, which resulted in a mild reprimand to the university. The course is still one of the most popular courses, the head of the women's studies programs, Sue Ellen Jacobs, told me and there be will no changes in its substance.

This raises the possibility that there are forms of sexual harassment other than those conceived of by feminists. Indeed, it is hard to see how feminism's fundamental assumption, that women are oppressed, can fail to lead to male-bashing. Could one not reasonably conclude that feminist studies, by their very nature, constitute a form of sexual harassment?

Yet, two wrongs do not make a right and the question of male harassment of women remains. It would be idle to deny that this constitutes a problem for some women. The fanaticism and, frankly, cruelty that seem to come so easily to feminists intent on slaying the dragon of sexual harassment, though, suggest that a more nuanced approach may be called for—one that does not see women as impotent and inevitable victims, and men as omnipotent and inevitable villains. Nothing could be clearer, to somebody who has lived a little, than that disappointed female lovers sometimes make real trouble for the men who reject them. Endless phone calls, threats, and even violence are hardly unknown behaviors for either gender. The scenario of the movie *Fatal Attraction* has been played out, albeit typically at a much lower level of violence, between countless men and women since the dawn of history, and perhaps especially since the sexual revolution. It is true that there may be a sex difference here: men are probably more prone to attempt coercion for sex, and women for love. This merely corresponds to a fundamental difference in sexual strategy that has been heavily documented by sociobiologists; it is hard to see what difference this makes to the victim.

Oddly enough, virtually all feminists will accept the foregoing statement if it is cast in terms of unisexism. Thus if you say to a feminist that women are just as powerful and strong-willed as men, and that they cannot be expected to take rejection lying down, she will readily accept the statement, even though, if consistently applied, it demolishes the notion that only men engage in harassing behavior in the sexual arena.

Here we approach the contradictoriness of the feminist position with re- 35
gard to sexual harassment. On the one hand, feminists have endlessly assured us, women are "strong," physically, mentally, and morally—just as tough as men, equally able to take part in military combat and to endure the torture that is often the fate of the prisoner of war, and not especially concerned with the likelihood of rape at the hands of their captors. To assert that there are sex differences—which means to a feminist, when she is standing on her unisexist foot, to assert that men do some things better than women, although it would make equal sense to conclude that women do some things better than men—is perceived as profoundly insulting. On the other hand, if women are as tough as men, as easily

able to stand up to abuse and resist pressure of all kinds, why do they need the protection of special "sexual harassment" laws? After all, could a woman not just say no?

Here we encounter the profound influence of socialism on feminist thinking. Feminists are prone to assume that a woman threatened with the loss of one job has little prospect of finding another. Employment is seen as a scarce commodity (whereas in a libertarian economy, labor itself is in short supply). This assumption of employment scarcity leads to the concept of a job as an entitlement, which in turn reclassifies the employer as a servant of the state. Gradually, the private sphere risks being subsumed within the public sphere. Not coincidentally, a standard leitmotif of sophisticated feminists is to criticize the very existence of the public/private dichotomy. Traditionalists may take heart, from a very long-range point of view, for the logical result of the annihilation of the private is a castification of society and the destruction of liberal institutions. The alternative would be to assume that individuals are substantially capable of taking care of themselves, and that it is futile and destructive to attempt to regulate the minutiae of human behavior through the crude instrument of law.

None of this is meant to imply that sexual harassment laws and regulations will do no good. Women will be treated with somewhat more respect; some overbearing men will be frightened into restraining their impulses; and from time to time a genuine victim will manage to obtain justice for a real slight. But the increased regulation of the minutiae of speech and behavior will far outweigh this limited benefit. The concept of sexual harassment has already begun to claim its victims. The looseness of the concept of sexual harassment, and the fact that its justifiable ambit has already been perverted beyond recognition, should be sufficient warning against its implementation.

Feminists, ever ready to play on male chivalry, which they elsewhere condemn, often ask: "How would you feel if your wife or daughter were sexually harassed by her superior?" We should remember to ask: "How would you feel if your husband or son were falsely accused of sexual harassment?"

Ultimately the feminist perspective must be rejected along with the destructive chimeras it generates, and we must go back to nature, where men and women, not unisexism and female chauvinism, circle each other like twin stars, in constant tension and mutual dependency. For that tension is the Dance of Life itself, and not an ideological ramble into the absurd.

Questions for Discussion

1. Feminists have been and continue to be active in organizing resistance to sexual harassment. But is it accurate to say without qualification, as Davidson does, that "sexual harassment is a feminist issue" (paragraph 1)?
2. The nature vs. nurture dispute—which is now argued as genetics vs. socialization—is centuries old. The outlook Davidson calls unisex takes the nurture or socialization side of the dispute. Based on your own experience and any information acquired through research, how would you respond to the asser-

tion that, in Davidson's words, "There are no inherent differences between the sexes, and . . . whatever differences exist are socially constructed" (paragraph 3)?
3. As concretely as you can, define what we associate with the category "feminine." Does the view that the feminine has been and continues to be undervalued in our culture necessarily lead to "female chauvinism"?
4. In paragraph 12 Davidson says, "Feminism is thus not either the belief that women are the same as men, nor the belief that women are different from men and superior to them, but it is both of these beliefs at once. In the final analysis, it is impossible to reject one of these beliefs and remain a feminist." How do you respond to these statements?
5. In paragraphs 26–30 Davidson describes a course taught at the University of Washington. Is his description necessary for and relevant to his case? If so, how? What impact does his account have on readers?

For Convincing or Persuading

Work out a feminist position that avoids the contradiction which, according to Davidson, afflicts all feminist thought. Then explain how your position relates to your larger view of sexual harassment—in terms of definition, prevention, procedures for handling accusations, and so forth. Conceive your essay as a rebuttal to Davidson, and present it in a way that will appeal to moderates, both men and women.

For Further Research and Discussion

1. Sexual harassment of students by faculty is only one dimension of the problem on campus. More common is the harassment of students by students. Do research on this dimension of the problem, including date and acquaintance rape. What can be done to eliminate or reduce sexual harassment of students by students?
2. Most of the literature about sexual harassment deals with the workplace rather than school settings. Do research in order to compare harassment in the workplace with harassment on campus. What special problems exist for the victims? What can be done to eliminate or reduce sexual harassment in the workplace?

Additional Suggestions for Writing

1. *Inquiry.* How can we understand and explain the behavior of harassers? Do research on the question of causation, including consultation with campus experts. Then write an exploratory essay analyzing the explanations you have found. Conclude with a statement and brief defense of your own conclusions about what motivates sexual harassment.
2. *Persuasion.* Perhaps the most formidable barrier to dealing with sexual harassment is getting the victims to admit to themselves that they have been harassed and to report the abuse to authorities.

Write an essay addressed to first-year students that will help them recognize what sexual harassment is and encourage them to take action against it. Be sure to be sympathetic in addressing reasons for not reporting harassment, but make as strong a case as you can for taking action.

3. *Negotiation*. Perhaps as your class read the articles in this section, did research, and discussed the topic of sexual harassment, certain factions took shape—probably a more or less "feminist" group versus a more or less "antifeminist" group.

   Offer a set of ethical principles to govern interaction between single men and women on college campuses. Phrase the principles and defend them so as to appeal both to feminist and antifeminist viewpoints.

CHAPTER FOURTEEN

Abortion and Religion

Roe v. Wade, the landmark Supreme Court decision that legalized most abortions, was handed down in 1973. In the twenty years since, the antiabortion movement has been active and highly visible, but with little in terms of concrete results. With polls showing that a considerable majority of Americans support legal access to abortion (at least under some circumstances), the chances of a Constitutional amendment outlawing abortion completely are very slight. During the 1980s antiabortion activists hoped that a conservative Supreme Court would overturn *Roe;* but, despite opportunities to do so, the Court has left *Roe* substantially intact. Now foes of abortion have shifted their attention to lobbying state legislatures and demonstrating outside abortion clinics.

The battle over legalized abortion is far from over. But the question of whether abortion should remain legal, while not quite moot, is also no longer at the center of thoughtful discussion. Abortion *is* legal and will almost certainly remain so for the foreseeable future. The question now is, Can we as a society come to terms with these existing conditions?

Many supporters of the right to abortion are hardly at ease with their position personally. Even as they strongly oppose government interference in the reproductive choices of women, they wonder whether abortion can be a moral choice, and, if so, under what circumstances? Another fundamental question is whether we can reach some sort of national consensus on abortion. Are we doomed to painful, perpetual conflict on this profoundly disturbing issue?

In sum, it is the moral and social questions surrounding abortion, rather than legal ones, that must occupy our attention now. To answer these questions, we will need to confront internal tensions, as we debate within ourselves, and external tensions, as we debate others.

This chapter is called "Abortion and Religion" because all the writers included frame their arguments from a consciously religious perspective. We do not mean to suggest that the only significant positions on abortion are religious. However, we do think that religion is ultimately the source of most of our deepest conflicts over abortion. The very desire to find some inner peace and genuine community on this divisive question has clear religious overtones. And even the nonreligious and antireligious must grant that understanding the struggle over abortion requires an understanding of the religious sources within the debate.

Note that the readings in this chapter expand on those in Chapter 8, which focuses on mediating between the two opposing sides of the abortion controversy.

RABBI ARYEH SPERO

Therefore Choose Life: How the Great Faiths View Abortion

Judaism is not only one of the world's great religions but also the indisputable historical fountainhead of two others—Christianity and Islam. It is fitting, then, that we begin with a Jewish view of abortion. But keep in mind that the following article, which first appeared in Policy Review, *is emphatically only one Jewish view of abortion: There is no single Jewish view just as there is no single Protestant view. Jews, in fact, have taken an especially prominent role in the movement for abortion rights, something that might surprise you after reading Rabbi Spero's historical survey of "how the great faiths view abortion." Rabbi Spero speaks here for only* some *Orthodox Jews, the most traditional of groups within Judaism and the group least likely to compromise their beliefs with contemporary moral attitudes toward elective abortion. His audience is also traditionalist,* Policy Review *being an organ of the Heritage Foundation, a prominent conservative research organization based in Washington, D.C.*

The great strength of this article is its honesty and its learning. Rabbi Spero does not conceal his very restrictive view of abortion behind a pretense to "objective" reporting, and he reminds us that all current views of abortion have a history that we should both know about and understand. He does, however, fail to acknowledge Catholic dissenters from the Vatican's extreme antiabortion stance, and he gives all-too-little attention to liberal views of abortion among Jews, Protestants, and Muslims. His account, therefore, is as much persuasive as informative, designed to support his thesis that "[t]he great faiths . . . share an abhorrence for elective abortions and a fundamental belief that, absent extreme conditions, abortion is wrong."

As they have wrestled with the question of abortion for the past 2,500 years, the great religions of the Western and Eastern worlds have sought to balance a concern for the mother with a concern for the fetus. With the prominent exception of Roman Catholicism, most of these religions have permitted abortion in a small number of circumstances. But for most of their history, the great religions have all strongly disapproved of abortion in the vast majority of circumstances in which it takes place today. The exceptions that religions have often permitted—for example, protection of the life and health of the mother, sometimes rape, incest, and serious fetal deformity—have been carefully delimited, and in no way predicated on the notion of a woman's right to do as she pleases with the fetus in her womb. And though the religious arguments against abortion have frequently been connected with prohibitions on birth control, they exceed in gravity the opposition to contraception, and deserve to be taken seriously by modern couples who may be disregarding the birth-control teachings of their faiths. The great religions oppose abortion because it snuffs out life or nascent life, or destroys souls, not simply because as birth control it contravenes the precept to "be fruitful and multiply."

The most widely sanctioned exception is the protection of the mother's life. Except under Catholicism, direct abortion of the fetus is allowable, and sometimes required, to save the mother. Even the Eastern Orthodox Churches, which otherwise consider abortion murder, allow it here, as do Judaism, Protestantism, and Islam.

While Catholicism prohibits abortion in situations where the mother's health is severely jeopardized, Judaism allows it—not only to avert, for example, blindness or deafness but in most situations where physical incapacitation is anticipated. The majority of Islamic denominations rule like Judaism. With the exception of some evangelicals and fundamentalists, almost every Protestant denomination considers protecting the mother's essential physical health grounds for abortion. The Mormon Church also takes this position.

The mother's psychological and emotional well-being is, according to conventional Orthodox Judaism, taken into account only when these conditions are expected to translate into a physical health risk or aberration in the mother. There are, however, some Orthodox authorities who share the Conservative and Reform position allowing abortion for reasons purely emotional and psychological. Like Judaism, Islam manifests a diversity of opinion in such cases. While many evangelical and fundamentalist churches do not sanction abortion to protect the mother's emotional well-being, such major Protestant denominations as the Presbyterian Church (U.S.A.) and United Methodist Church are amenable to abortion in such cases.

The Eastern Orthodox Churches, many fundamentalist and evangelical 5
Protestant denominations, and certainly the Roman Catholic Church do not consider rape or incest justification for abortion. Although most Protestant denominations do, some Protestant theologians recently have suggested that adoption redresses the burden of unwanted pregnancy and that abortion can itself be as traumatizing as pregnancy and delivery in these circumstances. Relying on a 300-year-old decision, most Orthodox Jewish authorities approve abortion in rape situations. The Conservative and Reform movements approve it without hesitation. Islam displays a variety of views.

While most religious denominations do not demand that heroic measures be taken to treat *in utero* a fetal deformity, many would condemn the active aborting of even a severely deformed fetus, viewing that as outside the rubric of therapeutic abortion. Still, most major nonfundamentalist and non-Catholic denominations do allow abortion in such cases.

The United Church of Christ, United Presbyterian Church, and many Methodist denominations now include social, economic, and familial concerns among their legitimate abortion considerations. A number of mainline religious groups belong to an organization called the Religious Coalition for Abortion Rights. However, the Southern Baptist Convention, America's largest Protestant denomination, has been retreating from an earlier permissive position. Other denominations have reevaluated their "pro-choice" positions, with the Lutheran

Church in America (now part of the Evangelical Lutheran Church) specifically excluding "abortion on demand," and the Episcopal Church approving a resolution "emphatically opposing abortion as a means of birth control, family planning, or any reason of mere convenience." Similar resolutions were passed last May at the convention of the American Baptist Churches.

All faiths agree that when abortion is to be performed, it should be done as early as possible. Over the centuries, religions have enunciated certain cut-off points. For example, Aristotle, the Catholic theologians Augustine and Aquinas, and Jewish and Islamic religious thinkers considered the fetus unformed, fluid-like until 40–46 days. The Talmud reckoned distinct organ formation as occurring immediately thereafter. Today we know that by the end of that period not only have the stomach, esophagus, and intestines been defined but that the primitive skeletal system has been completed and the major organ systems formed.

For most of the six centuries between Aquinas' death and Pope Pius IX's canon in 1869, Catholicism held that the fetus was unformed until approximately 80 days, near the end of the first trimester. And, 18th- and 19th-century Protestantism posited that quickening occurred at pregnancy's midpoint (135 days). Modern rabbinic authorities mention a first trimester cutoff point. Islam points to quickening, or the beginning of life, at 120 days. Today, we know that fetal movement occurs within the later stages of the first trimester.

Judaism

Judaism considers a fetus nascent life, indeed a life form, but it does not 10
regard the fetus as an actual human being, or *nefesh,* to use the Hebrew word. Unsanctioned abortion is therefore not murder, but it is a sin or crime.

Judaism's view originates in Exodus 21:22,23 where scripture refers to a mother's life as *nefesh* but not her fetus's:

> If two men struggle (with the intention of killing each other) and accidentally assault a woman so that she miscarries: if she herself is not killed, the combatants shall pay monetary damages for the dead fetus; if, however, she is killed, a *nefesh* [life] shall be given for a *nefesh.*

The scriptural prescription of capital punishment for murder, "Whosoever shall kill a *nefesh* (human) shall be put to death" (Leviticus 24:17), thus does not apply to abortion, since the fetus is not *nefesh.* The Talmud, the authoritative commentaries on the Torah, held that actual personhood does not begin until birth.[1]

If not actually *nefesh,* however, a fetus, according to the Torah, is a form of life, certainly life inchoate. The word for miscarried issue in Exodus 21:22 is *y'ladeha,* or children, instead of *u'bar* or *v'lad,* the appropriate Hebrew words for

[1] The Talmud is the book of traditional explanations and applications of Judaic law for everyday life and conduct. The Torah refers to the Law itself, the first five books of the Old Testament, traditionally ascribed to Moses.

embryo or fetus. The implication is that hominization has taken place—the fetus has human as opposed to vegetable or animal aspects.

One of the leading sages of the Talmud, Rabbi Yishmael, went further, and argued for the fetus's actual personhood. Reading Genesis 9:6 as, "Whosoever shall spill the blood of man in man, shall his blood be spilled," Rabbi Yishmael contended that "man in man" is a fetus, and accordingly, feticide is murder and warrants capital punishment. The majority of his Talmudic peers rebuffed this interpretation, holding instead that the correct reading of the verse is "Whosoever spills the blood of man, *by* man shall his blood be spilled." The possibility that Rabbi Yishmael was correct nevertheless produced an attitudinal reverence for the life-status of the fetus.

This reverence was so great that Jewish law modified various obligations in 15
order to protect the fetus's journey toward full human life. The Sanhedrin (the supreme tribunal of the ancient Jewish nation) allowed the Sabbath to be violated in behalf of the fetus, and deferred the trial of a pregnant woman charged with a capital-punishment offense until after she had given birth. Because the fetus was not *nefesh,* the Talmud permitted abortion to save the life or the health of the mother. But because the fetus was nascent life, abortion was prohibited in all other instances.

The Talmud held that the fetus is "one of the living limbs of the mother," but this did not give a woman the right "to control her own body." On the contrary, just as suicide or the amputation of one's limbs for non-health reasons was outlawed, so was the destruction of a woman's "fetus-organ" prohibited except in cases involving a grave threat to her health.

Maimonides, the 12th-century codifier of Jewish law, introduced an additional justification for destruction of a fetus when it poses a threat to the life or health of the mother: the mother's right of self-defense against her pursuer. The Talmud, centuries before, had invalidated such reasoning on grounds that a fetus is an unconscious being incapable of willful pursuit. Under the influence of Maimonides, however, subsequent scholars have taken seriously the self-defense thesis, which yields a host of implications for therapeutic abortions. For example, just as in other situations of self-defense where one can smite an aggressor of unknown dangerousness, so, too, may the mother abort even if it is uncertain whether the fetus will definitely kill her. Also, as in other cases of justifiable self-defense where one is duty-bound to defend oneself, the endangered mother should not construe her pregnancy as a "divine fate" mandating her surrender: She should abort.

Judaism permits abortion in any circumstance where the fetus threatens the mother's essential health, including her mental health. In Orthodoxy, the criterion is usually grave necessity. Aggravation of a heart condition by the fetus would be an example of grave necessity. Most Orthodox authorities allow abortion in cases of fetal deformity only when there is evidence that the mother's physical health will deteriorate as a result of her emotional distress.

The Conservative and Reform movements of Judaism, and a few recognized authorities in Orthodoxy, do not require such a grave-necessity litmus test but only "severe anguish."[1] Thus, the Conservative and Reform movements view deformity as, in and of itself, probable grounds for approved abortion because of the anguish caused parents. Abortion in the cases of rape and incest is also permitted if pregnancy in these circumstances leads to "severe anguish" or, in the Orthodox case, a deterioration of the mother's health.

Supporters of the "severe anguish" exceptions cite the Sanhedrin's practice of immediately executing all criminals convicted of capital-punishment offenses so as to spare them the inevitable severe anguish felt by prisoners waiting on death row. When it happened that a woman was first discovered to be pregnant *after* a death-penalty verdict had been handed her, the court still immediately executed her, reasoning that the need to spare her months of anxiety was more crucial than the months-later birth of the fetus. Thus the court placed the anxiety and suffering of one actually living (the mother) above the birth of potential, fetal life. Many, however, find such an analogy tenuous; they distinguish between the direct killing of a fetus and a warranted execution directed against a criminal with indirect consequences to the fetus.

Reform Judaism's Union of American Hebrew Congregations, a lay, congregational organization, stands alone among Jewish groups in its sweepingly permissive view allowing abortions purely on grounds of economic, social, and "freedom of choice" reasons. This contrasts to the position of the Reform movement's rabbinic body, the Central Conference of American Rabbis, which defers to the more traditional view expressed in conventional Jewish codes and regards abortion as an emergency procedure only. Abortion for economic or convenience reasons—such as escaping the financial drain of child-rearing or avoiding interruptions in career or education plans—is not sanctioned in Judaism.

In those cases where abortion is permitted, Jewish law dictates that abortion be done as early as possible, preferably before formation (40 days) and certainly before the point of quickening, at the end of the first trimester. After the first trimester, the fetus is considered as more than just a potential form of life although it still is not considered a human being.

CATHOLICISM

Among the faiths Roman Catholicism takes the strictest view of abortion. All abortion is considered murder, and direct fetal destruction is not allowed even to save the mother's life. The Catholic position on abortion is closely linked to its doctrine of ensoulment. From the Middle Ages until the middle of the 19th century, Catholicism held that the soul was not formed until 80 days after conception, and abortion before 80 days was then considered a crime but not murder. Since 1869, when the Church stated officially that actual hominization takes place at conception, its opposition to abortion has been absolute.

[1]Orthodox, Conservative, and Reform are names given to three branches of Judaism in current practice. Orthodoxy is the most traditional and authoritarian, Reform is the most liberal, and Conservative falls in between.

From its earliest stages Christianity was firmly opposed to abortion. Many Old and New Testament verses were cited to affirm the personhood of the fetus. In Luke 1:41–43, for example, the fetus of Elizabeth is already called a babe, and Mary is called the "mother of my Lord" while yet pregnant. Christian theologians also pointed to Old Testament verses such as "Before I formed thee in the belly I knew thee" (Jeremiah 1:5), referring to God's relationship with Jeremiah while yet a fetus, and Psalm 139:13–16, where David speaks of his "unformed substance" in the womb interacting with God.

While the New Testament makes no specific reference to abortion, Paul in his Epistle to the Galatians (5:20) condemned the use of *pharmakeia,* which many believe to be abortifacients. Similar condemnations occur in Revelations (9:21; 18:23; 21:8) in reference to sorceries.

Abortion was forbidden outright in the *Didache,* a second-century compilation of Christian law, and was called murder by the *Epistle of Barnabas,* an early Christian work. No distinction was then made between formed or unformed birth, that is, animation and non-animation. Both the *Apocalypse of Peter* and Clement of Alexandria's *Prophetic Selections,* two other early Christian works, pronounced abortionists doomed to Hell. Drawing from the Pythagoreans centuries before, they held that the fetus was given a soul at conception.

In the year 305 at the Council of Elvira, and later at the Council of Ancyra in 314, the Church made clear and formal its absolute opposition to abortion.

Augustine, who lived from 354–430 and whose teachings dominated Church thinking for almost a millennium, agreed that abortion was criminal, indeed murder; however, he distinguished between pre-formation and post-formation. Like Jerome[1] before him, he took Aristotle's position that the fetus was not human until animation (formation), which was 40 days for a male, 80 days for a female. With the advent of formation, Augustine theorized, the fetus obtained a soul and was therefore human, rendering the act of abortion murder. Before formation, in Augustine's view, abortion was a crime but not murder.

Augustine was influenced by a third-century B.C. Greek translation of the Torah known as the Septuagint, which became the most common text of the Five Books of Moses[2] in the non-Jewish world. In translating the previously mentioned verse in Exodus 21:22–23, the Septuagint departed from the conventional reading of the text. First, it focused not on the mother but only the fetus; second, it translated the Hebrew word *a'son* not as "death" but "formed":

> If two men struggle (with intention of killing each other) and accidentally assault a woman so that she miscarries: if the fetus is not formed, the combatants shall pay monetary damages for the dead fetus; if, however, the fetus is *formed* a *nefesh* [life] shall be given for a *nefesh.*

This reading, then, characterizes a formed fetus as *nefesh,* a person, with an accompanying penalty of death to whoever destroys it.

[1]St. Jerome (340?–420) was an early father of the Christian Church, a Latin scholar and theologian.

[2]The Five Books of Moses refer to the first five books of the Old Testament.

Under Augustine's influence, the Church condemned abortion for its birth-control implications—for voiding the conjugal act of procreative meaning, and for facilitating illicit sexual relationships. A more important objection, advanced by Augustine, was that abortion deprived the fetus of baptism. Abortion was thus even worse than conventional murder, since it denied a soul its entrance to Heaven, a consequence absent when killing a person already baptized. Such reasoning eventually led to papal edicts excommunicating abortion participants, but not the murderers of infants, children, and adults. Such excommunications ended centuries later, under the influence of Thomas Aquinas, who, while affirming Augustine's opposition to abortion, suggested the possibility of salvation even for the unborn.

Aquinas also distinguished between the formed and unformed fetus, and regarded abortion after formation as murder, and before formation as criminal. He held that formation occurs at 40 days, though for a different reason than the Talmud and the sixth-century Justinian Code, which took the same position. Those works settled on 40 days because of the impossibility of knowing if a fetus was male (40-day formation) or female (80-day formation). Aquinas, by contrast, anticipated male offspring, since "the male semen is the power of procreation and every agent tends to produce its like." For 600 years after Aquinas, however, most Catholics who subscribed to the delayed animation theory decided upon 80 days, close to the first trimester, as the animation point.

Thomas Sanchez, a 16th-century Jesuit theologian, wrote in favor of abortion, if done prior to animation, for cases of rape. "As a human being," he wrote, a mother "differs from 'mother earth' in that she need not nurture seed implanted within her forcibly. Like a property owner, she can expel an intruder—but only before the semen is ensouled, before formation."

In 1588, Pope Sixtus V made abortion at any stage a capital offense, dissolving the previous distinction between formed and unformed existence. Though Gregory XIV overturned this canon but three years later, Sixtus set in motion what was to become, centuries later, Catholicism's present position. Thomas Fienus, a 17th-century physician, argued that there are no gradations in a soul's existence. In other words, if the soul was extant post animation—and all concurred that it was—it had to be present always, from the moment of conception. Thus, Aristotle's thesis of successive souls—vegetative (conception), animal (until 40 days), rational-human (after formation)—and Augustine's subscription to delayed animation were discarded: Abortion was the murder of an ensouled human being from conception.

With Pope Clement XI's proclamation in 1701 hallowing the Immaculate Conception as a feast of universal obligation in the Church, a perception that ensoulment takes place at conception, as it had with Jesus, took root among the masses. And in 1869, 168 years later, Pius IX made the Church's position official: Hominization takes place at conception.

Thereafter, all canons and encyclicals on the subject, including *Humanae Vitae* of 1968, made no distinction between animate and inanimate fetuses, declaring "the fetus a human being in the same degree and by the same title as its mother, from the very first moment of conception" (Pius XII, 1930).

While Judaism accepted a principled ambiguity, holding that while a fetus is a form of life eminently deserving protection, it is not an actual person and is therefore secondary to the mother's survival—the Roman Catholic Church took an absolutist position, asserting, "We must again declare that direct interruption of the generative process already begun, and above all, directly willed and procured abortions, even for therapeutic reasons, are to be absolutely excluded. . . ." (*Humanae Vitae,* 1968). Therefore abortion to save the mother's life is not permitted, even when it is known that the fetus itself cannot survive the pregnancy. Although in this case destroying the fetus to save the mother is merely destroying that which is destined to die anyway, abortion is not allowed and both must perish, under the reasoning, "Better two deaths than one murder."

However, while the Catholic Church interdicts direct abortion of the fetus even to save the mother's life, it does allow remedial procedures to combat a variety of diseases afflicting her, though they may indirectly cause the fetus to die. For example, if a woman would die from a cancerous uterus, her pregnant uterus might rightfully be removed even though that results in the death of the fetus: The act is aimed at the cancer, not the fetus. This is known as the doctrine of "double effect," namely, allowing an action with an intended good effect (eradication of the disease) though it inevitably results in an evil effect (destruction of the fetus).

This doctrine, however, is not synonymous with the doctrine of "lesser of two evils" employed by other faiths as justification for choosing the mother over the fetus. The "lesser of two evils" principle allows the deliberate destruction of the fetus when the fetus's presence threatens the mother, while "double effect" allows only those actions necessary to remediate a threat coming from a source other than the fetus, but never, even indirectly, anything aimed at the fetus itself.

PROTESTANTISM

For most of their history, the leading Protestant denominations have con- 40
sidered abortion after animation criminal and an "act of sin and wickedness." Today Protestantism manifests the widest possible range of views on contemporary abortion questions. Many evangelicals and fundamentalists regard abortion as murder even in such circumstances as rape and incest, while some of the more liberal denominations essentially permit it on demand.

After the Reformation and the establishment of the Church of England, the Protestant and Anglican faiths continued living by the abortion position that had guided Christianity during its first 1,500 years. John Calvin and Martin Luther,[1] like Augustine and Aquinas before them, saw abortion as an affront to the procreative meaning behind conjugation, as well as a subterfuge for sexually immoral conduct, but their primary objection was the destruction of innocent

[1] John Calvin (1509–1564) was a Swiss Protestant theologian who stressed salvation through God's grace. Martin Luther (1483–1546) was a German monk and religious reformer closely associated with the birth of Protestantism.

life. Calvin wrote, "The fetus, though enclosed in the womb of the mother, is already a human being, and it is almost a monstrous crime to rob it of the life which it has not yet begun to enjoy." He compared abortion to killing a man in his house, his place of secure refuge, and "it seems more horrible to kill a man in his own house than in a field."

Luther, in *De homini,* wrote that the child in the womb has a soul from the moment of conception. As he was wont to do with many of Aristotle's propositions, which he felt had too heavy an influence on Augustine and Aquinas, Luther rejected Aristotle's theory of delayed animation.

Luther's successor, Melanchthon, also reviled abortion, but distinguished between embryo *formatus* and embryo *informatus,* as did the later 17th-century Anglicans and Puritans.

By the 18th century most Protestant countries marked animation, not at 40 or 80 days, but at the point of "quickening," halfway through gestation, when it was thought that independent fetal movement began. The 18th-century English jurist William Blackstone stated: "Life begins, in contemplation of law, as soon as the infant is able to stir in the mother's womb." Although Germany and England did not formally recognize and legislate according to quickening until the 18th century, the notion of quickening is traceable to early medieval times. The demarcation point between a felonious offense and capital offense was no longer formation but movement, pregnancy's midpoint. Abortion prior to quickening was considered a misprision, a felony; after quickening, it was a capital offense, though the death penalty was seldom implemented.

In 19th-century America, quickening was the criterion for determining 45
acceptable versus unacceptable abortion. Interestingly, in contrast to today, it was the medical profession, particularly the American Medical Association, which railed against pre-quickening abortions, while the Protestant clergy—and most Roman Catholic priests—remained generally silent. In 1868, for example, the Missouri State Medical Association wrote, "Our clergy, with some very few exceptions, have thus far hesitated to enter an open crusade against abortion," and in 1871 the AMA urged doctors to "visit every clergyman within their districts in an effort to persuade them to come out against abortion."

The exceptions to the prevailing silence were the Congregationalist churches, which in 1867 condemned pre-quickening abortion as "fashionable murder." Later, in 1871, the Old School branch of the Presbyterian Church committed itself to the antiabortion movement. Ironically, some Presbyterian denominations as well as the United Church of Christ, a concomitant of the Congregationalists, are among today's most liberal religious spokesmen regarding abortion.

Many reasons have been offered to explain the reticence of America's 19th-century Protestant clergy, ranging from not wanting to believe that abortion was widespread to squeamishness over openly and graphically talking and writing about matters sexual. The most probable reason was, however, that during the 19th century most clergy shared with their congregants the assumption that a fetus was not really alive prior to quickening: Abortion before quickening might be morally offensive, but it was qualitatively different from the destruction of human life.

With the advent of 20th-century scientific awareness of prenatal development, many eminent Protestant thinkers, in fidelity to the human-life yardstick, have begun viewing quickening as an erroneous barometer of when life begins. The late Paul Ramsey, a professor of Christian ethics at Princeton University, remarked that fetal movement begins not at pregnancy's midpoint but in the first trimester. Going even further, he agreed with John T. Noonan of the University of California, now a federal judge, that "a being with a human genetic code is already man," and "genetic coding occurs at conception."

Ramsey offered three stages at which life probably begins: conception, when the unique genotype originates; segmentation, when it is irreversibly settled whether there will be one child, twins, or triplets; and the early development of the fetus, when the "outline" cells contained in the fetus actualize in all essential respects, with only growth to come. This, he continued, transpires no later than eight weeks, after which it is no longer an embryo but a fetus: "By comparison with the achievements already made by the unborn life, traditional quickening refers to no change and birth to less significant change in the human life already present in the womb. There is growth, but the crucial development is already done."

Karl Barth, the preeminent 20th-century neo-orthodox Protestant ethicist, 50
wrote: "The unborn child is from the very first a child. It is still developing . . . but it is a man and not a thing. He who destroys germinating life kills man." While Barth would countenance abortion in cases where the mother's life and essential health are imperiled, he would not, according to scholars, allow abortion when a deformity is diagnosed, construing that as an act of "fetal euthanasia," that is, killing a fetus because of qualms about its future "substandard" quality of life.

Helmut Thielicke, an oft-quoted German theologian, stresses that the question of abortion is separate from that of contraception since, unlike contraception, abortion is the destruction of life. "The fetus," he writes, "has its own autonomous life, it is a human being. Therefore, here, in abortion, creation is infringed upon (an already bestowed gift is spurned) in a way that is completely different from that of the case of contraception."

Leading evangelical theologians have all strongly opposed abortion, with some differences about exceptions. Francis A. Schaeffer, who has had a major influence on the thinking of several televangelists, has written:

> The question of human life truly is a watershed issue. . . . [Abortion] results in the total devaluation of life. The unborn child is a human being created in the image of God, and to deny this is to deny the authority of the Bible. It is impossible to read Psalm 139 and truly believe what it says without realizing that life in the womb is human life. It is impossible to truly believe in the Incarnation and not realize that the child conceived in Mary by the power of the Holy Spirit was indeed the Son of God from the time of conception.

Carl F. H. Henry, the founding editor of *Christianity Today* and a leading evangelical scholar, has decried abortion on demand as "the most horrendous injustice" of this generation, and labeled as "monstrous" the "ready sacrifice of fetal life as a means of sexual gratification and of birth control." Nevertheless, he has also spoken for many evangelicals in countenancing a number of exceptions:

> When childbirth would endanger the mother's life abortion can be morally justifiable. The fetus seems less than human, moreover, in cases of extreme deformity in which rational and moral capacities integral to the *Imago Dei*[1] are clearly lacking. The scriptural correlation of sexual intercourse with marriage and the family, furthermore, implies an ethical basis for voluntary abortion in cases of incest and rape.

Other Protestant theologians, while affirming the life status of the fetus, incline toward more permissive abortion practices. For example, Paul K. Jewett, professor of theology at Fuller Christian Theological Seminary in Pasadena, California, considers the "conflicting personal and societal values to be weighed when making decisions about abortion," stressing that such decisions are ethically ambiguous. Robert P. Meye, dean of the School of Theology at Fuller Seminary, urges the possibility of and need for forgiveness in view of the "ambiguity of many situations faced in family life." James Gustafson, professor of Christian ethics at the University of Chicago, writes: "As the morally conscientious soldier fighting in a particular war is convinced that life can and ought to be taken 'justly but also mournfully,' so the moralist can be convinced that the life of the defenseless fetus can be taken, less justly, but more mournfully." Thus, although he says fetal life is to be preserved and protected in principle, he would case by case recognize social and emotional conditions affecting the woman and future child.

ISLAM

Islam considers the fetus a form of life, certainly potential personhood. Life 55
is made manifest with the arrival of *ruh,* breath from Allah, which divides mere physical formation from the human-spiritual formation: "And when I shall have fashioned him and breathed my spirit into him" (Koran; Sura 15:29).[2]

For many, this takes place at quickening, which Moslems calculate at 120 days after conception, though some see its arrival even earlier. In contrast to the physical breath mentioned by the Stoics, *ruh* is a transcendent, divine breath coming well in advance of the first breath taken at birth.

There is considerable debate within Islam about the permissibility of abortion prior to quickening. The more permissive Hanafi school allows it for any "good cause"; the stricter Ibadiyya school allows it only for grave necessity such as protection of the mother's life or health. Islam divides gestation into at least

[1] *Imago Dei* ("image of God") refers to the notion that we are all created in God's likeness.

[2] Allah is the Islamic name for God. The Koran is the Holy Book of Islam.

four stages: conception, conception to formation (40 days), formation to quickening (120 days), quickening (*ruh*) and onward. Abortion at each new stage brings a sanction of increasing severity, ranging from disfavor to prohibition to crime and, finally, murder, resulting, along the way, in payment of *ghurra* and *diya,* forms of "blood-money."

After quickening, abortion is allowed if needed to save the mother's life, since as *Shari'ah* (Islamic law) states, "necessity knows no law . . . and it is the lesser of two evils, she being the root and it a branch, she being the origin."

The legal commentaries called *Al-Fatawah* offer a sociological reason for choosing the mother's life over the fetus: "She is established in life with duties and responsibilities while the fetus has no responsibilities or obligations to fulfill." According to Islam, abortion for purely economic reasons is forbidden. Sura 17: 31 of the Koran states: "Kill not your children for fear of want. We shall provide sustenance for them as well as for you. Verily, the killing of them is a great sin." However, Ibn Wahban, the Hanafi scholar, says abortion before quickening is allowable if a current pregnancy interrupts the lactation necessary to nurse an already living baby, and the father is unable to hire a wet nurse.

Many Ibadiyya scholars regard the fetus as a complete, live human being, 60
the destruction of whom constitutes murder. They believe that *ruh* is akin to ensoulment. Yet they, too, would allow abortion in behalf of the mother's life since it is "the lesser of two evils."

Hinduism and Buddhism

Although the *Vedas* and *Vinayas*—the sacred texts of Hinduism and Buddhism, respectively—do not explicitly adjudge abortion, the age-old question of when life begins was indeed discussed by Eastern philosophers. Some saw life beginning at conception, others at first fetal movement, and still others at first breath.

Most held that *prana,* life, has no beginning nor end. It is simply a series of evolving births: egg, sperm, blastocyst, zygote, embryo, fetus, infancy, adulthood, and a death leading to a new *karmic* (reincarnated) life, with those whose chain of karma having ended finding their individual soul (*atman* in the Hindu) merging into the *brahman* or *nirvana* (cosmic soul). Though all agreed that the Conscious Self, akin to what Westerners might call soul, is not manifest until actual birth, life theoretically was present in previous existences.

Is personhood, for the Eastern religions, the *atman,* consciousness, which takes place only after birth, or does personhood reside in *prana,* life, which predates even conception? Based on the teachings of *ahimsa,* noninjury and nonviolence, as well as *kismet* and *karma,* fate and non-interference with the cycle, the Eastern religions produced a historical antipathy to elective abortions, resulting in a censure of abortion in the code of Manu (100 A.D.), which quotes from laws issued centuries before. It should be pointed out, however, that the concept of *ahimsa* (non-injury) is so general that included in it is the condemnation of killing even animals.

A Time To Be Born

The ancient Egyptians possessed a hymn, composed by Pharaoh Amenhotep IV, bespeaking "God's transference of life to a son while yet in the body of his mother," a sentiment found also in the Koran. The great religions have grappled with abortion within the age-old context framed by Ecclesiastes (3:2): "There is a time to be born, and a time to die; a time to plant, and a time to pluck up that which has been planted." The great faiths may differ as to when abortion is allowed and under what conditions. Yet they all share an abhorrence for elective abortions and a fundamental belief that, absent extreme circumstances, abortion is wrong. For in the words of Ecclesiastes (11:5), "Thou knowest not how the bones do grow in the womb of she that is with child."

Questions for Discussion

1. Look carefully at the key words in paragraph 64 of Rabbi Spero's article. For example, what exactly is an "elective abortion" (and how might it be distinguished from a "nonelective" abortion)? What exactly would qualify as "extreme circumstances"?
2. Divide into five groups, each to focus on one of the major faiths Rabbi Spero discusses. For the section of the article you are assigned to study, draft a summarizing statement that all members in the group can endorse; then share these summaries with the rest of the class. As you discuss your summaries, consider these questions: How exactly does each major faith distinguish itself from the others in its view of abortion? Is it true that *all* of "the great faiths . . . share an abhorrence for elective abortions"? Each group should also test the Spero's depiction of each religion's views against the experience of its practitioners, by interviewing local religious authorities, both on and off campus. Is Spero's account of each faith fair to the complexity and diversity of opinion? If not, exactly what does he omit or underemphasize? Remembering that no general survey can deal with everything, how much do his omissions and choices of emphasis distort the total picture?

For Convincing

One of the key issues in all debates about abortion is, of course, the status of the unborn. Reread Spero's article and take notes about each major religious conception of the embryo and fetus. Then decide what your own position is. (Your position need not be "religious" in any conventional sense.)

Write an essay addressed to your classmates defending your position and indicating why you find other interpretations unconvincing. If relevant, draw on what you know or can find out from medical science about the development of the unborn from conception to birth.

DAVID E. ANDERSON

Abortion and the Churches: "Clarification" or Rollback?

Any responsible engagement with the subject of abortion and religion should, of course, pay attention to the opinions of the major world faiths. However, in the United States it is Protestant opinion that is most important. This is true for several reasons. First, Protestants predominate here. Second, Protestant opinion is very diverse and presents a special challenge to understanding the issue. Third, Protestant opinion is probably the most volatile and hence most subject to change through argument.

David E. Anderson, a reporter for United Press International who specializes in issues of religion and society, wrote the following for Christianity and Crisis, *"a Christian journal of opinion" that favors a moderate to liberal position in theology and politics. We must emphasize that, like Rabbi Spero's "report" on the major faiths, Anderson's also has a definite persuasive aim: Anderson is as strongly in favor of a woman's right to abortion as Spero is against her right. More than simply assessing the current situation, Anderson is warning Protestants who favor legal abortion to beware of their own complacency and of efforts within their churches to take a more restrictive stance on abortion.*

We have also preserved here a statement by Vivian Lindermayer that prefaced Anderson's article. Lindermayer is the managing editor of Christianity and Crisis, *and her intention is to offer readers a context for the report. As you will see, her statement has as persuasive a purpose as Anderson's report and is meant primarily to urge us to see abortion within the context of present social conditions.*

An ecumenical grassroots effort has been launched to offer help to women facing a "crisis" pregnancy (Religious News Service, Jan. 28). Organizers of the effort—which includes mainline and evangelical Protestants as well as Roman Catholics—want to sidestep divisive abortion politics and provide direct help to women.

According to Stephen Wissler, director of the unofficial task force of United Methodists on abortion and sexuality, the effort is committed to reducing the number of abortions in the U.S. One aspect of abortion prevention has proved controversial: the use of contraceptives by single women who are sexually active. Organizers are more likely to stress traditional Christian views on sexuality and marriage. Says Wissler: "A deep religious experience and being in a committed marriage are the two most significant factors of a lifestyle unlikely to experience abortion violence."

We mention this news story because it resonates with and provides an important context for David Anderson's report on abortion politics within mainstream Protestant churches. Many, if not most, denominational statements support legal abortion but criticize abortion as a means of birth control or for reasons of "mere convenience," without actually specifying what these highly ambiguous terms mean. Some statements affirm the moral agency of women, but rarely do they speak of women outside the context of families, husbands, parents, and pastors.

Yet just over 80 percent of all women getting abortions in the U.S. in 1987 were unmarried, the majority in their teens or early 20s. Nearly all were either in school, or working. Two-thirds had annual family incomes of less than $25,000; two-thirds were white, even though abortion rates are higher for black and Hispanic women. As Rosalind Pollack Petchesky phrases it (*Abortion and Women's Choice*), "We are talking about young, single women . . . who are trying to stay in school, develop their skills, and maintain sexual lives." In other words, abortion has much to do with the reality of women having sex *without* having children, and outside their traditional dependencies.

David Anderson's article, in our judgment, raises these key questions for the churches: Phrases like "abortion as a means of birth control" and "mere convenience" are central to the current debate. Yet church statements do not define them. Nor do they come to grips with the ongoing cultural struggle over the meaning of procreation and sexuality in women's lives, and of gender more broadly. If denominational statements cannot speak a language that clarifies terms and addresses central issues, who are the denominations speaking to? Who are they speaking for?

VIVIAN LINDERMAYER

LAST JULY, as Louisiana's Governor Buddy Roemer agonized publicly before vetoing a bill that would have given the state one of the most restrictive abortion laws in the nation, a group of Louisiana's top clergy wrote him an unusual open letter.

"Theologies," they said, "differ dramatically on the question of whether the fetus is a person from the moment of conception and [on] when abortion may be a moral alternative for women facing problem pregnancies." But, they stressed, "laws banning abortion impose a particular theological perspective on all women, regardless of the teachings of their own faith."

The interfaith letter—signed by United Methodist, Episcopal, Jewish, Presbyterian, and United Church of Christ clergy—was unusual because it dealt with a controversial issue, and it dealt with it in an area of the country where conservative church members are thought to dominate. Equally important, it came at a time when the popular secular press has been hawking the notion that mainline Protestantism is retreating from its commitment to abortion rights.

Newsweek, for example, in an article written just after the Supreme Court's decision in *Webster v. Reproductive Services* (July, 1989) giving states much wider latitude in regulating abortion, said that the United Church of Christ (UCC) "stands almost alone in retaining its vigorous support of full abortion rights." A few months later, an Associated Press dispatch declared, "Most major Protestant denominations which once widely condoned abortions now either oppose it or specify limitations to it." And the *Los Angeles Times* argued that " 'pro-choice' churchgoers looking for moral encouragement are finding little leadership in mainline Protestant denominations."

These appraisals simplify and distort both the history and the current con- 5
text of the abortion debate in the mainline Protestant churches and the wider culture. Confusing questions of theology, morality, and ethics with questions of law and public policy, they suggest that the churches before *Webster* were of one mind on the morality of abortion. They were not. The UCC, for example, in a statement adopted in 1987, stated that General Synods, beginning in 1971, supported the legal availability of abortion "while recognizing its moral ambiguity and urging that alternatives to abortion must be fully and carefully considered."

Prior to 1973 and the Supreme Court's decision in *Roe v. Wade* making most abortions legal, mainline Protestant churches generally supported the repeal of restrictive abortion laws, arguing not that abortion was a moral good but that existing laws did more harm than good. This consensus was driven by a number of social factors, including a growing economy, and an expansive view of individual rights, fueling the movements for civil rights and women's equality. Women suffering and even dying from illegal and self-induced abortions also played a major role. Further impetus came from religious and secular concerns with preventing pregnancy and with the population crisis; both issues figure prominently in pre-1973 statements—in sharp contrast to the contemporary situation where the focus is more on infertility and the difficulties of conception.

The religious and the secular context has changed radically in the decade and a half since *Roe v. Wade.* But no strong indication exists that the churches' consensus on the *legality* of abortion has been reversed.

"I just don't see us falling back at all," said Mary Kuhns of the Justice for Women unit of the Presbyterian Church (USA). Instead, she said, "there has been a strengthening" of the Protestant consensus supporting basic abortion rights. Kuhns' view was seconded by John Evans, director of the state affiliates program of the Religious Coalition for Abortion Rights (RCAR). "There has been a total absence of any calls for change in the legality of abortion by mainstream church groups," Evans said.

RCAR, made up of some 35 Protestant and Jewish groups and agencies, has emerged as the major mainline Protestant voice in the national political debate; it is also playing an increasingly significant role at the state level. Because the nature of membership varies widely in accordance with the denomination's polity—four separate Episcopal groups belong, as do three United Church of Christ boards or agencies, while the Lutherans are represented by the Lutheran Women's Caucus—assessing the degree to which RCAR speaks for or to its denominational base is not easy. (That is less true of the Jewish groups, where membership is held by the national denomination such as the Union of American Hebrew Congregations or the National Federation of Temple Sisterhoods.) And because a diversity of views on abortion has always existed within the religious community, RCAR has consistently stressed "we do not advocate abortion; we advocate choices for women's lives."

While both Kuhns and Evans argue that pro-choice people have been mobilized by the *Webster* decision, they also acknowledge that churches—many with a new generation of leaders who were not part of the pre-1973 struggle—are going through what Evans calls "a process of clarification." With the legal right to abortion now established, churchpeople are arguing about when and under what circumstances abortion is a morally sound decision. 10

"Our policy," Kuhns said of the Presbyterian stance, "is a moderate policy. Yes, we are for choice, but abortion may not always be the best alternative for a problem pregnancy. Nor is it necessarily the worst. We would want to see good counseling and a decision based on a thorough examination of the choices."

Faith Johnson of the United Church Board for Homeland Ministries is equally adamant in drawing a distinction between an erosion of support for legal abortion and recognition of the moral complexity of abortion decisions. "I don't see any rollback," she said, noting that the UCC's General Synod "has consistently passed resolutions affirming a woman's right to abortion, to her right to choose if and when she will be a mother." Most recently, that stance has also included a stress on alternatives to abortion but, according to Johnson, that stress is more "by way of clarification than any retreat" from the support for legal abortion.

Nonetheless, many of the "clarifications" are being interpreted as a tightening of church stands or as a narrowing of church support for legal abortion, and many are being pushed by evangelical and conservative caucuses within mainstream denominations, such as the Good News movement in the United Methodist church, and elements of the Presbyterian Lay Committee within the Presbyterian Church (USA).

The fights over clarification reveal that mainline Protestants—like Roman Catholics, Southern Baptists, and society as a whole—hold diverse views on abortion, and their attitudes differ according to how the issue is presented.

The Episcopal church is a good example. Abortion opponents within the 3 million-member denomination hailed passage of legislation at the 1988 General Convention that opposed abortion as a means of birth control, sex selection, or for mere convenience. At the same time, however, the church called on national and state governments to "respect individual conscience and decision making." 15

As Presiding Bishop Edmond Browning said, "Our discussion of abortion must begin with an understanding that we are dealing with a tangled web of rights and wrongs, good and evil, and greater and lesser tragedies. . . . Our discussion of abortion must focus on finding what can be redemptive in a broken situation."

Still, in revising church statements of abortion to recognize the moral complexity of the issue and the diversity of views among church members, abortion opponents have made progress in undermining mainline Protestantism's embrace of abortion rights.

Remember that abortion opponents like the National Conference of Catholic Bishops and the National Right to Life Committee have virtually given up on efforts to overturn *Roe v. Wade* through a constitutional amendment or any other wholesale measure. Instead, they have turned their attention to the 50 state legislatures, pressing for a series of piecemeal reforms and restrictions: laws barring sex selection and birth control abortions; parental notification or consent requirements for minors; waiting periods; and toughened licensing laws for clinics and health facilities that perform abortions.

These reforms are also the points of contention within the churches. Once again, the Episcopal Church is a good example. The General Convention opposed abortion "as a means of birth control, family planning, sex selection or any reason of mere convenience" without calling for laws to ban such abortions.

"Sex selection" abortions, at least in the United States, are a red herring. 20
Few such abortions occur here. But abortion *is* a means of birth control and family planning. It is a way for women to deal with pregnancies that are unplanned, or devastating. Most abortions, in other words, *are* about women controlling their reproductive life and choosing when and under what circumstances to bear a child. That issue is no red herring.

Kuhns acknowledges the difficulty of defining terms such as "birth control." The Presbyterians' 1985 statement added language opposing abortion as a means of birth control. "What we are trying to say," she said, "is that abortion should not be used *merely* as a birth control *method.*" Rather, she said, abortion may be proper in some circumstances when other means of contraception have failed.

The Episcopal statement, Presiding Bishop Browning's view aside, did introduce the notion that birth control and family planning are somehow morally frivolous reasons for choosing abortion, and women should—literally—bear the consequences of mistakes and failures. Introducing that notion into the abortion debate, moreover, can be taken to imply that the fetus is of more value than the health and well-being of women and their families. "In recent years it has been easier for people to focus on the fetus," said Johnson. "We have to realize, keep realizing, that there is a woman involved, a woman and a fetus involved."

The battle over national mainstream church positions on abortion is likely to be centered in three church groups—the Evangelical Lutheran Church in America, which does not yet have a position; the Presbyterian Church (USA), which is undergoing an extensive process of reconsidering the issue; and the United Methodist Church, where conservatives are already working to make the issue a top priority at the General Conference in 1992.

Prior to *Roe v. Wade,* of course, little need existed for an antiabortion movement: Its tenets were inscribed in the law. But even after the 1973 ruling, it took more than a decade for anti-choice groups to become organized and powerful. Antiabortion groups were certainly boosted by the turn to the right and the cultural conservatism that marked the Reagan era, especially resurgent fundamentalism, which shares some theological principles with the conservatives in the mainline denominations. Fundamentalists used abortion as a means to politically organize masses of people turned off by the 1960s. Some of that organizing spilled over into the mainline, but at least among Methodists and Presbyterians they have met with limited success.

RCAR, meanwhile, reports slow but steady growth, especially at the state 25
and local level, as the fight over abortion moves away from Washington to the state legislatures.

Since the *Webster* decision, the coalition has picked up five new members—the Committee of Women of Color of the Presbyterian Church (USA); the Lutheran Women's Caucus; Women for Social Witness (Episcopal); Women's American Ort, a Jewish social service organization; and the Women's Rabbinic Network—bringing the number of national groups in the coalition to 35.

Still, RCAR's relation to the denominations is not all that clear. Frances Kissling, president of Catholics for a Free Choice, says that denominations have not supported RCAR in the way they should: "In some ways, the denominations have abdicated to RCAR without giving them the support—financial and staff—that is necessary to be effective. RCAR is their excuse for not doing anything. But RCAR has not existed as other church coalitions in Washington have, say, on the peace issue or the Middle East."

Johnson acknowledges the justice of Kissling's criticism: "The religious community still has a challenge to engage their own people. My feeling is that there is still a lot of complacency in the churches. They don't feel that there is any real threat to the basic right and therefore they don't need to struggle with the issue. . . . Bishops and conference ministers and other leaders are not going to put themselves on the line until confronted. Then they will make their choices of where they're going to stand." But Johnson also thinks that RCAR, after a period of turbulence and staff changes, "is moving in the right direction" and is stronger now than it has been in some time.

Perhaps the closest thing to a genuine rollback on abortion is likely to come from the newest of mainline Protestant denominations, the Evangelical Lutheran Church in America, formed from a merger of the Lutheran Church in America, the American Lutheran Church (ALC), and the Association of Evangelical Lutheran Churches.

Prior to the merger, the major groups in the uniting body—the ALC and 30
the LCA—had sharply differing political and theological stands on abortion, with the ALC underscoring the need for laws to protect "human life from the time of conception to birth" and the LCA seeking to make a "qualitative distinction . . . between the fetus' claims and the rights of a responsible person made in God's image who is in living relationship with God and other human beings."

In the fall of 1989, the ELCA's Commission for Church and Society set up a task force to prepare a social teaching statement on abortion by 1991. After a year of meetings, the task force sent an "unfinished" draft of its proposed statement to the churches. (Responses to the draft were incorporated into the final proposal the committee will bring to the ELCA commission's meeting later this month.)

The "unfinished" draft reports as wide a variety of views in the ELCA as in other denominations and society at large, ranging from adamant opposition to abortion under all circumstances to those who hold it is a "tragic option" but can be a "good in the life of the woman and those with whom she is related"—one of the few places abortion is ever talked about as a moral good.

On the public policy issue, the draft calls for making abortions after viability illegal "except for fetal medical or maternal medical indications." The difficulty lies in "determining what [legal] regulations may be appropriate in the case of abortions before the point of viability," it adds. But it does not recommend any particular restrictions or regulations and instead raises questions about such proposals without taking sides.

The moral and legal complexity that accompanies restrictions on abortion has fueled not only Protestant debate and discussion but politics at the state legislative level as well.

While most state action in the past year has consisted of efforts to restrict 35
abortion, in Connecticut abortion rights advocates sought, and won, passage of a state law firmly placing the right to an abortion in state law. According to news reports, RCAR and, in particular, the United Church of Christ's legislative lobbyist, Kim Harrison, played a key role in winning passage of the legislation.

Church advocates of abortion rights are also beginning to argue more forcefully that current efforts to restrict access to abortion are turning the issue into a race and class issue, since restrictions deny services most often to those who are poor women of color. (Class-based restrictions, in reality, have been with us since the first Hyde amendments were passed barring the use of federal Medicaid funds for abortion services.)

"RCAR has been moving on [the class] issue for years," said Johnson. "And we in the churches are becoming increasingly clear that abortion has to be addressed in part as a class issue." Kuhns was equally emphatic. "Abortion is already a class issue," she said. "We continue to remind ourselves that it is a justice issue. The middle class has a choice. Others don't, and it is becoming less and less of a choice for the poor."

"Another place the church needs to be active," said Johnson, "is in supporting the abortion providers. There is no question that the providers are weary. They have been affected by the picketing, by Operation Rescue, and pro-choice people have to find ways to support them and to encourage new people to enter the field."

Violence and disruptions directed at clinics and women's health facilities have been part of the abortion scene almost since *Roe*. By most accounts, the first clinic sit-in, or "rescue," as supporters prefer, occurred in 1975. Most early rescues were organized by Roman Catholics, often veterans of the anti-Vietnam War movement schooled in the tradition of pacifist nonviolent civil disobedience. In the mid-to-late 1980s, however, self-styled "born again" lay preacher Randall Terry organized Operation Rescue and with highly visible blockades and sit-ins in New York, Atlanta (during the 1988 Democratic convention), and Los Angeles, the movement took off and became a prominent player in the abortion debate, attracting money and endorsements from Jerry Falwell and Pat Robertson.

Few of Terry's adherents came from the ranks of mainline Protestantism 40
and none of the existing polls indicate that has changed. Most Protestant church

leaders have also rejected the rescue movement. The 1988 General Convention of the Episcopal Church specifically condemned "all actions of violence against abortion clinics" as well as "any act of violence against any of those persons seeking the services available at such clinics."

The movement has also been criticized and condemned by the United Church of Christ's Board for Homeland Ministries, the Women's Division of the United Methodist Church's Board of Global Ministries, the Unitarian Universalist Association, and the Washington Office of the Presbyterian Church (USA). That opposition has been firm and consistent throughout the debate and, while Operation Rescue has shut down its national operation and the flamboyant Terry romantically gone "underground" like some echo of the Weathermen, the invasion movement and ongoing picketing of facilities continues with some strength.

The new political and social climate, advocates stress, has deepened Protestant thinking about abortion; it has provided some moral nuances not always present in the drive to decriminalize the procedure and it has sought to underscore a multiplicity of choices without undermining the basic commitment to keeping abortion legal.

The churches' new stance *may* be more representative. But it entails political risks. Opponents of abortion are generally not willing either to compromise or to admit complexity and diversity of belief. For them, the goal remains criminalizing all abortions, and the piecemeal restrictions are the current strategy of choice. Such restrictions are also points of contention within the denominations.

"Sometimes it can be fairly depressing," said Kuhns. "The country is more conservative; likewise the church. In the church that has made us more realistic. But we have to keep vigilant."

Questions for Discussion

1. Vivian Lindermayer challenges the churches (and by implication her readers) to define what "abortion as a means of birth control" and "mere convenience" mean. What do these phrases mean to you? If a woman takes precautions but nevertheless gets pregnant and opts for an abortion (say, because she is a single college student in her first year), is it reasonable to claim that she is using abortion "as a means of birth control" or resorting to abortion as a "mere convenience"?
2. Along with Lindermayer, Anderson connects abortion with broader issues of gender, race, and class (paragraphs 36–37). Most influential churches in this country are controlled by white middle-class men; the policy they debate affects women, many of whom are poor and nonwhite. How do you respond to the implicit charge that some church thinking about abortion fails to reckon with gender, race, and class bias?
3. Is it true that "laws banning abortion impose a particular theological perspective on all women" (paragraph 2)? If so, what are the implications for freedom of religion and separation of church and state?

For Inquiry

In criticizing the popular media's interpretation of recent Protestant thinking on abortion, Anderson asserts that the media is "[c]onfusing questions of theology, morality, and ethics with questions of law and public policy" (paragraph 5). Write an essay that explores this distinction. Where abortion is concerned, to what extent can we separate theology, morality, and ethics from law and public policy? To what extent should we do so?

You might wish to consult with campus and other local authorities to help stimulate your own thinking.

For Persuasion

If the status of the unborn is a key issue in abortion, so also is the status of the woman carrying the child. If you favor legalized abortion, write an essay defending freedom of choice and arguing that abortion can be, in the words of the Evangelical Lutheran Church in America, "good in the life of the woman and those with whom she is related" (paragraph 32). If you are against legalized abortion, write an essay explaining why a woman should not have freedom of choice and refuting the assertion that abortion can be a moral good.

FRANCES KISSLING

Ending the Abortion War: A Modest Proposal

Writing in early 1990 in The Christian Century, *Frances Kissling, president of Catholics for a Free Choice, could say, "so far, my side, the side that favors legal abortion, is winning the war" (paragraph 6). No one can predict future policy, but if she were writing in the mid-1990s, during the Clinton presidency, she would probably be even more optimistic that her side will prevail.*

However, one seldom encounters a triumphant tone among thoughtful and sensitive advocates of choice, who like Kissling, worry that too many in the pro-choice camp "think and act in 30-second sound bites" and fail "to acknowledge the tragedy of abortion." In other words, if there is a victory for women in keeping abortion legal, any celebration must be tempered by the moral gravity such an option embodies. To speak glibly of winners and losers is to exhibit a very superficial grasp of the abortion issue.

Furthermore, winning the war is not the same as establishing a lasting peace. Kissling attempts here to open a dialogue about the values and goals that should guide policy within the framework of legal abortion. With this crucial step, she moves the argument beyond mere factionalism and slogans and beyond the increasingly pointless debate over whether or not abortion should be legal.

As we enter the 1990s with modest hopes for world peace, a particularly bitter and seemingly intractable domestic war continues unabated. The U.S. Supreme Court decision in *Webster v. Reproductive Health Services* has mobilized armies of supporters and opponents of legal abortion.

Explicitly, the court let stand a provision of a Missouri law that required testing to determine fetal viability in pregnancies of 20 weeks duration and longer (it should be noted that no such tests exist). The court further curtailed poor women's ability to choose abortion by substantially expanding its prior rulings on public funding. It ruled that states are free to prohibit abortions at any health-care facility that receives any public funding. Even private doctors who perform abortions on private patients with private funds will be affected by the ruling if their admission privileges happen to be at a hospital that receives public money or has contractual arrangements with state or local governments.

In a move troubling to most religious groups, the court also let stand the preamble to the Missouri law, which declared that life begins at conception, saying that the preamble represented a permissible value judgment by the state that would have no effect on the legality of abortion.

Implicitly, the five-justice plurality opinion warned that the court would no longer apply strict scrutiny to limitations on a woman's right to choose abortion. No longer would legislatures or regulatory bodies need to show a compelling state interest in order to intervene in women's decisions. The decision was interpreted by those who favor and those who oppose legal abortion as an open invitation to state legislatures to enact restrictive legislation designed to test further and possibly overturn *Roe.*

Both sides responded aggressively and passionately. Faye Wattleton, presi- 5
dent of the Planned Parenthood Federation of America, declared, "Make no mistake about it. This is war." Kate Michelman, director of the National Abortion Rights Action League, told elected officials, "Take our rights, lose your jobs." Randall Terry, leader of the controversial Operation Rescue, said: "We're calling on thousands of pro-life Americans to peacefully blockade these killing centers with their bodies to prevent children from dying and we will launch an equal force against state legislatures to chip away at *Roe.*" (By quoting Terry alongside Wattleton and Michelman, I do not mean to imply any philosophical or strategic equivalence in their viewpoints or actions. It is simply that these were the voices most frequently heard and quoted in the last half of 1989.)

By any reasonable measure, so far, my side, the side that favors legal abortion, is winning the war. On the electoral front, not only have candidates like Governor Douglas Wilder (Virginia) and Governor James Florio (New Jersey) made their pro-choice positions central to a winning strategy, but politicians considered pro-life are defecting to the pro-choice camp daily.

Perhaps more significant—and substantial—is that pro-choicers have partially shifted the terms of the debate from the question of whose rights will prevail, the woman's or the fetus's, to who will decide, women or the government. This is not to say that questions of rights or of the moral value of fetal life are insignificant in evaluating the act of abortion. However, to claim that the central conflict in the debate is between women and fetuses incorrectly and unfortunately casts a woman as the adversary of the fetus and in no way acknowledges her role as moral agent. Moreover, in light of the growing attempt to subordinate individual rights to a somewhat undefined "community," even opponents of legal abortion should exercise caution in making rights arguments paramount. In framing the question "who decides?" NARAL has moved subtly from the concept of "choice," a principle that has come to be seen as related to the trivial or selfish, to the concept of "decision making," which implies greater seriousness and complexity.

Webster's threat to legal abortion has also significantly increased the number of organizations, generally liberal to progressive, adding abortion to their portfolio of issues. The pro-choice coalition is bigger, stronger, more cohesive, and better financed than ever before. It is convinced that given enough time and money it has the capacity to build the political machine necessary to win the war and preserve *Roe.*

Pro-life leaders, while stung by the losses of 1989, are equally committed to the long war and will surely win some victories in the next (or some subsequent) foray into the courts or state legislatures. The Catholic bishops have reentered the political arena with a bang, declaring abortion—not the degradation of the planet, the economy, or racism—their number one concern. Catholic legislators got a hint of the kind of political muscle the bishops are prepared to use when Bishop Leo T. Maher of San Diego announced in the midst of a special election for the California state senate that candidate Lucy Killea could no longer receive communion in the Roman Catholic Church because of her pro-choice position. Catholic legislators in Montana, Rhode Island, Washington, Connecticut, and Minnesota have reported that their bishops have warned them that public pro-choice positions create "problems" for the church. With 28 professional statewide lobbying offices from Hartford to Sacramento, the bishops have a political machine capable of seriously restricting *Roe* at the state level.

How all this hardball political gamesmanship and bellicosity will contribute 10
to sound, stable public policy on abortion remains to be seen. If the past 20 years are any model for the next 20, we can expect abortion to remain both an issue that is ideologically shaped and a problem that is unsolved.

One would hope, however, that this new moment in the abortion debate could be seen not only as a time of crisis by those of us who are pro-choice (and I speak only to that group, having neither the right nor the interest to suggest a course of action for the opposition) but as an opportunity to examine our own beliefs in light of the signs of the times and the experience of 17 years of legal abortion. Perhaps it is time, as one good friend so aptly put it, for those of us who are pro-choice to "take the high dive"; that is, to resist the temptation to think and act in 30-second sound bites and engage instead in serious moral discourse on abortion.

Perhaps we need to listen to the wisdom of more than 50 percent of our population. They hold in creative tension a basic sense of fair play in wanting women, with consultation, to make the decision about abortion or childbirth and a concern for the value of fetal life and the quality of women's decisions. Only then will we be in a position to advocate public policy that respects each individual woman and expresses our concern for human life and the community at large.

Abortion is not fundamentally a political question; it deals with people's deepest, most unconscious feelings about life, the power of creation, and the survival of our species. Those in the so-called "muddled middle" understand this better than those at either end of the public opinion spectrum. They understand abortion—and reproduction—as both a private and a social phenomenon. They wait for one side or the other to answer such questions as: "How will we bring new life onto this planet?" "How will we treat the rest of life?" These elements are not unconnected. Just as we challenge pro-lifers to care about more than prenatal life, so must we challenge ourselves to talk about more than the life that is here. We must also talk with reverence of the life that is to come. Most important, this conversation cannot be viewed as a threat to the rights of women, but as an enhancement of the responsible exercise of those rights. We must not let our own justifiable fear of the opposition shape the dialogue.

Concretely, we must stop criticizing moderate pro-choice voices: public officials (like Governor Mario Cuomo) who speak of the "tragedy" of abortion; columnists (like Anna Quindlen of the *New York Times*) who express concerns about late-term abortions; and theologians (like Giles Milhaven of Brown University) who speak of women's sadness after abortion. All contribute a richness of spirit to the debate that needs to be encouraged, not crushed.

15 Our own inability to acknowledge the tragedy of abortion makes us suspect. Our continuous talk about *wanted* children does not inspire confidence but fear. We live in a world where our value is increasingly equated with wealth, brilliance, or success. Many rightly perceive that they are powerless and unwanted. For the powerless, the fetus is a ready symbol of their own vulnerability—a symbol exploited by right-wing leaders.

Acknowledging fetal life as valuable and as an important factor in decision making about abortion need not be linked to a specific religious doctrine. The Christian respect for life has never required the absolute protection of life. It does not require conferring personhood or rights on the fetus, nor does it suggest limiting the legal rights of women to decide whether to bring new life into the world or to have an abortion.

On the other hand, an enhanced sense of the value of fetal life should move us beyond the status quo on abortion and beyond an absolutist interpretation of the fundamental rights articulated in *Roe v. Wade.* On both principled and practical grounds, pro-choice advocates need to see *Roe* as a framework for good policy on abortion, not as a fortress against policy.

By no means should the pro-choice movement abandon, at this time, the rights framework implicit in *Roe.* Given the unrelentingly punitive, hostile approach to women in our society, we continue to need the strongest legal protection available to enable our full and equal participation in society. This includes legal control over fertility.

An equally compelling reason for maintaining a rights framework is the unprecedented assault on individual rights mounted by the Reagan administration. Individual rights for women are inseparable from individual rights for people of color. Efforts in both progressive and conservative circles (from Stanley Hauerwas to George Will) to portray individual rights as a threat to the community must be resisted. Individual rights, once they include women and people of color, are a threat not to the whole community but to the community of white men.

20 A theory of community that places unequal burdens on women in welcoming and respecting new life is inherently unjust and doomed to fail. That injustice is obvious in our society, and while lip service is paid to sharing the burden, there is little evidence that the architects of communitarian models or their admirers are moving toward a concrete embodiment of equality and responsibility.

Individual rights cannot, however, be slavishly pursued. Even the most fundamental rights are regulated under the Constitution. Many of us support even more regulation for any number of rights, such as the right to bear arms. Pro-choice advocates—not just those whose goal is prohibition—need to explore regulations that will enhance women's decision making in a manner that respects fetal life without making protection of fetal life absolute. (At the same time, we must strongly reject policy measures whose only purpose is to limit or prohibit access to legal abortion.) We must see that such regulations, once enacted, are enforced scrupulously and noncoercively and that penalties for deliberately misinforming, coercing, or unfairly influencing a woman's ability to make good decisions are promulgated and used.

Finally, all regulations need to be looked at individually and cumulatively to ensure that they do not prevent the poor or people of color from exercising their right to act as decision makers. Walter Dellinger, professor of law at Duke University, pointed out recently in the *University of Pennsylvania Law Review:*

> A 48-hour waiting period, for example, may not be an "undue burden" for affluent professional women, and a hospitalization requirement may only serve to make her abortion more expensive. But for an 18-year-old girl in the rural South, unmarried, pregnant, hoping to finish school and build a decent life, who has little or no access to transportation, a hospitalization requirement can mean an abortion that will cost nearly $1,000 and involve a trip of hundreds of miles; a waiting period can mean two long trips and an overnight stay in a strange and distant city. For such a woman, the burden would be absolute.

While it is premature to move from a brief exposition of some of the principles needed to inform public policy initiatives on abortion to a recommendation of specific measures, the state legislative season is upon us. Many legislators and advocates will not stop to reflect before running headlong to pass new laws. And it is important, as many rush to the "middle" on abortion, that those who seek to be consensus-builders or compromisers be held to a high standard of specificity. What do we think policy on abortion should be? Are we really listening to the middle or simply attempting to co-opt it?

Here, then, are some immediate guidelines and specific elements of a sound, stable public policy that can be implemented now and contribute to a balanced, long-term approach to the issue.

First, abortion laws need to acknowledge women's right—and need—to make reproductive health decisions free from coercion, as well as both women's and society's responsibility to create conditions for women to bring life into the world.

Either in the body of the law or by reference to other existing legislation, the community's reverence for life should be expressed in support of social and economic programs for children and families. A good model for this can be found in the legislative program of the Children's Defense Fund.

The balance between women's rights and reverence for life is best expressed by making resources available to assist women in good decision making and in preventing pregnancy. We should advocate a series of initiatives that signal government *involvement* as opposed to *intervention*. Among them: funding for voluntary nondirective, comprehensive, and confidential counseling services for women and their partners who are contemplating abortion (no funds should be made available to groups that favor one decision over the other or that preclude any legal option from the range of choices offered); funding for more measures designed to prevent pregnancy, including contraceptive research and testing as well as contraceptive education and services; and equitably distributing funds for adoption, abortion, childbearing, and child rearing.

These funding proposals represent a major shift in policy and would be a significant compromise for both sides of the debate. Pro-choice advocates will need to accept greater government involvement as an expression of community consensus; in turn, the community, through the government, will need to back up its involvement with resources.

Among the particularly thorny issues confronting legislatures this year are requirements for parental consent for minors' abortions, prohibitions on gender selection and postviability abortions, and so-called informed consent statutes.[1] Critical to the pro-choice movement's ability to forge consensus on the general question of legal abortion will be its ability to respond rationally and concretely to these issues. Up to now, a fundamental rights approach and our fear of the "slippery slope" has led us to reject outright all regulation in these areas. But a blanket No is simply not a sufficient response to these complex questions.

In the case of parental consent requirements, we need to acknowledge 30
young women's special need for adult involvement. Indeed, we want to protect teens from either coercive abortion or coercive childbearing. Form letters mailed to parents do not adequately or effectively discharge our obligation to these women. Neither does the absence of policy.

Provisions for nondirective, confidential counseling by health-care workers, ministers, and other qualified professionals would enhance decision making, and a record of such counseling could be kept as part of the medical file. Statutes similar to that passed in Maine, which demand involvement by a parent—or, when that is inappropriate, an adult family member, minister, teacher, or counselor—should be applauded.

While there is no evidence that some women seek abortions solely for gender selection, pro-lifers have seized on this possibility as a convenient and gruesome example of the extremes to which abortion liberty will drive us. But in fact the devaluation of women in society is the cause of gender-selection abortion. The few reports of abortion in which gender was a factor point to those communities, primarily Asian and African, where male children are still considered a necessity. Indeed, in Africa a woman is called infertile if she does not produce boys, while some Asian wives are abused and abandoned. As odious as I would find the practice of gender selection even in these hard cases, I would be loathe to take responsibility for any prohibition that could cost these women dearly.

However, the notion that women would seek abortions in the mid to late second trimester because the nursery is painted blue or hubby's family has had firstborn boys for generations is ludicrous. It really deserves no response. It also deserves no defense. I would seek no laws to prevent that which does not happen,

[1]"Informed consent" refers to the notion that women seeking an abortion should understand the physical process of abortion and should also be informed of alternatives to the procedure. Abortion rights activists fear that under informed consent statutes antiabortion propaganda will predominate.

but I would not oppose such laws. This is an area for self-regulation, and one hopes that responsible providers of abortion would decline their services in such cases.

In a similar vein, I think the question of postviability abortions is of little practical significance and of enormous symbolic importance. In practice, it is extremely difficult to find a physician who will perform such abortions unless there is a serious, physical, life-threatening condition for the woman, or the fetus is diagnosed with profound abnormalities. There is no evidence that the right to such abortions is necessary for women's well-being or full participation in society. These facts, combined with the growing sense that fetal life deserves increasing respect as it develops should lead pro-choice advocates to accept legislation limiting postviability abortions to life-threatening or disabling cases.

Another frequently cited set of regulations on abortions are those requiring 35
"informed consent." Up to now, the court has struck down such measures. In the post-*Webster* climate they will once again be raised. Without exception, all past informed consent laws were drafted by opponents of legal abortion—not to assist in good decision making but to prevent abortion. The information mandated was often biased, inaccurate, and simplistic: "Life begins at conception," "the heart beats at eight weeks," "abortion is dangerous and will make you sterile." Nondirective counseling is far more appropriate and respectful of women's capacity to make good decisions than existing informed consent approaches. Moreover, I cannot stress too strongly my belief that if the government is to be involved in the process of women's decision making, those who are entrusted with helping women need to be held to the highest standard of care.

For those whose interest is in outlawing abortion, the rather modest shift in both laws and values set forth here offers little. In the short run, these policy measures will not reduce the current number of abortions, which is troubling. It is important, however, that we not reduce abortion policy and values to a numbers game. The goal of caring people—eliminating all abortions—will require a radical transformation of society. We should focus our efforts on correcting the disease, not the symptom.

Questions for Discussion

1. Although access to abortion is commonly restricted during the last trimester, basically there can be no mediation over the legality of abortion: Either it is legal or illegal. As Kissling's article shows, however, the choices we have within a framework that assumes legal abortion are many and far from cut-and-dried. Beginning at paragraph 24, Kissling makes her proposals. What exactly is she calling for? How might her proposals appeal to each side in the abortion debate? Are they adequate to her high moral sense of the seriousness of abortion?
2. Compare Kissling's proposals with Roger Rosenblatt's in his article "How to End the Abortion War" (pages 179–187). How are they alike? How different? In your opinion, whose ideas offer the best chance for useful dialogue?

3. On most issues, consensus is not and cannot be 100 percent. Realistically, when we look for consensus we hope for agreement among significantly more than a simple majority, but we do not expect everybody to agree. We also hope that the consensus reached is truly satisfactory, uncoerced, and genuinely understood. Given your understanding of religion and abortion, and taking into account class discussion of Kissling's proposal, what chance do you see of a consensus forming around Kissling's views?

For Convincing or Persuading

Kissling admits that the policy measures she proposes "will not reduce the current number of abortions, which is troubling" (paragraph 36). It is unlikely that anyone is happy with the number of abortions performed in the United States each year. Write an essay addressing this problem and specifying what you think could be done—short of outlawing abortion—to reduce the number of abortions in the United States.

For Further Research and Discussion

Do some research on Randall Terry and Operation Rescue. How successful has this movement been in reducing access to abortion? What do you think about the methods Operation Rescue uses?

Additional Suggestions for Writing

1. *Persuasion.* Do some research into how abortion clinics operate. What sort of counseling is provided? If a clinic operates near you, try to talk with the staff, including doctors. Write a letter addressed to the head administrator of the clinic detailing any suggestions you may have for making sure that decision making is well-informed and rational.
2. *Convincing.* Some have argued that there ought to be a mandatory waiting period between seeking an abortion and the performance of the procedure. Write an essay supporting or attacking this proposal as being necessary or not. Be sure to find out about what actually happens when women seek abortions and about the process they go through prior to seeking an abortion.

CHAPTER FIFTEEN

Race Relations: Where Are We Now?

In the late 1950s and early 1960s, the struggle for racial justice was central to the drama of the times. The problem seemed clear: a social, economic, and political system that discriminated against all nonwhite people, but especially against blacks. The solution also seemed clear: the destruction of segregation and the guarantee of equal opportunity—in short, full civil rights for everyone that would lead eventually to a society in which the color of one's skin no longer mattered. Finally, the villains and heroes seemed clear as well: a reactionary white establishment with a guilty conscience, afraid of what was happening and resistant to change, in opposition to heroic civil rights leaders and their followers who risked their lives to win one small victory after another.

Of course, the racial drama of that earlier era was never quite as simple as it seems in memory, but the struggle at least had an identity and a direction, a coherence mostly lacking today. What has happened to the Civil Rights Movement? Where are we now in dealing with the question of race relations?

Some insist that the struggle is over or, at least, that it should be over: They point to the success of the Civil Rights Movement in ending legal segregation and to affirmative action programs, which helped blacks, other minorities, and women gain access to higher education and to jobs previously held almost exclusively by white males. If many blacks still languish in poverty, the argument goes, it is their fault for not taking advantage of the opportunities they now have. Racism can no longer be blamed for the plight of black Americans.

Others reject this view entirely. They point to episodes such as the 1992 beating of Rodney King by Los Angeles police officers to show that racism is far from over. They call attention to the desperate condition of our inner cities: massive unemployment, crime, drugs, and a pervasive sense of despair among the black underclass. They ask, Do civil rights matter if people are still impoverished? How much can integration or the privilege of voting mean to a ghetto gang member or to a single mother scraping by on welfare? Theoretical equality will not do, they argue; the struggle will not be over until minorities have real economic and political power.

These are the primary opposing viewpoints that structure the racial drama today, a drama that is less clear-cut because blacks themselves can be found on both sides of the struggle and because the issues are many and complicated. Among the questions being debated are the following:

To what extent does our society remain racist?
To what degree does racism, past and present, contribute to current conditions?
As far as public policy is concerned, what, if anything, should be done to further the cause of racial justice?
What must impoverished minorities do for themselves if they are to enjoy the fruits of prosperity?

To these key questions we can add at least two more. Looking deep inside, we must each ask, To what extent am I a secret racist in my attitudes and thinking? And, starting with our own surroundings, the college campus, we must also ask, To what extent is racial separation still the norm?

Much about race relations has changed since the 1960s. Some of these changes unquestionably have amounted to real progress. But many argue that during the 1980s the general condition of black America grew worse, that ground previously gained was lost again. Of one thing we can be sure: Problems between the races, older than the founding of the United States itself, have not been solved and will not go away. It seems that Americans are destined to wrestle with these questions again and again.

BRUCE YOUNG

Photograph

Before the Civil Rights Era of the 1960s, it was common to see blatant discrimination, especially in the South. This photograph of segregated restrooms reveals a great deal about the prejudices of an earlier time.

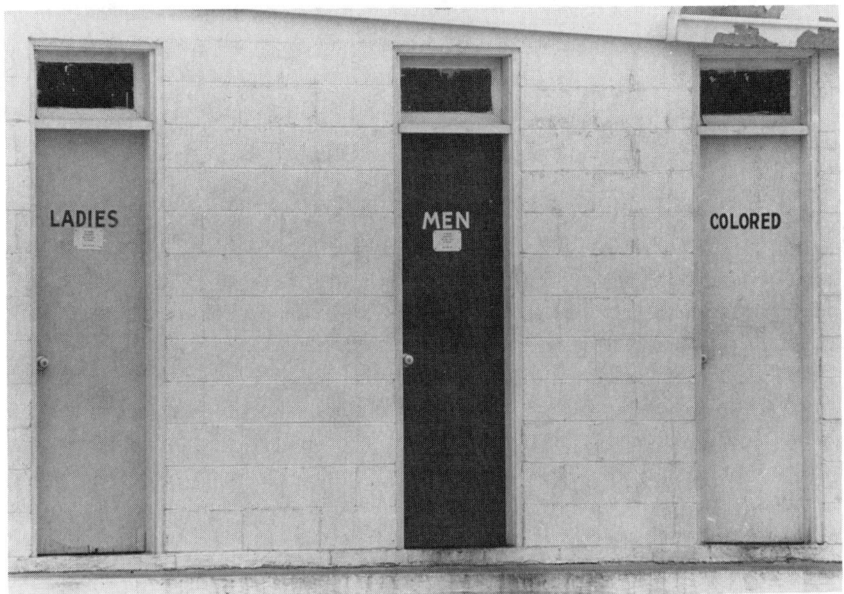

For Discussion

Rhetorically, the doors are an argument, made by the white majority to members of both white and black races. Discuss the argument in terms of rhetorical context, as described on page 17.

RYSZARD KAPUSCINSKI

Second Thoughts about America's Racial Paradise

The following two-part article appeared in New Perspectives Quarterly *(1991), published by the Center for the Study of Democratic Institutions. We include the headnote provided by the editors of* NPQ, *which explains the unusual circumstances of its composition.*

The article provides a European's perspective on racism in the United States. The author is clearly a prophet of sorts, focusing more on what might be or could be than on what is. And yet if we recognize that his vision is, as even he admits, "perhaps . . . overly naive and idealistic," we must yet grant its appeal—and its challenge. What do we see when we consider race in the United States? What perspective will allow us to understand best what is unfolding before our eyes?

Author most recently of the *The Soccer War,* Ryszard Kapuscinski has spent the last several decades reporting on the Third World for the Eastern European press.

In 1988, *NPQ* invited the acclaimed writer to Los Angeles to comment on a city that had become dubbed the "capital of the Third World." We reproduce a portion of his ode to LA's multiculturalism below.

After the beating of Rodney King by white cops, we asked Kapuscinski for his second thoughts, which he sent to us from Warsaw.

How is it, we asked him to ponder, that the same city celebrated for its inter-ethnic peace and remarkable cultural diversity—a city which attracts immigrants of color from all over the world seeking a new chance—was also the setting of the brutal beating of a black man by white police worthy of South Africa?

Is the multicultural paradise beginning to fray as the American economy falters? At the outset of the 1990s, LA's two major economic pillars—real estate and aerospace—have begun to crumble. Is violent inter-ethnic conflict on the horizon without the social glue of economic growth?

In such an eventuality, will Los Angeles remain, as Kapuscinski has postulated, a premonition of the future?

1988—TRADITIONAL HISTORY has been a history of nations. But for the first time since the Roman Empire, there is the possibility of creating the history of a civilization. Now is the first chance, on a new basis with new technologies, to create a civilization of unprecedented openness and pluralism. A civilization of the polycentric mind. A civilization that leaves behind forever the ethnocentric, tribal mentality. The mentality of destruction.

Los Angeles is a premonition of this new civilization. Linked more to the Third World and Asia than to the Europe of America's racial and cultural roots,

Los Angeles and Southern California will enter the 21st century as a multi-racial and multicultural society. This is absolutely new. There is no previous example of a civilization that is being simultaneously created by so many races, nationalities, and cultures. This new type of cultural pluralism is completely unknown in the history of mankind.

America is becoming more plural every day because of the unbelievable facility of the new Third World immigrants to put a piece of their original culture inside of American culture. The notion of a "dominant" American culture is changing every moment. It is incredible coming to America to find you are somewhere else—in Seoul, in Taipei, in Mexico City. You can travel inside Korean culture right on the streets of Los Angeles. Inhabitants of this vast city are veritable tourists in the place of their own residence.

There are large communities of Laotians, Vietnamese, Cambodians, Mexicans, Salvadorans, Guatemalans, Iranians, Japanese, Koreans, Armenians, Chinese. We find here Little Taipei, Little Saigon, Little Tokyo, Koreatown, Little Central America, the Iranian neighborhood in Westwood, the Armenian community in Glendale or Hollywood, and the vast Mexican-American areas of East Los Angeles. Eighty-one languages, few of them European, are spoken in the elementary school system of the city of Los Angeles.

This transformation of American culture anticipates the general trend in 5
the composition of mankind. Ninety percent of the immigrants to this city are from the Third World. At the beginning of the 21st century, nearly 90 percent of the world's population will be dark-skinned; the white race will be no more than 11 percent of all human beings living on our planet.

Usually, the contact between developed and underdeveloped worlds has the character of exploitation—just taking people's labor and resources and giving them nothing. And the border between races has usually been a border of tension, of crisis.

But this Pacific Rim civilization being created is a new relationship between development and underdevelopment. Here, there is openness. There is hope. And a future. There is a multicultural crowd. But it is not fighting. It is cooperating, peacefully competing, building. For the first time in 400 years of relations between the nonwhite Western world and the white Western world, the general character of the relationship is cooperation and construction, not exploitation or destruction.

Unlike any other place on the planet, Los Angeles shows us the potential of development once the Third World mentality merges with an open sense of possibility, a culture of organization, a Western conception of time.

In 1924, the Mexican philosopher Jose Vasconcellos wrote a book entitled *La Raza Cosmica*. He dreamt of the possibility that, in the future, mankind would create one human race, a mestizo race.[1] All races on the planet would merge into one type of man. *La Raza Cosmica* is being born in Los Angeles, in the cultural sense if not the anthropological sense. A vast mosaic of different races, cultures,

[1]Mestizo refers specifically to a person of mixed European and Native American blood; Vasconcellos's *La Raza Cosmica* (*The Cosmic Race*) envisions a world in which all races are blended.

religions and moral habits are working toward one common aim. From the perspective of a world submerged in religious, ethnic, and racial conflict, this harmonious cooperation is something unbelievable. It is truly striking.

For the destructive, paralyzed "Third World" where I have spent most of 10
my life, it is important, simply, that such a possibility as Los Angeles exists.

1991—Several thoughts crossed my mind almost simultaneously when I learned that white policemen in Los Angeles had beaten up a black man named Rodney G. King. The first thought—or, rather, feeling—was of surprise. Perhaps I have an overly naive and idealistic view of Los Angeles. My visit there left me with the impression of a city that, despite its indisputable problems with traffic jams, excessive pollution, and drugs, is nevertheless a model of the harmonious coexistence of people of various races, languages, and religions. I have widely voiced this positive assessment. Meantime, in my exemplar of racial harmony, white cops had beaten up a black man!

Because the whole unpleasant incident came to light through the sole fact that someone had recorded it on a videocamera, my second thought was of the revolution brought about in the world (a revolution that continues and develops) by this small, practically pocket-size object. Beware! Your every gesture can from now on be observed and registered without your knowledge or consent!

The vigilant eye of the meddlesome camera watches us from a thousand places—from windows, from balconies, from rooftops, from stationary or moving cars, from behind bushes. We can be filmed by someone who is standing at a bus stop, or sitting at a table in a bar. We can be filmed at all times, almost everywhere, and, potentially, by everyone. This is precisely what happened to the policemen who beat up Rodney King. They fell into the net of that ubiquitous lense, which has itself become a kind of weapon that is virtually universally accessible.

Next, as my attention was drawn to the enormous publicity given the deplorable incident by the American mass media, I thought—fortunate Americans! It is a fortunate country, a fortunate nation, that is able to call forth such a storm of anger and protests because somebody beat up somebody else.

After all, Los Angeles lies on the same planet on which on the very day, at the 15
very instant, that the policemen were beating up Rodney King, there perished in various wars or from hunger thousands upon thousands of people, in Ethiopia, in Mozambique, in Afghanistan, in Iraq; and it didn't occur to anyone to raise a voice of indignation and protest against these massive and cruel deaths. I thought—although it is an absurd thought—that it is fortunate to be one of the beaten in America, for afterwards one can demand a million dollars for every blow (as Rodney King has cleverly done), while the wretches in Africa and the Middle East, although they are harmed by fate in a truly horrible way, can't even count on a handful of rice and a few drops of water. (At that moment I found myself on slippery ground—for one cannot use a greater wrong to excuse a lesser one.)

Nevertheless, I decided to read once again what the American press had written about the incident. And upon rereading, one thing struck me—that the indignation did not result only from the fact of someone having been so badly beaten, but from the fact that *white* policemen had beaten up a *black* citizen. Whites beat up a black—that was the real cause of the press's anger and disapproval. While at first I was inclined to belittle and make light of the entire Rodney King incident, as I began to appreciate all its racial implications, the outrage of American public opinion started to seem understandable and justified. For today humanity is threatened by three powder kegs, variously dispersed around our planet: One keg is nationalism, the second, racism, and the third, religious fundamentalism.

The point is not to allow one of these kegs to explode in our own house, in our own country; for such an explosion would demolish our present order in its entirety. It would bring about its ruin. And the best way to prevent such an explosion is to snuff out even the smallest incident while it is still but a flicker.

For our increasingly irrational and unpredictable world, even something of seemingly little importance can serve as the catalyst of a larger and devastating conflict. That is why I understand the voice of criticism and censure raised against the Los Angeles policemen: They were playing with dangerous, easily spreading fire.

Questions for Discussion

1. What meanings would you attach to the terms "openness," "pluralism," and "the polycentric mind" (paragraph 1)? Are these "good" terms to you—that is, do they have positive connotations? How do you react to the extreme racial and ethnic diversity of cities like Los Angeles or New York? How do you account for your reaction?
2. Kapuscinski is attracted to Los Angeles because, in his view, it represents "a civilization that leaves behind forever the ethnocentric, tribal mentality. The mentality of destruction" (paragraph 1). How do you understand the notion of ethnocentricity? In your view, is the author justified in condemning the tribal mentality so completely? Is it "the mentality of destruction"?
3. With what is the author comparing the "racial paradise" of the United States? What can we learn from seeing our own racial problems in the context of, say, conflicts in the Middle East or what was formerly Yugoslavia? How do you react to the label "fortunate Americans" (paragraphs 14 and 15)?
4. In paragraph 16 Kapuscinski refers to "three powder kegs"—nationalism, racism, and religious fundamentalism. How would you define each of these "isms"? How do they figure in world problems? How do they figure in tensions and conflicts within the United States?

For Inquiry and Convincing

Find out all you can about the Rodney King episode, including the subsequent rioting, the trials of both the police officers involved and rioters arrested in other acts of brutality, and the aftermath for Los Angeles residents generally. Write an essay that agrees or disagrees (or does some of both) with Kapuscinski's evaluation of this event.

LEWIS M. KILLIAN

Race Relations and the Nineties: Where Are the Dreams of the Sixties?

The following scholarly study of the struggle for racial equity and the current condition of black Americans appeared in Social Forces, *published by the Department of Sociology at the University of North Carolina at Chapel Hill. (It is documented according to the stylistic conventions of that publication.) The text was originally an address delivered to the Southern Sociological Society in March of 1990, when the author, a professor at the University of West Florida, was president of that organization.*

ONE OF the most inspiring events of the 1960s occurred on August 28, 1963, when Martin Luther King, Jr., stood on the steps of the Lincoln Memorial and declared, "I have a dream my four little children will one day live in a nation where they will not be judged by the color of their skin but by the content of their character. I have a dream today!" (219). This was an era of brave, optimistic dreams. Those dreams began to take shape ten years before King's memorable speech, as the school desegregation decision of 1954 gave rise to brave hopes in the hearts of segregated, downtrodden blacks. The concept "a revolution of rising expectations" well described their situation. Victories over white southern resistance in Montgomery, Tallahassee, Little Rock, and New Orleans provided black Americans and their white allies with a sense of empowerment. The sit-ins of the early sixties, still nonviolent, still interracial, showed that the Movement could not be suppressed. As King said in his address, "Nineteen sixty-three is not an end, but a beginning. And those who hope that the Negro needed to blow off steam and will now be content will have a rude awakening if the nation returns to business as usual" (219). Yet as we stand on the brink of the nineties, the dreams have dimmed and the nation has indeed returned to business as usual. In his last presidential address to SCLC,[1] in 1962, King urged again, "Let us be dissatisfied until men and women, however black they may be, will be judged on the basis of the content of their character and not on the basis of the color of their skin" (251). How sorely pained he would be were he to witness the state of ethnic relations today!

A SUCCESSION OF DREAMS

The Civil Rights vision formulated by King and his lieutenants was the first of a series of dreams. It was symbolized by its famous slogan, "black and white together."

[1]King founded the Southern Christian Leadership Conference in 1956 as an organization committed to the advancement of civil rights.

Before the tragic end of his career, King did place greater and greater emphasis on economic equality, particularly as he saw segregation diminishing while black unemployment and poverty persisted. He called for full employment, a guaranteed annual income, redistribution of wealth, and skepticism toward the capitalistic economy. "A true revolution of values," he declared, "will soon look uneasily on the glaring contrast of poverty and wealth" (241).

During the height of the Civil Rights Movement the courage of the workers and the vicious violence of the white southern resistance engendered a national orgy of guilt and fear that provided the catalyst for the passage of the Civil Rights Act of 1964 and the Voting Rights Act the next year. The basic economic changes required if laws mandating desegregation and equal opportunity were to have more than a minimal effect had not come about, however. Moreover, the urban insurrections, brought to the forefront of the news by the Watts riot of 1965, awakened the nation to the fact that blacks were still far from content. King's dream of a revolution fueled by love and fought with nonviolence faded in the smoke of ghetto fires. The competing dream of Black Power dominated the last half of the decade.

The Black Power Dream

The vision of black power as the way out of inequality and stigmatization 5
had deep roots in black history in the United States. Even as King was emerging as a national black hero, the nationalistic message preached so eloquently by Malcolm X resonated in the consciousness of hundreds of impatient, angry black people who saw no chance of entering white middle-class society. As far back as the middle of the nineteenth century Black Nationalism had been a strong ideological undercurrent in the United States, surfacing, as William J. Wilson has argued, when intense frustration and disillusionment follow a span of heightened expectations (*Power,* 50).

As limited as its human and financial resources may have been, the Black Power Movement was, with the aid of a titillated white press, able to drown out the voices of the leaders of the Civil Rights Movement. "Power," not "love"; "defensive violence" and "any means necessary," not nonviolence; and "soul" or "blood," not "black and white together," were the cries resounding in the ghettos and repeated on the nation's television screens.

Even more so than do most social movements, the Black Power Movement failed to achieve its stated objectives. Blacks did not win even veto power in the politics of the nation, the states, or the cities. The sort of power they gained in predominantly black cities and congressional districts resulted from demographic changes, not from concessions to the demands of the movement. Neither the extravagant dream of a black republic in the South nor the moderate one of viable all-black municipalities, such as Soul City, North Carolina, was realized. Real advances in self-chosen separatism, going beyond the historically black churches and fraternal organizations, primarily took the form of black studies departments, black cultural centers, and a few all-black dormitories in predominantly white universities.

Despite its near failure, the significance of the short-lived black power movement has been greatly underestimated. First of all, its very demise dramatized the lengths that the white power structure, at all levels, would go to suppress blacks who did not remain meek and mild. Of even greater importance was the change in the terms of the ongoing debate between whites and blacks and within each community about the future of blacks in U.S. society. King's shining grail of integration had lost its luster, at least for the time being. Assimilation had long been the dominant theme among both black Americans and white liberals, but now both its feasibility and desirability were being questioned. Various forms of pluralism gained legitimacy. At best, assimilation was a dream to be deferred until after a period of benign race consciousness.

The theme of black consciousness underscored the pervasive persistence of ethnic diversity in the society. It was accompanied by a novel concept, that of ethnic group rights. The idea of civil rights, individual rights based on citizenship, was now supplemented by the idea of rights based on membership in an ethnic group with a collective claim to being or having been an oppressed minority.

This seed fell on fertile soil, for other ethnic groups, not only Latinos and 10
Native Americans, but also what Michael Novak called the "unmeltable white ethnics," began to advance their claims. A system of competitive pluralism coupled with what Barbara Lal has called "compulsory ethnicity" arose along with "the institutionalization of ethnic identification as a basis for the assertion of collective claims concerning the distribution of scarce resources" (167). In this connection we should note that since 1980 citizens filling out the schedule of the decennial census have been called on to specify the ancestral group with which they identify—application of the rule of descent has received bureaucratic sanction at the federal level. Yet those are probably the most inaccurate data to be found in the census volumes. Careful research has shown about one-third of respondents are likely to change their ethnic responses from year to year. And, ironically, Stanley Lieberson suggests that a new ethnic group is now growing in the United States—unhyphenated whites. He identifies them for statistical purposes as that one sixth of the population who, in 1980, identified themselves simply as "American" or refused to report any ancestry.

One of the last demands addressed to United States society in the spirit of black power was the call for reparations. The Black Manifesto read by James Forman on the steps of New York's Riverside Church on May 4, 1969, was not an angry, quixotic whim of Forman and the few associates who accompanied him. It was a document drawn up by the National Black Economic Development Conference at a meeting set up by the Interreligious Foundation for Community Organization. The latter was created by most of the mainline protestant denominations in the nation.

In the Manifesto Forman and others charged that the white Christian churches and the Jewish synagogues were part and parcel of the capitalistic system which had exploited the resources, the minds, the bodies, and the labor of blacks for centuries. The NBEDC was demanding $500 million in reparations. The melodramatic rhetoric of the Manifesto proclaimed that this came to "$15 per nigger," but the demand was not for the distribution of such a pittance to 30 million black individuals. Instead it called for the establishment of a southern land bank to enable displaced black farmers to establish farm cooperatives; black-controlled publishing houses and audio-visual networks; skills training centers; and other such collective enterprises. Whether such projects would have succeeded is beside the point. What is important is that the demand for reparations called for compensation to a group in the name of ethnic group rights; it was not a plea for the funding of "black capitalism."

The Dreams Fade

The principal outcome of the Manifesto was an outpouring of resolutions by churches. As Arnold Schucter observed, the "great orgy of American guilt" seemed to have subsided by that time, as had the urban insurrections (28). CointelPro was decimating the ranks of the Black Power Movement, and agents provocateurs were giving it a terrorist image. Even whites who had finally begun sympathizing with the goals of the Civil Rights Movement were asking, "Haven't we done enough for the blacks?"

Already the trend toward white acceptance of the principle of racial equality, particularly as applied to education and equal job opportunity, was discernible in public opinion polls. It was widely agreed that "white racism" was a terrible evil—but what did this mean?

The term "racism," usually meaning "white racism," became a catchword 15
after the Kerner Commission declared in the summary of its Report to the President on the causes of civil disorders, "White racism is essentially responsible for the explosive mixture which has been accumulating in our cities since the end of World War II" (203). But who are the white racists—particularly in the eyes of the majority of whites who now claim to accept the principle of racial equality? It is not they themselves but those Klansmen and American Nazis and Skinheads. They themselves are innocent, for they have accepted the victories of the Civil Rights Movement. They don't object to sharing public accommodations with blacks, and they will let their children go to school with them as long as there aren't too many. They believe that blacks should have equal job opportunities, and if a lot of them remain poor it must be because they don't take advantage of the changes open to them. Schucter was all too accurate when he wrote in 1970, "We are faced with a society in which racism has become institutionalized even though the majority of Americans vehemently protest their innocence" (28).

The Fruits of the Dreams

By the beginning of the 1970s both the Civil Rights Movement and the Black Power Movement were comparatively dormant. As pointed out earlier the

Black Power Movement had consequences of greater significance than is generally recognized. These consequences are seen primarily in the world view of blacks in the U.S., symbolized by the fact that the vast majority now call themselves "Black," not "Negro," and some even prefer "African American." Concretely, black power is seen only in the political realm and then only dimly. There is an important but still very small black congressional caucus, but there has been no black senator since the defeat of Edward Brook in 1972.[1] Numerous blacks have been elected to city, county, and state offices, but not until 25 years after the passage of the Voting Rights Act did a state elect a black governor. Black political power remains dependent upon a high degree of black residential concentration and the drawing of electoral boundaries to reflect that concentration.

The Civil Rights Movement, despite its apparent triumph with the passage of the Civil Rights Act and the Voting Rights Act, still won only intermediate objectives. *De jure* segregation was struck down. *De facto* segregation in public places was greatly reduced, but the illusion of equality created in the forum was not reflected at the hearth; American homes, neighborhoods, and private clubs remained highly segregated. King's dream of a society where people would not be judged on the basis of their color remained woefully unfulfilled. Even Latinos, a newer minority in many areas, find it easier to escape from the barrio than do blacks from the ghetto.

But what were the objectives unattained by either movement? Let us look again for a moment at the response of the white churches to the Black Manifesto. They placed new emphasis on preaching and teaching against "racism" and on welcoming blacks into the pews of white churches; they raised money—not a great deal—to put into the ghettos to aid the poor, the disenfranchised, and the uneducated. But the lesson of the failed dreams of the 1960s is that it is not sensitivity training, nor token integration, nor welfare that is needed to eradicate the destructive consequences of ethnic discrimination. It is drastic economic reform and that revolution of values that Martin Luther King said would "look uneasily on the glaring contrast of poverty and wealth." What the dreams did not produce was a society where black and white children would not only sit beside each other in school but also achieve equal gains in learning; a society where blacks would not only have equal rights to jobs but also have jobs; a society where poverty not only would ignore ethnic boundaries but also would actually diminish. How much closer are we to that sort of society than we were in 1970?

A Glass Half Empty

Many times after the publication of *The Impossible Revolution?,* I heard myself characterized as a chronic pessimist who would always see a glass as half empty, never as half full. The analogy itself is flawed, of course—in life good or bad is never stable but is always rising or falling.

[1]A black woman, Carol Moseley-Brawn of Illinois, was elected to the Senate in 1992.

Today when I look about me, particularly in the South, and see whites and 20
blacks eating, shopping, studying, working, and playing in each other's presence in places where once they were cruelly segregated, I think, "How great and wonderful the progress since 1954!" But when I look at the little clumps of black people sitting, talking, huddling together even in supposedly integrated settings, I wonder if we have not progressed only to that condition which Cayton and Drake called "the equality of anonymity" (102). When I drive through a still segregated and often very poor black residential area, and when I look at the economic indicators, I am even more pessimistic. Indeed, I am convinced that the glass is surely half empty, for the level of black well-being is falling.

Reports and Reports

Testifying before the Kerner Commission in 1968 Kenneth B. Clark said, "I read that report . . . of the 1919 riot in Chicago, and it is as if I were reading the report of the investigating committee on the Harlem riot of '35, the report of the investigating committee on the Harlem riot of '43, the report of the McCone Commission on the Watts riot. I must again in candor say to you members of this committee it is a kind of Alice in Wonderland—with the same moving picture shown over and over again, the same analysis, the same recommendations, and the same inaction" (ix).

Now we have the latest of the massive, comprehensive studies of how blacks are faring, *Blacks in American Society,* put together by a team of distinguished social scientists. It comes 70 years after the Chicago research, 45 years after *An American Dilemma,* and 20 years after the Kerner report. This volume starts out with refreshing honesty. While acknowledging many improvements, the authors declare, "We also describe the continuance of conditions of poverty, segregation, discrimination, and social fragmentation of the most serious proportions" (ix).

The analysis of trends since the great migration of blacks out of southern agriculture beginning in 1939 leads to the conclusion that the place of blacks in the American economy has been, and remains, that of a reserve army of labor. They have enjoyed some progress during periods of prosperity and high employment, usually war-induced. "But," says the study, "after initial reports of rising relative black economic status, black gains have stagnated on many measures of economic position since the early 1970s" (274). Two examples of this stagnation are given. Poverty rates for blacks increased from 29.7% in 1974 to 31% in 1985. Blacks' real per capita income in 1984 was one-third higher than in 1968 but still stood in the same relationship to white income as in 1971—57%. Yet it is important to note that poverty had increased among whites also, from 7.3% in 1974 to 11% in 1985.

There is no need to repeat the much cited evidence of the accentuated differences in status among blacks, with some segments gaining drastically relative to whites and others losing ground. The major source of inequality within the black community, the authors note, is the increased fraction of black men with no earnings at all. The major reasons for black economic inequality are (1) the concentration of black workers, particularly men, in low-paying jobs and (2) the relatively high proportion of unemployed blacks, many of them not even in the labor force. In fact, while between 1973 and 1986 black men with jobs continued to approach whites in position on the occupational ladder and in hourly wage rates, the gains were offset by employment losses. The optimistic reports about employment rates released almost every month from Washington rarely note that black unemployment still continues at a rate twice that of whites and that the rates are based on persons in the labor force, not including the bitter, discouraged dropouts.

Jaynes and his coauthors reject the explanation that it is transfer payments— 25
the much-maligned "welfare"—causing people to drop out of the labor force. They offer instead a structural explanation: "The shifting industrial base of the U.S. economy from blue-collar manufacturing to service industries, the slowdown in economic growth, and the consequent decline in real wages could be expected to produce a period of economic and social distress. For displaced and educationally or spatially misplaced workers, the rise in unemployment and increased competition for moderate-to-high-paying jobs might well lead to a rise in the number of discouraged workers" (310).

The most ominous of the statistics drawn together by this committee pertain to poverty rates. We have seen a dramatic decline from the unbelievably high rates, in 1939, of 93% and 65% for black and white people, respectively. By 1974 the rates were 30% for blacks and 9% for whites, but by 1986 rates for both groups were higher, 31% and 11%. Even more alarming is the prevalence of poverty among black children—44% in 1985, compared with 16% among white children.

The pessimistic conclusion of the chapter "Blacks in the Economy" reads, "The economic fortunes of blacks are strongly tied (more so than those of whites) to a strong economy and vigorously enforced policies against discrimination. Without these conditions, the black middle class may persist, but it is doubtful it can grow or thrive. And the position of lower status blacks cannot be expected to improve" (324).

To add my own pessimistic coda, a "strong economy" must achieve more than merely providing low-paying jobs in the service sector to replace those lost in the industrial sector through automation or export. Yet this seems to be what many secure people accept as a measure of solving the problem of unemployment. Moreover, with the insecurity felt by many whites, it cannot be expected that they will willingly share with blacks the risk of falling into poverty.

Hence the crescendo of rhetoric decrying growing white racism and calling for more affirmative action programs is simplistic, avoiding the main problems facing both blacks and the society. In addition to focusing on the economic nature of these problems, we must also consider the changes in the nature of what is now called "racism."

How Much and What Kind of "Racism"?

Although there is no doubt that "racism" subsumes a multitude of sins, the 30
term itself is very imprecise. Scholars defining it usually list a number of varieties.

Since the 1960s it seems to have replaced the older concepts "prejudice" and "discrimination" to denote those negative attitudes and behaviors that result in the subordination and oppression of some groups which are socially defined as "races."

Focusing on the attitudinal components of racism, Schuman, Steeh, and Bobo found a paradox in the attitudes of white Americans in public opinion surveys from 1942 through 1983. On the one hand, they found strong positive trends toward acceptance of the principle of racial equality and the rejection of absolute segregation. On the other hand, questions concerning governmental implementation of these abstract principles got relatively low levels of support, and there are few signs showing that such support has increased over time. In 1989 the authors of *Blacks in American Society,* who found no reason to disagree with this observation, added their own finding that measures of black alienation from white society suggest an increase from the late 1960s to the 1980s (Jaynes and Williams 131).

Many theoretical explanations have been advanced for the paradox disclosed by Schuman and his associates. One theory focuses on the level of abstract principles, seeing agreement with them as evidence of a strong progressive trend. It underplays the contradictory aspect of the findings as well as the absence of proportional structural changes in society, such as the persistence of massive residential segregation.

A sharply contrasting explanation holds that underlying "racist" attitudes have not changed. Agreement with abstract principles of racial equality constitutes only lip service conforming to a new cultural norm rendering crude, overt expression of racial prejudice less than respectable. Racial prejudice is now expressed symbolically. Opposition to school busing, open housing laws, and affirmative action, as well as failure to vote for a black candidate for public office, is to be explained primarily in terms of symbolic, covert racism. The more complex explanation of competing values such as objections to governmental intrusion, individualism, and genuine concern about what happens to one's children is rejected out of hand.

In *Racial Formation in the United States* Michael Omi and Howard Winant similarly give little credence to attitudinal expressions of support for abstract principles unless they are paralleled by support for implementation. Unlike other sociologists they offer a theory of how the persistence of covert racism has affected racial politics in what they define as still being a "racial state."

They concede that a great transformation in ideas about race took place in 35
the United States during the 1950s and 1960s. This had two major consequences. One was new, self-conscious racial identities which persisted even after the movements through which they were forged disintegrated. The second they call the "rearticulation of racial ideology" in reaction to the partial victories of the Civil Rights Movement and, I would add, of the Women's Liberation Movement. The conservative, right-wing trend in U.S. politics rests on racism, they suggest. "As the right sees it," they say, "racial problems today center on the new forms of racial injustice which originated in the great transformation. This new injustice

confers group rights on racial minority groups, thus granting a new form of privilege—that of preferential treatment" (114). Further developing this theme, Omi and Winant assert, "In this scenario, the victims of racial discrimination have dramatically shifted from racial minorities to whites, particularly white males" (114). They make a persuasive case that even though they were alluded to by code words, racial issues were central to support for President Reagan in his two elections and for President George Bush. Who can question that the Republican Party's "southern strategy" has included a strong component of this rearticulated racial ideology, one appealing not only to voters such as those who elected David Duke to the Louisiana legislature, but also to numerous white voters outside the South?

This pessimistic view of the United States as basically a racial state in which racism changes its face but does not disappear is frightening to anyone who hopes for movement toward greater equality in the 1990s. An even more ominous view of a majority of the electorate is offered by Edna Bonacich, who attaches more importance to class as a factor than do Omi and Winant. She asserts, "The United States is an immensely unequal society in terms of distribution of material wealth, and consequently in the distribution of all the benefits and privileges that accrue to wealth. . . . This inequality is vast irrespective of race." Granting that people of color suffer disproportionately, she goes on to say, "I believe that racial inequality is inextricably tied to overall inequality and to an ideology that endorses vast inequality as justified and desirable." She concludes, "And even if some kind of racial parity at the level of averages could be achieved, the amount of suffering at the bottom would remain undiminished, hence unconscionable" (80).

Bonacich cites dramatic statistics demonstrating the vastness of inequality and its frightening growth. In 1987, for example, 6.7 million American workers living on the minimum wage had incomes of $9,968 a year, while Lee Iacocca was paid over $20 million, or $9,615 an hour. In 1986 there were 26 billionaires in the country; in 1987, 49. "The Culture of Inequality" which Michael Lewis identified in 1978 is more entrenched than ever.

In the 1960s James Baldwin asked, "Who wants to be integrated into a burning house?" The house is still burning, being slowly consumed by the heat of greed and fear. Speculators gamble with the nation's wealth but pass the bill to the government when the dice roll against them. The CEOs of corporations have learned to live comfortably with affirmative action at the middle levels of the occupational scale but are equally comfortable with reductions in the total size of their work force. Often unnoted in optimistic studies of affirmative action is that increases in minority shares of employment are usually accompanied by contraction in the number of all persons employed. The size of the piece of the pie is not as critical in these times as is the shrinking of the fraction of the pie left for the have-nots in a class-polarized society.

The ideology of inequality Bonacich addresses is sustained also by the insecurities of people who have left the work force and are living on fixed incomes, either from interest and dividends or from those transfer payments now known as "entitlements." They do not see as their enemies the 0.5% of the families who in 1983 held 35% of the net wealth of the nation. Instead they fear the faceless people at the bottom of the heap. Have they not been told in campaign after campaign that it is the demands of the poor for welfare, social services, and higher wages that might cause higher taxes and increased prices? Polarization does not start near the top of the income distribution but near the bottom. One of Jonathan Rieder's subjects in *Canarsie* put it exactly, "We never join the have-a-littles with the have-nots to fight the haves. We make sure the have-a-littles fight the have-nots" (119).

Now, ironically, as the crisis of capitalism in America intensifies, the attention of American voters is distracted by the failures of socialist polities and economies abroad, as if that made their own plight less perilous and their own future more secure. The prospects for a radical rejection of the culture of inequality, with its concomitant acceptance of racial inequality, seem dim. To me, some pessimistic warnings from the past seem more appropriate today than do optimistic predictions for the 1990s.

Voices from the Past

When I look at the retreat of the Federal government from vigorous enforcement of civil rights laws, I am reminded of the warning of Frederick Douglass, issued as he witnessed a similar retreat. He wrote, "No man can be truly free whose liberty is dependent upon the thought, feeling, and actions of others, and who has himself no means in his own hands for guarding, protecting, defending, and maintaining that liberty" (539).

During the Civil Rights and Black Power movements, black Americans were catalysts in producing a national orgy of guilt, but they did not attain the sort of power Douglass described. After laws promising equal opportunity were passed, blacks lacked the political clout to get succeeding Congresses to pass laws to implement these promises. They were forced to depend, instead, on sympathetic bureaucrats in the executive branch and a narrow majority in a relatively friendly Supreme Court to promote implementation in the absence of majority popular support. Now we see the administrative and judicial support fading because of the growing strength of a political party that does not depend on minority voters for victory and often appears downright hostile to their interests. As inadequate as were the responses of the liberal Kennedy, Johnson, and Carter administrations, they were magnificent when compared to those of elected officials who use "liberal" as a code word signifying softness on crime, welfare fraud, pauperism, reverse discrimination, and the spread of communism in the Third World.

Yet the black middle class still prospers relative to its past condition as the gap between the haves and have-nots grows in the black community, just as in the white. Here I am reminded of Stokely Carmichael's quip in the 1960s: "To most whites Black Power seems to mean that the Mau Mau are coming to the suburbs at night" (5). Today we might say that, to most whites, actually accepting blacks as residents of their neighborhoods seems to mean that drug-ridden welfare recipients from the ghetto will be on their doorstep tomorrow. Julius Lester wrote at about the same time, "The black middle class is aware of its precarious position between the ghetto blacks and white society; and its members know that because they are black, they are dispensable" (34). Even the qualified black person who seems to have achieved equality is regarded as the "exceptional" black and even then is often suspected of reaching that level because of affirmative action. Until the plight of the underclass is alleviated its shadow will continue to blight the lives and fortunes of those blacks who have partially escaped the bonds of past discrimination.

Lester said that the black middle class knew that it was dispensable. Sidney Willhelm asked, "Who needs the Negro?" Although asked in 1970, his question is still horrendously relevant today. Writing before the export of semi-skilled jobs to Third World countries became another threat to workers in the United States, he warned about automation: "The Negro becomes a victim of neglect as he becomes useless to an emerging economy of automation. With the onset of automation, the Negro moves out of his historical state of oppression into one of uselessness. Increasingly, he is not so much economically exploited as he is irrelevant" (162).

Although he and Willhelm have been highly critical of each other's work, 45
William J. Wilson pointed to the same problem in *The Declining Significance of Race*. He observed, "Representing the very center of the New American economy, corporate industries are characterized by vertically integrated production processes and technologically progressive systems of production and distribution. The growth of production depends more on technical progress and increases in physical capital per worker than on the growth of employment." He added, "In short, an increasing number of corporate sector workers have become redundant because the demand for labor is decreased in the short run by the gap between productivity and the demand for goods" (96–97). Perhaps we must ask today, "Who needs people, except as consumers?" Willhelm characterized our situation as one in which "the new standard of living entails both production and distribution of goods without, however, involving either a producer or distributor through large-scale employment" (*Declining* 203). Hence this oft-disparaged but frighteningly accurate prophet among sociologists advanced a truly radical proposition: "It will be incumbent for a society relying upon automation and dedicated to the well being of human beings to accept a new economic gauge, namely: *services are to be rendered and goods produced, distributed and consumed in keeping with a designated standard of living*" (*Declining* 203). This is the sort of change in perspective of which Wilson said, in 1987, "It will require a radicalism that neither Democrat nor Republican parties have as yet been realistic enough to propose" (*Truly* 139). Instead what we continue to see is platforms that imply that if profits are kept high and taxes low so that investment is encouraged, plenty of jobs will be created. Then, if blacks will get an education and develop the right attitudes toward work and the family, they can enjoy that portion of the prosperity that trickles down to them. This, unfortunately, is the dream of many white voters today. It is not, however, an accurate vision of things to come but a rose-

tinted stereotype of an industrial era which is gone forever and was never good for minority workers.

Dreams or Nightmares for the 1990s?

During those years after 1940 during which I studied, taught, and lived race relations in the South, I had my own dream. It was that my fellow white southerners, most of whom I knew as good, kind people, would have peeled from their eyes the veil which kept them from knowing what they were doing to black people. Someday they would see, I hoped, how segregation and discrimination, no matter how paternalistic, left cruel injuries which would handicap both current and future generations.

During the decade after 1954, I thought I was beginning to see that veil thinning under the assault of the Civil Rights Movement. I did witness heartening changes, but then I saw new complacency, with white America asking, "How much more are we supposed to do for them?" Now I see a new veil blinding people whom I still believe to be good-spirited. They are blind to institutional discrimination and to the poverty increasing in our nation even more rapidly than 20 years ago. Ironically, the behavior of most white people, particularly in the South, has changed more than have their attitudes. Now they mix with their black fellow citizens, yet blacks still remain largely invisible to them. They admit selected, acceptable blacks to their company as individuals but ignore the tragedy of the masses who yearly become more separated and alienated from what appears to those on top as an affluent society. Poverty, black and white, is concealed in a way different from when the rich and the poor lived closer to each other. It is known to many Americans only by flitting images in the mass media. In the meantime defense of what security and prosperity one does enjoy, rather than concern for the social problems threatening the nation, anchors successful political appeals with the dominant theme, "no new taxes."

In 1961 James E. Conant wrote in *Slums and Suburbs,* "We are allowing social dynamite to accumulate in our large cities" (2). In the 1960s there were explosions of that dynamite, but its potential for destruction was far from exhausted. Now, in 1990, more dynamite is accumulating and in more cities.

Yet at this very time there appears to be a new basis for optimism. Many Americans are celebrating the end of the Cold War and looking forward to a "peace dividend." The case for deferring spending on domestic programs because of the demands for military defense loses its cogency. Journalists and novelists ask, "Who will be the enemy now that the Soviet Union is no longer the evil empire?"

There has been another cold war, however—a war of heartless neglect of the burgeoning needs of the truly disadvantaged in our own affluent society. A bright new dream would feature the end of this cold war and the beginning of a new war on poverty. We can expect increasingly urgent demands for a concerted attack on underemployment, undereducation, crime which preys on the poor, and the hopelessness that causes young people to drop out not only from school but also from the labor force. But these problems cannot be adequately addressed with the meager surplus left after the requirements for deficit reduction and new foreign aid are met. New taxes and a more equitable distribution of wealth will be required. But what if the response of the "haves" and the "have-littles" to this summons for self-sacrifice is a new wave of blaming the victim? If this is the case, the new enemy will be our own underclass.

WORKS CITED

Bonacich, Edna. "Inequality in America: The Failure of the American System for People of Color." *Sociological Spectrum* 9 (1989): 77–101.

Carmichael, Stokely. "What We Want." *New York Review of Books.* 22 September 1966.

Cayton, Horace W., and St. Clair Drake. *Black Metropolis.* New York: Harcourt, 1945.

Clark, Kenneth. Preface. *Commission Politics.* By Michael Lipsky and David J. Olson. New Brunswick, N.J.: Transaction, 1977.

Conant, James B. *Slums and Suburbs.* New York: McGraw Hill, 1961.

Douglass, Frederick. *Life and Times of Frederick Douglass.* 1845. New York: Collier, 1962.

Jaynes, Gerald, and Robin M. Williams. *Blacks and American Society.* Washington, D.C.: National Academy Press, 1989.

Kerner Commission, *Report of the National Advisory Commission on Civil Disorders.* New York: Bantam, 1968.

Killian, Lewis M. *The Impossible Revolution? Black Power and the American Dream.* New York: Random, 1968.

King, Martin Luther, Jr. *A Testament of Hope: The Essential Writings of Martin Luther King, Jr.* Ed. James M. Washington. New York: Harper, 1986.

Lal, Barbara Lallis. "Perspectives on Ethnicity: Old Wines in New Bottles." *Ethnic and Racial Studies* 6 (1983): 154–73.

Lewis, Michael. *The Culture of Inequality.* Amherst: Mass. Press, 1978.

Lieberson, Stanley. "A New Ethnic Group in the United States." *Majority and Minority,* 4th ed. Ed. Norman R. Yetman. Needham Heights, Mass.: Allyn & Bacon, 1982. 259–67.

Myrdal, Gunnar. *An American Dilemma.* New York: Harper, 1944.

Novak, Michael. *The Rise of the Unmeltable Ethnics.* New York: Macmillan, 1972.

Omi, Michael, and Howard Winant. *Racial Formation in the United States from the 1960's to the 1980's.* New York: Routledge & Kegan Paul, 1986.

Rieder, Jonathan. *Canarsie: The Jews and Italians of Brooklyn Against Liberalism*. Cambridge: Harvard UP, 1985.

Schucter, Arnold. *Reparations: The Black Manifesto and Its Challenge to White America*. Philadelphia: J. B. Lippincott, 1970.

Schuman, Howard, Charlotte Steeh, and Lawrence Bobo. *Racial Attitudes in America*. Cambridge: Harvard UP, 1985.

Willhelm, Sydney. *Who Needs the Negro?* Schenkman, 1970.

Wilson, William J. *Power, Racism, and Privilege*. New York: Macmillan, 1973.

______. *The Declining Significance of Race*. Chicago: U of Chicago P, 1980.

______. *The Truly Disadvantaged*. Chicago: U of Chicago P, 1987.

Questions for Discussion

1. How would you describe the general tone and outlook of Killian's article? What political and economic conditions at the time it was written in 1990 might help to explain its tone and outlook? What might the author say about conditions now?
2. How does the author interpret the achievements of the Civil Rights Movement? How does he understand the contribution of the Black Power Movement? The two clearly were in deep conflict. Is the same conflict still at work today? In what ways?
3. In paragraph 20, Killian refers to a phrase coined by two writers in 1945, "the equality of anonymity." Judging from the context of Killian's use of the phrase, what do you think it means? Do you see this kind of "equality" on college campuses? How do you evaluate it?
4. Summarize the viewpoint of Edna Bonacich, whom Killian cites in paragraph 36. How does her argument about inequality fit into Killian's argument about racism and its persistence in the United States? To what extent is the race problem part of a larger class problem?

For Persuasion

In paragraph 9 Killian discusses one of the most controversial notions of our time—"the idea of rights based on membership in an ethnic group with a collective claim to being or having been an oppressed minority." This idea, so different from the traditional concept of individual rights, has much to do with policies such as affirmative action.

For an audience of white, middle-class college students, write an essay attacking or defending the concept of group rights. If you oppose the concept, be sure to address the problems created by past and present discrimination against particular racial and ethnic groups. If you support the concept, be sure to address the problem of "reverse discrimination."

OSSIE DAVIS

Challenge for the Year 2000

A well-known actor, director, and playwright, Ossie Davis was also a significant figure in the Civil Rights Movement of the sixties. According to a note appended to the following article, "he was master of ceremonies at the March on Washington in 1963 [when Martin Luther King delivered his "I Have a Dream" speech] and delivered the eulogy at the funeral of Malcolm X."

The following passionate plea for racial justice appeared in 1989 in the weekly journal The Nation, *a liberal paper now almost 150 years old and published in New York City.*

The curse of poverty has no justification in our age. It is socially as cruel and blind as the practice of cannibalism at the dawn of civilization. . . . The time has come for us to civilize ourselves by the total, direct, and immediate abolition of poverty.
—MARTIN LUTHER KING JR. *Where Do We Go From Here: Chaos or Community?*

SYMBOLS AND myths—when emerging uncorrupted from human experience—are precious. Then it is the poetic voice and vision that informs and infuses—the poet-warrior's, the prophet-seer's, the dreamer's—reassuring us that truth is as real as falsehood. And ultimately stronger.

In *Chaos or Community?* (published one year before his death), King's was one such voice, which drew upon another to illustrate the debilitating toll of white oppression on black children. The words upon which King drew came from the pen of W.E.B. Du Bois in manifestation of that great poet-scholar's extraordinary ability to evoke stunning images powerful enough to strike deep into our souls.

"It is difficult," Dr. Du Bois writes in his autobiographical *Dusk of Dawn*, "to let others see the full psychological meaning of caste segregation":

> It is as though one, looking out from a dark cave in a side of an impending mountain, sees the world passing and speaks to it: speaks courteously and persuasively, showing them how the entombed souls are hindered in their natural movement, expression, and development: and how their loosening from prison would be a matter not simply of courtesy, sympathy, and help to them, but aid to all the world.
>
> One talks on evenly and logically in this way but notices that the passing throng does not even turn its head, or if it does, glances curiously and walks on. It gradually penetrates the minds of the prisoners that the people passing do not hear; that some thick sheet of invisible but horribly tangible plate glass is between them and the world. . . . Then the people within may become hysterical. They may scream and hurl themselves against the barriers, hardly realizing in their bewilderment that

> they are screaming in a vacuum unheard and that their antics may actually seem funny to those outside looking in. They may even, here and there, break through in blood and disfigurement, and find themselves faced by a horrified, implacable, and quite overwhelming mob of people frightened for their very own existence.

In 1967, King drew on Du Bois's 1940 analogy of the cave as background to his own tale of the months he spent living and working in the ghettos of Chicago to effect open-housing laws. Here he encountered racial hatreds and fury even greater than those he had experienced in the South.

The slum neighborhood in which he took an apartment was an "island of poverty" within a city enjoying one of the highest per capita incomes in the world. From behind the ghetto walls, the black entrapped were well aware of the white suburbanites speeding, via elevated skyways and elaborate expressways, past the vast pockets of black deprivation. Allowed only the hardest, ugliest, and most menial jobs, they were just as aware that they were as capable as anyone else of building the tall towers of the modern city—but were excluded by white labor unions.

King wrote in his depressing apartment, looking out on streets where hundreds of children played, lacking playground facilities, and the phone rang daily with "countless stories of man's inhumanity to man." Constantly he found himself, he said, forced to struggle "against the depression and hopelessness which the hearts of our cities pump into the spiritual bloodstream of our lives." Of the children, King wrote:

> When you go out and talk to them you see the light of intelligence glowing in their beautiful dark eyes. Then you realize their overwhelming joy because someone has simply stopped to say hello; for they live in a world where even their parents are often forced to ignore them. In the tight squeeze of economic pressure, their mothers and fathers both must work; indeed, more often than not, the father will hold two jobs, one in the day and another at night. With the long distances ghetto parents must travel to work and the emotional exhaustion that comes from the daily struggle to survive in a hostile world, they are left with too little time or energy to attend to the emotional needs of their growing children.
>
> Too soon you begin to see the effects of this emotional and environmental deprivation. The children's clothes are too skimpy to protect them from the Chicago wind, and a closer look reveals the mucous in the corners of their bright eyes, and you are reminded that vitamin pills and flu shots are luxuries which they can ill afford. The "runny noses" of ghetto children become a graphic symbol of medical neglect in a society which has mastered most of the diseases from which they will too soon die. There is something wrong in a society which allows this to happen.

King wrote *Chaos or Community?* to detail what was wrong; namely, that the most unconscionable horror of America's caves does not lie simply in the squalid housing, the woefully inadequate medical facilities (if any exist at all), the shockingly inferior educational facilities, the psychological violence of the environment promoting violent response among the caged, the lack of access to cultural institutions, or the absence of a "job network system" such as those that service communities outside.

No, the greatest horror lies in the fact that the purpose of the caves is to contain people within them: They are caverns of exclusion. No piecemeal and uncoordinated programs of education, welfare, jobs, or other aid will change the circumstances of the masses of people imprisoned within, King concluded. Rather, it is the very walls of the cave that must come tumbling down, and with them the notion of the acceptability of such implacable restraints on any people within society. Accordingly, the last crusade envisioned by King was a war by poor people and their allies against domestic poverty and a global campaign for the eradication of poverty, racism and militarism.

Significantly, it was at this stage of the prophet's development that King was himself eliminated, the ruthless who engage in such tactics failing to recognize that a man's body may be eliminated but his spirit marches on.

Twenty-two years later, not only have the conditions within the caves 10
worsened but in the current tenacious hold of the old rationalizations, some African-Americans sense white endorsement—if not explicit, then by default—of black genocide.

For African-Americans in the current era, something irrevocably changes in the face of such a realization. There comes a time in history when the lessons are plain, when no excuse exists any longer for old partners to waltz in each other's arms—or at arm's length—in the same old dance of monstrous domination by the one and dehumanizing subjugation of the other. At that moment both partners are free to make choices, and those choices will determine the character of the new relationship.

King himself stands as a symbol of why the old order can never return. No more heroic, no more loving crusade to change the nation for the better has ever come about than the nonviolent crusade he led. Yet before he died, he was perfectly aware that the moral imperative so briefly honored would not be translated into committed political action by the Federal government or by the people as a whole any more than had been true after the Revolutionary and the Civil Wars.

Before the end, he recognized that the struggle would have to be enlarged onto the world stage, and with uncanny foresight he laid out a new comprehensive strategy—and the choices—in *Chaos or Community?* On the eve of the twenty-first century, there seems to us little doubt that the most fundamental challenge facing the nation today is that of resurrecting the goal and pursuit of King's Poor Peoples Crusade and his quest for justice and peace worldwide.

Clearly, African-Americans must be in the vanguard in the building of such a movement. Not because we are inherently noble but because we have no choice if we are to save our children and thus have a future. To do this, those of us outside the caves must achieve solidarity with those within.

"Power, properly understood," King wrote, "is the ability to achieve pur- 15
pose. It is the strength required to bring about social, political, or economic changes. In this sense power is not only desirable but necessary in order to implement the demands of love and justice."

In whatever form power comes to the people, he indicates, it is most often by *organized* efforts to achieve it, essentially through three means: ideological, political, and economic.

Politically, we have recently witnessed a widening base of black voters and the successful implementation of alliances, as brilliantly pursued by Jesse Jackson and others on local and national levels, particularly in the South. Undoubtedly, that political base must specifically widen to catch the imagination and commitment of the masses of the ghetto disfranchised and disillusioned. Currently, as men in Washington decree that tens of thousands of young black women will enter the cheap labor market through "workfare,"[1] it is interesting to contemplate the possibility of organizing teen-age mothers into political units capable of exerting themselves to change their conditions on behalf of their children. Likewise, it is interesting to contemplate the possibility of organizing black male youth—currently under genocidal siege—on behalf of the same!

In the ideological arena, African-Americans occupy a position of uncommon and exciting advantage if we will only elevate our gaze high enough to recognize it. For, excluded from the ranks of the myth-makers in this land, we have historically had to deal with reality and with truth, in whatever form the truth came, if we were to survive and transcend. It is therefore we who are uniquely free to dream of a world without racism, poverty, war, sexism and all the other "isms" that plague humankind. Given our present condition, we would be foolish indeed if we did not act on the dream!

Our advantage is that untold millions of people long for such a world. Ideologically, our philosophy is rooted in the simple humanism that has always been our strength: that however much it often seems to the contrary, most people wish to be better than they are, and they wish the world to be better. Through the ages, people have been capable of dying for such beliefs (African-Americans have contributed substantially to that roster); in the twenty-first century, perhaps millions will be willing to live for them. "Cooperation," then, rather than "competition" is the essential principle that we propose should govern human affairs. Is it not possible that through application of such a principle, humankind could effect a quantum leap in ethics sufficient to match the awesome (and frequently terrifying) technological advances?

On the world scene, one thing is clear. It is time that African-Americans 20
do what Du Bois, Malcolm X, and King came to realize, each in his own time, had to be done: *elevate our struggle from the domestic arena of civil rights to the global*

[1]Workfare is a reform of the welfare system that requires any recipient of public assistance to work in an assigned job or to be enrolled in some sort of job training.

level of human rights. In doing so, we must bring history around full circle in reestablishing with the peoples of Africa the bonds of kinship severed so cruelly over four centuries. For the millions of black children occupying such terrible cages of war, poverty, and death in African lands are a phenomenon linked in history to the millions caged in America and other nations: the intolerable fruits of European plunder, colonialism, and neocolonialism extending into our times.

The most immediate responsibility faced by African-Americans is the restoration to black youth of their self-esteem and sense of place in a world so cruelly snatched from them every single day, and to encourage within them a visionary view.

A second great responsibility is that of teaching the nation, so that white Americans cannot continue to hide so grotesquely behind the myth of national equality while the relentless quiet and unquiet eradication of millions of their fellow citizens proceeds. The twentieth century has made such innocence obscene.

A century and a half ago, a free black from North Carolina living in Boston addressed an "Appeal . . . to the Colored Citizens of the World but in Particular and Very Expressly to Those of the United States of America." In four detailed parts, David Walker's appeal spelled out the crimes against African peoples, named the perpetrators, and called upon slaves to rise and cast off slavery, using whatever means they had to in order to end the monstrous system.

The document caused a sensation. The slave states unsuccessfully sought to suppress it, and Walker, in Boston, met a mysterious death. Walker's influence, however, as in the case of King, could not be curtailed. It was not William Lloyd Garrison's thunderous denunciation of slavery that initiated the organized abolitionist movement but Walker in his stirring call. At the close, Walker wrote that it seemed to him there had to be some purpose to all the suffering Africans had endured in their cruel transport from their homeland.

In the twentieth century, King must surely have agreed that at landmark 25
stages in history, it is incumbent upon human beings to declare their purpose. Do not be afraid, he surely charges African-Americans in the spirit of one of the old black spirituals upon which he loved to draw, "Walk together, children. Don'cha get weary":

> In the days ahead we must not consider it unpatriotic to raise certain basic questions about our national character. We must begin to ask, "Why are there forty million poor people in a nation overflowing with such unbelievable affluence?". . . Why have we substituted the arrogant undertaking of policing the whole world for the high task of putting our own house in order? . . . For its very survival's sake, America must reexamine old presuppositions and release itself from many things that for centuries have been held sacred. For the evils of racism, poverty, and militarism to die, a new set of values must be born. Our economy must become more person-centered than property-and-profit centered. Our government must depend more on its moral power than on its military power.

> Let us . . . be those creative dissenters who will call our . . . nation to a higher destiny, to a new plateau of compassion, to a more noble expression of humaneness.
>
> We are superbly equipped to do this. We have been seared in the flames of suffering. . . . We have learned from our have-not status that it profits a nation little to gain the whole world of means and lose the end, its own soul. We must have a passion for peace. . . . Giving our ultimate allegiance to . . . justice. . . . So in dealing with our particular dilemma, we will challenge the nation to deal with its larger dilemma.
>
> This is the challenge. If we will dare to meet it honestly, historians in future years will have to say there lived a great people—a black people—who bore their burdens of oppression in the heat of many days and who, through tenacity and creative commitment, injected new meaning into the veins of American life.

If the challenge to African-Americans is to lead, the challenge to the nation is surely to follow. We have only to envision the prospect and undertake the task with the same determination and commitment of resources.

Let us, accordingly—*all of us*—get about the business of demolishing the walls of the caves!

Questions for Discussion

1. W.E.B. Du Bois's metaphor of the cave dominates this article. "The purpose of the caves," Davis claims, "is to contain people within them: They are caverns of exclusion" (paragraph 8). Read or reread the preceding article by Lewis Killian. Does Killian's depiction of current racial conditions among poor blacks support Davis's interpretation of the purpose of the caves?
2. In paragraph 15, Davis cites Martin Luther King on the relation between power and civil rights. Judging from this quote alone, how did King view the relation? How does King's view differ from those of Malcolm X and other exponents of separatist black power? Which, in your opinion, is the more realistic view?
3. Commenting on King's description of black children in a Chicago ghetto (paragraph 6), Davis refers to "the psychological violence of the environment" (paragraph 7) in which they live. What does he have in mind by "psychological violence"? Have you experienced or observed any instances of it yourself? How is it depicted in films or books about ghetto life that you have seen or read? Does this psychological violence contribute significantly to the physical violence of the ghetto, to the killing of so many young black men mostly by other young black men, which Davis refers to as a "genocidal siege" (paragraph 17)?
4. In paragraph 20 Davis emphasizes the need for black Americans to link their struggle in the United States to the world-wide struggle for human rights, especially in Africa. Is such a global view really helpful or relevant to achieving

racial justice here? How, for example, did Alex Haley's *Roots* contribute to the cause of black Americans?

For Convincing or Persuasion

Lewis Killian—the white, southern professor of sociology who wrote the preceding article—and Ossie Davis come together in calling for fundamental economic change. Study both articles and make careful notes about what changes each recommends.

Write an essay addressed to your generation of college students that either supports traditional American capitalism or opts for Martin Luther King's call for "full employment, a guaranteed annual income, redistribution of wealth, and skepticism toward the capitalist economy" (see Killian, paragraph 3), basically a socialistic program.

Do you think another war on poverty is needed? Do you agree with Davis that "cooperation" rather than "competition" should be our primary principle for the economy of the future (paragraph 19)?

WILLIAM RASPBERRY

The Myth That Is Crippling Black America

The following article appeared in 1990 in Reader's Digest, *a highly influential journal. Offering condensed versions of books, essays, and speeches,* Reader's Digest *generally favors articles supportive of traditional American institutions, attitudes, and values.*

A widely-syndicated columnist for the Washington Post, *William Raspberry represents a growing chorus among middle- and upper-class blacks who say that blaming racism for the problems of poor, black Americans accomplishes nothing and may even be counterproductive because doing so draws attention away from what blacks themselves can do to improve their lot.*

A MYTH HAS crippled black America: the myth that racism is the dominant influence in our lives.

Two things flow from this racism-is-all myth. It puts the solution to our difficulties outside our control. And it encourages the fallacy that attacking racism as the source of our problems is the same as attacking our problems. As a result, we expend precious time, energy, and imagination searching (always successfully) for evidence of racism—while our problems grow worse.

Consider poor whites. They can vote, live where their money permits them, eat where their appetites dictate, work at jobs for which their skills qualify them. They have their civil rights. And yet they are in desperate straits. It doesn't seem to occur to us that the full grant of our civil rights would leave black Americans in about the same situation that poor whites are now in.

There is another minority whose situation may be more instructive. I refer to Asian-Americans. Neither the newly arrived Southeast Asians nor the earlier-arriving Japanese-Americans, Chinese-Americans, and Korean-Americans are loved by white people. But these groups have spent little time and energy proving that white people don't love them.

While our myth is that racism accounts for our shortcomings, their belief 5
is that their own efforts can make the difference, no matter what white people think. They have looked at America like children with their noses pressed to the candy-store window: If only I could get in there, boy, could I have a good time. And when they get in, they work and study and save and create businesses and jobs for their people.

But we, born inside the candy store, focus only on the maldistribution of the candy. Our myth leads us to become consumers when victories accrue to the producers.

This is a fairly recent phenomenon. Following the Civil War, free blacks and former slaves, though denied many of the rights we take for granted today, were entrepreneurs—artisans and inventors, shopkeepers and industrialists, bankers and financiers. The first female millionaire in America was a black woman, Madame C. J. Walker. Fifty years after emancipation, in 1913, as Robert L. Woodson observed in his book *On the Road to Economic Freedom,* black America "could take pride in owning 550,000 homes, 40,000 businesses, and 937,000 farms."

What has happened since? Hundreds of thriving restaurants, hotels, service outlets, and entertainment centers have gone out of business because we preferred integration to supporting our own painstakingly established institutions. Indeed, aside from black churches and black colleges, little remains to show for that entrepreneurial spurt early this century.

We over-learned the lessons of the civil-rights era. That courageous movement enabled black Americans, for the first time, to enjoy the full panoply of civil rights. Unfortunately, the movement also taught us to see in terms of civil rights things that might more properly be achieved by enterprise and exertion.

Even when we speak of business now, our focus is on set-asides and affir- 10
mative action. We insist on a fair distribution of jobs in businesses created and run by others. But the emphasis ought to be on getting more of us into our own businesses, creating jobs ourselves, and encouraging an entrepreneurial approach to our social problems.

I am not suggesting that government has no role. But we need government-backed programs that, instead of merely making our problems more bearable, help solve them. We are forever talking about the lack of day care as an impediment to work for welfare families. Why aren't we lobbying for legislation to permit some of the money now spent on public welfare to be used to establish child-care centers? Why aren't we looking for ways to create small jitney services to transport job seekers to distant jobs?

I leave to others the specifics. I will tell you only that increasing the economic success of black America can be done—and is being done by an encouraging number of us. When people believe that their problems can be solved, they tend to get busy solving them.

On the other hand, when people believe that their problems are beyond solution, they tend to position themselves so as to avoid blame. Take the woeful inadequacy of education in the predominantly black central cities. Does the black leadership see the ascendancy of black teachers, school administrators, and politicians as an asset to be used in improving those dreadful schools? Rarely. You are more likely to hear charges of white abandonment, white resistance to integration, white conspiracies to isolate black children, even when the schools are officially desegregated. In short, white people are accused of being responsible for the problem. But if the youngsters manage to survive those awful school systems and achieve success, leaders want to claim credit. They don't hesitate to attribute that success to the glorious civil-rights movement.

Many of us, of course, aren't succeeding. Teen-age pregnancy, dope trafficking, lawlessness, and lack of ambition make many doubt that we ever will succeed. But when we see failure among our people and have reason to believe the failure is permanent, our leaders say racism is the culprit. Mistakenly, we credit black pride for our successes and blame prejudice for our shortfalls. My simple suggestion is that we stop using the plight of the black underclass as a scourge for beating up on white racists.

I used to play a little game in which I'd tell black leaders: "Let's say you're 15
exactly right, that racism is the overriding reason for our situation and that an all-out attack on racism is our most pressing priority.

"Now let us suppose that we eventually win the fight against racism and put ourselves in the position currently occupied by poor whites—that is, in full possession of civil rights, but economically disadvantaged. What would you urge we do next?

"Pool our resources? Establish and support black businesses? Insist that our children take advantage of the opportunities that a society free of racism would offer?

"Well, just for the hell of it, why don't we pretend the racist dragon has been slain already—and take that next step right now?"

Questions for Discussion

1. In a previous reading in this chapter, Lewis Killian describes the aims of the Black Power Movement (paragraphs 5–12). In what ways does Raspberry's approach resemble that of the Black Power Movement? In what ways is it different?
2. In paragraphs 4–6 Raspberry contrasts the relative success of Asian immigrants with the plight of many black Americans. Is the comparison fair? How effective could it be in persuading black readers to accept his argument? How do you evaluate the candy store analogy?
3. Raspberry praises the Civil Rights Movement but also criticizes it for having "taught us to see in terms of civil rights things that might more properly be achieved by enterprise and exertion" (paragraph 9). Look over the statements by Martin Luther King cited in the two preceding readings by Killian and Davis. Do they provide any justification for Raspberry's criticism?
4. The standard accusation leveled against writers like Raspberry is that, because they are themselves successful, they have lost touch with most other blacks and that, consequently, they are blaming the victim rather than the system that exploits the victim. What is your response to this accusation?

For Inquiry and Negotiation

Raspberry differs sharply with Killian and Davis in his approach to solving the problems of the black underclass. Write an essay that explores these contrasting positions, evaluating both as potential solutions.

Is it possible that some aspects of both solutions might work together to improve the conditions of the poor, regardless of race? Attempt to mediate between Raspberry's position and the position of Killian and Davis, proposing a solution that pulls together the best of each and so might appeal to both.

SHELBY STEELE

The Recoloring of Campus Life

We conclude this chapter on race relations in the 1990s with a more personal and reflective essay that centers on what the author calls "concentrated micro-societies," our college campuses.

In recent years there has been much discussion of a "new racism" on campuses across the country. Shelby Steele, a professor of English at San Jose State University who attended college in the 1960s, argues that today's campus racism is indeed new and tries to explain why it exists and how it works. His essay appeared originally in 1989 in Harper's, *an eclectic monthly magazine offering essays on various current topics. Much discussed and often reprinted, "The Recoloring of Campus Life" may well be a contemporary classic.*

IN THE past few years, we have witnessed what the National Institute Against Prejudice and Violence calls a "proliferation" of racial incidents on college campuses around the country. Incidents of on-campus "intergroup conflict" have occurred at more than 160 colleges in the last three years, according to the institute. The nature of these incidents has ranged from open racial violence—most notoriously, the October 1986 beating of a black student at the University of Massachusetts at Amherst after an argument about the World Series turned into a racial bashing, with a crowd of up to 3,000 whites chasing twenty blacks—to the harassment of minority students, to acts of racial or ethnic insensitivity, with by far the greatest number falling in the last two categories. At Dartmouth College, three editors of the *Dartmouth Review,* the off-campus right-wing student weekly, were suspended last winter for harassing a black professor in his lecture hall. At Yale University last year a swastika and the words "white power" were painted on the school's Afro-American cultural center. Racist jokes were aired not long ago on a campus radio station at the University of Michigan. And at the University of Wisconsin at Madison, members of the Zeta Beta Tau fraternity held a mock slave auction in which pledges painted their faces black and wore Afro wigs. Two weeks after the president of Stanford University informed the incoming freshman class last fall that "bigotry is out, and I mean it," two freshmen defaced a poster of Beethoven—gave the image thick lips—and hung it on a black student's door.

In response, black students around the country have rediscovered the militant protest strategies of the Sixties. At the University of Massachusetts at Amherst, Williams College, Penn State University, UC Berkeley, UCLA, Stanford, and countless other campuses, black students have sat in, marched, and rallied. But much of what they were marching and rallying about seemed less a response to specific racial incidents than a call for broader action on the part of the colleges and universities they were attending. Black students have demanded everything from more black faculty members and new courses on racism to the addition of "ethnic" foods in the cafeteria. There is the sense in these demands that racism runs deep.

Of course, universities are not where racial problems tend to arise. When I went to college in the mid-Sixties, colleges were oases of calm and understanding in a racially tense society; campus life—with its traditions of tolerance and fairness, its very distance from the "real" world—imposed a degree of broad-mindedness on even the most provincial students. If I met whites who were not anxious to be friends with blacks, most were at least vaguely friendly to the cause of our freedom. In any case, there was no guerrilla activity against our presence, no "mine field of racism" (as one black student at Berkeley recently put it) to negotiate. I wouldn't say that the phrase "campus racism" is a contradiction in terms, but until recently it certainly seemed an incongruence.

But a greater incongruence is the generational timing of this new problem on the campuses. Today's undergraduates were born after the passage of the 1964 Civil Rights Act. They grew up in an age when racial equality was for the first time enforceable by law. This too was a time when blacks suddenly appeared on television, as mayors of big cities, as icons of popular culture, as teachers, and in some cases even as neighbors. Today's black and white college students, veterans of *Sesame Street* and often of integrated grammar and high schools, have had more opportunities to know each other—whites and blacks—than any previous generation in American history. Not enough opportunities, perhaps, but enough to make the notion of racial tension on campus something of a mystery, at least to me.

To try to unravel this mystery I left my own campus, where there have been 5
few signs of racial tension, and talked with black and white students at California schools where racial incidents had occurred: Stanford, UCLA, Berkeley. I spoke with black and white students—and not with Asians and Hispanics—because, as always, blacks and whites represent the deepest lines of division, and because I hesitate to wander onto the complex territory of other minority groups. A phrase by William H. Gass—"the hidden internality of things"—describes with maybe a little too much grandeur what I hoped to find. But it *is* what I wanted to find, for this is the kind of problem that makes a black person nervous, which is not to say that it doesn't unnerve whites as well. Once every six months or so someone yells "nigger" at me from a passing car. I don't like to think that these solo artists might soon make up a chorus or, worse, that this chorus might one day soon sing to me from the paths of my own campus.

I have long believed that trouble between the races is seldom what it appears to be. It was not hard to see after my first talks with students that racial tension on campus is a problem that misrepresents itself. It has the same look, the archetypal pattern, of America's timeless racial conflict—white racism and black protest. And I think part of our concern over it comes from the fact that it has the feel of a relapse, illness gone and come again. But if we are seeing the same symptoms,

I don't believe we are dealing with the same illness. For one thing, I think racial tension on campus is the result more of racial equality than inequality.

How to live with racial difference has been America's profound social problem. For the first 100 years or so following emancipation it was controlled by a legally sanctioned inequality that acted as a buffer between the races. No longer is this the case. On campuses today, as throughout society, blacks enjoy equality under the law—a profound social advancement. No student may be kept out of a class or a dormitory or an extracurricular activity because of his or her race. But there is a paradox here: On a campus where members of all races are gathered, mixed together in the classroom as well as socially, differences are more exposed than ever. And this is where the trouble starts. For members of each race—young adults coming into their own, often away from home for the first time—bring to this site of freedom, exploration, and now, today, equality very deep fears and anxieties, inchoate feelings of racial shame, anger, and guilt. These feelings could lie dormant in the home, in familiar neighborhoods, in simpler days of childhood. But the college campus, with its structures of interaction and adult-level competition—the big exam, the dorm, the "mixer"—is another matter. I think campus racism is born of the rub between racial difference and a setting, the campus itself, devoted to interaction and equality. On our campuses, such concentrated micro-societies, all that remains unresolved between blacks and whites, all the old wounds and shames that have never been addressed, present themselves for attention—and present our youth with pressures they cannot always handle.

I have mentioned one paradox: racial fears and anxieties among blacks and whites bubbling up in an era of racial equality under the law, in settings that are among the freest and fairest in society. And there is another, related paradox, stemming from the notion of—and practice of—affirmative action. Under the provisions of the Equal Employment Opportunity Act of 1972, all state governments and institutions (including universities) were forced to initiate plans to increase the proportion of minority and women employees—in the case of universities, of students too. Affirmative action plans that establish racial quotas were ruled unconstitutional more than ten years ago in *University of California Regents v. Bakke.*[1] But quotas are only the most controversial aspect of affirmative action; the principle of affirmative action is reflected in various university programs aimed at redressing and overcoming past patterns of discrimination. Of course, to be conscious of patterns of discrimination—the fact, say, that public schools in the black inner cities are more crowded and employ fewer top-notch

[1]Allan Bakke, a white applicant turned down for admission by a California State University medical school, sued the California system claiming discrimination because the school's policy of maintaining a 16 percent minority enrollment meant that minority applicants with lower grade point averages were admitted instead of him. The case was settled in 1978 when a divided U.S. Supreme Court ruled that specific quotas such as those in effect in the California system were not permissible; and Bakke was subsequently admitted to the program. However, the Court ruling also stated that race could be considered by college administrators in an effort to achieve a diverse student body. The full legal implications of the ruling have thus been ambiguous.

teachers than white suburban public schools, and that this is a factor in student performance—is only reasonable. However, in doing this we also call attention quite obviously to difference: in the case of blacks and whites, racial difference. What has emerged on campus in recent years—as a result of the new equality and affirmative action, in a sense, as a result of progress—is a *politics of difference,* a troubling, volatile politics in which each group justifies itself, its sense of worth and its pursuit of power, through difference alone.

In this context, racial, ethnic, and gender differences become forms of sovereignty, campuses become balkanized, and each group fights with whatever means are available. No doubt there are many factors that have contributed to the rise of racial tension on campus: What has been the role of fraternities, which have returned to campus with their inclusions and exclusions? What role has the heightened notion of college as some first step to personal, financial success played in increasing competition, and thus tension? Mostly what I sense, though, is that in interactive settings, while fighting the fights of "difference," old ghosts are stirred, and haunt again. Black and white Americans simply have the power to make each other feel shame and guilt. In the "real" world, we may be able to deny these feelings, keep them at bay. But these feelings are likely to surface on college campuses, where young people are groping for identity and power, and where difference is made to matter so greatly. In a way, racial tension on campus in the Eighties might have been inevitable.

10 I would like, first, to discuss black students, their anxieties and vulnerabilities. The accusation that black Americans have always lived with is that they are inferior—inferior simply because they are black. And this accusation has been too uniform, too ingrained in cultural imagery, too enforced by law, custom, and every form of power not to have left a mark. Black inferiority was a precept accepted by the founders of this nation; it was a principle of social organization that relegated blacks to the sidelines of American life. So when today's young black students find themselves on white campuses, surrounded by those who historically have claimed superiority, they are also surrounded by the myth of their inferiority.

Of course it is true that many young people come to college with some anxiety about not being good enough. But only blacks come wearing a color that is still, in the minds of some, a sign of inferiority. Poles, Jews, Hispanics, and other groups also endure degrading stereotypes. But two things make the myth of black inferiority a far heavier burden—the broadness of its scope and its incarnation in color. There are not only more stereotypes of blacks than of other groups, but these stereotypes are also more dehumanizing, more focused on the most despised of human traits—stupidity, laziness, sexual immorality, dirtiness, and so on. In America's racial and ethnic hierarchy, blacks have clearly been relegated to the lowest level—have been burdened with an ambiguous, animalistic humanity. Moreover, this is made unavoidable for blacks by the sheer visibility of black skin, a skin that evokes the myth of inferiority on sight. And today this myth is sadly reinforced for many black students by affirmative action programs, under which blacks may often enter college with lower test scores and high-school grade point averages than whites. "They see me as an affirmative action case," one black student told me at UCLA.

So when a black student enters college, the myth of inferiority compounds the normal anxiousness over whether he or she will be good enough. This anxiety is not only personal but also racial. The families of these students will have pounded into them the fact that blacks are not inferior. And probably more than anything, it is this pounding that finally leaves a mark. If I am not inferior, why the need to say so?

This myth of inferiority constitutes a very sharp and ongoing anxiety for young blacks, the nature of which is very precise: It is the terror that somehow, through one's actions or by virtue of some "proof" (a poor grade, a flubbed response in class), one's fear of inferiority—inculcated in ways large and small by society—will be confirmed as real. On a university campus, where intelligence itself is the ultimate measure, this anxiety is bound to be triggered.

A black student I met at UCLA was disturbed a little when I asked him if he ever felt vulnerable—anxious about "black inferiority"—as a black student. But after a long pause, he finally said, "I think I do." The example he gave was of a large lecture class he'd taken with more than 300 students. Fifty or so black students sat in the back of the lecture hall and "acted out every stereotype in the book." They were loud, ate food, came in late—and generally got lower grades than the whites in the class. "I knew I would be seen like them, and I didn't like it. I never sat by them." Seen like what? I asked, though we both knew the answer. "As lazy, ignorant, and stupid," he said sadly.

Had the group at the back been white fraternity brothers, they would not 15
have been seen as dumb *whites,* of course. And a frat brother who worried about his grades would not worry that he would be seen "like them." The terror in this situation for the student I spoke with was that his own deeply buried anxiety would be given credence, that the myth would be verified, and that he would feel shame and humiliation not because of who he was but simply because he was black. In this lecture hall his race, quite apart from his performance, might subject him to four unendurable feelings—diminishment, accountability to the preconceptions of whites, a powerlessness to change those preconceptions, and, finally, shame. These are the feelings that make up his racial anxiety, and that of all blacks on any campus. On a white campus a black is never far from these feelings, and even his unconscious knowledge that he is subject to them can undermine his self-esteem. There are blacks on every campus who are not up to doing good college-level work. Certain black students may not be happy or motivated or in the appropriate field of study—*just like whites.* (Let us not forget that many white students get poor grades, fail, drop out.) Moreover, many more blacks than whites are not quite prepared for college, may have to catch up, owing to factors beyond their control: poor previous schooling, for example. But the white who has to catch up will not be anxious that his being behind is a matter of his whiteness, of his being *racially* inferior. The black student may well have such a fear.

This, I believe, is one reason why black colleges in America turn out 34 percent of all black college graduates, though they enroll only 17 percent of black college students. Without whites around on campus the myth of inferiority is in abeyance and, along with it, a great reservoir of culturally imposed self-doubt. On black campuses feelings of inferiority are personal; on campuses with a white majority, a black's problems have a way of becoming a "black" problem.

But this feeling of vulnerability a black may feel in itself is not as serious a problem as what he or she does with it. To admit that one is made anxious in integrated situations about the myth of racial inferiority is difficult for young blacks. It seems like admitting that one *is* racially inferior. And so, most often, the student will deny harboring those feelings. This is where some of the pangs of racial tension begin, because denial always involves distortion.

In order to deny a problem we must tell ourselves that the problem is something different than what it really is. A black student at Berkeley told me that he felt defensive every time he walked into a class and saw mostly white faces. When I asked why, he said, "Because I know they're all racists. They think blacks are stupid." Of course it may be true that some whites feel this way, but the singular focus on white racism allows this student to obscure his own underlying racial anxiety. He can now say that his problem—facing a class full of white faces, *fearing* that they think he is dumb—is entirely the result of certifiable white racism and has nothing to do with his own anxieties, or even that this particular academic subject may not be his best. Now all the terror of his anxiety, its powerful energy, is devoted to simply *seeing* racism. Whatever evidence of racism he finds—and looking this hard, he will no doubt find some—can be brought in to buttress his distorted view of the problem, while his actual deep-seated anxiety goes unseen.

Denial, and the distortion that results, places the problem *outside* the self and in the world. It is not that I have any inferiority anxiety because of my race; it is that I am going to school with people who don't like blacks. This is the shift in thinking that allows black students to reenact the protest pattern of the Sixties. Denied racial anxiety-distortion-reenactment is the process by which feelings of inferiority are transformed into an exaggerated white menace—which is then protested against with the techniques of the past. Under the sway of this process, black students believe that history is repeating itself, that it's just like the Sixties, or Fifties. In fact, it is the not yet healed wounds from the past, rather than the inequality that created the wounds, that is the real problem.

This process generates an unconscious need to exaggerate the level of 20
racism on campus—to make it a matter of the system, not just a handful of students. Racism is the avenue away from the true inner anxiety. How many students demonstrating for a black "theme house"—demonstrating in the style of the Sixties, when the battle was to win for blacks a place on campus—might be better off spending their time reading and studying? Black students have the highest dropout rate and lowest grade point average of any group in American universities. This need not be so. And it is not the result of not having black theme houses.

It was my very good fortune to go to college in 1964, when the question of black "inferiority" was openly talked about among blacks. The summer before I left for college I heard Martin Luther King, Jr., speak in Chicago, and he laid it on the line for black students everywhere. "When you are behind in a footrace, the only way to get ahead is to run faster than the man in front of you. So when your white roommate says he's tired and goes to sleep, you stay up and burn the midnight oil." His statement that we were "behind in a footrace" acknowledged that because of history, of few opportunities, of racism, we were, in a sense, "inferior." But this had to do with what had been done to our parents and their parents, not with inherent inferiority. And because it was acknowledged, it was presented to us as a challenge rather than a mark of shame.

Of the eighteen black students (in a student body of 1,000) who were on campus in my freshman year, all graduated, though a number of us were not from the middle class. At the university where I currently teach, the dropout rate for black students is 72 percent, despite the presence of several academic-support programs; a counseling center with black counselors; an Afro-American studies department; black faculty, administrators, and staff; a general education curriculum that emphasizes "cultural pluralism"; an Educational Opportunities Program; a mentor program; a black faculty and staff association; and an administration and faculty that often announce the need to do more for black students.

It may be unfair to compare my generation with the current one. Parents do this compulsively and to little end but self-congratulation. But I don't congratulate my generation. I think we were advantaged. We came along at a time when racial integration was held in high esteem. And integration was a very challenging social concept for both blacks and whites. We were remaking ourselves—that's what one did at college—and making history. We had something to prove. This was a profound advantage; it gave us clarity and a challenge. Achievement in the American mainstream was the goal of integration, and the best thing about this challenge was its secondary message—that we *could* achieve.

There is much irony in the fact that black power would come along in the late Sixties and change all this. Black power was a movement of uplift and pride, and yet it also delivered the weight of pride—a weight that would burden black students from then on. Black power "nationalized" the black identity, made blackness itself an object of celebration and allegiance. But if it transformed a mark of shame into a mark of pride, it also, in the name of pride, required the denial of racial anxiety. Without a frank account of one's anxieties, there is no clear direction, no concrete challenge. Black students today do not get as clear a message from their racial identity as my generation got. They are not filled with the same urgency to prove themselves, because black pride has said, You're already proven, already equal, as good as anybody.

The "black identity" shaped by black power most powerfully contributes 25
to racial tensions on campuses by basing entitlement more on race than on constitutional rights and standards of merit. With integration, black entitlement was derived from constitutional principles of fairness. Black power changed this by skewing the formula from rights to color—if you were black, you were entitled.

Thus, the United Coalition Against Racism (UCAR) at the University of Michigan could "demand" two years ago that all black professors be given immediate tenure, that there be special pay incentives for black professors, and that money be provided for an all-black student union. In this formula, black becomes the very color of entitlement, an extra right in itself, and a very dangerous grandiosity is promoted in which blackness amounts to specialness.

Race is, by any standard, an unprincipled source of power. And on campuses the use of racial power by one group makes racial or ethnic or gender *difference* a currency of power for all groups. When I make my difference into power, other groups must seize upon their difference to contain my power and maintain their position relative to me. Very quickly a kind of politics of difference emerges in which racial, ethnic, and gender groups are forced to assert their entitlement and vie for power based on the single quality that makes them different from one another.

On many campuses today academic departments and programs are established on the basis of difference—black studies, women's studies, Asian studies, and so on—despite the fact that there is nothing in these "difference" departments that cannot be studied within traditional academic disciplines. If their rationale truly is past exclusion from the mainstream curriculum, shouldn't the goal now be complete inclusion rather than separateness? I think this logic is overlooked because these groups are too interested in the power their difference can bring, and they insist on separate departments and programs as a tribute to that power.

This politics of difference makes everyone on campus a member of a minority group. It also makes racial tensions inevitable. To highlight one's difference as a source of advantage is also, indirectly, to inspire the enemies of that difference. When blackness (and femaleness) becomes power, then white maleness is also sanctioned as power. A white male student at Stanford told me, "One of my friends said the other day that we should get together and start up a white student union and come up with a list of demands."

It is certainly true that white maleness has long been an unfair source of power. But the sin of white male power is precisely its use of race and gender as a source of entitlement. When minorities and women use their race, ethnicity, and gender in the same way, they not only commit the same sin but also, indirectly, sanction the very form of power that oppressed them in the first place. The politics of difference is based on a tit-for-tat sort of logic in which every victory only calls one's enemies to arms.

This elevation of difference undermines the communal impulse by making 30
each group foreign and inaccessible to others. When difference is celebrated rather than remarked, people must think in terms of difference, they must find meaning in difference, and this meaning comes from an endless process of contrasting one's group with other groups. Blacks use whites to define themselves as different, women use men, Hispanics use whites and blacks, and on it goes. And in the process each group mythologizes and mystifies its difference, puts it beyond the full comprehension of outsiders. Difference becomes an inaccessible preciousness toward which outsiders are expected to be simply and uncomprehend-

ingly reverential. But beware: In this world, even the insulated world of the college campus, preciousness is a balloon asking for a needle. At Smith College, graffiti appears: "Niggers, Spics, and Chinks quit complaining or get out."

Most of the white students I talked with spoke as if from under a faint cloud of accusation. There was always a ring of defensiveness in their complaints about blacks. A white student I spoke with at UCLA told me: "Most white students on this campus think the black student leadership here is made up of oversensitive crybabies who spend all their time looking for things to kick up a ruckus about." A white student at Stanford said: "Blacks do nothing but complain and ask for sympathy when everyone really knows they don't do well because they don't try. If they worked harder, they could do as well as everyone else."

That these students felt accused was most obvious in their compulsion to assure me that they were not racists. Oblique versions of some-of-my-best-friends-are stories came ritualistically before or after critiques of black students. Some said flatly, "I am not a racist, but. . . ." Of course, we all deny being racists, but we only do this compulsively, I think, when we are working against an accusation of bias. I think it was the color of my skin, itself, that accused them.

This was the meta-message that surrounded these conversations like an aura, and in it, I believe, is the core of white American racial anxiety. My skin not only accused them, it judged them. And this judgment was a sad gift of history that brought them to account whether they deserved such an accounting or not. It said that wherever and whenever blacks were concerned, they had reason to feel guilt. And whether it was earned or unearned, I think it was guilt that set off the compulsion in these students to disclaim. I believe it is true that in America black people make white people feel guilty.

Guilt is the essence of white anxiety, just as inferiority is the essence of black anxiety. And the terror that it carries for whites is the terror of discovering that one has reason to feel guilt where blacks are concerned—not so much because of what blacks might think but because of what guilt can say about oneself. If the darkest fear of blacks is inferiority, the darkest fear of whites is that their better lot in life is at least partially the result of their capacity for evil—their capacity to dehumanize an entire people for their own benefit, and then to be indifferent to the devastation their dehumanization has wrought on successive generations of their victims. This is the terror that whites are vulnerable to regarding blacks. And the mere fact of being white is sufficient to feel it, since even whites with hearts clean of racism benefit from being white—benefit at the expense of blacks. This is a conditional guilt having nothing to do with individual intentions or actions. And it makes for a very powerful anxiety because it threatens whites with a view of themselves as inhuman, just as inferiority threatens blacks with a similar view of themselves. At the dark core of both anxieties is a suspicion of incomplete humanity.

So the white students I met were not just meeting me; they were also 35
meeting the possibility of their own inhumanity. And this, I think, is what explains how some young white college students in the late Eighties can so frankly

take part in racially insensitive and outright racist acts. They were expected to be cleaner of racism than any previous generation—they were born into the Great Society. But this expectation overlooks the fact that, for them, color is still an accusation and judgment. In black faces there is a discomforting reflection of white collective shame. Blacks remind them that their racial innocence is questionable, that they are the beneficiaries of past and present racism, and that the sins of the father may well have been visited on the children.

And yet young whites tell themselves that they had nothing to do with the oppression of black people. They have a stronger belief in their racial innocence than any previous generation of whites, and a natural hostility toward anyone who would challenge that innocence. So (with a great deal of individual variation) they can end up in the paradoxical position of being hostile to blacks as a way of defending their own racial innocence.

I think this is what the young white editors of the *Dartmouth Review* were doing when they shamelessly harassed William Cole, a black music professor. Weren't they saying, in effect, I am so free of racial guilt that I can afford to ruthlessly attack blacks and still be racially innocent? The ruthlessness of that attack was a form of denial, a badge of innocence. The more they were charged with racism, the more ugly and confrontational their harassment became. Racism became a means of rejecting racial guilt, a way of showing that they were not ultimately racists.

The politics of difference sets up a struggle for innocence among all groups. When difference is the currency of power, each group must fight for the innocence that entitles it to power. Blacks sting whites with guilt, remind them of their racist past, accuse them of new and more subtle forms of racism. One way whites retrieve their innocence is to discredit blacks and deny their difficulties, for in this denial is the denial of their own guilt. To blacks this denial looks like racism, a racism that feeds black innocence and encourages them to throw more guilt at whites. And so the cycle continues. The politics of difference leads each group to pick at the sore spots of the other.

Men and women who run universities—whites, mostly—also participate in the politics of difference, although they handle their guilt differently than many of their students. They don't deny it, but still they don't want to *feel* it. And to avoid this *feeling* of guilt they have tended to go along with whatever blacks put on the table rather than work with them to assess their real needs. University administrators have too often been afraid of their own guilt and have relied on negotiation and capitulation more to appease that guilt than to help blacks and other minorities. Administrators would never give white students a racial theme house where they could be "more comfortable with people of their own kind," yet more and more universities are doing this for black students, thus fostering a kind of voluntary segregation. To avoid the anxieties of integrated situations, blacks ask for theme houses; to avoid guilt, white administrators give them theme houses.

When everyone is on the run from his anxieties about race, race relations 40
on campus can be reduced to the negotiation of avoidances. A pattern of demand and concession develops in which each side uses the other to escape itself. Black studies departments, black deans of student affairs, black counseling programs, Afro houses, black theme houses, black homecoming dances and graduation ceremonies—black students and white administrators have slowly engineered a machinery of separatism that, in the name of sacred difference, redraws the ugly lines of segregation.

Black students have not sufficiently helped themselves, and universities, despite all their concessions, have not really done much for blacks. If both faced their anxieties, I think they would see the same thing: Academic parity with all other groups should be the overriding mission of black students, and it should also be the first goal that universities have for their black students. Blacks can only *know* they are as good as others when they are, in fact, as good—when their grades are higher and their dropout rate lower. Nothing under the sun will substitute for this, and no amount of concessions will bring it about.

Universities and colleges can never be free of guilt until they truly help black students, which means leading and challenging them rather than negotiating and capitulating. It means inspiring them to achieve academic parity, nothing less, and helping them see their own weaknesses as their greatest challenge. It also means dismantling the machinery of separatism, breaking the link between difference and power, and skewing the formula for entitlement away from race and gender and back to constitutional rights.

As for the young white students who have rediscovered swastikas and the word "nigger," I think they suffer from an exaggerated sense of their own innocence, as if they were incapable of evil and beyond the reach of guilt. But it is also true that the politics of difference creates an environment which threatens their innocence and makes them defensive. White students are not invited to the negotiating table from which they see blacks and others walk away with concessions. The presumption is that they do not deserve to be there because they are white. So they can only be defensive, and the less mature among them will be aggressive. Guerrilla activity will ensue. Of course this is wrong, but it is also a reflection of an environment where difference carries power and where whites have the wrong "difference."

I think universities should emphasize commonality as a higher value than "diversity" and "pluralism"—buzzwords for the politics of difference. Difference that does not rest on a clearly delineated foundation of commonality not only is inaccessible to those who are not part of the ethnic or racial group but is antagonistic to them. Difference can enrich only the common ground.

Integration has become an abstract term today, having to do with little 45
more than numbers and racial balances. But it once stood for a high and admirable set of values. It made difference second to commonality, and it asked members of all races to face whatever fears they inspired in each other. I doubt the word will have a new vogue, but the values, under whatever name, are worth working for.

Questions for Discussion

1. Steele claims that "racial tension on campus [now] is the result more of racial equality than inequality" (paragraph 6). How does he support this contention? Do you find it convincing? Why, or why not? Test his assertion against what you see around you. Are blacks and other minority races treated equally on your campus?
2. Steele has much to say about what he calls a "politics of difference" (paragraph 8) on college campuses. How exactly does he depict it? In paragraphs 26–30, he presents an argument against it. What reasons make up the case? Judging from what you know of American history, is this politics of difference new? Is it restricted to college campuses?
3. How does Steele view the influence of black power? Compare his view to Lewis Killian's in a reading earlier in this chapter. How do their views differ? Why do they differ? Which do you find most persuasive? Why?
4. In many ways Steele's general perspective resembles Raspberry's in the preceding essay. How are these two writers alike in their general beliefs and values? How do you explain the similarities?
5. How does Steele explain the anxieties of black and white students? Do you agree that "[a]t the dark core of both anxieties is a suspicion of incomplete humanity" (paragraph 34)? How might this diagnosis apply to women on campus? To gay men and lesbians? To minority races other than blacks?

For Research, Discussion, and Convincing

Conduct research as Steele did—by interviewing students. (Appendix A provides guidelines for conducting interviews.) Talk to members of all races and significant ethnic groups on your campus. Pose the kind of questions Steele did, along with any questions his conclusions suggest to you. Record or take careful notes about what your interviewees say. Then meet as a class and discuss how to interpret the responses and how to explain them.

Finally, write an essay about some aspect of difference on your campus—it need not be black versus white. Attempt, as Steele does, to get to "the hidden internality of things" (paragraph 5), the deeper sources of tension and anxiety. Propose ways to cope better with the aspect of difference you isolate for analysis.

For Further Research and Discussion

1. For most of the history of the United States, racial conflict stemmed from the unequal balance of power between white Europeans on the one hand and Native Americans, blacks, and Hispanics on the other. But more recently racial tensions have been complicated by the influx of many new racial and ethnic minorities. Who are they? What do you know about them?

   Divide into groups, and with your group do intensive research on one of the United States' new minorities; summarize the results of your group research to the rest of the class. Then ask, How do the background and conditions of these new minorities resemble the older ones? How is each unique?

2. Much has been written about the breakdown of the American family—especially the black family. Find out as much as you can about what is happening to the black family, and why. How much of our present racial problems can be traced to the virtual disappearance of the traditional family, especially in urban ghettos?

Additional Suggestions for Writing

1. *Persuading.* Much has been written about so-called voluntary segregation, such as the black theme houses Steele mentions. Write an essay for your school paper or some other suitable publication arguing for or against such theme houses.
2. *Convincing.* Read or reread the articles in Chapter 17, "Political Correctness and Multiculturalism." In your view, do the ideologies of political correctness and multiculturalism make the "new racism" worse, or do they help the races understand and cope with difference better?
3. *Inquiry.* Examine yourself for traces of racism, new or old. In what ways and to what degree are you guilty of race stereotyping, avoidance of people of other races, and so forth? Do you sometimes feel the "racial anxiety" that Steele found in both black and white students? Where did you acquire whatever residual racism you have? What can you do to overcome it? What should universities do to help students and professors recognize and cope with latent racism?

CHAPTER SIXTEEN

Gay and Lesbian Rights

Homosexuality may not have increased in the last two decades, but society's awareness of it certainly has, largely because many gay men and women have become more open about their sexual orientation. Their "coming out" has brought many issues to the public's attention, most notably whether gay people should be protected against discrimination in employment, housing, accommodation, and insurance, and in custody cases and adoption. Indeed, many ask, why should they not be able to marry? In some communities, "domestic partnerships"—both homosexual and heterosexual—have recently been legally recognized as unions similar to marriage, and a small but growing number of employers extend benefits to the partners of homosexual employees; but in no state are homosexuals permitted to marry, and in a good number of states, sexual relations between members of the same sex are illegal.

While many homosexual men and women have decided to become activists, publicly pressing for protection against discrimination, others prefer to stay "in the closet," largely out of fear. According to the National Gay and Lesbian Task Force, over ninety percent of gay men and lesbians have been victims of some type of violence or harassment. One issue we take up here is *why* some heterosexuals react this strongly. "Homophobia" is often referred to as "the last acceptable prejudice," because so many heterosexuals think that discriminating against gay people—even exhibiting open hostility toward them—is defensible on moral grounds. Those who call homosexuality immoral usually turn to religion for support. But how strong are these religious arguments? And if homosexuality is judged immoral, what bearing does that judgment have on an individual's constitutional rights?

The causes of homosexuality have been much debated, and so far researchers have yet to agree on an explanation. From the nineteenth century until 1973, the medical community regarded homosexuality as a disease or pathology, something that could be cured, using treatments such as aversion therapy, electroshock, and neurosurgery—none of which succeeded. While many still conclude with former Vice President Dan Quayle that homosexuality is a choice, current biological research increasingly suggests that it is not. Recent work points to the role of hormones, especially hormones to which the fetus is exposed while in the womb. Research on twins reinforces the view that genetics play a significant role in sexual orientation.

Why and how people become homosexual, however, is not the primary concern of citizens debating public attitudes and policy regarding homosexuals and their rights. It is estimated that roughly ten percent of the American population is gay and lesbian, and, as a result, faces discrimination and harassment of one sort or another. The arguments in this section address the following questions:

Why do many heterosexual people react so strongly to homosexuality?

How does homophobia affect American society as a whole? Should people who disapprove of homosexuality be able to discriminate against homosexuals?

What might both gay and straight people do about homophobia?

Should sexual orientation be protected by civil rights legislation as race, gender, and religion now are?

The issues raised in these readings are central to the debates about more specific gay rights issues such as the role of homosexuals in the military service, the right of homosexuals to marry, and the need for antidiscrimination legislation.

JEFFREY NICKEL

Everybody's Threatened by Homophobia

Homophobia *is a term often used to describe the attitude of those who express hostility toward homosexuals. It suggests that heterosexuals' prejudice is actually rooted in fear. Whatever the cause, the prejudice too often results in acts of violence against gay men and lesbian women. The following argument appeared originally in* Christopher Street, *a literary magazine whose writers and readers are primarily homosexual; Jeffrey Nickel wants to show his readers that they can make a case against homophobia that will appeal to the interests of heterosexuals.*

Do I hate my brother because he reminds me of myself, or do I hate my brother because he reminds me of someone who is "not" myself? Whom do I hate; the one who is me, or the one who is anything but me?

—ELIE WIESEL

THE ANSWER is both. But knowing that would seem to be of little help. Our brothers *are* hated; sisters, too. We're right to tell America of the horrors that hatred visits upon us; of the humiliation, the isolation, and even the killings perpetuated, all in the name of heterosexual hegemony. These should be enough to convince this country that it's been terribly wrong about who we are. But there's more to the story. We can also tell about what homophobia—perhaps surprisingly—does to *others;* those who are perceived to be gay, those who are afraid they *might* be, and everyone else who clearly isn't but is nevertheless forced to feel bigotry's nasty bite. This is a lot of people—close to everyone, really. If only they could understand *these* things, too; maybe they would see.

As Allen Ginsberg wrote, "They can! They can! They can!" Practically every school child in America knows that a "faggot" is the worst thing they could be. How many wonder to themselves, is that *me*? Kids do have the vague perception that there are people in the world called homosexuals, though that's about all they know. How many boys who don't yet "like" girls think homosexuality is the explanation, when in fact for them, it's not? If gay weren't "bad" in their minds, they would feel no more anguish than that experienced by a child who discovers she's left-handed. But gay *is* bad in the country's consciousness, so children *do* worry a hell of a lot about being it. The "late-bloomer" thinks constantly of what might be "wrong" with him. Because the mere *possibility* that some of our children will be gay isn't even entertained, children who, in a freer society, would be relieved by that plausible conclusion are instead shut off from even *thinking* (much less talking) about it. It is awful that so many young gay people attempt, and often succeed in, killing themselves because of who they are.

It's just as awful that so many straight kids try and die for what they mistakenly *think*. How refreshing it would be for young people to be able to discover their sexuality without fear. But right now, that's only a fantasy. Kids in this country must not only be straight; they must make absolutely sure that they are *not* gay. They shouldn't *have* to make sure.

A straight friend of mine whom I came out to when I was seventeen confided in me that he occasionally had gay thoughts and dreams. I told him there was no cause to worry; that virtually all people have same-sex (and other-sex) fantasies to some degree or another. But as enlightened as he truly was about homosexuality, these thoughts *still* bothered him deeply. What would it be like for someone who believed the worst things about homosexuality? I know what it is to be gay and feel the guilt, but I have a hard time imagining what it's like to really be straight and feel it. As a gay person I've had the "coming out process" to sort out all the meanings, but what do straight people have? It doesn't lessen the pain of the gay person's coming-to-terms to admit that these feelings are probably excruciating for many heterosexuals as well. And as is true in our case too, it's all for nothing.

I remember, especially in boyhood, the amazing level of paranoia that surrounded any form of male-to-male physical contact—aside perhaps from sports—as well as any kind of inter-male emotional experience. Males can hardly touch each other in this culture, except, as always, by lashing out. Susan Trausch of the *Boston Globe* put it well when she said that many men (and boys too) are fighting desperately to continue breathing what she called "100 percent pure macho air." They wish to be super-men; super-aggressive, super-obnoxious, and super-ignorant. Their mentality has the dual disadvantage of making automatons of men, and figurines of women. A lot of this mentality is attributable to self- and other-directed homophobia. Men practically have to go to counseling just to be able to talk to each other in real ways. What a pointless chasm we've created, just to make sure that closeness isn't "misconstrued."

I've told before the awful story of what happened to a friend of mine while 5
we were in grade school. This boy hung around another boy so much and so ardently that it seemed he had a crush on him. He probably did. The other kids teased him for it a great deal, as I vaguely recall. But the teacher believed this was so intolerable that she had to do something about it, immediately. It really is unbelievable, but here's what she did: A "trial" was held in the classroom, with all members of the class present, at which this boy had to "defend" his feelings toward the other boy. The teacher herself served as the prosecutor. (He had no real defense.) My understanding is that this boy (now a man) really *isn't* gay. Yet he was totally humilated in front of all of his peers, in such a way that it took him several years to once again build up any semblance of his lost self-esteem. Dating was impossible for him for quite a long time. Some day, I would like to confront this teacher—whom theretofore I'd adored—and ask her what the hell she thought she was doing. It was child abuse of the worst kind, perpetuated against someone who didn't even possess the "demons" she most loathed.

Although I don't presume to know all of what this anxiety does to women, I imagine that it heightens an already well-inculcated sense that women are supposed to have no sexuality whatsoever. Women are taught to please men. Though they are, in a way, given more latitude to express affection for other women than men are for other men. Because women's sexuality is trivialized they're often prevented from knowing just what would constitute lesbianism and what would not. If there were no stigma to homosexuality, this stultifying paranoia just wouldn't exist. Prejudice against homosexuality sharply limits how all men and women may acceptably behave, among themselves and with each other.

I hadn't thought much about how homophobia hurts heterosexuals until I saw a piece on the TV show *20/20* about two or three years ago. They had fascinating stories about several straight people who were actually attacked—physically—because others thought they were gay. One heterosexual couple holding hands walking down the street was beaten repeatedly. It seems the woman's short hair made it seem from the back that they were two men. What an awful education in bigotry it must have been for these poor people. It's interesting to contemplate how these bigots reacted to the knowledge that they were pummeling a wife and her husband: "Oh—we're very sorry to have broken your bones, but we mistook you for someone else."

A similar event took place in Lewes, Delaware, just last year. A man walking down the street with his arm around the shoulder of his (male) friend was struck and seriously injured by a pickup truck, after the driver yelled "faggot" at him. A second man in the truck then hit him in the head with a beer bottle. Then, the driver backed the truck over a curb and onto the sidewalk where the man was standing, crushing the man's legs between the rear of the truck and three metal mailboxes. He then put the truck in reverse once again in order to run over this man a second time, apparently in order to finish him off. He was prevented from doing so only because he couldn't gain the necessary momentum in the space available to jump the curb. The man's legs were so severely injured that the doctors had to graft muscles, tendons, and skin from other parts of his body in order to repair them. During the entire incident the men on the sidewalk were pleading with their attackers: "We're just buddies; we're not gay." One of the men attacked was a married, heterosexual father. But it didn't matter.

And this year, three Pensacola teenagers who said they were out to beat up a gay person in order to get beer money, did so with a lead pipe, fatally, to a man named John Braun, who was a married (straight) father of four. It's incredible: Heterosexuals have actually *died* because of homophobia.

For John Braun and many others, it's too late to understand their stake in 10
eliminating prejudice against gay people. It's too late for him to join P-FLAG[1] and march on Gay Pride Day. But for most people, it isn't too late. Before their children kill themselves far from home; before they lie bleeding, mistaken, and prone; before their brothers die slowly alone; if we talk about it, they can understand. They can! They can! They can!

[1]P-FLAG is an acronym for the national organization Parents-Friends of Lesbians and Gays.

Questions for Discussion

1. Nickel divides his argument into three main sections, each focusing on a different segment of the heterosexual population hurt by homophobia: young people whose sexuality is just developing (paragraphs 2–3), men and women who do not feel comfortable expressing affection for friends of their own sex (paragraphs 4–6), and men and women who are attacked because they are mistaken for homosexuals: (paragraphs 7–9). Which do you think provides Nickel's strongest reason? Comment on his strategy for arranging and supporting these three reasons.
2. Do you agree that "[p]ractically every school child in America knows that a 'faggot' is the worst thing they could be"? If you agree, can you say how our society conveys this idea?
3. What do you think Nickel means when he says that in our society, women's sexuality is trivialized (paragraph 6)? Do you agree that society gives women more "latitude to express affection" for each other? Could this be related to the idea that their sexuality is not as powerful as that of men?
4. Notice that Nickel wants his readers to feel sympathetic to the problems of heterosexuals. How can you tell that his own sympathies are genuine?
5. What persuasive devices does Nickel use to urge his readers on to action?

For Inquiry

In an entry in your writer's notebook, assess the truth of Nickel's argument, based on your own experiences and observations.

PETE HAMILL

Confessions of a Heterosexual

Responding to acts of discrimination and violence, some gay rights activists make a point of displaying their pride and their anger through marches, demonstrations, and civil disobedience. In the selection printed below, Esquire *columnist Pete Hamill argues that some of the protesters have gone too far and are in fact creating a backlash among people who thought they had overcome their prejudices against gay people. As you read, consider whether Hamill is writing to militant homosexuals or to other heterosexuals—and what his purpose is.*

EARLY ONE evening in the spring, I left my apartment in Greenwich Village and went out to get a few things from the grocery store. The air was mild, the leaves were bursting from the trees. I paused for a moment on a corner, waiting for a light to change and the kamikaze traffic to come to a halt. Waiting beside me was a gray-haired man with a face the color of boiled ham and the thick, boxy body of an old dockwalloper. Before the light turned green, we heard distant chants, tramping feet, and suddenly, like a scene from a Chaplin movie, a small army of the night turned the corner. They came marching directly at us.

"Bash back!" they chanted. "Bash back!"

One of them looked at me and the other man and screamed: "You're fuckin' *killing* us! And we're not gonna *take it* anymore!"

Most of the members of this particular mob were young. A few were joking around, enjoying the fraternity of the march. But the faces of most of the demonstrators were contorted in fury as they raised clenched fists at the sky. While drivers leaned on auto horns and people came to their windows to watch, one wide-eyed kid spat in our direction and shouted, "Breeder shit!"

"What the hell *is* this?" the man beside me said. "Who *are* they?" 5

One marcher peeled off and explained. They were protesting gay-bashing and its most recent local manifestation, the planting of a bomb inside Uncle Charlie's, one of the more popular homosexual hangouts in the city. The marchers paraded off, and the man beside me said: "Tell ya the truth, I'd like to bash a few of these bastards myself."

With that brutal parting line, he stormed off. But as I watched him go, I felt an odd, uncomfortable solidarity with the man. He was my age, born in the Depression, raised in the '40s and '50s, and though we had probably led different lives, we almost surely came from the same roots. We were both out of the New York working class, children of immigrants, shaped by codes, geographies, and institutions now lost. We had thought the neighborhood triumvirate of church, saloon, and Tammany Hall would last forever; it didn't. We learned from our fathers and the older men (and not from television) what a man was supposed to do if he was to call himself a man: put money on the kitchen table, defend wife and children, pay his debts, refuse to inform, serve his country when called, honor picket lines, and never quit in a fight. Sexuality was crude and uncomplicated: Men fucked women. Period. So when my accidental companion had strangers curse him and spit at him, and above all, when he understood that they were gay, he reacted out of that virtually forgotten matrix. He wanted to give them a whack in the head.

But I was alarmed that a milder version of the same dark impulse rose in me. After all, I know that gay-bashing is real; homosexuals are routinely injured or murdered every day, all over the world, by people who fear or hate their version of human sexuality.

Yet what rose in me that night wasn't an instinct to hurt anyone in some homophobic spasm. It was more than simple irritation, and it was not new. In some fundamental way, I was bored by the exhibition of theatrical rage from the gay movement. I am tired of listening to people who identify themselves exclusively by what they do with their cocks. And I don't think I'm alone. Discuss the subject long enough with even the most liberal straight males of my generation, and you discover that twenty years of education, lobbying, journalism, and demonstrating by gays have had only a superficial effect; in some deep, dark pool of the psyche, homosexuals are still seen with a mixture of uneasiness and contempt.

10 Gay activists, of course, would laugh darkly at the above and think: *This is not news.* But most of them won't even listen to the reasons for these prejudices. Sadly, the folklore of the old neighborhood is not the only cause. Much of this persistent distaste is based on personal experience. Most males of my generation first encountered homosexuals during adolescence, and those men were not exactly splendid representatives of the gay community. When I was growing up, there were four known homosexuals in the neighborhood. All were in their forties. All singled out boys in the low teens. Two paid for sex, and in a neighborhood where poverty was common, a few dollars was a lot of money.

By all accounts, gay men, in those darkest years of The Closet, lived more dangerous and vulnerable lives than they do now. They were subject to blackmail, murder, beatings, and exposure on a more ferocious scale than today. But nothing so melodramatic seemed to happen in our neighborhood. Though everybody on the street knew about three of the four gay men, I don't remember any incidents of gay-bashing. Only one suffered public disgrace. One day, the police came to his door and took him off. A few days later his weeping wife and baffled children moved away, never to be seen again.

When I understood what these men actually *did,* I was horrified. For an Irish Catholic kid in those years, sex itself was terrifying enough; the homosexual variety seemed proof of the existence of Satan. Through all my years of adolescence, I believed that homosexuals were people who preyed exclusively on the very young, a belief strengthened by later experiences on subways, in men's rooms, and in the high school that I attended (where I met one of those tortured priests of the Catholic literary tradition). That belief was shared by most of the boys I grew up with, and when we left the neighborhood for the service (the working-class version of going off to college), we saw more of the same.

In the sailor joints of Norfolk or Pensacola, homosexuals were constantly on the prowl, looking for kids who were drunk, lonesome, naive, or broken-hearted over some Dear John letter shoved in their hip pockets. Again, older men taught us the code, demonstrating how Real Men were supposed to react. It was never very pretty: There was often violence, some gay man smashed and battered into the mud outside a tough joint after midnight. There was a lot of swaggering machismo, a triumphant conviction that by stomping such people we were striking a mighty blow against predators and corrupters. I'm still ashamed of some of the things I saw and did in those years.

It never occurred to us that some of these older gay men were actually looking for—and finding—other homosexuals, as driven in their search for love and connection as we were in our pursuit of lush young women. We were all so young that we arrogantly assumed that all of us were straight and they were bent; *we* were healthy, *they* were carriers of some sickness. It took me a while to understand that the world was more complicated than it was in the *Bluejackets' Manual.*[1]

The years passed. I grew up. I worked with homosexuals. I read novels and 15
saw plays written by homosexuals about the specifics of their lives. Gradually, the stereotypes I carried were broken by experience and knowledge. At the same time, I was roaming around as a reporter, seeing riots and wars, too much poverty and too many dead bodies. The ambiguities, masks, and games of human sexuality seemed a minor issue compared with the horrors of the wider world. Even after the gay-liberation movement began, in the wake of the 1969 Stonewall Riot, in New York, the private lives of homosexuals seldom entered my imagination. I didn't care what people did in bed, as long as they didn't wake up in the morning and napalm villages, starve children, or harm the innocent.

Some of my friends "came out" in the years after Stonewall. The process was more difficult for them than it was for me. On more than a few evenings, I found myself listening to a painful account of the dreadful angst that accompanied living in The Closet, and the delirious joy that came with kicking down its door forever. I apologized for any crudities I might have uttered while they were in The Closet; they forgave me. We remained friends.

In the years after Stonewall, I met gay men living in monogamous relationships, gay men of austere moral codes, gay men with great courage. I read interviews with gay cops, soldiers, and football players. I knew that there were thousands of gay men living lives of bourgeois respectability. There were even right-wing gay Republicans. Like many men my age, I thought, What the hell, there's room for everybody.

Then came AIDS.

[1]A bluejacket is an enlisted member of the U.S. Navy.

And for people like me, everything about homosexuals changed once more. Thousands have died from this terrible disease, but for people my age, the gulf between straight and gay seems to be widening instead of closing. I find myself deploring homophobia, like any good liberal, and simultaneously understanding why it seems to be spreading among otherwise decent people. A phobia, after all, is a fear. And AIDS terrifies.

Under the combined pressures of fear and pity, I've been forced to confront 20
my own tangled notions about gays. I cherish my gay friends, and want them to live long and productive lives. But while AIDS has made many millions even more sympathetic to and understanding of gay lives, I find myself struggling with the powerful undertow of the primitive code of my youth. I've lost all patience with much of the paranoid oratory of gay radicals. I can't abide the self-pitying aura of victimhood that permeates so much of their discussion. Their leaders irritate me with their insistence on seeing AIDS as if it were some tragic medieval plague of unknown origin instead of the result of personal behavior.

I know that AIDS cases are increasing among heterosexuals, and the virus is spreading wildly among intravenous drug users. For me, this knowledge is not abstract. I know one sweet young woman who died of the disease, picked up from her junkie husband; I was at her christening, and I'm still furious that she's dead. I also know that the rate of infection among homosexuals is down, the result of "safe sex" campaigns, education, and abstinence.

But when the gay militants in ACT UP go to St. Patrick's Cathedral and one of them crushes a Communion Host on the floor as a protest against the Church's traditional policies, I'm revolted. This is cheap blasphemy and even worse politics. I'm angered when the homosexual bedroom police force gays out of The Closet against their will while simultaneously opposing the tracing of AIDS carriers. When gay activists harass doctors, disrupt public meetings, and scream self-righteously about their "rage," my heart hardens.

I'm sure the government isn't doing enough to find a cure for AIDS. But it's also not doing enough to cure lung cancer, which kills 130,000 people every year, or acute alcoholism (57,000 every year), or to avert the ravages of cocaine addiction. Like AIDS (which has killed 81,000 Americans in a decade), these afflictions are spread, or controlled, by personal behavior. I've had more friends die of smoking, drinking, or doing dope than I have friends who died of AIDS. But I don't ever hear about the "rage" of the cigarette addict or the stone drunk or the crackhead, even though none of my stricken friends went gently into that good night. If anything, most current social rage is directed *against* such people, while the diseases continue to kill. And yet in most American cities, if you measured inches of type in newspapers, you might believe that all of the old diseases have been conquered and only AIDS remains.

I'm not among those who believe there is some all-powerful "Homintern" that manipulates the media while filling the museums with Robert Mapplethorpe photographs. But I don't feel I'm lining up with the unspeakable Jesse Helms when I say that I'm also fed up with the ranting of those gays who believe that all straights are part of some Monstrous Conspiracy to end homosexual life. One lie is not countered with another.

Certainly, as gay rhetoric becomes more apocalyptic, the entire public discussion is being reduced to a lurid cartoon, devoid of criticism, irony, nuance, and even common sense. Certainly, there is less room for tolerance. I know a few gay people who resent being told that if they don't follow the party line they are mere "self-hating gays." And as someone outside the group, I don't like being told that I must agree with the latest edition of the established creed or be dismissed as a homophobe. More than anything else, I'm angry with myself when some of the old specters come rising out of the psychic mists of my own generation. 25

In the face of the AIDS plague, gays and straights should be forging a union by cool reason. Instead, we are presented with cheap pity, romantic bullshit, or the irrational, snarling faces of haters. As in so many areas of our society, divisions are drawn in black and white; there are no shades of gray. Homophobia is countered by heterophobia; the empty answer to gay-bashing is a vow to bash back. There are sadder developments in American life, I suppose, but for the moment, I can't think of one.

Questions for Discussion

1. Using the "folklore" and experiences of his own working-class background, Hamill suggests that there was a connection between homophobia and economic class when he was growing up in the 1940s and 1950s. Do you think such a connection still exists?
2. Hamill refers to the 1940s and 1950s as "those darkest years of The Closet" (paragraph 11). Can you make any connection between homosexuals' staying in the closet and the experiences Hamill describes in paragraphs 10 through 13?
3. What made it possible for Hamill to overcome his prejudices? Have you had a similar experience in overcoming any form of prejudice?
4. Hamill defends his own recurring "homophobia" as a reaction to AIDS and the "ranting" of gay activists. What evidence does he offer to justify his new attitude? Is it all related to AIDS? How does Hamill use language as a way of persuading readers to see the militant activity as he does?
5. In paragraph 9, Hamill says that "twenty years of education, lobbying, journalism, and demonstrating by gays have had only a superficial effect" on public perceptions. What solution is he proposing to the problem of homophobia?

For Inquiry and Persuasion

Research any recent demonstrations by gay rights activists, such as those in ACT UP. What are these groups protesting, and what methods are they using? How confrontational are their protests? How often is civil disobedience involved? Why have they taken such a militant approach? Look also at what they are saying, the kind of language they are using. You might have to turn to periodicals aimed at the gay community, such as *The Advocate* and *Christopher Street,* which are indexed in Infotrac. Your campus may have an organization for gay and lesbian students, which could also supply you with some gay rights literature.

After inquiring thoroughly, if you feel Hamill's criticisms are justified, write persuasively to the militants, suggesting a cooler approach.

If you think their approach is justified, write to Hamill and others like him who have lost patience with the demonstrations; try to generate understanding and sympathy.

For Mediation

After inquiring into protests by militant homosexuals for the previous activity, write a mediatory essay aimed at both these militant demonstrators and an audience of men and women who feel as Hamill does. Before you write, create a brief of each side's position and reasons. In your mediatory essay, attempt to get each side to understand the other's emotions and interests. Suggest ways militant gays and straights might work together to eliminate homophobia.

TOM MEYER

Cartoon

In the preceding essay, Pete Hamill tells of his days in the U.S. Navy. He writes that he and other young sailors "arrogantly assumed that all of us were straight and they [gays] were bent" and that the sailors often responded to unwanted homosexual overtures with violence. This was the acceptable behavior of "real men" (paragraph 9). In 1991, U.S. Navy women complained that they were victims of unwanted heterosexual advances at the convention that year of Tailhook, an association of U.S. Navy aviators. In the cartoon below, Tom Meyer of the San Francisco Chronicle *comments on the irony of the Navy's position on military service for openly gay people.*

For Discussion

Read news accounts of the charges made by some of the women present at the September, 1991, Tailhook convention and accounts of other examples of sexual harassment against women in the military. Do you believe that sexual harassment is often overlooked in the military because it represents a "macho" attitude?

PETER J. GOMES

Homophobic? Reread Your Bible

Those who contend that homosexuality is immoral often cite the Bible for support. Although nonbelievers would find these arguments weak, the weight of biblical authority is unquestionable among many Christian audiences. During the crucial election year of 1992, fundamentalist Christians and others called upon Scripture to make their case that homosexuality is immoral and gay rights a threat to "traditional family values," defeating several gay rights measures in the process. In the following argument, a Baptist minister and professor of Christian morals at Harvard University challenges the fundamentalists' interpretation of the Bible.

OPPOSITION TO gays' civil rights has become one of the most visible symbols of American civic conflict this year, and religion has become the weapon of choice. The army of the discontented, eager for clear villains and simple solutions and ready for a crusade in which political self-interest and social anxiety can be cloaked in morality, has found hatred of homosexuality to be the last respectable prejudice of the century.

Ballot initiatives in Oregon and Maine would deny homosexuals the protection of civil rights laws. The Pentagon has steadfastly refused to allow gays into the armed forces. Vice President Dan Quayle is crusading for "traditional family values." And Pat Buchanan, who is scheduled to speak at the Republican National Convention this evening, regards homosexuality as a litmus test of moral purity.

Nothing has illuminated this crusade more effectively than a work of fiction, "The Drowning of Stephan Jones," by Bette Greene. Preparing for her novel, Ms. Greene interviewed more than 400 young men incarcerated for gay-bashing, and scrutinized their case studies. In an interview published in The Boston Globe this spring, she said she found that the gay-bashers generally saw nothing wrong in what they did, and, more often than not, said their religious leaders and traditions sanctioned their behavior. One convicted teen-age gay-basher told her that the pastor of his church had said, "Homosexuals represent the devil, Satan," and that the Rev. Jerry Falwell had echoed that charge.

Christians opposed to political and social equality for homosexuals nearly always appeal to the moral injunctions of the Bible, claiming that Scripture is very clear on the matter and citing verses that support their opinion. They accuse others of perverting and distorting texts contrary to their "clear" meaning. They do not, however, necessarily see quite as clear a meaning in biblical passages on economic conduct, the burdens of wealth, and the sin of greed.

Nine biblical citations are customarily invoked as relating to homosexuality. 5
Four (Deuteronomy 23:17, I Kings 14:24, I Kings 22:46, and II Kings 23:7) simply forbid prostitution, by men and women.

Two others (Leviticus 18:19–23 and Leviticus 20:10–16) are part of what biblical scholars call the Holiness Code. The code explicitly bans homosexual acts. But it also prohibits eating raw meat, planting two different kinds of seed in the same field, and wearing garments with two different kinds of yarn. Tattoos, adultery, and sexual intercourse during a woman's menstrual period are similarly outlawed.

There is no mention of homosexuality in the four Gospels of the New Testament. The moral teachings of Jesus are not concerned with the subject.

Three references from St. Paul are frequently cited (Romans 1:26–2:1, I Corinthians 6:9–11, and I Timothy 1:10). But St. Paul was concerned with homosexuality only because in Greco-Roman culture it represented a secular sensuality that was contrary to his Jewish-Christian spiritual idealism. He was against lust and sensuality in anyone, including heterosexuals. To say that homosexuality is bad because homosexuals are tempted to do morally doubtful things is to say that heterosexuality is bad because heterosexuals are likewise tempted. For St. Paul, anyone who puts his or her interest ahead of God's is condemned, a verdict that falls equally upon everyone.

And lest we forget Sodom and Gomorrah, recall that the story is not about sexual perversion and homosexual practice. It is about inhospitality, according to Luke 10:10–13, and failure to care for the poor, according to Ezekiel 16:49–50: "Behold, this was the iniquity of thy sister Sodom, pride, fullness of bread, and abundance of idleness was in her and in her daughters, neither did she strengthen the hand of the poor and needy." To suggest that Sodom and Gomorrah is about homosexual sex is an analysis of about as much worth as suggesting that the story of Jonah and the whale is a treatise on fishing.

10 Part of the problem is a question of interpretation. Fundamentalists and literalists, the storm troopers of the religious right, are terrified that Scripture, "wrongly interpreted," may separate them from their values. That fear stems from their own recognition that their "values" are not derived from Scripture, as they publicly claim.

Indeed, it is through the lens of their own prejudices and personal values that they "read" Scripture and cloak their own views in its authority. We all interpret Scripture: Make no mistake. And no one truly is a literalist, despite the pious temptation. The questions are, By what principle of interpretation do we proceed, and by what means do we reconcile "what it meant then" to "what it means now?"

These matters are far too important to be left to scholars and seminarians alone. Our ability to judge ourselves and others rests on our ability to interpret Scripture intelligently. The right use of the Bible, an exercise as old as the church itself, means that we confront our prejudices rather than merely confirm them.

For Christians, the principle by which Scripture is read is nothing less than an appreciation of the work and will of God as revealed in that of Jesus. To recover a liberating and inclusive Christ is to be freed from the semantic bondage that makes us curators of a dead culture rather than creatures of a new creation.

Religious fundamentalism is dangerous because it cannot accept ambiguity and diversity and is therefore inherently intolerant. Such intolerance, in the name of virtue, is ruthless and uses political power to destroy what it cannot convert.

It is dangerous, especially in America, because it is anti-democratic and is 15
suspicious of "the other," in whatever form that "other" might appear. To maintain itself, fundamentalism must always define "the other" as deviant.

But the chief reason that fundamentalism is dangerous is that, at the hands of the Rev. Pat Robertson, the Rev. Jerry Falwell, and hundreds of lesser-known but equally worrisome clerics, preachers, and pundits, it uses Scripture and the Christian practice to encourage ordinarily good people to act upon their fears rather than their virtues.

Fortunately, those who speak for the religious right do not speak for all American Christians, and the Bible is not theirs alone to interpret. The same Bible that the advocates of slavery used to protect their wicked self-interests is the Bible that inspired slaves to revolt and their liberators to action.

The same Bible that the predecessors of Mr. Falwell and Mr. Robertson used to keep white churches white is the source of the inspiration of the Rev. Martin Luther King, Jr., and the social reformation of the 1960's.

The same Bible that antifeminists use to keep women silent in the churches is the Bible that preaches liberation to captives and says that in Christ there is neither male nor female, slave nor free.

And the same Bible that on the basis of an archaic social code of ancient 20
Israel and a tortured reading of Paul is used to condemn all homosexuals and homosexual behavior includes metaphors of redemption, renewal, inclusion, and love—principles that invite homosexuals to accept their freedom and responsibility in Christ and demands that their fellow Christians accept them as well.

The political piety of the fundamentalist religious right must not be exercised at the expense of our precious freedoms. And in this summer of our discontent, one of the most precious freedoms for which we must all fight is freedom from this last prejudice.

Questions for Discussion

1. In paragraphs 5–9, Gomes offers his interpretations of the biblical passages usually cited as showing God's condemnation of homosexuality. How well does Gomes deflate the arguments from Leviticus and from the gospels written by St. Paul? To what extent does Gomes's own authority as a Baptist minister and Harvard theologian lend force to his view of these passages? (You may want to consult the biblical passages yourself before you respond.)
2. Gomes argues that all reading of Scripture involves interpretation (paragraph 11). What, for him, is the difference between right and wrong interpretation? How is "right" interpretation similar to Inquiry, as we describe it on pages 42–44? Must a "right" interpretation be apolitical—that is, influenced by no political viewpoint?

3. What argumentative and stylistic techniques do you see Gomes using in paragraphs 17–20 to support his point about right and wrong interpretations of the Bible?
4. In his criticism of the rhetorical, or persuasive, strategy of the religious right, Gomes says their use of the Bible "encourage[s] ordinarily good people to act upon their fears rather than their virtues" (paragraph 16). Do you agree? Is it always bad to use fear as an emotional appeal in persuasive argumentation?
5. What other issues can you think of in which people commonly call upon the authority of the Bible for support? Do you think Gomes would argue that any of these misuse Scripture in the way he describes here?

For Analysis and Persuasion

A classic example of persuasive argumentation that calls upon the Bible as a source of authority is the "Letter from Birmingham Jail" by Martin Luther King, Jr. (pages 114–125). After you have read King's "Letter" itself and our analysis of King's audience and purpose (pages 109–113), go back and locate all of King's references to the Bible. Write a paper in which you discuss King's use of the Bible, noting the specific fears or virtues of his audience to which he is appealing.

JONATHAN ALTER

Degrees of Discomfort

If someone has no tolerance for others of a particular race, that person is a racist. The following argument, originally published in Newsweek, *asks whether homophobia, or prejudice against homosexuals, is equivalent to racism. The question is important because defenders of homosexual rights argue that the two forms of discrimination are comparable, while those who oppose gay rights claim their own right to disapprove of people whose behavior is repugnant or even sinful according to their own moral standards. Note how Jonathan Alter's argument makes the case for civil rights for gay people but not for universal tolerance of homosexuality. Note, too, that Alter wrote his essay in response to an incident in which Martin Luther King's son first made, and then retracted, a statement critical of homosexuals.*

WHEN ANDY Rooney got in trouble last month, gay activists complained he was being publicly rebuked for his allegedly racist remarks and not for his gay-bashing.[1] They wanted to know why homophobia was viewed as less serious than racism. The case of Martin Luther King III last week brought the comparison into even sharper relief. After a speech in Poughkeepsie, N.Y., in which he said "something must be wrong" with homosexuals, the young Atlanta politician met with angry gay leaders and quickly apologized. His father's legacy, King said, was "the struggle to free this country of bigotry and discrimination." In that light, he added, he needed to examine his own attitudes toward homosexuals.

King will need to ask himself this question: Is homophobia the moral equivalent of racism? To answer yes sounds right; it conforms to commendable ideals of tolerance. But it doesn't take account of valid distinctions between the two forms of prejudice. On the other hand, to answer no—to say, homophobia is not like racism for this reason or that—risks rationalizing anti-gay bias.

Discrimination against homosex*uals* is not the same as personal distaste for homosex*uality.* The former is clearly akin to racism. There is no way to explain away the prejudice in this country against gays. People lose jobs, promotions, homes, and friends because of it. Incidents of violence against gays are up sharply in some areas. Hundreds of anti-sodomy laws remain on the books, and gays are shamelessly discriminated against in insurance and inheritance. The fact is, a lot of people are pigheaded enough to judge a person entirely on the basis of his or her sexuality. Rooney's mail—and that of practically everyone else commenting publicly on this issue—is full of ugly anti-gay invective.

But does that mean that anyone who considers the homosexual sex act sinful or repulsive is the equivalent of a racist? The answer is no. Objecting to it

[1]Rooney, a commentator on *60 Minutes*, was briefly suspended by CBS in 1990 after making remarks that offended blacks but not for comments critical of homosexuality.

may be narrow-minded and invasive of privacy, but it does not convey the same complete moral vacuity as, say, arguing that blacks are born inferior. There is a defensible middle position. Recall Mario Cuomo's carefully articulated view of abortion: personally opposed, but deeply supportive of a woman's right to choose. That tracks quite closely to polls that show how the majority of Americans approach the subject of homosexuality.

5 Like all straddles, this one offends people on both sides: straights who consider all homosexuality sinful, and gays who consider a hate-the-sin-but-not-the-sinner argument merely another form of homophobia. Moreover, the "personal opposition" idea rings more hollow on homosexuality than on abortion; after all, there is no third-party fetus—just consenting adults whose private behavior should not be judged by outsiders. Of course there are times when squeamishness is understandable. In coming of age, many gays have made a point of flaunting their sexuality, moving, as one joke puts it, from "the love that dare not speak its name" to "the love that won't shut up." Exhibitionism and promiscuity (less common in the age of AIDS) are behavioral choices that, unlike innate sexual preference, can be controlled. It's perfectly legitimate to condemn such behavior—assuming heterosexuals are held to the same standard.

Simply put, identity and behavior are not synonymous. A bigot hates blacks for what they *are;* a reasonable person can justifiably object to some things homosexuals *do.* The distinction between objecting to who someone is (unfair) and objecting to what someone does (less unfair) must be maintained. The worst comment about gays allegedly made by Rooney was that he would not like to be locked in a room with them. That would be a tolerable sentiment only if the homosexuals were *having sex* in the room. Otherwise it's a form of bigotry. Who would object to being locked in a room with cigarette smokers if they weren't smoking?

"Acting gay" often involves more than sexual behavior itself. Much of the dislike for homosexuals centers not on who they are or what they do in private, but on so-called affectations—"swishiness" in men, the "butch" look for women—not directly related to the more private sex act. Heterosexuals tend to argue that gays can downplay these characteristics and "pass" more easily in the straight world than blacks can in a white world.

This may be true, but it's also irrelevant. For many gays those traits aren't affectations but part of their identities; attacking the swishiness is the same as attacking *them.* Why the visceral vehemence, particularly among straight men? Richard Isay, a psychiatrist and author of the 1989 book "Being Homosexual," suggests that homophobia actually has little to do with the sex act itself. "This hatred of homosexuals appears to be secondary in our society to the fear and hatred of what is perceived as being 'feminine' in other men and in oneself."

Such fears, buried deep, are reminiscent of the emotional charge of racial feelings. At its most virulent, this emotion leads to blaming the victim—for AIDS, for instance, or for poverty. In its more modest form, the fear, when recognized, can be helpful in understanding the complexities of both homosexuality and race.

That consciousness is sometimes about language—avoiding "fag" and "nig- 10
ger." But the interest groups that expend energy insisting that one use "African-American" instead of "black" or "gay and lesbian" instead of "homosexual" are missing the point. Likewise, the distinctions between racism and homophobia eventually shrivel before the larger task at hand, which is simply to look harder at ourselves.

Questions for Discussion

1. In your own words, explain what Alter sees as "a defensible middle position" on the issue of discrimination against homosexuals (paragraph 4). How does he support and defend that position?
2. Evaluate Alter's argument in paragraph 6, which compares homosexuals to cigarette smokers. In context, how valid is this analogy?
3. In paragraphs 7–10, Alter points out that what many straight people call "affected" behavior in gay people is actually part of their identities, something that they may not be able to hide, even if they wanted to. Is one's sexual orientation something everyone should try to "downplay" in their public lives? Should, for example, heterosexual couples be expected to avoid romantic physical contact in public, as most homosexual couples feel they must do?
4. Alter seems to conclude that homophobia, or "personal distaste for homosex-*uality*," is not as severe a character flaw as racism (paragraphs 3 and 4). How does he support this point? Do you agree with him?
5. Alter quotes psychiatrist Richard Isay on a possible cause for homophobia (paragraph 8). What do you think of Isay's theory? Look at Pete Hamill's description of how "Real Men were supposed to react" if approached by a homosexual (paragraph 13 in his essay earlier in this chapter). Do you think Isay's theory might help to explain some of the violence committed against gay men?

For Inquiry

Alter acknowledges that his middle position would offend "people on both sides" (paragraph 5). Write a dialogue with Alter in which you examine the truth of his position, posing questions that would represent the viewpoints of both sides. See pages 43–44 for suggestions about what to ask.

MICHAEL LEVIN

A Case against Civil Rights for Homosexuals

While Jonathan Alter's argument acknowledges both similarities and differences between homophobia and racism, Michael Levin, a philosophy professor at the City University of New York, claims that discrimination based on sexual orientation is not at all analogous to discrimination based on race or religion; his concern is with the individual's right to act upon his or her private conscience.

Levin's argument against legally protecting the civil rights of homosexuals appeared originally as part of a rebuttal to the feminist position that abortion should be a woman's private decision, based on her individual conscience. Levin has pointed out that feminists want government protection from errors of conscience in employment, housing, pedagogy, and so on, but "[t]he only matter feminists are willing to entrust to private conscience . . . is the killing of fetuses." Levin asks, If acting according to one's private conscience is correct in the case of abortion, would it not also be correct in the case of discriminating against gay people?

PLEAS FOR the sovereignty of individual conscience become yet more puzzling when entered by supporters of laws banning private discrimination against homosexuals. The laws in question have nothing to do with guaranteeing homosexuals the right to do as they please in private; these laws, rather, would forbid the private use of "sexual preference" as a criterion for employment and housing decisions. These laws forbid third parties to refuse to associate with homosexuals on the basis of beliefs about and possible aversion to homosexual practices. It is unnecessary here to decide whether homosexuality is "unnatural" or whether distaste for homosexuals is "prejudice." The fact is that many people dislike homosexuals. They think homosexuality is intrinsically abhorrent, a violation of divine commands, a threat to their children. How is one to justify denying to such people the freedom to avoid homosexuals if they conscientiously feel that avoidance of homosexuality is desirable? Surely one's willingness to hire or rent to homosexuals can be seen as a matter of private conscience, one's "right to one's own body" (a landlord may not wish to rent rooms to a homosexual in the same building his own body is situated in), one's "right to choose."

The analogy often drawn between homosexuals, blacks, and Jews is obviously less than perfect. A black man cannot hide his race but a homosexual can hide his sexual impulses. True, a Jew can also remove his head cover if he is indoors with an anti-Semitic hiring officer, and perhaps has only himself to blame if he does not get the job—but if the Jew does choose to lose the job in preference to (as he sees it) offending God, that is a matter of religious conviction. It is hard to think of a comparable motive that could induce a homosexual to refuse to disguise his homosexuality from a prospective employer. The point is that the analogy impresses some people but not others. Blacks and Jews no doubt have their own opinion of it. Genuine respect for freedom of conscience would allow each person to make up his own mind about it, and about whether to ignore "sexual preference" in those situations in which he is required by law to ignore race and religion. Perhaps permitting freedom of conscience will permit mistakes; perhaps some people will choose (wrongly, in some eyes) to consider sexual preference important. Perhaps as a result of such choices, many homosexuals will be worse off than they would have been had freedom of conscience been forbidden. Anyone who considers this possibility too awful for the state to countenance, but also supports decriminalizing abortion, must consider the happiness of homosexuals more important than the lives of fetuses.

Questions for Discussion

1. Levin effectively turns the question of gay rights completely around, since what he is really looking at is the right of people who are not gay to refuse to associate with homosexuals. For Levin, why should laws against discrimination not apply to those who "dislike homosexuals"?
2. Is Levin suggesting that gay people can change their sexual orientation—or merely that they can conceal it?
3. Why would a homosexual refuse to disguise his or her sexual orientation? What would be the difficulties of living in "the closet"?

For Inquiry

Using the Questions for Inquiry on pages 44–45, write out a dialogue with Michael Levin, inquiring into the truth of his argument that private conscience can serve as the basis for discrimination against homosexuals. Pay particular attention to the two comparisons he makes in this argument.

RICHARD MOHR

The Civic Rights of Invisible Minorities

A person who is fired from a job because he or she is gay has no legal grounds for complaint, as people do have if they are fired because of their race or religion. This is why gay activists are demanding that the protections offered by the Civil Rights Act of 1964 be extended to them. In some communities, local ordinances have been passed to ensure the civil rights of gay men and lesbians; in others, such as the state of Colorado in 1992, legislation providing that protection has been bitterly contested and voted down. In the following argument, University of Illinois philosophy professor Richard Mohr makes the case that without civil rights, gay people also are denied civic rights—the right to the full use of our nation's court system. The selection is excerpted from Mohr's book Gays/Justice *(1988).*

THIS SECTION argues that civil rights legislation for gays is warranted as being a necessary precondition for gays having equitable access to civic rights. By civic rights I mean rights to the impartial administration of civil and criminal law in defense of property and person. In the absence of such rights there is no rule of law. An invisible minority historically subjected to widespread social discrimination has reasonably guaranteed access to these rights only when the minority is guaranteed nondiscrimination in employment, housing, and public services.

For an invisible minority, possessing civil rights has the same ethical justification as everyone's having the right when on criminal trial to have a lawyer at government expense. A lawyer through her special knowledge and skills provides her client with *access* to the substantive and procedural rights of the courts—rights to which a layman left to his own devices would not have reasonably guaranteed access. Without the guarantee of a lawyer, judicial rights are not equal rights but those of the well-to-do.

All would agree that everyone ought to have judicial rights, and moreover—as in the case of having a lawyer at state expense—ought to have in that strong sense of rights by which an individual can make demand claims based on them. All individuals must be assured the right to demand from government access to judicial procedures. Judicial rights ought not to be debased to the level where government may simply be prevented from prohibiting judicial access, but need not guarantee it. This debasement would give judicial access the same status that abortion now has in the U.S.; it cannot be prohibited, but is not guaranteed for those who want or even (in most cases) need it. Civic rights ought not to be mere immunities and they ought not to be restricted only to certain classes.

Imagine the following scenario. Steve, who teaches math in a suburban high school and coaches the swim team, on a weekend night heads to the city to try his luck at Up and Coming, a popular gay cruise bar. There he meets Tom, a self-employed contractor, who in his former life sired two sons by a woman who now hates him, but who is ignorant of his new life. Tom and Steve decide to walk to Tom's nearby flat, which he rents from a bigot who bemoans the fact that the neighborhood is going gay and refuses to rent to people he supposes to be gay; Tom's weekend visitations from his sons are his cover.

Meanwhile, at a nearby Children's Aid Home for teenagers, the leader of 5
the Anglo gang is taunting Tony, the leader of the Latino gang, by calling him a faggot. After much protestation to the contrary, Tony claims he will prove to the Anglos once and for all that he is not a faggot, and hits the streets with his gang members, who tote with them the blunt and not so blunt instruments of the queerbasher's trade. Like a hyena pack upon a wildebeest, they descend on Tom and Steve, downing their victims in a blizzard of strokes and blows. Local residents coming home from parties and others walking their dogs witness the whole event.

Imagine that two miracles occur. One, a squad car happens by, and two, the police actually do their job. Tony and another of the fleeing queerbashers are caught and arrested on the felony charges of aggravated assault and battery, and attempted murder. Other squad cars arrive and while witnesses' reports are gathered, Steve and Tom are taken to the nearest emergency room. Once Steve and Tom are in wards the police arrive to take statements of complaint from them, complaints which will engage the wheels of justice in what appears to be an open and shut case. But Steve knows the exposure of a trial will terminate his employment. And Tom knows the exposure of a trial would give his ex-wife the legal excuse she desires to deny his visitation rights and he knows he will eventually lose his apartment. So neither man can reasonably risk pressing charges. Tony is released, and within twelve hours of attempting murder, he returns to the Children's Aid Home hailed by all as a conquering hero. Gay rights are a necessary material condition for judicial access.

Any reader of gay urban tabloids, like Chicago's *Windy City Times,* San Francisco's *Bay Area Reporter,* Boston's *Gay Community News,* Toronto's *The Body Politic,* or *The Washington Blade,* knows that the events sketched here—miracles excepted—are typical. Every day gays are in effect blackmailed by our judicial system. Our judicial system's threat of exposure prevents gay access to judicial protections. The example given above of latter-day lynch law falls within the sphere of criminal justice. Even more obviously, the same judicial blackmail occurs in civil cases. Nor are the offending parties always outsiders to the group whose civic access is thus limited:

> Similarly, lesbians can be sexually harassed by other lesbians. Some lesbians may foist sexual attentions upon other lesbians who already have lovers, for example. To a large extent lesbians who are victims of nondiscriminatory [i.e., peer-on-peer] sexual harassment will be on their own. A lesbian will tend to reject any suggestion that she initiate a civil suit against her female harasser. Fearing that she will be laughed out of

> court, or doubting the wisdom of publicly proclaiming her sexual preference, the lesbian is apt to handle her problem in informal ways.[1]

These "informal ways," however, are bound to be unsatisfactory. For insofar as they try to circumvent the law and yet require for their warranted success the sort of justified coercion which is the exclusive preserve of the state's police powers, they will at a minimum result in violation of the law,[2] and more likely end in attempted usurpation of the law.[3]

It is unreasonable to expect anyone to give up that by which he lives, his employment, his shelter, his access to goods and services and loved ones in order for judicial procedures to be carried out equitably, in order to demand legal protections. Even if one were tempted to follow the libertarian and say that these are in fact reasonable expenses to pay for making the choice of living an open lifestyle, that a person always makes tradeoffs among his necessarily limited options, and that this condition does not warrant the state coercing *others* on his behalf—even if one believed all that, one would not, I think, go on and say that these costs are a reasonable price to pay to see one's assailants dealt justice or to enter a court of equity.

Now what is bitterly paradoxical about this blackmail by the judiciary is that it is a necessary concomitant of two major virtues of the fair administration of justice. The first is that trials are not star chamber affairs, but are open to scrutiny by public and press. The second is that defendants must be able to be confronted by the witnesses against them and have compulsory process for obtaining witnesses in their favor, while conversely prosecutors must have the tools

[1]Rosemarie Tong, "Lesbian Perspectives," in *Women, Sex, and the Law* (Totowa, N.J.: Rowman & Allanheld, 1984), p. 187. [Author's note.]

[2]Example: in December 1982, the only two women's bars in NYC—unwilling, not without reason, to rely on police protections—initiated a "women only" door policy to protect patrons from persistent harassment from nongay males. This action, of course, violated state liquor codes (among others) which bar gender discrimination. The result: both establishments lost their licenses and were closed by the state (Tong, *Women*, p. 186). I leave here as open questions whether such a door policy could be justified as a private sector affirmative action program or whether, given the historically central role of bars in the development and maintenance of lesbian and gay male culture and politics, the license revocations should be subject to successful challenge as violations of the constitutional right to (political) association. On this role, see John D'Emilio, *Sexual Politics, Sexual Communities: The Making of a Homosexual Minority in the United States, 1940–1970* (Chicago: University of Chicago Press, 1983), pp. 30–33, 49–51, and especially 97–99, 107, 186. [Author's note.]

Caveat emptor: usually, though not always, such Constitutional challenges to civil rights ordinances have worked against rather than in favor of gay male and lesbian interests, especially when religious rights have been invoked. See, for example, *Walker v. First Presbyterian Church,* 22 F E P Cases 762 (Cal. Super. Ct., 1980) (Free Exercise Clause voids application of municipal gay employment protections to gay church organist).

[3]For a grisly example of such vigilantism—a case of revenge over an alleged violation of personal rights in which the avenger is in no position to seek recourse in the law—see Tong, *Women,* p. 189; for further examples and analysis, see "Lesbian Battering" *Gay Community News,* January 14, 1984, II(25):13–17, and Kerry Lobel, ed., *Naming the Violence: Speaking Out About Lesbian Battering* (Seattle: The Seal Press, 1986). [Author's note.]

with which to press cases on behalf of victims. In consequence, determinations of guilt and innocence must be based on a full examination of the facts. The result of these two virtues is that trials cast the private into the public realm.

The Supreme Court itself has recognized that public exposure of the private realm necessarily attends the workings of justice; thus wrote Chief Justice Burger for a unanimous Court in *United States v. Nixon:*

> [A]ll the values to which we accord deference for the privacy of all citizens . . . must yield . . . to our [nation's] commitment to the rule of law. This is nowhere more profoundly manifest than in our view that "the twofold aim [of criminal justice] is that guilt shall not escape or innocence suffer." We have elected to employ an adversary system of criminal justice in which the parties contest all issues before a court of law. . . . The very integrity of the judicial system and public confidence in the system depend on full disclosure of all the facts.

That trials cast the private into the public realm puts the lie to those condescending (would-be) liberals who claim that what gays do in private is no one else's business and should not be anyone else's business, so that on the one hand gays do not need rights, and on the other hand they do not deserve rights, lest they make themselves public. If the judiciary system is to be open and fair, it is necessary that gays be granted civil rights. Otherwise judicial access becomes a right only for the dominant culture.

In being *de facto* cast beyond the pale of civic procedures, gays, when faced with assaults on property and person, are left with only the equally unjust alternatives of the resignation of the impotent or the rage of man in a state of nature. Societies may remain orderly even when some of their members are denied civic procedures. Many tyrannies do. But such societies cannot be said to be civil societies which respect the rule of law.[1]

In October 1984, the governor of California signed a bill making actionable as civil suits assaults on gays which are motivated by an animus against gays.[2]

[1]I have not here intended to address a complementary problem of criminal justice for gays: whether, when gays stand accused of crime or pursue civil litigation, they get fair treatment from police, bench, and jury. For some eye-opening examples of patently prejudicial and abusive treatment of gays from the bench, see Rhonda R. Rivera's magisterial "Our Straight-Laced Judges: The Legal Position of Homosexual Persons in the U.S.," *Hastings Law Journal* (1979) 30:799–955. . . .

To the extent that civil rights legislation for a group tends to legitimate that group in the eyes of society as a whole, gay civil rights legislation would in fact increase the likelihood of gays getting fair trials. The issue is complex, but I doubt that this benefit outweighs the general inappropriateness of government throwing its weight behind one or another lifestyle or class. There is no guarantee that the government's symbolic actions are a ratchet that turns only in the direction of the good, so gays would do well to remember that what government may bless government may curse. I am inclined to agree with neoconservatives that gay civil rights legislation is not warranted *if* its main purpose and effect is simply a symbolic legitimizing of gays. See Jean Bethke Elshtain, "Homosexual Politics: The Paradox of Gay Liberation," *Salmagundi* (1982–1983) 255. [Author's note.]

[2]While I think that all assaults (or at least highly aggravated ones, as queerbashings almost always are) should *qua* assaults be actionable as civil suits, I do not think that they should be actionable (especially with punitive

In March of the same year, he had vetoed a civil rights bill which would have protected gays from private employment discrimination. Given the lived experience of gays, the former legislation will prove virtually pointless in the absence of the latter.

Questions for Discussion

1. In paragraphs 4–6 Mohr provides a hypothetical example of a situation in which two gay men would be unable to go to court without becoming "visible" and thus jeopardizing their jobs, shelter, and other needs. Does he portray the two gay men in a way that would earn them his readers' sympathy? Why do you suppose he has them be casual acquaintances who just met at a gay cruise bar, rather than monogamous lovers with a long-standing relationship?
2. What are the similarities and differences between victims of gay bashing who decline to press charges against their attackers and women rape victims who also decide not to take their assailants to court?
3. Aside from the example of Steve and Tom, and the example of same-sex sexual harassment that Mohr offers in paragraph 7, can you think of other types of cases in which gay people might fear exposure by going to court?
4. Mohr makes one of his hypothetical victims a public school teacher, a profession in which gay people have frequently suffered discrimination. What are the standard arguments against hiring gay teachers? In class discussion, inquire into these reasons.
5. If you assume that homosexuality is immoral, could you make a case that gay people forfeit their right to the protection of the courts? Should other "immoral" people forfeit such protection as well?

For Inquiry and Persuasion

Mohr's argument seems aimed at convincing his readership that gay people can, in effect, be blackmailed out of court by their lack of civil rights. If you agree, try to make a more persuasive argument, aimed at moving an audience to support the gay rights movement. You might look into the issue of gay-bashing; in 1992, for example, the number of reported incidents of violence against gay people reached a record high. To what extent might fear of exposure make gay people susceptible to violent attacks?

For Inquiry and Convincing

Inquire into the incidence of discrimination against gay men and lesbians in nonmilitary employment and into the arguments for and against extending the Civil Rights Act to protect homosexuals in the workplace. (You may want to

damages) *simply in virtue* of some political dimension of the assault, such that the only distinguishing feature between actionable and nonactionable assaults is simply the assailant's social or political beliefs and attitudes. Indeed, to the extent that a law draws a distinction based solely on the political dimension of some violent act, the law should be declared unconstitutional on first amendment grounds.

focus on one occupation, such as school-teaching or police work.) Decide whether you think the discrimination warrants this additional legislation. Take a position on this issue, determine what audience might disagree with you, and make a case to convince that audience you are right.

JONATHAN RAUCH

Beyond Oppression

Some writers have claimed that gay men and lesbians are an oppressed class. Jonathan Rauch sets forth what he sees as criteria for claiming oppression, and he argues that gay men and lesbians in the United States do not meet these criteria. What is Rauch's purpose in denying victim status to gay people?

At 10:30 on a weeknight in the spring of 1991, Glenn Cashmore was walking to his car on San Diego's University Avenue. He had just left the Soho coffee house in Hillcrest, a heavily gay neighborhood. He turned down Fourth Street and paused to look at the display in an optician's window. Someone shouted, "Hey, faggot!" He felt pain in his shoulder and turned in time to see a white Nissan speeding away. Someone had shot him, luckily only with a pellet gun. The pellet tore through the shirt and penetrated the skin. He went home and treated the wound with peroxide.

Later that year, on the night of December 13, a 17-year-old named John Wear and two other boys were headed to the Soho on University Avenue when a pair of young men set upon them, calling them "faggots." One boy escaped, another's face was gashed and Wear (who, his family said, was not gay) was stabbed. Cashmore went to the hospital to see him but, on arriving, was met with the news that Wear was dead.

This is life—not all of life, but an aspect of life—for gay people in today's America. Homosexuals are objects of scorn for teenagers and of sympathy or moral fear or hatred for adults. They grow up in confusion and bewilderment as children, then often pass into denial as young adults and sometimes remain frightened even into old age. They are persecuted by the military, are denied the sanctuary of publicly recognized marriage, occasionally are prosecuted outright for making love. If closeted, they live with fear of revelation; if open, they must daily negotiate a hundred delicate tactical issues. (Should I bring it up? Tell my boss? My co-workers? Wear a wedding band? Display my lover's picture?)

There is also AIDS and the stigma attached to it, though AIDS is not uniquely a problem of gay people. And there is the violence. One of my high school friends—an honors student at Brophy Prep, a prestigious Catholic high school in Phoenix—used to boast about his late-night exploits with a baseball bat at the "fag Denny's." I'm sure he was lying, but imagine the horror of being spoken to, and about, in that way.

If you ask gay people in America today whether homosexuals are op- 5
pressed, I think most would say yes. If you ask why, they would point to the sorts of facts that I just mentioned. The facts are not blinkable. Yet the oppression diagnosis is, for the most part, wrong.

Not wrong in the sense that life for American homosexuals is hunky-dory. It is not. But life is not terrible for most gay people, either, and it is becoming less terrible every year. The experience of gayness and the social status of homosexuals have changed rapidly in the last twenty years, largely owing to the courage of thousands who decided that they had had enough abuse and who demanded better. With change has come the time for a reassessment.

The standard political model sees homosexuals as an oppressed minority who must fight for their liberation through political action. But that model's usefulness is drawing to a close. It is ceasing to serve the interests of ordinary gay people, who ought to begin disengaging from it, even drop it. Otherwise, they will misread their position and lose their way, as too many minority groups have done already.

"Oppression" has become every minority's word for practically everything, a one-size-fits-all political designation used by anyone who feels unequal, aggrieved, or even uncomfortable. I propose a start toward restoring meaning to the notion of oppression by insisting on *objective* evidence. A sense of grievance or discomfort, however real, is not enough.

By now, human beings know a thing or two about oppression. Though it may, indeed, take many forms and work in different ways, there are objective signs you can look for. My own list would emphasize five main items. First, direct legal or governmental discrimination. Second, denial of political franchise—specifically, denial of the right to vote, organize, speak, or lobby. Third—and here we move beyond the strictly political—the systematic denial of education. Fourth, impoverishment relative to the non-oppressed population. And, fifth, a pattern of human rights violations, without recourse.

Any one or two of those five signposts may appear for reasons other than 10
oppression. There are a lot of reasons why a people may be poor, for instance. But where you see a minority that is legally barred from businesses and neighborhoods and jobs, that cannot vote, that is poor and poorly educated, and that lives in physical fear, you are looking at, for instance, the blacks of South Africa, or blacks of the American South until the 1960s; the Jews and homosexuals of Nazi Germany and Vichy France; the untouchable castes of India, the Kurds of Iraq, the women of Saudi Arabia, the women of America 100 years ago; for that matter, the entire population of the former Soviet Union and many Arab and African and Asian countries.

And gay people in America today? Criterion one—direct legal or governmental discrimination—is resoundingly met. Homosexual relations are illegal in twenty-three states, at least seven of which specifically single out acts between persons of the same sex. Gay marriage is not legally recognized anywhere. And the government hounds gay people from the military, not for what they do but for what they are.

Criterion two—denial of political franchise—is resoundingly not met. Not only do gay people vote, they are turning themselves into a constituency to be reckoned with and fought for. Otherwise, the Patrick Buchanans of the world would have sounded contemptuous of gay people at the Republican convention last year, rather than panicked by them. If gay votes didn't count, Bill Clinton would not have stuck his neck out on the military issue during the primary season (one of the bravest things any living politician has done).

Criterion three—denial of education—is also resoundingly not met. Overlooked Opinions Inc., a Chicago market-research company, has built a diverse national base of 35,000 gay men and lesbians, two-thirds of whom are either not out of the closet or are only marginally out, and has then randomly sampled them in surveys. It found that homosexuals had an average of 15.7 years of education, as against 12.7 years for the population as a whole. Obviously, the findings may be skewed if college-educated gay people are likelier to take part in surveys (though Overlooked Opinions said that results didn't follow degree of closetedness). Still, any claim that gay people are denied education appears ludicrous.

Criterion four—relative impoverishment—is also not met. In Overlooked Opinions' sample, gay men had an average household income of $51,624 and lesbians $42,755, compared with the national average of $36,800. Again, yuppie homosexuals may be more likely to answer survey questions than blue-collar ones. But, again, to call homosexuals an impoverished class would be silly.

Criterion five—human rights violations without recourse—is also, in the 15
end, not met, though here it's worth taking a moment to see why it is not. The number of gay bashings has probably increased in recent years (though it's hard to know, what with reporting vagaries), and, of course, many gay-bashers either aren't caught or aren't jailed. What too many gay people forget, though, is that these are problems that homosexuals have in common with non-gay Americans. Though many gay-bashers go free, so do many murderers. In the District of Columbia last year, the police identified suspects in fewer than half of all murders, to say nothing of assault cases.

And the fact is that anti-gay violence is just one part of a much broader pattern. Probably not coincidentally, the killing of John Wear happened in the context of a year, 1991, that broke San Diego's all-time homicide record (1992 was runner-up). Since 1965 the homicide rate in America has doubled, the violent crime arrest rate for juveniles has more than tripled; people now kill you to get your car, they kill you to get your shoes or your potato chips, they kill you because they can do it. A particularly ghastly fact is that homicide due to gunshot is now the second leading cause of death in high school-age kids, after car crashes. No surprise, then, that gay people are afraid. So is everyone else.

Chances are, indeed, that gay people's social class makes them safer, on average, than other urban minorities. Certainly their problem is small compared with what blacks face in inner-city Los Angeles or Chicago, where young black males are likelier to be killed than a U.S. soldier was in a tour of duty in Vietnam.

If any problem unites gay people with non-gay people, it is crime. If any issue does not call for special-interest pleading, this is it. Minority advocates, including gay ones, have blundered insensitively by trying to carve out hate-crime statutes and other special-interest crime laws instead of focusing on tougher measures against violence of all kinds. In trying to sensitize people to crimes aimed specifically at minorities, they are inadvertently desensitizing them to the vastly greater threat of crime against everyone. They contribute to the routinization of murder, which has now reached the point where news of a black girl spray-painted white makes the front pages, but news of a black girl murdered runs in a round-up on page D–6 ("Oh, another killing"). Yes, gay-bashing is a problem. But, no, it isn't oppression. It is, rather, an obscenely ordinary feature of the American experience.

Of course, homosexuals face unhappiness, discrimination, and hatred. But for everyone with a horror story to tell, there are others like an academic I know, a tenured professor who is married to his lover of fourteen years in every way but legally, who owns a split-level condo in Los Angeles, drives a Miata, enjoys prestige and success and love that would be the envy of millions of straight Americans. These things did not fall in his lap. He fought personal and professional battles, was passed over for jobs and left the closet when that was much riskier than it is today. Asked if he is oppressed, he says, "You're damn straight." But a mark of oppression is that most of its victims are not allowed to succeed; they are allowed only to fail. And this man is no mere token. He is one of a growing multitude of openly gay people who have overcome the past and, in doing so, changed the present.

"I'm a gay person, so I don't live in a free country," one highly successful 20
gay writer said recently, "and I don't think most straight people really sit down and realize that for gay people this is basically a totalitarian society in which we're barely tolerated." The reason straight people don't realize this is because it obviously isn't true. As more and more homosexuals come out of hiding, the reality of gay economic and political and educational achievement becomes more evident. And as that happens, gay people who insist they are oppressed will increasingly, and not always unfairly, come off as yuppie whiners, "victims" with $50,000 incomes and vacations in Europe. They may feel they are oppressed, but they will have a harder and harder time convincing the public.

They will distort their politics, too, twisting it into strained and impotent shapes. Scouring for oppressions with which to identify, activists are driven further and further afield. They grab fistfuls of random political demands and stuff them in their pockets. The original platform for April's March on Washington[1] called for, among other things, enforced bilingual education, "an end to genocide of all the indigenous peoples and their cultures," defense budget cuts, universal health care, a national needle exchange program, free substance-abuse treatment on demand, safe and affordable abortion, more money for breast cancer "and other cancers particular to women," "unrestricted, safe and affordable alternative

[1]A major gay rights demonstration was held in Washington, D.C., on April 25, 1993.

insemination," health care for the "differently-abled and physically challenged," and "an end to poverty." Here was the oppression-entitlement mentality gone haywire.

Worst of all, oppression politics distorts the face of gay America itself. It encourages people to forget that homosexuality isn't hell. As the AIDS crisis has so movingly shown, gay people have built the kind of community that evaporated for many non-gay Americans decades ago. You don't see straight volunteers queuing up to change cancer patients' bedpans and deliver their groceries. Gay people—and unmarried people generally—are at a disadvantage in the top echelons of corporate America, but, on the other hand, they have achieved dazzlingly in culture and business and much else. They lead lives of richness and competence and infinite variety, lives that are not miserable or squashed.

The insistence that gay people are oppressed is most damaging, in the end, because it implies that to be gay is to suffer. It affirms what so many straight people, even sympathetic ones, believe in their hearts: that homosexuals are pitiable. That alone is reason to junk the oppression model, preferably sooner instead of later.

If the oppression model is failing, what is the right model? Not that of an oppressed people seeking redemption through political action; rather, that of an ostracized people seeking redemption through personal action. What do you do about misguided ostracism? The most important thing is what Glenn Cashmore did. After John Wear's murder, he came out of the closet. He wrote an article in the *Los Angeles Times* denouncing his own years of silence. He stepped into the circle of people who are what used to be called known homosexuals.

25 This makes a difference. *The New York Times* conducted a poll on homosexuals this year and found that people who had a gay family member or close friend "were much more tolerant and accepting." Whereas oppression politics fails because it denies reality, positive personal example works because it demonstrates reality. "We're here, we're queer, get used to it," Queer Nation's chant,[1] is not only a brilliant slogan. It is a strategy. It is, in some ways, *the* strategy. To move away from oppression politics is not to sit quietly. It is often to hold hands in public or take a lover to the company Christmas party, sometimes to stage kiss-ins, always to be unashamed. It is to make of honesty a kind of activism.

Gay Americans should emulate Jewish Americans, who have it about right. Jews recognize that to many Americans we will always seem different (and we are, in some ways, different). We grow up being fed "their" culture in school, in daily life, even in the calendar. It never stops. For a full month of every year, every radio program and shop window reminds you that this is, culturally, a Christian nation (no, not Judeo-Christian). Jews could resent this, but most of us choose not to, because, by way of compensation, we think hard, we work hard, we are cohesive, we are interesting. We recognize that minorities will always face special

[1]Queer Nation is a gay political organization, many members of which are in their twenties, that advocates a highly visible gay presence in society.

burdens of adjustment, but we also understand that with those burdens come rewards of community and spirit and struggle. We recognize that there will always be a minority of Americans who hate us, but we also understand that, so long as we stay watchful, this hateful minority is more pathetic than threatening. We watch it; we fight it when it lashes out; but we do not organize our personal and political lives around it.

Gay people's main weapons are ones we already possess. In America, our main enemies are superstition and hate. Superstition is extinguished by public criticism and by the power of moral example. Political activists always underestimate the power of criticism and moral example to change people's minds, and they always overestimate the power of law and force. As for hate, the way to fight it is with love. And that we have in abundance.

Questions for Discussion

1. Rauch acknowledges the arguments of his opposition in paragraphs 1–5, but he denies that any of the examples constitute "*objective* evidence" of oppression (paragraph 8). Would you agree?
2. Does Rauch offer enough evidence to show that homosexuals meet only one of his criteria for claiming oppression? Could you raise any questions about the five criteria that he sets up? Can you think of additional criteria?
3. In paragraph 24, Rauch argues that gay people work on the model that they are ostracized, not oppressed. What is the difference?
4. Rauch suggests that gay people can improve their situation through personal rather than political action. What is he advocating? Do you think his plan will work?

For Convincing

Many of the arguments in this chapter suggest or deny that parallels exist between racism and discrimination against homosexuals. Make your own case for or against this parallel, using some of the readings here as well as additional sources and evidence.

For Further Research and Discussion

1. One large area of debate related to homosexual rights involves marriage, or the legal benefits of marriage: Our society bestows many advantages on married couples in the form of tax breaks, employer-sponsored insurance coverage for spouses, inheritance rights, even the right not to be forced to testify in court against one's mate. There is, further, the symbolic statement that marriage makes about a couple's commitment to one another. In 1967, the Supreme Court called marriage "one of the basic civil rights of man," yet no state permits individuals of the same sex to marry. Inquire into this issue, and be ready to report to the class on the range of opinions about marriage and domestic partnerships. (Gay people themselves are divided on the question.)

2. Inquire into the latest research on the causes of homosexuality. What interpretation do most gay people seem to accept on this matter? Your class may want to discuss whether, if a clear case could be made for biological causation, that would be likely to influence any of the arguments about homophobia and gay rights.

Additional Suggestions for Writing

1. *Inquiry and Convincing.* Based on the research suggested previously regarding views of gay marriage, write an exploratory essay in which you discuss areas of agreement and disagreement. Conclude with a statement of your own position on this issue, indicating which reasons uncovered in your research best help you support that position. Then go on to draft and revise a case for an opposing audience.
2. *Persuasion.* Jeffrey Nickel (pages 486–488) points out that homophobia is something children learn at an early age in our society. Some school districts have devised curriculums aimed at encouraging greater tolerance for homosexuals, through, for example, storybooks that depict children who have "two mommies" or "two daddies." This aspect of New York City's "Rainbow Curriculum" was quite controversial.

   Do research into educational curriculums that deal with homosexuality. Find out where such curriculums have been tried, and what the pro and con arguments are. If you decide such curriculums would not be effective in reducing homophobia or that reducing homophobia should not be a function of the schools, write a persuasive argument against instituting one. If you decide that they are a good idea, make a persuasive argument for some specific course of action.
3. *Mediation.* The AIDS epidemic has focused public attention on questions of rights and responsibilities. Some gay advocates argue that it is the responsibility of the government and the medical community to find a vaccine to prevent AIDS so that people need not live in terror if they fail to follow all the guidelines for safe sex. At the other extreme, people argue that since AIDS is a preventable disease, it is the responsibility of each adult to see that he or she is not exposed through risky behavior, and the government and medical community ought to give their full attention to life-threatening diseases that strike at random. Do research into these arguments about AIDS research and spending, and the range of viewpoints in between. Write a mediatory essay that suggests a position all sides could find reasonable.

CHAPTER SEVENTEEN

Political Correctness and Multiculturalism

"Political correctness" and "multiculturalism" refer to distinct but closely related issues. The first, often abbreviated "p. c.," is at one level an effort to eliminate language offensive to women, racial and ethnic minorities, and other groups—such as the disabled and homosexuals—who have been misunderstood or shunned. At another, more complex level, political correctness raises questions about whether offensive and unpopular ideas ought to be expressed or discussed on college campuses. Political correctness, then, is usually conceived as a free speech or academic freedom issue.

In contrast, multiculturalism is usually debated as a curricular issue. The United States is and always has been a nation composed of many peoples. But until recently study of the history, literature, and culture of the United States has been biased toward Europe, especially northern Europe, and in particular toward the British heritage. Besides being, as the multiculturalists argue, Eurocentric, liberal studies are mostly taught by white males who assign mostly works by white males, so that the cultural bias toward the West is also a racial and gender bias as well. The contribution of women, blacks, native Americans, Latino culture, and Asian culture (among others) has been ignored or minimized. The thrust of multiculturalism is to create texts and syllabi that include the once excluded, to add to the canon significant works by women and minorities, and to encourage new programs devoted to women's and minority studies as well as multicultural approaches to traditional courses.

Although debated in different contexts, political correctness and multiculturalism are both rooted in economics, demographics, and social movements. Basically, the Civil Rights Movement of the sixties led to programs such as integration and affirmative action, which opened American society to groups excluded from social, economic, and political power. Ideals of diversity and nonprejudicial treatment took hold. At the same time, the population of minority groups has been growing much faster than the Anglo majority, so that sometime in the next century it is predicted white Americans will no longer be the majority.

Consequently, American business must look to women and minorities more and more as both employees and customers, and the demands of a world economy mean that how well we cope with difference in the United States and abroad will determine in part how competitive we will be able to remain.

Political correctness is an issue, then, because stereotypes and prejudices persist in an age when Americans are no longer segregated by race, class, and gender to anything like the degree they were only thirty years ago. Multiculturalism is an issue because the story of America can no longer be the story of a white, male-dominated society. Women and what we now call minorities should always have been a significant part of the story; understandably, the once ignored and marginalized want to learn about themselves and want others to know and value their past and present contributions.

But what exactly is at issue in the debates over political correctness and multiculturalism?

The central question is, What kind of society do we want? Traditional thinkers favor assimilation, based on the metaphor of the "melting pot." Their ideal is to create a common American culture out of the many cultures represented in American society, overcoming difference through unity. Others argue that assimilation has never included everyone, that what a "common American culture" really means is the continued dominance of white European culture; they believe that, rather than overcoming difference, we should preserve and celebrate difference as the source of the distinctive nature and strength of the United States.

Closely related to this general social question are questions about curriculum: What should be taught? Should students be required to take a course or courses in Western civilization? Should the curriculum include at least one mandatory course in a non-Western culture? What role should Women's Studies, African-American studies, and so forth play in the basic college curriculum?

If the content of the curriculum is widely debated, so also is the attitude of those teaching the courses. Some say, in fact, that the question of what should be taught matters less than two other questions: By whom, and in what manner? Traditional scholars tend to assume their courses are apolitical, their stances toward the subject matter essentially neutral and unbiased. Increasingly, however, this view has been called into question. Many instructors now contend that bias of some sort is unavoidable, that teachers should understand their biases, acknowledge them openly in class, and encourage dissent and the expression of other points of view. More radical academics argue further that all teaching is advocacy and see their role in the classroom as serving to further social, economic, and political change. Clearly this facet of the issue boils down to the question, What role or roles should teachers assume in class and in other interactions with students?

Finally, there is the issue of free speech itself. Many colleges now have speech codes, written statements prohibiting discriminatory language. Are such codes a violation of free speech? With or without codes and penalties for offensive language, what forms of expression ought to be condemned and discouraged?

Universities are supposed to be places where all ideas, popular or unpopular, can be aired and freely discussed. Does the current climate on college campuses discourage serious discussion of some topics? For example, can a white, male professor criticize a black or female colleague or oppose affirmative action or the Equal Rights Amendment without being accused of racism or sexism?

Although the context and focus of discussion are different, political correctness and multiculturalism come together in one enbracing question: What should education, especially higher education, be and do? As we think our way through the readings that follow we should return again and again to this difficult question.

ARTHUR SCHLESINGER, JR.

The Cult of Ethnicity, Good and Bad

We begin with a brief essay that addresses the broad question, What kind of society do we want? Developing his answer in the context of world-wide ethnic and racial conflict, Schlesinger argues that the United States must continue to function as a model of diverse people living together in relative harmony.

This essay is of interest on a number of counts. First, the essay itself is eloquent and powerful. Second, it appeared in Time, *the country's best-known news magazine, popular with a wide audience. Third, the author is an internationally renowned historian whose opinions carry more weight than most. And, finally, Schlesinger is a political moderate with liberal leanings, which means that his very traditional view of American society cannot be lightly dismissed as conservative posturing.*

THE HISTORY of the world has been in great part the history of the mixing of peoples. Modern communication and transport accelerate mass migrations from one continent to another. Ethnic and racial diversity is more than ever a salient fact of the age.

But what happens when people of different origins, speaking different languages, and professing different religions, inhabit the same locality and live under the same political sovereignty? Ethnic and racial conflict—far more than ideological conflict—is the explosive problem of our times.

On every side today ethnicity is breaking up nations. The Soviet Union, India, Yugoslavia, Ethiopia, are all in crisis. Ethnic tensions disturb and divide Sri Lanka, Burma, Indonesia, Iraq, Cyprus, Nigeria, Angola, Lebanon, Guyana, Trinidad—you name it. Even nations as stable and civilized as Britain and France, Belgium and Spain, face growing ethnic troubles. Is there any large multiethnic state that can be made to work?

The answer to that question has been, until recently, the United States. "No other nation," Margaret Thatcher has said, "has so successfully combined people of different races and nations within a single culture." How have Americans succeeded in pulling off this almost unprecedented trick?

We have always been a multiethnic country. Hector St. John de Crève- 5
coeur, who came from France in the 18th century, marveled at the astonishing diversity of the settlers—"a mixture of English, Scotch, Irish, French, Dutch, Germans, and Swedes . . . this promiscuous breed." He propounded a famous question: "What then is the American, this new man?" And he gave a famous answer: "Here individuals of all nations are melted into a new race of men." *E pluribus unum.*

The U.S. escaped the divisiveness of a multiethnic society by a brilliant solution: the creation of a brand-new national identity. The point of America was not to preserve old cultures but to forge a new, *American* culture. "By an intermixture with our people," President George Washington told Vice President John Adams, immigrants will "get assimilated to our customs, measures, and laws: in a word, soon become one people." This was the ideal that a century later Israel Zangwill crystallized in the title of his popular 1908 play *The Melting Pot*. And no institution was more potent in molding Crèvecoeur's "promiscuous breed" into Washington's "one people" than the American public school.

The new American nationality was inescapably English in language, ideas, and institutions. The pot did not melt everybody, not even all the white immigrants: Deeply bred racism put black Americans, yellow Americans, red Americans, and brown Americans well outside the pale. Still, the infusion of other stocks, even of nonwhite stocks, and the experience of the New World reconfigured the British legacy and made the U.S., as we all know, a very different country from Britain.

In the 20th century, new immigration laws altered the composition of the American people, and a cult of ethnicity erupted both among non-Anglo whites and among nonwhite minorities. This had many healthy consequences. The American culture at last began to give shamefully overdue recognition to the achievements of groups subordinated and spurned during the high noon of Anglo dominance, and it began to acknowledge the great swirling world beyond Europe. Americans acquired a more complex and invigorating sense of their world—and of themselves.

But, pressed too far, the cult of ethnicity has unhealthy consequences. It gives rise, for example, to the conception of the U.S. as a nation composed not of individuals making their own choices but of inviolable ethnic and racial groups. It rejects the historic American goals of assimilation and integration. And, in an excess of zeal, well-intentioned people seek to transform our system of education from a means of creating "one people" into a means of promoting, celebrating, and perpetuating separate ethnic origins and identities. The balance is shifting from *unum* to *pluribus*.

10 That is the issue that lies behind the hullabaloo over "multiculturalism" and "political correctness," the attack on the "Eurocentric" curriculum, and the rise of the notion that history and literature should be taught not as disciplines but as therapies whose function is to raise minority self-esteem. Group separatism crystallizes the differences, magnifies tensions, intensifies hostilities. Europe—the unique source of the liberating ideas of democracy, civil liberties, and human rights—is portrayed as the root of all evil, and non-European cultures, their own many crimes deleted, are presented as the means of redemption.

I don't want to sound apocalyptic about these developments. Education is always in ferment, and a good thing too. The situation in our universities, I am confident, will soon right itself. But the impact of separatist pressures on our public schools is more troubling. If a Kleagle of the Ku Klux Klan wanted to use the schools to disable and handicap black Americans, he could hardly come up with anything more effective than the "Afrocentric" curriculum. And if separatist tendencies go unchecked, the result can only be the fragmentation, resegregation, and tribalization of American life.

I remain optimistic. My impression is that the historic forces driving toward "one people" have not lost their power. The eruption of ethnicity is, I believe, a rather superficial enthusiasm stirred by romantic ideologues on the one hand and by unscrupulous con men on the other: self-appointed spokesmen whose claim to represent their minority groups is carelessly accepted by the media. Most American-born members of minority groups, white or nonwhite, see themselves primarily as Americans rather than primarily as members of one or another ethnic group. A notable indicator today is the rate of intermarriage across ethnic lines, across religious lines, even (increasingly) across racial lines. "We Americans," said Theodore Roosevelt, "are children of the crucible."

The growing diversity of the American population makes the quest for unifying ideals and a common culture all the more urgent. In a world savagely rent by ethnic and racial antagonisms, the U.S. must continue as an example of how a highly differentiated society holds itself together.

Questions for Discussion

1. Judging from the essay itself, what audience did Schlesinger have in mind? How does he try to persuade this audience? Do you think his attempt succeeds?
2. What does the word "cult" mean? What connotations does it have? Do you see any evidence of a "cult of ethnicity" in the United States?
3. In paragraph 9 Schlesinger refers to the traditional American value of individualism. Are people assimilated into society as individuals or as part of groups? Are we really "individuals making [our] own choices"? To what extent are our choices governed by our gender, class, race, or ethnic identity? Do you think an emphasis on ethnicity is antithetical to individualism?
4. In paragraph 12 Schlesinger refers to "romantic ideologues." What does he mean by "romantic"? He also refers to "unscrupulous con men." Can you think of any individuals that fit the description—"self-appointed spokesmen whose claim to represent their minority groups is carelessly accepted by the media"?

For Convincing

Find out as much as you can about the Afrocentric curriculum Schlesinger refers to in paragraph 11. Write an essay evaluating its content and significance. Will it, as Schlesinger claims, "disable and handicap black Americans"?

GARRY TRUDEAU

Cartoon

In a series of Doonesbury cartoons, Garry Trudeau followed the efforts of one professor to combat grade inflation at the mythical Walden College. In the strips below, Professor Deadman gives a B+ and finds himself confronted by one version of Arthur Schlesinger's "cult of ethnicity."

Doonesbury BY GARRY TRUDEAU

For Discussion

In what specific ways do Trudeau's cartoons make an argument similar to Schlesinger's?

WHOSE CULTURE IS IT, ANYWAY?

The two short essays that follow appeared originally on the op-ed pages of the New York Times *in 1991. Under the title "Dialogue: The Curriculum Wars," the editors arranged these two pieces as contrasting answers to the question "Whose Culture Is It, Anyway?"*

Professor Gates, a black scholar who is a distinguished critic and chair of African-American Studies at Harvard, holds that "culture is always a conversation among different voices" (paragraph 5). In his view, Western culture is only one of many cultures in "a community of civilizations."

Professor Kagan, a white scholar who is dean of Yale College (the undergraduate, liberal arts college of Yale University), holds that "Western culture and institutions are the most powerful paradigm in the world" (paragraph 10). For him, then, the West is not just one among many civilizations, but a model for the rest.

In these two essays we have, in miniature, the basic alternatives of thought about liberal arts curriculum today. Later essays in this chapter develop parts of these two views in greater detail.

HENRY LOUIS GATES, JR.

It's Not Just Anglo-Saxon

I RECENTLY asked the dean of a prestigious liberal arts college if his school would ever have, as Berkeley has, a 70 percent nonwhite enrollment. "Never," he replied. "That would completely alter our identity as a center of the liberal arts."

The assumption that there is a deep connection between the shape of a college's curriculum and the ethnic composition of its students reflects a disquieting trend in education. Political representation has been confused with the "representation" of various ethnic identities in the curriculum.

The cultural right wing, threatened by demographic changes and the ensuing demands for curricular change, has retreated to intellectual protectionism, arguing for a great and inviolable "Western tradition," which contains the seeds, fruit, and flowers of the very best thought or uttered in history. (Typically, Mortimer Adler has ventured that blacks "wrote no good books.") Meanwhile, the cultural left demands changes to accord with population shifts in gender and ethnicity. Both are wrongheaded.

I am just as concerned that so many of my colleagues feel that the rationale for a diverse curriculum depends on the latest Census Bureau report as I am that those opposed see pluralism as forestalling the possibility of a communal "American" identity. To them, the study of our diverse cultures must lead to "tribalism" and "fragmentation."

5 The cultural diversity movement arose partly because of the fragmentation of society by ethnicity, class, and gender. To make it the culprit for this fragmentation is to mistake effect for cause. A curriculum that reflects the achievement of the world's great cultures, not merely the West's, is not "politicized"; rather it situates the West as one of a community of civilizations. After all, culture is always a conversation among different voices.

To insist that we "master our own culture" before learning others—as Arthur Schlesinger Jr. has proposed—only defers the vexed question: What gets to count as "our" culture? What has passed as "common culture" has been an Anglo-American regional culture, masking itself as universal. Significantly different cultures sought refuge underground.

Writing in 1903, W.E.B. Du Bois expressed his dream of a high culture that would transcend the color line: "I sit with Shakespeare and he winces not." But the dream was not open to all. "Is this the life you grudge us," he concluded, "O knightly America?" For him, the humanities were a conduit into a republic of letters enabling escape from racism and ethnic chauvinism. Yet no one played a more crucial role than he in excavating the long buried heritage of Africans and African-Americans.

The fact of one's ethnicity, for any American of color, is never neutral: One's public treatment, and public behavior, are shaped in large part by one's perceived ethnic identity, just as by one's gender. To demand that Americans shuck their cultural heritages and homogenize themselves into a "universal" WASP culture is to dream of an America in cultural white face, and that just won't do.

So it's only when we're free to explore the complexities of our hyphenated culture that we can discover what a genuinely common American culture might actually look like.

10 Is multiculturalism un-American? Herman Melville didn't think so. As he wrote: "We are not a narrow tribe, no. . . . We are not a nation, so much as a world." We're all ethnics; the challenge of transcending ethnic chauvinism is one we all face.

We've entrusted our schools with the fashioning and refashioning of a democratic polity. That's why schooling has always been a matter of political judgment. But in a nation that has theorized itself as plural from its inception, schools have a very special task.

Our society won't survive without the values of tolerance, and cultural tolerance comes to nothing without cultural understanding. The challenge facing America will be the shaping of a truly common public culture, one responsive to the long-silenced cultures of color. If we relinquish the ideal of America as a plural nation, we've abandoned the very experiment America represents. And that is too great a price to pay.

DONALD KAGAN

Western Values Are Central

AMERICANS DO not share a common ancestry and a common blood. What they have in common is a system of laws and beliefs that shaped the establishment of the country, a system developed within the context of Western civilization.

It should be obvious, then, that all Americans need to learn about that civilization to understand our country's origins and share in its heritage, purposes, and character.

At present, however, the study of Western civilization is under attack. We are told we should not give a privileged place in the curriculum to the great works of its history and literature. At the extremes of this onslaught, the civilization, and its study, is attacked because of its history of slavery, imperialism, racial prejudice, addiction to war, its exclusion of women and people not of the white race from its rights and privileges.

Some criticize its study as narrow, limiting, arrogant, and discriminatory, asserting that it has little or no value for those of different cultural origins. Others concede the value of the Western heritage but regard it as only one among many, all of which have equal claim to our attention.

These attacks are unsound. It is necessary to place Western civilization and 5
the culture to which it has given rise at the center of our studies, and we fail to do so at the peril of our students, country, and the hopes for a democratic, liberal society.

The assault on Western civilization badly distorts history. Its flaws are real enough, but they are common to almost all the civilizations on any continent at any time in history.

What is remarkable about the Western heritage is the important ways in which it has departed from the common experience. More than any other, it has asserted the claims of the individual against those of the state, limiting its power and creating a realm of privacy into which it cannot penetrate.

By means of the philosophical, scientific, agricultural, and industrial revolutions in the West, human beings have been able to produce and multiply the things needed for life so as to make survival and prosperity possible for ever-increasing numbers, without rapacious ways and at a level that permits dignity and independence. It is the champion of representative democracy as the normal way for human beings to govern themselves. It has produced the theory and practice of the separation of church from state, protecting each from the other and creating a free and safe place for the individual conscience.

At its core is a tolerance and respect for diversity unknown in most cultures. One of its most telling characteristics is its encouragement of criticism of itself and its ways. The university itself, a specially sheltered place for such self-examination, is a Western phenomenon only partially assimilated in other cultures.

Western culture and institutions are the most powerful paradigm in the world. As they increasingly become the objects of emulation by peoples everywhere, their study becomes essential for those of all nations who wish to understand their nature and origins. 10

Happily, student bodies have grown vastly more diverse. Less happily, students see themselves increasingly as parts of groups, distinct from other groups. They often feel pressure to communicate mainly with others like themselves in the group and to pursue intellectual interests that are of particular importance to it. But a liberal education needs to bring about a challenge to the ideas, habits, and attitudes students bring with them.

Take pride in your family and in the culture they and your forebears have brought to our shores. Learn as much as you can about that culture. Learn as much as you can of what the particular cultures of others have to offer. But do not fail to learn the great traditions that are the special gifts of Western civilization.

Questions for Discussion

1. "The point of America," Arthur Schlesinger claims in the first essay in this chapter, "was not to preserve old cultures but to forge a new, *American* culture" (paragraph 6). Gates challenges the idea of a common culture by asking, "What gets to count as 'our' culture?" (paragraph 6). How does he answer his own question? Do you agree that "[w]hat has passed as 'common culture' has been an Anglo-American regional culture" pretending to be universal?
2. Kagan claims that the center of Western values "is a tolerance and respect for diversity unknown in most cultures" (paragraph 9). Drawing on your own experience of living in the United States, would you say we show tolerance and respect for difference? In the same paragraph Kagan also claims that Western culture encourages the "criticism of itself and its ways." Has your own education up to now helped you to develop a critical attitude in thinking about U.S. society and culture?
3. These two articles are billed as dialogue, but they are really two monologues. What does Gates say that Kagan might agree with? What does Kagan say that Gates might agree with? That is, what common ground or points of agreement exist that would permit genuine dialogue rather than a mere exchange of opinion?

For Research, Inquiry, and Convincing

Interview students and faculty involved in gender and ethnic studies on your campus. Based on these interviews and your own experience with college life, write an essay responding to the charge that such programs promote tribalism and fragmentation. Do students, as Kagan says, "see themselves increasingly as parts of groups, distinct from other groups" (paragraph 11)?

For Dialogue

Start a genuine dialogue with and between Gates and Kagan. Half the class should take Gates's statement, the other half Kagan's. Using the suggestions for dialogue in Chapter 5 (pages 44–46 and 48–52), interrogate each separately. Then, as a class or in groups, find questions Gates might ask of Kagan and vice versa.

Summarize the results of this dialogue in your writer's notebook.

DIANE RAVITCH

Multiculturalism Yes, Particularism No

The following essay appeared in The Chronicle of Higher Education, *a weekly newspaper intended for college teachers and administrators and a useful source of information about all matters that effect higher education. The last page of each issue, called "Point of View," is reserved for essays, like this one, which take a stance on some controversial question.*

A historian of education at Teachers College of Columbia University, Professor Ravitch has written extensively about multiculturalism, her perspective drawing fire from all sides. On the one hand, like Arthur Schlesinger and Donald Kagan, she defends the study of Western culture; but unlike most traditionalists, she stresses the multicultural background of American culture and supports multicultural education. On the other hand, like Henry Louis Gates, she defends democratic pluralism and sees our culture as "a diversity of voices"; but she is nevertheless critical of certain attitudes in cultural studies and clearly rejects what she calls particularism in education. In short, her argument falls somewhere in between traditionalist and reformer.

THE CONTROVERSY at Stanford in 1988 over changes in a required course in Western culture has grown into a national debate about the issue of multiculturalism. College campuses, school districts, and even state boards of education are presently examining what is taught and asking whether the history and literature that are offered reflect accurately the different cultural strands in our society and our world.

Unfortunately, the Stanford battle cast the argument in the wrong terms. Defenders of the existing Western-culture course opposed those who advocated adding works by women and members of minority groups and thus created the impression that Western culture excludes the voices of people who are female, black, Hispanic, and Asian. That image is, of course, ridiculous; we need only look around to see that all of these groups are very much part of Western culture and that their members have made important contributions to its literary and historical traditions.

The debate over multiculturalism follows a generation of scholarship that has enriched our knowledge about the historical experiences of women, blacks, and members of other minority groups in various societies. As a result of the new scholarship, our schools and our institutions of learning have in recent years begun to embrace what Catharine R. Stimpson of Rutgers University has called "cultural democracy," a recognition that we must listen to "a diversity of voices" to understand our culture, past and present. Teachers of history and literature have discovered that it is not very difficult, in fact that it is rewarding, to broaden their perspective beyond the one that they learned when they were in school.

Of course, students should still study Western culture, and they should learn about the emergence of the democratic ideology and the concept of individual freedom that have been so crucial in the history of the world. But they must also learn about the cultures of Asia, Africa, and Latin America. These all represent complex civilizations, containing many cultural groups and different languages.

But today, when educators argue about multiculturalism, they are usually 5
not talking about disciplined study of other major civilizations. They refer instead to American culture, which, because it is ours and because it is relatively new, is vulnerable to reconstruction, deconstruction, and revision. From which perspective should it be taught? Who should be included?

The real issue on campus and in the classroom is not whether there will be multiculturalism, but what kind of multiculturalism there will be. Two versions presently compete for dominance in the teaching of American culture. One approach reflects cultural pluralism and accepts diversity as a fact; the other represents particularism and demands loyalty to a particular group. The two coexist uncomfortably, because they are not different by degree. In fact, they are opposite in spirit and in purpose.

The pluralist approach to American culture recognizes that the common culture has been shaped by the interaction of the nation's many diverse cultural elements. It sees American culture as the creation of many groups of immigrants, American Indians, Africans, and their descendants. American music, art, literature, language, food, clothing, sports, holidays, and customs all demonstrate the comingling of diverse cultures in one nation. Paradoxical though it may seem, the United States has a common culture that is multicultural.

The particularist approach to American culture can be seen most vividly in ethnic-studies programs whose goal is to "raise the self-esteem" of students by providing role models. Such courses are animated by a spirit of filiopietism and by fundamentalist notions of racial and ethnic purity. Students are encouraged to believe that something in their blood or their race memory or their cultural D.N.A. defines who they are and what they may achieve. Particularists seek to attach their students to their ancestral homelands as the source of their personal identity and authentic culture.

The pluralists promote a broader interpretation of common American culture by recognizing first that there *is* a common culture, and second that it has been created by many different groups. At its most basic, our common culture is a civic culture, shaped by our Constitution, our commitment to democratic values, and our historical experience as a nation. In addition, our very heterogeneity sets us apart from most other nations and creates styles of expression that the rest of the world perceives as distinctively American. The pluralists seek due recognition for the ways in which the nation's many racial, ethnic, and cultural groups have transformed the national culture. They say, in effect, "American culture belongs to all of us, and we remake it in every generation." The cohesive element in the pluralistic approach is the clear acknowledgement that, whatever our differences, we are all human. The thread that binds us is our common humanity, transcending race, color, ethnicity, language, and religion.

Particularists have no interest in extending American culture: Indeed, they deny that a common culture exists. They do not appeal to the common good, because their idea of community is defined along racial or ethnic lines. They reject any accommodation among groups, any interactions that blur the distinct lines among them. They espouse a version of history in which everyone is either the descendant of victims or of oppressors. By doing so, ancient hatreds are fanned and recreated in each generation. 10

There is not a fine line that divides pluralism from particularism; they are as different as secularism and sectarianism. The pluralist approach to teaching culture accords with traditional academic ethics, in that students learn to approach their subject with a critical eye. They learn *about* the subject, and they know that they may criticize its strengths and weaknesses without offending the professor. For example, in a traditional academic setting, the object of learning about Confucianism or Islam or Judaism is to study its history and philosophy, not to become an adherent of the faith. Similarly, there is a valid place for special courses and programs in black studies, women's studies, gay studies, or any other kind of cultural studies, so long as they are taught critically and not as doctrinal faiths.

By contrast, particularism has spurred a separatist ethic in higher education. In the particularist classroom, students are taught to believe in the subject, to immerse themselves in its truths, and to champion them against skeptics. They are taught to believe, not to doubt or criticize. In this sense, particularism resembles a religious approach to teaching. Students are taught a faith, and the professor expects them to believe what he or she believes. In this sense, particularism resembles a sectarian approach to teaching.

On our campuses today, courses in black studies, Asian studies, and all other special cultural studies should welcome all students, not just in theory but in fact. The severing of such courses from established disciplines probably encourages separatism and ideological extremism. All too often, even though the catalogue implies that such courses are for everyone, the particularism of the professor or the department may discourage students who are not members of the in-group from signing up. The tendency to turn such courses into separatist enclaves violates a major purpose of higher education, which is to broaden one's understanding of the world. No special status should be accorded to students who are of the group being studied, nor should scholars be expected to specialize only in the culture of their ancestors.

The essential difference between pluralism and particularism is that the former actively combats ethnocentrism and the latter purposefully teaches it. Ethnocentrism is the specter that has been haunting the world for centuries—causing war, injustice, and civil conflict. Ethnocentrism tells people that they must trust and accept only members of their own group. It tells them that they must immerse themselves in their own culture and close their minds to others. It says to members of the group that they have nothing in common with people who are of a different race, a different religion, a different culture. It breeds hatred and distrust.

15 Ethnocentrism has no place in our schools and institutions of higher learning. Academic institutions have an obligation to introduce students to a larger culture than the one they learned at home.

The purpose of education is not to reproduce and reinforce the prejudices of our inherited culture. Education must prepare people to live in a world of competing ideas and values, to be able to work with people from different backgrounds, to be able to question their own beliefs.

The novelist Salman Rushdie's recent comments are germane to the ongoing debate about multiculturalism.[1] This past summer, he published an essay called "In Good Faith," his reflections on the events that forced him into isolation. Mr. Rushdie wrote that those who oppose his novel "are of the opinion that intermingling with a different culture will inevitably weaken and ruin their own." He goes on to say:

> *The Satanic Verses* celebrates hybridity, impurity, intermingling, the transformation that comes of new and unexpected combinations of human beings, cultures, ideas, politics, movies, songs. It rejoices in mongrelization and fears the absolutism of the Pure. Melange, hotchpotch, a bit of this and a bit of that is *how newness enters the world.*

True believers in all societies have never been comfortable with the kinds of ideas and activities found in the university. They have seen the university as a citadel of doubt, skepticism, nonconformity, unorthodoxy, and dissent; a place where young people learn to question the faith of the elders; a safe haven for those who criticize the conventional wisdom.

And so it should remain.

Questions for Discussion

1. According to Ravitch, "American culture belongs to all of us, and we remake it in every generation." She wants us to recognize a common humanity that rises above our differences (paragraph 9). Read or reread Gates's essay, paying special attention to paragraphs 7–11. How would Gates respond to what Ravitch says in paragraph 9?
2. Is it possible to set up a program in African-American studies, women's studies, gay and lesbian studies, or any other cultural studies, without some degree of separatism? Given the historic exclusion of these groups from higher education, is concern for self-esteem necessary or desirable? Can a critical attitude be combined with raising self-esteem and creating role models?
3. Ravitch calls those holding the position opposed to hers as "particularists." What persuasive impact does this label have? How might the opposition characterize itself?

[1]Indian-born Salman Rushdie's 1988 novel *The Satanic Verses* was denounced as blasphemy against Islam, and Iran's Ayatollah Khomeini called for Rushdie's assassination. Rushdie continues to live in hiding.

For Inquiry

Write an essay explaining how Ravitch's point of view corresponds with and departs from the views of Schlesinger, Gates, and Kagan. Conclude your analysis with a statement of your own point of view and your reasons for holding it.

See Chapter 5 for guidance on exploratory essays.

For Persuasion and Dialogue

All the writers represented in this chapter would agree with the point Ravitch makes in paragraph 16 of her essay. Has your education so far helped to prepare you "to live in a world of competing ideas and values, to be able to work with people from different backgrounds, [and] to be able to question [your] own beliefs"? If not, propose changes in the curriculum of your high school that would help achieve these ends. Direct your case to members of your high school faculty and administration; send a copy of your essay to them with a cover letter asking for a response. Discuss their response with them, if possible, and with your class.

JOHN E. VAN DE WETERING

Political Correctness: The Insult and the Injury

The following argument differs from the others in this chapter on several counts. Most importantly, it is not an essay but rather the text of a speech, probably read by its author. As a speech, it is adapted to a very specific audience and occasion—a group of business people at a Rotary Club meeting in Rochester, New York, on September 3, 1991.

Also different is the status of the author. Whereas Schlesinger, Gates, Kagan, and Ravitch are all prominent voices in the debate over political correctness and multiculturalism, John Van De Wetering is not. President of the State University of New York at Brockport, he is a university administrator whose task here was to explain and defend political correctness and multiculturalism to practical, fairly conservative business people whose knowledge of the issue was probably limited mainly to negative accounts in the popular press. His audience may be respectful of him but not likely to be favorably inclined toward a defense of political correctness and multiculturalism.

As I look around the room, I can see a flicker of recognition. How many of you have heard of the term political correctness? That's quite a few. And how many of you have read about political correctness in the news?

I'd like to spend the next ten minutes or so talking about what political correctness really means—what it is, and what it isn't—because I believe it's a concept that has been widely misrepresented and misunderstood.

Some of you may be wondering, what is this political correctness, and what does it have to do with us who are in business or the professions? It appears to be an issue on college campuses, and not one of corporate or governmental or professional significance. As I explain the history and essentials of political correctness, I'll also address the connection of it to business and professional people, for it is vitally important to all of us in Rochester, not only those in the academy.

Political correctness is a pejorative term. In its very modern usage, to be politically correct is to slavishly adhere to language that is neutral of any sexist, racist, ageist, or any other "ist" connotations. The politically correct person is one who is so sensitive to the feelings of minority groups that he or she exhibits no attitudes and uses no speech that may in any way insinuate offense upon any minority group. And the correct speech is very specific, to be used slavishly, and to fail to use it is to be a bigot. The definition of the politically correct is meant to be absurd; it is meant to carry with it the baggage of unwarranted and excessive sensitivity. It also bears with it the suggestion of sanctimoniousness and smug self-righteousness. As it has come to be used today, it is itself an epithet of conformity which nobody wishes to claim. It is meant to be a mockery of certain constricted behavior, usually by people who are perceived to be the most knee-jerk of liberals. This definition is unfortunate. It is unfortunate because it has a history which has led to attacks on some of the most fundamentally positive changes that have occurred socially in this country over the past three decades. The charge of politically correct is more specifically an attack upon certain campus policies of civil intercourse promoted by administrators like me who wish to make the campus community a community of civil exchanges of ideas, a community in which, despite debate, all people are encouraged and comfortable in their differences.

5 The politically correct, or rather the modern version of the politically correct, began, then, as a mockery of what was perceived by certain people to be the excesses of affirmative action programs on campus. It was affirmative action programs, after all, that engendered the spirit of careful, civil speech with respect to minority groups. Notions of the politically correct spread, especially in this state, to become not only a satire on affirmative action programs, but more seriously a grave attack on programs of multiculturalism. Several events coalesced in the past two years to bring political correctness satire to the forefront of *serious* discourse.

First was the series of articles in such magazines as *Newsweek, Time,* and *U.S. News & World Report* in which certain campus administrations of affirmative action were satirized for going overboard in their advocacy of civil behavior on campus. Students were told in handbooks what terms were considered offensive or taboo by minority groups, how these groups preferred to be addressed, what bodily terms were taken as disrespectful to women. Accordingly, we learned that both "black" and "African American" were acceptable, but "colored" was not; that "Asian" was preferred to "Oriental"; that women of thirty who worked as clerks in offices were not "the girls." These directives, obviously, are not without merit. Young men at college need to know, for their own sakes, what is acceptable behavior, for example, to women and what is not. People who have had no contact with African Americans or Asians were made aware not only of their preferences in names, but also of the history behind such preferences. It is not simple etiquette that requires that we not call Jewish people by a derisive name, but a long and dreadful history of rock-pelting, derision, and segregation that recommends it. Blacks remember lynch mobs as well. Asians remember the Yellow Peril associated with the word "Oriental." Nomenclature, in short, is not devoid of significant history and education.

In any case, politically correct language *began* to become part of the general public consciousness with these satires in widely published magazines. At the same time, as the public has come to perceive it, political correctness is not simply saying and writing about and doing the civil or "nice" thing in order to show respect for minorities. Political correctness has, today, become confused with issues of censorship and totalitarianism.

This occurrence is a strange twist of history. As far back as we can judge, the term was used first by Marxists and left progressives as a way of offering criticism to themselves for their own overbearing preachiness. It was to them a label for a person who mindlessly adhered to the party line, no matter how inappropriate the policy might be for the given occasion. Marxists, thus, who preached to tough and practical-minded American auto workers about the class revolution were called by their comrades "politically correct." What was left unsaid was "politically correct" but absolutely inappropriate. It wasn't until the late 1980s that politically correct was applied to a set of beliefs that sprang from campus policies of multiculturalism. PC, starting first as a satire of the excesses of the language of affirmative action and multiculturalism, became later, in the hands of frightened scholars and laymen, a convenient label for curricular changes which seemed threatening to the traditional and established structure of the white, masculine-dominated educational system. I've read headlines in publications that could be called anything from conservative to liberal equating politically correct with "Sensitivity Fascism," or the "New McCarthyism," or "Academic Thought Control." For the most part, the fears emanating from the suggestion of restrictions on freedom of speech, I believe, have been overblown and lack an historical foundation or perspective. The academy infrequently mandates anything, let alone restrictions on free speech.

But there is an almost universal search among campuses for an enlightened and invigorating ethos, a code of behavior following the straightforward precepts of some of the more noteworthy members of the law faculty at Harvard University. They argue that the best ethic is the one which seeks to do the least harm to others while preserving individual prerogative. We on the campus realize, without pretensions to great knowledge or insight, that although sticks and stones do break bones, words do, in fact, hurt as well.

We must remember that this so-called politically correct language did not 10
breed itself; it did not start in a vacuum. The rule that we now mock, that we now fear for its restraint on free speech, did not come as an invention of some bored bureaucrat. It came because damage was inflicted by the language of the advantaged upon the spirits of the deprived. My good friend and colleague, the president of St. John Fisher College, Bill Pickett, has perhaps put it best for all of us. He has outlined his defense of policies that answer to the slurs and mockeries of those who satirize serious attempts to construct an ethos of civility on our campuses. He reported thus:

> A student hangs a swastika on a banner out of a residence hall window; he is disciplined by college authorities. A student loudly and repeatedly uses racial epithets to refer to Jewish students but takes no overt action against them; she is expelled from her university. A female campus minister is subjected to harassment and those responsible must publicly apologize.

These are not peculiar or isolated incidents. Racial tensions have grown immeasurably in the past several years.

As another author, this time one of our students at SUNY Brockport, has documented,

> . . . eight Asian students at the University of Connecticut were harassed by a group of white students who hurled racial epithets and spit on them. At the University of San Diego a group of students burned a cross in May 1989 in front of a Black Student Union. At the University of Pennsylvania, a young black student, a woman, was harassed by racial slurs coming from two white men as she passed their dormitory. They then poured jars of urine on her. At the University of Montana several male athletes mercilessly harassed an admitted gay student until he moved out of his dormitory saying he feared for his life.

This is in addition to a rising incidence of date rape on campuses throughout the country. An ethic, a code of decent social behavior among peoples, is sorely needed on our campuses and communities. Politically correct did not emerge for no reason at all.

In this environment intolerance and the *test* of all kinds of freedoms of speech have proliferated on campuses as though student and/or professor and/or reporter and/or editor are all daring administrators to lay down rules and damning them if they do.

Simple humane rules of decent conduct have thus become targets for tests 15
of free speech, under the mocking aegis of politically correct. It is almost as though one were saying, "If I cannot speak exactly what is on my mind at the moment it occurs to me, in exactly the terms I wish, expressing honest hatred, then my first amendment rights have been violated." Let us not play games about this. Those who have made politically correct a political issue of free speech are saying just that. Perhaps they are right. There is much legal doctrine recommending this position. The protectionist view in opposition to campus regulations governing hate speech is represented best by those like Robert O'Neil, president of the Virginia School of Law, who has said, "The worthiest motives prompt efforts to restrict speech that may wound, or embarrass, or offend." Yet, the "enduring precepts of free expression that compel Americans to tolerate such speech" is legally upheld by the Supreme Court, even in its decision to strike down the flag desecration rulings that had been attempted in local jurisdictions.

On the other hand, we have legal precedents that argue for the 14th Amendment on the grounds that certain kinds of speech are harmful in its creation of an atmosphere in which equality is compromised. In *Brown vs. the Board of Education,* it was held that the fact of segregation affected the "hearts and minds" of black children, and that "racial epithets" similarly caused "deep emotional scarring" that rendered the atmosphere of the school room of black children unequal to the atmosphere of the school room of white children.

Perhaps the protectionists of unrestricted free speech are right. Perhaps we will once again have to say, "I hate what you are saying, but I will defend your right to say it." And perhaps it is right to defend the immunity that the Nazis enjoyed, when they marched down the streets of Skokie, Illinois, as a warrantable price for the pleasures of our freedom. If the issue of free speech surrounding politically correct had resolved itself simply into speaking the unpopular, speaking the hated, then that is probably the way I would have resolved the question myself. Let them speak without sensitivity in the hope that an ultimately educated population will reject them.

But that was not the whole story. There is more. Especially in New York there is more. The juxtaposition of the Board of Regents' recommendation on multiculturalism in the classroom with the publicity surrounding the "politically correct" has brought a grave connection with politically correct and multiculturalism to the foreground. Let me illustrate this by referring to a popular column in our daily newspaper to point out just how clearly the juxtaposition between politically correct and campus attempts at multiculturalism are perceived by the public as coterminous.

In the "Speaking Out" in the *Democrat & Chronicle* of June 23, 1991, a writer named Bill Kauffman gave voice to his real fears on this issue. His concern, and it may be a typical one, is that the mounting attempts to create regulations on campus and habituate students to a language of civility and super-sensitivity to diverse ethnic groups, will lead, he cried, "by decade's end, to an attempt by speech-controllers to outlaw harmful speech, for example, ethnic jokes." He said, without embarrassment, that an example of the "general deterioration of American political debate" would result in the demise of "ancient vaudevillians," who, in "telling the one about the Pole, the Italian, and the Irishman, will be hauled into court and subjected to grim harangue about Sensitivity and Diversity and the Trojan Horse concept of the year, multiculturalism."

20 In his angry diatribe over the potential loss of such Americanisms as the ethnic joke, the right to describe a woman's body as "cheesecake," and what he called the "frank speech" of personal insult, Kauffman rightly named his enemy: the advancing ethos of multicultural sensitivity. Kauffman is right. The so-called "politically correct" derives from the push on academic campuses to recognize the reality of a multicultural world in which their students will eventually live and earn their keep. It recognizes that it is necessary to understand and even to accommodate Asian conventions of correct intercourse and Middle Eastern conventions of correct intercourse, if for no other reason than we must live and do business with them. Campuses, of course, go further. They actually suggest it is ethical to behave in such accommodating ways, even if the result is a restriction on one's speech. Multiculturalism was born and bred, first, by political reality and, second, by a need to define a workable and honorable ethic for an ethics-hungry America. Those among the scholars of America, those like the revered Arthur Schlesinger, who fear that an emphasis on multicultural diversity will Balkanize America as it seems to be doing in central Europe, strangely ignore the straightforward truth that America, unlike homogeneous pockets of Europe, never was unified into a homogeneity, always was a squabbling, vocal, insistent bunch of haranguers. We were always diverse in this country; our attempts to carve unity have always come self-consciously because of the truth of our inherent differences. Before there were Asians and blacks to speak of, did not the Puritan deliberately separate himself from Anglican, from Methodist, from Roman Catholic? Did not the Virginian claim superiority over the Pennsylvanian

and vice versa? We have always been a nation of states, not a unified, univocal people. Is that not our strength, our great strength historically? That we failed at homogeneity?

Finally, there is the last concern with respect to multiculturalism and the politically correct. It is articulately presented by several historians in criticism of the new multicultural public school curriculum.

They want to prevent the change. A quick look at American history will make the point. When we were growing up, we certainly knew about Washington's crossing the Delaware and his refusal to be a king; monumental events without a doubt. We learned about a revolution of brave men for the privileges of independence. We learned about the battles of the Civil War. We chuckled over Ben Franklin's journals and autobiography if we were really educated. What we did not find on the pages of these works was anything that women were doing; or blacks were doing; or, indeed, what day laborers, school teachers, or volunteers were doing. But the critics say the new approach goes too far and is not accurate history.

I disagree. Our concern with multiculturalism is not to promote patriotism, or any particular ethnic position, but a true picture of who we are. We are not Puritan Pilgrim Nordic churchmen who transformed themselves into pioneers, cowboys, Indian fighters forever chanting democratic slogans and itching to go to war. We are diverse people struggling, groping to reach each other; not to fight but to recognize; not to defeat but to accommodate. That is what we were before, too; but only recently, through multiculturalism, are we beginning to recognize this. Multiculturalism is not a clever invention by college folk to appease ethnic sensibilities. It is an acknowledgement, not an invention, of who we are, who we have always been, and what makes us both strong and unique. Both extremes tend to ignore this in the debate.

I hope what I have said today has provided you with a context for abandoning the term politically correct because it is a pejorative that has been too closely associated with attacking change—change in the language we use, change in the curriculum our students and your children study, and change in the way we go about doing business day-to-day.

I think it's important to keep in mind that the development of sensitivity to 25
people of color and women and those who are physically challenged isn't limited to campus life. We're going to need that sensitivity in the business world, too.

Consider a few facts about the changing nature of our world. For example, I just read in the current issue of *American Demographics* magazine the not so surprising fact that Hispanics are one of the fastest-growing consumer segments and a major reason for America's growing ethnic diversity. In that article a gentleman named Robert Lattimer who is managing director of the firm Diversity Consultants in Atlanta pointed out:

> The company that gets out in front of managing diversity will have the competitive edge. Eighty-five percent of the labor force increase over the next decade will be minorities and women. If you intend to do

> business in the year 2000, you need to prepare for it now. Slower growth in the total work force will fuel the need to incorporate people from all walks of life.

That's certainly true of our own corner of the world. New York ranks third in the top twenty Hispanic states, for example. And in the five-county greater Rochester area, the white population will grow by a mere three percent from 1990 to 1995. Meanwhile, the Hispanic population will grow by a whopping 34 percent and the black population by almost 10 percent.

Rochester, in particular, is already experiencing globalization and its concurrent mingling with colleagues of other cultures. We're one of the top ten exporting regions in the country. And 40 percent of all New York state exports originate from the greater Rochester area. We're changing the way we do business—and the people we do business with. The culture of tomorrow's work force is going to be considerably different than it was a few years ago.

Multiculturalism is here to stay; political correctness or no political correctness. And each of us will have to muster the sensitivity to adapt to it. If I'm seeing growth in racial and ethnic diversity on the campus at SUNY Brockport, it won't be very long—less than four years from now—that you'll be seeing it in the office and on the assembly line. So, clearly, now is not the time, nor is it ever, to attack change in the name of political correctness or any other emotionally laden labels that only obscure the real issues. Now is the time for us to welcome change.

Thank you. 30

Questions for Discussion

1. Break Van De Wetering's speech down into sections. In each section, describe the sequence of strategic "moves" the author makes. How does he attempt to appeal to his audience in each of the essay's parts?
2. One of Van De Wetering's central points is that the United States has "failed at homogeneity," and that this failure is actually a strength (paragraph 20). Do you agree? How would Schlesinger, Gates, Kagan, and Ravitch respond to this assertion?
3. In paragraphs 15–17, Van De Wetering presents several views of the free speech issue. Which of the conflicting positions do you agree with? Why?

For Negotiation

In paragraph 9 Van De Wetering speaks of "an almost universal search . . . for an enlightened and invigorating ethos, a code of behavior" to guide campus life. He goes on to advocate an ethic "which seeks to do the least harm to others while preserving individual prerogative."

Attempt to understand this ethic and to resolve its tensions in a concrete proposal for a campus language code. What kinds of speech should be prohibited altogether? What kinds should be discouraged? What kinds ought to be promoted, encouraged to develop further? What kinds should be of no concern at all? A strong suggestion: Consider carefully the matter of context—who is speaking to whom, where, and for what reasons.

Present your proposal to your class or to some other group on campus concerned with the issue, such as the Panhellenic Council. Based on the response of others, revise your proposal until all or almost all of those responding to it are satisfied.

DINESH D'SOUZA

The Visigoths in Tweed

Articles and books critical of education in the United States appear daily and are hardly anything new. But until recently most of the attention has centered on our public schools, especially secondary or high schools. Colleges and universities have rarely been the target of serious and concentrated criticism, in part because our system of higher education is widely perceived as one of the best in the world.

Allan Bloom's 1987 The Closing of the American Mind*—a best seller—marked the beginning of an outpouring of books and shorter pieces sharply critical of higher education, especially the humanities and social sciences. Among the books to follow in Bloom's wake was* Illiberal Education: The Politics of Race and Sex on Campus, *by Dinesh D'Souza, whose basic point of view is summarized in this article from* Forbes.

A research fellow at the conservative American Enterprise Institute, D'Souza has appeared as a guest speaker on college campuses all over the United States.

"I AM a male WASP who attended and succeeded at Choate (preparatory) School, Yale College, Yale Law School, and Princeton Graduate School. Slowly but surely, however, my lifelong habit of looking, listening, feeling, and thinking as honestly as possible has led me to see that white, male-dominated, western European culture is the most destructive phenomenon in the known history of the planet.

"[This Western culture] is deeply hateful of life and committed to death; therefore, it is moving rapidly toward the destruction of itself and most other life forms on earth. And truly it deserves to die. . . . We have to face our own individual and collective responsibility for what is happening—our greed, brutality, indifference, militarism, racism, sexism, blindness. . . . Meanwhile, everything we have put into motion continues to endanger us more every day."

This bizarre outpouring, so reminiscent of the "confessions" from victims of Stalin's show trials, appeared in a letter to *Mother Jones* magazine and was written by a graduate of some of our finest schools. But the truth is that the speaker's anguish came not from any balanced assessment but as a consequence of exposure to the propaganda of the new barbarians who have captured the humanities, law, and social science departments of so many of our universities. It should come as no surprise that many sensitive young Americans reject the system that has nurtured them. At Duke University, according to the *Wall Street Journal,* professor Frank Lentricchia in his English course shows the movie *The Godfather* to teach his students that organized crime is "a metaphor for American business as usual."

Yes, a student can still get an excellent education—among the best in the world—in computer technology and the hard sciences at American universities.

But liberal arts students, including those attending Ivy League schools, are very likely to be exposed to an attempted brainwashing that deprecates Western learning and exalts a neo-Marxist ideology promoted in the name of multiculturalism. Even students who choose hard sciences must often take required courses in the humanities, where they are almost certain to be inundated with an anti-Western, anticapitalist view of the world.

Each year American society invests $160 billion in higher education, more 5
per student than any nation in the world except Denmark. A full 45 percent of this money comes from the federal, state, and local governments. No one can say we are starving higher education. But what are we getting for our money, at least so far as the liberal arts are concerned?

A fair question? It might seem so, but in university circles it is considered impolite because it presumes that higher education must be accountable to the society that supports it. Many academics think of universities as intellectual enclaves, insulated from the vulgar capitalism of the larger culture.

Yet, since the academics constantly ask for more money, it seems hardly unreasonable to ask what they are doing with it. Honest answers are rarely forthcoming. The general public sometimes gets a whiff of what is going on—as when Stanford alters its core curriculum in the classics of Western civilization—but it knows very little of the systematic and comprehensive change sweeping higher education.

An academic and cultural revolution has overtaken most of our 3,535 colleges and universities. It's a revolution to which most Americans have paid little attention. It is a revolution imposed upon the students by a university elite, not one voted upon or even discussed by the society at large. It amounts, according to University of Wisconsin-Madison Chancellor Donna Shalala, to "a basic transformation of American higher education in the name of multiculturalism and diversity."[1]

The central thrust of this "basic transformation" involves replacing traditional core curriculums—consisting of the great works of Western culture—with curriculums flavored by minority, female, and Third World authors.

Here's a sample of the viewpoint represented by the new curriculum. 10
Becky Thompson, a sociology and women's studies professor, in a teaching manual distributed by the American Sociological Association, writes: "I begin my course with the basic feminist principle that in a racist, classist, and sexist society we have all swallowed oppressive ways of being, whether intentionally or not. Specifically, this means that it is not open to debate whether a white student is racist or a male student is sexist. He/she simply is."

Professors at several colleges who have resisted these regnant dogmas about race and gender have found themselves the object of denunciation and even university sanctions. Donald Kagan, dean of Yale College, says: "I was a student during the days of Joseph McCarthy, and there is less freedom now than there was then."

[1]Shalala is currently President Clinton's Secretary of Health and Human Services.

As in the McCarthy period, a particular group of activists has cowed the authorities and bent them to its will.[1] After activists forcibly occupied his office, President Lattie Coor of the University of Vermont explained how he came to sign a 16-point agreement establishing, among other things, minority faculty hiring quotas. "When it became clear that the minority students with whom I had been discussing these issues wished to pursue negotiations *in the context of occupied offices* . . . I agreed to enter negotiations." As frequently happens in such cases, Coor's "negotiations" ended in a rapid capitulation by the university authorities.

At Harvard, historian Stephan Thernstrom was harangued by student activists and accused of insensitivity and bigotry. What was his crime? His course included a reading from the journals of slave owners, and his textbook gave a reasonable definition of affirmative action as "preferential treatment" for minorities. At the University of Michigan, renowned demographer Reynolds Farley was assailed in the college press for criticizing the excesses of Marcus Garvey and Malcolm X; yet the administration did not publicly come to his defense.

University leaders argue that the revolution suggested by these examples is necessary because young Americans must be taught to live in and govern a multiracial and multicultural society. Immigration from Asia and Latin America, combined with relatively high minority birth rates, is changing the complexion of America. Consequently, in the words of University of Michigan President James Duderstadt, universities must "create a model of how a more diverse and pluralistic community can work for our society."

No controversy, of course, about benign goals such as pluralism or diversity, 15
but there is plenty of controversy about how these goals are being pursued. Although there is no longer a Western core curriculum at Mount Holyoke or Dartmouth, students at those schools must take a course in non-Western or Third World culture. Berkeley and the University of Wisconsin now insist that every undergraduate enroll in ethnic studies, making this virtually the only compulsory course at those schools.

If American students were truly exposed to the richest elements of other cultures, this could be a broadening and useful experience. A study of Chinese philosophers such as Confucius or Mencius would enrich students' understanding of how different peoples order their lives, thus giving a greater sense of purpose to their own. Most likely, a taste of Indian poetry such as Rabindranath Tagore's *Gitanjali* would increase the interest of materially minded young people in the domain of the spirit. An introduction to Middle Eastern history would prepare the leaders of tomorrow to deal with the mounting challenge of Islamic culture. It would profit students to study the rise of capitalism in the Far East.

But the claims of the academic multiculturalists are largely phony. They pay little attention to the Asian or Latin American classics. Rather, the non-Western or multicultural curriculum reflects a different agenda. At Stanford, for

[1]Senator Joseph McCarthy (1909–1957) initiated Congressional investigations into the supposedly "un-American" activities of his liberal political opponents in the early 1950s, leading to considerable repression of leftist voices on college campuses.

example, Homer, Plato, Dante, Machiavelli, and Locke are increasingly scarce. But often their replacements are not non-Western classics. Instead the students are offered exotic topics such as popular religion and healing in Peru, Rastafarian poetry, and Andean music.

What do students learn about the world from the books they are required to read under the new multicultural rubric? At Stanford one of the non-Western works assigned is *I, Rigoberta Menchu,* subtitled "An Indian Woman in Guatemala."

The book is hardly a non-Western classic. Published in 1983, *I, Rigoberta Menchu* is the story of a young woman who is said to be a representative voice of the indigenous peasantry. Representative of Guatemalan Indian culture? In fact, Rigoberta met the Venezuelan feminist to whom she narrates this story at a socialist conference in Paris, where, presumably, very few of the Third World's poor travel. Moreover, Rigoberta's political consciousness includes the adoption of such politically correct causes as feminism, homosexual rights, socialism, and Marxism. By the middle of the book she is discoursing on "bourgeois youths" and "Molotov cocktails," not the usual terminology of Indian peasants. One chapter is titled "Rigoberta Renounces Marriage and Motherhood," a norm that her tribe could not have adopted and survived.

If Rigoberta does not represent the convictions and aspirations of Guate- 20
malan peasants, what is the source of her importance and appeal? The answer is that Rigoberta seems to provide independent Third World corroboration for Western left-wing passions and prejudices. She is a mouthpiece for a sophisticated neo-Marxist critique of Western society, all the more powerful because it seems to issue not from some embittered American academic but from a Third World native. For professors nourished on the political activism of the late 1960s and early 1970s, texts such as *I, Rigoberta Menchu* offer a welcome opportunity to attack capitalism and Western society in general in the name of teaching students about the developing world.[1]

We learn in the introduction of *I, Rigoberta Menchu* that Rigoberta is a quadruple victim. As a person of color, she has suffered racism. As a woman, she has endured sexism. She lives in South America, which is—of course—a victim of North American colonialism. She is also an Indian, victimized by Latino culture within Latin America.

One of the most widely used textbooks in so-called multicultural courses is *Multi-Cultural Literacy,* published by Graywolf Press in St. Paul, Minn. The book ignores the *Analects* of Confucius, the *Tale of Genji,* the Upanishads and Vedas, the Koran and Islamic commentaries. It also ignores such brilliant contemporary authors as Jorge Luis Borges, V.S. Naipaul, Octavio Paz, Naguib Mahfouz, and Wole Soyinka. Instead it offers 13 essays of protest, including Michele Wallace's autobiographical "Invisibility Blues" and Paula Gunn Allen's "Who Is Your Mother? The Red Roots of White Feminism."

One student I spoke with at Duke University said he would not study *Paradise Lost* because John Milton was a Eurocentric white male sexist. At the

[1]Menchu was awarded the Nobel Peace Prize in 1992, a year or so after this article appeared.

University of Michigan, a young black woman who had converted to Islam refused to believe that the prophet Muhammad owned slaves and practiced polygamy. She said she had taken courses on cultural diversity and the courses hadn't taught her that.

One of the highlights of this debate on the American campus was a passionate statement delivered a few years ago by Stanford undergraduate William King, president of the Black Student Union, who argued the benefits of the new multicultural curriculum before the faculty senate of the university. Under the old system, he said, "I was never taught . . . the fact that Socrates, Herodotus, Pythagoras, and Solon studied in Egypt and acknowledged that much of their knowledge of astronomy, geometry, medicine, and building came from the African civilization in and around Egypt. [I was never taught] that the Hippocratic Oath acknowledges the Greeks' 'father of medicine,' Imhotep, a black Egyptian pharaoh whom they called Aesculapius. . . . I was never informed when it was found that the 'very dark and wooly haired' Moors in Spain preserved, expanded, and reintroduced the classical knowledge that the Greeks had collected, which led to the 'renaissance.' . . . I read the Bible without knowing Saint Augustine looked black like me, that the Ten Commandments were almost direct copies from the 147 Negative Confessions of Egyptian initiates. . . . I didn't learn Toussaint L'Ouverture's defeat of Napoleon in Haiti directly influenced the French Revolution, or that the Iroquois Indians in America had a representative democracy which served as a model for the American system."

25 This statement drew wild applause and was widely quoted. The only trouble is that much of it is untrue. There is no evidence that Socrates, Pythagoras, Herodotus, and Solon studied in Egypt, although Herodotus may have traveled there. Saint Augustine was born in North Africa, but his skin color is unknown, and in any case he could not have been mentioned in the Bible; he was born over 350 years after Christ. Viewing King's speech at my request, Bernard Lewis, an expert on Islamic and Middle Eastern culture at Princeton, described it as "a few scraps of truth amidst a great deal of nonsense."

Why does multicultural education, in practice, gravitate toward such myths and half-truths? To find out why, it is necessary to explore the complex web of connections that the academic revolution generates among admissions policies, life on campus, and the curriculum.

American universities typically begin with the premise that in a democratic and increasingly diverse society the composition of their classes should reflect the ethnic distribution of the general population. Many schools officially seek "proportional representation," in which the percentage of applicants admitted from various racial groups roughly approximates the ratio of those groups in society at large.

Thus universities routinely admit black, Hispanic, and American Indian candidates over better-qualified white and Asian American applicants. As a result of zealously pursued affirmative action programs, many selective colleges admit minority students who find it extremely difficult to meet demanding academic standards and to compete with the rest of the class. This fact is reflected in the dropout rates of blacks and Hispanics, which are more than 50 percent higher than those of whites and Asians. At Berkeley a study of students admitted on a preferential basis between 1978 and 1982 concluded that nearly 70 percent failed to graduate within five years.

For affirmative action students who stay on campus, a common strategy of dealing with the pressures of university life is to enroll in a distinctive minority organization. Among such organizations at Cornell University are Lesbian, Gay, & Bisexual Coalition; La Asociacion Latina; National Society of Black Engineers; Society of Minority Hoteliers; Black Students United; and Simba Washanga.

Although the university brochures at Cornell and elsewhere continue to 30
praise integration and close interaction among students from different backgrounds, the policies practiced at these schools actually encourage segregation. Stanford, for example, has "ethnic theme houses" such as the African house called Ujaama. And President Donald Kennedy has said that one of his educational objectives is to "support and strengthen ethnic theme houses." Such houses make it easier for some minority students to feel comfortable but help to create a kind of academic apartheid.

The University of Pennsylvania has funded a black yearbook, even though only 6 percent of the student body is black and all other groups appeared in the general yearbook. Vassar, Dartmouth, and the University of Illinois have allowed separate graduation activities and ceremonies for minority students. California State University at Sacramento has just established an official "college within a college" for blacks.

Overt racism is relatively rare at most campuses, yet minorities are told that bigotry operates in subtle forms such as baleful looks, uncorrected stereotypes, and "institutional racism"—defined as the underrepresentation of blacks and Hispanics among university trustees, administrators, and faculty.

Other groups such as feminists and homosexuals typically get into the game, claiming their own varieties of victim status. As Harvard political scientist Harvey Mansfield bluntly puts it, "White students must admit their guilt so that minority students do not have to admit their incapacity."

Even though universities regularly accede to the political demands of victim groups, their appeasement gestures do not help black and Hispanic students get a genuine liberal arts education. They do the opposite, giving the apologists of the new academic orthodoxy a convenient excuse when students admitted on a preferential basis fail to meet academic standards. At this point student activists and administrators often blame the curriculum. They argue that it reflects a "white male perspective" that systematically depreciates the views and achievements of other cultures, minorities, women, and homosexuals.

With this argument, many minority students can now explain why they 35
had such a hard time with Milton in the English department, Publius in political science, and Heisenberg in physics. Those men reflected white male aesthetics, philosophy, and science. Obviously, nonwhite students would fare much better if the university created more black or Latino or Third World courses, the argument goes. This epiphany leads to a spate of demands: Abolish the Western classics,

establish new departments such as Afro-American Studies and Women's Studies, hire minority faculty to offer distinctive black and Hispanic "perspectives."

Multicultural or non-Western education on campus frequently glamorizes Third World cultures and omits inconvenient facts about them. In fact, several non-Western cultures are caste-based or tribal, and often disregard norms of racial equality. In many of them feminism is virtually nonexistent, as indicated by such practices as dowries, widow-burning, and genital mutilation; and homosexuality is sometimes regarded as a crime or mental disorder requiring punishment. These nasty aspects of the non-Western cultures are rarely mentioned in the new courses. Indeed, Bernard Lewis of Princeton argues that while slavery and the subjugation of women have been practiced by all known civilizations, the West at least has an active and effective movement for the abolition of such evils.

Who is behind this academic revolution, this contrived multiculturalism? The new curriculum directly serves the purposes of a newly ascendant generation of young professors, weaned in the protest culture of the late 1960s and early 1970s. In a frank comment, Jay Parini, who teaches English at Middlebury College, writes, "After the Vietnam War, a lot of us didn't just crawl back into our library cubicles. We stepped into academic positions. . . . Now we have tenure, and the work of reshaping the university has begun in earnest."

The goal that Parini and others like him pursue is the transformation of the college classroom from a place of learning to a laboratory of indoctrination for social change. Not long ago most colleges required that students learn the basics of the physical sciences and mathematics, the rudiments of economics and finance, and the fundamental principles of American history and government. Studies by the National Endowment for the Humanities show that this coherence has disappeared from the curriculum. As a result, most universities are now graduating students who are scientifically and culturally impoverished, if not illiterate.

At the University of Pennsylvania, Houston Baker, one of the most prominent black academics in the country, denounces reading and writing as oppressive technologies and celebrates such examples of oral culture as the rap group N.W.A. (Niggers With Attitudes). One of the group's songs is about the desirability of killing policemen. Alison Jaggar, who teaches women's studies at the University of Colorado, denounces the traditional nuclear family as a "cornerstone of women's oppression" and anticipates scientific advances enabling men to carry fetuses in their bodies so that child-bearing responsibilities can be shared between the sexes. Duke professor Eve Sedgwick's scholarship is devoted to unmasking what she terms the heterosexual bias in Western culture, a project that she pursues through papers such as "Jane Austen and the Masturbating Girl" and "How To Bring Your Kids Up Gay."

Confronted by racial tension and balkanization on campus, university lead- 40
ers usually announce that, because of a resurgence of bigotry, "more needs to be done." They press for redoubled preferential recruitment of minority students and faculty, funding for a new Third World or Afro-American center, mandatory sensitivity education for whites, and so on. The more the university leaders give in to the demands of minority activists, the more they encourage the very racism

they are supposed to be fighting. Surveys indicate that most young people today hold fairly liberal attitudes toward race, evident in their strong support for the civil rights agenda and for interracial dating. However, these liberal attitudes are sorely tried by the demands of the new orthodoxy: Many undergraduates are beginning to rebel against what they perceive as a culture of preferential treatment and double standards actively fostered by university policies.

Can there be a successful rolling back of this revolution, or at least of its excesses? One piece of good news is that blatant forms of racial preference are having an increasingly tough time in the courts, and this has implications for university admissions policies. The Department of Education is more vigilant than it used to be in investigating charges of discrimination against whites and Asian Americans. With help from Washington director Morton Halperin, the American Civil Liberties Union has taken a strong stand against campus censorship. Popular magazines such as *Newsweek* and *New York* have poked fun at "politically correct" speech. At Tufts University, undergraduates embarrassed the administration into backing down on censorship by putting up taped boundaries designating areas of the university to be "free speech zones," "limited speech zones" and "Twilight Zones."

Even some scholars on the political left are now speaking out against such dogmatism and excess. Eugene Genovese, a Marxist historian and one of the nation's most respected scholars of slavery, argues that "too often we find that education has given way to indoctrination. Good scholars are intimidated into silence, and the only diversity that obtains is a diversity of radical positions." More and more professors from across the political spectrum are resisting the politicization and lowering of standards. At Duke, for example, 60 professors, led by political scientist James David Barber, a liberal Democrat, have repudiated the extremism of the victims' revolution. To that end they have joined the National Association of Scholars, a Princeton, N.J.-based group devoted to fairness, excellence and rational debate in universities.

But these scholars need help. Resistance on campus to the academic revolution is outgunned and sorely needs outside reinforcements. Parents, alumni, corporations, foundations, and state legislators are generally not aware that they can be very effective in promoting reform. The best way to encourage reform is to communicate in no uncertain terms to university leadership and, if necessary, to use financial incentives to assure your voice is heard. University leaders do their best to keep outsiders from meddling or even finding out what exactly is going on behind the tall gates, but there is little doubt that they would pay keen attention to the views of the donors on whom they depend. By threatening to suspend donations if universities continue harmful policies, friends of liberal learning can do a lot. In the case of state-funded schools, citizens and parents can pressure elected representatives to ask questions and demand more accountability from the taxpayer-supported academics.

The illiberal revolution can be reversed only if the people who foot the bills stop being passive observers. Don't just write a check to your alma mater; that's an abrogation of responsibility. Keep abreast of what is going on and don't be afraid to raise your voice and even to close your wallet in protest. Our Western, free-market culture need not provide the rope to hang itself.

Questions for Discussion

1. D'Souza dismisses the letter to *Mother Jones* (paragraphs 1 and 2) as the result of "the propaganda of the new barbarians." Can the letter's concern over "our greed, brutality, indifference," and so forth be so easily dismissed as only a "bizarre outpouring" (paragraph 3)?
2. In paragraph 10 D'Souza cites a statement from a sociology teacher's manual by Becky Thompson claiming that, as a basic principle, all white students are racist and all males sexist. D'Souza apparently thinks her claim so ridiculous as to need no response on his part. Do you likewise reject her viewpoint out of hand? How would you respond to Thompson?
3. "At [the University of California at] Berkeley," D'Souza says, "a study of students admitted on a preferential basis between 1978 and 1982 concluded that nearly 70 percent failed to graduate within five years" (paragraph 28). What would we need to know to decide whether the percentage cited is significant?
4. Judging from how students associate at your school, would you agree with D'Souza that administrative policies actually encourage segregation (paragraph 30)?

For Research and Convincing

As a class research project, collect syllabi from courses at your college which adopt a multicultural approach. D'Souza claims that Western classics are losing out, not to classics from other cultures, but to inferior works from other cultures. Based on the class's assessment of syllabi at your school, write a group essay responding to his claim.

If you think his claim has merit, invite faculty teaching the courses to the class to discuss your assessment. If you think his claim lacks merit, write a short version of your assessment as a letter to the editor of *Forbes.*

ROSA EHRENREICH

What Campus Radicals?

Now a Marshall Scholar at Oxford University in England, Rosa Ehrenreich completed her undergraduate work at Harvard in 1991. This piece appeared under the title, "Cambridge Letter," in the December 1991 issue of Harper's.

Ehrenreich attempts to refute the charges of critics like D'Souza who claim that the radical left is dominating the liberal arts.

A NATIONAL SURVEY of college administrators released last summer found that "political correctness" is not the campus issue it has been portrayed to be by pundits and politicians of the political right. During the 1990–91 academic year, according to the survey's findings, faculty members complained of pressure from students and fellow professors to alter the political and cultural content of their courses at only *5 percent* of all colleges. So much for the influence of the radicals, tenured or otherwise.

The survey's findings came as no real surprise to me. The hegemony of the "politically correct" is not a problem at Harvard, where I've just completed my undergraduate education, or at any other campus I visited during my student years. But then none among those who have escalated the P.C. debate in the past year—Dinesh D'Souza and Roger Kimball, George Will and George Bush, *Time* and *New York* magazines—is actually interested in what is happening on the campuses. In all the articles and op-ed pieces published on P.C., multiculturalism, etc., very few student voices have been heard. To be a liberal arts student with progressive politics today is at once to be at the center of a raging national debate and to be completely on the sidelines, watching others far from campus describe you and use you for their own ends.

For instance: During the spring semester of my freshman year at Harvard, Stephan Thernstrom, an American history professor, was criticized by several black students for making "racially insensitive" comments during lectures. The incident made the *Harvard Crimson* for a few days, then blew over after a week or so and was quickly forgotten by most students. It continued a kind of mythic afterlife, however, in the P.C. debate. Here is how it was described last January in a *New York* magazine cover story by John Taylor on, in the author's words, the "moonies in the classroom" propagating the "new fundamentalism":

> "Racist." "Racist!" "The man is a racist!" A *racist!*"
>
> Such denunciations, hissed in tones of self-righteousness and contempt, vicious and vengeful, furious, smoking with hatred—such denunciations haunted Stephan Thernstrom for weeks. Whenever he walked through the campus that spring, down Harvard's brick paths, under the arched gates, past the fluttering elms, he found it hard not to imagine the pointing fingers, the whispers.

The operative word here is "imagine." Taylor seriously distorted what actually happened. In February of 1988, several black female students told classmates that they had been disturbed by some "racially insensitive" comments made by Professor Thernstrom. Thernstrom, they said, had spoken approvingly of Jim Crow laws, and had said that black men, harboring feelings of inadequacy, beat their female partners. The students, fearing for their grades should they anger Professor Thernstrom by confronting him with their criticisms—this is not an unusual way for college students to think things through, as anyone who's been an undergraduate well knows—never discussed the matter with him. They told friends, who told friends, and the *Crimson* soon picked up word of the incident and ran an article.

Professor Thernstrom, understandably disturbed to learn of the matter in 5
the *Crimson,* wrote a letter protesting that no students had ever approached him directly with such criticisms. He also complained that the students' vague criticisms about "racial insensitivity" had "launched a witch-hunt" that would have "chilling effect[s] upon freedom of expression." Suddenly, Professor Thernstrom was to be understood as a victim, falsely smeared with the charge of racism. But no one had ever accused him of any such thing. "I do not charge that [Thernstrom] is a racist," Wendi Grantham, one of the students who criticized Thernstrom, wrote to the *Crimson* in response to his letter. Grantham believed the professor gave "an incomplete and over-simplistic presentation of the information. . . . I am not judging [his] character; I am simply asking questions about his presentation of the material. . . ." As for the professor's comment that the criticisms were like a "witch-hunt," Grantham protested that Thernstrom had "turned the whole situation full circle, proclaimed himself victim, and resorted to childish name-calling and irrational comparisons . . . 'witch-hunt' [is] more than a little extreme. . . ." But vehement, even hysterical language is more and more used to demonize students who question and comment. Terms like "authoritarian" and "Hitler youth" have been hurled at students who, like Grantham, dare to express any sort of criticism of the classroom status quo.

• • •

In my four years as a student at Harvard, I found few signs of a new fascism of the left. For that matter, there are few signs of the left at all. The Harvard-Radcliffe Democratic Socialists Club collapsed due to lack of members, as did the left-wing newspaper, the *Subterranean Review.* As to the neoconservative charge that the traditional political left has been supplanted by a feminist-gay-multicultural left: In my senior year the African-American Studies department and the Women's Studies committee each had so few faculty that the same woman served as chair of both. I got through thirty-two courses at Harvard, majoring in the history and literature of England and America, without ever being required to read a work by a black woman writer, and of my thirty-two professors only two were women. I never even *saw* a black or Hispanic professor. (Fewer than 10 percent of tenured professors at Harvard are women, and fewer than 7 percent are members of minorities.)

Perhaps, as some conservatives have maintained, even a few radical professors can reach hundreds of students, bending their minds and sending them, angry and politicized, out into society upon graduation. To cure such fears, drop by Harvard's Office of Career Services. Most staffers there spend their days advising those who would be corporate execs, financial consultants, and investment bankers. Nearly 20 percent of the class of 1990 planned to go to law school. This compares with 10 percent who claimed that they would eventually go into government or one of what Career Services calls the "helping professions."

President Bush, speaking at the University of Michigan's commencement exercises last spring, went on about radical extremists on campus. It would be interesting to know how he calculated this rise in radicalism. Two thirds of Harvard students wholeheartedly supported the Gulf War, according to one *Crimson* poll. That's more support for the war than was found in the country at large. And during my years at Harvard I found that most women on campus, including those who consider themselves politically liberal, would not willingly identify themselves as feminists.

The very notion of "politicization" makes most Harvard students nervous. I discovered this in the fall of 1989, when I was elected president of Harvard's community service organization, Phillips Brooks House Association. I had been reckless enough to suggest that volunteers would benefit from having some awareness of the social and political issues that affected the communities in which they did their volunteer work. I was promptly attacked in the *Crimson* for trying to inappropriately "politicize" public service. The paper also suggested that under my leadership volunteer training might mimic a "party line" with Brooks House as a "central planning office." This used to be called red-baiting. (So much for the liberal campus media.)

• • •

Meanwhile—and unremarked upon by D'Souza, et al.—the campus right 10
thrives nationally. Two new right-wing vehicles have popped up on Harvard's campus in recent years. The Association Against Learning in the Absence of Religion and Morality (AALARM) initially made a splash with its uninhibited gay-bashing. The magazine *Peninsula,* closely tied to AALARM, bears an uncanny editorial resemblance to the notorious *Dartmouth Review,* claims to uphold Truth, and has a bizarre propensity for centerfold spreads of mangled fetuses. And older, more traditional conservative groups have grown stronger and more ideological. The Harvard Republican Club, once a stodgy and relatively inactive group, suffered a rash of purges and resignations as more moderate members were driven out by the far right. It is inactive no more.

There *are* those on the left who are intolerant and who could stand to lighten up a bit—these are the activists whom *progressive* and *liberal* students mockingly called "politically correct" years before the right appropriated the term, with a typical lack of irony. But on the whole, intolerance at Harvard—and, I suspect, elsewhere—is the province mostly of extreme conservatism. Posters put up at Harvard by the Bisexual, Gay, and Lesbian Students Association are routinely torn down. I don't recall any Republican Club posters being ripped up or removed.

The day after the bombing started in Iraq, I went to an event advertised as "a nonpartisan rally to support our troops," sponsored by the Republican Club. After the scheduled speakers—and several other non-scheduled speakers—had finished, I tried to speak. The rally organizers promptly turned off the microphone. I kept speaking, saying that I supported the troops but not the war. I added that I had been disturbed to hear it said by rally organizers—and applauded by the audience—that the time for debate was over. In a democracy, I said, the time for debate is never over.

I would have gone on, but at this point a group of men in the audience felt the need to demonstrate their conviction that there should be no debate. They began to loudly chant "victory" over and over, quite effectively drowning me out. By way of contrast, supporters of the war were listened to in polite silence by the crowd at an anti-war rally the next day.

• • •

In the classroom, too, right-wing political views are heard without disruption. One of Harvard's largest core courses, taken by nearly half of all undergraduates while I was there, is Social Analysis 10, Principles of Economics. It was taught, during my undergrad years, by two of President Reagan's top economic advisers, Martin Feldstein and Larry Lindsay. Students did not rise up *en masse* to protest the course's right-wing political bias; instead, they sat scribbling feverishly in their notebooks: Ec-10 had a notoriously steep grading curve. (No one seemed worried that each year some 750 innocent Harvard students were being lectured to by the engineers of what George Bush, in one of his more forthright moments, once referred to as "voodoo economics.")

There are many other politically conservative professors at Harvard whose 15
courses are quite popular—Richard Pipes on Russian history and Samuel P. Huntington on modern democracy, to name two of the most prominent—and in their classrooms, as in all undergrad classrooms I was in, free and open discussion did quite well. I took many classes in which fearless conservatives rushed to take part in entirely civil discussions about the efficacy and justice of affirmative action, about whether books like *Uncle Tom's Cabin* and Frederick Douglass's autobiography are "really *literature,*" as opposed to just interesting historical documents, and about whether it's at all fair or even interesting to condemn Jefferson for owning slaves even as he decried slavery. These are all valid questions, and all sides deserve a hearing—which, in my experience, is exactly what they always got.

And my experience was not unique. Most other Harvard students seemed to agree that there's no such thing as a cadre of P.C. thought police. Last winter the Republican Club laid huge sheets of poster board across several dining-hall tables and put up a sign asking students to scribble down their responses to the question "Is there free speech at Harvard?" The vast majority of students wrote things like "What's the big deal? Of course there's free speech here." And the lively, cheerful discussion going on among the students gathered around the tables attested to that fact.

• • •

Conservatives like D'Souza and Kimball charge that traditional Western culture courses barely exist anymore at schools like Harvard, because of some mysterious combination of student pressure and the multiculturalist, post-structuralist tendencies of radical professors. Writing in the *Atlantic Monthly* last year, Caleb Nelson, a former editor of the conservative *Harvard Salient,* complained that in the 1989–90 Harvard course catalogue:

> No core Literature and Arts course lists any of the great nineteenth-century British novelists among the authors studied, nor does any list such writers as Virgil, Milton, and Dostoevsky. In the core's history areas even students who . . . took every single course would not focus on any Western history before the Middle Ages, nor would they study the history of the Enlightenment, the Renaissance, the American Civil War, or a host of other topics that one might expect a core to cover.

Nelson's major complaint is that Harvard is not properly educating all of its students. I agree with him here; in Caleb Nelson, Harvard has let us all down by producing a student so poorly educated that he's unable even to read the course catalogue.

I have the 1989–90 catalogue in front of me as I write, and a quick sampling of some of the entries gives us, from the Literature and Arts and the Historical Study sections of the core curriculum, the following courses: Chaucer, Shakespeare, The Bible and Its Interpreters, Classical Greek Literature and 5th-Century Athens, The Rome of Augustus, The British Empire, The Crusades, The Protestant Reformation. Perhaps Chaucer and Shakespeare are somehow, to Caleb Nelson, not "such writers" as Milton and Dostoevsky and the Protestant Reformation is a historically trivial topic.

20 Nelson also worries that students will have "no broad look at . . . philosophy"—by which he really means Western philosophy. Yet in the Moral Reasoning section of the core, seven of the ten courses listed have at least four of the following authors on their primary reading lists: Plato, Aristotle, Thucydides, Machiavelli, Locke, Kant, Rousseau, Hume, Mill, Nietzsche, Marx, and Weber. There is one course devoted to a non-Western philosopher: Confucius. The remaining two Moral Reasoning courses focus, respectively, on the writings of "Aristotle . . . [and] Maimonides," and of "Jesus as presented in the Gospels."

These courses are far more representative of those taken by most Harvard undergraduates than the titillating and much denounced 1991 English course on Cross-Dressing and Cultural Anxiety—a graduate seminar listed in the course catalogue but ultimately never held. But then, if you are a right-winger looking for something to replace the commies on campus—remember them?—you aren't going to sell books or raise funds or win votes complaining about undergrads studying Confucian Humanism and Moral Community.

• • •

Many of the loudest complainers about P.C. thought police are those who are doing their best to curb free expression in other areas. It doesn't appear to bother Dinesh D'Souza that the word "abortion" cannot be uttered at a federally funded family clinic. More broadly, the brouhaha about political conformity on campus serves as a perfect smoke screen, masking from Americans—from ourselves—the rigid political conformity *off* campus: the blandness of our political discourse, the chronic silence in Washington on domestic matters, the same faces returned to office each year, the bipartisanship that keeps problems from becoming issues. During the Gulf War, the number of huge yellow bouquets in public places rivaled the number of larger-than-life photos of Saddam Hussein displayed on Iraqi billboards. Patriotically correct.

The campuses are no more under siege by radicals than is the society at large. It has been clever of the Kimballs and D'Souzas to write as if it were so. It is always clever of those in ascendance to masquerade as victims. Rebecca Walkowitz, the newly elected president of the *Harvard Crimson,* understands perfectly how this dynamic works. Referring to the 1988 incident involving Professor Thernstrom and several of his black students, Walkowitz has said: "People call the *Crimson* and ask what we 'did to that man.' It's important to remember who has the power here, because it's not students. Who would dare criticize a professor for political reasons now? In addition to fearing for your grade, you'd fear being pilloried in the national press."

Questions for Discussion

1. Ehrenreich alleges that "very few student voices have been heard" in the debate over political correctness and multiculturalism (paragraph 2). Based on your own reading and other exposure to the issue, would you agree? If so, how do you explain the lack of student voices?
2. Based on your own experience, do you agree with Ehrenreich that open discussion of issues in class, with all sides being encouraged to speak, is the norm in college (paragraph 15)? If not, why not?
3. In paragraph 22 Ehrenreich complains about "the rigid political conformity" in the United States generally, "the blandness of our political discourse, the chronic silence in Washington on domestic matters, the same faces returned to office each year. . . ." Do you agree with her evaluation? If so, how do you explain this rigid political conformity?

For Persuasion

The concept of academic freedom allows faculty at colleges and universities to teach without fear of censure by school administrators. That is, they may express personal political views, interpret texts according to their own biases, and, in many cases, design their own courses. Given the uneven power situation in the classroom, how do you think students should respond when they strongly disagree with a professor's views? Persuade an audience of students to act upon your suggested response.

CARLOS E. CORTÉS

Pluribus & Unum: The Quest for Community amid Diversity

A prominent Hispanic proponent of multiculturalism, Carlos Cortés is a professor of history at the University of California at Riverside. The following article appeared in the liberal journal Change *(September-October, 1991).*

The appeal of Cortés's article resides in the writer's voice as well as in his arguments. The popular press tends to depict multiculturalists, especially when they are minorities, as passionate extremists; Cortés brings a voice of reason and moderation to the debate, with powers of discrimination far beyond empty tolerance of everything and everyone. Further, because it covers many of the main concerns, "Pluribus & Unum" can also serve as a summary of the entire political correctness-multiculturalism issue.

"LIFE IS like a game of cards. The hand that is dealt you is determinism; the way you play it is free will." So said India's Nehru. Ethnic diversity comprises a critical aspect of America's future, including the future of our nation's colleges and universities. According to a 1989 Census Bureau projection, during the next four decades (1990–2030), the white population of the United States will grow by about 25 percent. During that same 40-year period, the African-American population will increase by 68 percent, the Asian-American, Pacific Island-American, and American Indian populations will grow by 79 percent, and the Latino or Hispanic population of the United States will leap by 187 percent. That's determinism!

The Population Reference Bureau has projected that, by the year 2080, the United States of America may well be 24 percent Latino, 15 percent African-American, and 12 percent Asian-American—more than half of the nation's population. Even recognizing that intermarriage complicates most racial and ethnic statistics and that all projections are merely informed guesswork, the United States has obviously reached merely the diversity take-off stage. What we now call "ethnic diversity" may well be viewed as relative homogeneity from a 21st-century perspective.

Which brings me to the second part of Nehru's wise adage. While this Diversity Revolution provides a major element of our nation's future determinism, the way that we play it involves a great degree of free will.

Colleges and universities face two main questions in addressing the Diversity Revolution. First, how can they help American society make the best of these inevitable demographic changes? Second, how can they deal more effectively with campus diversity in the quest for better institutional climate and community?

I would like to suggest one constructive response to both questions— 5
Multiculturalism, the omnipresent, often-celebrated, often-excoriated "M" word. Barbara Tuchman once wrote: "Bias is only misleading when it is concealed."

So let me unconceal my bias. I am a Multiculturalist. However, since so many scholars and pundits have been defining, redefining, and distorting this concept, and since not all Multiculturalists think alike, I need to further situate myself in the Multiculturalist cosmos.

I am an E Pluribus Unum (EPU) Multiculturalist. That is, I see the Diversity Revolution's opportunities and challenges in terms of the historical American Pluribus-Unum balancing act described incisively by R. Freeman Butts in *The Revival of Civic Learning.* Such Pluribus values as freedom, individualism, and diversity live in constant and inevitable tension with such Unum values as authority, conformity, and commonality. Constructive EPU Multiculturalism involves responding thoughtfully to both powerful Pluribus and necessary Unum imperatives, as well as carefully setting limits to Pluribus and to Unum when they become poisonous to climate and destructive to community.

The United States has been involved in this Pluribus-Unum balancing act since its inception. That's what federalism and the separation of powers are all about. That's what much of the Constitution, myriad laws, and many Supreme Court decisions have addressed. But the Diversity Revolution has added a major new dimension to the Pluribus-Unum relationship.

For colleges and universities, the Diversity Revolution has had Pluribus-Unum demographic and psychological ramifications for campus climate. Demographically, it has expanded the presence of women and persons of non-white backgrounds. Psychologically, it has led to a "revolution of rising expectations" that colleges and universities should not only welcome diversity, but also become more responsive to increasingly voiced ethnic and women's perspectives and concerns.

At one time happy just to be admitted to the higher education party, minorities and women now rightfully want a larger role in its planning and implementation. The result has been inevitable disagreements and ultimately a basic rethinking of the role and operation of higher education. While this diversity-impelled reconsideration of the college as an educational community has affected many areas of campus life, I will focus on the implications of four critical Pluribus-Unum areas for college climate:

1) multicultural curricular reform;
2) ethnic isolation and multicultural integration;
3) language and accent diversity; and
4) free speech and campus codes of conduct.

Multicultural Curricular Reform

The process of multicultural curricular reform provides the cornerstone 10
for EPU campus climate. Beginning in the 1960s, spurred by the civil rights movement and the growing minority presence on college campuses, the push

came for more curricular Pluribus—the establishment of minority content courses and ethnic studies programs, a call paralleled in the area of women's studies. Supporters of these Pluribus efforts saw such courses and programs as the most viable avenues for providing alternative scholarly interpretations and pedagogical perspectives seldom found in the traditional college curriculum. Although success has varied—some ethnic and women's studies programs have flourished, while others have collapsed—the new knowledge, insights, critical questions, and interpretive challenges generated by these scholarly and pedagogical movements have fueled the current second wave of multicultural reform.

While generally still supporting separate ethnic and women's studies programs as important loci of teaching and research about gender and ethnicity, EPU Multiculturalists no longer accept the sufficiency of Pluribus isolationist specialization. Rather, they have drawn upon new multicultural knowledge and insights to rethink the very bases of mainstream scholarship and to work toward a more capacious, future-oriented Unum curricular climate.

This curricular transformation has taken many forms: the establishment of required world civilization courses (incorporating, not defrocking, Western civilization); the institution of diversity-oriented course graduation requirements; and the greater integration of multicultural perspectives into mainstream courses in such areas as American history, literature, and society. In short, EPU Multiculturalists have championed the transformation of the Unum college curriculum to expose all students to national and world Pluribus in order to help better prepare them for the guaranteed future of ethnic diversity and global interdependence. For the Macbeths of traditionalist curricular Unum, Birnam wood, safely marginalized in the 1960s and '70s, has come to high Dunsinane hill.[1]

This multicultural transformation of curricular Unum is no clash between liberal, illiberal, and non-illiberal educators, no joust between accused closers and self-anointed openers of the American mind—as satisfyingly simplistic and journalistically marketable as these polarizing dichotomies may be. Highly publicized curricular debates and student demonstrations at a few major universities have dominated media attention. Yet, on most campuses such curricular changes have occurred not because of student protest or the imposition of supposed "political correctness" on spineless colleagues by campus radicals.

Curricular change has generally come through the serious, contemplative implementation of a new multicultural educational vision based on the desire to help students more effectively engage the future, in particular, the opportunities and challenges of the Diversity Revolution as well as growing global interdependence. Even American business in-service education has gone multicultural—witness the rapid rise of company-instituted diversity training—while some of K–12 education has progressed multiculturally far beyond colleges and

[1]In Shakespeare's play, an apparition tells Macbeth that he will not be vanquished until the trees of Birnam wood march upon his fortified castle at Dunsinane. In Act V the trees do march, as enemy soldiers carry cut boughs before them as camouflage.

universities. In carrying out such reforms, multicultural reformers have followed Charles Kettering's injunction: "My interest is in the future because I am going to spend the rest of my life there."

Overwhelmingly, this curricular reform has involved no rejection of Amer- 15
ican Unum, no repudiation of Western civilization, no adoption of valueless, nonjudgmental relativism. Rather, it has involved a serious recasting of the meaning of American Unum as a more Pluribus concept that recognizes the importance and value of engaging and considering previously marginalized voices and perspectives. In the words of Arnita Jones, executive secretary of the Organization of American Historians, multiculturalism is "not a problem. It's a wonderful opportunity to bring some excellent new scholarship to all levels of education." Multicultural reform-oriented college campuses have merely been heeding the advice of that old radical, Queen Victoria, when she admonished her followers: "Change must be accepted . . . when it can no longer be resisted."

Ethnic Isolation and Multicultural Integration

While the process of multicultural curricular reform has been one major influence on campus climate, it has been accompanied by other Pluribus-Unum issues, including ethnic isolation and multicultural integration. Colleges and universities have historically supported the right of *temporary* Pluribus group isolationism, emerging from the desire of people to spend time with others of shared concerns and interests.

Such isolationism has taken many forms. It encompasses students who feel like being around those of the same gender in sororities and fraternities. It involves persons who want to worship a deity together, usually within an isolationist religious setting, or to socialize with persons who share the same religious beliefs, like a Hillel or a Newman Club. It includes students who gather around common interests like a school newspaper, common pursuits like a football team, common pleasures like a chess club, or common social goals like working in a K–12 outreach tutorial program. And, of course, those groupings may be based on race, ethnicity, and culture, like African-American, Latino, American Indian, Asian-American, Italian-American, Arab-American, or Polish-American student associations, in which people gather periodically in ethnic comfort zones of shared experiences, identities, and concerns.

Yet, some campus denizens and off-campus critics, who accept, support, or even participate in other types of Pluribus isolationism without labeling them as "Balkanization" or "tribalism," become apoplectic about isolationism, no matter how transitory, involving race or ethnicity. When students, staff, or faculty of visibly similar ethnic appearance eat together in school cafeterias, sit together in classrooms, or, most terrifyingly, form organizations, such alarmist critics proclaim this as indisputable evidence of a collapsing Unum, even a disintegrating society.

But since all of us, at various times and places, function as Pluribus isolationists—even professors gather in their own disciplinary isolationism in department meetings or scholarly conventions—then there is nothing *intrinsically* wrong with temporary isolationism, even when based on race and ethnicity. The Unum problem for campus climate and, likewise, for society, occurs when racial, ethnic, cultural, religious, gender, political, disciplinary, or any other type of isolationism—what The Carnegie Foundation for the Advancement of Teaching report, *Campus Life: In Search of Community,* has called "little loyalties"—becomes an overly encompassing element of one's life. Isolationism becomes injurious to a sense of campus community when people decide that only their groups matter, when they lose (or fail to develop) concern and consideration for other individuals, other groups, the campus at large, and society as a whole.

20 The danger of Pluribus isolationism, then, lies not in its unavoidable existence, but in its avoidable extremism. The challenge for college campuses is to create a climate in which temporary Pluribus isolationism and continuous Unum integration operate in a mutually constructive fashion.

Language and Accent Diversity

Related to the isolation-integration issue is the growing controversy over foreign languages and accents. Bilingual students, staff, and faculty, many of whom speak English as a second language, are increasing on college campuses. While necessarily using English throughout most of their campus life, many bilingual speakers enjoy moments of non-English conversational respite from the demanding labor of listening to and speaking English. During these intervals they can relax by speaking their strongest language, a relief from the stresses and strains of operating continuously in a sometimes wearying "foreign-language" English environment.

Such actions are as natural and American as apple pie. When Americans run into each other in a foreign country, even if they speak that nation's language, they normally switch to English. Why? Because it is easier and more comfortable as well as emotionally relaxing and cognitively rejuvenating after hours of speaking and hearing the foreign language. Why shouldn't the same occur for English-as-a-second-language speakers on college campuses? Yet participants in such Pluribus speech behavior, particularly college employees, have become targets of extremist Unum criticism.

Now the U.S. Supreme Court has pushed the language issue one step further into the area of accents. In 1990, the Court let stand a Ninth Circuit Court of Appeals ruling in the case of *Fragante vs. the Honolulu Department of Motor Vehicles.* A Filipino immigrant, Manuel Fragante, had been denied a position with the Department not because of his command of English, which he had already demonstrated on the written examination, but on the grounds that his accent would restrict his ability to deal with the public. The Supreme Court upheld the Department, ruling that such discrimination is acceptable if an accent "interferes materially" with the ability to perform a job. (In the meantime, Fragante was hired by the state of Hawaii for a position in which he conducted telephone surveys—in English.)

Of course, the Court did not establish guidelines for determining when an accent "interferes materially" with job performance or what accents are acceptable or unacceptable for a particular endeavor. Did Henry Kissinger's thick accent "interfere materially" with his ability to teach history or serve as Secretary of State? *Everybody* speaks with an accent—just listen to a conversation between an American, a Jamaican, and a Kenyan, or throw in a couple of people from England or India. They all speak English, but each will notice the others' accents.

However, I don't want to trivialize the accent issue. I have had students— 25
mainly immigrant and refugee students—whose accents severely impeded their ability to communicate orally and probably rendered them less able to perform certain jobs where oral communication was important. Moreover, American universities are currently experiencing a sharp rise in student dissatisfaction with some foreign-born professors and teaching assistants—particularly in such areas as mathematics and the sciences—because of their accents and limited ability in oral English.

Such complaints raise perplexing Pluribus-Unum issues. Students have an Unum right to take courses from professors whose English they can understand, but professors also have a Pluribus right not to be victimized by students who simply don't like their accents. The *Fragante* case has added a new legal twist to this Pluribus-Unum issue, with serious implications for multicultural campus climate. In what respects do professorial accents actually "interfere materially" with student opportunities to learn? Or in what respects do some student complaints simply reflect "accentism," plain old Unum anti-accent nativist bigotry (maybe we should call it "AC"—accent correctness)?

Free Speech and Campus Codes of Conduct

This brings us inevitably to the most controversial current Pluribus-Unum issue spawned by the Diversity Revolution—the balancing of the Pluribus value of free speech and the Unum value of creating a campus climate of civility, in which people of diverse backgrounds can flourish. Racist, sexist, anti-religious, and homophobic incidents have hypertrophied in recent years—not only on college campuses, but also in society at large. How should colleges respond to these reprehensible acts, which poison campus climate and threaten campus community?

Some responses have increased polarization. On the one hand has come rising petulance by some students and faculty, who appear to be engaged in a never-ending search for statements and acts that they somehow can construe as racist, sexist, or other kinds of "ist." Moreover, some campuses have instituted ill-conceived speech codes that have reached ludicrous extremes of attempting to micro-manage the "unacceptable." Such actions have had the unfortunate side effect of trivializing the critical issue of continuing campus and societal bigotry, while at the same time casting a pall on the entire higher educational struggle against prejudice and for multicultural understanding: Witness the growing charges of supposed "political correctness" reigns of terror.

At the other extreme stand the anti-PC demonologists, who have etched mini-careers of modern academic witch-hunting, even branding the scarlet PC on moderate multiculturalist scholarly or curricular initiatives and reforms. Despite their self-righteous claims to being champions of societal Unum through unfettered Pluribus speech (provided, of course, that it is in English), they further polarize campus climate by disregarding variations in ethnic, gender, or multicultural perspectives.

As the *Los Angeles Times* pointed out in a May 13, 1991 editorial on PC, 30
"the label is often misused, for example, as the new acceptable way to denigrate laudable and necessary attempts to make the college curriculum inclusive of the history and achievements of women and minorities." Even the 1991 *Random House Webster's College Dictionary* has been accused of being PC because it has taken such steps as indicating that certain derogatory terms may be offensive. In truth, professional anti-PCers have personified H. L. Mencken's warning that "criticism is prejudice made plausible."

Caught in the middle, college administrators try to contend with the extremes of insult-hunters and anti-multiculturalism demagogues, as well as with the wearying expressions of individual hypersensitivity and the appalling expressions of continuing racism, sexism, and homophobia. But the issues are not simple.

Should campus free speech reign supreme as a Pluribus absolute? (Remember, the First Amendment has long been limited by libel, slander, and defamation laws.) Or should colleges take careful, limited, selective actions to restrict certain kinds of Pluribus expression that erode the Unum civility of campus climate by making some institutions unwelcome for certain groups of students? These EPU administrative dilemmas defy the types of facile answers currently colliding in the rhetorical arena.

Aesop once warned: "Beware lest you lose the substance by grasping at the shadow." The sound and fury over such overblown, media-hyped topics as political correctness have obscured the larger, deeper, more significant diversity-related issues facing higher education: the creation of a better E Pluribus Unum campus climate and the role that colleges and universities can play in contributing to our students' and our nation's successful response to the Diversity Revolution.

The challenge of building campus community in a multicultural society involves balancing Pluribus and Unum imperatives, avoiding Pluribus and Unum extremism, and rejecting the prophets of polarization. For the complex dilemmas raised by the Diversity Revolution, there are no simple solutions. However, as Einstein pointed out, "the formulation of a problem is often more essential than its solution."

By providing a framework for weighing and responding to both Pluribus 35
and Unum as basic, sometimes conflicting values of our society, EPU Multiculturalism can help colleges and universities reformulate, clarify, and thereby more effectively address these perplexing issues. Moreover, it also provides an

educational vision for better preparing college students to participate more constructively in what will inevitably be a multicultural future.

Questions for Discussion

1. Look at the article by Diane Ravitch earlier in this chapter. Would Cortés agree with her rejection of "particularism"? Is his multiculturalism the same as Ravitch's?
2. Cortés sees value in "ethnic comfort zones of shared experiences, identities, and concerns" (paragraph 17). But what exactly does he say in defense of "Pluribus isolationism"? Do you agree that such associations should be temporary, a matter of "little loyalties" (paragraph 19)? At what point can we say that such groups have become extremist?
3. In paragraph 26 Cortés satirizes "AC"—accent correctness. How can we distinguish between simple prejudice against an accent and genuine interference with communication? What should be done in cases of the former? Of the latter?

For Inquiry

Cortés conceives his entire article around the tension between what he terms "Pluribus" and "Unum." Choose three other articles in this chapter, and discuss how each writer deals with (or fails to deal with) this tension.

For Convincing or Persuading

Cortés invokes Aesop's adage "Beware lest you lose the substance by grasping at the shadow" (paragraph 33). Based on the articles in this chapter, any other reading you have done, and class discussion, attempt to distinguish substance from shadow in the debate over political correctness and multiculturalism. Write an editorial for your campus newspaper that states, explains, and defends your conclusions.

For Further Research and Discussion

1. Working with relevant resources listed in Appendix A on research, find three or four articles on the philosophy of education. Each member of the class should report back on what he or she has read. Then discuss the various viewpoints the class has found, compare them, and attempt to classify the writers in this chapter according to the philosophy of education each seems to entertain.
2. Find out about the attitudes, programs, and initiatives currently characteristic of local, state, and federal agencies concerned with education. What is the impact of these agencies on political correctness and multiculturalism? In your opinion, is government doing too much or too little? The right things or the wrong things?

Additional Suggestions for Writing

1. *Convincing.* Arthur Schlesinger argues that one of the roles of public schools in the United States has been to create a unified people out of the members of many races, nationalities, and religions that come to our shores. If you have had a public-school education, decide whether your experiences support such a role for U.S. schools. After doing additional field and library research, write an argument criticizing or defending the efforts of the public schools to forge a common culture and identity. You may choose to disagree with Schlesinger, arguing that this is not a necessary role for the schools.
2. *Persuasion.* At many colleges and universities, student groups organize programs that seek to raise the campus community's awareness of certain minorities. If your campus has held such "awareness" weeks or months, decide what purpose they are intended to accomplish and how effective they generally are. You might think in terms of Cortés's distinction between Unum and Pluribus: Do awareness weeks increase a sense of unity, a sense of difference or a sense of what Cortés calls "E Pluribus Unum Multiculturalism"? Write an argument that persuades groups that sponsor such events to either continue or drop their efforts.

APPENDIX A

Researching Arguments

This section is intended to help you with any argument you write. Research, which simply means "careful study," is essential to serious inquiry and most well-constructed cases. Before you write, you need to investigate the ongoing conversation that is "out there" on any given issue. As you construct your argument, you will need specific evidence and the support of authorities to make a convincing case for a skeptical audience.

Your experience in high school may have led you to regard the "research paper" as different from other papers, but this distinction between researched and non-researched writing does not usually apply to argumentation. An argument with no research behind it is generally a weak one indeed. Many of the arguments you read, including some that are reprinted in Part 2 of this text, may not appear to be "researched" because the writers have not cited their sources—most likely because they were writing for the general public rather than for an academic or professional audience. In college writing, however, students are usually required to document all sources of ideas used in a paper, as we will demonstrate later in this section.

Research for argumentation usually begins not as a search for evidence, but rather as inquiry into an issue that you have chosen or have been assigned. Your task in inquiry is to discover information about the issue but, more importantly, to find arguments that address the issue and to familiarize yourself with the range of positions and the cases people make for them. You should inquire into these arguments, using your critical reading skills and entering into dialogues with the authors until you feel satisfied and confident about a position you can take as your own.

However, sometimes research must begin at an even earlier stage if your instructor has asked you to select an issue to write about. So we begin with suggestions on how to find an issue.

FINDING AN ISSUE

Let's say you have been assigned an essay on any issue of current public concern, ranging from one debated on your campus to one rooted in international affairs. If you have no ideas for something to write about, what should you do?

Understand That an Issue Is More Than Just a Topic

You must look for a subject that people have genuine disagreements over. For example, homelessness is a topic: You could report on many different aspects of it from the number of homeless people in our country to profiles of individual homeless people. But this is not really an issue because virtually everyone agrees that the problem exists. However, once you start considering solutions to the problem of homelessness, you are dealing with an issue, because people will disagree about how to solve the problem.

Keep Abreast of Current Events

Develop the habit of reading newspapers and magazines regularly. This will keep you informed of debates on current issues. It is best to write on issues of genuine concern to you, rather than to manufacture concern at the last minute because a paper is due. If you keep a record of responses to your reading in your writer's notebook, you can use these now as a source of ideas.

Research the News

Visit the current periodicals shelves of your library or a local newsstand. Consult the front page and the editorial/opinion columns of your city's daily paper. In addition, most newsstands and all libraries carry the *New York Times* and other large-city dailies that offer thorough coverage of national and international events. Remember that you are looking for an issue, so if you find an article on the front page that interests you, think about how people might disagree over some question it raises. For example, an article announcing that health care costs rose a record 14 percent in the last year might suggest the issue of government control over the medical profession; an article about a traditionally African-American fraternity in your campus newspaper could raise the issue of the advisability of colleges tolerating racial segregation in the Greek system. In addition to newspapers, such magazines as *Time, Newsweek,* and *U.S. News and World Report* cover current events, and others, such as *Harper's, Atlantic Monthly, New Republic, National Review,* and *Utne Reader* offer essays, articles, and arguments on important current issues.

Research Your Library's Periodicals Indexes

Indexes are lists of articles in specific publications or groups of publications. You are most likely familiar with one index, the *Readers' Guide to Periodical Literature.* (For names of other indexes, see "Finding Sources" later in this section.) If you have a vague subject in mind, such as gender discrimination, consulting an index for articles and arguments on the topic can help you narrow your focus to a more concrete issue. Of course, if you don't have an issue in mind, looking through the *Readers' Guide* won't be very helpful, so we offer some suggestions for using indexes more efficiently.

You can, for example, look in a newspaper index (some are printed and bound, while others are computerized) under "Editorial" for a list of topics on which the editors have stated positions, or you can look under the name of a columnist—such as William F. Buckley, Anna Quindlen, or A. M. Rosenthal—whose views on current issues regularly appear in that paper. The bonus to using a newspaper index in this way is that it will lead you directly to arguments on an issue.

Another resource for finding arguments on an issue when you have a topic in mind is *InfoTrac,* a computerized index to magazines, journals, and selected current articles in the *New York Times.* After you type in an appropriate subject word or key word, InfoTrac allows you to narrow your search further. If you type in the key word of your subject followed by "and editorial" or "and opinion," the only articles called up will be argumentative columns and editorials.

A further possibility is to browse through an index listing only periodicals that specialize in social issues topics, such as the *Journal of Social Issues* and *Vital Speeches of the Day.* Finally, *Speech Index* will help you find speeches that have been printed in books.

Inquire into the Issue

Once you have determined an issue, you can begin your inquiry into the positions already articulated in the public conversation. You may yourself already hold a position, but during inquiry, you should be as open as possible to the full range of viewpoints on the issue, and you should look for articles that provide information as well as for arguments about the issue.

Inquiring into an issue also involves evaluating sources. Remember that research means "careful study," and being careful as you perform these initial steps will make all the difference in the quality of the argument you eventually write. An additional bonus is that care now will save you time in the long run.

FINDING SOURCES

Sources for developing an argument can be found through several kinds of research. Library research is usually essential, but don't overlook what social scientists call field research. (If you have access to computers, you can also draw on electronic mail and on the Internet of information networks, but because technology changes so rapidly in electronic research, we do not attempt to cover it here.)

Field Research

Research "in the field" means studying the world directly through observations, questionnaires, and interviews.

Observations

Do not discount the value of your own personal experiences as evidence in making a case. As you read the professional arguments in Part Two of this text, you will notice that many writers there offer as evidence what they themselves have seen, heard, and done.

Such experiences may be from the past. For example, Betty Friedan writes about her experiences as a wife and mother during the 1960s to support her point that she and other feminists were committed to their families (see pages 326–338). She mentions specific events—organizing a clambake on Long Island, taking her children to Gettysburg, making her husband a martini after work—and these make her writing both credible and interesting.

Alternatively, you may seek out a specific personal experience as you inquire into your topic. For example, a student writing about the homeless in Dallas decided to visit a shelter. She called ahead to receive permission and schedule the visit. Her paper was memorable because she was able to include the stories and physical descriptions of several homeless women, with details of their conversations.

Questionnaires and Surveys

You may be able to get information on some topics, especially if they are campus-related, by doing surveys or questionnaires. Be forewarned, however, that it is very difficult to conduct a reliable survey.

First, there is the problem of designing a clear and unbiased instrument to distribute. If you have ever filled out an evaluation form for an instructor or a course, you will know what we mean about the problem of clarity. A question might ask whether an instructor returns papers "in a reasonable length of time," while in fact what is "reasonable" to some students may be far too long for some other students. As for bias, consider the question, "Have you ever had trouble getting assistance from the library's reference desk?" To get a fair response, this questionnaire had better also ask how many requests for help were handled promptly and well. If you do decide to draft a questionnaire, we suggest you do it as a class project, so that students on all sides of the issue can contribute, and everyone can trouble-shoot for areas of ambiguity.

Second is the problem of getting a representative response. For the same reasons that we doubt the results of certain magazine-sponsored surveys of people's sex lives, we need to doubt the statistical accuracy of surveys targeting a group that may not be representative of the whole. For example, it might be difficult to generalize about all first-year college students in the United States based on a survey of just your English class—or even the entire first-year class at your college. Consider too that those who respond to a survey often have an ax to grind on the topic.

We don't rule out the value of surveys here, but we caution you to consider the difficulties of designing, administering, and interpreting one.

Interviews

You can get a great deal of current information about an issue as well as informed opinions by talking to experts. Just as when you go to your reference librarian, the first step in conducting an interview is to decide exactly what you want to find out. Write down your questions, whether you plan to conduct the interview over the telephone or in person.

Next, you need to find the right person to interview. This can take some effort and imagination, but many organizations and government and social agencies employ people whose primary responsibility is providing information to those who seek it. As you read about an issue, note the names (and the possible biases) of any organizations mentioned; these may have local offices, whose telephone numbers you could find in the directory. In addition, institutions such as hospitals, universities, and large corporations have offices of information and public relations. An excellent source of over 30,000 names and phone numbers of experts in almost any field is a book by Matthew Lesko, *Lesko's Info-Power.* Finally, do not overlook the expertise available from faculty members at your own school.

Once you have determined possible sources for interviews, you must begin a patient and courteous round of telephone calls until you are connected with the right person. According to Lesko, you can expect to make seven calls before you reach him or her. Remain cheerful and clear in your pursuit.

Whether your interview is face-to-face or over the telephone, begin by being sociable, but also by acknowledging that the person's time is valuable. Tell the person something about the project you are working on, but withhold your own position on any controversial matters. Try to sound neutral, and be specific about what you want to know. Take notes, and include the title and background of the person being interviewed as well as the date of the interview, which you will need when citing this source in the finished paper. If you want to tape the interview, be sure to ask permission. Finally, if you have the individual's mailing address, it is thoughtful to send a follow-up note thanking him or her for the assistance.

If everyone in your class is researching a single topic, and it is likely that more than one person would contact a particular expert on campus or in your community, organize a way to avoid flooding that person with requests for his or her time. Perhaps one or two students could be designated to interview the subject and report to the class, or the expert could be invited to visit the class, if that is convenient.

Library Research

University libraries are vast repositories of information. To use them most efficiently, consult with professional librarians. Do not hesitate to ask for help. Even college faculty can discover new sources of information by talking with librarians about current research projects.

Library of Congress Subject Headings

Finding sources will involve using your library's card or computerized catalog, reference books, and indexes to periodicals. Before using these, however, it makes sense to look first through a set of books every library locates near its catalog, the *Library of Congress Subject Headings.* This multi-volume set will help you know what terms to look under when you move on to catalogs and indexes. Consulting these subject headings first will save you time in the long run: It will help you narrow your search and keep you from overlooking potentially good sources because the *Library of Congress* listing also suggests related terms to look under. For example, if you look under the term "mercy killing," you will be directed to "euthanasia," where you can find the following helpful information:

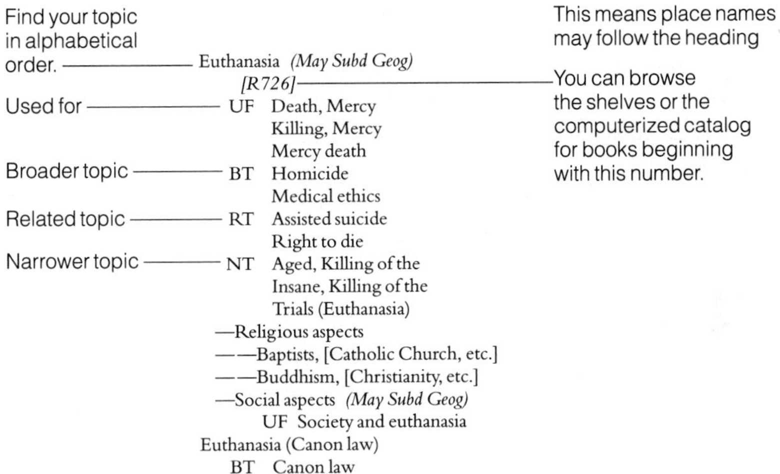

The Card or Computerized Catalog

Use your library's catalog primarily to find books or government documents. (For arguments and information on very current issues, however, keep in mind that the card or computer catalog is not the best source, because books take years to write and publish.) Library catalogs list all holdings and are referenced according to author, title, and subject. With a computerized catalog, it is also possible to find works according to key words and by Library of Congress number. Look under the subject headings you find in the *Library of Congress Subject Headings.* Because the Library of Congress system groups books according to subject matter, you may want to browse in the catalog (or on the shelves) for other books in the same range of call numbers.

Typically, the library's catalog card or screen will appear as illustrated at the top of page 574.

Indexes to Periodicals

Good libraries contain many indexes that list articles in newspapers, magazines, and journals. Some of these are printed and bound; others are computerized on CD-ROM. Once again, the *Library of Congress Subject Headings* can help you determine the best words to use in these indexes.

Newspaper Indexes *The New York Times Index* is printed and bound in volumes. Each volume indexes articles for one year, grouped according to subject and listed

```
Search Request: A=FALUDI SUSAN
BOOK - Record 2 of 3 Entries Found                                    Brief View
------------------------------- Screen 1 of 1 ----------------------------------
       TITLE:  Backlash : the undeclared war against American women
     EDITION:  1st ed.
      AUTHOR:  Faludi, Susan.

   PUBLISHER:  New York : Crown, c1991.
 DESCRIPTION:  xxiii, 552 p. : 25 cm.

    SUBJECTS:  Feminism--United States.
               Women--United States--Social conditions.
               Women--Psychology.
--------------------------------------------------------------------------------
        LOCATION:            CALL NUMBER:                     STATUS:
 1. Fondren Browsing      HQ1426 .F35 1991            Charged, Due: 04/02/93
    Coll.

--------------------------------------------------------------------------------
 COMMANDS:            LO Long View          I Index
                      N  Next Record        H Help
 O  Other Options     P  Previous Record

NEXT COMMAND:
```

according to the month and day of publication. The subject headings in the *New York Times Index* tend to be very general. For example, we could not find the heading "euthanasia," the term for mercy killing used in the *Library of Congress Subject Headings.* We had to think of a more general term, so we tried "medicine." There, we found the following:

MEDICINE AND HEALTH. See also
Abortion
Accidents and Safety
Acupuncture
Aged
Anatomy and Physiology
Anesthesia and Anesthetics
Antibiotics
Autopsies
Bacteria
Birth Control and Family Planning
Birth Defects
Blood
Death — The subject heading most likely to lead to articles on euthanasia.
Environment
Epidemics
Exercise
Faith Healers
First Aid
Food Contamination and Poisoning
Handicapped
Hormones
Immunization and Immunity
Implants
Industrial and Occupational Hazards
Malpractice Insurance
Mental Health and Disorders
Nursing Homes
Pesticides and Pests
Population
Radiation

Smoking
Spas
Surgery and Surgeons
Teeth and Dentistry
Transplants
Vaccination and Vaccines
Veterinary Medicine
Viruses
Vitamins
Water Pollution
Workmen's Compensation Insurance
X-Rays

We decided the term "death" on this list seemed most likely to lead us to articles on euthanasia, and we were correct. Following is a small selection of what we found.

Topic headings are listed in alphabetical order

DEATH. See also
Deaths

Several laws enacted in New York State in 1990 are set to take effect, including measure that will allow New Yorkers to designate another person to make health-care decisions on their behalf if they become unable to do so (M). Ja 1.1. 32:1

Articles are listed in chronological order.

Each entry contains an abstract.

Another right-to-die case emerges in Missouri, where Christine Busalacchi has been in persistent vegetative state as result of auto accident on May 29, 1987, when she was 17-year-old high school junior: her father, Pete Busalacchi, who has been seeking unsuccessfully to have his daughter transferred to Minnesota, where feeding tube may possibly be removed, says that Christine never discussed matters of life or death; Nancy Cruzan case recalled; photo (M). Ja 2. A.12:1

Missouri state court dismisses order preventing Pete Busalacchi from moving his comatose daughter Christine to another state where less strict rules might allow removal of feeding tube (S). Ja S.A.16:1

(S), (M), or (L) before date indicates whether an article is short, medium, or long.

In a case that medical ethicists and legal experts say is apparently a first, Minneapolis-based Hennapin County Medical Center plans to go to court for permission to turn off 37-year-old Helga Wanglie's life support system against her family's wishes; photos (L). Ja 10.A.1:1

Each entry concludes with the month, day, section, page, and column.

Probate Judge Louis Kohn of St. Louis County rules that Pete Busalacchi may move his daughter, Christine, from Missouri hospital where she has lain for more than three years with severe brain damage and take her to Minnesota where law might allow removal of her feeding tube (S). Ja 17.3.5:1

People wishing to avoid heroic medical treatment in event they become hopelessly ill and unable to speak for themselves are often poorly served by so-called "living wills" to achieve that end: many health care experts recommend a newer document, health care proxy, in which patients designate surrogate who has legal authority to make medical decisions if they are too sick to offer an opinion; others recommend combining living will with health care proxy; drawing (M). Ja 17.3.9:1

Missouri Judge Louis Kohn rules Pete Busalacchi has right to determine medical care of his daughter Christine, who has been severely brain-damaged for more than three years; gives him authority to have feeding tube removed (S). Ja 18.A.16:4

Missouri appeals court bars Pete Busalacchi from moving his comatose 20-year-old daughter Christine to Minnesota where laws governing removal of life-support systems are less restrictive (S). Ja 19.1.17:2

Editorial Notebook commentary by Fred M. Hechinger says his 94-year-old mother's last days were filled with needless suffering and fear because doctors ignored her, and her family's wish that no heroic efforts be taken to prolong her life; says inhumane legal restrictions have made doctors accomplices in torture, and medical profession has shown little courage in fighting them (M). Ja 24.A.22:1

You will also find a limited number of *New York Times* articles listed in the computerized periodicals index known as *InfoTrac,* which we discuss later.

Other printed and bound newspaper indexes carried by most libraries are the *Christian Science Monitor Index,* the *Times Index* (to the London *Times,* a good source for international issues), the *Wall Street Journal Index,* and the *Washington Post Index* (good for federal government issues).

Newsbank offers computerized indexes for hundreds of local and state newspapers. Your library is likely to subscribe to *Newsbank* for indexes of only one or two regional papers in your area. *Newsbank*'s CD-ROMs contain the entire text of each article indexed.

Indexes to Magazines, Journals, and Other Materials Many libraries have CD-ROM databases indexing journals in business and academic fields. *InfoTrac,* one such database, indexes current articles from the *New York Times* and many other periodicals, so you may want to begin your search here rather than with the printed and bound indexes discussed previously. Be aware, however, that *Info Trac* is a very selective index, far less comprehensive than the printed and bound indexes, which also go back much further in time. In addition, *Info Trac* will not include many articles that can be found in the specialized indexes that follow. *InfoTrac* is, however, constantly being upgraded, so check with your reference librarian to see how this database can help you research your issue.

1. General Interest Indexes

    Readers' Guide to Periodical Literature
    Public Affairs Information Service (PAIS)
    Essay and General Literature Index
    Speech Index

2. Arts and Humanities Indexes

    Art Index
    Film Literature Index
    Humanities Index
    Music Index

Philosopher's Index
Popular Music Periodical Index

3. Social Science, Business, and Law Indexes

Business Periodicals Index
Criminology Index
Education Index
Index to Legal Periodicals
Psychological Abstracts
Social Sciences Index
Sociological Abstracts
Women's Studies Abstracts

4. Science and Engineering Indexes

Applied Science and Technology Index
Biological and Agricultural Index
Current Contents
Environmental Index
General Science Index

Reference Books

Students tend to overlook reference books, often because they are unaware of their existence. You may find reference books useful early in the process of inquiring into your issue, but they will also be useful for locating supporting evidence as you develop your own argument.

Encyclopedias. Current, specialized encyclopedias are a good source of general background information. Find out which ones can help you by consulting *First Stop: The Master Index to Subject Encyclopedias,* which provides a subject index to 430 sources of background information.
Demographic Yearbook
Facts on File
Guide to American Law. This reference work explains legal principles and concepts in plain English.
Statistical Abstract of the United States
World Almanac and Book of Facts

Bibliographies

Books and articles sometimes include a Works Cited list or bibliography. These can open up numerous other sources. Library catalog entries and many indexes indicate whether a book or article contains a bibliography.

EVALUATING SOURCES

Before you begin to read and evaluate your sources, you may need to re-evaluate your issue. If you have been unable to find many sources that address the question you are raising, it is a good idea to step back and consider changing the focus of your argument, or at least expanding its focus.

For example, when offered the choice of any topic in the large area of issues involving the relationship between humans and other animals, one student, Michelle, decided to focus on the mistreatment of circus animals, based on claims made in leaflets handed out at the circus by protestors for animal rights. Even with a librarian's help, however, Michelle could find no subject headings that led to even one source in her university's library. Unable to find any materials in the library, she called and visited animal rights activists in her city, who provided her with more materials written and published by the animal rights movement. She realized, however, that researching the truth of their claims was more than she could undertake, so she had to acknowledge that her entire argument was based on inadequate inquiry and heavily biased sources.

Once you have re-evaluated your topic use the following method to record and evaluate sources.

Eliminate Inappropriate Sources

If you are a first-year college student, you will find that some books and articles are intended for audiences who have a much more specialized knowledge of the subject than you do. You will have trouble using a source that confuses you or shakes your confidence in your reading comprehension, so put it aside, at least temporarily.

Carefully Record Complete Bibliographic Information

For every source you are even considering using, be sure to record full bibliographic information. You should take this information from the source itself, not from an index, which may be incomplete or even inaccurate. If you make a record of this information immediately, you will not have to go back later to fill in careless omissions. We recommend that you use a separate small index card for each source, but whatever you write on, you must record the following:

For a book

Author's full name (or names)
Title of book
City where published
Name of publisher
Year published

For an article or essay in a book, record all of the information for a book, including the names of both the book's author or editor as well as the title and the author(s) of the article; include also the inclusive page numbers of the article or chapter (for example, "pp. 100–150").

For a periodical

Author's full name (or names)
Title of the article
Title of the periodical
Date of the issue
Volume number, if given
Inclusive page numbers

Read the Source Critically

As we say in Chapter 3, critical reading depends on having some prior knowledge of the subject and the ability to see a text in its rhetorical context. As you research a topic, your prior knowledge naturally becomes deeper with each article you read. But your sources are not simply windows onto your topic, giving you a clear view; whether argumentative or informative, they present a bias. Before looking through them, you must look *at* them. Therefore, it is essential that you devote conscious attention to the rhetorical context of the sources you find. As you read, keep these questions in mind.

Who Is the Writer and What Is His or Her Bias?

Is there a note that tells you anything about the writer's professional title or university or institutional affiliation? If not, a quick look in the *Dictionary of American Biographies* might help; or you can consult the *Biography and Genealogy Master Index,* which will send you to numerous specialized biographical sketches. If you are going to cite the writer as an authority in your argument, you need to be able to convince your audience of his or her credibility.

When Was This Source Written?

If you are researching a very current issue, you need to decide at what point sources may be too dated. Even for current issues, however, you may want to gather some earlier perspectives on your topic.

Where Did This Source Appear?

If you are using articles in periodicals, be aware of the periodical's readership and any editorial bias. For example, *National Review* has a conservative bent, while *The Nation* is liberal; an article in the *Journal of the American Medical Association* will usually defend the medical profession. Looking at the table of contents and scanning any editorial statements will help give you a feel for the periodical's political leanings. Also look at the page that lists the publisher and the editorial board. You would find, for example, that *New American* is published by the ultra right-wing John Birch Society. If you need help determining political bias, ask a librarian. A reference book that lists periodicals by subject matter and explains their bias is *Magazines for Libraries.*

Why Was the Book or Article Written?

While some articles are occasioned by events in the news, most books and arguments are written as part of an ongoing debate or conversation among scholars or journalists. Being aware of the issues and the participants in this conversation is essential, as you will be joining it with your own researched argument. You can check *Book Review Index* to find where a book has been reviewed and then consult some reviews to see how the book was received.

What Is the Author's Aim?

Be aware, first, whether the source is intended to inform or whether it is an argument with a claim to support. Both informative and argumentative sources are useful, and even informative works will have some bias. When your source is an argument, note whether it aims primarily to inquire, to convince, to persuade, or to mediate.

How Is the Source Organized?

If the writer hasn't done so for you with subheadings or chapter titles, try to break the text into its various parts, and note what function each part plays in the whole.

Inquire into the Source

Because we devote so much attention to inquiry in Chapters 4 and 5, we will not go into detail about this process here. However, you should identify the author's claim and evaluate the support offered for it. Look especially hard at arguments that support your own position; seeing weaknesses in such "friendly" arguments has caused many students to undergo an epiphany, or a moment of enlightenment, in which they change their whole stance on an issue.

Consider How You Might Use the Source

If you are fortunate, your research will uncover many authoritative and well-crafted arguments on your issue. The challenge you now face is to work out a way to use them in an argument of your own, with your own structure and strategy and suited to your own aim and audience.

A good argument results from synthesizing, or blending together, the results of your research. Your sources should help you come up with strong reasons and evidence, as well as ideas about opposing views. But it is unlikely that all your reasons will come from one source, or that each part of your argument will draw primarily upon a single source; and you don't want to create an argument that reads like a patchwork of other people's ideas. To avoid this, you must organize your sources according to your own argumentative strategy and integrate material from a variety of sources into each part of your argument.

We suggest that you review Chapter 6, where we discuss developing and refining a thesis (or claim) and constructing a brief of your argument. As you make your brief, identify those sources that will help you offer reasons or support, such as expert opinion or specific data.

USING SOURCES

How you use a source depends on what you need it for. After you have drafted an argument, you may simply need to consult an almanac for some additional evidence or look up John F. Kennedy's inaugural address to find a stirring quotation. But at earlier stages of the writing process, you may be unsure of your own position and even in need of general background information on the issue. What follows is some advice for those early stages, when you will be encountering a great deal of information and opposing viewpoints. As you research, remember to write down all of the bibliographical information for every source you might use (see pages 578–579).

Taking Notes

Photocopying machines make it possible to take the complete text of articles out of the library, just as we check out books. They also make it possible for us to mark up and annotate our own personal copy, which is particularly helpful.

However, if you do not take notes, preferably on large notecards, you will have to sort through the entire text of the article to find the idea you thought would work in your paper when you read the source two weeks before. So whether you are working with a book or an article, you will save time in the long run if you write down anything that strikes you as important or useful.

SUGGESTIONS FOR NOTETAKING

1. Note your source. Use the author's last name or an abbreviated title, or devise a code, such as "A," "B," "C," and so forth.
2. Note the exact page or pages where the information or quotation appears.
3. When you quote, be exact and put quotation marks around the writer's words, so you won't be guilty of plagiarism if you use them later in your paper.
4. Prefer paraphrase and summary to quotation, unless the writer's words are strongly opinionated or especially memorable.

Paraphrasing

Paraphrasing, which means restating a passage in different words, improves reading comprehension. When you put an idea, especially a complex one, into your own words, you are actually explaining the idea to yourself. When you feel sure of your grasp of an idea, you can write more confidently, with a sense of owning the idea rather than just borrowing it.

SUGGESTIONS FOR PARAPHRASING

1. Use the dictionary if any words in the original are not completely familiar to you.
2. Work with whole ideas, not word-by-word. Paraphrase involves more than keeping the original word order and just plugging in synonyms. Don't be afraid to make your paraphrase longer than the original, and to break a complex sentence into several simpler ones of your own. Take apart a difficult idea and rebuild it, using baby steps if necessary. Don't just echo the original passage thoughtlessly.
3. Don't be a slave to the original—or to the thesaurus. Read the passage until you think you understand it, or a part of it. Then write your version, without looking back at the original. Rearrange the order of ideas if doing so makes the passage more accessible.
4. Don't strain to find substitutes for words that are essential to the meaning of a passage.

We will illustrate paraphrasing with an excerpt from a source selected by one student, Patrick Pugh, who was researching the topic of euthanasia and planning to defend active euthanasia, or assisted suicide. In the university library Patrick found a book entitled *Suicide and Euthanasia: The Rights of Personhood,* a collection of essays written by doctors, philosophers, theologians, and legal experts. Published in 1981, the book was somewhat dated in 1991 when Patrick was working; but at the same time he felt the question of whether suicide is moral or immoral was a timeless one. He read an essay entitled "In Defense of Suicide" by Joseph Fletcher, a former professor at the Episcopal Divinity School and president of the Society for the Right to Die. Before taking notes on Fletcher's essay, Patrick made a bibliography card recording all the necessary information about this source, as shown at the top of p. 583.

The following passage from Fletcher's essay offers a crucial definition; it is the kind of passage that a researcher should paraphrase on a notecard rather than quote, so that the idea becomes part of one's own store of knowledge.

> We must begin with the postulate that no action is intrinsically right or wrong, that nothing is inherently good or evil. Right and wrong, good and evil, desirable and undesirable—all are ethical terms and all are predicates, not properties. The moral "value" of any human act is always contingent, depending on the shape of the action in the situation. . . . The variables and factors in each set of circumstances are the determinants of what ought to be done—not prefabricated generalizations or prescriptive rules. . . . No "law" of conduct is always obliging; what we ought to do is whatever maximizes human well-being.
>
> —JOSEPH FLETCHER, "In Defense of Suicide"

Fletcher's definition of ethical action:

The ethical value of any human action is not a quality inherent in the act itself. It is a judgment that we make about the act after examining the entire situation in which it takes place. Rather than relying on general rules about what is moral and immoral, we should make our decision on the basis of what is best for human well-being in any given set of circumstances.

Fletcher, pp. 38-39, in Wallace/Eser.

Patrick paraphrased this passage as follows. Note that on the card he names the author of the essay as well as the editors of the book and the exact pages on which the idea was found.

Fletcher, Joseph. "In Defense of Suicide." In Suicide and Euthanasia: The Rights of Personhood. Eds. Samuel E. Wallace and Albin Eser. Knoxville: U of Tennessee P 1981

Fletcher's article: pp. 38–50.

Following Through

From your own research, identify a passage of approximately one paragraph that presents a complicated idea. Write a paraphrase of the passage.

Alternatively, you may write a paraphrase of the following paragraph, also from Joseph Fletcher's "In Defense of Suicide":

> What is called positive euthanasia—doing something to shorten or end life deliberately—is the form [of euthanasia] in which suicide is the question, as a voluntary, direct choice of death. For a long time the Christian moralists have distinguished between negative or indirectly willed suicide, like not taking a place in one of the *Titanic's* lifeboats, and positive or directly willed suicide, like jumping out of a lifeboat to make room for a fellow victim of a shipwreck. The moralists mean that we may choose to allow an evil by acts of omission but not to do an evil by acts of comission. The moralists contend that since all suicide is evil, we may only "allow" it; we may not "do" it. (47)

Your instructor may ask you to compare your paraphrase with that of a classmate before revising it and handing it in.

Summarizing

While a paraphrased version may be either longer or shorter than the original passage, a summary is always considerably shorter. It ought to be at least one-third the length of the original and is often considerably less: You may, for example, reduce an entire article to one or two paragraphs.

A summary of an argument must contain the main idea or claim and the main points of support or development. The amount of evidence and detail you include depends upon your purpose for summarizing: If you just want to let your audience know (or remind yourself) about the gist of the original, a bare bones summary is enough; but if you plan to use the summary as part of making your case, you had better include the original's evidence as well.

SUGGESTIONS FOR SUMMARIZING

1. Read and reread the whole until you have identified the thesis and main points. You ought to be able to state these in your own words without looking back at the source.
2. Make it clear at the start whose ideas you are summarizing. Refer to the writer again only as necessary for clarity.
3. If you are summarizing a long passage, break it down into subsections, and work on summarizing each one at a time.

4. As with paraphrasing, work as independently as you can—from memory—as you attack each part. Then go back to the text to check your version for accuracy.
5. Try to maintain the original order of points, with this exception: If the author delayed presenting the thesis, you may want to move it forward.
6. Use your own words as much as possible.
7. Avoid quoting entire sentences. If you want to quote key words and phrases, try to incorporate them into sentences of your own, using quotation marks around just the borrowed words.
8. Write a draft summary; then summarize your draft.
9. Revise for conciseness and coherence; look for ways to combine sentences, using connecting words to show how ideas relate. See Appendix B, pages 624–625.

For an example of using a summary as part of an argument, we return to Patrick Pugh's investigation of euthanasia. In another book, *The End of Life: Euthanasia and Morality* by James Rachels, Patrick found what Rachels describes as the chief religious objections to euthanasia, with Rachels's rebuttals for each. Patrick decided to include this material, in summary, in his paper.

First read the original version that follows; then read Patrick's summarized version beginning on page 589.

JAMES RACHELS
from *The End of Life*

Religious Arguments

Social observers are fond of remarking that we live in a secular age, and there is surely something in this. The power of religious conceptions was due, in some considerable measure, to their usefulness in explaining things. In earlier times, religious ideas were used to explain everything from the origins of the universe to the nature of human beings. So long as we had no other way of understanding the world, the hold of religion on us was powerful indeed. Now, however, these explanatory functions have largely been taken over by the sciences: physics, chemistry, and their allies explain physical nature, while evolutionary biology and psychology combine to tell us about ourselves. As there is less and less work for religious hypotheses to do, the grip of religious ideas on us weakens, and appeals to theological conceptions are heard only on Sunday mornings. Hence, the "secular age."

However, most people continue to hold religious beliefs, and they especially appeal to those beliefs when morality is at issue. Any discussion of mercy-killing quickly leads to objections based on theological grounds, and "secular" arguments for euthanasia are rejected because they leave out the crucial element of God's directions on the matter.

Considering the traditional religious opposition to euthanasia, it is tempting to say: If one is not a Christian (or if one does not have some similar religious orientation), then perhaps euthanasia is an option; but for people who do have such a religious orientation, euthanasia cannot be acceptable. And the discussion might be ended there. But this is too quick a conclusion; for it is possible that the religious arguments against euthanasia are not valid *even for religious people.* Perhaps a religious perspective, even a conventional Christian one, does *not* lead automatically to the rejection of mercy-killing. With this possibility in mind, let us examine three variations of the religious objection.

What God Commands

It is sometimes said that euthanasia is not permissible simply because God forbids it, and we know that God forbids it by the authority of either scripture or Church tradition. Thus, one eighteenth-century minister, Humphrey Primatt, wrote ironically that, in the case of aged and infirm animals,

> God, the Father of Mercies, hath ordained Beasts and Birds of Prey to do that distressed creature the kindness to relieve him his misery, by putting him to death. A kindness which *We* dare not show to our own species. If thy father, thy brother, or thy child should suffer the utmost pains of a long and agonizing sickness, though his groans should pierce through thy heart, and with strong crying and tears he should beg thy relief, yet thou must be deaf unto him; he must wait his appointed time till his charge cometh, till he sinks and is crushed with the weight of his own misery.

5 When this argument is advanced, it is usually advanced with great confidence, as though it were *obvious* what God requires. Yet we may well wonder whether such confidence is justified. The sixth commandment does not say, literally, "Thou shalt not *kill*"—that is a bad translation. A better translation is "Thou shalt not commit *murder,*" which is different, and which does not obviously prohibit mercy-killing. Murder is by definition *wrongful* killing; so, if you do not think that a given kind of killing is wrong, you will not call it murder. That is why the sixth commandment is not normally taken to forbid killing in a just war; since such killing is (allegedly) justified, it is not called murder. Similarly, if euthanasia is justified, it is not murder, and so it is not prohibited by the commandment. At the very least, it is clear that we cannot infer that euthanasia is wrong *because* it is prohibited by the commandment.

If we look elsewhere in the Christian Bible for a condemnation of euthanasia, we cannot find it. These scriptures are silent on the question. We do find numerous affirmations of the sanctity of human life and the fatherhood of God, and some theologians have tried to infer a prohibition on euthanasia from these general precepts. (The persistence of the attempts, in the face of logical difficulties, is a reminder that people insist on reading their moral prejudices *into* religious texts much more often than they derive their moral views *from* the texts.) But we also find exhortations to kindness and mercy, and the Golden Rule proclaimed as the sum of all morality; and these principles, as we have seen, support euthanasia rather than condemn it.

We *do* find a clear condemnation of euthanasia in Church tradition. Regardless of whether there is scriptural authority for it, the Church has historically opposed mercy-killing. It should be emphasized, however, that this is a matter of history. Today, many religious leaders favour euthanasia and think the historical position of the Church has been mistaken. It was an Episcopal minister, Joseph Fletcher, who in his book *Morals and Medicine* formulated the classic modern defence of euthanasia. Fletcher does not stand alone among his fellow churchmen. The Euthanasia Society of America, which he heads, includes many other religious leaders; and the recent "Plea for Beneficent Euthanasia," sponsored by the American Humanist Association, was signed by more religious leaders than people in any other category. So it certainly cannot be claimed that *contemporary* religious forces stand uniformly opposed to euthanasia.

It is noteworthy that even Roman Catholic thinkers are today reassessing the Church's traditional ban on mercy-killing. The Catholic philosopher Daniel Maguire has written one of the best books on the subject, *Death By Choice.* Maguire maintains that "it may be moral and should be legal to accelerate the death process by taking direct action, such as overdosing with morphine or injecting potassium"; and moreover, he proposes to demonstrate that this view is "*compatible with historical Catholic ethical theory,*" contrary to what most opponents of euthanasia assume. Historical Catholic ethical theory, he says, grants individuals permission to act on views that are supported by "good and serious reasons," even when a different view is supported by a majority of authorities. Since the morality of euthanasia *is* supported by "good and serious reasons," Maguire concludes that Catholics are permitted to accept that morality and act on it.

Thus, the positions of both scripture and Church authorities are (at least) ambiguous enough so that the believer is not bound, on these grounds, to reject mercy-killing. The argument from "what God commands" should be inconclusive, even for the staunchest believer.

The Idea of God's Dominion

10 Our second theological argument starts from the principle that "The life of man is solely under the dominion of God." It is for God alone to decide when a person shall live and when he shall die; we have no right to "play God" and arrogate this decision unto ourselves. So euthanasia is forbidden.

This is perhaps the most familiar of all the theological objections to euthanasia; one hears it constantly when the matter is discussed. However, it is remarkable that people still advance this argument today, considering that it was decisively refuted over 200 years ago, when Hume made the simple but devastating point that *if it is for God alone to decide when we shall live and when we shall die, then we "play God" just as much when we cure people as when we kill them.* Suppose a person is sick and we have the means to cure him or her. If we do so, then we are interfering with God's "right to decide" how long the life shall last! Hume put it this way:

> Were the disposal of human life so much reserved as the peculiar providence of the Almighty that it were an encroachment on his right, for men to dispose of their own lives; it would be equally criminal to act for the preservation of life as for its destruction. If I turn aside a stone which is falling upon my head, I disturb this course of nature, and I invade the peculiar providence of the Almighty by lengthening out my life beyond the period which by the general laws of matter and motion he had assigned it.

We alter the length of a person's life when we save it just as much as when we take it. Therefore, if the taking of life is to be forbidden on the grounds that only God has the right to determine how long a person shall live, then the saving of life should be prohibited on the same grounds. We would then have to abolish the practice of medicine. But everyone (except, perhaps, Christian Scientists) concedes that this would be absurd. Therefore, we may *not* prohibit euthanasia on the grounds that only God has the right to determine how long a life shall last. This seems to be a complete refutation of this argument, and if refuted arguments were decently discarded, as they should be, we would hear no more of it.

Suffering and God's Plan

The last religious argument we shall consider is based on the idea that suffering is a part of God's plan for us. God has ordained that people should suffer; he never intended that life should be continually pleasurable. (If he had intended this, presumably he would have created a very different world.) Therefore, if we were to kill people to "put them out of their misery," we would be interfering with God's plan. Bishop Joseph Sullivan, a prominent Catholic opponent of euthanasia, expresses the argument in a passage from his essay "The Immorality of Euthanasia":

> If the suffering patient is of sound mind and capable of making an act of divine resignation, then his sufferings become a great means of merit whereby he can gain reward for himself and also win great favors for the souls in Purgatory, perhaps even release them from their suffering. Likewise the sufferer may give good example to his family and friends and teach them how to bear a heavy cross in a Christlike manner.
>
> As regard those that must live in the same house with the incurable sufferer, they have a great opportunity to practice Christian charity. They can learn to see Christ in the sufferer and win the reward promised in the Beatitudes. This opportunity for charity would hold true even when the incurable sufferer is deprived of the use of reason. It may well be that the incurable sufferer in a particular case may be of greater value

to society than when he was of some material value to himself and his community.

This argument may strike some readers as simply grotesque. Can we imagine this being said, seriously, in the presence of suffering such as that experienced by Stewart Alsop's roommate? "We know it hurts, Jack, and that your wife is being torn apart just having to watch it, but think what a good opportunity this is for you to set an example. You can give us a lesson in how to bear it." In addition, some might think that euthanasia is exactly what *is* required by the "charity" that bystanders have the opportunity to practise.

But, these reactions aside, there is a more fundamental difficulty with the argument. For if the argument were sound, it would lead not only to the condemnation of euthanasia but of *any* measures to reduce suffering. If God decrees that we suffer, why aren't we obstructing God's plan when we give drugs to relieve pain? A girl breaks her arm; if only God knows how much pain is right for her, who are we to mend it? The point is similar to Hume's refutation of the previous argument. This argument, like the previous one, cannot be right because it leads to consequences that no one, not even the most conservative religious thinker, is willing to accept.

We have now looked at three arguments that depend on religious assump- 15
tions. They are all unsound, but I have *not* criticized them simply by rejecting their religious presuppositions. Instead, I have criticized them on their own terms, showing that these arguments should not be accepted even by religious people. As Daniel Maguire emphasizes, the ethics of theists, like the ethics of all responsible people, should be determined by "good and serious reasons," and these arguments are not good no matter what world-view one has.

The upshot is that religious people are in the same position as everyone else. There is nothing in religious belief in general, or in Christian belief in particular, to preclude the acceptance of mercy-killing as a humane response to some awful situations. So, as far as these arguments are concerned, it appears that Christians may be free, after all, to accept the Golden Rule.

PATRICK PUGH

Summary of Excerpt from The End of Life

(The numbers in parentheses indicate the original pages where material appeared. We will explain this method of documentation later in this chapter.)

ACCORDING TO James Rachels, in spite of the fact that we live in a secular age, many objections to active euthanasia focus on religion, and particularly Christianity. However, even religious people ought to be able see that these arguments may not be valid. For example, one of the most often-stated objections is that, in the Ten Commandments, God forbids killing. Rachels counters by pointing out that the Sixth Commandment is more accurately translated as "Thou shalt not commit murder." Since we define murder as "wrongful killing," we will not call some killing murder if we do not see it as wrong. Thus, the Sixth Commandment "is not normally taken to forbid killing in a just war . . . since such killing is (allegedly) justified" (161–62). Rachels points out that while the scriptures do not mention euthanasia, and in fact affirm the "sanctity of human life," one also finds "exhortations to kindness and mercy" for fellow humans, principles which "support active euthanasia rather than condemn it" (162).

To those who claim that "[i]t is for God alone to decide when a person shall live and when he shall die," Rachels responds that "if it is for God alone to decide when we shall live and when we shall die, then we 'play God' just as much when we cure people as when we kill them" (163). He notes that philosopher David Hume made this argument over two hundred years ago.

A third common Christian argument is that since suffering is a part of God's plan for humans, we should not interrupt it by euthanasia. Rachels responds to this with the question, How can we then justify the use of any pain-relieving drugs and procedures? (165). He concludes that "[t]here is nothing in religious belief in general, or in Christian belief in particular, to preclude the acceptance of mercy-killing as a humane response to some awful situations" (165).

Following Through

Write a summary of the argument opposing euthanasia entitled "Rising to the Occasion of Our Death" by William F. May, on pages 29–31. Or summarize any other argument that you are considering using as a source for a project you are currently working on.

Creating an Annotated Bibliography

To get an overview of the sources they have compiled, many writers find it useful to create an annotated bibliography. A bibliography is simply a list of works on a particular topic; it can include any kind of source—from newspaper articles to books to government documents. The basic information of a bibliography is identical to that in a Works Cited list: author, title, publisher, date, and, in the case of articles, periodical name, volume, and page numbers. (See pages 597–601 for examples.) Like a Works Cited list, a bibliography is arranged in alphabetical order, based on author's last name.

To annotate a bibliography means to include critical commentary about each work on the list, usually in the form of one or two short paragraphs. Each annotation should contain the following:

A sentence or two about the rhetorical context of the source. Is it an informative news article, an opinion column, a scholarly essay? Is it intended for lawyers, the public, students, the elderly? What is the bias?
A capsule summary of the content.
A note about why this source seems valuable and how you might use it.

Sample Annotated Bibliography Entry

Ames, Katrine. "Last Rights." *Newsweek* 26 Aug. 1991: 40-41. This is a news article for the general public about the popularity of a book called *Final Exit,* on how to commit suicide. Ames explains the interest in the book as resulting from people's perception that doctors, technology, and hospital bureaucrats are making it harder and harder to die with dignity in this country. The article documents with statistics the direction of public opinion on this topic, and also outlines some options, beside suicide, that are becoming available to ensure people of the right to die. Ames shows a bias against prolonging life through technology, but she includes quotations from authorities on both sides. This is a good source of evidence about public and professional opinion.

Following Through

Write an annotated bibliography of the sources you are using for a researched argument of your own.

INCORPORATING AND DOCUMENTING SOURCE MATERIAL

We turn now to the more technical matter of how to incorporate source material into your own writing and how to document the material you include. You incorporate material through direct quotation or through summary or paraphrase; you document material by naming the writer and providing full publication details of the source—a two-step process. In academic writing, documenting sources is essential, even for indirect references, with one exception: You do not need to document your source for factual information that could easily be found in many readily available sources, such as the current number of women in the U.S. Senate or the decision of the Supreme Court in a particular case.

Different Styles of Documentation

Different disciplines have different formal conventions regarding how to document sources in scholarly writing. In the humanities, the most common style is that of the Modern Language Association (MLA). In the social sciences, the American Psychological Association (APA) style is most often used. We will illustrate both in the examples that follow. Unlike the footnote style of documentation, MLA and APA use parenthetical citations in the text and simple, alphabetical bibliographies at the end of the text, making revision and typing much easier.

In both MLA and APA formats, you provide some information in the body of your paper and the rest of the information in a *Works Cited* (MLA) or *References* (APA) list at the end of your paper.

MLA Style

1. In parentheses at the end of both direct and indirect quotations, supply the last name of the author of the source and the exact page number(s) where the quoted or paraphrased words appear. If the name of the author appears in your sentence that leads into the quotation, you can omit it in the parentheses.

   A San Jose University professor who is black argues that affirmative action ''does not teach skills, or educate, or instill motivation'' (Steele 121).

   Shelby Steele, a black professor of English at San Jose State University, argues that the disadvantages of affirmative action for blacks are greater than the advantages (117).

2. In a Works Cited list at the end of the paper, provide complete bibliographical information in MLA style, as explained and illustrated on pages 597–601.

APA Style

1. In parentheses at the end of the directly or indirectly quoted material, place the author's last name, the date of the cited source, and the exact page number(s) where any quoted material appears. If the author's name appears in the sentence, the date of publication should follow the name directly, in parentheses. The page number still comes in parentheses at the end of the sentence.

Unlike MLA, the APA style uses commas between the parts of the citation, and *p.* or *pp.* before the page numbers.

> **A San Jose University professor who is black argues that affirmative action ''does not teach skills, or educate, or instill motivation'' (Steele, 1990, p. 121).**

> **Shelby Steele (1990), a black professor of English at San Jose State University, argues that the disadvantages of affirmative action for blacks are greater than the advantages (p. 117).**

2. In a References list at the end of the paper, provide complete bibliographical information in APA style, as explained and illustrated on pages 597–601.

GUIDELINES FOR USING MLA AND APA STYLE

Avoid plagiarism by being conscious of whether you are quoting or paraphrasing. Any time that you take exact words from a source, even if it is only a phrase or a significant word that expresses an author's opinion, you are quoting. You must use quotation marks in addition to documenting your source. If you make any change at all in the wording of a quotation, you must indicate the change with ellipses or brackets. Even if you use your own words to summarize or paraphrase any portions of a source, you must still name that source in your text and document it fully. Be careful about using your own words when paraphrasing and summarizing. See the discussion of how to paraphrase and how to summarize, pages 581–590.

At the very least, use an attributive tag such as "According to . . ." to introduce quotations, both direct and indirect. Don't just drop them in to stand on their own.

Name the person whose words or idea you are using. Give the person's full name on first mention.

Give some identifying information, so readers will know why what he or she has to say matters. Omit this if the speaker is someone readers would recognize without your help.

Transitions into and out of quotations should link the ideas they express to whatever point you are making—that is, to the context of your essay.

(*continued*)

GUIDELINES FOR USING MLA AND APA STYLE *(continued)*

If your lead-in to a quotation is a simple phrase, follow it with a comma. But if your lead-in can stand alone as a sentence, follow it with a colon.

The period at the end of a quotation or paraphrase comes after the parenthetical citation, except with block quotations.

Direct Quotations

Direct quotations are exact words taken from a source. The simplest direct quotations are whole sentences, worked into your text, as illustrated in the following excerpt from a student essay.

MLA Style

In a passage that echos Seneca, *Newsweek* writer Katrine Ames describes the modern viewpoint: "Most of us have some choices in how we live, certainly in how we conduct our lives" (40).

This source is listed in the Works Cited list as follows:

Ames, Katrine. "Last Rights." *Newsweek* 26 Aug. 1991: 40-41.

APA Style

In a passage that echos Seneca, *Newsweek* writer Katrine Ames (1991) describes the modern viewpoint: "Most of us have some choices in how we live, certainly in how we conduct our lives" (p. 40).

This source is listed in the References list as follows:

Ames, K. (1991, Aug. 26). Last rights. *Newsweek,* pp. 40-41.

Altering Direct Quotations with Ellipses and Brackets

While there is nothing wrong with quoting whole sentences, you will probably find it more economical to quote selectively, working some words or parts of sentences from the original into sentences of your own. When you do this, use ellipses (three spaced periods) to delete words from the original that are not essential to your use of the quote; use brackets to substitute words, to add words for purposes of clarification, and to change the wording of a quotation so that it fits gracefully into your own sentence.

The following passage from a student paper illustrates quoted words integrated into the student's own sentence, using both ellipses and brackets. The citation is in MLA style.

> **Robert Wennberg, a philosopher and Presbyterian minister, explains that "euthanasia is not an exclusively modern development, for it was widely endorsed in the ancient world. [It was] approved by such respected ancients as . . . Plato, Sophocles, . . . and Cicero" (1).**

The source appears in the Works Cited list as follows:

> **Wennberg, Robert N. *Terminal Choices: Euthanasia, Suicide, and the Right to Die*. Grand Rapids, Mich.: William B. Eerdamans Publishing Co., 1989.**

Using Block Quotations

If a quoted passage takes up more than four lines of text in your essay, you should indent it ten spaces from the left margin, double-space it as you do the whole paper, and omit quotation marks. In block quotations, a period is placed at the end of the final sentence, followed by two spaces and the parenthetical citation.

> **The idea of death as release from suffering was expressed by Seneca, a Stoic philosopher of Rome, who lived during the first century C.E.:**
>
> > **Against all the injuries of life, I have the refuge of death. If I can choose between a death of torture and one that is simple and easy, why should I not select the latter? As I chose the ship in which I sail and the house which I inhabit, so will I choose the death by which I leave life. . . . Why should I endure the agonies of**

disease . . . when I can emancipate myself from all my torments? (qtd. in Wennberg 42–43)

Note that the source of the Seneca quotation is the book by Wennberg. In the parenthetical citation, *qtd.* is an abbreviation for *quoted.* The entry on the Works Cited page would be the same as for the previous example.

Indirect Quotations

Indirect quotations are paraphrases or summaries of material, either fact or opinion, taken from a source.

Following is an example of a direct quotation on a student notecard.

Expert's opinion — pro:

"It is time to rethink many of our attitudes toward death and dying.... I feel that society is ready to take a giant step toward a better understanding of the dignity of death, and in the attainment of that dignity, if necessary, through the acceptance of euthanasia."

— Barnard in Barnard, p.8

Here is how this quotation might be incorporated into a paper as an indirect quotation. Note that the author of the book is the same as the person indirectly quoted, so it is not necessary to repeat his name in parentheses.

MLA Style

One cannot help but agree with pioneer heart-transplant surgeon Christiaan Barnard that death should involve dignity, and that society may have to accept the practice of euthanasia as a means to death with dignity (8).

The entry on the Works Cited list would appear as follows:

Barnard, Christiaan. *Good Life, Good Death.* Englewood Cliffs: Prentice-Hall, 1980.

APA Style

One cannot help but agree with pioneer heart-transplant surgeon Christiaan Barnard (1980) that death should involve dignity, and that society may have to accept the practice of euthanasia as a means to death with dignity (p. 8).

The entry on the References list would appear as follows:

Barnard, C. (1980). *Good life, good death.* Englewood Cliffs, N.J.: Prentice-Hall.

CREATING A *WORKS CITED* OR *REFERENCES* LIST

At the end of your paper, include a bibliography of all sources that you quoted, paraphrased, or summarized. If you are using MLA style, your heading for this list will read Works Cited; if you use APA style, the heading will read References. In either case, the list is in alphabetical order based on either the first author's (or editor's) last name, or—in the case of anonymously written works—the first word of the title, not counting articles (*a, an, the*). The entire list is double spaced, both within and between entries. See the Works Cited page at the end of the sample student paper, page 612, for the correct indentation and spacing.

The following examples illustrate the correct form for the types of sources you will most commonly use.

Books

Book by One Author

MLA: **Crusius, Timothy W. *Discourse: A Critique & Synthesis of Major Theories.* New York: MLA, 1989.**

APA: **Crusius, T. W. (1989). *Discourse: A critique & synthesis of major theories.* New York: Modern Language Association.**

(Note that APA uses initials rather than first names, and capitalizes only the first words and proper nouns in titles of books.)

Two or More Works by the Same Author

MLA: **Crusius, Timothy W. *Discourse: A Critique & Synthesis of Major Theories.* New York: MLA, 1989.**

---. *A Teacher's Introduction to Philosophical Hermeneutics.* Urbana, Ill. NCTE, 1991.

(Note that MLA arranges works alphabetically by title and uses three hyphens to show that the name is the same as the one directly above.)

APA: **Crusius, T. W. (1989). *Discourse: A critique & synthesis of major theories.* New York: Modern Language Association.**

Crusius, T. W. (1991). *A teacher's introduction to philosophical hermeneutics.* Urbana, IL: National Council of Teachers of English.

(Note that APA repeats the author's name and arranges works in chronological order.)

Book by Two or Three Authors

MLA: **Deleuze, Gilles, and Felix Guattari. *Anti-Oedipus: Capitalism and Schizophrenia.* New York: Viking, 1977.**

APA: **Deleuze, G., & Guattari, F. (1977). *Anti-Oedipus: Capitalism and schizophrenia.* New York: Viking.**

Book by Four or More Authors

MLA: **Bellah, Robert N., et al. *Habits of the Heart: Individualism and Commitment in American Life.* New York: Harper, 1985.**

(Note that the Latin abbreviation *et al.*, meaning "and others," stands in for all names after the first.)

APA: Bellah, R., Madsen, R., Sullivan, W., Swidler, A., & Tipton, S. (1985). *Habits of the heart: Individualism and commitment in American life*. New York: Harper & Row.

(Note that APA does not use the *et al.* abbreviation.)

Book Prepared by an Editor or Editors

MLA: Connors, Robert J., ed. *Selected Essays of Edward P.J. Corbett*. Dallas: Southern Methodist UP, 1989.

APA: Connors, R. J. (Ed.). (1989). *Selected essays of Edward P.J. Corbett*. Dallas: SMU Press.

Work in an Edited Collection

MLA: Jackson, Jesse. "Common Ground: Speech to the Democratic National Convention." *The American Reader*. Ed. Diane Ravitch. New York: HarperCollins, 1991. 367-371.

APA: Jackson, J. (1991). Common ground: Speech to the Democratic national convention. In D. Ravitch (Ed.), *The American reader* (pp. 367-371). New York: HarperCollins.

Translated Book

MLA: Vattimo, Gianni. *The End of Modernity: Nihilism and Hermeneutics in Postmodern Culture*. Trans. Jon R. Snyder. Baltimore: Johns Hopkins UP, 1988.

APA: Vattimo, G. (1988). *The end of modernity: Nihilism and hermeneutics in postmodern culture*. (J. R. Snyder, Trans.). Baltimore: Johns Hopkins U.P.

Periodicals

Article in a Journal with Continuous Pagination in Each Volume

MLA: **Herron, Jerry. "Writing for My Father."** ***College English*** **54 (1992): 928-37.**

APA: **Herron, J. (1992). Writing for my father.** ***College English, 54,*** **928-937.**

(Note that in APA style the article title is not fully capitalized, but the journal title is.)

Article in a Journal Paginated by Issue

MLA: **McConnell, Margaret Liu. "Living with Roe v. Wade."** ***Commentary*** **90.5 (1990): 34-38.**

APA: **McConnell, M. L. (1990). Living with Roe v. Wade.** ***Commentary, 90*** **(5), 34-38.**

(In both these examples, *90* is the volume number, and *5* is the number of the issue.)

Article in a Magazine

MLA: **D'Souza, Dinesh. "Illiberal Education."** ***Atlantic*** **Mar. 1990: 51+.**

(Note that the plus sign indicates the article runs on discontinuous pages.)

APA: **D'Souza, D. (1990, March). Illiberal education.** ***Atlantic,*** **pp. 51-58, 62-65, 67, 70-74, 76, 78-79.**

Anonymous Article in a Newspaper

MLA: **"Clinton Warns of Sacrifice."** ***Dallas Morning News*** **7 Feb. 1993: A4.**

APA: **Clinton warns of sacrifice. (1993, Feb. 7).** ***The Dallas Morning News,*** **p. A4.**

(In both these examples the *A* refers to the newspaper section in which the article appeared.)

Editorial in a Newspaper

MLA: **Lewis, Flora. "Civil Society, the Police and Abortion." Editorial. *New York Times* 12 Sept. 1992: A14.**

APA: **Lewis, F. (1992, Sept. 12). Civil society, the police and abortion [Editorial]. *The New York Times,* p. A14.**

Nonprint Sources

For an Interview

MLA: **May, William. Personal interview. 24 Apr. 1990.**

Note that APA style documents personal interviews only parenthetically within the text: "According to William May (personal interview, April 24, 1990), . . ." They are not included on the References list.

For a recording:

MLA: **Glass, Philip. *Glassworks.* CBS, MK 37265, 1982.**

APA: **Glass, P. (1982). *Glassworks* [CD Recording No. MK 37265]. CBS.**

For a Film

MLA: **Scott, Ridley, dir. *Thelma and Louise.* With Susan Sarandon, Geena Davis, and Harvey Keitel. MGM/UA Home Video, 1991.**

APA: **Scott, R. (Director). (1991). *Thelma and Louise* [Film]. Culver City, CA: MGM/UA Home Video.**

(Note that with nonprint media, APA asks you to identify the medium—CD, cassette, film, and so forth. MLA includes the principal actors, but APA does not. APA specifies the place of production, but MLA does not.

Pugh 1

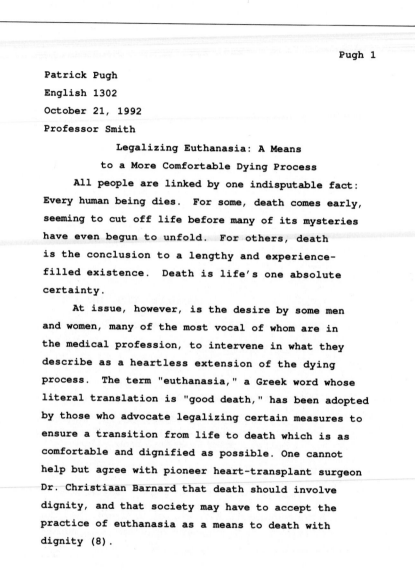

Patrick Pugh
English 1302
October 21, 1992
Professor Smith

Legalizing Euthanasia: A Means
to a More Comfortable Dying Process

All people are linked by one indisputable fact: Every human being dies. For some, death comes early, seeming to cut off life before many of its mysteries have even begun to unfold. For others, death is the conclusion to a lengthy and experience-filled existence. Death is life's one absolute certainty.

At issue, however, is the desire by some men and women, many of the most vocal of whom are in the medical profession, to intervene in what they describe as a heartless extension of the dying process. The term "euthanasia," a Greek word whose literal translation is "good death," has been adopted by those who advocate legalizing certain measures to ensure a transition from life to death which is as comfortable and dignified as possible. One cannot help but agree with pioneer heart-transplant surgeon Dr. Christiaan Barnard that death should involve dignity, and that society may have to accept the practice of euthanasia as a means to death with dignity (8).

Pugh 2

To me, having watched both my grandfather and my aunt spend months dying slow, torturous deaths from incurable lung cancer, there can be little doubt that euthanasia would have provided a far more humane close to their lives than the painful and prolonged dying that the ultimately futile regimens of chemotherapy and radiation caused them to suffer. My family members' experiences were far too common, for "80 percent of Americans who die in hospitals are likely to meet their end . . . in a sedated or comatose state; betubed nasally, abdominally, and intravenously, far more like manipulated objects than moral subjects" (Minow 124).

Advocates of euthanasia can turn to history for support of their arguments. Robert Wennberg, a philosopher and Presbyterian minister, explains that "euthanasia is not an exclusively modern development, for it was widely endorsed in the ancient world. [It was] approved by such respected ancients as . . . Plato, Sophocles, . . . and Cicero" (1). The idea that we have a right to choose death was expressed by Seneca, a Stoic philosopher of Rome, who lived in the first century C.E.:

> Against all the injuries of life, I have the refuge of death. If I can choose between a death of torture and one that is simple and easy, why should I not select

> the latter? As I chose the ship in which I sail and the house which I inhabit, so will I choose the death by which I leave life. In no matter more than death should we act according to our desire. . . . Why should I endure the agonies of disease . . . when I can emancipate myself from all my torments? (qtd. in Wennberg 42-43)

In a passage that echos Seneca, *Newsweek* writer Katrine Ames describes the modern viewpoint: "Most of us have some choices in how we live, certainly in how we conduct our lives. How we die is an equally profound choice, and, in the exhilarating and terrifying new world of medical technology, perhaps almost as important" (40).

Regardless of historical precedents and humane implications, euthanasia in both of its forms remains a controversial issue for many. In the first kind, known as passive, or indirect, euthanasia, death results from such measures as withholding or withdrawing life-support systems or life-sustaining medications. Passive euthanasia is often equated with simply "letting someone die," in contrast to the far more controversial active, or direct, euthanasia in which life is ended by direct intervention, such as giving a patient a lethal dose of a drug or assisting a patient in his or her suicide.

During the past two decades, the so-called Right to Die movement has made great strides in the promotion of passive euthanasia as an acceptable alternative to the extension of impending death.

> There seems to be a clear consensus that the competent adult has the right to refuse treatments. . . . This legal recognition of the right to reject medical treatment is grounded in a respect for the bodily integrity of the individual, for the right of each person to determine when bodily invasions will take place. (Wennberg 116)

Passive euthanasia, as an extension of the stated wishes of the dying patient, has become a widely accepted practice, a fact confirmed by medical ethicist and theologian Joseph Fletcher:

> What is called passive euthanasia, letting the patient die . . . , is a daily event in hospitals. Hundreds of thousands of Living Wills have been recorded, appealing to doctors, families, pastors, and lawyers to stop treatment at some balance point of the pro-life, pro-death assessment. (47)

The case for passive euthanasia has withstood, for the most part, the arguments of those who claim that life must be preserved and extended at all costs.

The euthanasia debate that is currently being waged focuses on active, or direct, euthanasia, where another person, notably a physician, assists a terminally ill patient in dying by lethal injection or provides the dying patient with the means to commit suicide. The case for active euthanasia is strong. For example, active euthanasia is preferable to passive euthanasia in cases of chronic and incurable diseases which promise the patient pain and suffering for the duration of his or her life. As Robert K. Landers explains, with the advance of AIDS and diseases such as Alzheimer's affecting our aging population, Americans are paying more attention to the idea of "giving death a hand" (555). Surely, many terminally ill patients, whose only hope for release from agonizing pain or humiliating helplessness is death, would welcome the more comfortable and dignified death that physician-assisted suicide can bring.

Still, there are those who argue that while passive euthanasia is moral, the active type is not. Ethically, is there a difference between passive and active euthanasia? Christiaan Barnard thinks not:

> Passive euthanasia is accepted in general by the medical profession, the major religions, and society at large. Therefore, when it is permissible for treatment to be stopped or not instituted in order to allow the patient to die, it makes for small mercy and less sense when the logical step of actively terminating life, and hence suffering, is not taken. Why, at that point, can life not be brought to an end, instead of extending the suffering of the patient by hours or days, or even weeks? . . . Procedurally, there is a difference between direct and indirect euthanasia, but ethically, they are the same. (68-69)

Barnard's ethics are supported by Joseph Fletcher's definition of ethical action, which holds that the ethical value of any human action is not a quality inherent in the act itself, but rather a judgment that we make about the act after examining the entire situation in which it takes place. We should decide what is moral and immoral on the basis of what is best for human well-being in any given set of circumstances (38-39).

While Fletcher is an Episcopal theologian, many other Christians do make arguments against active euthanasia on religious grounds. However, according to ethicist James Rachels, even religious people ought to be able to see that these arguments may not be valid. For example, one of the most often-stated objections is that, in the Ten Commandments, God forbids killing. Rachels counters by pointing out that the Sixth Commandment is more accurately translated as "Thou shalt not commit murder." Since we define murder as "wrongful killing," we will not call some killing murder if we do not see it as wrong. Thus, the Sixth Commandment "is not normally taken to forbid killing in a just war . . . since such killing is (allegedly) justified" (161-162). Rachels points out that while the scriptures do not mention euthanasia, and in fact affirm the "sanctity of human life," one also finds "exhortations to kindness and mercy" for fellow humans, principles which "support active euthanasia rather than condemn it" (162).

To those who claim that "[i]t is for God alone to decide when a person shall live and when he shall die," Rachels responds that "if it is for God alone to decide when we shall live and when we shall die, then we 'play God' just as much when we cure people as when we kill them" (163). He notes that philosopher David Hume made this argument over two hundred years ago.

Pugh 8

A third common Christian argument is that since suffering is a part of God's plan for humans, we should not interrupt it by euthanasia. Rachels responds to this with the question, How can we then justify the use of any pain-relieving drugs and procedures? (165). He concludes that "[t]here is nothing in religious belief in general, or in Christian belief in particular, to preclude the acceptance of mercy-killing as a humane response to some awful situations" (165).

In fact, there is increasing support for the legalization of active euthanasia, specifically physician-assisted euthanasia, as an alternative to a lingering death for terminal patients. Landers reports that a July 1990 poll showed half the respondents believed someone suffering from incurable disease had a "moral right to commit suicide" (560). In October 1991, a poll sponsored by the Boston Globe and the Harvard School of Public Health found that 64 percent of Americans sampled favor the legalization of physician-assisted suicide, and 52 percent think they would actually consider it themselves. The public interest in suicide as a way out of suffering is also evident in the popularity of *Final Exit,* a detailed guide on how to commit suicide, published in March 1991. By August, that book was at the top of the *New York Times'* best-seller list in the category of how-to books.

Some states have put the question of legalizing active euthanasia before their voters. For example, the issue was placed on the Washington state ballot, as Initiative 119, in November of 1991 after 223,000 people signed petitions to place it there. The most controversial section of Initiative 119 stated that a conscious adult patient, who had been diagnosed with a terminal disease and who was deemed to have no more than six months to live, could ask a doctor to hasten death. The doctor had no obligation to comply, nor must the hospital allow it. But if the doctor and/or the hospital refused the patient's request, the patient had the right to be referred to a doctor or a hospital which would honor the request. Although voters in Washington rejected Initiative 119 by a 54 to 46 percent margin, the issue is far from decided. Citizens in Oregon, Florida, California, and Washington, D.C., will soon vote on similar initiatives.

At this point, there is no way to predict whether active euthanasia will be legalized in the near future. One thing is reasonably certain, however. Any compassionate person, who has sat helplessly by as a fellow human being has spent his or her final days thrashing around on a sweat-soaked bed, or who has observed a once-alert mind that has become darkened by the agony of inescapable pain,

Pugh 10

will give consideration to the eventual fate that awaits him or her. In times like these, frightened humans are united in the universal prayer, "God, spare me from this when my time comes," and even the most stubborn anti-euthanasia minds are opened to the option of an easier journey between life and death, an option that can be made a reality by the legalization of physician-assisted euthanasia.

Pugh 11

Works Cited

Ames, Katrine. "Last Rights." *Newsweek* 26 Aug. 1991: 40-41.

Barnard, Christiaan. *Good Life, Good Death.* Englewood Cliffs: Prentice, 1980.

Fletcher, Joseph. "In Defense of Suicide." *Suicide and Euthanasia: The Rights of Personhood.* Eds. Samuel E. Wallace and Albin Eser. Knoxville: U of Tennessee P, 1981. 38-50.

Landers, Robert. "Right to Die: Medical, Legal, and Moral Issues." *Editorial Research Reports* 1.36 (1990): 554-64.

Minow, Newton. "Communications in Medicine." *Vital Speeches of the Day.* 1 Dec. 1990: 121-25.

Rachels, James. *The End of Life.* Oxford: Oxford UP, 1987.

Wennberg, Robert N. *Terminal Choices: Euthanasia, Suicide, and the Right to Die.* Grand Rapids, Mich.: William Eerdamans Publishing Co., 1989.

APPENDIX B

Editing and Proofreading

Editing and proofreading are the final steps in creating a finished piece of writing. Too often, these steps are fast ones, as writers race to meet a deadline, but ideally, you should distinguish between the acts of revising, editing, and proofreading. Because each requires that you pay attention to something different, you cannot reasonably expect to do them well if you try to do them all at once.

Our suggestions for revising appear in each of Chapters 5–8 on the aims of argument. Revising means shaping and developing the whole argument, with an eye to audience and purpose; when you revise, you are ensuring that you have accomplished your aim. Editing, on the other hand, means making smaller changes within paragraphs and sentences. When you edit, you are thinking about whether your prose will be a pleasure to read. Editing improves the sound and rhythm of your voice. It makes complicated ideas more accessible to readers and usually makes your writing more concise. Proofreading means eliminating errors. When you proofread, you correct everything you find that will annoy readers, such as misspellings, punctuation mistakes, faulty grammar, and typos.

In this appendix, we offer some basic advice on what to look for when editing and proofreading. For more detailed help, you should consult a handbook on grammar and punctuation and a good book on style, such as Joseph Williams's *Ten Lessons in Clarity and Grace* or Richard Lanham's *Revising Prose.* Both of these texts guided our thinking in the advice that follows.

EDITING

Most ideas can be phrased in a number of ways, each of which gives the idea a slight but distinctive twist.

In New York City, about 74,000 people die each year.

In New York City, death comes to one in a hundred people each year.

Death comes to one in a hundred New Yorkers each year.

To begin an article on what becomes of the unknown and unclaimed dead in New York, Edward Conlon wrote the final of these three sentences. We can only speculate about the possible variations he considered, but because openings are so crucial, he almost certainly cast these words quite deliberately.

For most writers, such deliberation over matters of style occurs during editing. In this late stage of the writing process, writers examine choices made earlier, perhaps unconsciously, while drafting and revising. They listen to how sentences sound, to patterns of rhythm both within and among sentences. Editing is like an art or craft; it can provide you the satisfaction of knowing you've said something gracefully and effectively. To focus on language this closely, you will need to set aside enough time after you have revised.

Below, we list some things to look for when editing your own writing. Don't forget, though, that editing does not always mean looking for weaknesses. You should also recognize passages that work well just as you wrote them, that you can leave alone or play up more by editing passages that surround them.

Editing for Clarity and Conciseness

Even drafts revised several times may have wordy and awkward passages: These are often places where a writer struggled with uncertainty or felt less than confident about the point being made. Introductions often contain such passages. In editing, you have the opportunity to take one more stab at clarifying and sharpening your ideas. Following are some suggestions for doing so.

Express Main Ideas Forcefully

Emphasize the main idea of a sentence by stating it as directly as possible, using the two key sentence parts (*subject* and *verb*) to convey the two key parts of the idea (*agent* and *act*).

As you edit, first look for sentences that state ideas indirectly rather than directly; such sentences may include (1) overuse of the verb *to be* in its various forms (*is, was, will have been,* and so forth); (2) the opening words "There is . . ." or "It is . . ."; (3) strings of prepositional phrases; (4) many vague nouns. Then ask, "What is my true subject here, and what is that subject's action?" Here is an example of a weak, indirect sentence:

> It is a fact that the effects of pollution are more evident in lower-class neighborhoods than in middle-class ones.

The writer's subject is pollution. What is the pollution's action? Limply, the sentence tells us its "effects" are '"evident." The following edited version makes pollution the agent that performs the action of a livelier verb, *fouls.* The edited sentence is more specific—without being longer.

> *Pollution* more frequently *fouls* the air, soil, and water of lower-class neighborhoods than of middle-class ones.

Editing Practice The following passage, about a plan for creating low-income housing, contains two weak sentences. In this case the weakness results from wordiness. (Note the overuse of vague nouns and prepositional phrases.) Decide for each sentence what the true subject is, and make that word the subject of the verb. Your edited version should be much shorter.

> As in every program, there will be the presence of a few who abuse the system. However, as in other social programs, the numbers would not be sufficient to justify the rejection of the program on the basis that one person in a thousand will try to cheat.

Choose Carefully between Active and Passive Voice

Active and passive voice indicate different relationships between subjects and verbs. As we have noted, ideas are usually clearest when the writer's true subject is also the subject of the verb in the sentence—that is, when it is the agent of the action. In the passive voice, however, the agent of the action appears in the predicate, or not at all. Rather than acting as agent, the subject of the sentence *receives* the action of the verb.

The following sentence is in the passive voice:

> The air of poor neighborhoods is often fouled by pollution.

There is nothing incorrect about the use of the passive voice in this sentence, and in the context of a whole paragraph, passive voice may be the most emphatic way of making a point. (Here, for example, it allows the word *pollution* to fall at the end of the sentence, a strong position.) But, often, use of the passive voice is not a deliberate choice at all, but rather a way of stating a point vaguely and unspecifically. Consider the following sentences, in which the main verbs have no agents:

> It *is believed* that dumping garbage at sea is not as harmful to the environment as *was* once *thought*.

> Ronald Reagan *was considered* the "Great Communicator."

Who thinks such dumping is not so harmful? Environmental scientists? Industrial producers? Who considered Reagan a great communicator? Speech professors? News commentators? Such sentences are clearer when they written in the active voice:

> Some environmentalists believe that dumping garbage at sea is not as harmful to the environment as they used to think.

> Media commentators considered Ronald Reagan the "Great Communicator."

In editing for the passive voice, look over your verbs. Passive voice verbs are easily recognized because they always contain (1) some form of *to be* (*is, was, were, will be, has been,* and so on) as a helping verb; and (2) the main verb in its past participle form (which ends in *ed, d, t,* or *en,* or may in some cases be irregular: *drunk, sung, lain,* and so on).

When you have found a sentence containing a passive voice verb, decide who or what is performing the action; the agent may appear after the verb, or not at all. Then decide if the sentence and the sound of the whole passage that surrounds it will be improved if you change the voice to active.

Editing Practice

1. The following paragraph from a student's argument needs editing for emphasis. It is choking with excess nouns and forms of the verb *to be,* some as part of passive constructions. You need not eliminate all use of the passive voice, but do look for instances when it is vague and ineffective. Your edited version should be not only stronger, but also much shorter.

   Although emergency shelters are needed in some cases (for example, a mother fleeing domestic violence), they are an inefficient means of dealing with the massive numbers of people they are bombarded with each day. The members of a homeless family are in need of a home, not a temporary shelter into which they and others like them are herded, only to be shuffled out when their thirty-day stay is over to make room for the next incoming herd. Emergency shelters would be sufficient if we did not have a low-income housing shortage, but what is needed most at present is an increase in availability of affordable housing for the poor.

2. Select a paragraph of your own writing to edit with an eye to finding strong verbs and subjects to carry the main idea of your sentences.

Editing for Emphasis

When you edit for emphasis, you make sure that your main ideas stand out and that you have expressed them so that your reader will take notice. Following are some suggestions to help.

Emphasize Main Ideas by Subordinating Less Important Ones

Subordination refers to distinctions in rank or order of importance. Think of the chain of command at an office: The boss is at the top of the ladder, and all those lower are subordinates, with employees at each lower level subordinate to those on the rung above.

In writing, subordination means placing less important ideas in less important positions in sentences, thus throwing greater emphasis on the main ideas that should stand out. Writing short on subordination treats all ideas equally, giving each a sentence of its own or joining ideas with coordinators like *and, but,* and *or.* Such a passage follows, with its sentences numbered so we can refer to them later.

> (1) It has been over a century since slavery was abolished, and a few decades since lawful, systematic segregation came to an unwilling halt. (2) Truly, blacks have come a long way from the darker days that lasted for more than three centuries. (3) Many blacks have entered the main-

> stream, and there is a proportionately large contingent of middle-class blacks. (4) Yet an even greater percentage of blacks are immersed in truly pathetic conditions. (5) The inner city black poor are enmeshed in devastating socioeconomic problems. (6) Unemployment among inner city black youths has become much worse than it was even five years ago.

Three main ideas are most important here—that blacks have been free for some time, that some have made economic progress, and that others are trapped in poverty—and of these three, the last is probably intended to be the most important. Yet, as we read the passage, these key ideas do not stand out. In fact, each point receives equal emphasis and sounds about the same, with the repeated subject-verb-object syntax. The result seems monotonous, even apathetic, though the writer is probably truly disturbed about the subject. The following edited version that subordinates some of the points is more emphatic. We have italicized the main points.

> *Blacks have come a long way* in the century since slavery was abolished and in the decades since lawful, systematic segregation came to an unwilling halt. Yet, while many blacks have entered the mainstream and the middle class, *an even greater percentage are immersed in truly pathetic conditions.* To give just one example of these devastating socioeconomic problems, *unemployment among inner city black youths is much worse now than it was even five years ago.*

While different editing choices are possible, this version plays down sentences 1, 3, and 5 in the original, so that sentences 2, 4, and 6 stand out.

As you edit, look for passages that sound wordy and flat because all the ideas are expressed with equal weight in the same subject-verb-object pattern. Then single out your most important points, and try out some options for subordinating the less important ones. The key is to put main ideas in main clauses, and modifying ideas in modifying clauses or phrases.

Modifying Clauses Like simple sentences, modifying clauses contain a subject and verb. They are formed in two ways: with relative pronouns and with subordinating conjunctions.

Relative pronouns introduce clauses that modify nouns, with the relative pronoun relating the clause to the noun it modifies. There are five relative pronouns:

> that
> which
> who
> whose
> whom

The following sentence contains a relative clause:

> Alcohol advertisers are trying to sell a product *that is by its very nature harmful to users.*
>
> —JASON RATH (student)

Relative pronouns may also be implied:

> I have returned the library book *you loaned me.*

Relative pronouns may also be preceded by prepositions such as *on, in, to,* or *during:*

> Drug hysteria has created an atmosphere *in which civil rights are disregarded.*

Subordinating conjunctions show relationships among ideas. It is impossible to provide a complete list of subordinating conjunctions in this short space, but here are the most common and the kinds of modifying roles they perform:

To show time: after, as, before, since, until, when, while
To show place: where, wherever
To show contrast: although, though, whereas, while
To show cause and effect: because, since, so that
To show condition: if, unless, whether, provided that
To show manner: how, as though

By introducing it with a subordinating conjunction, you can convert a sentence into a dependent clause that can perform a modifying role in some other sentence. Consider the following two versions of the same idea:

> Pain is a state of consciousness, a "mental event." It can never be directly observed.
>
> Since pain is a state of consciousness, a "mental event," it can never be directly observed.
>
> —PETER SINGER, "Animal Liberation"

Modifying Phrases Unlike clauses, phrases do not have a subject and a verb. Prepositional phrases and infinitive phrases are most likely already in your repertory of modifiers. (Consult a handbook if you need to review these.) Here, we remind you of two other useful options.

Participial phrases modify nouns. Participles are created from verbs, so it is not surprising that the two varieties represent two verb tenses. *Present participles* end in *-ing:*

> *Hoping to eliminate harassment on campus,* many universities have tried to institute codes for speech and behavior.
>
> The desperate Haitians fled here in boats, *risking all.*
>
> —CARMEN HAZAN-COHEN (student)

Past participles end in *-ed* or *-en:*

> Women themselves became a resource, *acquired by men much as the land was acquired by men.*
>
> —GERDA LERNER

> *Linked more to the Third World and Asia than to the Europe of America's racial and cultural roots,* Los Angeles and Southern California will enter the 21st century as a multi-racial and multicultural society.
>
> —RYSZARD KAPUSCINSKI

Notice that these modifying phrases should be placed close to the nouns they modify.

An **appositive** is a noun or noun phrase that restates another noun, usually in a more specific way. Appositives can be highly emphatic, but more often they are tucked into the middle of a sentence or added to the end, allowing a subordinate idea to be slipped in. When used like this, appositives are usually set off with commas:

> Rick Halperin, *a professor at Southern Methodist University,* noted that Ted Bundy's execution cost Florida taxpayers over six million dollars.
>
> —DIANE MILLER (student)

Editing Practice

1. Edit the following passage as needed for emphasis, clarity, and conciseness, using subordinate clauses, relative clauses, participial phrases, appositives, and any other choices that occur to you. If some parts are effective as they are, leave them alone.

   > The monetary implications of drug legalization are not the only reason it is worth consideration. There is reason to believe that the United States would be a safer place to live if drugs were legalized. A large amount of what the media has named "drug-related" violence is really prohibition-related violence. Included in this are random shootings and murders associated with black market transactions. Estimates indicate that at least 40 percent of all property crime in the United States is committed by drug users so they can maintain their habits. That amounts to a total of 4 million crimes per year and $7.5 billion in stolen property. Legalizing drugs would be a step toward reducing this wave of crime.

2. Edit a paragraph of your own writing with an eye to subordinating less important ideas through the use of modifying phrases and clauses.

Vary the Length and Pattern of Sentences

Even when read silently, your writing has a sound. If your sentences are all about the same length (typically fifteen to twenty words) and all structured according to a subject-verb-object/complement pattern, they will roll along with the regular rhythm of an assembly line. Obviously, one solution to this problem is to open some of your sentences with modifying phrases and clauses, as we discussed in the previous section. Here, we offer some other suggestions. All add emphasis by introducing something unexpected.

Use a Short Sentence after Several Long Ones

> [A] population's general mortality is affected by a great many factors over which doctors and hospitals have little influence. For those diseases and injuries for which modern medicine can affect the outcome, however, which country the patient lives in really matters. Life expectancy is not the same among developed countries for premature babies, for children born with spina bifida, or for people who have cancer, a brain tumor, heart disease, or chronic renal failure. *Their chances of survival are best in the United States.*
>
> —JOHN GOODMAN

Interrupt a Sentence

> The position of women in that hippie counterculture was, *as a young black male leader preached succinctly,* "prone."
>
> —BETTY FRIEDAN

> Symbols and myths—*when emerging uncorrupted from human experience*—are precious. Then it is the poetic voice and vision that infoms and infuses—*the poet-warrior's, the prophet-seer's, the dreamer's*—reassuring us that truth is as real as falsehood. And ultimately stronger.
>
> —OSSIE DAVIS

Use an Intentional Sentence Fragment The concluding fragment in the previous passage by Ossie Davis is a good example.

Invert the Order of Subject-Verb-Object/Complement

> Further complicating negotiations is the difficulty of obtaining relevant financial statements.
>
> —REGINA HERZLINGER

> This creature, with scarcely two thirds of man's cranial capacity, was a fire user. Of what it meant to him beyond warmth and shelter, we know nothing; with what rites, ghastly or benighted, it was struck or maintained, no word remains.
>
> —LOREN EISELY

Use Special Effects for Emphasis

Especially in persuasive argumentation, you will want to make some of your points in ways that are deliberately dramatic. Remember that, as the crescendos stand out in music because the surrounding passages are less intense, so in rhetoric, the special effects work best when you use them sparingly.

Repetition Deliberately repeating words, phrases, or sentence patterns has the effect of building up to a climactic point. In Chapter 7 we noted how Martin

Luther King, Jr., in the emotional high point of his "Letter from Birmingham Jail," used repeated subordinate clauses beginning with the phrase "when you" to build up to his main point: ". . . then you will understand why we find it difficult to wait" (paragraph 14, page 116). Here is another example, from the conclusion of an argument linking women's rights with environmental reforms:

> Environmental justice goes much further than environmental protection, a passive and paternalistic phrase. *Justice requires that* industrial nations pay back the environmental debt incurred in building their wealth by using less of nature's resources. *Justice prescribes that* governments stop siting hazardous waste facilities in cash-poor rural and urban neighborhoods and now in the developing world. *Justice insists that* the subordination of women and nature by men is not only a hazard; it is a crime. *Justice reminds us that* the Earth does not belong to us; even when we "own" a piece of it, we belong to the Earth.
>
> —H. PATRICIA HYNES

Paired Coordination Coordinators are conjunctions that pair words, word groups, and sentences in a way that gives them equal emphasis and that also shows a relationship between them, such as contrast, consequence, or addition. In grade school you may have learned the coordinators through the mnenomic *FANBOYS,* standing for *for, and, nor, but, or, yet, so.*

Paired coordinators emphasize the relationship between coordinated elements because each serves as a marker word to introduce one of the coordinated elements. Some paired coordinators are:

both ____________ and ____________

not ____________ but ____________

not only ____________ but also ____________

either ____________ or ____________

neither ____________ nor ____________

The key to effective paired coordination is to keep the words that follow the marker words as grammatically similar as possible. Pair nouns with nouns, verbs with verbs, prepositional phrases with prepositional phrases, whole sentences with whole sentences. (Think of paired coordination as a variation on repetition.) Here are some examples:

> Feminist anger, or any form of social outrage, is dismissed breezily—*not* because it lacks substance *but* because it lacks "style."
>
> —SUSAN FALUDI

> Alcohol ads that emphasize "success" in the business and social worlds are useful examples *not only* of how advertisers appeal to people's envy *but also* of how ads perpetuate gender stereotypes.
>
> —JASON RATH (student)

Emphatic Appositives While an appositive (a noun or noun phrase that restates another noun) can subordinate an idea (page 619), it can also emphasize an idea if it is placed at the beginning or the end of a sentence where it will command attention. Here are some examples:

> *The poorest nation in the Western hemisphere,* Haiti is populated by six million people, many of whom cannot obtain adequate food, water, or shelter.
>
> —SNEED B. COLLARD III

> [Feminists] made a simple, though serious, ideological error when they applied the same political rhetoric to their own situation as women versus men: *too literal an analogy with class warfare, racial oppression.*
>
> —BETTY FRIEDAN

Note that at the end of a sentence, an appositive may be set off with a colon or a dash.

Emphatic Word Order The opening and closing positions of a sentence are high-profile spots, not to be wasted on weak words. The following, for example, begins weakly with the filler phrase "there are":

> *There are* several distinctions, all of them false, that are commonly made between rape and date rape.

A better version would read:

> My opponents make several distinctions between rape and date rape; all of these are false.

Even more important are the final words of every paragraph and the opening and closing of the entire argument.

Editing Practice

1. Find a passage of one or two paragraphs in a piece of published writing that you have recently read and admired. Be ready to share it with your class, explaining how the writer has crafted the passage to make it work.
2. Take a paragraph or two from one of your previous essays, perhaps even an essay from another course, and edit it to improve clarity, conciseness, and emphasis.

Editing for Coherence

Coherence refers to what some people call the "flow" of writing. Writing flows when the ideas connect smoothly, one to the next. When writing is incoherent, the reader must work to see how ideas connect and infer points that the writer, for whatever reason, has left unstated.

Incoherence is a particular problem in paragraphs that contain many direct or indirect quotations from sources. In using sources, be careful always to lead into the quotation with some words of your own, showing clearly how this new idea connects with what has come before.

Finding incoherent passages in your own writing can be difficult; you might ask a friend to read your draft looking for gaps in the presentation of ideas. Here are some suggestions for improving coherence.

Move from Old Information to New Information

Coherent writing is easy to follow because the connections between old information and new information are clear. Sentences refer back to previously introduced information and set up reader expectations for new information to come. Notice how, in the following excerpts from an argument on animal rights by Steven Zak, every sentence fulfills your expectations.

> The credibility of the animal-rights viewpoint . . . need not stand or fall with the "marginal human beings" argument.

Next, you would expect to hear why animals do not have to be classed as "marginal human beings"; and you do:

> Lives don't have to be qualitatively the same to be worthy of equal respect.

At this point you might ask upon what else we should base our respect. Zak answers this question in the next sentence:

> One's perception that another life has value comes as much from an appreciation of its uniqueness as from the recognition that it has characteristics that are shared by one's own life.

Not only do these sentences fulfill reader expectations, but each also makes a clear connection by referring specifically to the key idea in the sentence before it, forming an unbroken chain of thought. We have underlined the words that accomplish this linking up:

> The credibility of the animal-rights viewpoint . . . need not stand or fall with the "*marginal human beings*" argument.
>
> Lives don't have to be *qualitatively the same* to be worthy of *equal respect.*
>
> One's perception that *another life has value* comes as much from an *appreciation of its uniqueness* as from the recognition that it has characteristics that are shared by one's own life.
>
> One can imagine that the lives of various kinds of animals *differ radically.* . . .

In the following paragraph, reader expectations are not so well fulfilled:

> We are presently witness to the greatest number of homeless families since the Great Depression of the 1930s. The cause of this phenomenon is a shortage of low-income housing. Mothers with children as young as

two weeks are forced to live on the street because there is no room for them in homeless shelters.

While these sentences are all on the subject of homelessness, the second leads us to expect that the third will take up the topic of shortages of low-income housing. Instead, it takes us back to the subject of the first sentence, and offers a different cause—no room in the shelters.

Looking for ways to link old information with new information will help you find problems of coherence in your own writing.

Editing Practice

1. In the following paragraph, underline the words or phrases that make the connections backward to the previous sentence and forward to the next, as we did earlier with the passage from Zak.

> The affluent, educated, liberated women of the First World, who can enjoy freedoms unavailable to any women ever before, do not feel as free as they want to. And they can no longer restrict to the subconscious their sense that this lack of freedom has something to do with—with apparently frivolous issues, things that really should not matter. Many are ashamed to admit that such trivial concerns—to do with physical appearance, bodies, faces, hair, clothes—matter so much. But in spite of shame, guilt, and denial, more and more women are wondering if it isn't that they are entirely neurotic alone but rather that something important is indeed at stake that has to do with the relationship between female liberation and female beauty.
>
> —NAOMI WOLF

2. The following student paragraph lacks coherence. Read through it, and put a slash (/) between sentences where you sense a gap between ideas. You may try to rewrite the paragraph, rearranging sentences and adding ideas to make the connections tighter.

> Students may know what AIDS is and how it is transmitted, but most are not concerned about AIDS and do not perceive themselves to be at risk. But college age heterosexuals are the number one high risk group for this disease (Gray and Sacarino 258). "Students already know about AIDS. Condom distribution, public or not, is not going to help. It just butts into my personal life," said one student surveyed. College is a time for exploration and that includes the discovery of sexual freedom. Students, away from home and free to make their own decisions for maybe the first time in their lives, have a "bigger than life" attitude. The thought of dying is the farthest from their minds. Yet at this point in their lives, they are most in need of this information.

Use Transitions to Show Relationships between Ideas

Coherence has to be built into a piece of writing; as we discussed earlier, the ideas of sentences must first cohere. However, sometimes readers need help in making the transition from one idea to the next, so you must provide signposts to help them see connections more readily. For example, a transitional word like *however* can prepare readers for an idea in contrast to the one before it, as in the second sentence in this paragraph. Transitional words can also bring to the foreground the structure of an argument, referring explicitly to "another reason" or "an example." Here are some examples of transitional words and phrases:

> *To show order:* first, second, next, then, last, finally
> *To show contrast:* however, yet, but, nevertheless
> *To show cause and effect:* therefore, consequently, as a result, then
> *To show importance:* moreover, significantly
> *To show an added point:* as well, also, too
> *To show an example:* for example, for instance
> *To show concession:* admittedly
> *To show conclusion:* in sum, in conclusion

The key to using transitional words is similar to the key to using special effects for emphasis: Don't overdo it. Your writing can become choked with these words. Anticipate where your reader will genuinely need them.

Editing Practice Underline the transitional words and phrases in the following passage of published writing:

> When people believe that their problems can be solved, they tend to get busy solving them.
>
> On the other hand, when people believe that their problems are beyond solution, they tend to position themselves so as to avoid blame. Take the woeful inadequacy of education in the predominantly black central cities. Does the black leadership see the ascendancy of black teachers, school administrators, and politicians as an asset to be used in improving those dreadful schools? Rarely. You are more likely to hear charges of white abandonment, white resistance to integration, conspiracies to isolate black children, even when the schools are officially desegregated. In short, white people are accused of being responsible for the problem. But if the youngsters manage to survive those awful school systems and achieve success, leaders want to claim credit. They don't hesitate to attribute that success to the glorious Civil Rights movement.
>
> —WILLIAM RASPBERRY

PROOFREADING

Proofreading is truly the final step in writing a paper. After proofreading, you ought to be able to print your paper out one more time; but if you do not have time, most instructors will be perfectly happy to see the necessary corrections done neatly in ink on the final draft.

Following are some suggestions for proofreading.

Spelling Errors

If you have used a word processor, you may have a program that will check your spelling. If not, you will have to check your spelling by reading through again carefully, with a dictionary at hand. Consult the dictionary whenever you feel uncertain. You might consider devoting a special part of your writer's notebook to your habitual spelling errors: Some students always misspell "athlete," for example, while others leave the second "n" out of environment.

Omissions and Jumbled Passages

Read your paper out loud, even if you have to do so very softly. Physically shaping your lips around the words can help you find places where you have left out a word, where you have typed "saw" instead of "was," or where the remnants of some earlier version of a sentence did not get fully deleted. Place a caret in the sentence, and write the correction or addition above the line.

Punctuation Problems

Apostrophes and commas give writers the most trouble. If you have habitual problems with these, you should record your errors in your writer's notebook.

Apostrophes

Apostrophe problems usually occur in forming possessives, not contractions, so here we discuss only the former. If you have problems with possessives, you may also want to consult a good handbook or seek a private tutorial with your instructor or your school's writing center.

Here are the basic principles to remember.

1. Possessive pronouns never take an apostrophe.

   his, hers, yours, theirs, its

2. Singular nouns become possessive by adding *-'s.*

   A single parent's life is hard.
   A society's values change.
   Do you like Mr. Voss's new car?

3. Plural nouns ending in *-s* become possessive by simply adding an apostrophe.

   Her parents' marriage is faltering.
   Many cities' air is badly polluted.
   The Joneses' house is up for sale.

4. Plural nouns that do not end in *-s* become possessive by adding *'s.*

   Show me the women's (men's) room.
   The people's voice was heard.

If you err by using apostrophes where they don't belong in non-possessive words ending in "s," remember that a possessive will always have a noun after it, not some other part of speech such as a verb or a preposition. You may even need to read with a ruler under every line of print to help yourself focus on this problem.

Commas

Because commas indicate a pause, reading your paper aloud is a good way to decide where to add or delete them. A good handbook will elaborate on the basic principles below. The example sentences here and following have been adapted from an argument by Mary Meehan, who opposes abortions.

1. Use a comma when you join two or more main clauses with a coordinating conjunction.

   Main clause, (*and, but, or, nor, so, yet*) main clause.

   Feminists want to have men participate more in the care of children, but abortion allows a man to shift total responsibility to the woman.

2. Use a comma after an introductory phrase or dependent clause.

   Introductory phrase or clause, main clause.

   To save the smallest children, the Left should speak out against abortion.

3. Use commas around modifiers such as relative clauses (see pages 617–618) and appositives (see page 619) unless they are essential to the noun's meaning. Be sure to put the comma at both ends of the modifier.

   ____________, appositive, ____________

   ____________, relative clause, ____________

   One member of the 1972 Presidential commission on population growth was Graciela Olivarez, a Chicana who was active in civil rights and anti-poverty work. Olivarez, who later was named to head the Federal Government's Community Services Administration, had known poverty in her youth in the Southwest.

4. Use commas with a series.

   ____________ x, y, and z ____________

   The traditional mark of the Left has been its protection of the underdog, the weak, and the poor.

Semicolons

Think of a semicolon as a strong comma. It has two main uses.

1. Use a semicolon to join two main clauses when you choose not to use a conjunction. This works well when the two main clauses are closely related or parallel in structure.

Main clause; main clause.

Pro-life activists did not want abortion to be a class issue; they wanted to end abortion everywhere, for all classes.

When speaking with counselors at the abortion clinic, many women change their minds and decide against abortion; however, a woman who is accompanied by a husband or boyfriend often does not feel free to talk with the counselor.

As a variation, you may wish to add an introductory adverb to the second main clause. The adverb indicates the relationship between the clauses, but it is not a conjunction, so a comma preceding it will not be correct.

Main clause; (*however, therefore, thus, moreover, consequently, etc.*), main clause

2. Use semicolons between items in a series if any of the items themselves contain commas.

__________ x; y; and z __________

A few liberals who have spoken out against abortion are Jesse Jackson, a Civil Rights leader; Richard Neuhaus, a theologian; the comedian Dick Gregory; and politicians Mark Hatfield and Mary Rose Oakar.

Colons

The colon has two common uses.

1. Use a colon to introduce a quotation when both your own lead-in and the words quoted are complete sentences that can stand alone. (See pages 594–596 for more on introducing quotations.)

Main clause of your words: "Quoted sentence(s)."

Mary Meehan criticizes liberals who have been silent on abortion: "If much of the leadership of the pro-life movement is right-wing, that is due largely to the default of the Left."

2. Use a colon before an appositive that comes dramatically at the end of a sentence, especially if the appositive contains more than one item.

__________ : appositive, appositive, and appositive.

Meehan argues that many pro-choice advocates see abortion as a way to hold down the population of certain minorities: blacks, Puerto Ricans, and other Latins.

Grammatical Errors

Grammar mistakes can be hard to find, but once again we suggest reading aloud as one method of proofing for them. Grammar errors tend not to "sound right" even if they look like good prose. Another suggestion is to recognize your habitual errors and then look for particular grammatical structures that lead you into error.

Introductory Participial Phrases

Constructions such as these lead writers to create dangling modifiers. (See the discussion of participial phrases on pages 618–619.) Remember that an introductory phrase dangles if it is not immediately followed by the noun it modifies.

> *Incorrect:*
>
> Using her conscience as a guide, our society has granted each woman the right to decide if a fetus is truly a "person" with rights equal to her own.
>
> *Corrected:*
>
> Using her conscience as a guide, each woman in our society has the right to decide if a fetus is truly a "person" with rights equal to her own.

Paired Coordinators Such As **Not Only . . . But Also**

If the words that follow each of the coordinators are not of the same grammatic structure, then an error known as nonparallelism occurs. Think of the paired items as lined up beneath one another, and you will see what you need to do to correct this error. The correction often involves simply adding a word or two to one side of the pair or deleting some words.

> ____________ not only ____________
> ____________ but also ____________
>
> *Incorrect:*
>
> Legal abortion not only protects women's lives, but also their health.
>
> *Corrected:*
>
> Legal abortion not only protects women's lives; it also protects their health.
>
> *Another correct version:*
>
> Legal abortion protects not only women's lives but also their health.

Split Subjects and Verbs

If the subject of a sentence contains long modifying phrases or clauses, by the time you get to the verb you may make an error in agreement (using a plural verb, for example, when the subject is singular) or even in logic (for example, having a subject that is not capable of being the agent that performs the action of the verb). These are some typical such errors:

> The *goal* of the courses grouped under the rubric of "Encountering Non-Western Cultures" *are*. . . .

Here, the writer forgot that *goal,* the subject, is singular; it is an agreement error.

> During 1992, *the Refugee Act of 1980,* with the help of President Bush and Congress, *accepted* 114,000 immigrants into our nation.

The writer here should have realized the the agent doing the accepting would have to be the Bush administration, not the Refugee Act. A better version would read:

> During 1992, the Bush administration accepted 114,000 immigrants into our nation under the terms of the Refugee Act of 1980.

Proofreading Practice Proofread the following passage for errors of grammar and punctuation.

> The citizens of Zurich, Switzerland tired of problems associated with drug abuse, experimented with legalization. The plan was to open a central park, Platzspitz, where drugs and drug use would be permitted. Many European experts felt, that it was the illegal drug business rather than the actual use of drugs that had caused many of the cities problems. While the citizens had hoped to isolate the drug problem, foster rehabilitation, and curb the AIDS epidemic, the actual outcome of the Platspitz experiment did not create the desired results. Instead, violence increased. Drug-related deaths doubled. And drug users were drawn from not only all over Switzerland, but from all over Europe as well. With thousands of discarded syringe packets lying around, one can only speculate as to whether the spread of AIDS was curbed. The park itself was ruined and finally on February 10, 1992, it was barred up and closed. After studying the Swiss peoples' experience with Platzspitz, it is hard to believe that some advocates of drug legalization in the United States are urging us to participate in the same kind of experiment.

INDEX

Boldfaced numbers indicate page on which term is defined.

ACKNOWLEDGMENTS

Text Credits

HENRY J. AARON, "The Worst Health Care Reform Plan . . . Except for All the Others." Reprinted with permission of publisher, M. E. Sharpe, Inc., 80 Business Park Drive, Armonk, NY 10504, from the November–December 1991 issue of CHALLENGE.

JONATHAN ALTER, "Degrees of Discomfort." From *Newsweek*, March 12, 1990. Copyright © 1990 Newsweek, Inc. All rights reserved. Reprinted by permission.

DAVID E. ANDERSON, "Abortion and the Churches: 'Clarification' or Rollback?" from *Christianity & Crisis*, 3/4/91.

JOHN ATLAS AND PETER DREIER, "The Phony Case Against Rent Control," from *The Progressive*, April 1989. Reprinted by permission from *The Progressive*, 409 East Main Street, Madison, WI 53703.

CHRISTOPHER AWALT, "Brother, Don't Spare a Dime." Reprinted by permission of the author.

SUSAN BROWNMILLER, "Pornography Hurts Women" from *Against our Will: Men, Women and Rape*. Copyright © 1975 by Susan Brownmiller. Reprinted by permission of Simon and Schuster, Inc.

SNEED B. COLLARD III, "The Environment: Us Versus It?" first appeared in the November/December 1992 issue of *The Humanist*. Reprinted with permission.

MATTHEW CONOLLY, "Euthanasia Is Not the Answer" from a speech delivered at the Hemlock Society's Second National Voluntary Euthanasia Conference, February 9, 1985. Reprinted with permission of the author.

CARLOS E. CORTÉS, "The Quest for Community amid Diversity," from *Change*, September/October 1991. Reprinted with permission of the Helen Dwight Reid Educational Foundation. Published by Heldref Publications, 1319 Eighteenth St., N.W., Washington, D.C. 20036–1802. Copyright © 1991.

CONSUMER REPORTS, "Health Care in Crisis: Does Canada Have the Answer?" Copyright 1992 by Consumers Union of U.S., Inc., Yonkers, NY 10703–1057. Reprinted by permission from CONSUMER REPORTS, September 1992.

NICHOLAS DAVIDSON, "Feminism and Sexual Harassment" from *Society*, May/June 1991. Copyright © 1991. Reprinted by permission of the publisher.

OSSIE DAVIS, "Challenge for the Year 2000," from the July 24/31, 1989 issue of *The Nation*. Copyright © The Nation Company, Inc.

DINESH D'SOUZA, "The Visigoths in Tweed," from *Forbes*, April 1, 1991. Reprinted by permission of the author.

BILLIE WRIGHT DZIECH, "Sexual Harassment on Campus." From THE LECHEROUS PROFESSOR by Billie Wright Dziech. Copyright © 1984 by Billie Wright Dziech and Linda Weiner. Reprinted by permission of Beacon Press.

ROSA EHRENREICH, "What Campus Radicals?" Copyright © 1991 by *Harper's Magazine*. All rights reserved. Reprinted from the December issue by special permission.

KAY EBELING, "The Failure of Feminism," *Newsweek*, November 19, 1990. Reprinted by permission of the author.

SUSAN FALUDI, "The Backlash Against Feminism," from BACKLASH. Copyright © 1991 by Susan Faludi. Reprinted by permission from Crown Publishers, Inc.

JOHN FIRE/LAME DEER AND RICHARD ERDOES, "Talking to the Owls and Butterflies" from *Lame Deer: Seeker of Visions*. Copyright © 1972 by John Fire/Lame Deer and Richard Erdoes. Reprinted by permission of Simon & Schuster, Inc.

BETTY FRIEDAN, "The Half-Life of Reaction" from *The Second Stage*. Copyright © 1981, 1986 by Betty Friedan. Reprinted by permission of Simon & Schuster, Inc.

HENRY GATES, JR., "Whose Culture Is It, Anyway? It's Not Just Anglo-Saxon," *The New York Times*. May 4, 1991. Copyright © 1991 by The New York Times Company. Reprinted by permission.

PETER J. GOMES, "Homophobic? Reread Your Bible," *The New York Times*, August 17, 1992. Copyright © 1992 by The New York Times Company. Reprinted by permission.

JOHN C. GOODMAN, "An Expensive Way to Die," from *National Review*, 4/16/90. Copyright © 1990 by National Review, Inc., 150 East 35th Street, New York, NY 10016. Reprinted by permission.

ANGELA J. GRELLHESL, "Mediating the Speech Code Controversy." Reprinted by permission of the author.

PETER HAMILL, "Confessions of a Heterosexual," from *Esquire*, August 1990. Reprinted by permission of International Creative Management, Inc. Copyright © 1990 by Pete Hamill.

REGINA E. HERZLINGER, "Health Competition," from *The Atlantic*, August 1991. Reprinted by permission.

SIDNEY HOOK, "In Defense of Voluntary Euthanasia," from *The New York Times*. Copyright © 1987 by The New York Times Company. Reprinted with permission.

H. PATRICIA HYNES, "Beyond Global Housekeeping," *Ms. Magazine*, July/August 1990. Copyright © 1990 Ms. Magazine. Reprinted by permission.

DONALD KAGAN, "Whose Culture Is It, Anyway? Western Values Are Central," *The New York Times*, May 4, 1991. Copyright © 1991 by The New York Times Company. Reprinted by permission.

RYSZARD KAPUSCINSKI, "Second Thoughts About America's Racial Paradise," from *New Perspectives Quarterly*, Summer 1991. Reprinted by permission of the publisher.

LEWIS KILLIAN, "Race Relations and the Nineties: Where are the Dreams of the Sixties?" Reprinted from *Social Forces*, 69(1), September 1990. Copyright © The University of North Carolina Press.

MARTIN LUTHER KING, JR., "Letter from Birmingham Jail." Reprinted by arrangement with the Heirs of the Estate of Martin Luther King Jr., ℅ Joan Daves Agency as agent for the proprietor. Copyright 1962 by Dr. Martin Luther King, Jr., copyright renewed 1991 by Coretta Scott King.

FRANCES KISSLING, "Ending the Abortion War: A Modest Proposal." Copyright 1990 Christian Century Foundation. Reprinted by permission from the February 21, 1990 issue of *The Christian Century*.

MICHAEL LEVIN, "The Case for Torture," from *Newsweek*, June 7, 1982. Reprinted with permission of the author. "Sex, the Family, and the Liberal Order," from *Feminism and Freedom*, Transaction. Copyright © 1987 by Transaction, Inc. Reprinted by permission.

PETER MARIN, "Virginia's Trap," from *Mother Jones*, July/August 1992. Reprinted by permission of the author.

WILLIAM F. MAY, "Rising to the Occasion of our Death." Copyright 1993 Christian Century Foundation. Reprinted by permission from the 7/11/93 issue of *The Christian Century*.

MARGARET LIU MCCONNELL, "Living with Roe v. Wade," *Commentary*, November 1990. Reprinted with permission of the author.

RICHARD MOHR, "Civic Rights of Invisible Minorities" from *Gays/Justice*. Copyright © 1988 Columbia University Press, New York. Reprinted with the permission of the publisher.

GORDON T. MOORE, MD, MPH, "Caring for the Uninsured and Underinsured—Let's Provide Primary Care to All Uninsured Americans—Now!" from *JAMA*, 4/24/91. Copyright © 1991, American Medical Association. Reprinted by permission.

WILLIAM MURCHISON, "Should Dallas Drop Ban: City Shouldn't Ignore Morality," from *The Dallas Morning News' Viewpoint*, January 17, 1992. Reprinted with permission of The Dallas Morning News.

NEW REPUBLIC, "Talking Dirty," from the issue of 11/4/91. Reprinted by permission of THE NEW REPUBLIC. Copyright © 1991, The New Republic, Inc.

JEFFREY NICKEL AND C. S. ESSAY, "Everybody's Threatened by Homophobia." Reprinted from *Christopher Street*, Issue 185, August 17, 1992, with permission.

ANNE MARIE O'KEEFE, "The Case Against Drug Testing." Reprinted with permission from *Psychology Today* Magazine. Copyright © 1987 Sussex Publishers, Inc.

VIRGINIA POSTREL, "The Environmental Movement: A Skeptical View," from *Chemtech*, August 1991.

PATRICK W. PUGH, "Legalization of Euthanasia: A Means to a More Comfortable Dying Process." Reprinted by permission of the author.

ANNA QUINDLEN, "Mother's Choice," from *Ms. Magazine*, February 1988. Reprinted by permission of the author.

WILLIAM RASPBERRY, "The Myth That is Crippling Black America," from *Imprimis*, March 1990. Reprinted by permission of *Imprimis*, Hillsdale College.

JAMES RACHELS, "The End of Life," from *The End of Life: Euthanasia and Morality* by James Rachels. Copyright © 1986 by James Rachels. Reprinted by permission of Oxford University Press.

JONATHAN RAUCH, "Beyond Oppression," *New Republic*, May 10, 1993. Reprinted by permission of The New Republic. Copyright © 1993, The New Republic, Inc.

DIANE RAVITCH, "Multiculturalism Yes, Particularism No," from *Chronicle of Higher Education*, October 24, 1990. Reprinted by permission of the author.

ROGER ROSENBLATT, "How to End the Abortion War." Copyright © 1992 by The New York Times Company. Reprinted by permission.

ARTHUR SCHLESINGER, JR., "The Cult of Ethnicity, Good and Bad," *Time*, July 8, 1991. Copyright © 1991 Time Inc. Reprinted by permission.

JOEY SHANKS, "An Uncomfortable Position." Reprinted by permission of the author.

RABBI ARYEH SPERO, "Therefore Choose Life: How the Great Faiths View Abortion," from *Policy Review*, Spring 1989. Reprinted by permission of the publisher.

SHELBY STEELE, "The Recoloring of Campus Life." Copyright © 1989 by *Harper's Magazine*. All rights reserved. Reprinted from the February issue by special permission.

CINDY TARVER, "An Appeal to Prejudice." Reprinted by permission of the author.

WILLIAM TUCKER, "How Housing Regulations Cause Homelessness," from *The Public Interest*, Winter 1991. Reprinted by permission.

UNION OF CONCERNED SCIENTISTS, "World Scientists' Warning to Humanity." Reprinted by permission.

UNIVERSITY OF MINNESOTA, "Policy Statement on Sexual Harassment." Reprinted by permission of the University of Minnesota.

JOHN E. VAN DE WETERING, "Political Correctness: The Insult and the Injury," from *Vital Speeches of the Day*. Reprinted by permission.

ELLEN WILLIS, "Abortion: Whose Rights to Life Is It Anyway?" Copyright © 1985 by Ellen Willis. Reprinted by permission of the Charlotte Sheedy Literary Agency.

NAOMI WOLF, "The Beauty Myth." Copyright © 1991 by Naomi Wolf. Reprinted by permission of William Morrow & Company, Inc.

JAMES D. WRIGHT, "Address Unknown: Homelessness in Contemporary America," from *Society*, September/October 1989. Copyright © 1989. Reprinted by permission of the publisher.

AMBER YOUNG, "Capital Punishment: Society's Self-Defense," reprinted with permission of the author.

Illustration Credits

Page 146 Silver Jeans, *Peace on Earth*, Christmas 1993 campaign U.S. by permission of Brainstorm.

Page 148 Courtesy of Department of Defense.

Page 151 (Top) Scott Stantis. Courtesy of Grand Rapids Press, Grand Rapids, MI. (Bottom) By permission of Mike Luckovich and Creators Syndicate.
Page 234 Courtesy of Guy Badeaux.
Page 241 Reuters/Bettmann.
Page 297 Reprinted by permission: Tribune Media Services.
Page 357 Kirk Anderson, Ladysmith, WI.
Page 368 Request Jeans ad by permission of Request Jeans.
Page 369 Lawman Jeanswear ad by permission of Lawman Sportswear Inc.
Page 439 Photo Researchers, Inc., New York City.